About the Authors

Top Universities Guide 2008 is co-authored by
John O'Leary, Nunzio Quacquarelli and Martin Ince

John O'Leary is former editor of the Times Higher Education Supplement (now Times Higher Education) and editor of The Times Good University Guide, UK. Previously, John was education editor at The Times. John has a degree from Sheffield University.

Nunzio Quacquarelli is managing director of QS. Nunzio is director of research of the Times Higher-QS World University Rankings, assisted by Ben Sowter, head of research at QS. Nunzio is editor in chief of TopUniversities.com, TopMBA.com and TopGraduate.com, and writes regularly on education and careers topics for The Times (London), The Times of India, Die Zeit, South China Morning Post and other newspapers worldwide. Nunzio has an MA from Cambridge University and an MBA from The Wharton School, University of Pennsylvania.

Martin Ince is a contributing editor of Times Higher Education and coordinator of the Times Higher-QS World University Rankings. He works as a freelance journalist and media adviser and is author of ten books, most recently the Rough Guide to the Earth (2007).

Discover more about the world's top 500 universities and the Times Higher-QS World University Rankings at **www.topuniversities.com**

2nd revised and updated edition exclusively featuring the

THE QS World University Rankings Top 500

TOP UNIVERSITIES GUIDE

John O'Leary, Nunzio Quacquarelli, Martin Ince

In association with

ETS TOEFL

ETS GRE

DUBAI INTERNATIONAL ACADEMIC CITY

IELTS English for International Opportunity

Published by Quacquarelli Symonds Limited

QS

Top Universities Guide
Published by QS Quacquarelli Symonds Limited
First published in 2006 as Guide to the World's Top Universities
2nd revised and updated edition 2008

QS Quacquarelli Symonds Limited
1 Tranley Mews, Fleet Road
London NW3 2DG
United Kingdom
www.qsnetwork.com

ISBN: 978-0-9558157-0-6

Acknowledgements
Sponsors: ETS-TOEFL®, ETS-GRE®, Dubai International Academic City, IELTS™.
The authors would like to thank the many individuals who have contributed to this edition. In particular Ben Sowter, head of research, QS, who has compiled and processed the data behind the Times Higher-QS World University Rankings, assisted by Baerbel Eckelmann. Other contributing QS colleagues include Marie Field, Tony Martin, Mandy Mok, David Nelkin, Jason Newman, Tim Rogers, Elke Schwarz, Ed Winder. Additional conributions from Michael Chan, Philip Fine, Michael Leidig, Jane Marshall, Geoff Maslen, Jon Marcus and Tom McGrenery. The authors would also like to thank Gerard Kelly, editor of Times Higher Education.

Special thanks are owed to Scopus™ for the provision of the citation data used in the compilation of the Times Higher-QS World University Rankings 2007. The authors would also like to thank all the universities that provided data and the numerous governmental and research agencies worldwide that supplied information.
Contact details for many of the universities and agencies can be found in the data sources tables and Directory of this book.

Editorial and project coordinator: Emma Simmons
Design: Sarah Hudson at Room 13 Ltd. Cover: Anna Martin
Print management: Spixel Design Communications, Singapore
Printed on: 100gsm GoldEast Matt Artpaper
Printed by: SNP Security Printing Pte Ltd, Singapore
Distribution: QS, OCS

Contents

Times Higher-QS World University Rankings: worldwide media reaction

"One of the two big international measures of university performance — The Times Higher/QS Rankings, which assigns 40 per cent of its weighting to peer review, placed 11 Australian universities in its global top 200." *The Australian*

"Many Asian universities have higher scores in 2007 than previously. Their governments may regard this as more important than the number of appearances for their own country. The Asia-Pacific region now has five of the world's top 30 universities, two fewer than the UK but four more than France."
Daily Times, Pakistan

"Just two institutions make annual attempts to compare universities round the world…both these indices…are closely watched by participants in a fickle and fast-expanding global education market." *The Economist, UK*

"The education company Quacquarelli Symonds compiles the data used to produce the...THES-QS World University Rankings... For the fourth consecutive year,… has named Harvard the world's leading university." *Harvard Crimson, US*

"The increasing internationalisation of universities is one of the emerging themes in recent years, through strategic global partnerships, joint teaching and research initiatives and increased international student recruitment activities. The THES-QS World University Rankings 2007 reflects the internationalisation of higher education around the world, with 27 universities from 14 different countries entering the top 200 for the first time." *The Nation, Thailand*

"The world's most comprehensive international university rankings, the THES-QS World University Rankings 2007, show a strong performance by New Zealand's universities, competing with the world's best." *Scoop, New Zealand*

"Hong Kong's good showing in the latest The Times Higher Education Supplement-QS world university rankings is an encouraging achievement."
South China Morning Post

"Rankings and ratings seem an inevitable aspect of today's higher education scene in most parts of the world. And while there is much debate about them, they can provide a useful basis for comparison of institutions. As such, the publication of the Times Higher-QS World University Rankings has been awaited with interest in recent years." *The Star, Malaysia*

"UCT is one of only four universities from the developing world in the rankings. 'International rankings are becoming increasingly important in a global education market,' says Vice-Chancellor…, Professor Njabulo S Ndebele... 'And I believe the rating bears out our mission to be an African university of international repute'."
UCT Daily News, South Africa

"...while the US is still the global higher education "superpower", China will soon be knocking it off top spot if current trends continue… In the latest THES-QS World University Rankings… China now has three universities in the top 100 plus another two if you include Hong Kong. Across Asia…the number of universities in the top 100 has risen to 13… The importance of higher education to economic success is now increasingly recognised around the world." *www.bbc.co.uk/news*

Welcome

Welcome to Top Universities Guide. This book will provide all the information and practical guidance you (and your parents) need to set you off on your home or worldwide search and successful application to a top university and program of study.

Who should use this guide?

Are you bright, well educated, aiming for a successful international career after university? Are you a parent looking to give your son or daughter an edge in his or her choice of higher education? Are you taking your first degree and considering a masters, PhD, or study abroad program? Are you an employer/ researcher refining your choice of universities to target for recruitment? Are you an academic looking to change institution? If you are any of these, there is something in this guide for you.

What's in the book?

This is your starting point for choosing a top university at home or abroad. As you begin your investigation into one of the most important and exciting decisions of your life, Chapter 1 guides you through the best way to choose a university and course that is right for you. Chapter 2 introduces you to the many benefits of taking the step to study abroad. The attitudes of international employers to recruiting graduates at every level and salary expectations are investigated in Chapter 3. Bearing all these aspects in mind, Chapter 4 offers you practical advice on making a university application, anywhere in the world. Chapter 5 looks at the potential costs you (and your parents) will face to study around the world and Chapter 6 explores options available in the search for funding and scholarships.

This second, updated, edition exclusively includes the latest Times Higher-QS World University Rankings. Beyond the detailed ranking table of the top 200 (Chapter 7) and a detailed analysis of how this ranking is carried out and how to read and interpret the data tables, the guide has profiles of the top 100 institutions worldwide in Chapter 8, and a directory of facts and contact details of the top 500 universities worldwide (Chapter 11). Chapter 9 looks at the top 100 institutions worldwide in each of the main subject areas: arts and humanities, life sciences and biomedicine, natural sciences, social sciences, and engineering and IT and it surveys the many varied employment choices you will have after completing your study, depending on which course you decide to select. The top ten study abroad destinations worldwide are investigated in Chapter 10 with a presentation of the pros and cons of each, a look at the university system and the lifestyle and opportunities you might experience there.

How to use Top Universities Guide

You can read this book through from start to finish or use it as a reference work, dipping in at points relevant to where you are in your university search. When reviewing the rankings tables, do not rely on them out of context. A university should not be selected purely based on its worldwide ranking, when relatively small variations in data can account for large positional movements. You should cross reference the overall ranking position of each university, with its strength in the subject area ranking relevant to your study interests. There can be some major differences because universities are never equally good at everything.

Your university selection should also be strongly influenced by your career goals. Study the sections of the book that look at employer attitudes and that suggest the different career paths possible after studying different subjects. Aim to identify universities and study destination countries that measure up to your study and career goals and provide a feasible option in terms of cost and financial aid. Once you have drawn up a list of top universities that meet your basic criteria, you can further investigate entry requirements, culture and specific subjects offered. You can read a profile of those universities ranked in the top 100 worldwide in this book and visit school websites. You will find all necessary contact details for the worldwide top 500 institutions in the Directory (Chapter 11). QS, the publishers of this book also provide www.topuniversities.com, which is a supplementary source of worldwide university information and includes direct web links to all the institutions featured in this book. Additional information on the rankings is also available at www.timeshighereducation.co.uk.

Once you have short listed target universities, the sections of this book on how to apply to university and how to fund your studies will, hopefully, make a difference and help you to gain a place to study your chosen subject, at the university of your choice.

International study

Competition for the best university places worldwide is growing. Around the world, governments are one-by-one ending the free provision of local university education and, instead, are encouraging students to seek out the best university education, at home or abroad. Many are providing grants for international student mobility. In the USA, recent Abraham Lincoln Study Abroad legislation aims to encourage one million students to study overseas, annually by 2016. Europe's Bologna Accord will make room for over 500,000 first-degree graduates to study in other EU nations for a masters degree, by 2010. Over three million Asians are expected to study outside their home country by 2020. The majority of all these students will aim to study at one of the 500 top universities featured in this guide.

Graduates of these universities are consistently among the most highly paid young professionals in every country in the world. Government and industry leaders in every country considered here, come overwhelmingly from these same universities. A report for the UN has identified that 80 per cent of the world's 18-24 year olds are unemployed, while only 10 per cent of the world's graduates are unemployed. But for many high-flyers, it is no longer enough to have a first degree from a local university. From knowledge based industries like consulting and banking, to global concerns like the automotive, and technology industries, as well as governments seeking to establish a globally minded cadre of young administrators, QS research finds that employers are increasingly focused on the best universities, internationally, to recruit graduates and, increasingly, willing to pay a premium for those with higher degrees.

In addition to making fascinating reading, we hope this guide will help change for the better your life and that of tens of thousands of other high achievers, worldwide. We hope it will help direct you to the top performing universities in the world, help you identify the best subject and destination for you, assist you in finding funding, and guide you into career paths which will allow you to achieve your full potential. Good luck!

(ETS) **TOEFL®**

TOEFL® Scores Open More Doors.

Unmatched quality with scores *you can trust*

The **TOEFL® test is the world's most popular test** because score users can select from more than 750,000 candidates in 180 countries.

Scores you can TRUST

More than 6,000 institutions in 110 countries, including most of the world's best universities, use TOEFL scores because they are:

- **Secure** – ETS ensures the security of scores and will cancel any that are questionable
- **Unbiased** – Multiple raters score the test and are constantly monitored (as opposed to single raters who are checked periodically)
- **Reliable** – Scores are consistent among all forms of the TOEFL test
- **Meaningful** – Full-range score scales to better distinguish ability

Sign up NOW

ETS is your partner in international education and invites you to join our official recognition list. The benefits are:

- **Increased visibility**
- **Convenient online score reporting**
- **Yearly performance data:** www.ets.org/toefldata.html
- **Score user helpline** (+1-609-283-2008)
- **The latest TOEFL test news** at TOEFLNews@ets.org

ETS – *Listening. Learning. Leading.*

Join our recognition list at www.ets.org/toefl/topgrad.

1

How to choose a university and course

In this chapter you will find advice on how to approach the daunting task of looking worldwide to find the best university for you. We look at the research necessary to make an informed choice and introduce rankings as a starting point. This chapter also surveys some the issues that are developed in the rest of this book such as subject choices, university location, facilities and funding.

Choosing a university, whether for an undergraduate, masters or exchange program is one of the biggest decisions you will take in your life. It will fundamentally affect the type of work you will do, many of the friends you will have in later life, the cultures you will understand. Increasingly, people choose a university to influence the country in which they seek to live and work. There are many factors to consider when choosing a university. The decision should be complex and will take time and effort to research. We believe this book can save you a great deal of time in the process of researching your options and will open your eyes to many new opportunities, both at home and abroad.

Aim high

In modern complex society, a good education is the most reliable route to a well-paid and interesting career, in almost any field. A report for the UN identified that 80 per cent of the world's 18-24 year olds were unemployed, while only ten per cent of the world's graduates in the same age range were unemployed. The vast majority of students around the world still settle for a local university, based on the convenience of being 'close to home'. It is easier to research and carries less apparent risk. However, some local universities may lack the global prestige to attract top employers, or the quality of programs to provide a route to a future masters or PhD and a wider search is always to be recommended before deciding.

When choosing a university you should always aim for the best institution that will accept you. If you have the academic ability to gain a top university place, you should be able to arrange the funding you need through either scholarships, student loans, part-time jobs or, perhaps, your family.

Using this guide

One of the best starting points for anyone, worldwide, serious about a top quality university education, is the tables within this book. These represent a guide to the world's top 500 universities. The prestige of these institutions is unmatched and is passed on to alumni of their programs and degrees, who reap the benefits throughout their professional careers. However, rankings can only ever give an overview. Every decision to apply for a university place is a highly individual one and is based on a number of personal priorities and criteria. Rankings may give you an overview of position and a snapshot of expertise but you should always follow this with extensive and detailed research into any institutions and courses that interest you.

The data contained in the rankings in this guide and the methods used to analyze them have been subject to a great deal of expert scrutiny. But the information needs to be used with thought, as is true of all rankings. We encourage you to read the detailed introduction to Chapter 7 on how the universities are ranked in the Times Higher-QS World University Rankings and to dig deeper into the data to help assess whether a university might be right for you. The rankings include evidence of excellence in teaching and research, as well as the opinions of academics and employers. In addition, they incorporate measures of the international commitment of universities by taking account of percentages of overseas staff and students. Not everyone should study at Harvard, or Cambridge, Australian National, Tokyo or Peking universities. Every university has different departmental strengths, cultures and networks. (Chapter 9 looks at subject area strengths across the world). All these aspects have to be considered in the light of your personal talents and aspirations.

Profiles and directory

The main data tables in this book are supplemented by additional sources of information. Each of the world's top 100 universities is profiled in Chapter 8. These profiles do not aim to duplicate the information you would find on university websites, though a factfile of basic data is included with each profile, but are intended to give a flavour of each university with interesting aspects and recent developments. For example, is the institution you are considering rural or in the city? What is its culture and history? Has it produced famous alumni? What are its main strengths? What current plans does it have to develop particular areas? This sort of thing is important for the overall ethos of an institution and for the experience you will have as a student. The profiles also contain more tangible information, much relating to subject specializations. The world's top 100 institutions tend to be good at a broad range of subjects, and excellent in many. But if your first love is philosophy, you might not be happy on a campus dominated by engineers or medics. To give a human face, many profiles also include quotes that capture the anecdotal essence of one student's experience. In addition, there is some information on the way in which universities support their students, for example in terms of accommodation and finance.

Chapter 11, the directory is a further valuable resource to support your worldwide search. The directory provides outline information on the world's top

500 universities including full contact details and websites, which will allow you to access more information quickly and easily. Additional information on all 500 institutions can also be found with direct links at www.topuniversities.com.

How to read the rankings tables

All the universities in this book are top institutions. They educate the leaders in every activity from medicine to politics, and produce new knowledge at an increasing pace in all fields. Chapter 7 includes a full presentation of the methodology behind the rankings, but some initial pointers follow here to help. Rankings are based on a selection of carefully chosen criteria. A final ranking of the institution is given but the columns of data reveal how each institution performs according to the individual criteria. It is well worth looking carefully at these because an institution may perform highly in one particular aspect important to you and less well in others.

The biggest component (40 per cent) is an academic peer review: the regard in which universities are held by a statistically robust sample of other top academics worldwide. Information comes from all over the world and from all fields of academic life, so an institution is likely to do well in this respect by being good in most, or all, subject areas. Prestigious specialist institutions may require specialist consideration in the context of their expertise to get a fuller picture of their relative position in the world.

An employer peer review, based on a sample of top international graduate employers worldwide captures universities' attractiveness to top recruiters. This is a factor of acute interest to many students. However, all 500 of the universities we analyze here produce graduates who are in high demand. This measure is mainly designed to assess universities' attractiveness to employers operating on a global basis. If you already know the kind of employer, career and location you intend to seek out locally, this measure might not be so valuable to you. Its main use is for students wanting a higher education that will make them visible to worldwide enterprises.

International attractiveness to staff and students is assessed to gauge a university's commitment to globalization. The US has so many top ranked institutions overall, but this is one area in which it does not have a world lead. Europe and Asia have the world's most international universities. It has been argued that the large size of the US makes it difficult for universities to be highly international. In the Netherlands or Switzerland, for example, whose universities have a large percentage of foreign staff and students, there are several other countries within a day's drive. In the US Midwest, there are none. Nevertheless, the authors consider this to be a valuable measure of the seriousness with which universities take their international role. Australia is, after all, an island continent but still brings in overseas students and academics in impressive numbers. By contrast, universities in some other Asian countries, such as South Korea and Japan, perform less well in this measure of their international orientation. Many universities now regard it as a priority to change, for example by teaching more courses in English. Such institutions may move radically in this part of the table in future years. Overall, we think that this factor is important in assessing the likely experience of overseas students. As a rule of thumb, a university with a low percentage of international students and faculty is likely to offer fewer facilities and provide less of a social network for overseas students.

The research performance of universities is measured based on the number of times faculty work is cited in publications. This measure is intended to capture research capacity as a function of university size. (We use the number of citations per staff member, partly to prevent very large universities dominating the table, and partly to allow us to measure the density of top research intellect in institutions.) This measure is a good one for would-be research students. It might also be of value for internationally mobile lecturers and organizations thinking of homes for their research budgets. However, it has a number of inevitable biases such as the fierce publishing ethos of the biomedical sciences. A big medical school is a massive plus in terms of generating both papers and citations. This data is also known to favour English language publications and the arts and humanities show less strongly. Anyone with an interest in these subjects might pay less attention to this criterion.

One of the aspects measured in the rankings, which is of most interest to prospective students, is the staff to student ratio. This aims to be a direct look at commitment to teaching. It might matter less for potential researchers than to would-be undergraduates. It is also prone to subtle influences, which you might want to research further. Oxford and Cambridge universities in the UK both teach for several weeks a year less than other nearby institutions. Some universities make extensive use of postgraduate students to teach undergraduates (which are not included in faculty numbers) while others frown on the practice. In some top institutions, students may never see the renowned scholars whose pictures adorn the prospectus, while in others these individuals give their fair share of lectures. Again, it is worth looking beyond these figures, for example at the institution profiles and websites, to get a fuller picture.

Search for the best department and course

It is not just the institution at which you study that is important. Finding the right program of study is vital to your enjoyment of university and your future career. Chapter 9 includes a detailed ranking of the 100 best institutions in five major subject categories: arts and humanities, life sciences and biomedicine, natural sciences, social sciences, and engineering and IT. This will help you identify a university in the field you are interested in. The chapter also includes an overview of the variety of career options that may be open to you if you follow each of the different subject areas, many of which may be new to you. The profiles of the top 100 institutions worldwide in Chapter 8 also include the top subjects at those universities.

Overall, rankings contain little subject-specific information because of the sheer volume of detailed data that would be involved. University prospectuses and websites are the right place to find out this sort of detail. However, every university featured in this guide has a searchable course listing available on www.topuniversities.com You are well advised to add research from subject associations, professional societies, research institute websites and other specialist sources, in order to find out as much as possible about the suitability of courses and programs for your future ambitions.

Consider the location

Identifying the right country in which to study is also a major task. Chapter 10 provides detailed country reviews for the world's ten most popular overseas study destinations: US, UK, Australia, Canada, France, Germany, the Netherlands, Singapore, Japan and the Nordic countries. These reviews will help you identify which country best suits your study needs in terms of quality, culture, cost and financial aid. Sometimes there are particular considerations, which affect the country you choose. For example, most large US medical schools teach the subject to postgraduates. They may have studied the life sciences as undergraduates, but many have not, and there are doctors in the US with first degrees in mathematics or languages. It works well, but if you want to start studying medicine at age 18, the US system may not be for you.

Student exchanges

One increasingly popular way of expanding your experience and getting a flavour of overseas study is through your university's exchange program. Typically this might involve spending anything from a few weeks in summer to a complete year in a foreign country. Therefore, it can be useful to look at the exchange schemes offered by any university to which you are thinking of applying. Are they in countries that interest you? Do they major on the US and Europe, or has the university recognized the growing importance of Asia? Which institutions are involved in the other countries? Use this book to identify how well ranked the exchange institutions on the list are. If your interest is in engineering, you might look for an exchange with MIT rather than a less prestigious university. Further information on student exchanges is also available at www.topuniversities.com.

How good are facilities?

The facilities offered by universities can vary enormously. This can have a big impact on your enjoyment of university. All the universities featured in this guide offer an excellent academic experience, but you should also check the availability of computer centres, sports facilities, arts activities, career services and even social clubs. University websites provide varying levels of information on these topics. However, the best source of this information is current students and alumni. The profiles of the top 100 universities in Chapter 8 also provide some insights. Student accommodation is always an important factor when considering studying abroad and the availability of campus accommodation is also summarized in many profiles.

Identify cost and funding options

Study at university all over the world continues to increase in cost. This factor alone underlines how important it is to make the right choice of university and program of study to ensure an adequate return on investment in your future career. Chapter 5 includes a detailed review of average university course fees, for domestic and international students. These vary from completely free at many Scandinavian universities, to more than US$50,000 per year at some private US universities, not including living costs.

Fees act as a constraint on many people wanting to study at a top university, especially the expensive private universities. However, don't forget, the graduates of the world's top universities tend to earn enough in their careers to pay back their student debts within a few short years. If you can gain entry to one of these top institutions, you will benefit from higher earnings for the rest of your life.

Will you be accepted?

No standard comparison of university entry standards across borders exists. Each university website will provide a guide to its own entry requirements, which are usually based on the local education system, though these can vary greatly within one country. The government statistical sources listed at the end of this chapter can help you with comparisons within and between countries. What is in your control is to submit the best application you are capable of. Chapter 4 of this guide helps you make your best university application. It explains the different parts of many application procedures and offers you tips to ensure that you are as well prepared to make it as possible.

University visits and education fairs

There is no substitute for face-to-face contact. If a university is nearby, or within reach of a cheap airfare or as a detour on holiday or business travel, there is absolutely nothing better than to visit it, and if at all possible, meet the people who will be teaching you, and some students. This can happen when you visit for an interview, on an open day, or at your individual request.

Education fairs can be a time efficient way to meet the admissions officers of target universities, gather brochures and obtain answers to your personal questions. Many undergraduate education fairs take place around the world and they can easily be found through an online search. QS, the publisher of this book organizes the annual QS World Grad School Tour (www.topgraduate.com) in more than 25 countries, enabling you to meet with more than 150 universities offering postgraduate masters and PhD programs. At the world leading QS World MBA Tour (www.topmba.com), you can meet many business schools from around the world.

Talk to staff and alumni

If you cannot arrange a visit, perhaps because of distance, remember that telecommunications is not expensive these days. What happens when you ring up a university that looks good on paper, or send them an email? You will need the right answers to questions on topics such as finance, accommodation and employment prospects. But in addition, you will be able to form an impression of how important you are to them. Given the amount of time and money you are about to commit to the next stage of your studies, this is a substantial consideration.

Most universities with a significant international student body have an alumni association with branches around the world. Contacting them will put you in touch with recent (and not so recent) graduates whose experiences you might want to hear about. But their testimony should be treated with some caution. Activists in such groups are self-selected and probably had a better than average time at the university in question.

Further research

This guide, its rankings tables and chapters with information on all topics relating to university search and application are one of the best starting packs you will find for a top international university search. However, as pointed out throughout this chapter, you will need to commit time and energy to much further research, online, on the phone and in person. Finally, if you seek comparatively objective college data, many countries have institutions that collect it on a national scale. In the UK and the US respectively, there are the Higher Education Statistics Agency (HESA) and the National Center for Education Statistics (NCES). In Japan, Australia, Hong Kong and elsewhere, such data tends to be gathered by government statistics agencies many of which are listed in Chapter 7. In either case, a few hours online will yield basic numbers on topics such as course completion. Many countries have information sites about the education in their country and the table on the next page lists some of these.

Information sources for study worldwide

Australia	IDP Education Australia www.idp.com
Austria	ÖAD Austrian Exchange Service www.oead.ac.at
Canada	Canadian Education Centre Network www.studycanada.ca
Denmark	CIRIUS Study in Denmark www.studyindenmark.dk
Finland	CIMO Centre for International Mobility www.studyinfinland.fi
France	Agence EduFrance www.edufrance.fr
Germany	DAAD German Academic Exchange Service www.daad.de
India	University Grants Commission www.ugc.ac.in
Ireland	Education Ireland www.educationireland.ie
Italy	MIUR/CIMEA www.study-in-italy.it www.cimea.it
Japan	JASSO Japan Student Services Organization www.jasso.go.jp
Malaysia	Study Malaysia www.studymalaysia.com
Netherlands	NUFFIC www.studyin.nl
New Zealand	Education New Zealand www.newzealandeducated.com
Norway	SIU www.studyinnorway.no
Singapore	Singapore Education www.singaporeedu.gov.sg
South Korea	NIIED www.studyinkorea.go.kr
Spain	Eduespaña www.eduespa.org
Sweden	The Swedish Institute www.studyinsweden.se
Taiwan	Ministry of Education www.studyintaiwan.org
Turkey	Study Turkey www.studyturkey.metu.edu.tr
UK	The British Council www.educationuk.org
US	Education USA www.educationusa.state.gov

2

The benefits of studying abroad

This chapter considers some of the many benefits of a period of study abroad: academic, personal, cultural and language. It includes reflections by students and alumni on how it has helped their personal and professional development.

Nowadays, international experience often forms part of an undergraduate degree. For many students, this will be a semester or term on an organized exchange program, with a partner university in another country. However, for approaching three million students a year, worldwide, international experience means an entire program of study being followed away from home, sometimes in a neighbouring country, but very often on the other side of the world. Though almost 70 per cent of all tertiary-level students studying abroad are currently enrolled in programs in North America or Europe, more and more are seeking different destinations. Location, subject choice, mode of delivery, length of study, cost of program and teaching style are all areas of concern for students thinking of pursuing an undergraduate or postgraduate degree abroad.

So what are the benefits of studying abroad and why might you consider a period away from home for part, or all, of your degree? Listening to students who already have experienced the benefits of study abroad is one of the best ways of finding out. Many choose to study abroad because the academic program they wish to pursue is not available at home, the emphasis or teaching method is different or simply because of the reputation of a particular institution. Remember, not all education systems are set up the same way and many adopt a very traditional way of teaching and assessment that might not fulfill your ambitions or strengths. Jackie Wong, the Senior Education Advisor at the Australian Education Consultancy and graduate of the University of Melbourne, chose to study abroad for two main reasons: firstly, "because of the flexibility of choice in the subjects I wanted to study. In Hong Kong I would have had to study a large number of options with very little opportunity to choose", and secondly, "as there were only 20 or so students in each class, the professors actually remembered my name!" Such reasons for studying abroad are common and underline the importance many attach to the different learning experience you may find abroad.

International quality and recognition

One of the most compelling reasons for studying abroad, however, involves the perceived quality of the degree itself. This is a very complex area that such tools as the Times Higher-QS World University Rankings seek to help unravel. In many societies, anything that is regarded as international is synonymous with quality and prestige. Education is no different, yet the sheer number of universities in the world today means that the notion that all are of the same quality is nonsense. Universities in many different countries benefit from excellent government support, good infrastructure and a policy of strict quality control. This ensures that the degree programs offered are of an agreed and reputable standard with international reference points. However, there is an equal number that do not have such good policies and simply offer a degree that meets a local need and has little or no significant value in the international context. True benefit for an international student is derived from studying at an institution that fulfils certain universal standards and is, at a very minimum, quality assured by a national agency and, at best, recognized by an international body such as a professional association.

The international recognition of your degree is one of the foremost reasons why you might seek a period of study abroad and is certainly one of the major benefits of the experience. Albert Luk, an Assistant Technical Analyst at OOCL, an international logistics company in Hong Kong, chose the University of York in the UK for his degree in Software Engineering for two key reasons: "firstly because UK higher education has an excellent reputation over most other countries in the world and, secondly, because the recognition of the degree in Hong Kong is very high." With so many people now travelling overseas for their education, the current labour market is also far more mobile than ever before. The more recognized your degree is, the farther you will be able to travel with it. Recognition, however, is not always focused on an individual name such as Harvard or Cambridge, but can simply indicate a more general reputation of a country's system of higher education or vocational training.

Personal development, life skills and culture

Sameera Suri is typical of many students who have studied internationally. An Indian national, Sameera now resides in Geneva, an employee of the World Health Organization. In her role as a communications officer for the Diabetes Unit she utilizes both the skills she gained in her degree from the London School of Economics and her experiences of being an international student in London. "There were so many advantages of my period of study abroad. I learnt to become self-sufficient and much more independent than I was in India. More importantly, I started to understand how many common elements there are, irrespective of where you come from and where you live."

Anuradha Bajaj, also from India, studied in the UK for reasons as important as any related to quality or reputation. "I wanted to get a blend of different academic approaches and the opportunity of living and working in another country. The chance to manage my life away from home: open a bank account, speak another language, cook different food and see a different history were things

I thought were important to help me develop." Such reasons compel many to study overseas and many international students rank experiences outside of the classroom as important as those at university. The ability to adapt to a different culture, manage everyday life, often in a foreign language and gain an insight into a completely new way of life are as valid reasons as any academic ones for a period of international study and, in some ways, benefit the individual much more directly. Employers, too, recognize these reasons for studying abroad and consistently employ graduates who have the ability to understand different cultures so that they can bring these skills to the business. In a shrinking world, the need to be more international in outlook and understanding is something all employers want and so the need for graduates of this kind is likely to grow.

A Macedonian MSc student of International Relations at the London School of Economics who also studied in Kuwait feels that, "learning from another culture/society is the greatest benefit of study abroad and benefits the country of study as well. Many international students who return to their own country with a positive impression assume positions of responsibility in their government or society. Meeting people from all over the world is a bonus and adds a whole new dimension to your thinking. You really begin to appreciate being able to compare different mentalities, traditions, politics, and the best method of crossing boundaries, as well as fostering international dialogue and consensus."

Future employment and language

With the global labour market placing more importance on further educational experience, getting the decision right on where and what to study is increasingly complex. A recent report by the Finnish Government indicates that employers assess studying and training abroad in three different ways: firstly, from the perspective of occupational skills and whether the international experience increases students' skills in their field of studies; secondly, how the experience affects students' personal growth; and thirdly, what kind of skills and abilities are developed abroad that will help them perform in an international setting. The report suggests that the second and third issues provide very strong arguments for study abroad, particularly the development of language skills and the ability to deal with people from other countries.

"I studied overseas primarily to enhance my future career opportunities," says Tommy So, a personal portfolio consultant at Credit Suisse. His experience working in another language, he believes, has certainly enabled him to progress in his chosen career path. "For me, the benefits of studying abroad are not only about the gaining of an international exchange experience but the improvement of my spoken and written English. Studying abroad helped me to get opportunities at some large international companies." Kenneth Lai, assistant to the general manager of a Japan joint venture manufacturing firm investing in China, completed a degree in the UK. He concurs: "Studying in English was important. In fact, grasping English in the UK was even more important in helping me develop an international career."

These experiences touch on a centrally important reason for the enormous interest in study abroad. The growth in qualifications taught exclusively in the

English language at all levels reflects the continuing importance of the language in every contemporary international sphere. Universities that wish to attract more international students must increasingly adapt their academic offerings. Developments in such diverse countries as Finland, the Netherlands and South Korea, where degrees of all kinds are now being taught in English, underline the importance of language in the choice of some international study destinations. However, international choice is still great and as relevant to careers in certain country situations for students with particular and non-English language ambitions. An Argentinean who studied both at Tufts University, US and the University of Plymouth, UK and is now president of an Argentine shipping company sums up the benefits of studying overseas. "In my line of work, the ability to communicate fluently in English is fundamental. Studying abroad has helped me greatly in shipping. Being international in nature, the experience of studying and working with people from different parts of the world has been most beneficial."

Ambition and adventure

There are many reasons for seeking an international education, all of which ultimately revolve around personal ambition and circumstances. The benefits are similarly individual but can be summed up in a number of areas: personal development and growth, general experience, cultural experience and future employment opportunities. Jackie Wong reports the wide spectrum of benefits. "Since graduating, I have worked in different fields including banking, finance, and now education consulting. The network I have built from my time abroad has really helped in my career. I have also learnt to become independent, to multi-task and I am able to work in an English-speaking environment."

You may find yourself in the position where you know precisely what your ambitions are and what you need to do to achieve them and so pursue your period of international study in a more single-minded fashion. Or, you may understand the more general benefits of studying abroad and embark on it as more of an adventure. Either way, you will discover many things: about yourself, the country and the world, and you will remember and use the experiences for the rest of your life. Ross McCalden's experience of researching, applying for and enjoying a degree overseas is typical. "I was drawn to the College of Europe because of the prestige of the institution, the quality of the degree and the fact that being abroad gave me a perspective on people from different cultures." Ross may never have studied abroad if it wasn't for a personal contact and now he sees only advantages in his experience, "I think you definitely get to know yourself better and being away from familiar concepts really opens your mind to new ideas and ways of doing things. It also builds character and language skills. It made me a more rounded person." Whatever your reasons for studying abroad, you can be certain that the experience will be one that you never regret and will value for the rest of your life.

DUBAI INTERNATIONAL ACADEMIC CITY

3

A top degree, international study and your career

This chapter looks at the impact a degree from a top university and international experience can have on your career. It looks at trends of international student mobility and employment and from the point of the view of international employers and what they are looking for in graduate recruitment. We survey the career aspirations and expectations of international job applicants.

Studying at a top university and especially time spent abroad can have a dramatic influence on your future career prospects and professional mobility in the globalized world. From the attraction of learning new languages and adopting and embracing different cultures, to the more functional benefits of developing occupational and personal skills and seeking prospective employment abroad, gaining an internationally recognized qualification from a top university is always going to be a life changing and enhancing experience.

The UNESCO Institute of Statistics reported that between 1999 and 2004, the number of mobile students worldwide surged by 41 per cent. That number is now estimated to be close to three million. This reflects both the rapid expansion of higher education around the world and the sustained growth in demand for top quality graduates by employers around the world.

What benefits can students with international experience offer employers and what can they expect from them? Views will naturally vary from country to country, employer to employer, and person to person, but the overriding view of employers is that these students can offer tangible added value if their skills and knowledge are applied in the most effective way.

International graduate recruitment

As part of the Times Higher-QS World University Rankings, QS conducted a survey of almost 400 international employers of graduates and postgraduates around the world in addition to 450 employers of MBAs. The employer views in this chapter are drawn from this annual research program, as well as from other sources.

More and more companies have global operations, without ties to any one region. Many of these have human relations managers with global or regional responsibility for hiring graduates, postgraduates and MBAs from the best universities and business schools in the world. In addition, many recruiters headquartered in one location have responsibility for regions elsewhere in the world. For example, many graduates and postgraduates in Asia, Latin America and Eastern Europe are hired through head offices in North America or Western Europe.

38 per cent of responding recruiters in this employer survey are based in the North American region, but 40 per cent of these have some responsibility for recruiting globally or in Europe, Asia or Latin America. Similarly, European recruiters make up 28 per cent of the sample, but 36 per cent also have some responsibility for recruiting globally or in North America, Asia or Latin America. This should be good news for mobile graduates, whatever your country of origin or study, and your preference for international mobility.

Salary benefits of a top degree

Though future salary may not be the overriding factor in your choice of university or first degree course, a sense of your potential future earnings nevertheless helps in determining the feasibility of study abroad. The Association of Graduate Recruiters in the UK publishes a report on graduate salaries compared to non-graduates, which reveals that graduates, on average, achieve a 50 per cent premium over non-graduates' earnings. QS' research suggests that the premium for graduate education spans all professional sectors and continues to increase as each further degree is added.

The tables below indicate average reported salaries across the EU and North America, at four stages of higher education: first degree, masters, PhD and MBA. First degree salaries vary significantly by industry sector. Consulting/professional

Average reported salaries by sector in EU and North America at different levels of higher education US$

	First degree	Masters	PhD	MBA
Aerospace/defense	47,618	70,000	97,500	85,000
Consulting/professional services	58,968	65,121	77,415	99,154
Energy	52,059	65,074	70,761	83,100
Financial services/banking	58,460	62,937	73,002	93,515
FMCG	39,388	45,286	52,710	87,329
Manufacturing/automotive	35,079	60,716	70,466	86,988
Media/entertainment	42,838	46,927	63,745	97,295
Pharma/healthcare	49,901	71,287	72,346	89,671
Public sector/non-profit	37,211	66,478	73,188	82,398
Retail	38,125	63,541	72,388	79,833
Telecoms/high tech	48,183	72,500	75,000	82,500

services, financial services/banking and energy pay the highest starting salaries averaging in all three sectors above US$50,000. The manufacturing/automotive, public sector/non-profit and retail sectors report the lowest average graduate starting salaries in the range of US$35-38,000 per annum.

Starting salaries are not always indicators of long-term earnings potential, though there is some correlation between the two. Nor is the average length of service of staff in different companies and sectors always the same.

Decisions on future career will always be based on more than just salary, with quality of work-life balance, a stimulating environment and assignments and travel being factors which interest more and more people in the workplace.

Premium value of further study

Employers place a high premium on further higher education: masters, PhDs and MBAs, as the following table from the QS research reveals. Masters degrees can achieve anything between an eight and a 79 per cent premium on a first degree, with some of the lower paid sectors at first degree level, such as the public sector/non-profit and manufacturing/automotive, putting a particularly high premium on masters degrees and PhDs, which are no longer just a route to a professorship. Many employers actively seek to recruit PhDs and offer salary premiums. This QS research is one of the first studies to quantify this PhD premium, which varies between 25 and 105 per cent, over and above first degree starting salaries. The aerospace/defense industries offer the highest premium for PhDs, followed by manufacturing/automotive, and the public sector/non-profit.

Percentage variation in average salaries in EU and North America by qualification, relative to first degree

	First degree	Masters	PhD	MBA
Aerospace/defense	100	147	205	179
Consulting/professional services	100	110	131	168
Energy	100	125	136	160
Financial services/banking	100	108	125	160
FMCG	100	115	134	222
Manufacturing/automotive	100	173	201	248
Media/entertainment	100	110	149	227
Pharma/healthcare	100	143	145	180
Public sector/non-profit	100	179	197	221
Retail	100	167	190	209
Telecoms/high tech	100	150	156	171

A discussion of higher education salaries would not be complete without referring to the world's most popular postgraduate course, the MBA. Employers continue to place the greatest salary premium on the MBA qualification, with salaries of between 160 and 248 per cent of equivalent first degree salaries. The sector with the highest average reported MBA starting salary is consulting/ professional services, at over US$99,000.

The fight for top international graduates

International graduates are seen as huge assets by international employers in many sectors from knowledge based industries like consulting and banking, to global industries like healthcare, consumer products and automotive, as well as government, all seeking to establish a globally minded cadre of young administrators. Many international employers now focus on building relationships with universities and business schools to target the crème-de-la-crème of international graduates. The most straightforward source of entry for international students into companies is through internship programs. This allows employees to become familiar with a company and its culture, and gives employers the opportunity to view candidates at close hand, without having to complete all the formal visa requirements for full-time hiring.

The global company Procter & Gamble (P&G), for example, hires international graduates in most countries in which it operates. P&G has an extensive internship program, which often leads to full-time hiring. P&Gs diverse workforce demonstrates the multi-cultural nature of business in today's society and the opportunities for international graduates. "Procter & Gamble has an amazingly diverse intake of international graduates" according to Alexa Barker, director of diversity. In P&Gs UK & Ireland head office alone, there are staff representing 73 different nationalities. This holistic approach to operations, an approach reflected by many blue-chip companies, opens up a wealth of opportunity for international graduates. As an example of the success of this international policy, Ms Barker cites one team of 13 people, made up of 13 different nationalities, which was recently the company's most successful division.

Other companies hire international graduates directly. Take, for example, DSM, that, in its own words, is "embracing the international market of young academics." This multinational manufacturing company based in the Netherlands had, until recently, focused on recruiting Dutch-based nationals. This focus has now shifted towards the attraction of international graduates to help diversify the company's management population. DSM hires directly into structured programs, in which employees have the opportunity to work in an international environment. "We are broadening our international talent population more than ever before. We want our graduate employees to grow to become tomorrow's executives," says Jackie Cuthbert, vice president of executive resourcing.

For employers around the world in any industry, success ultimately lies in the skills of the workforce. In a world, now international by nature, occupational and life skills can be accrued through international student mobility. The importance of this mobility as perceived by governments is also evident, with schemes such as the Abraham Lincoln Study Abroad Act of 2006 implemented by the US Senate, which calls for a national program to study abroad. The program will create fellowships and scholarships for individual students and establish partnerships with colleges and universities. The goal of the program is to create and sustain annual growth rates to achieve one million US students studying abroad, annually, by 2016.

Business wants international skills

Irma Garam of CIMO, the government education agency of Finland summarized in her report, 'Study on the relevance of international student mobility to work and employment', three major benefits that international graduates offer: occupational skills, personal growth, and internationalization. It is the combination of these three skill sets, which is the attraction for employers. Occupational skills relate to increased skills in the students' field of study, personal growth to such factors as cross-cultural communication skills, an understanding of local customers and cultures and the ability to deal well with new circumstances, while internationalization is the attribute that will allow him or her to operate in an international environment. International graduates are expected to bring new energy, new ideas and concepts to a business and they tend to have good, all round, business acumen. Irma Garam believes that "international experience gives students the self-confidence, the ability to 'survive', and other general skills highly valued in the labour market". Irma Garam adds that "there is a strong belief amongst employers that studying abroad teaches students to handle different situations, gives them a broader perspective and a greater sense of proportion."

P&G agrees with the view that personal growth from international mobility is a valuable asset. "International candidates bring a good dimension to our workforce, which helps with our holistic approach. We do not expect, and do not disadvantage, those who do not have particular language experience in a particular country. We can offer them that with the job, and working with such global products, understanding of different cultures on the job will enable employees to pick up skills which will enable them to be transferred to our offices throughout the world," says Alexa Barker.

DSM focuses on Europe and Asia-Pacific where they forecast the most substantial business growth. Jackie Cuthbert at DSM says that the attractiveness of international graduates lies in their ability to translate local values on a global scale: "Employees who have studied or worked abroad bring with them an international mindset. Different geographies have different ways of doing business, and, as with all firms, we must ensure that our corporate values remain. Our graduate employees are able to work in a global marketplace, but with a cultural sensitivity that ensures our values stay true. They are much more business savvy than in yesteryear."

International mobility

QS also conducts surveys of international applicants for postgraduate study to identify what motivates them and how they can best meet their career/education objectives. In the last 12 months, more than 6,000 postgraduate applicants have been surveyed. You may have a variety of motivations for deciding to study abroad: curiosity, learning and developing language skills, opportunities of taking courses your home country may not offer, or perhaps you did not get into the university of your choice at home. The QS Postgraduate Applicants Survey is the largest poll of international postgraduate candidates. It becomes abundantly clear that most applicants seeking an international education, whether masters, PhD or MBA, are also seeking to work abroad for a period of time.

Study abroad can certainly improve your employment prospects. Of paramount importance are ensuring that you apply yourself and your skills in the most effective way, and that you know where, and how, to find the opportunities. It is also worth looking at what you expect in return, and how you feel that international mobility will aid your career development. Also important, is how to convey your international experience as a valuable marketing tool for yourself. If an employer was torn between two like-for-like candidates, this could prove to be a deciding factor.

On job applications and in interviews, it is important to point out that your choice to study abroad was a beneficial career decision and will add to your personal and occupational attributes. How did you decide upon your location? What skills have you learned that will help in your role? How have you grown on a personal level? And how did the placement tie in with your degree? In layman's terms, you need to prove that it has given you added value and was not just fulfilling your backpacking dream. It is a common desire for young people to want to travel, so it is important to stand out from the crowd and show what you have adopted and embraced from your time abroad.

What applicants want

Criteria for selecting an MBA or postgraduate employer

Criterion	Rank	Importance (%)
Job satisfaction	1	68
Training & development	2	64
Career progression	3	62
International opportunities	4	61
Salary & benefits	5	48
Job type/function	6	46
Corporate ethics	7	36
Corporate culture	8	32
Industry sector	9	26

The QS Postgraduate Applicants Survey identifies that international mobility remains important to people seeking a post study employer. 'International opportunities' stands alongside 'career progression', 'job satisfaction' and 'training and development' as the most important employer selection criteria for postgraduate applicants.

Preferred sectors to work in

A correlation exists between the industry in which students aspire to work, and the country they come from. Figures for all levels of degree are fairly uniform, indicating a trend dependent on country of origin. According to the QS research, among postgraduate applicants from the US & Canada, consulting was the most desirable industry sector, with 74 per cent choosing this as a preference. Financial services, and banking and accounting were close behind in popularity. Respondents from Latin America favour consulting, with 56 per cent of respondents selecting this option followed by a preference for a career in industry and engineering. In Western Europe, financial services and accounting was the most popular career path, followed by consulting, then industry and then IT. By contrast, in Asia-Pacific, applicants favour a career in IT and telecommunications ahead of consulting, financial services or industry.

The career advantage of study abroad

Demand for international graduates by employers is set to continue to rise, with a particular emphasis on postgraduate degrees. Candidates graduating will generally be well remunerated, so funding your studies should not be an area of concern, if you possess the sought after skills and attend a top university.

However, graduates should not expect to simply walk into a great job just because they have qualified with a first degree, masters or PhD. Valid experience and other personal attributes must still fit in with the employment role. Today's graduates live in a world of global mobility and opportunity, but, everywhere, they will face competition from increasing numbers of other top graduates from around the world. So, it is how you convey your skills and demonstrate your ability to apply them to the employment opportunity that will see you succeed.

The overriding view from employers is that if you have an excellent academic track record, your nationality is no barrier to your future employment. In fact, if you can demonstrate a real passion to work in an international environment, and bring with you a degree from a top university and the mindset and outlook that can help drive a business forward, you will very often be more attractive to employers than locally educated graduates.

LSE

4

How to make your best university application

This chapter surveys the things you may have to arrange and provide when applying to university, anywhere in the world. It offers tips and advice and gives you background on what admissions staff would like, and expect, to see in a potential student's application. This guidance can help maximize your chances of gaining a place at the university of your choice.

Applying to your local university or to an international institution is not something that should be taken lightly. The competitive world in which we live makes the process of university application extremely significant for those who wish to enter the best and most suitable university for their own abilities. Whether you choose to apply to one of the world's top universities in the US or a smaller college in Denmark, the time and effort you will need to invest in the application procedure is great. Advice is available from various sources, some unexpected, to make the process more manageable and to increase your chances of making a successful application. Teachers, lecturers, careers counsellors, parents and current students are potentially all able to provide you with tips before you submit your application. All of them may be able to improve your chances of admission to your chosen university.

However, with increasing competition for top university places, the need to make the best of your application becomes ever greater. The application form and related materials consist of a number of common elements, irrespective of the university you are applying to. Each of these elements plays a role in your admissions decision and should be considered individually to ensure that you submit a complete, well-rounded and thorough application.

Basic application materials

The content of basic application forms tends to be consistent across all countries. You need to provide your name, age, address, schooling, academic achievements, including those that have yet to provide results (eg final exams) and the program of study that you are interested in. These sections require precision and honesty and are regarded by admissions staff as the most basic information that qualifies your application for further consideration. Many institutions now ask you to submit online application forms, so the need to remember to write legibly is no longer relevant, though the care you must take in completing the online forms and attaching the correct documents is as important, no matter how your application is submitted.

Many university application procedures require you to submit an application form and additional documentation. This material can take many different forms, but generally includes attested or original copies of your academic exam and assessment results and qualifications, the results of any standardized tests that you might have to take such as IELTS www.ielts.org or TOEFL www.ets.org/toefl and one or more letter(s) of recommendation. Often, an application fee is payable at the same time these materials are submitted.

There are exceptions. For example, the UK's Universities and Colleges Admissions Service (UCAS) system is based on a single completed form and there is, officially, no opportunity to send additional material through the administrative process. Application materials vary from system to system, but is universally important to provide admissions staff with as much information as possible to enable them to make an informed decision on the quality of your application. If you are unsure of exactly what material is required, contact the institution you are interested in directly to get the correct information. There is no point in failing in a university application because you did not provide the right documents.

References

Depending on the system of education you are applying to, and the individual university, 'reference letters' or 'letters of support' are often requested to substantiate your academic record, what you have written about yourself and to help the university make a judgement on your potential to benefit from the program of study that you have applied for. UK undergraduate programs require one reference, whereas most US degrees require two and some Australian universities do not require any at all. Two main issues arise with references. Firstly, and in many ways most importantly, there is the issue of who actually writes your reference. Secondly, there is the question of what the references should say about you as a student and as a person.

Choosing someone to be a referee is an extremely important task and one that may have a significant impact on the success or failure of your application. Referees have to possess a good knowledge of you as a person and as a student and, as such, be able to write in support of your application in a very honest, open and direct manner. Most universities expect to receive references from teachers, tutors or counsellors, though in some situations, it will be relevant to ask your employer or someone that you have had contact with in another context, such as an extracurricular activity. Most members of admissions staff will not examine who the person actually is, though they will note the relationship between you and the referee. Their main focus will be the content of the supporting comments in the reference and so there are no particular advantages in asking well-known people to be your referees. Above all, those who write your references should know you well and be able to describe you in a way that reflects the best of your abilities and the qualities that make you unique. Comments on your academic and intellectual strengths are particularly important in the more competitive universities. At smaller institutions, a description of the way in which you work or interact with others may be particularly important.

The style in which a reference should be written is very much dependent on the individual university. Many US institutions will provide a pro-forma reference sheet that allows referees to indicate your academic abilities in relation to those in your graduating class, for example. Others will allow a more free flowing approach, encouraging referees to express exactly what they feel about you as an applicant and as a potential member of the university. In either case, guidelines are issued along with other application materials so that the people you choose to be your referees are fully aware of exactly what is expected from the admissions staff at the institution you are interested in. Your references are important because they help give a flavour of you as an individual and separate you from other students with very similar entry qualifications. References that are written positively and informed with examples of your work, your activities or your characteristics, are more likely to help your application be successful than those that are routine and simply list your attributes.

Statement of purpose and essays

All students intending to study at university will have heard countless stories about the importance of the statement of purpose or the application essay or essays. As one of the most talked about aspects of an application, it is commonly and consistently the most misunderstood part of the application process and, as such, causes the greatest amount of concern. One common problem is identifying the purpose of such a piece of writing within a university application process. Irrespective of the country or university you wish to apply to, the opportunity to write about something at relative length is often the only chance you have to deviate from, what is essentially, a rather mundane and list-like process. In the US, Canada and throughout Asia, this piece of writing is called the application essay and serves two purposes: to demonstrate your command of the written word in English and to give an insight into you as a person.

It is common practice for universities to give you topics or questions as a basis for the application essay(s). This enables admissions staff to learn about your personal qualities and the way in which you think and behave. Topics might be, for example, 'Describe the defining moment of your childhood' or, 'Describe how a failure in your life made you a better person.' More often than not, international students interested in applying to universities that operate this kind of scenario type essay will not be asked for an interview and therefore this essay can serve the purpose of an 'interview on paper.' These essays need to be worked on carefully and can take a great deal of time. Many universities that favour this approach will ask you to write several essays of this kind, making the effort needed to make your application much greater than you might anticipate and so you should make sure you leave enough time for it.

In other parts of the world, the approach is different. The UK, Australia, the Netherlands and other countries in Europe operate a more limited essay type format for their applicants. In the UK, for example, this is known as a 'personal statement' on the UCAS application form and one page of A4 paper is allowed for the purpose. Because space is limited, the intention is to test the applicant to see whether he or she is able to express him or herself in a succinct fashion, capturing the important aspects of his or her personality and interest in an individual academic subject area. Again, because few of these universities will be in a position to interview you, admissions staff will want to see a blend of what makes you unique and what kind of contribution you will make to your chosen program of study, or university.

Deciding what to include in this kind of essay is very difficult indeed and requires a lengthy period of preparation before you submit the finished piece of writing. Some universities will expect you to demonstrate knowledge of their programs or reputation, while others will want you to exhibit strong extracurricular interests to complement your academic record. The only way of knowing what the right approach is for your application is to contact the admissions staff of the university you are interested in and asking what they expect in these documents. Talking about the application with students already at the university, or alumni, may also help with this part of the application process.

As a national or international student, the importance of the application essay cannot be underestimated. Different universities view the importance, however, in quite unique ways. Some of the most competitive universities in Australia, the UK and the US, use this extended piece of writing as the defining element that separates applications from one another and ensures that some are accepted while others are rejected. This certainly occurs in cases where many applications are received from students with very similar academic records and the university has little alternative but to use other measures to select. Other universities such as smaller institutions in Europe and the US, with limited student numbers and applications, also focus a great deal of their admissions effort on the assessment of the extended piece(s) of writing. Their emphasis is often on building a particular community or atmosphere on campus and, therefore, how different individuals might be able to contribute is extremely important.

Wherever you are applying, your approach to writing one of these extended elements of an application is important. It goes without saying that honesty in all that you commit to paper is essential. It is not uncommon for students to inflate their achievements or interests, only to have them questioned by a member of admissions staff via email or telephone contact, thus bringing their entire application into doubt. Many of the more complex scenario type essays require a great deal of preparation and thought and should not be undertaken lightly. Your school or college counsellor may well be an excellent resource to help you develop a coherent argument in one of these essays. He or she may allow you to draft a number of versions so that the final result reflects not only your character but also your best effort. The shorter kind of essays or personal statements will expect you to balance concrete examples of your interest in the academic subject area you are applying for, as well as demonstrating that you have qualities outside of the classroom that the institution would benefit from. As a general rule, irrespective of the kind of essays expected, you should be confident that, once written, your friends reading your statement would be able to both recognize you and be interested in learning a little more!

Interviews

It used to be very common for many of the world's top universities to insist on interviewing all likely candidates by asking then to attend a face-to-face session at the university itself. With more students choosing to leave their home country and study abroad, however, the position of interviews as part of the application process has become more complicated. Many universities recognize that it is often unreasonable to expect candidates to fly overseas for an interview in addition to the potentially high tuition fees they will have to pay when accepted, and have stopped requesting an interview.

Some institutions, however, continue to interview applicants because they believe it is the fairest way of selecting the most appropriate students for their programs. Occasionally, this will require you to fly to the university, at your own expense, to undergo one or more interviews as part of your application. In other cases, the institution is willing to travel to you for the purpose of interview, conducted either by admissions or international staff, or often by local alumni who have already graduated from the institution in question.

Depending on the institution, the purpose of the interview is to make a final selection based on the material you have already submitted as part of your application. Interviews can focus on a number of areas, including the subject that you have applied for, your extracurricular interests or the reasons behind wanting to come and study at that particular university. In an interview, an institution tends to be looking for a number of qualities in your answers that indicate that you would be an asset to them. Firstly, they will be looking for a passion for, and knowledge of, your academic subject. Secondly, they will want to see that you have the ability to think independently and critically, and grasp any complex or new issues raised in the discussion. Thirdly, they will want to assess whether you are a good fit for their environment. Finally, they will want to assess your confidence and your all-round abilities.

Preparing for an interview is not always easy and you will be guided by staff at the institution as to what they expect from you. If you are given this opportunity to meet admissions or other staff, be sure of the reasons for your application, your own unique qualities and what you might be able to bring to the university. Make sure that you have fully studied all sources of information such as university websites and talked to any relevant people you can before your interview.

Deadlines

Take application deadlines very seriously. Irrespective of what and where you wish to study, it is essential that you inform yourself of all deadlines that are relevant to your application process. In almost all country systems of education, whether the application process is managed by a central administrative service or direct with the universities, deadlines exist for all or certain categories of students. All institutions publish these deadlines at least one year in advance and make the consequences of missing any of these dates very clear to applicants. Deadlines really are exactly what they indicate: the very last line past which you cannot move. Many institutions around the world will simply not review your application at all if it is received after the published date, which is a terrible situation if all of the other elements of your application are very strong and would normally qualify you for a place.

The timing of your application can have a significant impact on whether you are successful or not. In many of the very popular programs, such as economics, law and management, the earlier you submit a completed application the better your chances of gaining a place are, if you have met the minimum entry requirements. Similarly, in the most popular universities, programs fill up quickly and so applications received early can increase the chances of a positive decision. The process obviously varies from country to country, but, as a general rule, submitting your application early will be beneficial to you.

In some cases, applying to university can take more than a year and the thorough preparation of all of your application materials can take some time. Within the application process, there is never one single area that is more important than any other. Universities regard applications holistically and, as such, your preparation must be thorough and consistent to ensure that all of the elements are your very best efforts and reflect your highest standards.

5

Study costs worldwide: guide for students and parents

The text and tables in this chapter provide an overview of the relative study and living costs of studying around the world and of the fees at the top 200 universities worldwide. There are great variations from country to country, between universities and within individual universities (in this case, averages are used in the tables, so further investigation is recommended in every case). This chapter offers a starting point for a discussion of potential costs applicable to study destinations that future students, as well as their parents, will find useful.

With over 4,000 universities in the world and more than 17 million students, it is little surprise that the availability and participation in higher education differs greatly in countries around the world and so do the relative costs of study and living: you will face tuition and living costs that can vary, quite dramatically, throughout the world. Today, smart students and parents can shop around the world to look for the best value education, to fit within a career strategy. Studying at university is a major investment, one of the most important of your life, and we have seen in earlier chapters the positive impact studying at a top worldwide institution can have on future earnings potential. Having to study hard for several years and accumulate significant debt may seem like a bad bargain, but when you review the career options for today's graduates, it becomes apparent that a good degree is almost priceless. However, for any prospective student and his or her parents, it is important to know and understand the costs associated with educational institutions, as well as their quality, in order to assess budgets, return on investment and make the best choice.

An end to free universities

The world of higher education is undergoing great change. Ron Perkinson of the International Finance Corporation (World Bank) describes the "perfect storm of forces changing the shape of international education: increased importance of knowledge and credentials in the employment market, demographic increases in numbers of young people aged 18-24 around the world, reduced government funding and globalization." These forces are creating many changes, but the overwhelming change is that university education is no longer going to be free for the majority of people, even in their home countries. Most institutions today are either charging, or about to introduce charges for tuition. Private and public universities alike have passed on some of the study costs to their students for many years, but the implementation of full-cost tuition fees is now commonplace throughout Europe, Asia and North and Latin America. A free university education is rapidly becoming a thing of the past, worldwide. As a consequence, many young people are shopping overseas for the best deals; not necessarily the lowest overall cost, but the best price for a given quality. This calculation will vary according to the type of program that is chosen, the country of choice, the length of stay, as well as other factors that can be evaluated with the help of the Times Higher-QS World University Rankings, which provide a guide to institutional quality — and there are other indicators that should also be taken into account.

Average university study costs by country

Study costs do vary considerably throughout the world, which could play a part in your choice of university, but these costs should always be considered alongside the quality of the university and course. The following table provides a quick basis for comparison for prospective students (and their parents) considering study at home or abroad. It shows average tuition costs for domestic and international students for undergraduate and postgraduate programs by country. The data collected from the 500 universities in this book forms the basis of these figures.

University fees in the US are the highest, on average, in the world. By contrast, a number of Scandinavian countries charge no university fees, though this policy is under review and expectations are that most countries will introduce fees in the coming years. There are a number of other European countries where fees remain modest.

The UK and Ireland are more expensive than European counterparts. The level of UK tuition fees for domestic students is dependent upon personal circumstances including family income. Nevertheless, the UK remains a very popular overseas study destination. A Norwegian report, for example, (Norway and Iceland have the highest number of students abroad relative to population) identified that, in 2005, there were 21,484 Norwegian students at foreign universities, with the UK as the top choice with 2,905 studying full-time and an additional 530 returning to the UK for part of their studies, eg exchange programs. According to AimHigher, the UK government-backed website for higher education, 30,000 international students begin undergraduate courses each year in the UK, the vast majority of whom are full fee paying students.

There are many variations in the approach to tuition costs worldwide. Singapore, for example, has a unique arrangement. If a student is accepted for study, he or she will be eligible for a Ministry of Education grant if he or she signs a deed of covenant agreeing to work in Singapore for three years after graduation, reducing considerably the net cost of study.

Average annual university tuition costs by country US$

Country	Domestic undergraduate	Domestic postgraduate	International undergraduate	International postgraduate
Argentina	3,603	4,206	4,203	4,439
Australia	12,133	12,608	16,350	17,034
Austria	845	845	1,011	1,011
Belgium	902	936	1,923	936
Canada	4,284	5,522	12,647	9,984
Chile	4,478	11,660	4,478	11,660
China	2,196	-	3,600	-
Denmark	0	0	15,856	15,856
Finland	0	0	0	0
France	1,899	7,361	2,718	5,035
Germany	1,137	2,714	1,142	1,202
Hong Kong	5,874	9,571	8,965	11,595
Hungary	0	-	-	-
India	1,698	4,579	2,000	2,000
Indonesia	352	1,369	3,094	3,500
Ireland	5,116	6,982	20,287	15,366
Israel	1,653	2,222	5,738	6,331
Italy	2,284	2,872	2,398	3,355
Japan	5,056	5,082	4,967	4,979
Malaysia	399	1,475	1,554	2,395
Netherlands	1,826	2,421	6,430	10,788
New Zealand	3,581	7,046	14,227	16,581
Pakistan	1,945	1,865	6,709	5,300
Poland	-	-	4,940	6,175
Portugal	0	-	-	-
Russia	3,250	-	-	-
Singapore	4,209	-	4,628	-
South Africa	2,793	4,927	18,949	8,745
South Korea	7,288	8,533	6,830	7,412
Spain	2,816	4,302	3,052	4,418
Sweden	0	0	0	0
Switzerland	970	890	900	914
Taiwan	1,411	1,106	2,066	1,174
Thailand	833	1,695	12,842	6,514
Turkey	14,890	-	-	-
United Kingdom	5,407	9,524	21,181	21,264
United States	22,065	18,599	24,375	20,352

Costs are calculated based on the average of the numbers supplied by or for institutions in each country, (exchange rate to US$ as at 27.07.07). An average has only been calculated where a minimum of two separate values are available for that country in that column. The table is marked with a dash (-) where satisfactory information was not available. Any data updates will be published on www.topuniversities.com.

Tuition fees at the world's top 200 universities

In most countries, private universities typically charge higher fees than public universities. The top 200 universities in the Times Higher-QS World University Rankings consist of both private and public institutions, explaining some of the wide variation in fees, even within countries. Not surprisingly, many of the most expensive universities in the world are some of the top ranked US private institutions. Looking at these costs together with the information in the Times Higher-QS World University Rankings table in Chapter 7, the profiles of the top 100 worldwide in Chapter 8 and the subject rankings in Chapter 9, will help put them in perspective relative to the quality of the course and the institution.

Tuition fees can vary for different program types within universities, for example, many professional graduate degrees are more expensive than the averages quoted; equally, other courses are less expensive. The table is intended to give outline guidance. Further research in relation to specific programs at particular institutions should always be carried out at an early stage. Decisions to study should always involve direct confirmation from the university of choice of the exact tuition fees you will be liable to pay for the program you will study.

The tuition fees in the table have been compiled (exchange rate to US$ as at 27.07.07) using many sources including published information, websites and telephone interviews. Where no clear information was available, the following table is marked with a dash (-). Any data updates will be published on www.topuniversities.com.

Times Higher-QS top 200 universities annual tuition fees US$

Rank	Institution	Country	Domestic undergraduate	Domestic postgraduate	International undergraduate	International postgraduate
1	HARVARD University	United States	30,275	32,518	-	-
2=	University of CAMBRIDGE	United Kingdom	6,294	10,949	21,806	21,995
2=	University of OXFORD	United Kingdom	6,294	6,400	21,078	22,155
2=	YALE University	United States	33,030	26,800	-	-
5	Imperial College LONDON	United Kingdom	6,294	7,388	34,357	31,608
6	PRINCETON University	United States	33,000	29,910	-	-
7=	CALIFORNIA Institute of Technology (Caltech)	United States	29,940	25,355	-	-
7=	University of CHICAGO	United States	33,336	31,680	-	-
9	UCL (University College LONDON)	United Kingdom	6,294	6,643	26,890	24,911
10	MASSACHUSETTS Institute of Technology (MIT)	United States	33,600	33,600	33,600	33,600
11	COLUMBIA University	United States	35,166	30,532	-	-
12	MCGILL University	Canada	3,296	2,491	13,751	6,513
13	DUKE University	United States	34,335	33,990	34,335	33,990
14	University of PENNSYLVANIA	United States	35,916	29,386	-	-
15	JOHNS HOPKINS University	United States	35,900	30,140	-	-
16	AUSTRALIAN National University	Australia	4,611	14,289	16,935	19,581
17	University of TOKYO	Japan	4,332	4,443	4,321	4,443
18	University of HONG KONG	Hong Kong	7,803	21,735	10,225	24,157
19	STANFORD University	United States	31,200	31,200	31,200	31,200
20=	CARNEGIE MELLON University	United States	36,950	28,200	-	-
20=	CORNELL University	United States	34,231	30,000	-	-
22	University of California, BERKELEY	United States	6,730	7,457	23,828	22,396
23	University of EDINBURGH	United Kingdom	3,557	8,919	23,476	20,503
24	King's College LONDON	United Kingdom	6,294	11,244	25,400	24,174
25	KYOTO University	Japan	4,375	4,375	4,375	4,375

Rank	Institution	Country	Domestic undergraduate	Domestic postgraduate	International undergraduate	International postgraduate
26	Ecole Normale Supérieure, PARIS	France	-	-	-	-
27	University of MELBOURNE	Australia	18,020	21,565	21,698	21,169
28	ÉCOLE POLYTECHNIQUE	France	-	15,094	9,605	15,094
29	NORTHWESTERN University	United States	33,408	29,940	-	-
30	University of MANCHESTER	United Kingdom	6,294	-	-	-
31	The University of SYDNEY	Australia	16,080	11,986	17,708	18,055
32	BROWN University	United States	35,584	30,672	-	-
33=	University of BRITISH COLUMBIA	Canada	3,994	10,459	16,538	12,056
33=	University of QUEENSLAND	Australia	18,211	15,284	22,120	22,626
33=	National University of SINGAPORE	Singapore	4,397	3,042	4,834	4,166
36	PEKING University	China	3,706	-	-	-
37	University of BRISTOL	United Kingdom	6,294	-	-	-
38=	The CHINESE University of Hong Kong	Hong Kong	5,381	5,381	10,225	5,381
38=	University of MICHIGAN	United States	16,000	-	-	-
40	TSINGHUA University	China	686	-	3,842	-
41	University of CALIFORNIA, Los Angeles (UCLA)	United States	19,068	14,694	27,066	-
42	ETH Zurich (Swiss Federal Institute of Technology)	Switzerland	1,070	1,070	1,070	1,070
43	MONASH University	Australia	18,002	15,547	21,536	21,627
44	University of NEW SOUTH WALES	Australia	15,384	16,120	15,384	19,280
45	University of TORONTO	Canada	875	1,698	3,360	3,209
46	OSAKA University	Japan	4,465	5,582	4,465	5,582
47	BOSTON University	United States	34,930	29,988	-	-
48	University of AMSTERDAM	Netherlands	2,110	-	12,350	-
49	NEW YORK University (NYU)	United States	35,283	23,304	-	-
50	The University of AUCKLAND	New Zealand	3,759	11,008	14,500	18,905

51=	SEOUL National University	Korea, South	5,761	7,130	5,761	7,130
51=	University of TEXAS at Austin	United States	4,173	11,952	13,352	-
53=	HONG KONG University of Science & Technology	Hong Kong	5,385	9,937	8,974	9,937
53=	TRINITY College Dublin	Ireland	6,963	6,020	13,928	10,757
55=	University of WASHINGTON	United States	5,985	8,818	21,283	20,641
55=	University of WISCONSIN-Madison	United States	6,730	9,184	20,730	24,454
57	University of WARWICK	United Kingdom	2,409	29,879	29,366	33,979
58	University of CALIFORNIA, San Diego	United States	7,446	-	27,066	-
59	LONDON School of Economics and Political Science	United Kingdom	6,294	-	-	-
60	HEIDELBERG University	Germany	1,372	-	1,372	-
61	Katholieke Universiteit LEUVEN	Belgium	732	-	6,861	-
62	University of ADELAIDE	Australia	5,151	4,763	16,847	16,935
63	DELFT University of Technology	Netherlands	2,112	3,480	2,367	8,095
64	University of WESTERN AUSTRALIA	Australia	12,200	9,350	15,300	16,150
65=	University of BIRMINGHAM	United Kingdom	6,294	-	-	-
65=	Ludwig-Maximilians-Universität München (MUNICH)	Germany	-	-	-	-
67	Technische Universität MÜNCHEN	Germany	1,372	1,372	1,372	1,372
68	University of SHEFFIELD	United Kingdom	6,294	-	-	-
69	NANYANG Technological University	Singapore	4,020	-	4,421	-
70	University of NOTTINGHAM	United Kingdom	6,150	7,575	17,382	17,884
71=	DARTMOUTH College	United States	33,501	33,342	33,501	33,342
71=	UPPSALA University	Sweden	0	0	0	0
73	University of ILLINOIS	United States	13,140	15,362	31,950	-
74=	EMORY University	United States	32,100	27,770	-	-
74=	University of YORK	United Kingdom	6,294	6,642	18,758	18,758

Rank	Institution	Country	Domestic undergraduate	Domestic postgraduate	International undergraduate	International postgraduate
76	University of ST ANDREWS	United Kingdom	3,557	-	-	-
77=	University of PITTSBURGH	United States	24,000	-	-	-
77=	PURDUE University	United States	6,092	6,092	18,700	18,700
79	University of MARYLAND	United States	7,906	-	21,345	-
80=	University of LEEDS	United Kingdom	6,294	6,642	19,867	18,680
80=	University of SOUTHAMPTON	United Kingdom	6,294	-	-	-
82	VANDERBILT University	United States	1,359	1,359	1,359	1,359
83	University of GLASGOW	United Kingdom	3,557	-	-	-
84	LEIDEN University	Netherlands	2,058	2,058	2,058	15,094
85=	CASE WESTERN RESERVE University	United States	32,800	25,400	-	-
85=	FUDAN University	China	-	-	3,358	3,838
85=	University of VIENNA	Austria	498	498	498	498
88	QUEEN'S University	Canada	4,182	6,033	14,152	10,143
89	UTRECHT University	Netherlands	2,058	2,058	6,404	9,148
90=	PENNSYLVANIA STATE University	United States	23,152	16,654	-	-
90=	TOKYO Institute of Technology	Japan	4,465	4,465	4,465	4,465
92	RICE University	United States	28,400	25,600	-	-
93=	University of COPENHAGEN	Denmark	0	0	14,686	14,686
93=	University of MONTREAL	Canada	1,668	2,502	11,628	14,067
95	University of ROCHESTER	United States	31,297	31,297	31,297	31,297
96	University of CALIFORNIA, Davis	United States	7,446	14,694	27,066	-
97=	University of ALBERTA	Canada	4,484	3,156	15,566	6,592
97=	GEORGIA Institute of Technology	United States	5,642	6,444	23,366	23,334
99	CARDIFF University	United Kingdom	6,294	-	-	-
100	University of HELSINKI	Finland	0	0	0	0
101	University of LIVERPOOL	United Kingdom	6,150	19,475	24,600	24,600

102=	GEORGETOWN University	United States	35,568	27,528	-	-
102=	National TAIWAN University	Taiwan	872	887	872	887
102=	TOHOKU University	Japan	4,316	4,242	1,745	1,331
105	University of GENEVA	Switzerland	813	878	813	878
106	LUND University	Sweden	0	0	0	0
107	University of COLORADO	United States	24,797	20,592	27,000	-
108	MCMASTER University	Canada	5,368	4,968	14,597	12,525
109	DURHAM University	United Kingdom	6,294	-	17,286	19,977
110	University of VIRGINIA	United States	38,235	18,672	-	-
111	MAASTRICHT University	Netherlands	2,084	2,084	10,978	15,780
112=	NAGOYA University	Japan	4,465	4,465	4,465	4,465
112=	University of WATERLOO	Canada	4,400	5,700	16,100	14,400
114=	University of AARHUS	Denmark	-	16,741	16,741	16,741
114=	University of BASEL	Switzerland	583	583	583	583
114=	University of OTAGO	New Zealand	3,861	10,400	14,412	16,071
117=	University of CALIFORNIA, Santa Barbara	United States	7,277	7,501	25,961	22,462
117=	Ecole Polytechnique Fédérale de LAUSANNE	Switzerland	1,050	660	1,050	660
119	University of SOUTHERN CALIFORNIA	United States	16,657	24,240	-	-
120	OHIO STATE University	United States	8,406	9,177	20,301	22,530
121	University of SUSSEX	United Kingdom	6,294	-	-	-
122	TEXAS A&M University	United States	6,966	6,969	15,400	13,753
123	Université Catholique de LOUVAIN (UCL)	Belgium	1,068	1,068	1,068	1,068
124	University of GHENT	Belgium	-	-	-	-
125	NANJING University	China	-	-	-	-
126=	HUMBOLDT-Universität zu Berlin	Germany	-	-	-	-
126=	University of WESTERN ONTARIO	Canada	4,809	5,575	14,815	2,501
128	Hebrew University of JERUSALEM	Israel	201	514	10,000	9,100

Rank	Institution	Country	Domestic undergraduate	Domestic postgraduate	International undergraduate	International postgraduate
129	NEWCASTLE University, NEWCASTLE Upon Tyne	United Kingdom	6,150	7,175	21,269	21,269
130=	Technical University of DENMARK	Denmark	-	-	18,000	18,000
130=	EINDHOVEN University of Technology	Netherlands	-	-	-	-
132=	KOREA Advanced Institute of Science & Technology	Korea, South	16,340	18,519	16,340	18,519
132=	Université Pierre-et-Marie-Curie - PARIS VI	France	494	778	494	778
134	University of ARIZONA	United States	-	13,228	-	-
135	University of FLORIDA	United States	3,370	7,478	17,150	22,603
136	KYUSHU University	Japan	4,375	4,411	4,375	4,411
137=	University of ABERDEEN	United Kingdom	3,557	6,642	28,358	26,906
137=	INDIANA University Bloomington	United States	7,837	10,334	22,316	15,465
139	SIMON FRASER University	Canada	4,337	13,368	13,888	13,368
140=	University of CALIFORNIA, Irvine	United States	7,446	14,694	27,066	-
140=	University of ZURICH	Switzerland	1,146	981	1,312	1,147
142=	University of MINNESOTA	United States	-	-	-	-
142=	Universität TÜBINGEN	Germany	1,372	-	1,372	1,372
144	Universität FREIBURG	Germany	686	686	686	686
145	University of BATH	United Kingdom	6,294	-	-	-
146	Freie Universität BERLIN	Germany	-	-	-	-
147	University of LANCASTER	United Kingdom	6,294	6,888	21,115	19,834
148	WAGENINGEN University	Netherlands	-	-	-	-
149=	CITY University of Hong Kong	Hong Kong	5,400	5,400	7,700	10,800
149=	Queen Mary, University of LONDON	United Kingdom	6,294	-	-	-
151=	HOKKAIDO University	Japan	4,465	4,465	4,465	4,465
151=	University of NORTH CAROLINA	United States	-	-	-	-

151=	TEL AVIV University	Israel	2,210	2,772	7,550	9,200
154	Université Libre de BRUXELLES (ULB)	Belgium	1,081	1,081	1,081	1,081
155=	University of Science and Technology of China	China	-	3,800	-	-
155=	University of NOTRE DAME	United States	29,070	28,970	29,070	28,970
157	Ecole Normale Supérieure de LYON	France	222	343	222	343
158	CRANFIELD University	United Kingdom	-	-	-	-
159=	MICHIGAN STATE University	United States	6,540	7,296	17,336	15,168
159=	TUFTS University	United States	35,900	33,672	35,900	33,672
161=	KEIO University	Japan	8,726	6,499	8,726	6,499
161=	WASHINGTON University in St. Louis	United States	35,524	-	35,524	-
163=	ERASMUS University Rotterdam	Netherlands	2,058	2,058	7,547	15,094
163=	SHANGHAI JIAO TONG University	China	-	-	-	-
165	Universität STUTTGART	Germany	-	-	-	-
166=	University of CALGARY	Canada	5,210	5,408	15,630	10,816
166=	VIENNA University of Technology	Austria	998	998	998	998
168=	Universität GÖTTINGEN	Germany	1,372	1,372	1,372	1,372
168=	MACQUARIE University	Australia	13,669	17,199	16,035	18,541
170	HELSINKI University of Technology - TKK	Finland	0	0	0	0
171=	University of DUNDEE	United Kingdom	3,557	3,235	17,425	17,425
171=	Universität KARLSRUHE	Germany	1,372	1,372	1,372	1,372
173=	University of BOLOGNA	Italy	1,939	1,015	1,939	1,015
173=	University of GRONINGEN	Netherlands	2,127	3,094	3,819	9,804
175=	University of MASSACHUSETTS, Amherst	United States	9,921	8,455	20,499	12,967
175=	University of SAO PAULO	Brazil	-	-	-	-
177=	University of CAMPINAS (Unicamp)	Brazil	-	-	-	-
177=	University College DUBLIN	Ireland	0	6,106	24,700	12,213
177=	RUTGERS, The State University of New Jersey	United States	19,783	-	-	-
180=	University of READING	United Kingdom	6,294	-	-	-

Rank	Institution	Country	Domestic undergraduate	Domestic postgraduate	International undergraduate	International postgraduate
180=	WASEDA University	Japan	9,000	9,500	9,000	9,500
182	Rheinisch-Westfälische Technische Hochschule AACHEN	Germany	1,784	1,784	1,784	1,784
183	Università degli Studi di ROMA - La Sapienza	Italy	988	-	988	-
184	Université Louis Pasteur - STRASBOURG I	France	243	486	243	486
185=	University of LEICESTER	United Kingdom	6,304	-	19,475	18,450
185=	University of TWENTE	Netherlands	2,111	2,111	2,744	3,431
187	University of ANTWERP	Belgium	731	731	731	731
188=	University of CANTERBURY	New Zealand	3,238	3,369	12,943	-
188=	University of OSLO	Norway	-	-	-	-
190	University of SURREY	United Kingdom	6,294	-	-	-
191	RENSSELAER Polytechnic Institute	United States	35,878	36,702	35,878	36,702
192=	KTH, ROYAL Institute of Technology	Sweden	0	0	0	0
192=	Universidad Nacional Autónoma de México (UNAM)	Mexico	-	65	450	1,000
194	University of BARCELONA	Spain	1,029	2,882	1,029	2,882
195=	Radboud Universiteit NIJMEGEN	Netherlands	-	-	-	-
195=	QUEENSLAND University of Technology	Australia	10,584	12,348	14,112	15,876
197=	CHALMERS University of Technology	Sweden	0	0	0	0
197=	KOBE University	Japan	4,465	4,465	4,465	4,465
199	University of WOLLONGONG	Australia	5,167	16,700	15,434	18,057
200=	University of CAPE TOWN	South Africa	1,586	6,432	6,847	2,136
200=	RMIT University	Australia	13,068	11,256	16,218	17,158

Living costs

In addition to tuition fees, you will need to take into consideration a variety of costs when budgeting and deciding on where to study. The living costs of moving abroad, or even moving out of the family home to study at a domestic university, will form a large part of your expenditure. You will often find, especially with US institutions, that these variables are grouped into a single figure, so, it is very important that students or parents research what costs are included in quoted figures and what additional costs will be incurred. Costs include essentials such as accommodation, food, travel and study books. Don't forget that you will also need a budget for extracurricular activity and travel, especially if you are studying overseas. It is also important to remember that exchange rates will fluctuate and therefore affect your budget.

So how can you find out about these costs of living? Where is the most expensive place to study? And where can you afford? There are numerous public sources and publications providing you with tables of the costs of living throughout the world. These tend to have slightly varied results, as differing criteria are used for each, but they generally present a similar 'big picture', so browsing any of the widely published ones will give you a good idea of the expenses you may face.

According to research by the Economist Intelligence Unit (EIU), in February 2007, Oslo maintains its place as the world's most expensive city, with both Paris and Copenhagen climbing the table. The EIU ranks the world's ten most expensive cities as follows (2006 position in brackets): 1 (1) Oslo, 2 (4) Paris, 3(6) Copenhagen, 4(7) London, 5(2) Tokyo, 6=(3) Reykjavik, 6=(8) Zurich, 8 (4) Osaka, 9=(-) Frankfurt, 9=(10) Helsinki. This follows the trend of eight of the most expensive locations being in Europe, whilst the USA has significantly dropped, with the highest city New York in 28th place. Websites such as www.citymayors.com provide this and much other data on living in cities worldwide.

This kind of information can act as a guide to the cost of study abroad, but actual costs will also be dependent upon your lifestyle and ability to budget. You are, however, not just comparing like for like goods, as different cultures will encourage you to spend in different ways, and student environments usually have lower cost accommodation, restaurants, sports facilities and entertainment, than the city as a whole. In many cities, students are also eligible for large concessions on transport and other items. Reading online blogs and real-life accounts can give a more real picture of the costs you may face. Some of the profiles of the top 100 universities in Chapter 8 give information on the cost of living for a student on particular campuses.

Salaries are likely to be commensurate with the costs, so a part-time job could be a solution to supporting your time at university and a more comfortable lifestyle and working part-time is becoming more of an accepted international trend for students. A survey in 2006 by the Royal Bank of Scotland, published by the BBC, shows that students in the UK work an average of 16 hours a week (with 20% doing more than 20 hours), and almost half of the UK's students take on part-time work in term-time, in a £2.3bn a year industry.

Foreign currency influences

Another good way to compare living costs, taking into account currency fluctuations, is the annual Big Mac Index, published by The Economist. This, in effect, measures the purchasing power parity (PPP) between currencies and the US$ and provides a basis for showing how market exchange rates affect a similar basket of goods (eg Big Mac hamburger) in different countries. As a general rule, the cost of living is higher where the US dollar is weak relative to the local currency and vice versa. In most of Asia living costs are low in dollar terms, with currencies being undervalued against the dollar from minus 0.86 per cent in South Korea to minus 53.92 per cent in China, according to the 2007 index. Central Europe also has low living costs in dollar terms, with Poland undervalued at minus 13.84 per cent and Russia at minus 37.88 per cent. Latin America shows quite a substantial variation in its rating of countries compared to other regions, with Argentina undervalued by minus 19.71 per cent and Brazil overvalued at 13.39 per cent. At the other end of the spectrum, the UK has a high cost of living in dollar terms being overvalued by 29.01 per cent, and the Euro area is even more expensive, being overvalued by 33.4 per cent. Heading the list, Switzerland at 74.56 per cent is the most costly region in which to live according to this method of calculation, with Sweden, next, overvalued by 57.1 per cent. Websites such as www.oanda.com are sources of such information and other tools for understanding the important consideration of foreign currency fluctuations in calculating costs in other countries.

Understanding the bigger picture

Broadly speaking, study in developed countries will be more costly than in developing countries. However, the reputation of universities tends to far outweigh tuition and living costs, as a factor when people make their study choices. Few students choose to move from developed countries to study in developing countries. By contrast, huge numbers of students from developing countries choose to study abroad. In spite of the higher study and living costs they realize the importance of the comparatively higher quality of education away from their homeland and the high recognition their qualification will carry for their future career. Indeed, the OECD publication Education at a Glance 2007, reports that tertiary students from sub-Saharan Africa are the most mobile in the world, while less than one per cent of US students studies overseas, making this group one of the least mobile in the world.

Costs will vary according to your destination country, the type and length of your program, what is included in the program cost, and costs that may include your passport, visa, airfare, medical costs, transportation, meals, books, insurance and accommodation, to name but a few. However, if you are planning to study abroad, do not let these facts scare you off. You would encounter many of these costs at home, and those extra ones involved will generally be worth the outlay, especially with the level of financial aid available for international students and the fact that you will, more than likely, be well remunerated upon employment (see Chapter 3). The true cost of your study will be dependent upon a multitude

6

Financing and scholarships

This chapter looks at options for funding study at home and abroad and surveys some available options for scholarships, loans and financial aid in several of the most popular study destinations worldwide.

How do people pay for their studies?

How to fund study at university is an issue that faces prospective students worldwide. With fees for international students often being higher than those for domestic students, organizing adequate funding is particularly important when considering study abroad. Parents often prepare to fund the first degree of many 18 year olds. QS recently surveyed 4,000 applicants to university graduate schools around the world and for those with no work experience, parents and scholarships were the most frequently cited sources of funding. However, a rapidly growing proportion of graduate students around the world return to university after a period of work experience. These students are willing to use their personal savings and loans from global financial institutions to fund their study abroad. In fact, worldwide, 70 per cent of respondents in the QS survey reported that they would use personal savings or loans to fund their studies.

International funding organizations

The Rotary Foundation is one of the largest scholarship providers in the world. Since 1947 nearly 38,000 men and women from 100 nations have studied abroad with Ambassadorial Scholarships. Today, it is the world's largest privately funded international scholarship program. Nearly 800 scholarships for undergraduate and graduate students, as well as for qualified professionals pursuing vocational studies, were awarded for study in more than 70 nations in 2005-06, totalling approximately US$500 million. While abroad, scholars serve as ambassadors of goodwill to the people of the host country and give presentations about their homelands to Rotary clubs and other groups. Upon returning home, scholars share with Rotarians and others the experiences that led to greater understanding of their host countries. www.rotary.org/foundation/educational/amb_scho/. The Ford Foundation provides an International Fellowship Program for PhD students and other potential leaders, targeting individuals in countries without systematic access to higher education www.fordfound.org/grants/fellowships/individuals.

The Bill & Melinda Gates Foundation, funds educational scholarships through various programs and partnerships with specific universities. In the US, the Foundation awards a variety of scholarships to promising students who don't have the financial means to attend college www.gatesfoundation.org/UnitedStates/Education/Scholarships/. On an international level, the Gates Cambridge Trust established in 2000 is an extensive international scholarship program to enable outstanding graduate students from anywhere (outside the UK) to study at the University of Cambridge. The Trustees are required to award scholarships on the basis of a person's intellectual ability, leadership capacity and desire to use their knowledge to contribute to society throughout the world by providing service to their communities and applying their talents and knowledge to improve the lives of others. The Trust seeks to elect approximately 100 new scholars annually www.gates.scholarships.cam.ac.uk/.

University scholarships for overseas students

Many of the universities featured in this book offer scholarships or other forms of financial aid to international students. These awards are based on various criteria and administered by each of the individual universities. Some scholarships are intended to reward academic merit, others are for different subject concentrations or some are specifically for students from particular countries. Information on scholarships is available from university websites and admissions offices and is also generally made available to students who gain a place to study there. Competition for all such financial awards is always tough.

Student loans

Commercial banks are geared towards providing student loans for domestic study in most countries of the world, but they can be more wary about funding overseas study. There is a risk that candidates will not return home and it will prove difficult to collect the outstanding loan. A bank may ask for some form of parental guarantee, before providing a student loan, but this, at least, avoids the need for parents to have the cash ready and available from day one.

In the US, www.fedmoney.org is the most comprehensive, free, online resource giving details of all US government grants and student financial aid programs. Federal Direct Student Loans and Federal Family Student Loans are available for people seeking to study within the US. SallieMae offers loan facilities for people to study abroad and at home, for undergraduate and graduate studies. www.salliemae.com In addition there are private loan providers who will underwrite high potential candidates who meet selection criteria (usually based on acceptance by a top tier institution).

In Europe most of the major banks provide student loans, but will require some form of guarantees for study abroad. The UK is probably the most mature market in this respect. By contrast, in Germany banks are still getting used to the idea of student loans and are only just beginning to offer these types of products.

Scholarships for study in the US

An attraction for international students is the large number of scholarships and financial aid packages available at the many universities in the US. Despite this large availability of scholarships, competition is fierce.

The World Bank estimates that 70 per cent of foreign students in the US pay full fees. The US also offers the most sophisticated financial support, including discounted rates for delayed payment and other solutions to meet the needs of people with lesser financial means. Many US universities'financial aid departments ask for a statement of your family's financial situation. If they decide that your family can only contribute US$1,000 per year, that is all you will have to pay; if they want you to study with them.

There are, however, many charitable bodies that can provide partial scholarships. The most prominent provider of scholarships for study in the US is the Fulbright Commission, which supports educational exchanges at the graduate level that strengthen understanding and communication between the US and over 140 countries worldwide. The work of the program is developed and facilitated by the US Department of State and binational Fulbright Commissions and US embassies overseas. Selection is carried out in the student's home country with applications via the local Fulbright office. Information on this scholarship program is provided on a country-by-country basis and an internet search will reveal the Fulbright organization nearest to you.

There are also a large number of corporate sponsored scholarship schemes for study in the US. For example, the Adobe Multi-National Scholarship Program, funded by Adobe Systems, provides scholarship awards to meritorious secondary school students attending a post-secondary degree program in business, design studies, education, engineering, graphic art, graphic design, mathematics or science and who need financial assistance to achieve their educational goals www.iiesf.org/new/programs/corporate.htm. USAID provides scholarships for women in technology, sponsored by CISCO www.iie.org/wcoast/wit.html.

Scholarships for study in the UK

The British Council provides a comprehensive website of scholarships available on a university-by-university basis in the UK www.educationuk.org. Oxford University offers Rhodes Scholarships, and the Bill & Melinda Gates Foundation funds numerous scholarships at Cambridge.

In addition there are the Chevening Scholarships that are available for outstanding graduate applicants to British institutions. These scholarships, funded by the British Foreign and Commonwealth Office, enable overseas students to study in the UK. Scholarships are offered in over 150 countries and enable talented graduates and young professionals to become familiar with the UK and gain skills that will benefit their countries. The Chevening program currently provides around 2,500 new scholarships each year for postgraduate studies or research at UK institutions www.chevening.com.

Marshall Scholarships finance young Americans of high ability to study for a degree in the UK. At least 40 scholars are selected each year to study either at graduate, or occasionally undergraduate, level at an UK institution in any field of study. Each scholarship is held for two years www.marshallscholarship.org.

The Association of Commonwealth Universities www.acu.ac.uk administers the Commonwealth Scholarship and Fellowship Plan and a number of other awards. The Plan was designed as a system of awards to men and women from all Commonwealth countries chosen for their high intellectual promise and their capacity to return to make a significant contribution to life in their own countries. Other scholarships include the Commonwealth Shared Scholarship Scheme and a limited number of smaller awards for study abroad and exchange students.

Scholarships for study in the EU

There are three main sources of scholarship funding within the European Union (EU); national associations geared towards encouraging study in each home country, individual universities and the EU itself.

National bodies such as DAAD in Germany, CampusFrance, Nuffic in the Netherlands and other national organizations around Europe all offer some scholarship funding. The DAAD concerns itself primarily with funding living costs for overseas students or international mobility programs for German students. It offers a comprehensive database of its scholarships available for study in Germany www.daad.de/deutschland/foerderung/stipendiendatenbank/00462.en.html. One very large individual university scholarship scheme is offered in Italy by Politecnico di Milano for candidates entering their graduate programs in design, architecture and management.

The French government makes approximately 22,000 grant awards each year to foreign students. There are scholarships offered under bilateral assistance programs between French and overseas governments, accounting for about 80 per cent of the 22,000 grants. Information can be obtained from French embassies in each country www.diplomatie.gouv.fr/en/. The French Ministry of Foreign Affairs also provides grants for specific programs, run from its head office in Paris.

The EU is also a major provider of scholarships for study within EU member states. The program Alßan aims at the reinforcement of EU/Latin American co-operation in the area of Higher Education and covers studies for postgraduates as well as higher training for Latin American professionals and future decision-makers, in institutions or centres in the EU www.programalban.org.

The EU also offers programs such as Erasmus and EuropeAid, which include scholarship funding at various levels for educational institutions and individuals. The websites are not particularly user friendly and, in the best EU tradition, change frequently, so it is best to use search engines to search for up to date information.

Scholarships for study in Australia

According to IDP Education Australia, the official representative body supporting the recruitment of international students to Australia, most international students in Australia are full-fee paying students who are not covered by any form of scholarship or financial aid. The number of scholarships available for international students is limited and the competition is intense. IDP manages a range of scholarships for the Australian Government, foreign governments and private organisations, the focus of which varies from subject-to-subject.

The Commonwealth Learning Scholarships Program was introduced in 2004 to assist students from poor backgrounds, particularly those from regional and remote areas and indigenous students, who are Australian citizens or holders of permanent humanitarian visas. Both are awarded on a competitive basis, are non-repayable and target students from low socio-economic status backgrounds. Over a five-year period, 2005 to 2009, the AU$406 million that the Government will provide will help approximately 43,000 students meet the costs associated with participating in higher education www.dest.gov.au. There are also AusAID scholarships for students from partner countries, deemed to require financial support. These countries include, but are not limited to, Pacific-Rim and African nations.

Scholarships for study in Asia

The Ministry of Education in Singapore has one of the most extensive scholarship programs in Asia. The ASEAN Scholarships aim to provide the young people of the region with opportunities to develop their potential and train them in the skills that will enable them to step confidently through the new millennium www.moe.gov.sg/aseanscholarships/.

Malaysia also offers a wide range of education scholarships for postgraduate and undergraduate study www.malaysia-scholarship.com.

South Korea is making a concerted effort to attract more foreign students. In part, this is through cooperative arrangements with overseas universities. Scholarships and grants are available through KOICA (Korea international Cooperation Agency) www.koica.go.kr. Additional information can also be found from KAFSA (Korean Association of Foreign Student Administrators www.kafsa.or.kr.

Japan has one of the largest communities of foreign students in Asia. Some 65,000 students from approximately 160 countries and regions around the world have studied in Japan under the Japanese government Monbukagakusho scholarship program, established in 1954 with nearly 10,000 foreign students a year studying in Japan as Japanese government scholarship students www.studyjapan.go.jp/en/toj/toj0302e.html.

Other Asian countries are following. China and Thailand are embarking on major expansion plans to attract overseas students and will be making funds available for scholarships to attract the best and most talented international students to their systems of education.

7

Top 200 universities in the world

This chapter begins with a look at the growing phenomenon of cross-border university rankings and their use. Following the table of the top 200 universities worldwide in 2007 from the Times Higher-QS World University Rankings, the methodology and sources used for the rankings are explained and discussed in detail and pointers given for your own further research.

Whatever the nature of their search, students and research managers want to be sure that their chosen university is truly world class. And those institutions with international ambitions need to be able to demonstrate their quality in the round. Until recently, however, there had been no way to compare universities internationally. League tables have now become commonplace in virtually every substantial higher education system, but they have been constrained by national boundaries.

The World University Rankings, produced by Times Higher Education (THE) and QS, represents an attempt to fill this gap. Published in 2007 for the fourth time (and for the second time in this book form), it has aroused huge interest and no little controversy. Millions of people have viewed the rankings online, www.timeshighereducation.co.uk and www.topuniversities.com and debate within the academic community has been incessant. A UNESCO experts' group spent more than a year poring over the methodology and there have been several international conferences devoted entirely to the ranking process.

What has become clear is that the need for international comparisons is growing all the time. The travelling scholar dates back to the Middle Ages, but never before have such numbers been crossing national boundaries. There were great leaps forward in student mobility in the late 1970s, when numbers rose by 30 per cent, and at the beginning of the 1990s, when the increase was even larger. But they were as nothing compared with the almost 50 per cent growth that has taken place since the 2000. UNESCO now estimates total student numbers worldwide to be beyond 132 million, almost three million of whom are studying abroad.

More than half of this travelling band go to four countries: France, Germany, the UK and the US (which takes by far the largest share, despite fluctuations in recent years.) Australia, Canada and Japan are the other three big student destinations, although countries such as China have set their sights on joining this group. The Times Higher-QS World University Rankings illustrates vividly why this is the case since these are the countries (with some honorable additions) that dominate the leading positions. US universities have consistently occupied more than a third of the top 100 places, but this is less than many critics predicted. Famous American names, led in all three years by Harvard University, take a majority of places in the top 20, but their grip is soon loosened. European universities are neck and neck with the US contingent in the top 100, led by UK institutions, and Australasia is not far behind.

Widespread excellence

In fact, the rankings have shown that excellence in higher education is distributed more widely than many in the West have presumed. The high standing of Australian universities in Asia, for example, has helped propel six of them into the top 50, while no fewer than 20 different countries are represented in the top 100. Several nations have only one such institution, but it has become a matter of economic and cultural importance, as well as national pride, to compete at this level. In Germany, for instance, which has 11 universities in the top 200 but none in the top 50, the government has set about identifying a group of elite research institutions which will benefit from considerable extra investment.

The 2006 edition of the Organisation for Economic Cooperation and Development's (OECD) annual Education at a Glance report focused particularly on international student mobility as one of the defining characteristics of 21st century activity. It recorded an eight per cent increase in traffic in 12 months and expressed concern that some countries might be both overexposed to the international market and nearing their effective capacity in some academic areas. More than a third of postgraduates at UK universities were from overseas, for example, while foreign students accounted for 39 per cent of masters' places in Australia and 41 per cent of PhDs in Switzerland.

Such figures illustrate not only the scale of international demand for higher education, but also the need for prospective applicants to do their homework on likely destinations. Large concentrations of foreign students, especially representing a single nationality, can dilute the experience of working and living in another country.

The OECD's statistics underline the dominance of English language tuition and the ability of universities in developed countries to both attract and cater for more foreign students than their counterparts elsewhere. There is no sign yet of any slowing of the trend to internationalization, but it is easy to imagine students' choices narrowing for reasons of cost or the availability of places. Rankings should never be the sole source of information behind the choice of university, but they can be an invaluable starting point.

Global trends

Global rankings of universities are less than five years old and are used by students, employers, research funders and the universities themselves. Although still controversial, rankings such as the Times Higher-QS World University Rankings in this book have been now recognized by bodies such as the International

Association of Universities (IAU) as a permanent fixture on the international academic scene. An editorial in the IAU's journal said: "The strength of the market seems unavoidable and rankings are its most resonant indicator at the moment."

Recently, the debate has intensified on how rankings should be compiled. Discussions have taken place on every continent and numerous research papers have been published on the subject. But few people deny that there is a need for international comparisons of some sort.

The world's leading universities are no longer content to be recognized as pre-eminent in their own country. Higher education has become such a global enterprise that the best institutions are often more interested in comparing themselves with rivals thousands of miles away. In the UK, Manchester University, for example, set itself the target of breaking into the top 25 in the world; Bristol University wanted to be in the top 50 and achieved that.

It is easy to see why this should be. Companies and governments mount global searches before placing valuable research contracts, top academics frequently move continents to further their careers and students, too, are increasingly mobile, particularly at postgraduate level. For some students, a move abroad may be the only way to find top quality tuition and academic facilities in their particular subject; for others, to experience a different culture and a new way of thinking is valuable enough in itself.

The world class university

As might be expected, given the nature of the project, there is still no consensus. Some, such as Philip Altbach, Director of the Center for International Higher Education, at Boston College, continue to insist that a world ranking of universities cannot be done. "Everyone wants a world class university. No country feels it can do without one," he wrote when the 2005 rankings were published. "The problem is that no one knows what a world class university is, and no one has figured out how to get one."

In all probability, there never will be agreement on a single method of comparing universities worldwide. But there has been widespread support for the objectives set in compiling the Times Higher-QS World University Rankings: to produce an up-to-date view of the strengths of the leading institutions as they impact on research and teaching and giving credit for an international outlook. They reflect the qualities seen in almost all of the universities recognized informally as international powerhouses; institutions rooted in research, but also, justly proud of their teaching prowess.

Richard Levin, president of Yale University, listed in the magazine Newsweek the same priorities in his account of what makes a global university: "In response to the same forces that have propelled the world economy, universities have become more self-consciously global: seeking students from around the world who represent the entire spectrum of cultures and values, sending their own students abroad to prepare them for global careers, offering courses of study that address the challenges of an interconnected world and collaborative research programs to advance science for the benefit of all humanity. Of the forces shaping higher education, none is more sweeping than the movement across borders," he wrote.

However, there are many other types of university, equally valuable and fit for purpose, that do not aspire to international status. They may serve their local communities, usually with an emphasis on teaching, rather than research, or they may be determinedly national institutions with an eye to knowledge transfer. The universities in the Times Higher-QS World University Rankings (and other similar rankings) tend to judge themselves internationally on the power of their research, often as members of the growing number of global higher education networks, and they recruit both students and staff from many parts of the world.

Times Higher-QS World University Rankings

The table of the top 200 universities worldwide, according to the 2007 Times Higher-QS World University Rankings, begins on the following page. A discussion of the methodology behind these rankings begins on page 85 after the table.

The world's top 200 universities

2007 rank	2006 rank	Name	Country	Peer review score	Recruiter review score	Faculty student score	Citations per faculty score	International faculty score	International student score	Overall score
1	1	HARVARD University	United States	100	100	100	96	93	91	100.0
2=	2	University of CAMBRIDGE	United Kingdom	100	100	99	83	98	91	97.6
2=	3	University of OXFORD	United Kingdom	100	100	100	82	97	96	97.6
2=	4=	YALE University	United States	100	98	100	91	84	75	97.6
5	9	Imperial College LONDON	United Kingdom	99	99	100	81	98	100	97.5
6	10	PRINCETON University	United States	100	94	95	97	83	75	97.2
7=	7	CALIFORNIA Institute of Technology (Caltech)	United States	100	55	100	100	100	91	96.5
7=	11	University of CHICAGO	United States	100	97	100	86	71	90	96.5
9	25	UCL (University College LONDON)	United Kingdom	96	97	100	82	91	98	95.3
10	4=	MASSACHUSETTS Institute of Technology (MIT)	United States	100	99	85	98	34	94	94.6
11	12	COLUMBIA University	United States	100	96	94	91	34	89	94.5
12	21	MCGILL University	Canada	100	97	99	72	73	96	93.9
13	13	DUKE University	United States	98	97	100	92	16	74	93.4
14	26	University of PENNSYLVANIA	United States	97	96	88	92	83	65	93.3
15	23	JOHNS HOPKINS University	United States	99	77	98	96	35	69	92.9
16	16	AUSTRALIAN National University	Australia	100	91	100	66	68	91	91.6
17	19=	University of TOKYO	Japan	100	92	96	88	25	44	91.1
18	33=	University of HONG KONG	Hong Kong	95	90	85	79	100	89	90.7
19	6	STANFORD University	United States	100	99	66	100	25	94	90.6
20=	35=	CARNEGIE MELLON University	United States	96	94	76	87	67	96	90.0
20=	15	CORNELL University	United States	100	98	74	93	36	69	90.0
22	8	University of California, BERKELEY	United States	100	98	59	92	73	88	89.7
23	33=	University of EDINBURGH	United Kingdom	96	98	82	76	71	80	88.8

2007 rank	2006 rank	Name	Country	Peer review score	Recruiter review score	Faculty student score	Citations per faculty score	International faculty score	International student score	Overall score
24	46=	King's College LONDON	United Kingdom	90	95	91	70	93	84	88.2
25	29=	KYOTO University	Japan	99	89	83	90	29	24	87.2
26	18	Ecole Normale Supérieure, PARIS	France	91	60	83	98	61	81	87.1
27	22	University of MELBOURNE	Australia	100	99	64	70	64	95	85.9
28	37	ECOLE POLYTECHNIQUE	France	76	94	100	78	70	94	85.1
29	42	NORTHWESTERN University	United States	88	97	77	91	35	68	85.0
30	40	University of MANCHESTER	United Kingdom	88	99	77	70	84	85	84.7
31	35=	The University of SYDNEY	Australia	99	95	51	71	100	95	84.6
32	54=	BROWN University	United States	90	77	74	89	75	58	84.5
33=	50=	University of BRITISH COLUMBIA	Canada	100	91	70	74	35	63	84.3
33=	45	University of QUEENSLAND	Australia	95	94	70	68	79	76	84.3
33=	19=	National University of SINGAPORE	Singapore	100	93	34	84	100	100	84.3
36	14	PEKING University	China	100	98	98	53	32	26	84.2
37	64=	University of BRISTOL	United Kingdom	81	98	85	77	88	72	84.1
38=	50=	The CHINESE University of Hong Kong	Hong Kong	83	79	80	80	100	85	83.8
38=	29=	University of MICHIGAN	United States	99	96	53	89	41	52	83.8
40	28	TSINGHUA University	China	95	92	100	59	20	36	83.3
41	31	University of CALIFORNIA, Los Angeles (UCLA)	United States	100	92	56	91	20	36	82.8
42	24	ETH Zurich (Swiss Federal Institute of Technology)	Switzerland	92	75	61	74	100	92	82.5
43	38	MONASH University	Australia	98	97	53	57	99	99	82.1
44	41	University of NEW SOUTH WALES	Australia	97	98	39	76	89	91	81.8
45	27	University of TORONTO	Canada	100	96	21	93	86	50	80.6
46	70=	OSAKA University	Japan	83	75	86	91	17	29	80.0
47	66	BOSTON University	United States	91	89	49	88	29	88	79.7
48	69	University of AMSTERDAM	Netherlands	84	81	81	70	76	32	78.6
49	43	NEW YORK University (NYU)	United States	95	93	48	77	29	49	77.8

50	46=	The University of AUCKLAND	New Zealand	95	83	38	61	100	99	77.5
51=	63	SEOUL National University	Korea, South	92	54	80	79	16	24	77.1
51=	32	University of TEXAS at Austin	United States	95	94	22	92	66	47	77.1
53=	58=	HONG KONG University of Science & Technology	Hong Kong	84	82	28	92	100	96	76.9
53=	78	TRINITY College Dublin	Ireland	80	92	70	58	99	77	76.9
55=	84	University of WASHINGTON	United States	84	50	73	92	44	33	76.7
55=	79=	University of WISCONSIN-Madison	United States	94	81	31	95	50	44	76.7
57	73	University of WARWICK	United Kingdom	80	98	62	58	89	96	76.4
58	44	University of CALIFORNIA, San Diego	United States	98	39	51	95	23	30	76.3
59	17	LONDON School of Economics and Political Science	United Kingdom	89	100	65	29	100	100	75.7
60	58=	HEIDELBERG University	Germany	84	63	61	78	42	87	75.5
61	96	Katholieke Universiteit LEUVEN	Belgium	88	83	39	84	51	55	75.0
62	105=	University of ADELAIDE	Australia	75	86	66	65	77	96	74.7
63	86	DELFT University of Technology	Netherlands	75	80	66	72	83	67	74.4
64	111=	University of WESTERN AUSTRALIA	Australia	72	88	56	78	96	78	74.3
65=	90=	University of BIRMINGHAM	United Kingdom	71	93	62	75	84	70	74.1
65=	98	Ludwig-Maximilians-Universität München (MUNICH)	Germany	80	60	70	72	58	71	74.1
67	82=	Technische Universität MÜNCHEN	Germany	68	71	88	69	59	83	73.9
68	102=	University of SHEFFIELD	United Kingdom	69	96	71	69	81	67	73.7
69	61=	NANYANG Technological University	Singapore	81	82	37	72	100	99	73.6
70	85	University of NOTTINGHAM	United Kingdom	69	98	64	65	84	88	73.2
71=	61=	DARTMOUTH College	United States	60	89	91	83	26	53	73.0
71=	111=	UPPSALA University	Sweden	85	34	81	72	51	26	73.0
73	77	University of ILLINOIS	United States	94	64	29	86	34	51	72.6
74=	56	EMORY University	United States	61	75	99	85	13	39	72.4
74=	124=	University of YORK	United Kingdom	62	91	77	69	76	83	72.4
76	109=	University of ST ANDREWS	United Kingdom	57	95	78	69	91	99	72.3
77=	88	University of PITTSBURGH	United States	62	45	94	85	78	38	72.2

2007 rank	2006 rank	Name	Country	Peer review score	Recruiter review score	Faculty student score	Citations per faculty score	International faculty score	International student score	Overall score
77=	127	PURDUE University	United States	87	79	24	82	76	64	72.2
79	111=	University of MARYLAND	United States	71	62	71	85	48	45	72.1
80=	121	University of LEEDS	United Kingdom	74	97	56	69	76	59	72.0
80=	141=	University of SOUTHAMPTON	United Kingdom	60	90	71	76	88	74	72.0
82	53	VANDERBILT University	United States	55	81	99	87	28	41	71.9
83	81	University of GLASGOW	United Kingdom	71	84	71	75	42	54	71.8
84	90=	LEIDEN University	Netherlands	81	63	35	93	78	40	71.7
85=	60	CASE WESTERN RESERVE University	United States	59	50	99	85	18	80	71.6
85=	116=	FUDAN University	China	87	96	45	68	31	31	71.6
85=	87	University of VIENNA	Austria	86	80	12	90	63	89	71.6
88	176	QUEEN'S University	Canada	74	88	49	79	87	34	71.2
89	95	UTRECHT University	Netherlands	80	55	65	80	38	24	70.9
90=	99=	PENNSYLVANIA STATE University	United States	84	82	63	64	18	24	70.5
90=	118	TOKYO Institute of Technology	Japan	67	86	59	91	34	42	70.5
92	102=	RICE University	United States	65	45	80	88	39	58	70.3
93=	54=	University of COPENHAGEN	Denmark	82	55	51	70	66	62	70.1
93=	181=	University of MONTREAL	Canada	88	50	31	80	89	41	70.1
95	48=	University of ROCHESTER	United States	58	38	100	84	24	63	69.3
96	170=	University of CALIFORNIA, Davis	United States	83	34	60	82	31	26	69.1
97=	133=	University of ALBERTA	Canada	88	30	23	87	88	62	68.8
97=	145	GEORGIA Institute of Technology	United States	79	77	25	93	18	74	68.8
99	141=	CARDIFF University	United Kingdom	62	84	70	65	72	75	68.6
100	116=	University of HELSINKI	Finland	79	45	28	93	56	78	68.2
101	139	University of LIVERPOOL	United Kingdom	55	85	70	76	83	64	68.1
102=	102=	GEORGETOWN University	United States	57	94	69	80	28	73	68.0
102=	108	National TAIWAN University	Taiwan	86	68	39	79	18	24	68.0

102=	168=	TOHOKU University	Japan	53	59	96	84	40	32	68.0
105	39	University of GENEVA	Switzerland	62	54	39	91	100	100	67.2
106	122	LUND University	Sweden	76	41	43	81	77	52	66.9
107	211=	University of COLORADO	United States	60	15	100	85	33	31	66.8
108	155	MCMASTER University	Canada	84	49	31	89	28	37	66.6
109	132	DURHAM University	United Kingdom	59	98	49	74	92	61	66.5
110	130=	University of VIRGINIA	United States	63	94	52	86	22	36	66.4
111	172=	MAASTRICHT University	Netherlands	43	72	80	81	68	99	66.2
112=	128=	NAGOYA University	Japan	53	74	83	85	25	30	66.1
112=	204=	University of WATERLOO	Canada	82	82	17	75	63	49	66.1
114=	126	University of AARHUS	Denmark	65	19	89	69	59	37	65.6
114=	75	University of BASEL	Switzerland	52	20	99	67	89	81	65.6
114=	79=	University of OTAGO	New Zealand	69	61	39	66	100	92	65.6
117=	141=	University of CALIFORNIA, Santa Barbara	United States	88	31	25	89	43	21	65.5
117=	64=	Ecole Polytechnique Fédérale de LAUSANNE	Switzerland	58	58	97	29	100	100	65.5
119	101	University of SOUTHERN CALIFORNIA	United States	62	77	52	80	25	78	65.4
120	219=	OHIO STATE University	United States	69	77	39	79	67	38	65.3
121	105=	University of SUSSEX	United Kingdom	58	51	58	77	90	83	65.2
122	150=	TEXAS A&M University	United States	76	75	27	81	41	39	64.9
123	76	Université Catholique de LOUVAIN (UCL)	Belgium	78	60	28	73	50	74	64.8
124	141=	University of GHENT	Belgium	63	29	88	69	47	30	64.5
125	180	NANJING University	China	74	72	45	69	59	14	64.4
126=	105=	HUMBOLDT-Universität zu Berlin	Germany	71	38	71	57	44	68	64.3
126=	215=	University of WESTERN ONTARIO	Canada	68	90	30	80	72	30	64.3
128	119	Hebrew University of JERUSALEM	Israel	86	20	18	91	83	14	64.0
129	133=	NEWCASTLE University, NEWCASTLE Upon Tyne	United Kingdom	45	87	74	67	80	80	63.9
130=	194	Technical University of DENMARK	Denmark	47	23	86	84	91	59	63.8
130=	67	EINDHOVEN University of Technology	Netherlands	48	48	99	69	60	48	63.8

2007 rank	2006 rank	Name	Country	Peer review score	Recruiter review score	Faculty student score	Citations per faculty score	International faculty score	International student score	Overall score
132=	198=	KOREA Advanced Institute of Science & Technology	Korea, South	65	27	64	85	53	28	63.7
132=	93=	Université Pierre-et-Marie-Curie - PARIS VI	France	60	5	90	73	20	92	63.7
134	224=	University of ARIZONA	United States	69	57	37	88	28	45	63.1
135	226=	University of FLORIDA	United States	62	41	77	74	27	32	63.0
136	128=	KYUSHU University	Japan	50	68	80	82	17	31	62.8
137=	195	University of ABERDEEN	United Kingdom	45	64	78	67	91	73	62.7
137=	232=	INDIANA University Bloomington	United States	67	79	28	85	45	37	62.7
139	282=	SIMON FRASER University	Canada	72	72	22	67	97	62	62.6
140=	198=	University of CALIFORNIA, Irvine	United States	79	30	38	82	27	30	62.5
140=	109=	University of ZURICH	Switzerland	71	32	13	95	99	58	62.5
142=	187=	University of MINNESOTA	United States	76	43	28	89	26	35	62.3
142=	170=	Universität TÜBINGEN	Germany	60	52	46	79	76	65	62.3
144	219=	Universität FREIBURG	Germany	57	23	93	61	24	76	62.2
145	153	University of BATH	United Kingdom	46	96	49	71	91	91	62.0
146	149	Freie Universität BERLIN	Germany	79	16	31	70	70	81	61.9
147	228=	University of LANCASTER	United Kingdom	49	80	65	57	88	81	61.7
148	97	WAGENINGEN University	Netherlands	39	28	88	87	46	97	61.5
149=	154	CITY University of Hong Kong	Hong Kong	62	51	37	76	100	51	61.2
149=	99=	Queen Mary, University of LONDON	United Kingdom	55	65	81	30	94	92	61.2
151=	133=	HOKKAIDO University	Japan	49	69	76	82	19	21	61.1
151=	123	University of NORTH CAROLINA	United States	72	86	28	74	22	20	61.1
151=	147=	TEL AVIV University	Israel	81	36	26	89	13	13	61.1
154	165=	Université Libre de BRUXELLES (ULB)	Belgium	56	52	57	69	43	96	61.0
155=	165=	University of Science and Technology of CHINA	China	75	77	28	76	16	11	60.9
155=	152	University of NOTRE DAME	United States	56	88	43	81	25	50	60.9
157	72	Ecole Normale Supérieure de LYON	France	42	45	100	67	41	58	60.8

158	140	CRANFIELD University	United Kingdom	31	74	100	57	74	100	60.7
159=	163	MICHIGAN STATE University	United States	63	71	33	76	65	45	60.6
159=	130=	TUFTS University	United States	42	78	61	90	46	44	60.6
161=	120	KEIO University	Japan	52	88	91	45	25	16	59.9
161=	48=	WASHINGTON University in St. Louis	United States	72	62	100	1	27	48	59.9
163=	92	ERASMUS University Rotterdam	Netherlands	51	97	28	88	64	45	59.7
163=	179	SHANGHAI JIAO TONG University	China	72	92	38	55	35	11	59.7
165	201=	Universität STUTTGART	Germany	47	81	71	50	52	90	59.4
166=	266=	University of CALGARY	Canada	67	61	28	81	24	37	58.9
166=	138	VIENNA University of Technology	Austria	53	44	68	52	75	88	58.9
168=	156=	Universität GÖTTINGEN	Germany	66	-	73	59	41	54	58.8
168=	82=	MACQUARIE University	Australia	61	89	23	52	85	99	58.8
170	291	HELSINKI University of Technology - TKK	Finland	52	17	94	57	56	44	58.7
171=	238	University of DUNDEE	United Kingdom	44	51	65	71	84	66	58.3
171=	222=	Universität KARLSRUHE	Germany	45	60	73	59	56	85	58.3
173=	207=	University of BOLOGNA	Italy	78	66	24	62	21	26	58.2
173=	232=	University of GRONINGEN	Netherlands	48	51	69	74	62	29	58.2
175=	124=	University of MASSACHUSETTS, Amherst	United States	62	45	34	90	24	31	57.9
175=	284=	University of SAO PAULO	Brazil	65	59	51	63	24	14	57.9
177=	448	University of CAMPINAS (Unicamp)	Brazil	52	30	78	73	43	16	57.8
177=	219=	University College DUBLIN	Ireland	56	85	29	63	89	58	57.8
177=	215=	RUTGERS, The State University of New Jersey	United States	72	33	30	73	60	24	57.8
180=	190=	University of READING	United Kingdom	45	67	52	69	78	78	57.7
180=	158=	WASEDA University	Japan	68	92	64	25	26	23	57.7
182	172=	Rheinisch-Westfälische Technische Hochschule AACHEN	Germany	40	80	80	48	53	81	57.5
183	197	Università degli Studi di ROMA - La Sapienza	Italy	79	63	11	71	15	21	57.3
184	161=	Université Louis Pasteur - STRASBOURG I	France	58	64	19	82	45	77	57.1
185=	239=	University of LEICESTER	United Kingdom	37	60	60	76	77	86	57.0

2007 rank	2006 rank	Name	Country	Peer review score	Recruiter review score	Faculty student score	Citations per faculty score	International faculty score	International student score	Overall score
185=	115	University of TWENTE	Netherlands	46	42	61	76	75	51	57.0
187	252=	University of ANTWERP	Belgium	41	7	99	67	57	59	56.9
188=	333=	University of CANTERBURY	New Zealand	62	77	30	55	55	66	56.6
188=	177	University of OSLO	Norway	61	25	54	62	51	55	56.6
190	258=	University of SURREY	United Kingdom	33	79	61	64	95	92	56.4
191	255=	RENSSELAER Polytechnic Institute	United States	44	44	44	90	70	58	56.2
192=	172=	KTH, ROYAL Institute of Technology	Sweden	49	17	51	70	90	99	56.1
192=	74	Universidad Nacional Autónoma de México (UNAM)	Mexico	74	78	64	13	28	13	56.1
194	190=	University of BARCELONA	Spain	69	46	22	78	17	36	55.9
195=	137	Radboud Universiteit NIJMEGEN	Netherlands	40	19	82	75	83	31	55.8
195=	192=	QUEENSLAND University of Technology	Australia	66	87	28	39	64	63	55.8
197=	147=	CHALMERS University of Technology	Sweden	51	23	42	83	74	59	55.5
197=	181=	KOBE University	Japan	51	67	60	65	22	27	55.5
199	196	University of WOLLONGONG	Australia	45	89	31	58	99	99	55.3
200=	257	University of CAPE TOWN	South Africa	54	69	28	68	27	91	54.8
200=	146	RMIT University	Australia	63.5	88.3	22.5	32.4	73.7	99.9	54.8

Methodology: what does the Times Higher-QS World University Rankings measure and how?

The real difficulty facing those who seek to rank universities worldwide is not how to define them, but where to find the data that will make for reliable comparisons. Different national systems collect the data that matter to them and in the form that suits their purpose. The limited number of measures in the Times Higher-QS World University Rankings reflect just how few indicators there are that transfer across borders, and even they can present problems, as outlined below.

The main rankings table evaluates six key aspects of university activity using the most recent data available at the time of initial publication: 1. Peer review, 2.Citations per faculty (research quality); 3. Student faculty ratio (teaching quality); 4. Recruiter review (graduate employability); numbers of 5. International faculty, and, 6. International students (international outlook).

It is not easy to measure international activity. Some universities have whole campuses overseas, others have numerous partnership programs and exchange schemes. But it is possible to be globally active and internationally minded without such formal initiatives. The proportions of international students and staff have been selected as the most universally applicable indicators, although both have been accorded a low weighting in the Times Higher-QS World University Rankings so as not to overplay their importance.

Z-scores — a balancing tool

A statistical technique called the z-transformation, (sometimes known as normal or standard scores), has been applied to each measure. This is a statistical way of ensuring that each measure contributes the intended amount to the overall score. (For the statistically minded, it involves subtracting the mean score from each individual score and then dividing by the standard deviation of the scores. The percentile ranks of the z-scores are then plotted using a standard normal distribution table). This change in methodology in 2007 will add to the reliability of the ranking by ensuring that high performers on a single indicator do not gain a disproportionate advantage, and will bring the ranking into line with other similar assessments. In future years, the use of z-scores will lessen volatility in the ranking.

In previous years, scores for each indicator have been scaled against the top performer on that measure; the leading institution awarded 100 and subsequent institutions' scores scaled against that maximum. Where there was a steep curve in the distribution of scores, universities at the head of lowly weighted indicators, such as the proportion of international students, could benefit by the equivalent of up to 50 places in the top-weighted peer review section. Applying z-scores effectively 'flattens' the curve, normalizing the scores throughout the ranking to iron out such ripple effects. The change benefits universities that are strong across the board and explains some of the larger falls in this year's ranking. In 2007, the London School of Economics, for example, has lost the benefit of a large lead in the proportion of international students, while the methodological change has had a similar effect on Macquarie University, Australia, which had a big lead on international faculty.

Weightings

Weightings are applied to the data results as set out in the chart below. (All decisions regarding the allocation of weightings are the responsibility of Times Higher Education).Finally, the total scores were transformed to a scale where the top score was set at 100 with the remainder being a proportion of the top score.

Times Higher–QS World University Rankings criteria/weights

Criterion	Indicator	Description	Weight
Research quality	1. Peer review	Composite score drawn from peer review (in five subject areas) 5,101 responses	40%
	2. Citations per faculty	Score based on research performance factored against the size of the research body	20%
Teaching quality	3. Student faculty ratio	Score based on student/ faculty ratio	20%
Graduate employability	4. Recruiter review	Score based on responses to recruiter survey 1,482 responses	10%
International outlook	5. International faculty	Score based on proportion of international faculty	5%
	6. International students	Score based on proportion of international students	5%

Further potential indicators of university quality

Academic opinion was already considered a vital element if the rankings were to paint the most current picture of international higher education, rather than reflecting past glories. Even citations inevitably credit universities for work, which may have been carried out several years previously; Nobel prizes, which form a substantial part of the global university rankings published by Shanghai Jiao Tong University, often relate to research done far in the past. The thousands of academics who take part in the peer review exercise conducted by QS for the Times Higher-QS World University Rankings are judging universities in their own discipline as they are today. By aggregating the views of subject experts, we avoid impressionistic judgments of overall quality and provide material for the separate faculty-level rankings.

Other possible indicators have been considered and either discarded as impractical or shelved until enough data can be collected to make them reliable sources of comparison. This was the case initially with the employers' survey, which was omitted from the first edition of the rankings, in 2004, because the sample was considered too small. Now that the pool of international employers is larger and more diverse, it is considered a valuable addition and one that will continue to grow in the years to come.

Among the other indicators considered for inclusion in the rankings have been various spending measures. Many domestic tables measure the amount spent on libraries, for example, but it was decided that, even if genuinely comparable data could be collected, too great an advantage would be conferred upon wealthy nations for the results to be meaningful. Similar objections have been raised to the use of graduate employment rates: there is a danger of comparing economies more than universities.

Entry standards provide another obvious area of comparison and one much used in national league tables. But while business schools have an international entry standard, most areas of university life do not. Much work has been done on the equivalence of different qualifications, but it is not yet clear how this can be incorporated into a system of rankings such as these. No doubt other measures will be developed such as the proportion of staff with PhDs, or the number of PhDs awarded by each university, but, despite frequent appeals for workable additions, no glaring omission has yet emerged.

Major universities are complex and while attempting to encapsulate their quality by a few simple measures, the process of ranking inevitably involves simplification. Many US state universities, for example, or the Indian Institutes of Technology have a number of campuses and centres, but it is often beyond data-gathering feasibility to distinguish adequately between them. If handled separately, fewer of them would appear in the rankings and in lower positions. The units analysed in the rankings relate to universities, as they exist in practice. For example, the various colleges of the universities of London and California, which have their own management structures and in some cases award their own degrees are treated individually.

Understanding the ranking indicators

Each indicator was calculated as follows with some observations on how to interpret the results:

1. Peer review

Peer review is a measure of the average reputation for research of a given institution amongst academics in each of five broad subject areas. It is the method used to assess academic quality in universities all over the world and it has formed a part of US university league tables for many years. In the absence of more precise statistical data on activities such as teaching and more up-to-date comparisons of research, it has become the central element of the Times Higher-

QS World University Rankings. It is, after all, partially a matter of opinion, which are the best universities in the world. Who better to ask than the people who work in them?

QS operates an international survey of academics asking them to identify institutions they consider best for research in the subject area(s) they identify themselves as knowledgeable in. Respondents are sourced from previous survey respondents and third-party databases. 5,101 results were considered for the 2007 rankings.

Respondents are asked to identify the subject area(s) with which they have most familiarity from the following: arts and humanities, life sciences and biomedicine, natural sciences, social sciences, and engineering and IT. They are also asked to identify which of three large geographical areas: 1. Americas, 2.Europe, Middle East & Africa, 3. Asia Pacific, they have most awareness of. Respondents are asked to identify up to 30 institutions they consider excellent in each subject area they have selected, from a list of institutions in the region(s) they have selected. They are not asked to rank those institutions; performance is based on the number of occurrences of each institution's name. Responses are weighted by region and compiled into five separate peer reviews for each of the five subject areas which are combined with equal weighting to yield the final result. Respondents are not able to respond in favour of their own institution. An analysis of 2007 respondents is available on www.topuniversities.com.

The peer review is based on an average of about 20 responses from over 5,000 respondents, resulting in a statistical universe of over 100,000 data points to evaluate just over 500 institutions. Whilst being statistically robust, since it is a reputation survey, it is sensitive to certain bias. For example, big name universities and universities in the world's largest cities may perform beyond expectations and respondents may identify institutions as strong in fields they may not even have.

As the response is growing dramatically each year the rankings are carried out, the influence of such bias will diminish. Whilst any evaluation of university research strength is likely to be skewed in favour of universities operating in widely spoken languages, the peer review is more resistant to this problem than citations' scores, resulting in many universities from non-English speaking countries performing more strongly in the peer review evaluation. In addition, the peer review reflects no bias between any of the five main subject areas, so if you're interested in arts, humanities or social sciences, which are, relatively, under-represented by citations, this measure reflects a more even balance.

2. Citations per faculty

Citations in leading academic journals are a conventional measure of institutional research strength and the most common source of international academic comparisons. Dividing these by the number of faculty staff, takes into account the size of the institution.

Citation numbers come from Scopus™ www.scopus.com. Faculty numbers come either from central statistics bodies, (many of which are listed for reference at the end of this chapter), from the universities directly, from institutions' websites or, in a few unusual cases, from an extrapolated average.

Scopus™ supplies QS with the latest five complete years of publication data with citation counts. QS maps all of the names from the rankings exercise into the Scopus™ data. In 2007, over 14,500 name variants for the 566 institutions considered for the rankings were found. It is expected that this number will increase for 2008 as we invite institutions to help identify additional names. The faculty number used is total and not purely restricted to research faculty. While it would be ideal to factor research output purely by those involved in its production, this level of data has proved difficult to collect globally and may constitute a future enhancement to the methodology.

In general, the breakdown of faculty is reasonably consistent across the sample institutions, but there are exceptions where a given institution may have a particular concentration of either teaching or research faculty. These institutions may be at an advantage or disadvantage in any indicator involving faculty numbers. Institutions with strong medical schools are at a particular advantage since citations are a more prolific practice in science and particularly in medical subject areas than in any other.

Also, citations data yields a strong language bias towards English and a strong cultural bias towards countries where academics place a stronger emphasis on publication; little consolation to institutions that work in other languages and whose academics stand correspondingly less chance of building up a competitive body of citations. The US is the most profound beneficiary of these last two factors as it is clearly, by far, the most significant nation in terms of the publication of academic research in English. Furthermore, the research culture in the US and the sheer volume of citations registered by US universities suggests that their academics also cite each others' work more regularly than is the case in most of Europe or Asia. There is no suggestion of corruption, merely of a difference in normal academic practice.

3. Student faculty ratio

This is the most universally available metric that indicates commitment to teaching. There is no international measurement of teaching quality — and almost certainly never will be. Most countries do not even attempt national comparisons. The nearest proxy, however imperfect, is the faculty student ratio. Despite the onward march of technology, there is no substitute in conventional universities for face-to-face contact. Students value small teaching groups and the opportunity to consult tutors.

Both student and faculty numbers come either from central statistics bodies, from the universities directly, from institutions' websites or, in a few unusual cases from an extrapolated average.

Separate numbers are collected for undergraduate and postgraduate students from each institution. In most cases, the sum of the two is used. In a scenario where separate metrics are not available, total student numbers are requested. The lower the number for a student faculty ratio, the better; which makes its inclusion in an index, based on high scores, a challenge. So, for purposes of the ranking, the ratio is reversed, thus essentially evaluating the number of faculty per student.

In a similar way to the citations indicator, the faculty score used is total without identifying and eliminating faculty not contributing to research. As a result, universities with typical faculty demographics may be at an advantage or disadvantage. While this may remain the best universally available indicator of commitment to teaching, it is a far from perfect measure of teaching quality. In fact, measuring teaching quality remains one of the greatest challenges for international rankings. If you are concerned about teaching quality in particular, it may be worth your while to refer to country-specific rankings, a list of which can be found on www.topuniversities.com Speaking to staff and alumni of the institution, either through your personal network or at an education fair, is also highly recommended as a way to gauge teaching quality at a particular institution.

4. Recruiter review

Recruiter review is a measure of the quality of graduates from particular institutions, from the perspective of global employers.

QS conducts an annual survey of global graduate employers. Prospective respondents are sourced from QS' comprehensive databases, from a selection of partner and other organizations. 1,482 responses were considered for the results in 2007.

The recruiter review is conducted along very similar lines to the peer review. There is no distinction between different subject areas and it is operated in a near identical way to a single subject area peer review. Regional weightings are still applied. The international respondents come from a very diverse range of businesses in terms of scope, sector, size and nature.

No weighting is applied on the basis of the seniority of respondent, or the scope of their recruitment base. While the international spread of the responding sample is rapidly improving year-on-year, the response and, thus, the results still show some bias towards English speaking nations in 2007.

5. Number of international faculty

The ability of an institution to attract, retain and adequately compensate international faculty members could be considered a measure of quality. The proportion of international faculty also gives prospective students an impression of the diversity of an institution and, perhaps, some feeling for its progressiveness, in terms of globalization.

All faculty and international faculty data is collected via the same means as discussed for the student faculty indicator (3. above).

Raw scores are simply a proportion of the faculty that is international (ie hold a foreign passport). The higher the proportion, the higher the eventual score.

Very high international faculty numbers may not necessarily be a good thing; poor quality faculty may be forced to seek employment outside their home nation and a poor quality institution may find it difficult to attract faculty from its own country. Understanding the nature of an institution from an international perspective is of value, however, it is best considered only in the context of other indicators of quality. It is important to take a balanced and comprehensive view of this kind of aspect of an institution, one that extends far beyond the scope of these rankings. This book helps reveal the first steps.

6. Number of international students

The proportion of international students also gives prospective students an impression of the diversity of an institution and perhaps some indication of its commitment to international students and ability to provide them with adequate academic and other support.

All student and international student data is collected via the same means as discussed for the student faculty indicator (3. above).

The raw scores are simply a proportion of the full time student body that is international. Exchange students are not currently included. The higher the proportion, the higher the eventual score.

Very high international student numbers may not necessarily be a good thing: a poor quality institution may find it difficult to attract students from its own country and, thus, focus on the overseas market. More students are able to engage in full program study abroad, if those programs are taught in a language they understand. This gives institutions in English-speaking countries an advantage for both of these international indicators. In the future, including, separately, exchange students in this consideration may help add balance and may, perhaps, become feasible as institutions, year on-year, furnish the exercise with more complete data.

Conclusions

The position of an institution in the Times Higher-QS World University Rankings is, clearly, not only influenced by its activities and performance in the last 12 months, but by reputation, effort and achievements over years and decades and, in some cases, centuries. There are many factors outside direct institutional control that may have influenced the current position of a university, such as language, politics, economics, and culture, for example.

The ranking of the top 200 or 500 can provide an interesting basis for initiating your research into university choice worldwide. However, rankings do not replace the need for that research entirely, but simply, perhaps, help make it more incisive.

These tables do not, for example, consider institutional strength in many specific fields. The following chapter takes a more in-depth look at the top 100 institutions and highlights some specific areas of excellence. For a student considering economics or marine engineering, for example, a more detailed analysis will be required by looking at the subject area rankings for social sciences, and engineering and IT (Chapter 9). There are certainly many institutions worldwide that offer real excellence in specific fields, but may not do so across an entire broad subject area and thus may not be revealed in these rankings.

The continuing research work involved in this ranking exercise is not exhaustive, nor is it, obviously, customised to any single person's specific quest for the right program or course. Your own personal university ranking, evolved according to your own personalized criteria, combined using your own weightings and only looking at institutions that meet your own search requirements would yield very different results.

The Times Higher-QS World University Rankings, this book, Top Universities Guide and www.topuniversities.com are designed to provide a good starting point for your journey. Visiting the websites of the institutions listed (non-exhaustively) on the following pages is also a good starting point for your own further research on higher education in particular countries across the world.

Higher education data sources worldwide

Australia
Department of Education, Science & Training www.dest.gov.au
Government Education Portal www.education.gov.au
Australian Education International www.aei.dest.gov.au/AEI

Brazil
MEC Ministry of Education Portal http://portal.mec.gov.br/

Canada
Statistics Canada www.statcan.ca
Canadian Education Statistics Council www.cesc.ca
The University Presidents' Council of British Columbia www.tupc.bc.ca

China
National Bureau of Statistics of China www.stats.gov.cn/english/index.htm
Ministry of Education of the People's Republic of China www.moe.edu.cn/english/index.htm

Finland
Statistics Finland - Finland in Figures www.stat.fi/tup/suoluk/index_en.html
KOTA - statistical data on universities and fields of education http://kotaplus.csc.fi:7777/online/Etusivu.do?lng=en

France
Ministry of Education www.education.gouv.fr
INSEE - National Institute for Statistics and Economic Studies www.insee.fr
The French Official Statistics Portal www.statistique-publique.fr

Germany
Federal Statistical Office Germany www.destatis.de
Bayerisches Landesamt für Statistik und Datenverarbeitung www.statistik.bayern.de

Greece
National Statistical Service of Greece www.statistics.gr
Ministry of National Education and Religious Affairs www.ypepth.gr

Hong Kong
Census and Statistics Department www.censtatd.gov.hk
Education Bureau www.edb.gov.hk

India
Department of Secondary and Higher Education www.education.nic.in
Government of India - Ministry of Statistics and Programme Implementation www.mospi.nic.in

Ireland
Central Statistics Office www.cso.ie
Higher Education Authority www.hea.ie
Department of Education and Science www.education.ie

Israel	Central Bureau of Statistics www.cbs.gov.il/engindex.htm
Italy	Italian National Institute of Statistics www.istat.it/english Ministero dell'Università e della ricerca http://statistica.miur.it/
Japan	Statistics Bureau Ministry of Internal Affairs www.stat.go.jp/english Ministry of Education www.mext.go.jp/english/ KNSO - Korea National Statistical Office www.nso.go.kr
Malaysia	Department of Statistics Malaysia www.statistics.gov.my
Mexico	INEGI - Instituto Nacional de Estadística Geografía e Informática www.inegi.gob.mx
Netherlands	CBS - Central Bureau of Statistics - Statistics Netherlands www.cbs.nl/en-GB
Norway	Statistics Norway www.ssb.no/www-open/english/
Russia	Federal State Statistics Service www.gks.ru
Singapore	Statistics Singapore www.singstat.gov.sg
South Africa	Statistics South Africa www.statssa.gov.za
South Korea	Ministry of Education & Human Resources Development http://english.moe.go.kr/
Spain	Instituto Nacional de Estadística www.ine.es/en/welcome_en
Sweden	Swedish National Agency for Higher Education www.hsv.se Statistics Sweden www.scb.se
Switzerland	CRUS - Rectors' Conference of the Swiss Universities www.crus.ch Swiss Federal Statistical Office www.bfs.admin.ch
Turkey	Ministry of National Education www.meb.gov.tr
Thailand	Ministry of Education www.moe.go.th Commission on Higher Education www.inter.mua.go.th
Taiwan	Ministry of Education http://english.moe.gov.tw/
US	National Center for Education Statistics www.nces.ed.gov Common Data Set (CDS) http://cds.berkeley.edu
UK	Higher Education Statistics Agency www.hesa.co.uk

"As financial resources become more scarce, it is more critical to identify research and researchers who are the most productive and on the right track."
Peter Brimblecombe
Professor, Atmospheric Chemistry
School of Environmental Sciences
University of East Anglia, UK
How does your institution measure up?
Scopus is the optimal data source for research performance measurement.
No other database has so much breadth of content covering so many authors.
With Scopus you can identify authors' papers, track their citations and analyze their influence using the Scopus h-index. And, to evaluate the performance of journals, research projects and groups of researchers you can measure the performance of a specified collection of articles.
Now it's easy to:
• Evaluate and prioritize resource allocation by departments or fields
• Make informed decisions about tenure and promotion
• Promote your institution for funding and recruitment
www.scopus.com
refine your research
SCOPUS™

KERANA TUHAN UNTUK MANUSIA
UNIVERSITI TEKNOLOGI MALAYSIA
UNIVERSITI TEKNOLOGI MALAYSIA
Malaysia's Premier University in Engineering and Technology

8

Profiles of the world's top 100 universities

The following pages profile, in order, each of the top 100 universities in the Times Higher-QS World University Rankings, starting with Harvard University at number one. Each profile introduces you to the institution and looks at some of the reasons you might wish to consider it as a study choice. The profiles identify some of the unique features, latest developments and subjects the institution is known for. Renowned former students are mentioned and, in most cases, a more personal face is portrayed through anecdotal comments of a recent student. A factfile summarizes useful information about each institution and outline maps show the position of each university in its country context.

Profiles

The profiles in this chapter have been compiled by an international network of experts and journalists, located close to the respective institutions, who have collected information from a multitude of public sources. The intention of these profiles is to give you more of a realistic flavour of the top 100 universities than can be obtained through reading a rankings table. However, in the space of two pages, even a profile, can only provide a snapshot from one writer's perspective, and any included student comments are highly individual and may reflect opinions not shared by all who study there. Nevertheless, these profiles are a starting point for your further research. They may help form the basis for your own questions about an institution that you may address to its staff or students, as you search for your ideal program and study destination. Reading a profile may also awaken your interest in an institution that you had previously not considered.

Factfiles

The factfiles have been compiled by the dedicated research team behind the Times Higher-QS World University Rankings 2007. The factfile for each institution is designed to give you a user-friendly overview of the information behind the Rankings, which can be found in the various chapters of this book for each of the top 100 institutions. Each factfile brings together the rankings information collected during the 2007 exercise and the average tuition fee data and subject area information in one place. Full contact details of the university, including web address, are included, as are the foundation dates, where available. The factfiles are positioned in the profiles in such a way to facilitate comparison between the top 100 ranked universities. While many of the profile texts refer to costs a student may face in local currencies, the factfiles use US$ throughout (exchange rates as at 27.07.07) to facilitate comparison.

Any disparity between numbers in the factfiles and numbers in the text is a consequence of different data collection dates, sources or data definitions. For example, the student numbers listed in the factfiles are for full time equivalent (FTE) students, which counts students who do not take a full course load only as the fraction of a full time student that they represent, rather than as individual students. It is also a fact that many universities have students that are neither undergraduate nor postgraduate students, such as foundation year, diploma and some language students. Universities also all have different ways of counting distance learning and exchange students, among others, and this can lead to numbers published on university websites, for example, being sometimes quite different from the official statistics of registered students provided for an official rankings exercise.

These issues underline the imperative of your own research beyond this information and the need for you to verify all important data, especially precise tuition fees, for example, for your chosen course directly with the institution, before you take action based upon it. Any factual clarifications received by the publisher will be posted on www.topuniversities.com as appropriate, which also has electronic links to all the universities profiled in this chapter.

1 Harvard University

Why this university?

So stubbornly independent of one another are the colleges that make up Harvard University, the school is creating an entire new campus largely to encourage the interdisciplinary study that other universities have long ago enthusiastically adopted. And like most everything that Harvard does, the scheme is ambitious almost beyond precedent, a small city in Boston's Allston section, just a short footbridge's walk across the Charles River from Harvard's longtime Cambridge home.

The Allston campus of America's oldest and the planet's richest university — Harvard's endowment wealth now tops US$35 billion — will vastly expand its science and technology programs and will be anchored by two 500,000-square-foot research facilities. One will house the Harvard Stem Cell Institute, the first noncommercial enterprise in the United States to create disease-specific stem-cell lines to develop treatments for, now, incurable conditions.

It will take a decade for the new campus to take shape. Harvard isn't waiting around. It already conducts ground-breaking medical research, largely in its affiliated hospitals, which are among the world's best. Beginning with the 19th-century introduction of anaesthesia, Harvard scientists were the first to synthesise chlorophyll and cholesterol, invented the pacemaker, performed the first human kidney transplant, developed the defibrillator, learned how to decode the structure of genes, discovered nuclear magnetic

FACTFILE

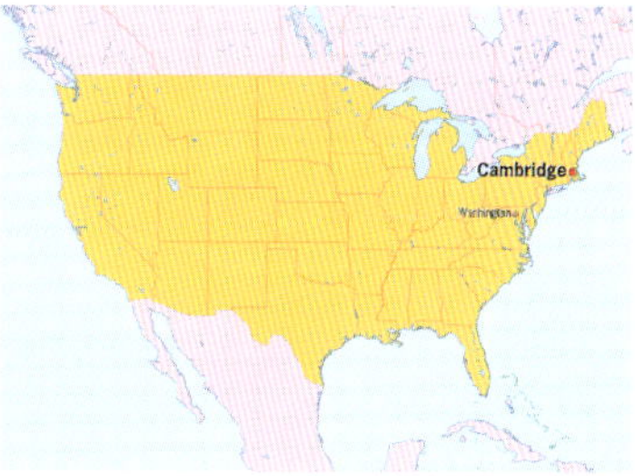

HARVARD University

Country	United States
Foundation Year	1636
World Ranking	1 (1)

Faculty Area Rankings

Arts & Humanities	1
Engineering & IT	15
Life Sciences & Biomedicine	1
Natural Sciences	4
Social Sciences	1

Survey Performance

Peer Review	2
Recruiter Review	4

Contact Details

1350 Massachusetts Ave
Cambridge
MA 2138
www.harvard.edu
+1 617 495 1000

People

Student Faculty Ratio	4.7:1
International Faculty	31.0%
Undergraduates	3,593
Postgraduates	10,237
International Students	23.0%

Course Fees For Domestic Students

Average Undergraduate	$30,275
Average Postgraduate	$32,518

Overall Research Strength

Papers (Scopus 2002-2006)	132,611
Citations (Scopus 2002-2006)	1,164,052
Impact	8.8

Research Impact By Faculty Area

Engineering & IT	5.1
Life Sciences & Biomedicine	9.1
Natural Sciences	11.1
Social Sciences	5.6

resonance and bred the first transgenic mouse. Harvard's faculty, which has produced 43 Nobel laureates (its alumni have won another 32 Nobels), also developed the modern theory of magnetism based on quantum mechanics and proved that the universe will go on expanding forever. Harvard's library is the largest at any academic institution in the world, with nearly 16 million volumes.

The university has also been serious about fulfilling its mission of serving the public good while commercializing technology. A deal it signed for licensing a new, less expensive process to develop vaccines, for instance, includes a proviso with its commercial partner that the vaccine be sold at affordable prices in poor and developing countries, and for Harvard to forgo its royalties for such uses. In all, the university's 2,500 non-medical and 11,000 medical school faculty conduct about US$400 million a year in research. The university is actively trying to increase the number of women on that faculty after a controversy in which its confrontational former president was quoted (largely out of context) theorizing that women did not have the innate ability to succeed in the sciences. Now the university has its first woman president and an initiative to support tenure-track women.

Nine applicants vie for every seat in the entering class. A university review has recommended improving the quality of teaching and rewarding successful teachers by encouraging faculty to share course materials and teaching practices and linking good teaching to salaries and career advancement. This follows complaints that teaching is an afterthought for faculty more concerned with research and writing.

People

Harvard's alumni have served as leaders in every field, from seven US presidents (including George W Bush, who went to Harvard Business School) to Benazir Bhutto and Al Gore. Some of the most famous, however, are the ones who dropped out, including Microsoft's Bill Gates (he reportedly quit when Harvard objected to his use of university computers for private business). Other Harvard dropouts: Polaroid founder Edwin Land, publishing magnate William Randolph Hearst, and actor Matt Damon.

What students say

It was the generous financial aid that made Harvard possible for Wojtek Kaszynski, an undergraduate from Poland who is majoring in applied mathematics. But what attracted him in the first place, he said, was the idea of a liberal arts undergraduate education — "this idea of going to school, yes to learn something, but more to just to go to school and figure things out." Mr. Kaszynski doesn't dispute that students aren't always delighted with the teaching at Harvard. "The best researchers are not always the best teachers. And the faculty will not seek out actively to get in touch with you. It's on the side of the students to be proactive and meet the faculty." But he added, "My experience is that if I wanted to meet a particular professor, I certainly could. I've met a number of famous professors. I just emailed and set up an appointment."

Good at

Everything. Top of the world for the arts and humanities, social sciences and the life sciences and biomedicine, improving on last year's stellar performance.

2= Cambridge University

Why this university?

Only one university outperforms Cambridge in our ranking — and, importantly in the context of Britain's most enduring academic rivalry, it is not Oxford. But this year, for the first time, the ancient universities are tied with Yale in second place. Cambridge has tended to score more highly in national assessments of teaching and research over recent years. Traditionally supreme in the sciences, where it was ranked best in the world in successive years, Cambridge has also strengthened the arts and social sciences.

Cambridge is preparing to celebrate its 800th anniversary with a £1 billion fundraising campaign. There have been plenty of high-profile developments in recent years — from attracting Microsoft's first research base outside the United States to securing £60 million from the government for an innovative link with the Massachusetts Institute of Technology — but overall funding levels have remained a concern. The campaign is intended to at least narrow the gap with the US Ivy League.

Some 3,200 of the 18,000 students are from outside the European Union and the proportion may rise in the next few years. Already a third of the places are taken by postgraduates — more than half of whom are from overseas — and this is where any growth is likely to come.

The university dominates the small city of Cambridge, 50 miles north-east of London in East Anglia. All students belong to one of the 31

FACTFILE

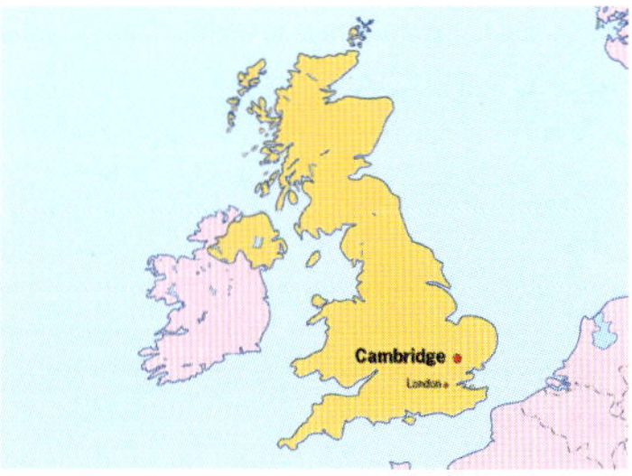

University of CAMBRIDGE

Country.. United Kingdom
Foundation Year 1209
World Ranking .... 2= (2)

Faculty Area Rankings

Arts & Humanities 4
Engineering & IT... 5
Life Sciences & Biomedicine................................ 2
Natural Sciences... 3
Social Sciences 7

Survey Performance

Peer Review 3
Recruiter Review 1

Contact Details

Trinity Lane
Cambridge
CB2 1TN
www.cam.ac.uk
+44 1223 337 733

People

Student Faculty Ratio..................................... 4.9:1
International Faculty.................................. 39.0%
Undergraduates 12,699
Postgraduates 5,611
International Students 23.0%

Course Fees For Domestic Students

Average Undergraduate.............................. $6,294
Average Postgraduate $10,949

Overall Research Strength

Papers (Scopus 2002-2006)......................... 96,598
Citations (Scopus 2002-2006) 592,627
Impact 6.1

Research Impact By Faculty Area

Engineering & IT... 3.4
Life Sciences & Biomedicine.............................. 7.5
Natural Sciences.. 6.2
Social Sciences 4.1

colleges which, with a handful of exceptions, are dotted around the city centre. Many boast historic buildings, several along the banks of the River Cam, where students and tourists go punting when the weather allows. Three colleges are for women only, while the rest are mixed.

Overseas students are guaranteed university-owned accommodation if they want it. A limited number of scholarships are available to overseas students and research students may be offered a small amount of teaching work.

People

The 81 "affiliates" of the university who have won Nobel prizes are divided among every category. They include Francis Crick and James Watson, who mastered the structure of DNA, and, more recently, Amartya Sen for his work in development economics, and geneticist John Sulston. Stephen Hawking has become one of the world's best-known scientists, while the student drama company Footlights has produced a stream of stars for the cinema and theatre.

What students say

Denise Law, a second year engineering student from Hong Kong, applied to Cambridge because she felt it is one of the few UK universities that can compete with the US institutions. She has encountered a lot of positive aspects to studying at Cambridge: "It's a lovely city with great heritage and very nice and helpful people. Plus the education and facilities are first class."

However, she acknowledged that the workload involved took her by surprise: "You're expected to make the most of supervisions by asking questions and taking the initiative, as opposed to the 'spoonfeeding' in A Levels. The learning curve is steep".

But, reassuringly, she added: "I was told that no one was ever kicked out for finding the material difficult. You won't get into trouble unless you adopt a 'can't be bothered' attitude or give up."

Good at

Every academic area is in the top ten in our rankings. Cambridge is in the top three for the life sciences and biomedicine, the natural sciences and the arts and humanities.

2= Oxford University

Why this university?

Oxford is the oldest university in the English-speaking world, dating back nine centuries, and also probably the best known. It has now caught Cambridge in our rankings, tying for second place with its ancient rival and with Yale. Oxford comes out on top in some UK league tables, but the two are invariably mentioned in the same breath when leading universities are discussed.

The 39 Oxford colleges select their own students and are responsible for much of the teaching, especially in the arts and social sciences. The Vice-Chancellor, Dr John Hood, who arrived from Auckland University in 2004, has been trying to push through reforms aimed at helping Oxford to compete not only with Cambridge but with the American Ivy League. The changes may include increasing the proportion of postgraduates and overseas students. At the moment, nearly two-thirds of the 18,000 students are undergraduates and about a fifth are from outside the European Union. Some 130 nationalities are represented in the student body and among an increasingly cosmopolitan faculty.

Traditionally, Oxford's strengths have been in the arts and social sciences, which have provided most of the 25 UK prime ministers educated at the university. But the sciences have been growing in quality — a £60 million development houses the world's largest chemistry department, for example — and the Saïd Business School, established only in 1996, has already carved out a strong reputation.

FACTFILE

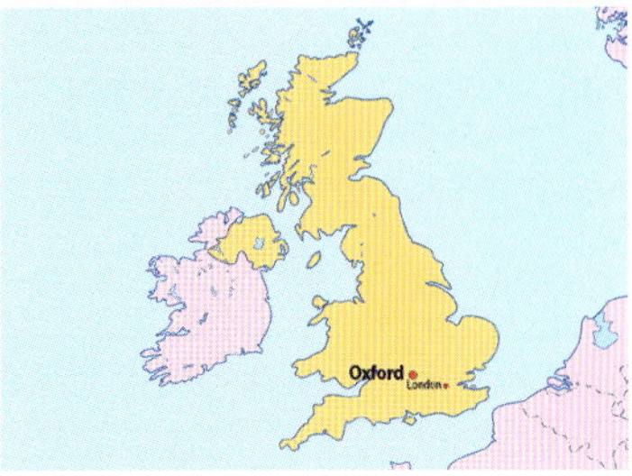

University of OXFORD

Country	United Kingdom
Foundation Year	1096
World Ranking	2= (3)

Faculty Area Rankings

Arts & Humanities	3
Engineering & IT	12
Life Sciences & Biomedicine	3
Natural Sciences	8
Social Sciences	6

Survey Performance

Peer Review	5
Recruiter Review	2

Contact Details

Wellington Square
Oxford
OX1 2JD
www.ox.ac.uk
+441865 270 000

People

Student Faculty Ratio	4.7:1
International Faculty	36.0%
Undergraduates	12,310
Postgraduates	6,357
International Students	27.0%

Course Fees For Domestic Students

Average Undergraduate	$6,294
Average Postgraduate	$6,400

Course Fees For International Students

Average Undergraduate	$21,078
Average Postgraduate	$22,155

Overall Research Strength

Papers (Scopus 2002-2006)	88,869
Citations (Scopus 2002-2006)	588,445
Impact	6.6

Research Impact By Faculty Area

Engineering & IT	3.7
Life Sciences & Biomedicine	7.8
Natural Sciences	6.3
Social Sciences	4.2

Most of the colleges and other university buildings are in or close to the centre of the city of Oxford, which is within reach of some of England's most picturesque countryside but only an hour by train from London. Although best known for the university, the city is large enough to have a life of its own.

Overseas students are guaranteed residential accommodation if they want it. Several hundred international students each year benefit from a range of scholarships and bursaries, the biggest of the schemes being the Rhodes Scholarships and the Clarendon Fund Scholarships. Details appear in the university's International Student Guide. Postgraduate fees for overseas students range from £9,235 in the social sciences to £40,000 for an Executive MBA, while Oxford puts average living costs at £9,750 a year.

People

Among scores of famous alumni are Erasmus, the philosopher Thomas Hobbes, the playwright Oscar Wilde, the author JRR Tolkein and the chemist Dorothy Hodgkin, the only British woman to win a Nobel prize. More recent alumni include President Bill Clinton and Tim Berners Lee, inventor of the World Wide Web.

What students say

Jenny Rigterink, a third-year English language and literature undergraduate: "The pros are the unparalleled teaching and resources at your fingertips, but the cons are a stagnant social scene that seems far too old for its audience." She says "Oxford will transform your life. The majority of people seem willing to let Oxford change them, but Oxford is begging for a generation that will turn things upside down."

She suggests to potential overseas applicants: "If you're foreign, make contact with potential tutors before you apply."

Good at

Only engineering and IT are outside the top ten in our rankings — and then only just. Oxford is in the top three for the arts and humanities and for the life sciences and biomedicine.

2= Yale University

Why this university?

A university that numbers both George H W Bush and Bill Clinton, as well as both George W Bush and John Kerry, among its graduates, must be providing a broad education. In fact, Yale does have one of the broadest curricula in American higher education, requiring its undergraduates to take at least three classes in each of four groups — languages, culture, social sciences, and science and maths. All students are required to speak a foreign language and to submit a senior essay or project, unusual in American higher education.

The university also seeks to make itself affordable for the broadest possible range of students, easing the financial burden on long-squeezed middle-class families. Beginning in the 2005-06 school year, families with combined incomes below US$45,000 a year were no longer required to pay any portion of the cost of their children's education at the school, a groundbreaking shift being watched closely by other universities. (International students are eligible for the same financial aid as US citizens.) There is also a loan-forgiveness program for law school graduates who go into public service.

Many of the programs at Yale centre around small classes; nearly a third of the classes enrol fewer than 10 students, and three-quarters have fewer than 20. The law school, for example, has 115 full- and part-time faculty for its 650 students. Yale has 11,483 students — about half of them undergraduates — and 3,333 faculty. Only one in 10 applicants is

FACTFILE

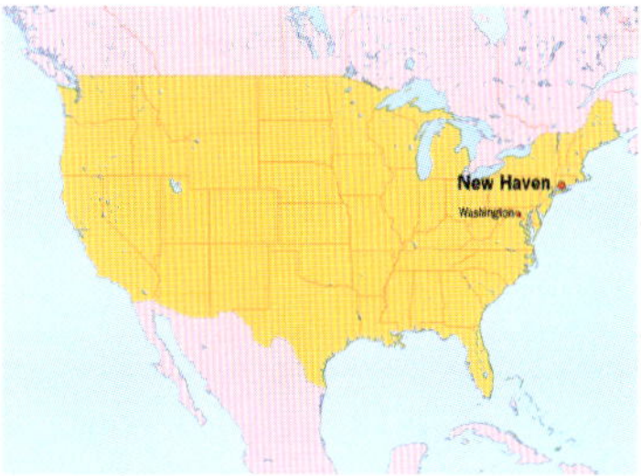

YALE University

Country	United States
Foundation Year	1701
World Ranking	2= (4=)

Faculty Area Rankings

Arts & Humanities	5
Engineering & IT	46
Life Sciences & Biomedicine	8
Natural Sciences	10
Social Sciences	4

Survey Performance

Peer Review	8
Recruiter Review	13

Contact Details

P.O. Box 208236
New Haven
CT 06520
www.yale.edu
+1 203 432 4771

People

Student Faculty Ratio	3.4:1
International Faculty	24.0%
Undergraduates	5,218
Postgraduates	4,383
International Students	16.0%

Course Fees For Domestic Students

Average Undergraduate	$33,030
Average Postgraduate	$26,800

Overall Research Strength

Papers (Scopus 2002-2006)	98,729
Citations (Scopus 2002-2006)	710,313
Impact	7.2

Research Impact By Faculty Area

Engineering & IT	4.5
Life Sciences & Biomedicine	7.5
Natural Sciences	8.8
Social Sciences	4.3

admitted, the lowest proportion in the country. (16 per cent of students are international — top countries of origin are China, Canada, South Korea, India, the UK, Germany, Italy, and Japan.) Undergraduates are divided into 12 small residential colleges of 450 students each. The most popular undergraduate majors are history, political science, and economics.

Named for Elihu Yale, who gave the young school 417 books and a portrait of King George I in 1716, Yale is in New Haven, Connecticut, a small city plagued with problems of urban poverty. This economic decline appears to be slowly reversing, helped in part by the role of the university in attracting biomedical and pharmaceutical companies. Some US$428 million a year in research is conducted at the university itself.

People

Alumni include both President Bushes and President Clinton, but also Presidents William Howard Taft and Gerald Ford and Senator Hillary Rodham Clinton; actors Jodie Foster, Sigourney Weaver, Sam Waterston, and Meryl Streep; former and current CEOs of FedEx and Coca Cola; 12 Nobel laureates; and Samuel F.B. Morse, the inventor of the telegraph.

What students say

"The biggest advantage of Yale is that it represents a sort of bubble of ideas from different perspectives," said Komli-Kofi Atsina, a student from Ghana who just received his undergraduate degree in molecular biophysics and biochemistry and is going on to medical school at the University of Pittsburgh. "It is a place that is so representative of the wide diversity around the world, a melting pot for crazy ideas, genius ideas, different kinds of ideology. In that respect, it's a great place for learning."

Good at

Only engineering and IT are outside the top 20 in our rankings. Yale is in the top ten for social science and the arts and humanities.

5 Imperial College London

Why this university?

Almost a third of Imperial College's students are from outside the European Union — 3,630 out of 12,129. Its specialisms of science, technology, medicine and engineering also make it the most male-dominated university institution in Britain. Female students, however, did double during the 1990s and are now up to a third.

Imperial College is an academic powerhouse in its chosen fields and is considered to be a rival to Oxford and Cambridge. Its 2,970 academic and research staff include Nobel prizewinners and 61 Fellows of the Royal Society. Three quarters of the academics entered in the latest research assessment exercise were in departments considered internationally outstanding — the highest proportion in any UK university — and almost all were in one of the top two categories.

On top of the traditional strengths of science and engineering, Imperial has built one of the largest and most powerful medical schools in Britain and a management school that is making its mark internationally. Language courses are available as joint degrees with management or science subjects. Like many London institutions, Imperial has not done particularly well in the annual National Student Survey, but those in electronic engineering and computer science were the most satisfied with their courses.

Imperial College can claim the invention of penicillin and of magnetically-levitated trains among its successes. The college is also respected for its

FACTFILE

Imperial College LONDON

Country.. United Kingdom
Foundation Year 1907
World Ranking 5 (9)

Faculty Area Rankings

Arts & Humanities 170
Engineering & IT.. 6
Life Sciences & Biomedicine 7
Natural Sciences.. 13
Social Sciences 73

Survey Performance

Peer Review 23
Recruiter Review 7

Contact Details

South Kensington Campus
London
SW7 2AZ
www3.imperial.ac.uk
+44 20 7589 5111

People

Student Faculty Ratio...................................... 4.1:1
International Faculty.................................... 39.0%
Undergraduates 7,927
Postgraduates 4,098
International Students 37.0%

Course Fees For Domestic Students

Average Undergraduate.............................. $6,294
Average Postgraduate $7,388

Course Fees For International Students

Average Undergraduate............................ $34,357
Average Postgraduate $31,608

Overall Research Strength

Papers (Scopus 2002-2006).......................... 83,046
Citations (Scopus 2002-2006) 430,570
Impact 5.2

Research Impact By Faculty Area

Engineering & IT... 2.7
Life Sciences & Biomedicine 6.2
Natural Sciences... 5.3
Social Sciences 6.3

strong links with both government and industry, boasting the largest external research income in the UK. Many distinguished scientists and engineers make a significant contribution to the direction of UK business and policy.

Many eyes have been on Imperial College since it announced that it was to leave the University of London in time for its centenary in 2007. The decision was made to trade on a reputation that puts the college in the top five universities in our world rankings — up four places from last year. The student services that were provided by the federal university are being replicated by the college, which was making little use of some shared facilities.

Imperial's headquarters could hardly be in a more glamorous part of London. South Kensington's cosmopolitan vibe and museums show off London at its best. That can increase the cost of living, but overseas students are guaranteed college-owned accommodation. London remains by far the most popular location for those coming the the UK to study.

People

Famous alumni include the four-minute miler and academic Sir Roger Bannister, politicians Rajiv Gandhi and Trevor Philips, the writers Simon Singh and HG Wells and pop star Brian May.

What students say

Natsuko graduated with an MSc in biochemistry in 2004 and went on to study for a PhD at Imperial College.

She said: "I chose Imperial because of its worldwide reputation for teaching and research excellence. I also liked the fact that it is located in the centre of London.

"London was scary at first as I had never lived in such a large city before, but I soon got used to it and discovered that it is an exciting place to live as a student. There is an endless supply of entertainment, so you can always find things to do. It's very cosmopolitan and I got to meet lots of people from so many different countries and backgrounds! I spent most of my spare time with my friends. We often went out to restaurants, pubs and cinemas and visited the famous tourist spots.

"Imperial does work you hard, so you need to be committed and disciplined to be successful. But it really does pay off in the end. A lot of employers are interested in the graduates from Imperial College and you get a great network of people who can help you in your future career, whatever it is that you want to do."

Good at

Imperial is ranked by other academics in the top ten in the world for engineering and IT and the natural sciences. It is 13th for life sciences and biomedicine and 73rd for social sciences, on the strength of its management courses.

6 Princeton University

Why this university?

Second-smallest of the Ivy League universities, with 4,790 undergraduate and 2,010 graduate students, Princeton has a reach far beyond its size. It accepts fewer than one in 10 applicants (some no doubt attracted by the pioneering 'no-loan' financial-aid policy, replacing loans with outright grants even for international students). It has see-sawed with Harvard in the American league tables, and even stolen some top faculty from its rival. Princeton's full-time faculty numbers about 850, all of whom must teach in addition to doing research — another tweak at Harvard, where students have complained that their professors are more interested in what they're doing in the lab than in the classroom. Ten Princeton faculty members are Nobel laureates. In turn, all undergraduates are required to submit a senior thesis, an option most other US universities make optional. All must also successfully complete two courses each in literature and the arts, science and technology, and social analysis, and one course each in epistemology and cognition, ethical thought and moral values, historical analysis, and quantitative reasoning. Even engineering students have to take at least seven humanities and social sciences courses.

The emphasis on teaching doesn't mean that Princeton doesn't have a robust tradition of research. Some US$220 million a year in research is conducted there, US$77 million of it at the Princeton Plasma Laboratory, which the university administers on behalf of the US Department of Energy.

FACTFILE

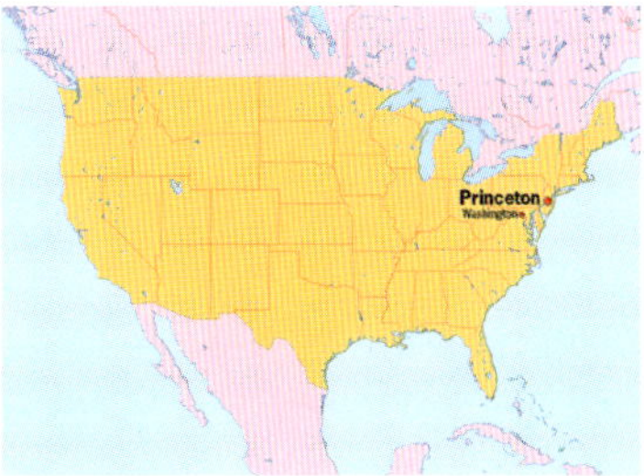

PRINCETON University

Country	United States
Foundation Year	1746
World Ranking	6 (10)

Faculty Area Rankings

Arts & Humanities	7
Engineering & IT	14
Life Sciences & Biomedicine	29
Natural Sciences	5
Social Sciences	9

Survey Performance

Peer Review	7
Recruiter Review	46

Contact Details

Princeton
NJ 08544
www.princeton.edu
+1 609 258 3000

People

Student Faculty Ratio	6.2:1
International Faculty	24.0%
Undergraduates	4,783
Postgraduates	2,012
International Students	16.0%

Course Fees For Domestic Students

Average Undergraduate	$33,000
Average Postgraduate	$29,910

Overall Research Strength

Papers (Scopus 2002-2006)	52,882
Citations (Scopus 2002-2006)	465,820
Impact	8.8

Research Impact By Faculty Area

Engineering & IT	4.7
Life Sciences & Biomedicine	7.5
Natural Sciences	12.2
Social Sciences	4.5

Since the millennium alone, it has established the Lewis-Sigler Institute for Integrative Genomics to encourage interdisciplinary collaboration between biologists and scientists in physics, chemistry, chemical engineering, molecular biology, and other fields; the Princeton Neuroscience Institute, which does the same thing in the area of brain and nervous system studies; and the Princeton Center for Theoretical Physics, which combines various departments to do research on everything from the Big Bang to quantum computing. The university's engineering school specializes in dissecting the connection between technology and economics, politics, the arts, and other fields.

In addition to an endowment that helps support PhD candidates, Princeton also gives three months of paid leave from research and teaching to new mothers and child-care grants to doctoral students who become parents.

People

Princeton alumni include US presidents James Madison and Woodrow Wilson, after whom the university named its Woodrow Wilson School of Public and International Affairs.

What students say

"It's a small university for the Ivy League, and there's a lot of focus on the undergraduates," said Ritu Kamal, an undergraduate from India studying bioengineering. "The faculty are willing to take undergraduates into their labs and give them a lot of personal attention. In science departments, students do a lot of hands-on lab work alongside grad students who are doing research that will probably be published."

For her part, Ms Kamal is doing hands-on work with stem cells. "It doesn't get much more cutting-edge than that," she said.

Good at

Princeton makes the top 30 in every academic area and is in the top five for the natural sciences, arts and humanities and the social sciences.

7= California Institute of Technology

Why this university?

One of America's smallest major research universities, with only 2,100 students, Caltech is also one of its best. Those students boast the highest average scores in the nation on the SAT university entrance examination, and with almost 1,300 faculty, visiting faculty, and postdocs, they enjoy a cozy student-faculty ratio of only three-to-one. (There are about 60 international students, and two and a half times as many men as women.) 30 per cent of classes have fewer than 10 students. Research is closely integrated with education.

Expectations here are high. Every student has to take at least five terms of mathematics, two of chemistry, one of biology and five of physics, including quantum mechanics, special relativity, and statistical mechanics.

To deal with the stress of this, collaboration is encouraged. So is a sense of humor. During final examination weeks, Wagner's "Ride of the Valkyries" is broadcast from loudspeakers across the campus every day at 7 am Caltech students also delight in playing pranks on their cross-country rival, the Massachusetts Institute of Technology, once manipulating that university's name as inscribed above the entrance of the MIT main building to read: "That Other Institute of Technology."

FACTFILE

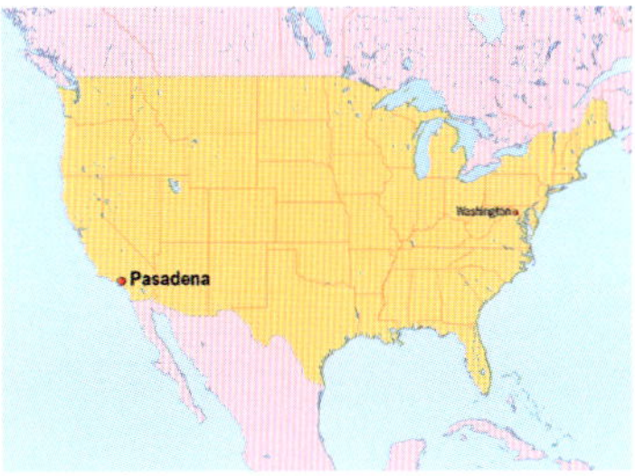

CALIFORNIA Institute of Technology (Caltech)

Country	United States
Foundation Year	1891
World Ranking	7= (7)

Faculty Area Rankings

Arts & Humanities	153
Engineering & IT	4
Life Sciences & Biomedicine	21
Natural Sciences	6
Social Sciences	70

Survey Performance

Peer Review	21
Recruiter Review	227

Contact Details

1200 East California Boulevard
Pasadena
California 91125
www.caltech.edu
+1 626 395 6811

People

Student Faculty Ratio	2.9:1
International Faculty	46.0%
Undergraduates	890
Postgraduates	1,307
International Students	23.0%

Course Fees For Domestic Students

Average Undergraduate	$29,940
Average Postgraduate	$25,355

Overall Research Strength

Papers (Scopus 2002-2006)	71,049
Citations (Scopus 2002-2006)	535,175
Impact	7.5

Research Impact By Faculty Area

Engineering & IT	3.7
Life Sciences & Biomedicine	10.4
Natural Sciences	9.1
Social Sciences	3.4

People

14 Caltech professors, 17 alumni, and four professors, who were also alumni, have won the Nobel prize for breakthroughs in almost every major scientific field. They made the first astronomical survey of the entire sky visible from the Northern Hemisphere, for example, and virtually invented seismology. It was Caltech physicist Carl Anderson who discovered anti-matter, chemist Linus Pauling who showed how atoms link up to form molecules, psychobiologist Roger Sperry who devised the left brain-right brain theory, and geophysicist Charles Richter who invented the scale for measuring earthquakes (which occasionally shake the ground beneath the campus, just north of Los Angeles). The university also operates the famous Jet Propulsion Laboratory under contract to NASA. Among its international alumni are former Israeli foreign and defence minister Moshe Arens and Steingrimur Hermannsson, the former prime minister of Iceland. Alumni also include Chester Carlson, the inventor of photocopying; Intel chairman Gordon Moore; and Frank Capra, director of the film classic It's a Wonderful Life.

What students say

Todd Gingrich, an undergraduate, was drawn to Caltech because he wanted a challenge; he had already jumped ahead to university courses while he was still in high school. Mr. Gingrich wasn't disappointed. "There's sort of this perception, which now that I'm here I can verify, that it's reasonably hardcore," he said.

The school's small size is mostly an advantage, he said. "People all know each other, you're living with a group of your good friends, and people are always looking out for you in a way that doesn't happen in a bigger school. I have this amazing network of peers in every field of math and science and I use it all the time."

Many of these students live in small residential houses. "It's almost as if a bunch of nerds had taken over all the frats," said Mr Gingrich.

Most come naturally to the university's tradition of humor, he said. "The student body is pretty quirky. It's a very tight-knit group of students, and most of the people here have this mode they can switch into where they can relax."

There can be a downside to this, too. "It's a school that's highly focused on a very small subject and a very small area of study, so as a consequence you get a group of students who are all quite similar. Often times I love that, but there are times where people wish there were more people here, different types of people — like girls."

Good at

Caltech is in the top six in the world for engineering and IT and for the natural sciences, and just outside the top 20 for life sciences and biomedicine.

7= University of Chicago

Why this university?

"We are uncommon." That's the motto on T-shirts donned by students at the University of Chicago critical of the school's controversial decision to accept the common application, an online time-saver that makes it possible for applicants to vie for seats in any of 300 US universities. Their protests persuaded the school to preserve the unique essay questions for which it's famous — asking that prospective students devise a brunch menu and a guest list for historical, literary "or other disreputable persons" and include dialogue from the meal that reveals something about themselves, for example, or write an essay inspired by a giant jar of mustard.

It's just one way that University of Chicago students have been fiercely protective of their school's intellectual seriousness. This school's heady credo: "Dedicated to the primacy of research, the intimate relationship of research to teaching, and the amelioration of the condition of humankind." After all, it was at this university that the first controlled, self-sustaining nuclear reaction was produced in 1942. So influential is the economics taught here that it has given rise to an entire field known as the Chicago School, combining basic theory with the psychology of what makes individuals and companies behave the way they do. Several members of the vaunted economics faculty are among the 80 Nobel laureates that have been affiliated with the university, including America's first: Albert Michelson, who calculated the speed of light. Other research at Chicago has demonstrated that

FACTFILE

University of CHICAGO

Country	United States
Foundation Year	1890
World Ranking	7= (11)

Faculty Area Rankings

Arts & Humanities	9
Engineering & IT	107
Life Sciences & Biomedicine	37
Natural Sciences	11
Social Sciences	8

Survey Performance

Peer Review	15
Recruiter Review	21

Contact Details

5801 S. Ellis Avenue
Chicago
IL 60637
www.uchicago.edu
+1 773 702 1234

People

Student Faculty Ratio	4.6:1
International Faculty	19.0%
Undergraduates	4,509
Postgraduates	7,228
International Students	22.0%

Course Fees For Domestic Students

Average Undergraduate	$33,336
Average Postgraduate	$31,680

Overall Research Strength

Papers (Scopus 2002-2006)	62,458
Citations (Scopus 2002-2006)	472,931
Impact	7.6

Research Impact By Faculty Area

Engineering & IT	5.5
Life Sciences & Biomedicine	6.6
Natural Sciences	13.8
Social Sciences	4.4

cancer is genetic, verified black holes and the "big bang" theory, developed the malaria pill and discovered the jet stream. The university also has the oldest sociology department in the United States, and was an early practitioner of interdisciplinary scholarship. The Graduate School of Business, second-oldest business school in the world and consistently ranked among the best, has campuses in London and Singapore and a European studies program based in a satellite center in Paris.

This is a place that takes higher education very seriously. Its 10-week quarters accelerate a learning process divided elsewhere into much longer semesters. Students are constantly subjected to examinations that test them on the rigorous core academic requirements. Updated in 1998 — also with some controversy — these requirements have been extended to include a foreign language and greater international and cross-cultural studies.

The university also conducts US$375 million a year in research and is building US$2 billion worth of new facilities including a Center for Integrative Science and a 10-storey biomedical research center. It is setting aside US$400 million, including US$100 million from a single anonymous donor, for student financial aid, entirely eliminating the need for loans for its middle-class students.

The flip side of Chicago's notorious seriousness is that it's not an especially fun place. "Our un-fun-ness has been the subject of both mirth and pride," a task force on the matter put it. "Although students take immense pride in the excellence of the academic program here, many feel that this comes at a high price, citing excessive academic pressure, lack of time, and competitiveness, as the biggest difficulties they encounter." Some say Chicago is the only school in America where the undergraduates are under more stress than the graduate students.

People

Alumni include former US Attorney General John Ashcroft, former World Bank President Paul Wolfowitz, authors Kurt Vonnegut Jr and Philip Roth, composer Philip Glass, astronomer Edwin Hubble, the Reverend Jesse Jackson, director Mike Nichols, and the current or former presidents of other universities on this list, including Northwestern and Caltech.

What students say

It was Chicago's competitiveness that attracted Bonginkhosi Mzileni, a student from Swaziland majoring in chemistry. "It is tough," Mr Mzileni said. "I found it even harder than I expected. We do get a lot of work every week and the quarter system puts you under a lot of pressure." But in the end, he said, succeeding at a school known for being so competitive is likely to serve him well in his career.

Mr. Mzileni agrees that, as he puts it, "People are a bit too serious most of the time. Even outside class people like to talk about mostly academics, about their homework, about how hard it is and how much work it is."

Good at

Chicago is in the top ten for the social sciences and the arts and humanities, and only just outside it for the natural sciences.

9 University College London (UCL)

Why this university?

University College London is a firm favourite with overseas students who make up almost a third of its student population — indeed, the college describes itself as 'London's Global University'. It is developing courses in global citizenship and leadership to be integrated into all undergraduate programs. Nearly 4,000 students come from outside the European Union and 2,000 from within it. These numbers are expected to grow still further in the next few years.

Apart from its cosmopolitan feel, UCL shares many other similarities with Oxford and Cambridge. The college is committed to teaching in small groups, especially in the second and subsequent years of degree courses. This may well explain its high levels of achievement: almost three-quarters leave with a first or an upper second class degree. Its drop-out rate is also low: barely 3 per cent, according to the latest figures. This is well below the national average for the courses it offers and the entry grades it demands.

UCL has even overtaken Oxford and Cambridge in the past for the amount of research support it has been allocated by the British Government's funding council. The university prides itself on excellence in biomedicine, Slavonic and East European Studies, among many other subjects. It pioneered degrees in architecture and law and has an excellent reputation for fine arts.

FACTFILE

UCL (University College LONDON)

Country	United Kingdom
Foundation Year	1826
World Ranking	9 (25)

Faculty Area Rankings

Arts & Humanities	27
Engineering & IT	94
Life Sciences & Biomedicine	26
Natural Sciences	70
Social Sciences	32

Survey Performance

Peer Review	34
Recruiter Review	22

Contact Details

Gower Street
London
WC1E 6BT
www.ucl.ac.uk
+44 20 7679 2000

People

Student Faculty Ratio	4.4:1
International Faculty	29.0%
Undergraduates	11,471
Postgraduates	5,646
International Students	29.0%

Course Fees For Domestic Students

Average Undergraduate	$6,294
Average Postgraduate	$6,643

Course Fees For International Students

Average Undergraduate	$26,890
Average Postgraduate	$24,991

Overall Research Strength

Papers (Scopus 2002-2006)	96,548
Citations (Scopus 2002-2006)	567,055
Impact	5.9

Research Impact By Faculty Area

Engineering & IT	3.1
Life Sciences & Biomedicine	6.2
Natural Sciences	5.3
Social Sciences	7.6

With 4,280 academic and research staff, UCL is comfortably the largest of the University of London's colleges and has now begun to award its own degrees. At the end of the 1990s it took in a number of specialist schools and institutes, most of which were medical or dental, adding to an already large medical school. The college has launched the biggest-ever fundraising effort at any UK university to support further developments.

Although parts of UCL are in north London, such as the Royal Free Hospital, most of campus life is based in busy, but beautiful, Bloomsbury, in the centre of the city. Here the academic pace is frantic with its close proximity to the West End. Students have immediate access to London University's underused central students' union facilities. The main outdoor sports facilities are a coach ride away in leafy Hertfordshire.

People

Former alumni include Indian leader Mahatma Gandhi (Law, 1889), TV presenter Jonathan Dimbleby (Philosophy, 1969), Japanese Prime Minister Junichiro Koizumi (Economics, 1969) and the inventor of the telephone Alexander Graham Bell (Phonetics, 1860s).

What students say

Erik Moore, from Australia is studying part-time for an MSc in environmental design and engineering. He said: "By offering the flexibility of working and studying at the same time, I feel I've really got the most I could from my degree at UCL. It's been the right mix of academic work twinned with practical work — with loads of extra guest lectures for those that want to learn more. The standard of teaching has been exceptional and with a mix of international students from a range of different backgrounds, I've learnt a lot about how design works in different sectors."

Good at

UCL is ranked in the top 30 for the arts and humanities and the life sciences and biomedicine, and is only just outside it for social science. It is in the top 100 in every academic area.

10 Massachusetts Institute of Technology (MIT)

Why this university?

Every January, the Massachusetts Institute of Technology runs an "Independent Activities Period" during which students can select such non-credit subjects as yoga, folk-dancing, chocolate sculpture-making, magic, palmistry, effective speaking, the symbolism of the Star Wars films, and how to make chain mail.

It is a whimsical break from the intensity of the demanding academics at a school whose students are required to take two semesters each of calculus and physics, one each of biology and chemistry, and various courses in the humanities, arts, and social sciences.

What makes MIT so tough, beyond the pressure its high-achieving students famously put on themselves, is the concept of the "teaching laboratory", which was pioneered there, combining teaching with applied research. It also makes the university one of the leading research institutions in America, where 3,500 scientists and scholars in addition to the 1,000 faculty (and 2,500 graduate students employed as research assistants) work on more than US$1 billion a year of research.

Just in the last few years, research teams at MIT, which is in the small city of Cambridge across the Charles River from Boston, have developed a single-electron transistor, invented a process similar to photosynthesis to produce hydrogen, and invented a gas with super-high temperature fluidity. Undergraduates, too, work with faculty on research into fields including cancer

FACTFILE

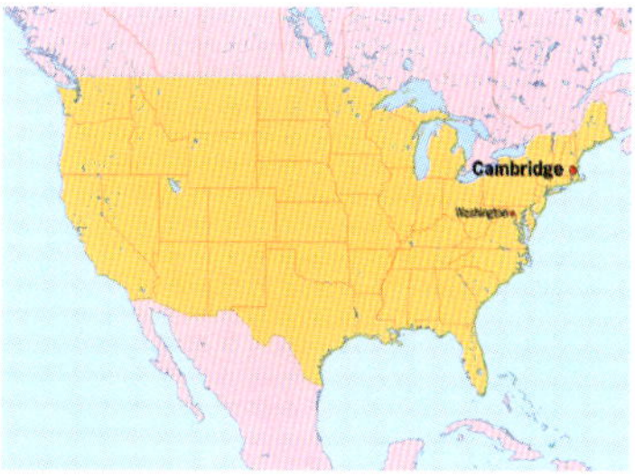

MASSACHUSETTS Institute of Technology (MIT)

Country.......United States
Foundation Year.......1861
World Ranking.......10 (4=)

Faculty Area Rankings

Arts & Humanities.......25
Engineering & IT.......1
Life Sciences & Biomedicine.......9
Natural Sciences.......2
Social Sciences.......11

Survey Performance

Peer Review.......6
Recruiter Review.......6

Contact Details

77 Massachusetts Avenue
Cambridge
MA 02139-4307
web.mit.edu
+1 617 253 1000

People

Student Faculty Ratio.......7.6:1
International Faculty.......0.0%
Undergraduates.......4,088
Postgraduates.......5,991
International Students.......25.0%

Course Fees For Domestic Students

Average Undergraduate.......$33,600
Average Postgraduate.......$33,600

Course Fees For International Students

Average Undergraduate.......$33,600
Average Postgraduate.......$33,600

Overall Research Strength

Papers (Scopus 2002-2006).......102,290
Citations (Scopus 2002-2006).......718,744
Impact.......7.0

Research Impact By Faculty Area

Engineering & IT.......4.0
Life Sciences & Biomedicine.......11.3
Natural Sciences.......7.8
Social Sciences.......4.9

treatment, solar power, and molecular biology through the Undergraduate Research Opportunity Program. The university has about 4,000 undergraduate and 6,000 graduate students, including 2,792 from other countries — the largest contingent from Asia. More than half the undergraduates who have declared a major are enrolled in engineering, the field in which MIT is indisputably preeminent.

This work is conducted in a collection of radically innovative buildings added in a just-completed building spree, including the Frank Gehry-designed Ray and Maria Stata Center for Computer, Information, and Intelligence Sciences and a huge new brain and cognitive sciences complex.

They are physical proof that the 140-year-old university is not resting on its laurels. Its new president, Susan Hockfield — a neuroscientist and the first woman to hold the post—has challenged MIT to find solutions to the world's energy crisis in a campaign involving all five of its schools — science, engineering, management, architecture, and the humanities. The university is also the first to put all of the teaching materials used in its courses onto the Internet without charge, and has set up a biomedical institute in collaboration with nearby Harvard to specialize in genomic medicine.

In addition to its science disciplines, MIT has a top-flight business school, the Sloan School of Management, which attracts mostly mid-career managers. The average age of students in Sloan's MBA program is 28, and the average age in its first-in-the-world university-based executive education program is 38. Students in the Sloan School come from more than 60 countries.

People

Sixty-one past and present MIT faculty and alumni have won the Nobel prize, 31 have received the National Medal of Science, and four have been awarded the Kyoto Prize. MIT leads all universities in America in patents granted.

What students say

Even chocolate sculpture-making fails to completely lighten the mood at a place where the stakes are so high. "In the dorm that I live in, people tend to keep to themselves. They're generally not outgoing. It's a little cold," said Dzikimaki Matara, a junior from Zimbabwe who is majoring in mechanical engineering. He, like many others, alleviates his stress by playing intramural sports (among other things, Matara takes part in an ice-hockey league for students who don't know how to skate). Some 65 per cent of all students play intramural sports, and among the university's many new facilities is a fitness centre with two swimming pools and international-scale squash courts. "The workload is really much heavier than anywhere else," he said. "I talk to friends at other schools and when they're given homework, they can start it the day before it's due. You can't do that here. It took me a while to get used to that." Then again, he said, "After you graduate from MIT, because of all the pressure we have here, when you start working, it's probably won't seem as hard."

Good at

Technology, science, medicine (one, five and 13 in the world) and not bad at social sciences (12) and arts and humanities (21).

11 Columbia University

Why this university?

One of America's oldest universities, opened in 1754 under a royal charter from King George II, is now undergoing one of the most ambitious expansions in the history of American higher education: a US$7.4 billion explosion out of its fortress-like Morningside Heights campus in Manhattan and into the neighboring Harlem section. The expansion will take 30 years and add 6.5 million square feet of labs, classrooms, offices, and housing, 1.5 million of it underground.

But it's what's on the surface that puts Columbia in such high demand: New York. The only Ivy League school in the city, Columbia attracts so many applicants that it's become one of the hardest American universities to get into, and can pick from the cream of the student crop.

There are 24,420 graduate and undergraduate students in all, more than 5,200 — or one in five — from countries outside the United States, the fourth-largest proportion of international scholars at any American university. Most of these are Asian and nearly 90 per cent are attached to the graduate and professional schools. Students from abroad most commonly enroll in engineering, public affairs, business, and social sciences programs.

Some 3,392 faculty teach these students and conduct some US$700 million a year in research, bringing in another US$230 million annually through an aggressive licensing program that has resulted in the awarding of some 110 patents a year for Columbia

FACTFILE

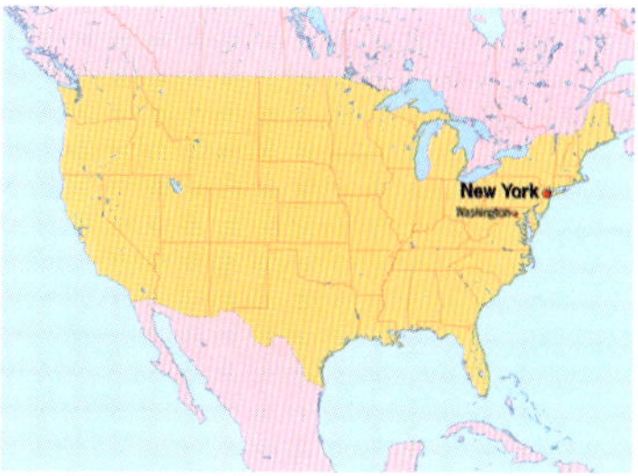

COLUMBIA University

Country	United States
Foundation Year	1754
World Ranking	11 (12)

Faculty Area Rankings

Arts & Humanities	6
Engineering & IT	59
Life Sciences & Biomedicine	25
Natural Sciences	21
Social Sciences	10

Survey Performance

Peer Review	13
Recruiter Review	29

Contact Details

2960 Broadway
New York
United States
NY 10027-6902
www.columbia.edu
+1 212 854 1754

People

Student Faculty Ratio	6.3:1
International Faculty	8.0%
Undergraduates	7,296
Postgraduates	11,433
International Students	22.0%

Course Fees For Domestic Students

Average Undergraduate	$35,166
Average Postgraduate	$30,532

Overall Research Strength

Papers (Scopus 2002-2006)	119,361
Citations (Scopus 2002-2006)	788,512
Impact	6.6

Research Impact By Faculty Area

Engineering & IT	4.0
Life Sciences & Biomedicine	6.8
Natural Sciences	9.0
Social Sciences	4.3

discoveries and breakthroughs. (Rival Harvard, by comparison, makes about US$21 million a year from licensing.) The modern science of anthropology was invented here, as was the field of modern genetics, the laser, and system initial protocol, or SIP, the basis for instant messaging. Columbia physicists I I Rabi, Enrico Fermi, and Polykarp Kusch conducted groundbreaking work into the atom, splitting the uranium atom for the first time in North America. The School of International and Public Affairs founded in the wake of World War II, is among the world's best, and the highly selective Graduate School of Journalism is considered the best in America.

Columbia, like the city it calls home, is a comparatively noisy place. Its early graduates included some of the leaders of the American Revolution. Its students were in the forefront of the 1960s antiwar movement. And it remains a hotbed of controversy involving its Middle Eastern scholars, who have been criticized as being anti-Israel by politicians who have urged the university to fire them, even though a university investigation found these faculty had never pressed their views on students. Columbia administrators did, however, agree to allow students to file grievances against faculty for promoting political causes in the classroom.

People

Among Columbia's prominent alumni have been many who may have made King George regret his royal charter. They include John Jay, the first chief justice of the United States; Alexander Hamilton, the first secretary of the treasury; Gouverneur Morris, the author of the final draft of the US Constitution; and Robert Livingston, who helped draft the Declaration of Independence. More recent graduates have included Presidents Theodore Roosevelt, Franklin D. Roosevelt, and Dwight D. Eisenhower, US Senator Barack Obama, former Secretary of State Madeleine Albright, author Isaac Asimov, and anthropologist Margaret Mead.

What students say

Columbia's best asset is New York, said Stephanie Lew, an undergraduate. "The only thing that's a negative here is housing. They just don't have the best housing. I guess that's New York City for you."

Ms. Lew also appreciates the school's diversity. "It's an environment that's very accepting. Everyone expresses themselves and their cultures."

A major in neuroscience and behavior who plans to become a physical therapist, Ms. Lew found the pre-med classes she took to be comparatively large. "But the professors are always accessible. They have office hours and they answer your emails right away."

Good at

Columbia is in the top 100 in all areas, but its strengths are in the social sciences and arts and humanities, where it is in the top ten.

12 McGill University

Why this university?

McGill University's big research pillars have traditionally been and remain medicine and law. Those two faculties have given the university a reputation in the fields of neurosciences, genomics, cancer, human rights and social policy.

The engineering faculty has spawned specialties in nanotechnology and biomedical engineering. It also has a dental faculty, a school of environmental sciences, a large music faculty and a full complement of arts and sciences.

In terms of those studying full time, last year, the Montreal university enrolled almost 24,000 undergraduate and nearly 7,400 graduate students, with more than 1,300 post-docs, residents and fellows. Last autumn, over 2,200 of its international students came from the US, by far the most common nationality of its non-Canadian contingent. France and China were number two and three, respectively, for countries that McGill attracts. Last year, 119 UK students attended the university.

McGill counts 1,600 tenured or tenure-track professors, with a high proportion being new to both the university and the country. Since January 2000, McGill has hired almost 800 new faculty members, with over 450 recruited from outside Canada.

People

In 1948, John Humphrey, a McGill graduate and law professor, authored

FACTFILE

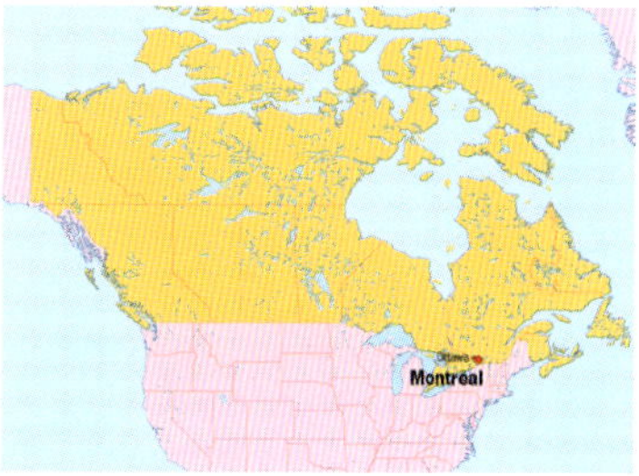

MCGILL University

Country .... Canada
Foundation Year 1821
World Ranking 12 (21)

Faculty Area Rankings

Arts & Humanities 12
Engineering & IT 27
Life Sciences & Biomedicine 10
Natural Sciences 26
Social Sciences 12

Survey Performance

Peer Review 12
Recruiter Review 25

Contact Details

845 Sherbrooke Street West
Montreal
Quebec
H3A 2T5
www.mcgill.ca
+1 514 398 4455

People

Student Faculty Ratio 5:1
International Faculty 20.0%
Undergraduates 17,361
Postgraduates 5,233
International Students 27.0%

Course Fees For Domestic Students

Average Undergraduate $3,296
Average Postgraduate $2,491

Course Fees For International Students

Average Undergraduate $13,751
Average Postgraduate $6,513

Overall Research Strength

Papers (Scopus 2002-2006) 86,694
Citations (Scopus 2002-2006) 415,026
Impact 4.8

Research Impact By Faculty Area

Engineering & IT 2.4
Life Sciences & Biomedicine 5.5
Natural Sciences 4.4
Social Sciences 3.8

the first draft of the Universal Declaration of Human Rights. Four McGill graduates have won Nobel prizes: Andrew Victor Schally (Medicine, 1977), Val Fitch (Physics, 1980), David Hubel (Medicine, 1981) and Rudolph Marcus (Chemistry, 1992). Ernest Rutherford uncovered the alpha particle, which earned him the 1908 Nobel prize in Chemistry, while on the staff of McGill; and Norman Bethune designed the world's first mobile medical unit and became a hero in China during the Second World War for training thousands of Chinese medics and doctors.

Other notable alumni include poet and literary icon Leonard Cohen; and William Shatner, best known as Captain James T Kirk of Star Trek, though the university can also lay claim to real astronauts Dave Williams, Robert Thirsk and Julie Payette.

McGill is one of Canada's most research-intensive universities, with the country's highest per-faculty research funding in three of the past four years. Among some of its current crop, Wendy Thomson, Director of the School of Social Work, spearheaded public service reform in Britain focussing on education, health and local government; Henry Mintzberg is among the most distinguished contemporary management authors; Michael Meaney and Moshe Szyf are proving that maternal behaviour in rats can have a profound impact on the genetics of offspring; legal scholar Payam Akhavan is an authority on human rights and genocide; Mark Wainberg is an internationally recognized scientist in the field of HIV/AIDS research; environmental scientist Nigel Roulet is a contributing author to the 2007 Nobel prize winning International Panel on Climate Change; and Michel Tremblay's research has provided breakthroughs in the genetics of breast cancer, diabetes and obesity.

What students say

Astrophysics student Andrew McCann was attracted from Dublin by McGill's reputation and a very active and lively department. "Very few universities in the world research my particular area of study, and there are many talks and seminars of interest, as well as highly motivated students and teachers."

Mr McCann had been disappointed by what he believes was too little information provided on financial aid for international students. But he says that did not mar the academic excellence he saw at the university.

Good at

McGill is in the top 30 in all academic areas and in the top ten for the life sciences and biomedicine. The arts and humanities and the social sciences only just miss out on that accolade.

13 Duke University

Why this university?

Considered one of the preeminent universities of the American South, Duke has gone through some soul-searching in the wake of, what turned out to be, unfounded allegations that members of one of its sports teams raped a black woman. Raising the spectre of racism and elitism as it did — even after the players were exonerated and it turned out to be the prosecutor who was disbarred for unethical conduct — the case provoked some introspection that promises to forever change Duke. It has begun a US$30 million "civic engagement program" under which all undergraduates will be pushed to perform community service over a summer or semester, many of them in the surrounding city of Durham, North Carolina, including with an organization that promotes awareness about sexual health, rape prevention, and alcohol and drug use.

The controversy distracted deserved attention from Duke's decidedly forward-looking work in the sciences. Anchoring the so-called Research Triangle in North Carolina's Piedmont region (its other corners are North Carolina State University and the University of North Carolina), Duke has sprouted cutting-edge facilities on its Gothic revival-style campus — endowed originally by the Duke family tobacco fortune — that have given the university a lead in fast-growing and emerging fields more closely associated with rivals in the North. They include the new US$97 million Fitzpatrick Center for Interdisciplinary Engineering, US$41 million Institute for Genome Sciences and Policy,

FACTFILE

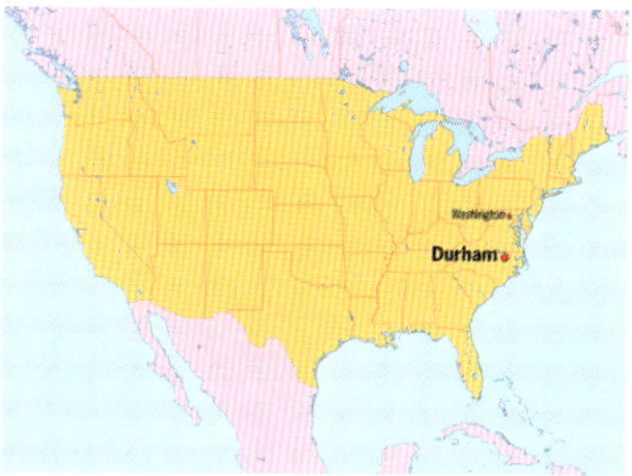

DUKE University

Country	United States
Foundation Year	1838
World Ranking	13 (13)

Faculty Area Rankings

Arts & Humanities	20
Engineering & IT	107
Life Sciences & Biomedicine	19
Natural Sciences	54
Social Sciences	25

Survey Performance

Peer Review	28
Recruiter Review	23

Contact Details

2138 Campus Drive
Box 90586
Durham
NC 27708
www.duke.edu
+1 919 684 8111

People

Student Faculty Ratio	4.4:1
International Faculty	2.0%
Undergraduates	5,452
Postgraduates	4,855
International Students	16.0%

Course Fees For Domestic Students

Average Undergraduate	$34,335
Average Postgraduate	$33,990

Course Fees For International Students

Average Undergraduate	$34,335
Average Postgraduate	$33,990

Overall Research Strength

Papers (Scopus 2002-2006)	104,923
Citations (Scopus 2002-2006)	666,692
Impact	6.4

Research Impact By Faculty Area

Engineering & IT	3.4
Life Sciences & Biomedicine	7.0
Natural Sciences	6.2
Social Sciences	5.2

and US$115 million French Sciences Building, which includes laboratories for biological chemistry, materials science, nanoscience, physical biology, and bioinformatics. Duke's Levine Science Research Center is the largest single-site interdisciplinary research facility at any American university.

In all, Duke conducts nearly half a billion dollars a year in research. Its medical school is a leader in the science (and, as is inevitable in America, the politics) of stem cells. Many of the students at Duke are pre-med, intending to go on to medical school; many of the rest are engineering majors. All undergraduates enroll in either the Trinity College of Arts & Sciences or the Pratt School of Engineering, and half study abroad at some point, five times the US average. A self-described "global gateway," Duke requires its students to take foreign language and international courses. One-fifth of its 6,600 graduate and professional students (and five per cent of its 6,200 undergraduates) are international, and more than 400 international post-doctoral fellows do research at Duke. In all, the university has 2,664 faculty.

People

Prominent alumni have included President Richard Nixon, Senator Elizabeth Done, and the former president of Chile, Ricardo Lagos; Melinda Gates, cofounder of the Bill and Melinda Gates Foundation; and the current or former heads of companies including Bear Stearns, Boston Scientific, Cisco Systems, ExxonMobil, General Motors, Northwest Airlines, PepsiCo, and Pfizer.

What students say

"It's still a growing university," said Shian Ling Keng, an undergraduate from Malaysia who is majoring in biology. In just the three years I've been here, there has been so much expansion going on."

Ms. Keng said,"My experience as an international student is that it was difficult for me to fit into the social environment here, maybe because of the cultural differences. Partying, drinking — people feel like that's the main way of social interaction, and I just don't party or do those things. But after a while I found that there are people who share my interests and I found my niche."

Some good has also come out of the sports team controversy, she said. "These issues have been underlying many campuses, maybe Duke especially, and this has really put them on the table where people can discuss them."

Good at

In the top 100 in every area except engineering and IT, Duke's best positions are in the arts and humanities and the life sciences and biomedicine, where it is in the top 20.

14 University of Pennsylvania

Why this university?

Penn was founded by Benjamin Franklin and boasts that it carries on his principles of entrepreneurship, innovation, invention, and the pursuit of practical knowledge. It has 174 research centers and institutes and conducts US$790 million a year in research. The 4,800 faculty include 11 Nobel laureates (there is a like number of alumni with Nobels). An ongoing US$3.5 billion fundraising campaign aims to add a nanoscale research building and new clinical, research, and educational facilities for the school of medicine, America's oldest. It will also help pay for more faculty, student financial aid, and new programs and research.

Like Franklin, a statue of whom sits at the center of the campus, Penn is well-rounded. Its Wharton School, the world's first collegiate school of business and largest global business school, is consistently regarded among the top three in America. Its School of Nursing ranks in the top two and its School of Arts and Sciences and graduate schools of education, law, medicine, and veterinary medicine in the top 10.

There are 10,000 undergraduates and 10,000 graduate students; fewer than one in five applicants is accepted and 20 per cent of students are from outside the United States. The university also ranks first in the Ivy League and seventh nationally in the number of its students who study overseas.

The university's global emphasis also applies to the programs on its home

FACTFILE

University of PENNSYLVANIA

Country	United States
Foundation Year	1740
World Ranking	14 (26)

Faculty Area Rankings

Arts & Humanities	50
Engineering & IT	79
Life Sciences & Biomedicine	35
Natural Sciences	35
Social Sciences	22

Survey Performance

Peer Review	30
Recruiter Review	32

Contact Details

3451 Walnut Street
Philadelphia,
Pennsylvania 19104
www.upenn.edu
+1 215 898 5000

People

Student Faculty Ratio	7.2:1
International Faculty	24.0%
Undergraduates	13,626
Postgraduates	9,901
International Students	14.0%

Course Fees For Domestic Students

Average Undergraduate	$35,916
Average Postgraduate	$29,386

Overall Research Strength

Papers (Scopus 2002-2006)	135,476
Citations (Scopus 2002-2006)	895,007
Impact	6.6

Research Impact By Faculty Area

Engineering & IT	4.9
Life Sciences & Biomedicine	6.6
Natural Sciences	10.3
Social Sciences	4.2

campus. Its Solomon Asch Center for the Study of Ethnopolitical Conflict advises foreign governments. Medical school faculty and students treat HIV-infected patients in Botswana. Penn's Graduate School of Education has teamed up with Beijing and East China Normal universities to offer the first education doctorates in China. The school has close ties to India, and its Center for the Advanced Study of India is the only research institute of its kind in the United States.

Penn suffers somewhat from its West Philadelphia setting, separated from the city's center by an industrial wasteland to the east that even a university task force described as 'unattractive.' Urban blight afflicts the residential neighborhood to the west. The university hopes to transform both with an ambitious expansion, starting with a new 'East Campus.'

People

Nine signers of the American Declaration of Independence and 11 signers of the Constitution are associated with the University of Pennsylvania. Eadweard James Muybridge, who pioneered motion photography, began his experiments under the university's auspices.

What students say

"It is not the best feeling in the world to be at the edge of West Philly, but I sincerely believe that the campus has become a lot safer than it was a couple of years ago or when my sister went here," said Schuchi Kothari, an undergraduate business major from India who also has a minor in psychology and has taken classes in subjects including photography and political science. "There have been a few incidents but everyone has come out safe. I do not feel unsafe walking around campus alone. There are security officers at every corner and street and the campus is well protected. The university does a great job of dealing with an area that most people would perceive as less than ideal."

Ms. Kothari said she meets people at Penn from all over the world. In some of her classes at the Wharton School of Business, she said, at least 40 per cent of the students come from other countries. "It's a great way to gain a different perspective of a question or argument, especially in classes where class discussion is stressed."

Good at

Penn is in the top 100 in all academic areas, with the social sciences top-ranked, at 22nd in the world.

15 Johns Hopkins

Why this university?

Among the many breakthroughs that have occurred at Johns Hopkins University is this one: The university's school of public health has imposed a ban on taking money for research from the tobacco industry. Hopkins — it's named for a Baltimore merchant who left his fortune for the purpose as he died on Christmas Eve in 1873 — can afford it. It receives by far the most government research funding in America. Its Bloomberg School of Public Health alone gets one-quarter of all federal research money awarded to the 28 US schools of public health.

No wonder such a disproportionate number of Johns Hopkins undergraduates (there are 4,480 of them) are pre-med, planning for careers in medicine. (There are 3,100 faculty, and Hopkins faculty and alumni have won 32 Nobel prizes.) The university's Whiting School of Engineering is also highly selective, and bioengineering is a popular major that spans both of the university's principal strengths. Its Applied Physics Laboratory, founded during World War II to improve the effectiveness of Allied anti-aircraft shells, today conducts research in fields including national security and space exploration, and has developed more than 100 biomedical devices in conjunction with Johns Hopkins medical faculty and graduate students. Seventy per cent of engineering students and 50 per cent of other undergraduates work with faculty on primary research for pay or academic credit.

This tradition of close student-faculty interaction dates from Johns Hopkins' legacy as America's first university modelled after the European research

FACTFILE

JOHNS HOPKINS University

Country.........United States
Foundation Year.........1876
World Ranking.........15 (23)

Faculty Area Rankings

Arts & Humanities.........21
Engineering & IT.........52
Life Sciences & Biomedicine.........4
Natural Sciences.........37
Social Sciences.........38

Survey Performance

Peer Review.........24
Recruiter Review.........132

Contact Details

3400 N Charles St.
Baltimore
Maryland
21218-2688
www.jhu.edu
+1 410 516 8000

People

Student Faculty Ratio.........5.5:1
International Faculty.........8.0%
Undergraduates.........5,610
Postgraduates.........10,611
International Students.........15.0%

Course Fees For Domestic Students

Average Undergraduate.........$35,900
Average Postgraduate.........$30,140

Overall Research Strength

Papers (Scopus 2002-2006).........164,647
Citations (Scopus 2002-2006).........1,148,289
Impact.........7.0

Research Impact By Faculty Area

Engineering & IT.........3.8
Life Sciences & Biomedicine.........7.1
Natural Sciences.........10.1
Social Sciences.........4.1

institution, teaching through seminars instead of solely through lectures. With the proceeds of a US$2 billion fundraising campaign that surpassed its goal two years early and now stands to infuse the university with US$3.2 billion, it's constructing the first academic building on its home campus dedicated to interdisciplinary research, the Computational Science and Engineering Building, where cross-departmental programs in, among other subjects, robotics and computational medicine will be housed. Its renowned School of Advanced International Studies is named for Cold War architect Paul Nitze, who cofounded it in 1943. That division is based in Washington, 45 minutes by train from the university's park-like, Georgian-style main campus in Baltimore.

But the medical school is the main reason for Johns Hopkins' fame. It was there that neurosurgery, urology, endocrinology, paediatrics, renal dialysis, and CPR were developed. The Bloomberg School of Public Health, the oldest and largest of its kind in the world, has research under way in 40 countries and attracts students from 78 countries. 13 per cent of students come from outside the United States.

Johns Hopkins has been aggressive about extending its reach globally. Its Bologna campus houses the only full-time, resident American graduate school of international relations in Europe. It has a center in Florence for its Italian studies program, another in Nanjing, and two in Singapore, one a collaboration between its Peabody Institute of Music and the National University of Singapore to establish a music conservatory.

People

The university's alumni have included President Woodrow Wilson, Vice President Spiro Agnew, novelist John Barth, New York Mayor Michael Bloomberg, pianist Andre Watts, Nobel economics winner Merton Miller, Nobel Peace Prize winner Jody Williams, IBM CEO Samuel Palmisano, horror film director Wes Craven (A Nightmare on Elm Street, Scream), biologist and author Rachel Carson, and Hamilton Smith, the Nobel laureate who helped discover those restriction enzymes.

What students say

"If you're interested in doing research, it's right there. You just have to ask," said Kristy Gangaram, an undergraduate from Trinidad and Tobago majoring in public health. "As you walk along campus, you're able to look in the windows and see students working in the labs until well into the night." One thing that's less popular with students is the neighbourhood surrounding the main undergraduate campus. "Baltimore is the inner city so you have to be always cautious," said Ms Gangaram, who is president of a self-defense instruction group. "But we have a blue light system and when you feel unsafe, you press the button under a blue light and a security officer is there in 30 seconds." Extra lighting has also been installed around the university, and escorts are available at night.

Good at

Johns Hopkins is ranked fourth in the world for biomedicine. It is just outside the top 50 for engineering and IT and within that elite group in all other academic areas.

16 Australian National University

Why this university?

The Australian National University was the first to be created by an act of the federal parliament in 1946 and the first university founded in the national capital, Canberra. The ANU is the only Australian member of the International Alliance of Research Universities and one of the nation's Group of Eight research-intensive institutions.

The university is consistently placed among the best in the world by a range of international ranking systems. ANU finishes above all its Australian peers, as it did in this year's rankings by the Shanghai Jiao Tong University.

The ANU campus spreads over 145 hectares adjacent to the city centre of Canberra but there are also smaller sites, including the astronomy observatories at Mt Stromlo west of Canberra and Siding Spring near Coonabarabran in western New South Wales.

Academics at the ANU carry out research and teaching in seven colleges that cover the arts, Asian and Pacific studies, economics and business, engineering and IT, science, medicine and health sciences, and law.

People

The ANU has four Nobel laureates among many of its distinguished scholars who have achieved international recognition: John Eccles, John C Harsanyi and, joint-winners, Rolf Zinkernagel and Peter Doherty. It also has more Federation Fellows -

FACTFILE

AUSTRALIAN National University

Country	Australia
Foundation Year	1946
World Ranking	16 (16)

Faculty Area Rankings

Arts & Humanities	10
Engineering & IT	39
Life Sciences & Biomedicine	28
Natural Sciences	19
Social Sciences	16

Survey Performance

Peer Review	16
Recruiter Review	63

Contact Details

Canberra
ACT 0200
www.anu.edu.au
+61 2 6125 5111

People

Student Faculty Ratio	4.5:1
International Faculty	18.0%
Undergraduates	7,213
Postgraduates	3,440
International Students	23.0%

Course Fees For Domestic Students

Average Undergraduate	$4,611
Average Postgraduate	$14,289

Course Fees For International Students

Average Undergraduate	$16,935
Average Postgraduate	$19,581

Overall Research Strength

Papers (Scopus 2002-2006)	37,527
Citations (Scopus 2002-2006)	167,342
Impact	4.5

Research Impact By Faculty Area

Engineering & IT	2.4
Life Sciences & Biomedicine	4.9
Natural Sciences	5.5
Social Sciences	2.4

lucrative fellowships awarded by the Australian Research Council — than any other Australian university and also claims more members of the Royal Society on its staff than any of its Australian counterparts.

What students say

Many of Australia's brightest young people apply to join the 12,500 students enrolled at the ANU. There are also 1,470 postgraduate international students and 1,260 undergraduates who come from 100 other countries.

Malaysian Yew Kuen Tan, known as Kenny, recently graduated with a bachelor of medical science. Mr Tan was president of the Malaysian Students Association and acted as a mentor for new students through a scheme linking first-years with those in later years to learn from their knowledge and experience of campus life.

He was awarded a full scholarship to the ANU but says one of main reasons he opted for Canberra was that it was quiet and good for study. He praises the university's student support services and says his course consisted of a well-balanced system of assignments and examinations.

"I think the lecturers are fantastic," he says. "The ones I know are well aware that many international students have English as a second language so they speak slowly and are very approachable. They know that Asian students particularly tend not to question authority and do not speak out but, because they are so approachable, they help overcome that limitation."

Good at

ANU is in the top 40 in every academic area. The arts and humanities are in the top ten in the world, with the social and natural sciences both in the top 20.

17 University of Tokyo

Why this university?

Tokyo University is the oldest in Japan and still stands out today as the most prestigious in the country. Perhaps it is in reflection of its unrivalled political status that the university received the biggest direct government grant of ¥95.7 billion (£445 million) in 2005, comprising just under 50 per cent of its total income of ¥193.3 billion that year. However, faced with a one per cent cut in the subsidies over the next four years, the university has set the target of raising ¥13 billion in endowment.

The university has five campuses — two in the heart of Tokyo. It first started out in 1872 as a law school, largely for Mandarines, before setting up science and liberal arts departments to be fully established as a tertiary education institution in 1877. The legacy of a mandarine training institution in a country of powerful bureaucracy persists to this day. Its law graduates dominate the top civil service posts. "The university provides training in law in the way civil servants should see it," says a law graduate.

However, in the country where Nobel prize triumphs make huge newspaper headlines, Tokyo University's record has not been illustrious, with only a single winner in 2002, in physics, by Professor Emeritus Masatoshi Koshiba.

President Hiroshi Komiyama is careful not to specify any particular area of strength, emphasizing instead the university's pursuit of excellence in all aspects of education and research. A university spokesman echoes this

FACTFILE

University of TOKYO

Country	Japan
Foundation Year	1877
World Ranking	17 (19=)

Faculty Area Rankings

Arts & Humanities	24
Engineering & IT	9
Life Sciences & Biomedicine	13
Natural Sciences	12
Social Sciences	24

Survey Performance

Peer Review	14
Recruiter Review	53

Contact Details

7-3-1, Hongo, Bunkyo-ku
Tokyo
113-8654
www.u-tokyo.ac.jp
+81 3 3812 2111

People

Student Faculty Ratio	5.9:1
International Faculty	5.0%
Undergraduates	14,241
Postgraduates	15,018
International Students	9.0%

Course Fees For Domestic Students

Average Undergraduate	$4,332
Average Postgraduate	$4,443

Course Fees For International Students

Average Undergraduate	$4,321
Average Postgraduate	$4,443

Overall Research Strength

Papers (Scopus 2002-2006)	237,025
Citations (Scopus 2002-2006)	1,073,564
Impact	4.5

Research Impact By Faculty Area

Engineering & IT	2.1
Life Sciences & Biomedicine	4.8
Natural Sciences	5.6
Social Sciences	2.2

view: "It is not our policy to single out any specific areas."

As stated in its objectives, the university is striving to raise its international profile attracting overseas students and researchers, which in itself is the Educational Ministry's own objective. In 2006, however, only 2,269 of the university's 29,000 students were foreign nationals, although 2,700 foreign researchers came on short or extended visits. The university closest to Japan's power centre looks very much a Japanese male dominated institution, with only nine per cent of the faculty women. But in other ways, it is a highly successful global institution, continuing its progress this year up the top 20 of the World University Rankings.

People

Faculty members include architect Tadao Ando, winner of the 1995 Pritzker Architecture Prize, and Masatoshi Koshiba.

Notable alumni include six prime ministers since 1946; mathematician Kunihiko Kodaira (Fields Medal winner); Nobel literature laureates Yasunari Kawabata and Kenzaburo Oe; writer Yukio Mishima; Nobel Physics laureates Leo Esaki and Masatoshi Koshiba; and industrialist Eiji Toyoda.

What students say

"International atmosphere is definitely lacking," says a 2nd year student of literature. "I have yet to come across any undergraduates with a powerful personality — they all seem to be obedient people who follow the rule without a question."

Good at

Tokyo is in the world's top ten for engineering and IT, and in the top 20 for natural sciences and biomedicine. No area falls outside the top 25.

18 University of Hong Kong

Why this university?

The University of Hong Kong, Hong Kong's first university, was founded in 1911 and incorporated the Hong Kong College of Medicine, which was established in 1887. Its 10 faculties include medicine, engineering, arts, social sciences, dentistry, architecture, education, law and business and economics

From the student population of 22,000, 3,250 students are from outside Hong Kong, representing some 65 different countries from six continents. Over half are undergraduates, 35% in taught postgraduate programs and 10% in research postgraduate programs. They are served by a teaching staff of over 2,000, of which around half are international faculty.

Its ethos of providing "outstanding teaching and world-class research" and its international outlook is signified by its Coat of Arms. It features two Chinese phrases from Confucius: "Illustrious Virtue" and "The investigation of things," combined with the Latin motto "Sapientia et Virtus" meaning "wisdom and virtue."

The university's commitment to research excellence was demonstrated in 2003 when the influenza research team at its Faculty of Medicine identified the coronavirus that triggered the 2003 SARS epidemic. While the faculty members and its researchers worked to discover the origins of the virus and its mode of transmission, they also met with local and international media to explain its causes and educate the public on keeping the virus at bay.

FACTFILE

University of HONG KONG

Country	Hong Kong
Foundation Year	1911
World Ranking	18 (33=)

Faculty Area Rankings

Arts & Humanities	44
Engineering & IT	68
Life Sciences & Biomedicine	36
Natural Sciences	61
Social Sciences	31

Survey Performance

Peer Review	40
Recruiter Review	66

Contact Details

Pok Fu Lam Road
Hong Kong
www.hku.hk
+852 2859 2111

People

Student Faculty Ratio	7.5:1
International Faculty	55.0%
Undergraduates	8,974
Postgraduates	6,792
International Students	22.0%

Course Fees For Domestic Students

Average Undergraduate	$7,803
Average Postgraduate	$21,735

Course Fees For International Students

Average Undergraduate	$10,225
Average Postgraduate	$24,157

Overall Research Strength

Papers (Scopus 2002-2006)	59,814
Citations (Scopus 2002-2006)	263,239
Impact	4.4

Research Impact By Faculty Area

Engineering & IT	2.2
Life Sciences & Biomedicine	5.4
Natural Sciences	4.5
Social Sciences	2.1

From the experience, the university was subsequently appointed by the Chinese government to establish a State Key Laboratory of Emerging Infectious Diseases and a State Key Laboratory of Brain and Cognitive Sciences — the only such laboratories outside the Mainland.

The MBA program offered by the faculty of business and economics also has a highly-regarded reputation, particularly in Asia. Its curriculum was further enhanced by partnerships that will allow students to take classes at the London Business School and Columbia Business School.

The university's international outreach is reflected in numerous joint initiatives and programs with overseas institutions. It has academic links with more than 400 overseas universities and ongoing student exchanges with over 180 partner institutions in 25 different countries and in Mainland China.

The university has big expansion plans as it approaches its centennial year in the form of a new Centennial Campus. Due to be completed in 2011 at the cost of over HK$2.4 billion (£170 million), the new 42,000 square-meter state-of-the-art campus will allow the university to enhance its teaching and research facilities as well as increase its student numbers by over 3,000 in preparation for the territory-wide introduction of a 4-year degree structure in 2012.

People

As Hong Kong's pre-eminent research institution, the university receives the lion's share of government research grants. Its strength in scientific research is internationally recognised with members of the faculty being elected as Fellows of the Royal Society; 10 faculty elected to the Chinese Academy of Sciences; 82 of its faculty have been ranked as being among the world's top one per cent of scientists based on the impact of their publications; and one of its academics became the first Hong Kong scientist to receive the First Class Prize in the National Natural Science Awards in China.

What students say

Alexander Schindler from Germany, who is in year three of his LLB at the Faculty of Law, was initially surprised by the diversity and competitiveness of his fellow-students. He says: "The program exceeded all my expectations. Scholars from all major jurisdictions offered a rich learning experience with special priority on business and financial law due to Hong Kong's position as an international trade centre."

Good at

In the top 70 in all academic areas, the university's best placings are for social sciences and biomedicine, both of which are in the top 40.

19 Stanford University

Why this university?

Stanford's US$1 billion a year in research and its small-scale teaching have made it an incubator for the likes of Google, Yahoo!, Cisco Systems, eBay, Sun Microsystems, and 350 other cutting-edge companies that have, in turn, helped fuel California's high-tech boom. This at a school with decidedly low-tech origins, whose benefactor made his fortune selling provisions to miners during the 1850s California gold rush. Leland Stanford, who grew even richer by investing in the first transcontinental railroad, also gave the school his ranch — students still call the university 'the farm' — making it one of the largest campuses in America, whose distinctive red-tile-roofed buildings sit on 8,000 roomy acres in the otherwise densely populated San Francisco Bay area.

It may be a big place, but Stanford boasts small classes with individualized instruction. In all, there are 6,690 undergraduates and 8,200 graduate students (6 per cent come from outside the United States), yet nearly three-quarters of the classes have fewer than 20 students in them. First- and second-year students also can select from the Stanford Introductory Seminars, each focused on a narrow topic and none with more than 16 students. Classes are small at the graduate level, too. And it's an impressive faculty, at that. Stanford's 1,800 faculty members include 16 Nobel laureates. The university's Undergraduate Research Program not only encourages students to work with faculty on research; it funds them to design their own research projects, to the tune of more

FACTFILE

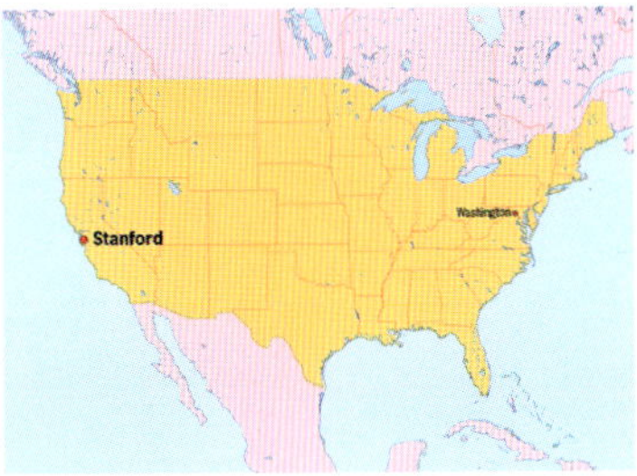

STANFORD University

Country	United States
Foundation Year	1891
World Ranking	19 (6)

Faculty Area Rankings

Arts & Humanities	11
Engineering & IT	3
Life Sciences & Biomedicine	6
Natural Sciences	7
Social Sciences	5

Survey Performance

Peer Review	4
Recruiter Review	7

Contact Details

Montag Hall
Stanford
CA 94305-3020
www.stanford.edu
+1 650 723 2300

People

Student Faculty Ratio	9.8:1
International Faculty	5.0%
Undergraduates	5,785
Postgraduates	9,132
International Students	25.0%

Course Fees For Domestic Students

Average Undergraduate	$31,200
Average Postgraduate	$31,200

Course Fees For International Students

Average Undergraduate	$31,200
Average Postgraduate	$31,200

Overall Research Strength

Papers (Scopus 2002-2006)	161,287
Citations (Scopus 2002-2006)	1,042,882
Impact	6.5

Research Impact By Faculty Area

Engineering & IT	4.3
Life Sciences & Biomedicine	7.7

than US$4 million a year. More than 4,000 undergraduates and graduate students are involved in research.

Stanford has been the site of such breakthroughs as the laser, the musical synthesizer, magnetic resonance imaging, and global positioning systems. The two-mile-long Stanford Linear Accelerator, used in the study of particle physics, is run by the university under contract to the US Department of Energy. The medical school was the first to synthesize DNA-like material, and it was where segments of DNA from two species were joined and made to replicate, leading to the creation of the biotechnology industry. A Stanford surgeon performed the first human heart transplant in the United States and the world's first heart/lung transplant, and it was a lab at Stanford that was the first to isolate stem cells. The Stanford Institute for Stem Cell Biology and Regenerative Medicine is today among the top such research centers in the world. The National Research Council also ranks Stanford's programs the best in America in computer science, electrical engineering, and mechanical engineering, and rates it highly in aeronautics and astronautics and civil engineering. Among undergraduates, the most popular majors are biology, computer science, economics, English and psychology.

Fully one-quarter of the more than US$4 billion being collected in an ambitious fundraising campaign is earmarked to encourage multidisciplinary research, in which Stanford has already launched several initiatives. The new Initiative on Human Health combines biology, engineering, and medicine to solve health problems, for example. The new Initiative on the Environment and Sustainability combines faculty from several departments.

People

Alumni include Hewlett Packard cofounders William Hewlett and David Packard; Nike CEO Philip Knight; the developer of the Google search engine; the cofounder of Yahoo!; the cofounder of The Gap; the cofounder of Sun Microsystems; the chairman and CEO of Pfizer; the chairman of Intel; four US Supreme Court justices; US President Herbert Hoover; former Israeli Prime Minister Ehud Barak; Dolby Laboratories founder Ray Dolby; golfer Tiger Woods; Sally Ride, the first American woman in space; and the presidents of Johns Hopkins, Caltech, and Yale, and the provost and dean of engineering at MIT.

What students say

"Stanford has good resources, it has good libraries, it has good research, and the professors are very easy to approach," said Pumsaran Tongliemnak, a doctoral candidate from Thailand who is studying education economics. "They're world-class, but they're unassuming and students can approach them more easily than at other institutions." As for the students, Mr Tongliemnak said, "They have the mentality of work hard, play hard, and they have a lot of creativity. They're just not the type that go to the library all the time. They have some fun."

Good at

Despite Stanford's fall in the overall ranking this year, it remains among the top dozen universities in every academic area. The university is ranked third in the world for engineering and IT and in the top five for social sciences.

20= Carnegie Mellon University

Why this university?

While other universities plead with their faculties to collaborate across disciplines, Carnegie Mellon has been doing it for years. Unconventional partnerships among seemingly unrelated fields — arts management, behavioral economics — are part of the university's culture, made possible by its comparatively small size (5,580 undergraduates and 4,450 graduate students, 13 per cent of them from outside the United States). Most known for science and technology, Carnegie Mellon has top drama and business programs. It has an Art Conservation Research Center that studies scientific methods of preserving paintings, books, and paper, and another program that combines engineering, social sciences, economics, and the arts to help restore contaminated industrial spaces to productive use.

The enthusiasm generated by these combinations has helped double the number of applications for admission in the last 10 years to Carnegie Mellon, which was founded in 1900 as a technical school by the Scottish-American industrialist Andrew Carnegie (members of the band, which includes bagpipers, still wear kilts) to train the children of the working-class poor in industrial Pittsburgh. Its School of Computer Science is one of the best in the world and includes the pre-eminent Robotics Institute, the largest at any US university, which developed robots to clean up nuclear waste at Three Mile Island and Chernobyl. Its Science and Technology Center for Light Microscope Imaging and Biotechnology is developing tools such as microscopy

FACTFILE

CARNEGIE MELLON University

Country	United States
Foundation Year	1900
World Ranking	20= (35=)

Faculty Area Rankings

Arts & Humanities	98
Engineering & IT	7
Life Sciences & Biomedicine	99
Natural Sciences	50
Social Sciences	28

Survey Performance

Peer Review	32
Recruiter Review	41

Contact Details

5000 Forbes Avenue
Pittsburgh
PA 15213-3890
www.cmu.edu
+1 412 268 2000

People

Student Faculty Ratio	8.7:1
International Faculty	18.0%
Undergraduates	5,359
Postgraduates	3,535
International Students	27.0%

Course Fees For Domestic Students

Average Undergraduate	$36,950
Average Postgraduate	$28,200

Overall Research Strength

Papers (Scopus 2002-2006)	40,530
Citations (Scopus 2002-2006)	197,959
Impact	4.9

Research Impact By Faculty Area

Engineering & IT	3.6
Life Sciences & Biomedicine	4.7
Natural Sciences	8.0
Social Sciences	4.5

workstations for biological research. It has 15 Nobel Laureates on its faculty of 1,421, and maintains a branch campus in California's Silicon Valley.

Carnegie Mellon's highly regarded business school also takes advantage of its presence at a university that specializes in technology, pioneering management science to replace the conventional case-study method, and developing hybrid programs in such areas as information technology and operations management. Its Heinz School of Public Policy and Management, named for the ketchup family, founded in the turbulent 1960s, studies urban and social issues with an equally interdisciplinary approach, combining statistics, economics, technology, and psychology. Its Human-Computer Interaction Institute integrates computer science, design, social science, and learning science.

Not surprisingly, the campus, neighbor to the University of Pittsburgh, is among America's most wired, and the home to a 10-teraflop Cray XT3 computer called Big Ben, capable of 10 trillion calculations per second, or as much processing capacity as 30,000 personal computers. Scientists have used it to model earthquake soil vibration, forecast severe thunder-storms, map blood flow in the heart in three dimensions, forecast Comet Shoemaker-Levy 9's impact with Jupiter, and create a super-lightweight aluminum used in soda cans.

Concerned about public perceptions that universities with robust research programs neglect undergraduate teaching (it spends US$315 million a year on research) Carnegie Mellon was also one of the first universities in America to establish a center aimed at helping faculty improve their classroom teaching.

People

Alumni include James Gosling, creator of the Java programming language; Sun Microsystems cofounders Andy Bechtolsheim and Vinod Khosla; and astronaut Judith Resnik, who died in the Challenger disaster. Carnegie Mellon's conservatory-style drama program has graduated the likes of George Peppard, Jack Klugman, Holly Hunter, Ted Danson, Blair Underwood, and producer Steven Bochco.

What students say

"When I told people I was going to Carnegie Mellon, they all thought that I was going to be an engineer," said Jen Johnson, an undergraduate who describes herself as technologically unskilled and who is actually majoring in anthropology. "And when they told them I wasn't, they assumed I must be in the drama school. In fact, you get to know a lot of people outside of your field. We all feed off of each other's energies that way. You're surrounded by a wide array of different types of thinking."

Ms Johnson, who comes from a small town in Montana near the Canadian border, said, "A lot of the professors really do take a lot of interest in you as a person. Although they are obviously very bright and doing research of their own, they're able to bring that down into the classroom level. They're really accessible. I never feel that I'm being lectured to."

Good at

In the top 100 in every academic area, Carnegie Mellon's best position is seventh for engineering and IT.

20= Cornell University

Why this university?

Its ambitious partnerships with schools in India, Singapore, and China, and a medical campus in Qatar — the first American medical school outside the United States — have started Cornell calling itself the world's first transnational university. But its attention is also firmly rooted at home, where it has been working to move back up after dropping slightly in the pre-eminent American league tables. Its principal selling point? That Cornell's large size makes it by far the most comprehensive in the elite Ivy League, with 70 undergraduate specialities. So far, the marketing campaign is paying off; both applications for admission and financial contributions are up.

Part of Cornell's need to sell itself comes from its unique status in a country whose universities are divided between public and private. Cornell is both. Partly private it is also partly run and financially underwritten by the state of New York, in whose rural (and often very cold and snowy) west central reaches it's set. Founded after the American Civil War, it is not only far bigger than most other Ivy League schools, but far newer, and is less readily identified among them.

It also has specialties unusual among the Ivies. Its College of Agriculture and Life Sciences is the third largest in the United States, and usually rated the best. So is its School of Hotel Management, which has the largest faculty and curriculum of any program of its kind and attracts a sizeable international enrolment representing, at last count, 28 countries. Its School

FACTFILE

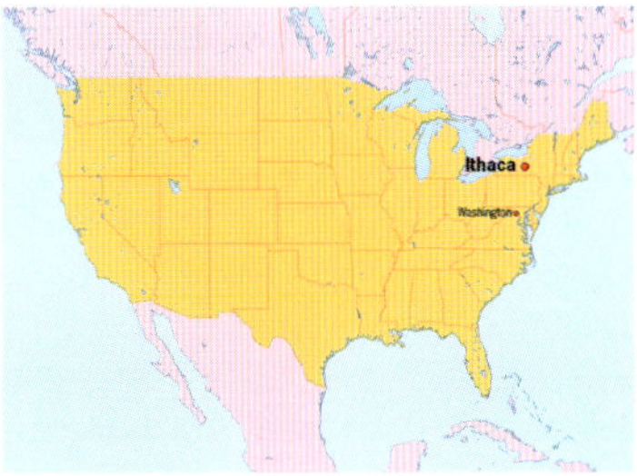

CORNELL University

Country	United States
Foundation Year	1865
World Ranking	20= (15)

Faculty Area Rankings

Arts & Humanities	16
Engineering & IT	20
Life Sciences & Biomedicine	16
Natural Sciences	9
Social Sciences	17

Survey Performance

Peer Review	11
Recruiter Review	17

Contact Details

Day Hall Lobby
Ithaca
NY 14853
www.cornell.edu
+1 607 254 4636

People

Student Faculty Ratio	8.8:1
International Faculty	8.0%
Undergraduates	13,926
Postgraduates	4,475
International Students	15.0%

Course Fees For Domestic Students

Average Undergraduate	$34,231
Average Postgraduate	$30,000

Overall Research Strength

Papers (Scopus 2002-2006)	109,419
Citations (Scopus 2002-2006)	641,418
Impact	5.9

Research Impact By Faculty Area

Engineering & IT	4.4
Life Sciences & Biomedicine	5.9
Natural Sciences	7.2
Social Sciences	3.9

of Industrial and Labor Relations offers the only four-year undergraduate degree in America devoted to workplace issues. And its College of Veterinary Medicine is the nation's most respected; among other things, it's where Salmonella was discovered.

Despite its location a distant five hours' drive northwest of New York City, Cornell is one of America's most international campuses. Of the 20,630 students — just under two thirds of them undergraduates — 18 per cent are from other countries..

An enormous amount of research is conducted at Cornell. Annual research expenditures there exceed US$600 million. The university ranks first in National Science Foundation funding for academic science and engineering. Forty Nobel laureates have been affiliated with Cornell, and there are three on the current faculty of 2,722.

Cornell has set out to raise US$4 billion to build on these strengths, a significant amount of it for a new biomedical research center attached to its satellite Weill Cornell Medical College in New York City.

People

Alumni include US Supreme Court Justice Ruth Bader Ginsburg, former US Attorney General Janet Reno, the former presidents of Taiwan and Cuba and the former prime minister of Iran, the men who invented the iPod, the pacemaker and the Heimlich maneuver, and the founders or heads of businesses including Citigroup, Grumman Aerospace Corporation, and Burger King.

What students say

Undergraduate Arthur Change said he was attracted to come to Cornell from Hong Kong because "I wanted a business degree, but I wanted the whole Ivy League experience. It has exceeded my expectation. With the connections you gain from Cornell, you can really do anything you want. Definitely the weather is tough, but everybody survives it." And while Cornell is part of the Ivy League, he said, it's less stuffy than its smaller counterparts.

Good at

Cornell is in the top 20 in every academic area and in the top 10 for the natural sciences.

22 University of California at Berkeley

Why this university?

The first and flagship campus of the University of California system, Berkeley can trace its origins to the California gold rush era, when the nascent state was seeking cultural legitimacy. With a generous amount of space set aside for its campus in the hills above San Francisco Bay, and a curriculum modelled after Harvard's and Yale's, Berkeley was an ambitious place. It still is. 35 of its 36 graduate programs are ranked in the top 10 in their fields by the National Research Council, or NRC, including the best overall in chemistry, English, German, mathematics, and statistics. That's the highest score in America. It produces more PhDs than any other US university, its library holdings are the nation's fourth largest, and it also ranks first in the number of its research programs the NRC considers "distinguished."

Research has always been Berkeley's great strength, particularly in the sciences. It was here that the first cyclotron, or circular particle accelerator, was developed by physicist Ernest O Lawrence, who, along with other Berkeley scientists, went on to help produce the atomic and hydrogen bombs at a secret base in Los Alamos, New Mexico. Berkeley researchers also discovered the anti-proton and elements including plutonium, isolated the polio virus, and contributed to the invention of the laser. 20 members of the faculty have won the Nobel prize — seven laureates still work there — and 14 have

FACTFILE

University of California, BERKELEY

Country	United States
Foundation Year	1868
World Ranking	22 (8)

Faculty Area Rankings

Arts & Humanities	2
Engineering & IT	2
Life Sciences & Biomedicine	5
Natural Sciences	1
Social Sciences	2

Survey Performance

Peer Review	1
Recruiter Review	11

Contact Details

110 Sproul Hall
Berkeley
California
CA 94720
www.berkeley.edu
+1 510 642 6000

People

Student Faculty Ratio	10.8:1
International Faculty	20.0%
Undergraduates	20,129
Postgraduates	7,277
International Students	21.0%

Course Fees For Domestic Students

Average Undergraduate	$6,730
Average Postgraduate	$7,457

Course Fees For International Students

Average Undergraduate	$23,828
Average Postgraduate	$22,396

Overall Research Strength

Papers (Scopus 2002-2006)	121,815
Citations (Scopus 2002-2006)	733,151
Impact	6.0

Research Impact By Faculty Area

Engineering & IT	-
Life Sciences & Biomedicine	-
Natural Sciences	-
Social Sciences	-

received the National Medal of Science.

Complaints about security lapses and other problems have cost Berkeley its prized management of the Los Alamos and Lawrence Livermore national nuclear science laboratories, which it operated under contract to the government, though faculty and students continue to work in these along with 65 university research centers that conduct US$516 million a year in research, a number that has begun to rebound after years of budget cuts. Berkeley continues to manage the Lawrence Berkeley National Laboratory, which has an annual budget of an additional US$500 million and 3,800 employees, including 500 students, and which specializes in quantitative biology, nanoscience, and 15 other disciplines.

Research opportunities aren't limited to the university's 8,800 graduate students. Its 22,880 undergraduates can apply to take part in the Undergraduate Research Apprentice Program and work side-by-side with faculty in any discipline. Just over three per cent of Berkeley students come from countries other than the United States.

In addition to groundbreaking science, Berkeley is famous as a center of the Free Speech Movement, which began there in the 1960s, and for student and faculty activism.

People

Alumni include former Pakistan President Zulfikar Ali Bhutto, Vietnam-era Defense Secretary Robert McNamara, California governor and onetime US presidential candidate Jerry Brown, Apple Computer cofounder Steve Wozniak, Intel CEO Paul Otellini, MySpace creator Tom Anderson, Vodafone CEO Arun Sarin, Korean Airlines president Choon Kun Chom, The Gap CEO Don Fisher, and Stephen Bechtel, founder of the controversial worldwide engineering firm that bears his name.

What students say

"What I find most remarkable about Berkeley is that it is a public university and yet it is doing so well academically, especially in a right-wing society like America," said Arpita Roy, a doctoral student in cultural anthropology from India. "It just tells me that money is not everything, and that good research can be accomplished even under financial constraints."

Good at

Every academic area is in the world's top ten, with engineering and IT, the social sciences and arts and humanities all second-placed and the natural sciences top in the world.

23 University of Edinburgh

Why this university?

Edinburgh was founded in 1583 as the 'Tounis (Town's) College,' but its local roots are matched by an international outlook. It is Scotland's most research-intensive university, with more than 96 per cent of its researchers in units carrying out work of international quality, according to the most recent Research Assessment Exercise. Its cutting edge research in medicine has been boosted by the opening of the £49 million Queen's Medical Research Institute. This brings together hundreds of elite researchers in inflammation research, cardiovascular medicine and reproductive biology, who will work together on conditions from diabetes and heart disease to cancer and menstrual disorders.

Edinburgh is also increasing its existing strength in informatics, a discipline covering computer science, artificial intelligence, cognitive science and linguistics, by bringing together researchers who are currently scattered across the city.

Commercialisation is seen as increasingly important. Edinburgh has pledged its commitment to boosting the Scottish economy, and in the wake of political devolution in 1999, has helped to create more than 50 companies.

The university recently restructured itself from nine faculties into three American-style colleges: humanities and social science, medicine and veterinary medicine, and science and engineering, which it believes will foster interdisciplinary work. It is also a prominent player in Scotland's

FACTFILE

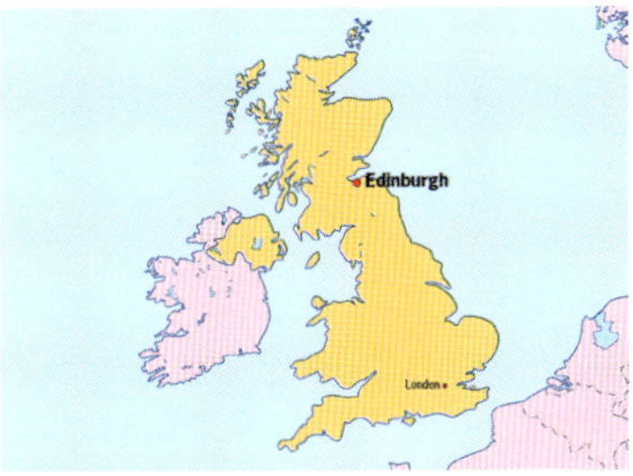

University of EDINBURGH

Country	United Kingdom
Foundation Year	1582
World Ranking	23 (33=)

Faculty Area Rankings

Arts & Humanities	28
Engineering & IT	56
Life Sciences & Biomedicine	30
Natural Sciences	65
Social Sciences	47

Survey Performance

Peer Review	33
Recruiter Review	14

Contact Details

Old College
South Bridge
Edinburgh
EH8 9YL
www.ed.ac.uk
+44 131 650 1000

People

Student Faculty Ratio	8:1
International Faculty	19.0%
Undergraduates	15,917
Postgraduates	4,523
International Students	18.0%

Course Fees For Domestic Students

Average Undergraduate	$3,557
Average Postgraduate	$8,919

Course Fees For International Students

Average Undergraduate	$23,476
Average Postgraduate	$20,503

Overall Research Strength

Papers (Scopus 2002-2006)	52,487
Citations (Scopus 2002-2006)	291,085
Impact	5.5

Research Impact By Faculty Area

Engineering & IT	2.9
Life Sciences & Biomedicine	6.0
Natural Sciences	6.7
Social Sciences	3.6

pioneering 'research pooling' ventures in physics, chemistry, geosciences, and engineering and mathematics. These ensure critical mass by letting researchers in different universities work together and share expensive equipment. And Edinburgh hopes it will also prove an attractive lure to international research stars.

It is also drawing on American experience to develop an ambitious £350 million fundraising campaign. This is headed by Young Dawkins III, previously vice-principal of development, and latterly president, of the University of New Hampshire Foundation. He says one of its top priorities will be scholarships and bursaries for both undergraduate and postgraduate students. Edinburgh is often stereotyped as Scotland's Oxbridge, attracting wealthy, privately educated English students. But it has been strenuously combating its elitist image with widening access schemes, and is already putting some £15 million into scholarships. Edinburgh is Scotland's largest university, with around 4,000 academic and related staff and more than 22,000 students. There are roughly 17,000 undergraduates and 5,000 postgraduates, more than 4,000 of whom are international students from 130 different countries.

Edinburgh offers a blend of innovation and tradition: Old College, designed by alumnus Robert Adam, dates from the late 18th century and is in the centre of a World Heritage Site. Similarly, the historic city is a magnet for tourists, especially during the Edinburgh Festival, but its leisure facilities are thoroughly up-to-date.

People

Notable Edinburgh graduates include Charles Darwin, David Hume, James Hutton and writers Sir Walter Scott, Robert Louis Stevenson and Sir Arthur Conan Doyle. Two of today's best known Scottish writers have Edinburgh connections: Ian Rankin, creator of detective John Rebus, is an Edinburgh graduate, while Alexander McCall Smith, author of the "No. 1 Ladies' Detective Agency" series, was professor of medical law until he retired two years ago to concentrate on writing.

What students say

Wen Hao Zou from China, in the final year of a business and accountancy degree, said: "My father runs a small business so I want to learn some new things. I realize here [the course] is more practical and I think it's very useful. I enjoy the course and the teachers are good. The first time I came to Edinburgh, I was carrying my bags and someone stopped in a car and gave me a lift. I could never imagine this happening in London. It's friendly. Edinburgh University has a lot of international students and we have a lot of fun."

Good at

Everything. Ranked 30th in the life sciences and biomedicine, 28th in arts and humanities, 47th in the social sciences, 56th in engineering and IT, and 65th in the natural sciences.

24 King's College London

Why this university?

For the second year in succession, King's has shot up the world rankings and has done the same in domestic league tables. The college set itself the goal of reaching the top 25 in the world by 2016, but has already achieved this feat with a leap of more than 20 places.

At one time King's was known primarily for science, but it now also excels in Portuguese, Byzantine Greek, Law and War Studies. History, philosophy, psychiatry, developmental biology and dentistry were also given the title "internationally outstanding" and a 5* grade in the latest research assessments. These accolades, coupled with its prime location on London's Strand, are proving an obvious attraction for the high proportion of students from outside Britain who apply to King's. Of the college's 19,000 students, more than one in five are from overseas. Nearly nine per cent are from other parts of the European Union, but they are outnumbered by students from farther afield.

The outlook at King's is truly international. The college was among the first to follow the example of American universities by submitting to a credit rating, which took account of its academic and financial standing. It received an 'AA minus' — better than that awarded to many. Its academics' achievements include discovering the structure of DNA, in collaboration with a Cambridge team.

A £500 million redevelopment of the college's estate is nearly completed, concentrating its activities on five

FACTFILE

King's College LONDON

Country	United Kingdom
Foundation Year	1829
World Ranking	24 (46=)

Faculty Area Rankings

Arts & Humanities	36
Engineering & IT	154
Life Sciences & Biomedicine	32
Natural Sciences	102
Social Sciences	64

Survey Performance

Peer Review	48
Recruiter Review	40

Contact Details

Strand
London
WC2R 2LS
www.kcl.ac.uk
+44 20 7836 5454

People

Student Faculty Ratio	6.8:1
International Faculty	30.0%
Undergraduates	12,554
Postgraduates	4,607
International Students	20.0%

Course Fees For Domestic Students

Average Undergraduate	$6,294
Average Postgraduate	$11,244

Course Fees For International Students

Average Undergraduate	$25,400
Average Postgraduate	$24,174

Overall Research Strength

Papers (Scopus 2002-2006)	43,277
Citations (Scopus 2002-2006)	214,385
Impact	5.0

Research Impact By Faculty Area

Engineering & IT	2.7
Life Sciences & Biomedicine	5.0
Natural Sciences	6.1
Social Sciences	5.2

sites close to the River Thames. They include the largest university building in London, where 2,800 study health and life sciences. Biomedical sciences, medicine and dentistry have also acquired new buildings.

Science students dominate, but they are offered a wide range of interdisciplinary combinations. Alongside their degree, all students can take lectures on ethics, philosophy, theology, biblical studies and Christian doctrine. Health subjects have been the fastest-growing in recent years: King's is the only UK university to have five Medical Research Council centres and boasts Europe's largest centre for medical and professional healthcare education.

A member of the Russell Group of 20 leading research universities, King's is the fourth-oldest institution in UK higher education, but it is embracing the expanded role of the modern university. Research earnings top £110 million, of which £13 million came from commercial enterprises, and the college's annual turnover is approaching £390 million.

People

Famous alumni include the Romantic poet John Keats, Archbishop Desmond Tutu, and John Eliot Gardiner. An array of distinguished staff is headed by Rosalind Franklin and Maurice Wilkins, the discoverers of DNA, Lord Lister, pioneer of antiseptic surgery, and Sir Edward Appleton, whose work on atmospheric layers paved the way for modern telecommunications. Florence Nightingale established the first professional school of nurse training at St Thomas's Hospital, now also part of the large medical school at King's.

What students say

Joanne Ooi, a Malaysian student studying medicine, said: "I'd chosen to study medicine at King's based on the strength of its international reputation, so naturally I started at university with very high hopes.

"Two years on, I'm delighted to say the King's experience has far exceeded my expectations. In a typical day I am fortunate enough to sample the best of all the worlds that college life could possibly offer. I attend lectures by world-class academics with students from diverse backgrounds in history-rich surroundings. I enjoy the excellent social and cultural opportunities of the capital by taking just a short walk down the Thames. I may have travelled halfway across the globe to get to King's, but I feel right at home here!"

Good at

King's is in the top 40 in our rankings for both biomedicine and the arts and humanities. It is also 64th in the social sciences.

25 Kyoto University

Why this university?

Kyoto University was founded in 1897 in the ancient capital of Japan, only 10 years after Tokyo University was established.

Initially, the university consisted of science and engineering, medicine and law, but it has since expanded to cover nearly all aspects of education and research including medicine and nuclear energy. The university's commitment to academic freedom has long been a hallmark of the institution — even in pre-war Japan under a military government.

But the overseas composition of this prestigious university is limited. Language is a major barrier as nearly all lectures and seminars are in Japanese, as at Tokyo and other universities in the country. In 2007, only 1,300 of 13,300 undergraduates and 9,300 postgraduate students were from outside Japan. In postgraduate courses, many faculties accept theses in English. This is one of the reasons for the higher ratio of foreign students at the postgraduate level. As at Tokyo, competition for getting an undergraduate place is intense, awarded only to those who pass the national entrance exams as well as the university's own entrance exam, which are both set in Japanese, though there is now a special selection process for foreign students and foreign educated Japanese.

Kyoto, like Japan's 81 other former national universities, faces a one per cent subsidy cut for the next four years. In 2005, 54 per cent of its total income of ¥119.13 billion (£554

FACTFILE

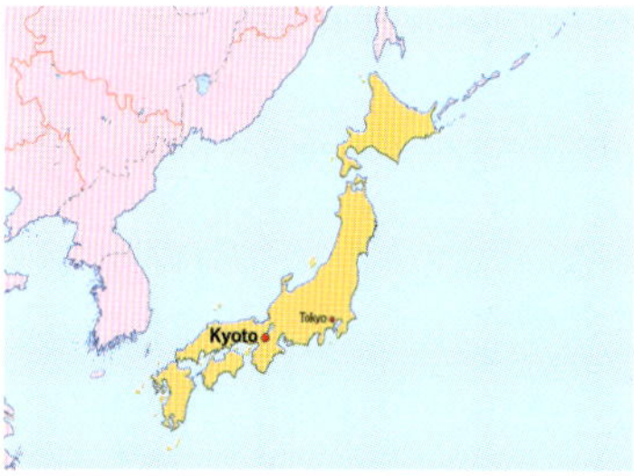

KYOTO University

Country	Japan
Foundation Year	1897
World Ranking	25 (29=)

Faculty Area Rankings

Arts & Humanities	34
Engineering & IT	29
Life Sciences & Biomedicine	27
Natural Sciences	17
Social Sciences	57

Survey Performance

Peer Review	26
Recruiter Review	70

Contact Details

Yoshida-Honmachi, Sakyo-ku,
Kyoto
606-8501
www.kyoto-u.ac.jp
+81 75 753 7531

People

Student Faculty Ratio	7.8:1
International Faculty	7.0%
Undergraduates	13,216
Postgraduates	9,228
International Students	4.0%

Course Fees For Domestic Students

Average Undergraduate	$4,375
Average Postgraduate	$4,375

Course Fees For International Students

Average Undergraduate	$4,375
Average Postgraduate	$4,375

Overall Research Strength

Papers (Scopus 2002-2006)	161,632
Citations (Scopus 2002-2006)	687,213
Impact	4.3

Research Impact By Faculty Area

Engineering & IT	2.0
Life Sciences & Biomedicine	4.6
Natural Sciences	5.0
Social Sciences	1.9

million) was government grant. Like Tokyo, Kyoto too has begun actively seeking endowment, for the first time in its over 100 year history.

The university has an even lower ratio of foreign faculty members than Tokyo. In 2005, less than one per cent of 2,900 faculty members was a foreign national.

Subsidy cuts prompted by denationalisation in 2004 are forcing Kyoto, like all other Japanese universities, to rely on the private sector for research grants, which many academics fear could erode the university's autonomy. So far, the fact that Kyoto is more than 500 kilometres — or two hours' bullet train ride away — from the capital has somewhat shielded the university from political influences, academics say. Only a handful of Kyoto university lecturers and professors are on government advisory panels. However, young ambitious academics seeking media exposures are seeking positions at Tokyo-based universities — often of less prestige.

People

Perhaps it is because of its liberal tradition that the university has produced more Nobel and Fields Medal winners than any of its Japanese rivals. In 1949 Physicist Hideki Yukawa, a Kyoto professor, was the first Japanese ever to win a Nobel prize. Since then, it has produced two winners in physics and science. In 1999, mathematician Shigefumi Mori won the Fields Medal.

What students say

"It's a liberal school," says a US PhD student, who completed a thesis on British-Japanese relations in late 19th century. "I think analysis approaches are not as strong as at American universities."

Good at

Only the social sciences are outside the top 50 — and then not by much. The natural sciences are top-ranked, at 17 in world.

26 École Normale Supérieure (ENS)

Why this university?

The École Normale Supérieure in Paris is one of the great institutions of revolutionary France, a pioneering grande école created in 1794 to train university and lycée teachers for the agrégation, the competitive high-level teaching examination. Today the school — also known as ENS, ENS-Paris, Normale Sup', ENS-Ulm — is France's elite training-ground not only for academics and researchers, but for those seeking careers in the upper echelons of the civil service, business or politics. The present establishment, based in the Latin Quarter of Paris, is the result of a merger in the mid-1980s between the original school and the École Normale Supérieure de Jeunes Filles in Sèvres, founded in 1880 to provide secondary education for young women. Entry is generally by the traditional concours — competitive exams — preceded by two years' post-baccalauréat study in preparatory classes. Pupils selected by concours ("normaliens") have civil servant status and are paid about €1,250 a month during their studies if they undertake to serve France for 10 years. There are alternative entry methods for students preparing for the ENS diploma or for foreign applicants.

On its three Parisian sites ENS caters for a total of over 1,300 normaliens and other students up to doctorate level, with 291 teachers including 18 members of the French Academies of Sciences, France and Inscriptions et Belles-Lettres. As well as 150 school-employed researchers there are 1,004 associated researchers from other institutions such as the CNRS, the

FACTFILE

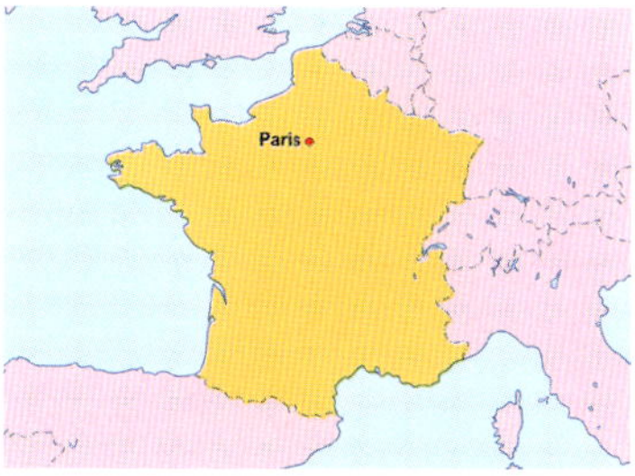

Ecole Normale Supérieure, PARIS

Country	France
Foundation Year	1794
World Ranking	26 (18)

Faculty Area Rankings

Arts & Humanities	33
Engineering & IT	102
Life Sciences & Biomedicine	137
Natural Sciences	20
Social Sciences	143

Survey Performance

Peer Review	46
Recruiter Review	201

Contact Details

45, rue d'Ulm
Paris Cedex 05
75230
www.ens.fr
+33 1 44 32 30 00

People

Student Faculty Ratio	7.8:1
International Faculty	16.0%
Undergraduates	242
Postgraduates	883
International Students	19.0%

Overall Research Strength

Papers (Scopus 2002-2006)	13,487
Citations (Scopus 2002-2006)	76,140
Impact	5.6

Research Impact By Faculty Area

Engineering & IT	3.2
Life Sciences & Biomedicine	6.3
Natural Sciences	6.9
Social Sciences	2.5

national scientific research centre, and Inserm, the national medical research institute.

ENS is the only grande école catering for both humanities and science students. Its watchwords are "interdisciplinarity" and "education through research". Courses and research are organized between 14 departments: biology, chemistry, cognitive studies, computer sciences, geography, history, literature and languages, history of art, pure and applied mathematics, philosophy, physics, sciences of antiquity, social sciences and earth-atmosphere-ocean; and four interdisciplinary structures and departments covering Cognitive studies: History and philosophy of the sciences, Environment and society, and Languages and cultures for non-specialists. Studies last three or four years leading to a licence (bachelors equivalent) and masters, awarded jointly with another higher education establishment. Many students, including most on humanities courses, take the agrégation. ENS graduates might otherwise continue at other grandes écoles to train as senior technocrats or follow careers in sought-after fields such as the media or publishing. The school has agreements with about 60 universities worldwide through which it exchanges about 150 students each year. About 60 foreign academics visit annually for month-long visits; and nearly 300 international researchers stay for periods of up to two years. The ENS International Division was created about five years ago for foreign students. Candidates are rigorously tested by a panel of professors from French and foreign universities who evaluate their capacity for analysis, conceptualisation and synthesis, scientific and literary knowledge, intellectual curiosity and relevance of their chosen projects. About 20 foreigners were accepted for the 2007 session.

People

Among ENS alumni (archicubes) are numerous eminent scientists, writers, philosophers, social scientists and politicians, including many winners of Nobel prizes, Fields medals and CNRS gold medals. Graduates include Louis Pasteur, Jean-Paul Sartre, Michel Foucault, Jacques Derrida, Simone Weil; Pierre Bourdieu; Romain Rolland, Charles Péguy; Jean Jaurès, Léon Blum and Georges Pompidou. Samuel Beckett taught here.

What students say

Klaus Speidel, 27 was admitted to ENS to study for a masters in philosophy after studying philosophy for two years at Munich University. He says interdisciplinarity and a close relationship with lecturers are the school's strong points. "The ENS has a system of personal tutors — you choose them at the beginning of your time there, and they sustain you in your choices, discuss and correct your work, and so on." But he regrets that students are not encouraged more to talk during their studies. "Class participation is nearly impossible in France, and I miss it," he says. "It's clear people who attend the ENS are clever, but the teachers mainly give lectures even if the courses are called seminars."

Good at

Two areas stand out: the natural sciences, where ENS is ranked 20 in the world, and the arts and humanities, where it is 33rd.

27 University of Melbourne

Why this university?

Being large, venerable and of high prestige, the University of Melbourne has huge financial, intellectual and locational assets. Its centralised campus, a few minutes' tram ride from the central business district, is in the heart of cosmopolitan Carlton. There are other small campuses dotted around Victoria that focus on agriculture, forestry and rural medicine.

Melbourne is Australia's second oldest university and, as with its counterparts in the other state capitals, it attracts a large number of students from socially advantaged homes and top private schools. But it claims to offer the nation's largest scholarship scheme — 8000 scholarships worth AU$100 million over three years for highly-able school students.

Next year, Melbourne will become the first in Australia to introduce a comprehensive graduate school system, with the aim of transforming itself along the lines of the Bologna model for European universities. Students will enrol in a new set of six broad undergraduate degrees leading to professional graduate programs such as architecture, law and teaching, or to the workplace, or research higher degrees such as PhDs.

In 2008, law, architecture, building and planning, as well as nursing and some education courses will be offered only as graduate programs. Other professional degrees, such as medicine, dentistry and engineering, will also become graduate-entry only.

FACTFILE

University of MELBOURNE

Country	Australia
Foundation Year	1853
World Ranking	27 (22)

Faculty Area Rankings

Arts & Humanities	17
Engineering & IT	21
Life Sciences & Biomedicine	17
Natural Sciences	33
Social Sciences	17

Survey Performance

Peer Review	20
Recruiter Review	10

Contact Details

Parkville
Victoria 3010
www.unimelb.edu.au
+61 3 8344 4000

People

Student Faculty Ratio	10.1:1
International Faculty	17.0%
Undergraduates	25,255
Postgraduates	8,680
International Students	26.0%

Course Fees For Domestic Students

Average Undergraduate	$18,020
Average Postgraduate	$21,565

Course Fees For International Students

Average Undergraduate	$21,698
Average Postgraduate	$21,169

Overall Research Strength

Papers (Scopus 2002-2006)	66,676
Citations (Scopus 2002-2006)	287,252
Impact	4.3

Research Impact By Faculty Area

Engineering & IT	2.9
Life Sciences & Biomedicine	4.5
Natural Sciences	5.2
Social Sciences	3.7

From its current 44,000 students, Melbourne expects to peak at around 50,000 but towards 2015 it will drop to current levels or below. Some 20 per cent of these students will be in new graduate schools and a further 10-15 per cent engaged in post-graduate research.

People

Many of Melbourne's 3,200 academics are among Australia's most accomplished and sought-after scholars and they account for 250 memberships of the four Australian learned academies. Melbourne has three Nobel Laureates on its staff — Peter Doherty, Sir Clive Granger and Sir James Mirrlees. The university has led the recent Thomson Scientific Australian citation survey making 'Top Three' appearances in 21 fields (11 by total citations and 10 by impact) and in both citations and impact in five fields — neurosciences, physics, microbiology, pharmacology and psychology/psychiatry.

What students say

The university enrols 10,000 international students of whom some 2,700 are undertaking postgraduate studies. One of them is Nicklas Sandstrom who travelled from Sweden to start as a first-year medical student at Melbourne in 2006 after finishing school at home and then completing a year's military service.

"I wanted to try something different," Mr Sandstrom says. "I saw the problem-solving approach that Melbourne uses in its medical course and thought I'd like to try that form of learning."

The cost of a six-year medical degree at Melbourne amounts to around AU$200,000 (£88,000) but Mr Sandstrom says his tuition is paid for by the Swedish government although he must repay the loan after he graduates.

"I've learnt a lot more than I expected and have no complaints about the teaching so far," he says. "The problem-based approach and tutorials are different to the teaching back home where they don't have the small discussion groups. You remember more and learn more while interacting, rather than just looking at slides in a lecture."

Good at

Melbourne is in the top 40 in all five areas covered by our rankings. Social science, the arts and humanities and the life sciences and biomedicine are all ranked 17th in the world.

28 École Polytechnique

Why this university?

France's most prestigious engineering grande école, École Polytechnique has for over two centuries trained distinguished scientists, captains of industry, military chiefs and political leaders, as well as engineers.

Founded as the École Centrale des Travaux Publics in 1794 by Lazare Carnot and Gaspard Monge, it was renamed a year later. In 1804 Napoleon established it as a military academy, with the motto "Pour la patrie, les sciences et la gloire" ("For the nation, sciences and glory.").

The Defence Ministry is its supervisory authority. Students have military status and wear a distinctive uniform on special occasions. Women were first admitted in 1972. Entrance is through competitive exam after two years' studies in post-baccalauréat preparatory classes, though nowadays there is an alternative selection procedure for foreign students.

The school — nicknamed 'X' — has an undergraduate program, graduate school and many research laboratories mostly run in association with other institutions such as CNRS, the national centre for scientific research.

Polytechnique specializes in biology, chemistry, computer science, economics, pure and applied mathematics, mechanical engineering, physics and social sciences. But all students must study a broad range of subjects including two languages and general cultural courses, and follow several work placements.

Reforms in 2000 extended by a year the

FACTFILE

ÉCOLE POLYTECHNIQUE

Country	France
Foundation Year	1794
World Ranking	28 (37)

Faculty Area Rankings

Engineering & IT	34
Life Sciences & Biomedicine	202
Natural Sciences	31
Social Sciences	261

Survey Performance

Peer Review	92
Recruiter Review	43

Contact Details

rue de Saclay
Palaiseau
91128
www.polytechnique.fr
+33 1 69 33 33 33

People

Student Faculty Ratio	3.7:1
International Faculty	19.0%
Undergraduates	1,000
Postgraduates	1,464
International Students	25.0%

Course Fees For International Students

Average Undergraduate	$9,605
Average Postgraduate	$15,094

Overall Research Strength

Papers (Scopus 2002-2006)	19,357
Citations (Scopus 2002-2006)	80,842
Impact	4.2

Research Impact By Faculty Area

Engineering & IT	2.3
Life Sciences & Biomedicine	3.4
Natural Sciences	5.2
Social Sciences	1.8

traditional three-year undergraduate engineering program — one year each military service, common studies and specialisation — and introduced a civilian service option. A year is spent at another university, possibly abroad.

Annual intake is 500, with foreigners of 40 nationalities representing a fifth of the 2,000 undergraduates. There are 170 master's students, half from abroad, and 400 studying for doctorates, including 33 per cent international students. Twelve per cent of the school's 400 teachers are from abroad. There are 145 agreements with universities in other countries.

About 15 patents are registered annually. Areas of research include an asymmetric anti-noise wall; a proton-therapy laser for cancer treatments; an original procedure allowing easy access to compounds for cardiac therapies; a model for forecasting air quality.

Among Polytechnique-related high-technology projects are the TGV, France's high-speed train; Ariane rocket launchers; Airbus planes; and France's nuclear reactor system.

In 1976 the school moved from its historic site in Paris's Latin Quarter to its present campus at Palaiseau, south of the capital, where all students are housed.

People

Alumni include Presidents Sadi Carnot and Valéry Giscard d'Estaing, astronauts Jean-François Clervoy and Philippe Perrin, scientists André-Marie Ampère, Paul Lévy, Henri Poincaré and Nobel prize-winner for economics, Maurice Allais. Alfred Dreyfus and Generals Foch and Joffre are among military Polytechniciens. Numerous heads of industry, corporations and companies include André Citroën, Charles Bébéar, Jean-Marie Messier, Serge Dassault, Jacques Attali.

What students say

British student Harry Robertson is taking the undergraduate program. For his six-month stage de formation humaine — "roughly a leadership-development work placement" — he "worked as a full-time teacher for inmates at a Paris prison, which was an incredible experience." His final diploma will be equivalent to a French engineering degree and an MSc.

His "very high expectations of both the quality of the education and the student lifestyle" were "more than lived up to. I was pleasantly surprised at just how much freedom students have in picking their courses, and at how cosmopolitan the campus is." He spent a month last summer working in Beijing, after studying Chinese for a year.

He identifies the school's strengths as "the diversity and quality of its education, its budget per student – Polytechnique is very highly subsidised; and the student lifestyle – there's an incredible amount of clubs, activities and sport". He says weaknesses are that "it is little known abroad, especially compared to the top British and American universities, and its relatively small size".

Good at

Polytechnique's strengths are in science and technology: 31st in the world for the natural sciences and 34th for engineering and IT.

29 Northwestern University

Why this university?

A major private research university, Northwestern has the feel of a small college, with a comparatively small enrollment of 7,800 undergraduates (there are some 9,300 graduate students) and a foundation in the liberal arts with a curriculum challenging enough that at exactly 9 pm on the Sunday before finals week each term, students traditionally lean out their windows and collectively unleash a primal scream. Nearly three-quarters of classes have fewer than 20 students in them, and the 1,000 undergraduate faculty teach more than 95 per cent of the courses — not graduate teaching assistants. Undergraduates can also do research or independent study.

And the research agenda at Northwestern is ambitious. Founded in 1850 in an office over a hardware store by Chicago civic leaders anxious to win respect for their gritty frontier town, it now has five doctoral programs ranked in the top 10 per cent in America by the National Research Council and 10 others in the top 25 per cent. Some US$400 million annually in research is conducted here.

Many international students come to Northwestern to attend its top-rated Kellogg School of Business; one-third of the business school's students are international, representing 50 countries. Like the university as a whole, the school has moved more nimbly than its peer institutions to incorporate such new programs as internet marketing and entertainment management. More than 50 new courses in all have been introduced at Kellogg in the

FACTFILE

NORTHWESTERN University

Country	United States
Foundation Year	1851
World Ranking	29 (42)

Faculty Area Rankings

Arts & Humanities	110
Engineering & IT	67
Life Sciences & Biomedicine	74
Natural Sciences	87
Social Sciences	29

Survey Performance

Peer Review	54
Recruiter Review	26

Contact Details

633 Clark Street
Evanston,
IL 60208
www.northwestern.edu
+1 847 491 3741

People

Student Faculty Ratio	8.5:1
International Faculty	8.0%
Undergraduates	8,079
Postgraduates	6,021
International Students	15.0%

Course Fees For Domestic Students

Average Undergraduate	$33,408
Average Postgraduate	$29,940

Overall Research Strength

Papers (Scopus 2002-2006)	74,748
Citations (Scopus 2002-2006)	416,650
Impact	5.6

Research Impact By Faculty Area

Engineering & IT	4.4
Life Sciences & Biomedicine	5.6
Natural Sciences	7.2
Social Sciences	3.8

last 10 years. Its Global Initiatives in Management includes two weeks of field study in such places as Central Europe, China, Russia, and Vietnam.

Northwestern's School of Law is small (240 students) and unusually supportive, rather than competitive like many other US law schools. It includes a nine-month master's program for graduates of foreign law schools to learn American law and legal processes. The university's Center for International Human Rights, headed by former US Ambassador at Large for War Crimes Issues David Scheffer, prepares students to argue before international criminal tribunals. It also has a unique program in corporate responsibility for human rights. And its Center for Wrongful Conviction, staffed largely by students from the law school and the university's Medill School of Journalism, famously proved innocent nine inmates on Illinois's death row, causing the state's governor to declare a moratorium on executions. The Medill curriculum is being overhauled to respond to declining American newspaper circulation in a controversial move; traditional faculty governance has been suspended for more than three years while the new plan is being implemented.

There are many changes under way on the Northwestern campus, now alongside Lake Michigan. New facilities have been completed or are under way, including a Molecular Therapeutics and Diagnostics Building.

The university's McCormick School of Engineering is among the top-rated in America, with a program that gives first-year students the chance to work with real engineers on projects at partner companies including BP-Amoco, Ford, Motorola, and DuPont. The "Engineering First" idea stemmed from concern that engineering education previously emphasised scientific analysis at the expense of practical design.

People

The theater program has graduated the likes of Charlton Heston, Warren Beatty, Cloris Leachman, Ann-Margret, Patricia Neal, Clancy Brown, Shelley Long, Lulia Louis-Dreyfus, Tony Roberts. There are 60 student theater productions each year. Other prominent alumni include the chairman and CEO of General Dynamics, the president and CEO of the Campbell Soup Company, and the president of Cornell University.

What students say

"You find people from all over the world, and they're definitely some of the smartest people to get in here," said Ruchit Duggal, an undergraduate from India who is majoring in both economics and computer engineering. Fewer than one in three applicants to the university are accepted; just under seven per cent are international. "It's a good mix of cultures," Mr Duggal said. "It's not inside the city, but if you need to go into the city, it takes maybe 30 minutes," he said. "You have close-knit communities, in spite of it being a big university. The only negative I've found is the weather in the winter, which gets you down a bit."

Good at

In the top 100 for everything except the arts and humanities, Northwestern's best placing is in the social sciences, where it is ranked in the top 30.

30 University of Manchester

Why this university?

England's oldest civic university became Britain's first chartered university of the 21st century and the largest single-site institution in the country when Victoria University of Manchester merged with UMIST to form the University of Manchester in 2004.

Since the merger, Manchester has set its sights on becoming a world giant by 2015 in terms of academic achievement and reputation, bringing its size, significant human capital, impressive facilities, and half a billion pounds annual income to bear on the challenge.

It is already well on its way to achieving its aims, albeit with work still to do in balancing the books. Manchester was voted University of the Year in Times Higher Education's annual awards of 2005. Its 4,500 academic and research staff notched up international-class rankings in 41 out of the university's 52 discipline areas in the last UK Research Assessment Exercise. Such impressive results have helped make Manchester the UK's most popular university among British students applying for places on undergraduate courses, and the second most popular institution among international students. The latter now make up 7,400 of Manchester's 37,000 student population, coming from a total of 180 different countries.

There are more than 50 specialist research centres and groups at Manchester, each undertaking pioneering research into areas ranging from cancer treatments and genetic

FACTFILE

University of MANCHESTER

Country.. United Kingdom
Foundation Year 1824
World Ranking 30 (40)

Faculty Area Rankings

Arts & Humanities 59
Engineering & IT 43
Life Sciences & Biomedicine 64
Natural Sciences 116
Social Sciences 68

Survey Performance

Peer Review 50
Recruiter Review 5

Contact Details

Oxford Road
Manchester
M13 9PL
www.manchester.ac.uk
+44 161 306 6000

People

Student Faculty Ratio 8.5:1
International Faculty 25.0%
Undergraduates 24,783
Postgraduates 7,499
International Students 20.0%

Course Fees For International Students

Average Undergraduate $6,294

Overall Research Strength

Papers (Scopus 2002-2006) 79,020
Citations (Scopus 2002-2006) 329,330
Impact 4.2

Research Impact By Faculty Area

Engineering & IT 2.6
Life Sciences & Biomedicine 4.8
Natural Sciences 4.5
Social Sciences 3.6

disorders to artificial intelligence and aeronautics. The university boasts the world-famous Jodrell Bank Observatory, the £35 million Manchester Interdisciplinary Biocentre, the Photon Science Institute, and the recently-opened £40 million Integrative Centre for Molecular Cell Biology. Other new facilities include the Brooks World Poverty Institute and a new centre for cancer research.

Manchester is funding these developments with a £360 million capital investment program — the largest ever seen in British higher education. As well as improving academic facilities, the money is being used to further enhance the university's city-centre campus. This it describes as a "mini-metropolis", with its own shops, accommodation, and social and sporting facilities.

Manchester guarantees university-managed accommodation, with more than 9,000 beds to choose from, throughout the duration of a course for all paying overseas student fees. Manchester's students union, the biggest in the UK, provides additional student support along with societies and social events.

Its huge student population helps to make the city of Manchester one of the most vibrant in the UK. It sees itself as the capital of the north of England and has the facilities to justify the claim.

People

More than 20 Nobel prize winners include Ernest Rutherford, who split the atom. WS Jevons formulated the principles of modern economics, while AJP Taylor was the best-known historian of his generation. Tom Kilburn and Sir Freddie Williams were among the pioneers of computers in the 1940s.

What students say

Tomomi Kimura, a life sciences PhD student from Japan, said she felt the convenient, compact, and comprehensive facilities on campus and in the city were among the university's greatest assets, along with its strong academic reputation. She said: "It is easy to get whatever you need at Manchester, and the facilities are excellent. The student accommodation is very good and conveniently located, and arranged so that it is easy to make friends. Manchester itself is a convenient place from which to visit anywhere in England and to travel internationally from the airport. Sometimes the transport system is not very reliable, but other than that I have had no real disappointments."

Good at

Manchester is in the top 70 in every subject area except the natural sciences. Its best position this year is 43rd in engineering and technology.

31 University of Sydney

Why this university?

Australia's oldest university celebrated its 150th anniversary with the Sydney Olympics in 2000. As with other long-established inner-city universities, the University of Sydney has a big reputation for research and its 2,500 academics are involved in hundreds of collaborative research projects with Australian governments and other organizations, and with colleagues overseas.

Founded in 1850 "to promote useful knowledge and to encourage the residents of New South Wales to pursue a regular course of liberal education", classes at the University of Sydney started two years later with 24 students enrolled in the Faculty of Arts. The course required three years study of Greek, Latin, mathematics and science.

The university began operating on its main campus on the edge of the Sydney Central Business District in 1860. Sweeping lawns and Gothic Revival sandstone architecture give the campus a sense of old world higher learning that continues within the grand quadrangle and the Great Tower, now a focal point.

As secondary education had hardly begun in the 1850s, it was 30 years before Sydney had attracted more than 100 students. Over the next century, numbers slowly and then rapidly increased so that by this year total enrolments exceeded 46,000, including nearly 9,000 international students. Sydney places a great emphasis on providing students with the complete university experience

FACTFILE

The University of SYDNEY

Country.....Australia
Foundation Year.....1850
World Ranking.....31 (35=)

Faculty Area Rankings

Arts & Humanities.....15
Engineering & IT.....41
Life Sciences & Biomedicine.....23
Natural Sciences.....43
Social Sciences.....27

Survey Performance

Peer Review.....25
Recruiter Review.....37

Contact Details

Sydney
NSW 2006
www.usyd.edu.au
+61 2 9351 2222

People

Student Faculty Ratio.....12:1
International Faculty.....46.0%
Undergraduates.....27,394
Postgraduates.....8,580
International Students.....26.0%

Course Fees For Domestic Students

Average Undergraduate.....$16,080
Average Postgraduate.....$11,986

Course Fees For International Students

Average Undergraduate.....$17,708
Average Postgraduate.....$18,055

Overall Research Strength

Papers (Scopus 2002-2006).....67,165
Citations (Scopus 2002-2006).....264,577
Impact.....3.9

Research Impact By Faculty Area

Engineering & IT.....2.3
Life Sciences & Biomedicine.....4.3
Natural Sciences.....4.4
Social Sciences.....2.7

on campus through more than 250 sporting and cultural clubs.

Sydney is a member of Australia's Group of Eight research-intensive universities and has formal links with many of the world's leading research institutions. The global network of partners covers research collaboration, joint teaching projects as well as staff and student exchanges across 37 countries in Europe, North America and Asia.

The University is one of only three Australian institutions in the Association of the Pacific Rim Universities which comprises members from Asia, the United States and South America.

In 2007 the university offered 36 full fee scholarships with stipends to cover living expenses to outstanding international candidates for the Doctor of Philosophy program, and may increase this to 60 in 2008. Merit scholarships are also offered to international students completing Australian final year high school examinations in Australia and abroad, as well as to continuing undergraduate students. Some 50 such scholarships are awarded to students who have completed at least one year of an undergraduate degree program.

All Sydney undergraduates are eligible for scholarships awarded on the basis of outstanding academic achievement.

The University offers on-campus accommodation ranging from self-catered apartments to fully catered residential colleges and halls of residence. The University's Accommodation Service assists students seeking independent and shared accommodation off-campus.

People

Graduates who have gained international recognition include Nobel laureates Professor Russell Robinson, Sir John Cornforth and Dr John Harsanyi, former president of the World Bank James Wolfensohn, academic and businesswoman Jill Ker Conway, film makers Phil Noyce, Jane Campion and Bruce Beresford, writers such as Germaine Greer and Clive James, and three Prime Ministers, including Australia's first — Andrew Barton — and the Governor of NSW and Chancellor of the University, Her Excellency Professor Marie Bashir.

What students say

Diego Poveda from Bogota in Colombia initially hoped to study in America or Britain. The cost was more than his parents could afford so he opted for Australia. A chemical engineering graduate, Mr Poveda finds it hard to think of anything to complain of about his lecturers, his studies or the University.

"When I saw the curriculum the University of Sydney had to offer, I realized that it had a balanced program between theoretical classes and problem-based learning," he says. "I'd say that in large part it has met my expectations. The mix of theoretical subjects and problem based learning really put a smile on my face as I could see how learning about systems could be applied in a chemical plant."

Good at

In the top 50 in all areas. The arts and humanities take pride of place, at 15th in the world, but social science and biomedicine are also in the top 30.

32 Brown University

Why this university?

Fretful about its standings in American league tables, Brown has embarked on an ambitious, US$1.4 billion plan to increase the size of its faculty, expand research, and improve facilities. "Largely because of a lack of resources — most notably reflected in the too-small size of the faculty and insufficient faculty support — our programs are not recognized as leaders as consistently as many in other great research universities," a task force studying the issue there concluded. Brown is even reviewing its so-called New Curriculum, under which there are no distribution requirements and grades are optional, meaning students get to choose from any of 2,000 courses in 40 departments while forgoing the ruthless competition characteristic of other Ivy League schools.

Whatever insecurities might have prompted these self-evaluations, students continue to flock to Brown. Less than 14 per cent of applicants are accepted. More than 18,300 applicants apply for the 1,460 seats in each year's entering class. Once enrolled, a survey found, these students are the happiest in America. They enjoy not only the New Curriculum, but the atmosphere of a comparatively small school, with 5,900 undergraduates and 1,900 graduate students, nine per cent of them international.

Founded in 1764 on College Hill, overlooking the resurgent onetime manufacturing city of Providence, Rhode Island (four of whose top office-holders, including the governor and the mayor, are alumni), Brown was the

FACTFILE

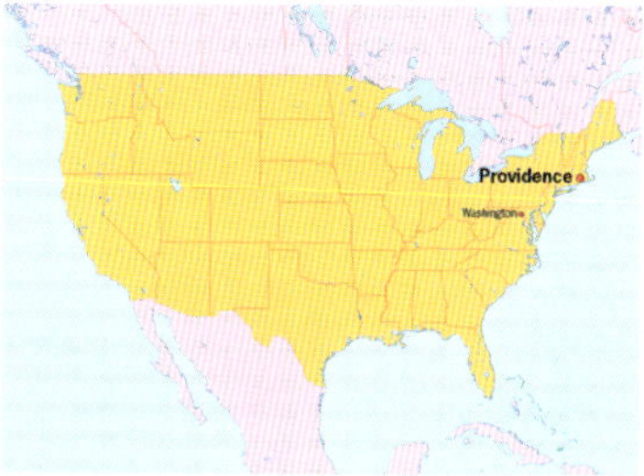

BROWN University

Country	United States
Foundation Year	1764
World Ranking	32 (54=)

Faculty Area Rankings

Arts & Humanities	31
Engineering & IT	89
Life Sciences & Biomedicine	59
Natural Sciences	62
Social Sciences	66

Survey Performance

Peer Review	47
Recruiter Review	130

Contact Details

Providence
RI 02912
www.brown.edu
+1 401 863 1000

People

Student Faculty Ratio	8.9:1
International Faculty	21.0%
Undergraduates	5,737
Postgraduates	1,601
International Students	12.0%

Course Fees For Domestic Students

Average Undergraduate	$35,584
Average Postgraduate	$30,672

Overall Research Strength

Papers (Scopus 2002-2006)	33,687
Citations (Scopus 2002-2006)	180,896
Impact	5.4

Research Impact By Faculty Area

Engineering & IT	4.2
Life Sciences & Biomedicine	4.9
Natural Sciences	8.2
Social Sciences	4.5

first US school to admit students of all religious persuasions and the first Ivy League university to be headed by a black woman president. Its undergraduate engineering program is the oldest in the Ivy League and it has the only undergraduate egyptology department in the Western Hemisphere and an undergraduate program in the history of mathematics that was, until recently, the only one of its kind in the world.

Brown conducts a relatively modest US$138.5 million in sponsored research. Researchers there have developed an implantable neuroprosthetic device four millimetres square that may help paralyzed people control electric wheelchairs, use email, and surf the Internet by using their thoughts. It's now being tested. The university's interdisciplinary Population Studies and Training Center conducts research into fertility, mortality, migration, and population and environment. Brown's relatively young medical school integrates premedical and medical education into a seamless, eight-year program; Brown also ranks in the top five for students accepted to other medical schools. Its "Boldly Brown" campaign has already resulted in the Sidney E Frank Hall for Life Sciences, the most expensive building in university history, with 30 laboratories designed to encourage scientific collaboration.

The university has also appointed its first-ever vice president for international affairs, whose job will be to enhance its global reputation as a major research institution.

People

Alumni include former US Secretary of State and Chief Justice Charles Evans Hughes, Prince Faisal Ben Al Hussein of Jordan, Prince Nikolaos and Princess Theodora of Greece and Denmark, Lady Gabriella Windsor, daughter of Prince Michael of Kent, John D Rockefeller Jr, and Allegra Versace.

What students say

The students are competitive with themselves, not with other people, said Guy Bloembergen, an undergraduate from the Netherlands. "I have friends who are very artsy people and aren't particularly good at science, but they can take a science course and not have to worry too much about the grade. They can focus on the class." Bloembergen said he was drawn to Brown by the openness of the curriculum. "That was probably the biggest pull for me."

Good at

In the top 100 in every area, Brown's highest position is in the arts and humanities, where it is just outside the top 30.

33= University of British Columbia

Why this university?

Out on Canada's West Coast, the University of British Columbia offers a full range of undergraduate, graduate and professional programs in the arts, sciences, medicine, law, commerce and other faculties.

Over 23,500 full-time undergraduate students, 6,900 full-time graduate students and approximately 13,300 part-time students attend its main campus in Vancouver, while its small campus in the province's Okanagan valley counts just under 4,600 full- and part-time students. There are over 6,000 international students from 143 countries at UBC.

As for those who teach and research at the university, UBC employs 4,504 faculty members, with quite an internationally educated contingent. Forty-three per cent of them earned their first degrees from institutions outside Canada

Neurosciences has become a leading discipline at the university, with UBC's Brain Research Centre bringing together 175 interdisciplinary investigators to form a powerhouse neuroscience research facility. Its physics and astronomy researchers are among the most cited in Canada.

In terms of research commercialisation, New Scientist in 2005 ranked it ninth in North America for life-science patents — the only Canadian university on the list. One of the products that had been developed in a UBC lab was Visudyne, the leading treatment for age-related blindness.

The university also boasts a strong

FACTFILE

University of BRITISH COLUMBIA

Country .... Canada
Foundation Year 1908
World Ranking .... 33= (50=)

Faculty Area Rankings

Arts & Humanities 14
Engineering & IT 30
Life Sciences & Biomedicine 20
Natural Sciences 30
Social Sciences 14

Survey Performance

Peer Review 18
Recruiter Review 60

Contact Details

2329 West Mall
Vancouver, B.C.
Canada
V6T 1Z4
www.ubc.ca
+1 604 822 2211

People

Student Faculty Ratio 9.3:1
International Faculty 8.0%
Undergraduates 30,786
Postgraduates 7,235
International Students 14.0%

Course Fees For Domestic Students

Average Undergraduate $3,994
Average Postgraduate $10,459

Course Fees For International Students

Average Undergraduate $16,538
Average Postgraduate $12,056

Overall Research Strength

Papers (Scopus 2002-2006) 89,496
Citations (Scopus 2002-2006) 417,356
Impact 4.7

Research Impact By Faculty Area

Engineering & IT 2.6
Life Sciences & Biomedicine 5.0
Natural Sciences 5.8
Social Sciences 3.4

creative writing program, and is particularly proud of the fact that its runs Canada's largest program in Asian Studies and counts the largest Asian library collection in the country. Its Museum of Anthropology is known internationally for a strong Pacific Northwest Collection.

Its mission it says is to "prepare students to become exceptional global citizens, promote the values of a civil and sustainable society, and conduct outstanding research to serve the people of British Columbia, Canada, and the world". It says its values are of excellence in research and teaching, global citizenship, sustainability and civil society.

People

The late Michael Smith, a Nobel laureate in chemistry taught for decades at UBC, while physics researcher Carl Wieman, recently hired to spearhead reforms in the teaching of science, is their newest Nobel laureate. World famous opera singer Ben Heppner is a graduate of its School of Music, while former Canadian Prime Ministers Kim Campbell and John Turner also call UBC their alma mater.

What students say

Deniz Kuran, of Istanbul, Turkey, chose to pursue her studies at UBC primarily "because I knew it was one of the top universities in Canada and their business program was one of the hardest to get into".

She also viewed its location as one of the school's strong points. "I had heard Vancouver was one of the best cities to live in the world." It also has some of the mildest weather in the country. Ms Kuran says her Bachelor of Commerce in Human Resources Management and International Business program enjoys "strong company connections and good professors". While UBC met her expectations both academically and socially, she says the large population can pose problems: "(That kind of size) can be too much for some students and they might feel lost sometimes."

Good at

UBC is in the top 30 for every academic area. Its top placings are in the arts and humanities and the social sciences, both of which are ranked 14 in the world.

33= University of Queensland

Why this university?

The University of Queensland is the oldest and most highly respected of the state's seven universities. It was founded in 1909 and its first lectures held two years later when 83 students, including 23 women, turned up for classes at Government House in the centre of the city. Today, the main campus is located on a tranquil site on the bend of the Brisbane River about six kilometres from the central business district. But UQ also operates on 50 locations across the state in hospitals, on tropical islands and even has its own experimental mine.

Around the world, UQ is probably best known for its unprecedented series of research institutes and centres which attract funding of about AU$700 million (£309 million). Its world-class institutes specialize in molecular bioscience, bioengineering and nanotechnology, social science, sustainable minerals, magnetic resonance capabilities and neuroscience.

The university is a founding member of Australia's Group of Eight research-intensive universities and also of Universitas 21. UQ is the first Australian university to accept year-round research scholarship applications, usually conducted in two rounds in March and October.

With AU$ 215 million (£95 million) in total research income, UQ accounts for about 70 per cent of Queensland's research as well as being one of the top three universities in Australia in this regard.

FACTFILE

University of QUEENSLAND

Country .... Australia
Foundation Year 1909
World Ranking .... 33= (45)

Faculty Area Rankings

Arts & Humanities 45
Engineering & IT 62
Life Sciences & Biomedicine 31
Natural Sciences 54
Social Sciences 34

Survey Performance

Peer Review 36
Recruiter Review 45

Contact Details

Brisbane
QLD 4072
www.uq.edu.au
+61 7 3365 1111

People

Student Faculty Ratio 9.3:1
International Faculty 22.0%
Undergraduates 22,477
Postgraduates 6,205
International Students 17.0%

Course Fees For Domestic Students

Average Undergraduate $18,211
Average Postgraduate $15,284

Course Fees For International Students

Average Undergraduate $22,120
Average Postgraduate $22,626

Overall Research Strength

Papers (Scopus 2002-2006) 61,583
Citations (Scopus 2002-2006) 239,851
Impact 3.9

Research Impact By Faculty Area

Engineering & IT 2.0
Life Sciences & Biomedicine 4.4
Natural Sciences 4.2
Social Sciences 3.1

People

More than 2,600 academics are researching and teaching in UQ's seven faculties where 37,000 students from 121 countries are enrolled. The university is large by Australian standards and is the biggest in Queensland. It is also the state's only provider for many disciplines, including dentistry, medicine, mining and minerals processing, pharmacy, space engineering, speech pathology and pharmacy.

Because it heads the academic and student status hierarchies in Queensland, UQ attracts the state's top school leavers, although this inevitably means that private school students are over-represented. Foreign students are also keen to study at the university and more than 6,600 are studying for their degrees.

Its alumni include Nobel prizewinner Professor Peter Doherty as well as former state premiers, a Governor-General and chief justices as well as Oscar-winning actor Geoffrey Rush and a list of famous business people, writers, artists, doctors and engineers.

What students say

Camryn Allen was drawn to UQ in 2002 as a study abroad student from California's San Diego. She says she felt so at home that she stayed on to complete her PhD in a study of koalas and plans to continue her research there.

Ms Allen says because the university was flexible about her studies and offered unique research opportunities in her particular area of interest, it was her "number one choice". At the school of animal studies, she spent her time with a koala research group that created a ground-breaking artificial insemination technique for the animals.

Her particular focus was on researching wild koalas to select the best males for breeding based on a range of physical characteristics and time of the year. "It was about getting more information on males' fertility to better the koala artificial insemination technique," she says.

Good at

The life sciences and biomedicine are UQ's main strength, finishing just outside the top 30, but the university hardly drops below the top 60 in any discipline.

33= National University of Singapore

Why this university?

The National University of Singapore, founded in 1905, has forged a global reputation since independence from Malaysia in 1965 and now ranks in the top quartile of the world's universities. Set on a 1.5 square kilometre campus at Kent Ridge, scene in February 1942 of the heroic last stand by the Malay Regiment, NUS is a beacon for the huge investment in education at all levels made by the government of the Republic of Singapore. The law school has moved to a new site at Bukit Timah in the centre of the island.

Privatised on April 1 2006, the university continues to receive a government subsidy as the island-state seeks to maintain the highest all-round standards in education.

Current student enrolment is around 24,000 undergraduates and 7,000 postgraduate students, with about 2,000 faculty. Sellapan Ramanathan, Singapore's president, is the university's chancellor.

Student intake is from a wide spectrum of countries. In the Law School more than two dozen nationalities are represented while student exchange programs take Singaporean students to a number of countries including China, Canada, Australia and the US.

Active on an international level, NUS plays a leading role in the Association of Pacific Rim Universities(APRU), whilst consolidating its existing position at the forefront of the International Alliance of Research Universities. The university has five

FACTFILE

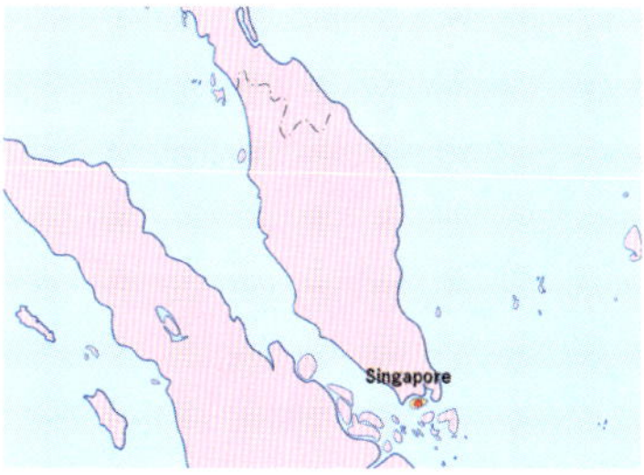

National University of SINGAPORE

Country	Singapore
Foundation Year	1905
World Ranking	33= (19=)

Faculty Area Rankings

Arts & Humanities	21
Engineering & IT	10
Life Sciences & Biomedicine	12
Natural Sciences	25
Social Sciences	20

Survey Performance

Peer Review	17
Recruiter Review	52

Contact Details

21 Lower Kent Ridge Road
Singapore
119077
www.nus.edu.sg
+65 6516 6666

People

Student Faculty Ratio	16:1
International Faculty	52.0%
Undergraduates	22,689
Postgraduates	6,617
International Students	36.0%

Course Fees For Domestic Students

Average Undergraduate	$4,397
Average Postgraduate	$3,042

Course Fees For International Students

Average Undergraduate	$4,834
Average Postgraduate	$4,166

Overall Research Strength

Papers (Scopus 2002-2006)	86,318
Citations (Scopus 2002-2006)	312,060
Impact	3.6

Research Impact By Faculty Area

Engineering & IT	2.9
Life Sciences & Biomedicine	4.4
Natural Sciences	4.1
Social Sciences	2.1

overseas colleges; Bio Valley (USA), Silicon Valley, Shanghai, Stockholm and Bangalore. A recent initiative has seen NUS enter the film-making world through the establishment of the NUS Hollywood Lab in co-operation with the University of Southern California School of Cinema and Television.

Facilities in Singapore are of the highest international standards and include six libraries and four museums, including the Raffles Museum of Biodiversity Research, which showcases over 500,000 specimens of flora and fauna.

Great all-round emphasis is placed on research at NUS. Current government reorientation of the republic's economy sets goals in new areas such as biotechnology and biomedicine, where NUS also plays a leading role.

People

Among its leading graduates NUS can number Goh Chok Tong, former Prime Minister of Singapore, Kishore Mahbubani, dean of the Lee Kuan Yew School of Public Policy at NUS and Choo San Goh, prominent choreographer of the Washington Ballet. Of the current staff, Wong Lim Soon of the school of computing has established an international reputation in data base theories.

What students say

Reben Ng, who has recently graduated in psychology and intends to read for a masters at NUS, exemplifies the university's international approach. He has qualified for an international award usually made to academics who have completed a PhD and five years' research on the basis of his undergraduate research paper.

Mr Ng wrote up his undergraduate internship with the Singapore police after only two years at NUS, becoming the first to qualify for the award from the International Council of Psychologists on the strength of his undergraduate work.

He says: "When I first stepped into NUS, I never expected that my university life would be so rich. In retrospect I realize I was given the opportunity to learn in three ways: from books, through travels and by interacting with people who were totally different from me.

"I now have friends from all over the world, and, more importantly, they are friends who are passionate about the same kinds of things."

Good at

Academics rank NUS in the top 25 in every academic area. It is in the top 10 for engineering and technology, and only just outside it for the life sciences and biomedicine.

36 Peking University

Why this university?

Founded in 1898, Peking University (Beijing Daxue, or Bei Da) is one of the oldest universities in China. Originally known as the Imperial Capital University, it was renamed the National Peking University in 1912, following the Xinhai Revolution. In 1919, students from the university formed the bulk of the protesters in the May Fourth Movement. In 1920, it became the second Chinese university to accept female students, after Nanjing University.

During the Second World War, the university moved to Kunming, where it formed the National Southwestern United University along with Tsinghua and Nankai. It returned to Beijing in 1946. After the founding of the People's Republic of China in 1949, it merged with Yenching University and dropped the "National" from its name, moving from central Beijing to the Yenching campus on the city's north-west outskirts. It remains there today, literally across the road from its rival Tsinghua.

Today, Peking is one of China's designated "national key universities" and competes with Tsinghua in the country's affections to be regarded as the best university in China. At present, Peking has over 46,000 students enrolled, of whom some 15,000 are undergraduates, 8,000 master's students and 4,000 doctoral candidates, with the remainder on correspondence or night courses.

Peking University also has one of the largest intakes in China of international students, with almost 2,000 currently enrolled from 62 different countries.

FACTFILE

PEKING University

Country .... China
Foundation Year 1898
World Ranking 36 (14)

Faculty Area Rankings

Arts & Humanities 18
Engineering & IT 36
Life Sciences & Biomedicine 18
Natural Sciences 15
Social Sciences 23

Survey Performance

Peer Review 19
Recruiter Review 18

Contact Details

Yiheyuan Road, Haidian District
Beijing
China
100871
www.pku.edu.cn
+86 10 6275 2114

People

Student Faculty Ratio 5.6:1
International Faculty 7.0%
Undergraduates 14,272
Postgraduates 16,666
International Students 5.0%

Course Fees For Domestic Students

Average Undergraduate $3,706

Overall Research Strength

Papers (Scopus 2002-2006) 96,294
Citations (Scopus 2002-2006) 244,224
Impact 2.5

Research Impact By Faculty Area

Engineering & IT 1.8
Life Sciences & Biomedicine 2.4
Natural Sciences 3.2
Social Sciences 2.1

Approximately 40 per cent of the international students are from South Korea.

While offering a comprehensive range of study courses, Peking University is known mostly for arts and science, and is heavily geared towards scientific research. It has 216 research institutions at present, including two national engineering research centres, 81 key national disciplines and 12 national key laboratories.

Though Peking concentrates on research, in recent years it has committed to improving its teaching standards. The university's goal is to combine continued research with the training of the specialized personnel needed for China's skill-hungry workforce. Peking is a member of Universitas 21, an international collaboration network of research-intensive universities.

People

Peking University has many famous alumni. Perhaps its most notable faculty member was Lu Xun, the godfather of modern Chinese literature, though early chancellor and May Fourth Movement leader Cai Yuanpei is a strong contender. Chinese Communist Party co-founders Chen Duxiu and Li Dazhao both worked there — the former was Dean of Letters, the latter head librarian.

A young Mao Zedong was a part-time student there whilst working as an assistant in the university library. Former full-time students include early Communist Party leader Zhang Guotao, the writer and journalist Mao Dun, and noted linguist Michael Halliday.

Current academics of note at Peking University include the environmental scientist Tang Xiaoyan, who recently won the Vienna Convention Award for her contributions towards ozone layer protection; leading geoscientist Dong Shenbao; cellular biologist Zhai Zhonghe; and Xu Guangxian, head of the Applied Quantum Chemistry Group of the State Key Laboratory of Rare Earth Materials Chemistry and Applications.

What students say

He Qinzhou from Tianjin, China, who is studying computing, said: "The special thing about here is that it is a very comprehensive university. Almost anything you want to study, Peking University can provide it at a good level. For me, it was a great honour to be able to study here.

"However, like all Chinese universities at the moment, we are very undeveloped — there is a big disparity between China and the West. China definitely needs to keep improving. I believe that it will not be long before we can get the same level as the best universities in the world."

Good at

Everything: eighth in life sciences

37 University of Bristol

Why this university?

Bristol has been moving steadily up the World University Rankings since they were first published and has now broken into the top 40. With more than 10 applicants for every undergraduate place, it is one of the UK's most popular universities. In total the institution has only 11,500 full-time undergraduates, and 5,000 postgraduate students — including 2,000 international students from 100 countries — but there are more than 5,000 staff.

Bristol is an old, city-based institution. A prominent member of the Russell group of research-intensive universities, the university has a strong research reputation across a wide variety of traditional disciplines. In the UK Research Assessment Exercise in 2001, 36 departments received the top 5 or 5* ratings. This means that just over three-quarters of all academic staff work in departments rated world class or internationally excellent for research. Areas of particular strength include mathematics, chemistry, biological sciences, civil engineering, drama, geography, clinical dentistry, veterinary science, law, classics and modern languages.

Bristol is pushing hard on knowledge transfer, spinning out a number of successful companies from University research. Bristol was awarded the highest level of confidence in the last institutional audit by the Quality Assurance Agency for Higher Education.

The university owns 400 hectares of land and 370 buildings. It is in the

FACTFILE

University of BRISTOL

Country	United Kingdom
Foundation Year	1876
World Ranking	37 (64=)

Faculty Area Rankings

Arts & Humanities	88
Engineering & IT	119
Life Sciences & Biomedicine	48
Natural Sciences	98
Social Sciences	121

Survey Performance

Peer Review	76
Recruiter Review	12

Contact Details

Senate House, Tyndall Avenue
Bristol
BS8 1TH
www.bris.ac.uk
+44 117 928 9000

People

Student Faculty Ratio	7.6:1
International Faculty	27.0%
Undergraduates	12,229
Postgraduates	3,590
International Students	16.0%

Course Fees For Domestic Students

Average Undergraduate	$6,294

Overall Research Strength

Papers (Scopus 2002-2006)	50,208
Citations (Scopus 2002-2006)	244,895
Impact	4.9

Research Impact By Faculty Area

Engineering & IT	3.0
Life Sciences & Biomedicine	4.9
Natural Sciences	6.3
Social Sciences	4.0

middle of a £250 million investment program which will cover new buildings, equipment and staff appointments. Major investments are planned in physics, mathematics, biological sciences, library and IT facilities, as well as new premises for the students' union and student support services. Bristol currently has a turnover of £300 million.

The city of Bristol, the largest in the south-west of England, is attractive and prosperous. Although relatively expensive by UK standards, it is also generally popular with students. London is less than two hours away by train and international air links are good.

People

Four Nobel Laureates have worked at Bristol: Paul Dirac (1933), a Bristol graduate; Cecil Frank Powell (1950); Hans Albrecht Bethe (1967); and Sir Neville Francis Mott (1977). There are 30 fellows of the Royal Society and nine fellows of the British Academy on the active and emeritus staff. Sir Winston Churchill became Chancellor in 1929 and continued in the role for more than a quarter of a century.

Other famous Bristol alumni include: Sir Liam Donaldson, chief medical officer of England; Will Hutton, chief executive of The Work Foundation, author of The State We're In and The State to Come; (Owen) Josh Lewsey, the rugby union international; and Lembit Opik, Liberal Democrat Member of Parliament for Montgomeryshire.

Distinguished faculty members now include Professor Michael Berry, one of the world's top physicists, and Professor Peter Fleming, whose work is credited with saving the lives of 100,000 babies worldwide.

What students say

Matthew Seow, a fourth year Electrical & Electronic Engineering student said: "The university's biggest strength is that it's managed to get that tricky balance between academic achievement, activities outside academia and social life, close to perfection. It's quite hard to think of weaknesses but I guess it could do a bit more to integrate international students into the general student body and vice-versa.

"Studying at Bristol University was the best thing that's ever happened to me, and the whole experience has definitely exceeded my expectations."

Good at

Bristol's best finish in this year's rankings was for life sciences and biomedicine, where it was ranked in the top 50. It also made the top 100 for the arts and humanities and the natural sciences.

38= The Chinese University of Hong Kong

Why this university?

The Chinese University of Hong Kong (CUHK) is a comprehensive research university with philosophical foundations built on the traditions of bilingualism and multiculturalism.

Established in 1963 through the amalgamation of three colleges with the addition of a fourth college in 1986, the university is the only one in Hong Kong that follows a collegiate structure and a bilingual policy that places equal emphasis on English and Chinese.

The teaching faculty is organized around eight Faculties/School: Arts, Business Administration, Education, Engineering, Medicine, Science, Social Science, and the School of Law. CUHK has a student population of 13,310 in undergraduate programs (77 per cent) and postgraduate programs (23 per cent). There are also several thousand students in professional and continuing education leading to higher degrees. With the largest campus in Hong Kong (134 hectares) the university provides over 6,000 hostel places and its member colleges play important roles in fostering an intellectual community and providing pastoral care and support. Of the 10 previous Rhodes Scholars from Hong Kong, seven are from the university.

The university has an internationally-mixed faculty. Of its 1,957 faculty members, nearly half are of foreign nationalities and 93 per cent hold overseas qualifications. Many of the academics have distinguished

FACTFILE

The CHINESE University of Hong Kong

Country	Hong Kong
Foundation Year	1963
World Ranking	38= (50=)

Faculty Area Rankings

Arts & Humanities	106
Engineering & IT	85
Life Sciences & Biomedicine	62
Natural Sciences	125
Social Sciences	48

Survey Performance

Peer Review	68
Recruiter Review	123

Contact Details

Shatin, N.T
Hong Kong SAR
The People's Republic of China
www.cuhk.edu.hk
+852 2609 7000

People

Student Faculty Ratio	8.2:1
International Faculty	51.0%
Undergraduates	10,197
Postgraduates	2,863
International Students	20.0%

Course Fees For Domestic Students

Average Undergraduate	$5,381
Average Postgraduate	$5,381

Course Fees For International Students

Average Undergraduate	$10,225
Average Postgraduate	$5,381

Overall Research Strength

Papers (Scopus 2002-2006)	53,912
Citations (Scopus 2002-2006)	211,932
Impact	3.9

Research Impact By Faculty Area

Engineering & IT	2.9
Life Sciences & Biomedicine	4.3
Natural Sciences	4.3
Social Sciences	2.5

themselves with research in the medical and scientific fields, including the first successful cloning of the plant gene, the development of the world's smallest Bluetooth communications module, the formulation of network coding theory, and breakthroughs in minimally invasive surgery and detection of foetal DNA in maternal plasma.

The university's MBA programs are also highly-regarded and have several notable firsts in Hong Kong: the first full-time MBA in 1966, the first part-time MBA in 1977, and the first EMBA in 1993. The Faculty of Business Administration of CUHK was accredited by AACSB in 1999, among the first in Asia to be accredited by AACSB. The Faculty is highly regarded internationally in management and organizational research on Greater China and its international recognition is reflected in a student composition where more than 70 per cent are from Asia, Europe and North America.

Five new colleges will be built in the next few years as the university aims to increase its undergraduate intake by 3,000 in preparation for Hong Kong's move towards a four-year degree structure in 2012.

The university's bilingual education policy offers a unique advantage as it extends itself internationally to attract more overseas students and faculty, and to position itself as a university of choice in Asia.

People

The university is the only one in Hong Kong to ever have Nobel Laureates among its staff, such as C. N. Yang, 1957 Nobel Laureate in Physics and Sir James Mirrlees, 1996 Nobel Laureate in Economics.

What students say

Sarah Moore worked in London for seven years before her decision to take a full-time MBA at CUHK. Motivated by China's integration into the world economy and a truly multicultural learning environment at the university, she has no regrets about relocating to Hong Kong: "Given China's increasing importance as a global economic power Hong Kong is an ideal place to develop myself and gain invaluable experience that will benefit my career."

Good at

The university's best positions in our rankings are in social sciences and biomedicine, both of which enjoyed top 50 placings.

38= University of Michigan

Why this university?

More than 107,000 people — the population of a small city — can fit inside the football stadium at the University of Michigan. And there's seldom an empty seat. Michigan fields some of the most dominant university sports teams in America, it has more alumni (420,000) than any other U.S. school, and its stadium is the largest built for American football at any university anywhere.

But while athletics garners much of the attention here, Michigan also conducts an almost unrivalled US$750 million a year in research, a tradition that began with Cold War- and space race-era government grants and in the days when nearby Detroit was the world center of the automotive industry. It was at Michigan that the polio vaccine and the EKG were developed. One in five undergraduates specializes in engineering, which is also the pre-eminent graduate program. The university's Phoenix Memorial Laboratory studies the peaceful uses of nuclear energy, and Michigan has top-flight laboratories for research into manufacturing engineering, manufacturing systems, and, not surprisingly, transportation. Today, as the American auto industry is struggling, Michigan has announced the University Research Corridor, along with Michigan State and Wayne State universities, to help reinvigorate the area economy by incubating technology and alternative energy companies that will be based there.

The first American university to use the seminar method of study, Michigan

FACTFILE

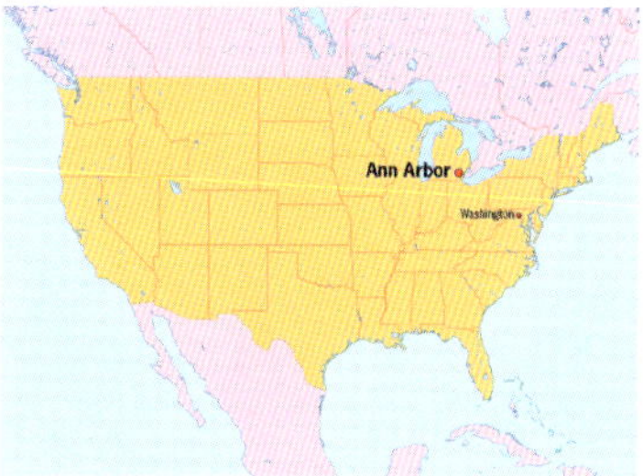

University of MICHIGAN

Country	United States
Foundation Year	1817
World Ranking	38= (29=)

Faculty Area Rankings

Arts & Humanities	19
Engineering & IT	32
Life Sciences & Biomedicine	33
Natural Sciences	24
Social Sciences	19

Survey Performance

Peer Review	22
Recruiter Review	35

Contact Details

Ann Arbor
Michigan
48109
www.umich.edu
+1 734 764 1817

People

Student Faculty Ratio	11.7:1
International Faculty	10.0%
Undergraduates	34,001
Postgraduates	13,059
International Students	11.0%

Course Fees For Domestic Students

Average Undergraduate	$16,000

Overall Research Strength

Papers (Scopus 2002-2006)	161,315
Citations (Scopus 2002-2006)	903,111
Impact	5.6

Research Impact By Faculty Area

Engineering & IT	3.6
Life Sciences & Biomedicine	6.4
Natural Sciences	6.1
Social Sciences	4.1

offers more than 70 seminars for first-year students, each capped at an enrolment of 20. This despite the fact that there are 39, 954 undergraduates and 14,470 graduate students. Those high numbers take a toll later on, when students find themselves in huge lecture classes or in courses taught by graduate students and not by one of the 4,635 faculty. But undergraduates do have a chance to work with faculty on research, and some 900 of them each year take advantage of the opportunity.

About four per cent of students come from outside the United States, allowing for diversity that has otherwise been diminished slightly by a court battle in which Michigan was put in the position of defending affirmative action in admissions. Where non-whites once were given an advantage over white applicants, the controversy was resolved with voters demanding that the race and gender of prospective students no longer be considered.

A multibillion-dollar fundraising campaign, whose goal wasreached months ahead of time, will underwrite nearly 170 more endowed professorships along with student financial aid and buildings including a hospital, drama center, the new Gerald R Ford School of Public Policy, and a new home for the school of public health.

People

Ford, the late ex-president, went to Michigan, where he played football. Many other Michigan athletes have gone on to high-profile professional careers in sports, and so many astronauts have been graduates that there is an alumni chapter on the moon, marked by a plaque left on the lunar surface by the all-Michigan crew of Apollo 15. Other alumni include the playwright Arthur Miller, actors James Earl Jones and Lucy Liu, Madonna, Iggy Pop (although he never graduated), and Swedish Holocaust hero Raoul Wallenberg.

What students say

"The research facilities are sensational," said Simon Schenk, an Australian who just received his doctorate in kinesiology with articles published about his groundbreaking research into exercise, obesity, and diabetes in high-profile scientific journals. "That's one of the fortunate things at Michigan. Typically people might think of kinesiology as teaching physical education or something. But we were really at the cutting edge of basic science."

Good at

In the top 40 in every field except the social sciences, where it is still in the top 100. The arts and humanities are top-rated, at 19th in the world.

40 Tsinghua University

Why this university?

Established in 1911, with reparation money paid to the US after the Boxer Uprising, as a preparatory school for Chinese graduates pursuing further studies at American universities, Tsinghua became a university in 1925, offering four year undergraduate and postgraduate programs.

The university's staff currently includes 2,877 teachers, of whom 1,069 are professors, 1,087 are associate professors and nearly 700 are doctoral advisers. Tsinghua's faculty has 34 members of the Chinese Academy of Sciences and 28 members of the Chinese Academy of Engineering, more than any other college or university in China.

Tsinghua has over 20,000 students, including 12,000 undergraduates, 6,200 masters degrees candidates and 2,800 doctoral candidates. This includes just over 1,000 foreign students, about half of whom are Korean — the rest are from more than 50 different countries.

Within China, Tsinghua is usually rated as one of the top two universities in the country. Located on the site of Qing dynasty royal gardens in the northwest of Beijing, it is usually considered the best university in China for engineering and business. Tsinghua has extensive business ties with companies in China's burgeoning high-tech sector. Arts and languages are comparatively weak, being mostly a support system for science and engineering students to get through the government-mandated tests in various subjects outside their major, necessary to

FACTFILE

TSINGHUA University

Country........China
Foundation Year........1911
World Ranking........40 (28)

Faculty Area Rankings

Arts & Humanities........91
Engineering & IT........16
Life Sciences & Biomedicine........52
Natural Sciences........34
Social Sciences........44

Survey Performance

Peer Review........36
Recruiter Review........55

Contact Details

Tsinghua Garden No.1, Haidian District
No.9, Dong Dan San Tiao, Dongchen District
Institute of Nuclear and New Energy Technology, Changping District
Beijing
100084
www.tsinghua.edu.cn
+86 10 6278 1943

People

Student Faculty Ratio........3.7:1
International Faculty........3.0%
Undergraduates........14,127
Postgraduates........3,110
International Students........7.0%

Course Fees For Domestic Students

Overall Average........$350

Course Fees For International Students

Overall Average........$4,517

Overall Research Strength

Papers (Scopus 2002-2006)........147,623
Citations (Scopus 2002-2006)........252,001
Impact........1.7

Research Impact By Faculty Area

Engineering & IT........1.2
Life Sciences & Biomedicine........2.4
Natural Sciences........2.5
Social Sciences........1.3

obtain their degrees. Tsinghua is keen to remedy this situation, and acquired an independent art college in Beijing in 2005.

Tsinghua also recently became the first Chinese university to offer a Master of Laws program in US law, and its law school now ranks as one of the best in China. While at the moment its appeal to overseas students and researchers is limited, Tsinghua is keen to improve to the point where it can compete at the international level, turning national prestige into global recognition. However, while it is lauded for its innovative attitude towards improving its teaching methods and subject provision, the university has been criticised as hidebound and a poor climate for creative thought.

People

Many of China's top scientists, engineers and politicians are Tsinghua alumni. Among them are former premier Zhu Rongji, present Chinese President Hu Jintao, and the Nobel prize for Physics laureate Chen Ning Yang. The present faculty includes such luminaries as former Goldman Sachs president John L. Thornton and computer scientist Andrew Yao, who received the Turing Prize in 2000.

What students say

Indrayani Joe from Pernatang Siantar in Northern Sumatra, in Indonesia, is studying graphic design.

"Tsinghua is the most popular and famous university in China, which people say is the best. If we graduate from there, we can be very proud. It does have a very nice campus. But the school is not always honest with its students, both foreign and Chinese. The fees are four times more expensive for foreigners than for Chinese students, but the facilities and teaching we get are not as good as the Chinese students receive.

"Also, the teaching is not as good as I expected — it's a university but it is like going to high school. A lot of teachers dislike foreigners, which can make life difficult."

Good at

Technology 14th in world, science 41st.

41 University of California at Los Angeles (UCLA)

Why this university?

You've already been to UCLA if you've ever watched an American movie. Convenient to the Hollywood film studios, the university has been the backdrop for such classics as Legally Blonde and American Pie 2. But UCLA's real contribution to the entertainment industry has been with its School of Theater, Film, and Television, whose undergraduate division is usually ranked first in the nation. It encompasses the largest university-based film and television archive in the world and boasts an impressive roster of alumni who have worked in every aspect of the business centered on its doorstep. The director, co-executive producer, and actress who provides the voice of Bart Simpson on the animated television show The Simpsons all attended UCLA. So did film directors Francis Ford Coppola and Rob Reiner, actors James Dean and Tim Robbins, and agent Mike Ovitz.

The benefits of being at the center of the entertainment world have worked both ways. Record executive and Dreamworks cofounder David Geffen gave UCLA $200 million for what is now called the David Geffen School of Medicine. The medical school is now in the top of the ranks of American medical schools, ninth in research funding from the National Institutes of Health and third in research dollars from all sources; it was UCLA physicians who identified the first AIDS cases. With money from the state — the national government won't pay for research that uses new

FACTFILE

University of CALIFORNIA, Los Angeles (UCLA)

Country	United States
Foundation Year	1919
World Ranking	41 (31)

Faculty Area Rankings

Arts & Humanities	13
Engineering & IT	18
Life Sciences & Biomedicine	15
Natural Sciences	14
Social Sciences	15

Survey Performance

Peer Review	10
Recruiter Review	54

Contact Details

405 Hilgard Avenue
Los Angeles
California
90095
www.ucla.edu
+1 310 825 4321

People

Student Faculty Ratio	11.2:1
International Faculty	4.0%
Undergraduates	25,423
Postgraduates	9,946
International Students	7.0%

Course Fees For Domestic Students

Average Undergraduate	$19,068
Average Postgraduate	$14,694

Overall Research Strength

Papers (Scopus 2002-2006)	136,172
Citations (Scopus 2002-2006)	803,745
Impact	5.9

Research Impact By Faculty Area

Engineering & IT	4.1
Life Sciences & Biomedicine	5.6
Natural Sciences	7.8
Social Sciences	4.9

embryonic stem-cell lines — UCLA has established the Institute for Stem Cell Biology and Medicine. It's also home to the California Nanosystems Institute, paid for with state, federal, and industry money. In all, there are nearly 300 research centers, labs, and institutes at UCLA, including a prestigious civil rights research center it stole from Harvard by offering more money and free space. Five of the 4,000 UCLA faculty (and four of the school's alumni) have won the Nobel prize, a distinction considered important enough that two have campus buildings named in their honor.

UCLA receives some US$800 million a year in research funding across all disciplines, and money also has been flowing for construction. Some US$2 billion worth of new facilities are going up, including buildings by the architects Cesar Pelli, I M Pei, and Rafael Vinoly, prompting wags to call the school the University of Construction at Los Angeles. Students, nine in 10 of whom come from California, have their own version: University of Construction, Like, Always.

People

There are 25,400 undergraduates and 11,200 graduate students, the largest enrolment of any university in California. UCLA has more applicants than any other university in the United States — more than 50,000 every year. The voluntary General Education Cluster Program allows entering students to work on research with faculty on interdisciplinary topics by combining lecture classes with lab work and discussion sessions. Or they can take a Fiat Lux Freshman Seminar — an honors-style course meant to encourage intellectual discourse by investigating a specific question or topic, with no grades or homework, in groups of 20 or less.

What students say

"Los Angeles is a place where strange encounters occur, something I happen to like without being able to say that you can be prepared for it in advance," said Stanislav 'Stas' Shvabrin, a graduate student from Russia who was drawn to the university's highly regarded Slavic Studies department. "It's an inscrutable, impossible city that grows on you the way very few places do."

Good at

UCLA is in the top 20 in every academic area. The arts and humanities are highest-placed, but there is little to choose between them.

42 ETH Zurich (Swiss Federal Institute of Technology)

Why this university?

The Eidgenössische Technische Hochschule (ETH Zurich) – Switzerland's largest and oldest Federal university — was founded in 1855 as the 'Eidgenössisches Polytechnikum'. To mark its 150th anniversary in 2005, the chair for the history of technology of ETH Zurich produced the «ETHistory 1855–2005» web site.

Its departments of architecture, civil engineering, mechanical engineering, chemistry, forestry, plus a department including mathematics, natural sciences, literature and social and political sciences were key players in the modernisation of Switzerland and in the brilliant engineering works, especially roads, railways, bridges and tunnels which marked the late 19th and early 20th centuries.

Alfred Escher, the prominent Swiss politician, railway entrepreneur and founder of what is today Credit Suisse, was a co-founder of ETH. It was the Confederation's only federal higher education institution until 1969, when Lausanne's École Polytechnique also acquired federal status.

There are about 12,700 undergraduate and graduate students and 350 professors in 16 departments. Including technical and administrative staff, a total of 18,000 people from 80 nations work and study at ETH. It was among the first European universities to adopt the three-plus-two degree structure of the Bologna process, and

FACTFILE

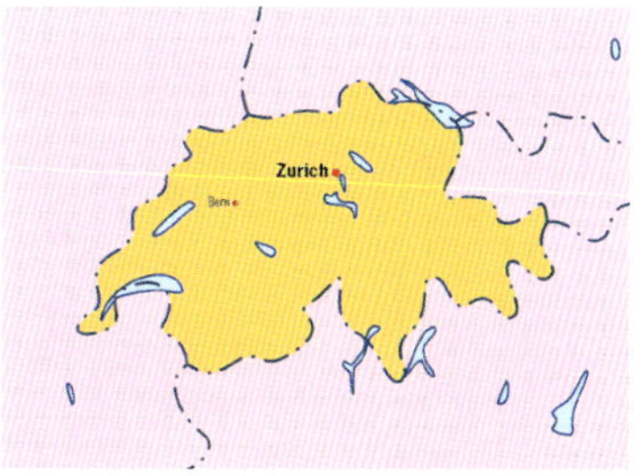

ETH Zurich (Swiss Federal Institute of Technology)

Country .... Switzerland
Foundation Year 1855
World Ranking 42 (24)

Faculty Area Rankings

Arts & Humanities 269
Engineering & IT 13
Life Sciences & Biomedicine 57
Natural Sciences 18
Social Sciences 170

Survey Performance

Peer Review 43
Recruiter Review 138

Contact Details

Rämistrasse 101
Zürich
8092
www.ethz.ch
+41 44 632 1111

People

Student Faculty Ratio 10.5:1
International Faculty 53.0%
Undergraduates 6,996
Postgraduates 6,416
International Students 23.0%

Course Fees For Domestic Students

Average Undergraduate $1,070
Average Postgraduate $1,070

Course Fees For International Students

Average Undergraduate $1,070
Average Postgraduate $1,070

Overall Research Strength

Papers (Scopus 2002-2006) 39,453
Citations (Scopus 2002-2006) 129,025
Impact 3.3

Research Impact By Faculty Area

Engineering & IT 2.5
Life Sciences & Biomedicine 3.6
Natural Sciences 4.0
Social Sciences 1.9

the changeover from four and five year degrees appears to have been untraumatic.

ETH claims its work in chemistry, physics and architecture is among the most advanced in the world, and that the Department of Biology is rapidly reaching the same level. A basic element of research policy is the creation of inter-disciplinary "platforms" for work on a specific field.

Entrance to ETH is open to all Swiss citizens who have passed the Matura school-leaving exam, while foreign students have to sit an admission exam. For all, there is a rigorous selection after the first two semesters.

People

ETH has an impressive list of 21 Nobel prize winners. Albert Einstein, who studied there from 1896 to 1900, returned to teach physics from 1912 to 1916. Others include Wilhelm Conrad Röntgen (Physics 1901) and Felix Bloch (Physics 1952), while the most recent is ETH professor Kurt Wüthrich (Chemistry 2002).

What students say

Laila Hossain is a British PhD with a chemistry degree from Bristol University. At the ETH she is working in the department of chemistry and applied biosciences.

"The ETH is very multi-cultural, very inter-disciplinary. You meet and work with people from many different countries, and one's own research group often works with people from research groups in completely different fields. There are lots of lectures by key speakers from around the world. Not just on one's own subject, but on all kinds of themes.

"The atmosphere here is very focused, very professional. Everyone seems eager to help, but the standards are very high and they expect a great deal of effort and dedication."

Good at

In a May 2006 ranking of German-speaking universities by the German CHE organization, by 'peer review' and "reputation" ETH came out on top in all natural, engineering and computer sciences. It is in this year's top 12 for natural sciences and for engineering and IT in our rankings.

43 Monash University

Why this university?

The biggest university in Australia has more students, more staff and more campuses around the world than any other. Monash University was established by the Victorian parliament in 1958 and was the first university created in that state since the University of Melbourne 105 years earlier. In 2008, Monash celebrates its 50th anniversary.

From an initial intake of 347 students in 1961, Monash grew rapidly in size and student numbers. The university also developed a wide range of courses in arts, commerce, engineering, education, law, medicine and science, and in 1990 began expanding, first around Melbourne, then outside the city and finally beyond Australia.

In 1998, the Malaysian Ministry of Education invited Monash to set up a campus near Kuala Lumpur jointly with the Sunway Group. The creation of Monash University Malaysia was followed by a second offshore in South Africa in 2001 while study centres were later established in London and in Prato, Italy.

Monash is now a network of eight campuses and has partnerships with 110 institutions around the world.

In 45 years, enrolments have grown from less than 400 to nearly 55,000 students from more than 100 countries. In 2006, there were more than 17,000 international students studying in Australia and overseas at Monash campuses — about 30 per cent of the total student population. More than 3100 students are based at

FACTFILE

MONASH University

Country..........Australia
Foundation Year..........1958
World Ranking..........43 (38)

Faculty Area Rankings

Arts & Humanities..........30
Engineering & IT..........44
Life Sciences & Biomedicine..........22
Natural Sciences..........68
Social Sciences..........26

Survey Performance

Peer Review..........29
Recruiter Review..........24

Contact Details

Victoria
3800
www.monash.edu.au
+61 3 9902 6000

People

Student Faculty Ratio..........11.8:1
International Faculty..........43.0%
Undergraduates..........32,072
Postgraduates..........8,537
International Students..........34.0%

Course Fees For Domestic Students

Average Undergraduate..........$18,002
Average Postgraduate..........$15,547

Course Fees For International Students

Average Undergraduate..........$21,536
Average Postgraduate..........$19,280

Overall Research Strength

Papers (Scopus 2002-2006)..........49,534
Citations (Scopus 2002-2006)..........178,215
Impact..........3.6

Research Impact By Faculty Area

Engineering & IT..........2.0
Life Sciences & Biomedicine..........4.2
Natural Sciences..........4.2
Social Sciences..........2.1

the Malaysian campus and 1100 at the Johannesburg campus.

The university has more than 1,900 beds on its campuses in Australia available for domestic and international students. The cost of accommodation ranges from AU$109 to AU$189 depending on the campus location and facilities provided. Monash can also arrange homestay accommodation with local families for AU$217 a week, which includes a room and three meals a day.

International students are encouraged to apply for scholarships including International scholarships for excellence, which provide up to AU$6,000 a year and Monash Global scholarships, which provide a AU$6,000 one-off grant.

People

Monash is one of the Group of Eight research-intensive universities and is home to 75 research centres. Three large projects have positioned the university at the epicentre of national and international science and technology breakthroughs: a AU$300 million Science, Technology, Research and Innovation Precinct, an Australian Stem Cell centre which is one of the major tenants of the precinct, and a AU$207 million synchrotron, the first to be built in Australia.

What students say

Shyamala Nataraj came from India in 2005 to complete a masters degree in bioethics at Monash's main campus in Melbourne and is now doing a PhD in public health. Ms Nataraj has been nominated as one of the 1000 "Women for Nobel Peace Prize 2005" for her work on HIV/AIDS related issues. After learning about the masters course, she thought it fitted exactly with the work she had been doing in the Tamil Nadu region over the past 18 years.

"Melbourne is such a lovely city to live in," she says. "I spent some time in the US and considered studying there but found I didn't want my son growing up in that country so I brought him with me while my daughter is studying in America."

Ms Nataraj says the teaching at Monash varies between "good and very good": none of the lecturing is poor, she says, and most is good while some is excellent. The only limitation is that the content and context of the curriculum is "very western".

"That comes from the fact that I'm studying in an area that encompasses ethics and philosophy in the context of health. International students come from different cultures and many of us expect to go back and work in own countries so the curriculum should look at other what is produced in other places such as Asia where Australia has close ties."

Good at

Monash is in the top 50 for four of the five areas covered in our rankings. The highest placing is 22nd for the life sciences and biomedicine, but social science and the arts and humanities are also in the top 30.

44 University of New South Wales

Why this university?

Although the origins of the University of New South Wales can be traced back to the founding of the Sydney Mechanics Institute in 1843, it was not until 1949 that it became a university.

The original Sydney institute had sought "the diffusion of scientific and special knowledge" and UNSW continues to apply those precepts today. Initially, the university's core focus was on teaching and research in science and technology but the courses also included humanities and commerce subjects and they are still a crucial component today, along with engineering, law and medicine.

UNSW is one of the heavyweights of Australian higher education. It enrols 40,000 students, nearly one in four of them from more than 130 countries, employs 2,300 academics, offers more than 665 programs in 75 schools to undergraduates and postgraduates, and has the biggest engineering course in Australia.

The university's main campus is in Kensington, an inner suburb of Sydney, but six others are scattered around the city. One of its most famous colleges, the Australian Defence Force Academy, is the nation's principal military training institute, based in Canberra.

As one of Australia's top research-intensive universities, UNSW is focused on developing world-class research centres. Construction has begun on the Lowy Centre for Cancer Research to bring together Australia's leading childhood and adult cancer

FACTFILE

University of NEW SOUTH WALES

Country	Australia
Foundation Year	1949
World Ranking	44 (41)

Faculty Area Rankings

Arts & Humanities	35
Engineering & IT	28
Life Sciences & Biomedicine	50
Natural Sciences	58
Social Sciences	30

Survey Performance

Peer Review	31
Recruiter Review	20

Contact Details

Sydney
NSW
2052
www.unsw.edu.au
+61 2 9385 1000

People

Student Faculty Ratio	14.4:1
International Faculty	27.0%
Undergraduates	21,601
Postgraduates	6,866
International Students	23.0%

Course Fees For Domestic Students

Average Undergraduate	$15,384
Average Postgraduate	$19,280

Course Fees For International Students

Average Undergraduate	$13,569
Average Postgraduate	$17,005

Overall Research Strength

Papers (Scopus 2002-2006)	53,257
Citations (Scopus 2002-2006)	217,357
Impact	4.1

Research Impact By Faculty Area

Engineering & IT	2.5
Life Sciences & Biomedicine	4.4
Natural Sciences	5.4
Social Sciences	3.7

researchers — making it the largest integrated cancer research institute in the Southern Hemisphere.

UNSW has identified environmental sustainability as one of its strategic priorities. In 2007 it established the UNSW Climate Change Research Centre — bringing together more than 60 researchers from various disciplines across the university and making it one of the largest centres of its kind. The university is also 'walking the talk' with sustainability initiatives aimed at making the UNSW campus the greenest in Australia.

People

As well as a member of Australia's Group of Eight research-intensive universities, UNSW is also a founding member of Universitas 21, the international alliance of 20 leading universities in 11 countries. Its researchers maintain more than 2,000 separate international and academic links with 500 universities and research organizations across 90 countries.

What students say

UNSW is a prime destination for overseas students keen to study in Australia. Catherine Nawangpalupi came with her four-year-old daughter and husband from the Indonesian island of Java last year, to undertake a PhD in the faculty of built environment after completing a master's degree in engineering at the university in 2001.

"I initially decided on UNSW after comparing the ranking of its engineering course with others and it was one of the best," she says. "My supervisors and other staff give me a great deal of support and I find that excellent although the library resources are not as good as when I did my master's."

Ms Nawangpalupi says as well as receiving help with her studies, she also has the opportunity to tutor undergraduate students. She believes the experience in conducting her research and tutoring will be of great use when she returns to teach at a private university in Java in another three years time.

Good at

UNSW does not drop below the top 60 in any area. The social sciences and engineering and IT are both in the top 30.

45 University of Toronto

Why this university?

The University of Toronto aims high with its stated mission and purpose: "It is this human right to radical, critical teaching and research with which the University has a duty above all to be concerned; for there is no one else, no other institution and no other office, in our modern liberal democracy, which is the custodian of this most precious and vulnerable right of the liberated human spirit."

That bold statement is an indication of the role the university has assumed. Canada's biggest university has over 60,000 full-time students attending classes on its three campuses, with the majority at its 180-year-old downtown location. It employs over 11,000 faculty and staff and boasts 75 PhD programs and 17 professional faculties, including medicine, law and management.

In its latest figures, it accumulated C$623 million (£316 million) in research grants and contract support and has spun off 103 companies. Its research library is one of the top four in North America and has more than 15 million holdings.

Research achievements have also been mammoth. It developed the first electronic heart pacemaker, artificial larynx, single-lung transplant, nerve transplant and artificial pancreas. It even created the infant cereal Pablum.

People

Alumni include authors Margaret Atwood and Michael Ondaatje, film directors David Cronenberg and

FACTFILE

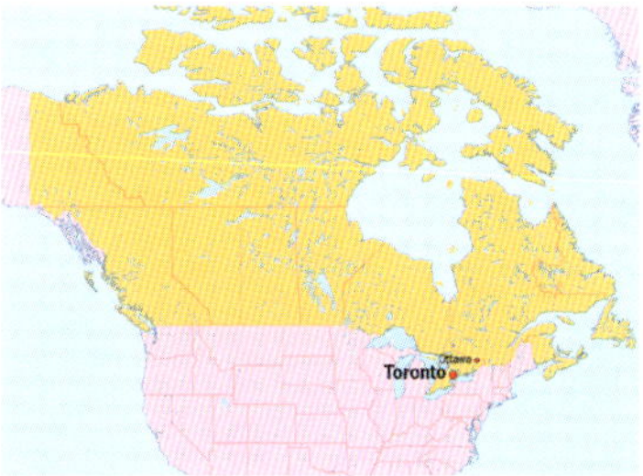

University of TORONTO

Country	Canada
Foundation Year	1827
World Ranking	45 (27)

Faculty Area Rankings

Arts & Humanities	8
Engineering & IT	11
Life Sciences & Biomedicine	14
Natural Sciences	16
Social Sciences	13

Survey Performance

Peer Review	9
Recruiter Review	34

Contact Details

Toronto
Ontario
M5S 1A1
www.utoronto.ca
+1 416 978 2011

People

Student Faculty Ratio	22.3:1
International Faculty	26.0%
Undergraduates	50,220
Postgraduates	10,991
International Students	11.0%

Course Fees For Domestic Students

Average Undergraduate	$875
Average Postgraduate	$1,698

Course Fees For International Students

Average Undergraduate	$3,360
Average Postgraduate	$3,209

Overall Research Strength

Papers (Scopus 2002-2006)	148,849
Citations (Scopus 2002-2006)	843,332
Impact	5.7

Research Impact By Faculty Area

Engineering & IT	3.5
Life Sciences & Biomedicine	6.3
Natural Sciences	6.1
Social Sciences	3.6

Norman Jewison, eBay's Jeff Skoll and former Canadian Prime Ministers Paul Martin and Lester B. Pearson.

Sir Frederick Banting and J J R Macleod won the Nobel prize in 1923 for their work with Charles Best in the discovery of the role of insulin in controlling diabetes.

Communications guru Marshall McLuhan was a faculty member. John C Polanyi won the 1986 Nobel prize in Chemistry for pioneering work that led to the development of the laser. Geneticist Tak Mak was the first to clone a T-cell gene, a key part of the immune system. Medical biophysicist Lap-Chee Tsui led the team of researchers who discovered the cystic fibrosis gene.

What students say

Audre Kapacinskas from Chicago is studying peace and conflict studies, psychology and economics. She appreciates the size and scope that she has seen in the institution. "I wanted a large university in a cosmopolitan city with a diverse student body." Kapacinskas says she also appreciated the variety of courses and found the flexibility attractive. She says requirements to complete credits in diverse academic areas like humanities and science meant she could try something different while focusing on what she was interested in. "It's a nice cross between European and US systems and allows you to combine different areas of study."

Weak points for her have been a frustrating student web service and a lack of student involvement in bolstering school spirit. But the university far exceeded her expectations: "I came for a fantastic city, nice campus, and variety of courses. The people I've met and the professors I've had have made it an exceptionally positive experience. You develop a friendly, caring community around you, but you still have the resources of a large research institution at your disposal."

Good at

Toronto is in the top 20 in the world in all five academic areas. The arts and humanities make the top ten, with engineering and IT only just missing out.

46 Osaka University

Why this university?

The sixth-oldest national university in Japan, Osaka University was established in 1931 in the heart of one of the commercial centres of Japan, 500 kilometres south west of Tokyo. Its roots lie in a local medical college founded in 1869.

At the outset the university consisted only of medical and science faculties. Today, medicine and science studies are considered the backbone of the university, which operates its own hospital. However, all undergraduates take liberal arts programs for the first three semesters.

The latest stage in its development came in October 2007, when the university merged with Osaka University of Foreign Studies. After the integration, Osaka University has 11 schools, 15 graduate schools, five research institutes and two hospitals. There are three campuses: in Suita, Toyonaka and Minoh cities and Nakanoshima, with about 5,150 teaching and administrative staff and 25,000 students, including about 1,400 overseas students.

Most Japanese students are from south west Japan. Before the merger, European students comprised 8.6 per cent of Osaka's students, including four Britons. About half of all foreign students receive grants through the university, including some from the Japanese government.

The university has the motto "Live locally, grow globally", underlining the international ambitions which have been at the heart of its activities since

FACTFILE

OSAKA University

Country	Japan
Foundation Year	1931
World Ranking	46 (70=)

Faculty Area Rankings

Arts & Humanities	180
Engineering & IT	68
Life Sciences & Biomedicine	39
Natural Sciences	57
Social Sciences	206

Survey Performance

Peer Review	70
Recruiter Review	139

Contact Details

1-1 Yamadaoka, Suita
Osaka
565 - 0871
www.osaka-u.ac.jp
+81 6 6879 7037

People

Student Faculty Ratio	7.4:1
International Faculty	2.0%
Undergraduates	11,876
Postgraduates	7,685
International Students	6.0%

Course Fees For Domestic Students

Average Undergraduate	$4,465
Average Postgraduate	$5,582

Course Fees For International Students

Average Undergraduate	$4,465
Average Postgraduate	$5,582

Overall Research Strength

Papers (Scopus 2002-2006)	163,483
Citations (Scopus 2002-2006)	706,219
Impact	4.3

Research Impact By Faculty Area

Engineering & IT	1.9
Life Sciences & Biomedicine	5.3
Natural Sciences	4.3
Social Sciences	1.8

the "semi-privatisation" of Japanese universities two years ago. Plans are afoot to send more Japanese students abroad with the aim of giving a third of the university's undergraduates overseas exposure. Osaka already has exchange programs with numerous European and American institutions, including Nottingham University and University College London.

The former Osaka University of Foreign Studies specialized in studies of more than 20 modern languages, including Urdu and Swahili, making it the largest national university in Japan, with a total of more than 25,000 students.

People

Among the university's most cited scientists is Shizuo Akira, 54, winner of the 2004 Robert Koch Prize for his discovery of the "toll-like receptor" that activates immune system cells upon recognition of pathogenic organisms. He was also recently named "the hottest researcher" by Thomson Scientific for outnumbering his peers in citation. Professor Akira currently leads a government-funded project that seeks to combine microbiology with immunology at the university's Research Institute of Microbial Disease. "We have great facilities for medical research that is backed by our long tradition. We also get a lot of bright students in our department," says Profesor Akira, who also cites robotic engineering as an area of strength for the university.

Alumni include Manga author Osamu Tezuka, Sony founder Akio Morita, and Nobel physics laureate Hideki Yukawa.

What students say

"The university provides an excellent atmosphere for research," says Ngan Chew Yee, a Malaysian student currently researching into anticancer drug mechanisms. "The graduate school of medicine provides an almost unlimited source of information and excellent student guidance by the 'sensei' (professors)."

Good at

Academics rank the life sciences and biomedicine in the top 50 in the world, with the natural sciences and engineering and IT close behind.

47 Boston University

Why this university?

Long in the shadow of MIT and Harvard just across the Charles River, Boston University has taken the head-down approach of the also-ran that has to work harder. It lobbies aggressively for the government money that has paid for such things as a new building dedicated to the study of photonics, largely for military applications, including an acoustic direction detection system that can ferret out snipers. It pushed through a new high-security, government-funded National Emerging Infectious Diseases Laboratory near its medical school to study the world's deadliest diseases, despite concerted opposition from the densely populated neighborhood. Its new high-rise residence halls and state-of-the-art fitness center and arena were partly underwritten by — and are named for — an insurance company rather than an academic or alumnus. It has a venture-capital arm that invests in startup companies as a way of making money toward operating costs.

But BU also has a tradition of social activism. Alexander Graham Bell was a professor at BU when he invented the telephone. Alumni include the civil rights leader Martin Luther King Jr. The School of Education took over the management of a nearby failed public school system in an attempt to turn it around, and its medical school merged with a city hospital that largely serves urban, low-income patients. BU was the first university to award a PhD to a woman, and the first to open all of its divisions to women. Today, 59 per cent of the 32,000 students — the fourth-

FACTFILE

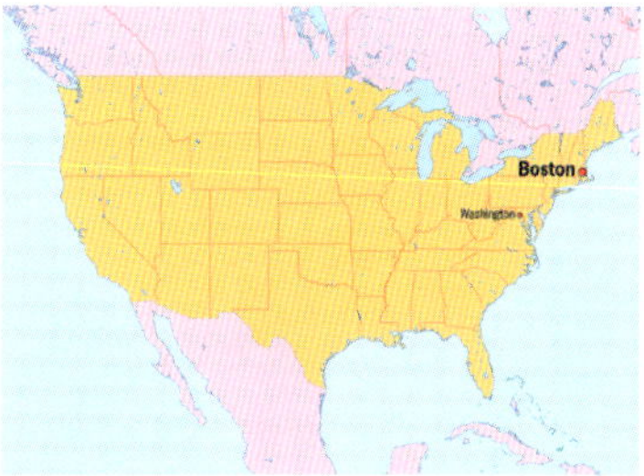

BOSTON University

Country	United States
Foundation Year	1839
World Ranking	47 (66)

Faculty Area Rankings

Arts & Humanities	54
Engineering & IT	98
Life Sciences & Biomedicine	44
Natural Sciences	69
Social Sciences	36

Survey Performance

Peer Review	45
Recruiter Review	74

Contact Details

One Sherborn Street
Boston
MA 02215
www.bu.edu
+1 617 353 2000

People

Student Faculty Ratio	12.4:1
International Faculty	6.0%
Undergraduates	19,692
Postgraduates	6,958
International Students	21.0%

Course Fees For Domestic Students

Average Undergraduate	$34,930
Average Postgraduate	$29,988

Overall Research Strength

Papers (Scopus 2002-2006)	63,257
Citations (Scopus 2002-2006)	446,574
Impact	7.1

Research Impact By Faculty Area

Engineering & IT	5.1
Life Sciences & Biomedicine	6.6
Natural Sciences	11.6
Social Sciences	4.5

largest enrollment among US private universities — are women. One-sixth of the students, or more than 4,500, come from outside the United States.

Many of them are drawn by the business school, housed in a brand-new, state-of-the-art building, which offers an unusual combined MS-MBA degree rooted in the connection between information technology and business management. BU also is pre-eminent in engineering, within which the most popular speciality is the emerging discipline of biomedical engineering. It is also where much of the US$312 million a year worth of research at the university is now under way, including in a new US$83 million life sciences and engineering building.

And yet, bucking the trend of other universities to focus on the sciences, BU has now turned to the arts. One of the few major research universities to also house a conservatory for the performing and visual arts, the university is renovating its College of Fine Arts.

People

Alumni of the College of Fine Arts include actors and actresses Faye Dunaway, Geena Davis, and Olympia Dukakis. The business school has graduated Benetton Group chairman Alessandro Benetton and Shin Yong-Il, CEO of Deutsche Asset Management. Among BU's other alumni are Ishrat Husain, governor of the State Bank of Pakistan, and Faisal al-Fayez, former prime minister of Jordan.

BU's nearly 4,000 faculty include Nobel prize winners Derek Walcott and Elie Wiesel. In all, six faculty have received Nobels.

What students say

Despite its size, students say, BU offers personal attention; the ratio of students to professors is a relatively low 15:1. "It has a 'community' feeling," says Masayo Nishida, a student from Japan who is working toward her doctorate in sociology. "In general, the professors are very approachable."

Like many students, she was also drawn by the university's location. "Boston is especially attractive because it is not a huge city but also not a typical college town in the middle of nowhere so that I can concentrate on my studies and also enjoy cultural life from time to time," Ms Nishida said. "The concentration of academic institutions is also a plus."

Good at

In the top 100 in every area, Boston is in the top 50 for the life sciences and biomedicine and for the social sciences, and just outside it for the arts and humanities.

48 University of Amsterdam

Why this university?

The Universiteit van Amsterdam prides itself on its ancient roots, which stretch back to the Athenaeum Illustre founded in 1632 to educate students in trade and philosophy. This became a university in 1877, and has since spread through the city, taking over old buildings and putting up its own modern structures along the canals and courtyards that make Amsterdam famous. Current excellence has propelled the university into the top 50 this year for the first time.

The university emphasises its comprehensive approach, taking in every discipline except technology, and offering a classical education that, it boasts, does not just cram students for the job market. It has seven faculties, from the humanities and social and behavioural sciences, to economics and business, medicine and dentistry, and science.

In 2006-7 the university had 25,000 students enrolled, 1,500 of whom were from outside the Netherlands. It offers 62 bachelor programs taught in Dutch and over 100 international study programs taught in English. It has more than 3,500 academic staff (including PhD students), of whom 230 are associate professors and 360 full professors. About 15 per cent are from outside the Netherlands.

People

The golden age of science at the university was between 1901 and 1910, when three of its professors won Nobel prizes: Jacobus van 't Hoff

FACTFILE

University of AMSTERDAM

Country	Netherlands
Foundation Year	1632
World Ranking	48 (69)

Faculty Area Rankings

Arts & Humanities	41
Engineering & IT	186
Life Sciences & Biomedicine	80
Natural Sciences	128
Social Sciences	48

Survey Performance

Peer Review	66
Recruiter Review	111

Contact Details

Spui 21
Amsterdam
1012 WX
www.uva.nl
+31 20 525 9111

People

Student Faculty Ratio	8:1
International Faculty	21.0%
Undergraduates	15,628
Postgraduates	9,450
International Students	6.0%

Course Fees For Domestic Students

Average Undergraduate	$2,110

Course Fees For International Students

Average Undergraduate	$12,350

Overall Research Strength

Papers (Scopus 2002-2006)	50,971
Citations (Scopus 2002-2006)	267,802
Impact	5.3

Research Impact By Faculty Area

Engineering & IT	3.9
Life Sciences & Biomedicine	5.6
Natural Sciences	6.6
Social Sciences	3.4

in chemistry, and Pieter Zeeman and Johannes van der Waals in physics. Now the university's strengths are very much on the mathematical side and where maths touches on physics and astronomy. In recent years it has picked up several Spinoza awards — the Dutch Nobels — for work in these disciplines. Particularly distinguished is Edward van den Heuvel, of the university's Anton Pannekoek Astrophysical Institute, who also led an international team researching the origins of gamma-ray bursts, which won an EU Descartes award in 2002.

The university can also claim Spinoza awards for Daan Frenkel, in macromolecular simulations, and Ronald Plasterk in molecular biology. Meanwhile Willem Saris, of the social and behavioural science faculty, was part of the team that won a Descartes award in 2005 for cross-national social surveys.

In the arts and humanities, Amsterdam is particularly strong in European studies, philosophy, film and television studies, linguistics and several areas of language and literature. Among the noted faculty are John Neubauer, specialist in comparative literature, Latin scholar Harm Pinkster, and Mieke Bal, professor of theory of literature and a founding director of the Amsterdam School for Cultural Analysis.

Unlike the rest of the university, the laboratories and research institutes of the medical faculty have been extracted from the city and united with three hospitals under the single roof of the Academic Medical Centre. In 2005 a graduate school for the medical sciences was created to raise the profile of this part of the medical centre's work. It has over 100 PhD graduations per year, divided over seven research institutes and 80 individual science programs, ranging from genetic factors in cancer biology to public health screening projects.

The AMC has the largest permanently exhibited collection of post-war Dutch visual art in the world. Intensive collecting, with government support, began in the early 1980s, and the collection now includes some 5,000 paintings, works on paper, graphic art and photography, with a generous selection of work from the CoBrA, Mixed-Media Art, Zero Art and New Figuration movements.

Good at

The arts and humanities and the social sciences are in the top 50 in this year's rankings. Amsterdam is also 80th in life sciences and biomedicine.

49 New York University (NYU)

Why this university?

The largest private, nonprofit university in the United States, with 19,400 undergraduates and 19,000 graduate students — 10 per cent of them from other countries — NYU is growing even bigger. It's merging with the Polytechnic University, giving it an instant engineering school. And it's opening a branch in Abu Dhabi, in the United Arab Emirates — the first complete liberal-arts campus developed abroad by a US research university, it says — which will infuse money into the main campus in exchange for borrowing members of the faculty on a rotating basis. This on top of US$2.5 billion NYU is raising to make more financial aid available to students, expand its campus, and add programs and faculty. NYU already has 3,100 faculty and 16,000 employees overall — more employees than most universities have students. Many members of that faculty remain active in the disciplines they teach, serving as advisors to government and industry, editors for publishing houses, and consultants to the global institutions with which they share the city of New York. Eleven NYU faculty members and an equal number of alumni have won the Nobel prize.

Despite NYU's huge enrolment, most classes are of a reasonable size; 82 per cent have fewer than 30 students. The university is regarded highly in business, law, the sciences, and the performing arts. Its law school, housed in a newly refurbished building, and Stern School of Business are among the nation's most distinguished. Its Institute of Fine Arts specializes in not

FACTFILE

NEW YORK University (NYU)

Country..United States
Foundation Year..1831
World Ranking..49 (43)

Faculty Area Rankings

Arts & Humanities..23
Engineering & IT..205
Life Sciences & Biomedicine..47
Natural Sciences..42
Social Sciences..21

Survey Performance

Peer Review..35
Recruiter Review..51

Contact Details

70 Washington Square South, 12S
New York
NY 10012
www.nyu.edu

People

Student Faculty Ratio..12.6:1
International Faculty..7.0%
Undergraduates..21,449
Postgraduates..13,573
International Students..10.0%

Course Fees For Domestic Students

Average Undergraduate..$35,283
Average Postgraduate..$23,304

Overall Research Strength

Papers (Scopus 2002-2006)..57,912
Citations (Scopus 2002-2006)..332,126
Impact..5.7

Research Impact By Faculty Area

Engineering & IT..5.2
Life Sciences & Biomedicine..5.6
Natural Sciences..11.3
Social Sciences..4.0

only the history of art and archaeology, but the conservation and technology of works of art, collaborating with New York's superlative museums. And its Gallatin School of Individualized Study lets students design their own program of study and create their own curriculum. The university also is developing a new science building for its life sciences departments. In what is believed to be the largest royalties deal by an academic institution, NYU will receive US$650 million for selling a portion of its rights to a drug developed by researchers there that fights rheumatoid arthritis and other autoimmune diseases.

NYU's interest in international affairs goes beyond its significant proportion — fifth highest in America—of students from abroad. The undergraduate division of its business school requires, and pays for, all its students to go on an international business trip. The law school's "global faculty" includes leading legal thinkers from all over the world who come there for at least a term. NYU has 11 campuses overseas.

The university's main campus wraps around Washington Square in bohemian Greenwich Village, the very center of Manhattan and itself a center of political and cultural activism, entertainment, and relatively constant, harmless urban lunacy.

People

Some of NYU's best-known alumni attended the Tisch School of the Arts, one of the nation's leading centers of undergraduate and graduate study in the performing and cinematic arts and the best film program east of southern California. They include Spike Lee, Oliver Stone, Alec Baldwin, Amy Heckerling, Ang Lee, Tony Kushner, Marcia Gay Harden, and M. Night Shyamalan. Among the university's other graduates have been Woody Allen, Angelina Jolie, Burt Lancaster, Martin Scorcese, Billy Crystal, John Cusack, Lou Gossett, Ethan Hawke, Meg Ryan, presidential candidate and former New York City Mayor Rudy Giuliani and John F. Kennedy Jr.

What students say

"It is all very well to read about globalization but NYU is about living it," said Devyani Prabhat, a doctoral candidate in sociology from India, who was drawn to the law school's Global Public Service Law Project, which trains activist lawyers in human rights and social justice. "A tremendous diversity of ideas and forward thinkers from all over the planet converge here."

NYU, he said, "is always thinking ahead and not resting on its past glories. Like New York City, it is always two steps ahead of the rest. It is not scared to try new things and does not hide behind tradition." As for Greenwich Village, Mr. Prabhat said, it is "historical, artistic, and global, so the university, which does not have a demarcated campus as such, merges with that and is steeped in its values."

Good at

NYU is in the top 50 for everything except engineering and IT. The university's strengths are in the social sciences and arts and humanities, where it is just outside the top 20.

50 University of Auckland

Why this university?

The gothic ogee pinnacles and crockets that cap the University of Auckland's distinctive clock tower are now surrounded by functional multi-storey structures — an apt symbol of the university's concerted effort in recent years to assert a reputation based not on tradition, but the quality of its research.

Auckland describes itself as New Zealand's 'pre-eminent research-led university'. This bold statement is given credence by the university's lion's share of money awarded through the New Zealand's Performance-Based Research Fund.

The first PBRF assessment, carried out in 2003, reported that 'on virtually any measure, the University of Auckland is the country's leading research university'. Of the 41 subject areas assessed, Auckland gained first or second place in 26.

Engineering and medical research were particular areas of excellence, but anthropology, philosophy, music, geology, sociology and theology also scored well.

With six campuses situated throughout the greater Auckland region, Auckland is New Zealand's largest university. It employs nearly 3,000 academic staff and 2,800 support staff. About a third of the academic staff are from oveseas. In 2006, 38,000 students were enrolled in eight faculties: Business and Economics, Arts, and Science are the largest with more than 7,000 students apiece. Education has about 6,000, while there are 3,500 students

FACTFILE

The University of AUCKLAND

Country	New Zealand
Foundation Year	1883
World Ranking	50 (46=)

Faculty Area Rankings

Arts & Humanities	32
Engineering & IT	51
Life Sciences & Biomedicine	41
Natural Sciences	78
Social Sciences	35

Survey Performance

Peer Review	38
Recruiter Review	100

Contact Details

Private Bag 92019
Auckland Mail Centre
Auckland
1142
www.auckland.ac.nz
+64 9 373 7999

People

Student Faculty Ratio	14.8:1
International Faculty	59.0%
Undergraduates	23,222
Postgraduates	5,087
International Students	34.0%

Course Fees For Domestic Students

Average Undergraduate	$3,759
Average Postgraduate	$11,008

Course Fees For International Students

Average Undergraduate	$14,500
Average Postgraduate	$18,905

Overall Research Strength

Papers (Scopus 2002-2006)	29,726
Citations (Scopus 2002-2006)	115,928
Impact	3.9

Research Impact By Faculty Area

Engineering & IT	2.5
Life Sciences & Biomedicine	4.5
Natural Sciences	4.1
Social Sciences	2.9

enrolled in Medical and Health Sciences and a couple of thousand each in Engineering, and Creative Arts and Industries. Law is the smallest of the faculties with 1,500 students, and there is a small School of Theology.

Almost 5,000 of Auckand's students are international, a substantial increase from 2002 when there were only about 1,000. China accounted for 2,700 of these students in 2005; the next largest source was the US with just 487 students. Overseas students account for 16 per cent of the postgraduate population.

People

Notable Auckland alumni include New Zealand's incumbent Prime Minister Helen Clark and Chief Justice Sian Elias, as well as the novelist Maurice Gee and Tom Schnackenberg, design coordinator for New Zealand's America's Cup wins in 1995 and 2000. Sir Graham Liggins, who pioneered the treatment of babies in the womb, is remembered by the university's Liggins Institute which carries out research on fetal and child health, and brain development and function. The institute works closely with the local biotechnology industry.

What students say

Heikki Hansen, a PhD candidate at the Yacht Research Unit in the Mechanical Engineering Department, says Auckland has taken great strides in its support for international students in the four years he has been there.

"The whole postgraduate experience wasn't perfect initially," he says. "But a lot has changed — the university is much more popular with international students now and the university has greatly improved its facilities and support."

Mr Hansen says locating external funding for research can be an issue compared with European universities, something he puts down to New Zealand's comparatively small size and lack of large businesses. But the quality of research does not suffer.

"I have been really impressed with the quality of research that is produced here, given the relative limitations of money and equipment," he says.

Mr Hansen attributes this to a "do it yourself" ethos of problem solving among the university's academic and technical support staff.

Good at

Only the natural sciences are placed far outside the top 50 in this year's rankings – and even they are in the top 80. Social science and the arts and humanities are both in the top 40.

51= Seoul National University

Why this university?

Few universities have their own on-campus cobbler. But the staff and students at Seoul National University have enjoyed the benefits of their own shoe-repairer for 45 of its 60 years of history.

Ha Yong Jin (74) is now the oldest person still working on the campus of Korea's first national university, founded in 1946.

Seoul National now has 14,000 full-time undergraduate and 9,000 graduate students enrolled in 16 colleges with 84 departments, one graduate school with 98 departments and six professional schools, staffed by 5,000 faculty.

Just 5 per cent of students are from overseas. They come from 33 different countries but more than half are from China. Only a small proportion of courses are offered in English. The overwhelming majority of its 56 foreign professors are from the US, while 67 of its own professors are teaching and researching overseas.

The number of foreign universities with which SNU has developed academic exchanges rose from 46 four years ago to 98 in 2005. It has academic exchange agreements with Yale, Princeton, Vienna, Tokyo and Toronto and has plans for a joint doctoral degree with Paris-Sud University.

SNU claims to have contributed significantly to the country's spectacular economic progress, while spearheading democratization efforts

FACTFILE

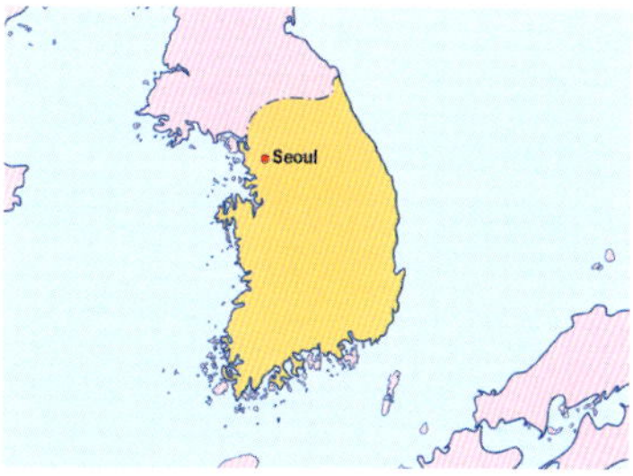

SEOUL National University

Country	Korea, South
Foundation Year	1946
World Ranking	51= (63)

Faculty Area Rankings

Arts & Humanities	91
Engineering & IT	56
Life Sciences & Biomedicine	46
Natural Sciences	38
Social Sciences	57

Survey Performance

Peer Review	44
Recruiter Review	232

Contact Details

San 56-1, Shillim-dong, Gwanak-gu
Seoul
151 742
www.useoul.edu
+82 2 880 2555

People

Student Faculty Ratio	8.2:1
International Faculty	2.0%
Undergraduates	17,488
Postgraduates	9,700
International Students	5.0%

Course Fees For Domestic Students

Average Undergraduate	$5,761
Average Postgraduate	$7,130

Course Fees For International Students

Average Undergraduate	$5,761
Average Postgraduate	$7,130

Overall Research Strength

Papers (Scopus 2002-2006)	129,440
Citations (Scopus 2002-2006)	425,837
Impact	3.3

Research Impact By Faculty Area

Engineering & IT	2.3
Life Sciences & Biomedicine	3.3
Natural Sciences	4.3
Social Sciences	2.6

on the peninsula. The proportion of high-ranking government officials with SNU degrees has declined from 81.7 per cent to a still-remarkable 68.8 per cent.

SNU has 28 dormitory buildings with 2,600 rooms accommodating 4,500 students.

People

Among its alumni, diplomat and former international relations student Ban Ki-moon has been tipped as a front runner to replace Kofi Annan as UN secretary-general. Its philosophy department produced Kim Young-sam, president of South Korea from 1993 to 1998.

The university was required to weather an international storm when one of its top research sicentists, Hwang Woo-suk, was dismissed after claims that his team had produced the first stem cells from human cloned embryos were shown to have been fabricated.

What students say

Wei-yi Sun, from Qingdao, China, is reading for a masters in Korean language education after majoring in Korean language education with Chinese literature.

"SNU is the one of the most prestigious universities in Korea, especially when it comes to Korean language education. Plus, the campus is really beautiful.

But the process of being accepted and coming to SNU was long and painful. In 1999, SNU didn't receive applications through the Internet, so everything had to be done through airmail, which is quite expensive and very time consuming. I even had to take my English and Korean test the school had requested on the phone, due to visa problems. Even though these experiences were really strenuous, I got to appreciate my life in Korea and at SNU even more thanks to them.

"The biggest problem is that SNU has only one Korean class for foreign students. So after attending the language education institute, there are no alternative classes foreigners can take to improve their Korean skills."

Good at

Seoul National is in the top 100 in every academic area. It is in the top 50 for the natural sciences and the life sciences and biomedicine.

51= University of Texas at Austin

Why this university?

Everything is bigger in Texas, or so the saying goes, and that includes its flagship university. Its 11,000 graduate students make it one of the largest graduate schools in America; there are also 39,000 undergraduates and 2,500 faculty on a vast campus centered around the 27-story UT Tower, six feet higher than the nearby Texas capitol building. The university's slogan is nothing less than, "What Starts Here Changes the World."

Thanks in part to the pull of Texas politicians — President Lyndon Johnson, for example, whose papers are kept in an archive on the campus along with a robot version of him that leans on a fence and tells jokes — UT has enjoyed federal grants for work in space flight, defense, nuclear physics, and other fields. It conducts research so secret at a satellite property, the J.J. Pickle Research Campus (named for an alumnus and former congressman), that much of the area is off limits to the public. The university is also a center of nanotechnology research, spurred on by the demands of the semiconductor industry. Seventy-five percent of the American semiconductor industry has a presence in Texas. In all, the university boasts more than $410 million a year worth of research and has spun off 400 patents and 65 companies that together generate $1.2 billion a year in revenue.

Appropriately for a university that was partly funded by oil discovered on its campus, UT's College of Engineering's graduate program in petroleum engineering is considered the best

FACTFILE

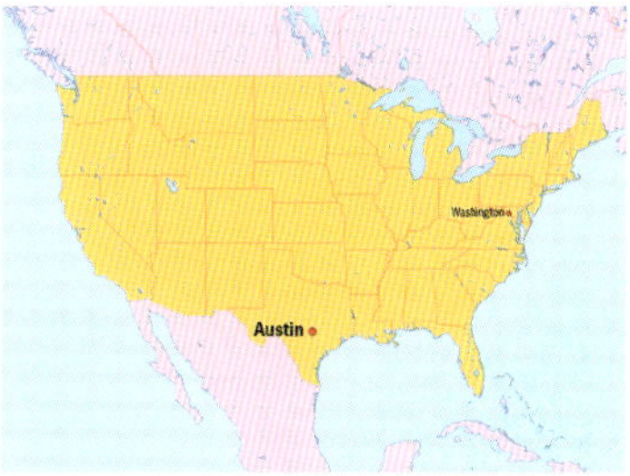

University of TEXAS at Austin

Country	United States
Foundation Year	1883
World Ranking	51= (32)

Faculty Area Rankings

Arts & Humanities	42
Engineering & IT	30
Life Sciences & Biomedicine	91
Natural Sciences	23
Social Sciences	81

Survey Performance

Peer Review	39
Recruiter Review	48

Contact Details

1 University Station
Austin
Texas
78712
www.utexas.edu
+1 512 471 3434

People

Student Faculty Ratio	21.4:1
International Faculty	17.0%
Undergraduates	34,172
Postgraduates	11,442
International Students	10.0%

Course Fees For Domestic Students

Average Undergraduate	$4,173
Average Postgraduate	$11,952

Overall Research Strength

Papers (Scopus 2002-2006)	112,268
Citations (Scopus 2002-2006)	590,915
Impact	5.3

Research Impact By Faculty Area

Engineering & IT	2.9
Life Sciences & Biomedicine	6.2
Natural Sciences	6.3
Social Sciences	3.6

in America. But it also has top-rated divisions of aerospace, chemical, civil, computer, electrical, environmental, and mechanical engineering.

UT also has one of the biggest cultural archives in the world, including a Gutenberg Bible and the world's earliest known photograph, while its new museum of art is, of course, the largest at any university in America and its academic library is the nation's fifth-largest.

The College of Communication, the largest and most comprehensive of its kind, has 4,200 students and 120 faculty teaching advertising, communication studies, journalism, and radio, television, and film. At the McCombs School of Business, more CEOs of companies ranked in the top 500 by the Standard & Poors bond-rating agency graduated than from any other business school.

Classes for undergraduates are large — introductory classes have as many as 400 students, with discussion sessions taught by graduate teaching assistants. Blacks, Asians, and Hispanics make up one-third of the enrollment, and there are more than 5,000 international students, about 10 per cent of the total. The surrounding city of Austin, known for its innovative music scene, is a lively setting.

Athletics is a central, and successful, facet of UT. Its American football team has won four national championships, while all UT teams combined have taken 40.

People

Alumni include First Lady Laura Bush, First Daughter Jenna Bush, Nobel laureate for literature J. M. Coetzee, actors Farrah Fawcett, Jayne Mansfield, Tex Ritter, Matthew McConaughey, and Renée Zellweger, singer Janis Joplin, filmmaker Wes Anderson, Dell Computer founder Michael Dell, and Rex Tillerson, chairman and chief executive officer of ExxonMobil.

What students say

"It's a huge university," said Assem Nasr, a doctoral student in international communications from Beirut. "I've never seen that many students at one time. I wondered, was I going to be lost in this place?"

He said, "Fortunately, I'm lucky to be in the department of radio, TV, and film, where the professors get to know at least the graduate students on a personal basis, and what you're doing in terms of research and such."

Mr. Nasr said the faculty are focused on the practical uses of his academic work, offering seminars about such things as how to look for a job. "They keep us on track and they're very motivating," he said.

Good at

In the top 100 in all academic areas, UT's highest placing is 23rd in natural sciences.

53= Hong Kong University of Science and Technology

Why this university?

Established in 1991, The Hong Kong University of Science and Technology (HKUST) is a young, dynamic research-intensive university, conceived with the goal of propelling Hong Kong towards a knowledge-based economy. The university has already won a global reputation and presence.

The teaching faculty is organized around four schools: science, engineering, business & management, and humanities & social science. A fifth school, the HKUST Fok Ying Tung Graduate School in Nansha, Guangzhou is now opened and is expected to be fully operational in the near future. The university has a student population of about 9,000, with 64 per cent in undergraduate programs, 23 per cent in taught masters programs and 13 per cent in post-graduate research. About 1,500 (17 per cent) are non-local students. Every year a few hundred undergraduates of the University participate in student exchange programs with over 100 institutions overseas.

The university's 3,200 postgraduates work in either research-postgraduate programs leading to an MPhil or a PhD degree, or in taught postgraduate programs leading to an MA, MBA, MTM or MSc degree. HKUST's EMBA program, run jointly with the Kellogg School of Management, is consistently ranked among the best in the world. Its reputation is reflected in its international makeup of students: over

FACTFILE

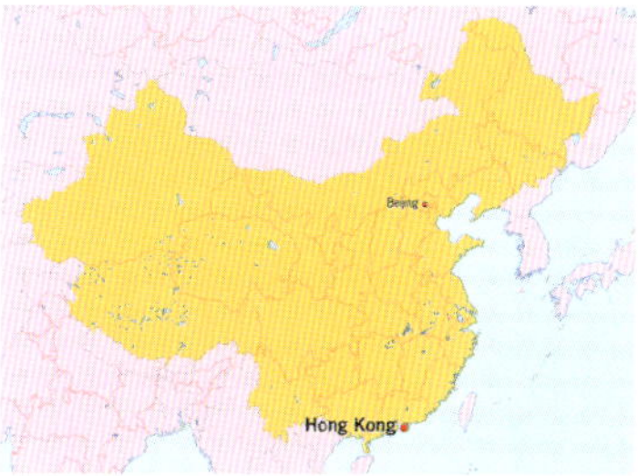

HONG KONG University of Science & Technology

Country .... Hong Kong
Foundation Year 1991
World Ranking .... 53= (58=)

Faculty Area Rankings

Engineering & IT 23
Life Sciences & Biomedicine 80
Natural Sciences 52
Social Sciences 63

Survey Performance

Peer Review 64
Recruiter Review 106

Contact Details

Clear Water Bay, Kowloon
Hong Kong
www.ust.hk
+852 2358 6000

People

Student Faculty Ratio 18:1
International Faculty 69.0%
Undergraduates 5,772
Postgraduates 2,488
International Students 26.0%

Course Fees For Domestic Students

Average Undergraduate $5,385
Average Postgraduate $9,937

Course Fees For International Students

Average Undergraduate $8,974
Average Postgraduate $9,937

Overall Research Strength

Papers (Scopus 2002-2006) 32,522
Citations (Scopus 2002-2006) 128,463
Impact 4.0

Research Impact By Faculty Area

Engineering & IT 3.1
Life Sciences & Biomedicine 4.4
Natural Sciences 5.0
Social Sciences 3.7

50 per cent of these students "fly in" to Hong Kong to take classes.

In 2007, the university started the MSc in Global Finance. Offered jointly with the Leonard N. Stern School of Business of New York University, it is the first such executive format finance program in the Asia-Pacific Region.

The university has an international faculty mix, with 450 faculty members from 28 countries. More than half of the faculty members (52 per cent) are from outside Hong Kong and Mainland China. Professors from North America account for 22 per cent of the faculty size.

HKUST laboratories have made many groundbreaking discoveries, including the fabrication and characterization of the world's smallest carbon nanotubes, genetic associations in schizophrenia, anti-aging drug development, and fast motion estimation algorithms for the MPEG4 standard. Two departments in the engineering school are ranked among the world's top leaders in the number of papers published in key international journals.

The university maintains close links to business and industry for collaborative R&D and commercialization of research outcomes. It has established a branch campus and R&D bases in southern China, capitalizing on the region's dynamic growth and emerging opportunities for technology and knowledge transfer.

People

In 2006 the Institute for Advanced Study was inaugurated at HKUST, with a mission to further scientific advancement by inviting the world's foremost scientists to work in partnership with local academics in the fields of nanotechnology and nanoscience, biotechnology and bioscience, information technology, the environment and sustainable development. The 13-member international advisory board consists of nine Nobel Laureates. Its inaugural lecture was delivered by Stephen Hawking in June 2006.

What students say

Gesche Haas, from Bonn, was heavily influenced by HKUST's proximity to China when she chose to join a BBA in Global Business program in 2005 over other offers in Germany and the UK. But even she was surprised by the quality of the university and the study and living environment.

"All professors at HKUST received their PhDs and other qualifications from prestigious universities all over the world," she says. "They also have a lot of work experience and are well connected to many companies."

She added that the university still has a lot to do to make itself better known to an international audience, saying that "HKUST's real potential does not seem to be fully realized by the entire world yet".

Good at

Good overall. Technology and executive training programs ranked particularly highly.

53= Trinity College Dublin

Why this university?

Trinity College Dublin is Ireland's oldest university: it was established in 1592 and is the sole constituent college of the University of Dublin.

Most of the college's activities are based on the 47 acre city centre campus which contains much of Dublin's finest architecture. The west end of the campus is laid out in five quadrangles with buildings from the Eighteenth Century including the Old Library which houses the priceless Book of Kells, written in the ninth century. The magnificent legal deposit library is also an invaluable resource to scholars.

The construction of a new building for nanoscience which will house Ireland's first Science Gallery is underway. At the heart of Trinity's strategy to meet the goal of a world reference point in key themes is a focus on interdisciplinarity. Its flagship interdisciplinary institutes are in areas such as nanostructures/ nanodevices; molecular medicine; neuroscience; and international integration studies.

The Irish government is pouring money into science and research and wants to double the number of PhD students within the next few years. The college was well poised to tap some of the additional funds and now almost one in three students in Trinity is studying at postgraduate level.

However, funding at undergraduate level is a problem and the average student:staff radio of 18:1 is high by international standards. Trinity plans to hold its undergraduate student

FACTFILE

TRINITY College Dublin

Country	Ireland
Foundation Year	1592
World Ranking	53= (78)

Faculty Area Rankings

Arts & Humanities	37
Engineering & IT	211
Life Sciences & Biomedicine	87
Natural Sciences	122
Social Sciences	103

Survey Performance

Peer Review	81
Recruiter Review	56

Contact Details

College Green
Dublin 2
www.tcd.ie
+353 1 896 1000

People

Student Faculty Ratio	9.3:1
International Faculty	42.0%
Undergraduates	9,811
Postgraduates	2,746
International Students	17.0%

Course Fees For Domestic Students

Average Undergraduate	$6,963
Average Postgraduate	$6,020

Course Fees For International Students

Average Undergraduate	$13,928
Average Postgraduate	$10,757

Overall Research Strength

Papers (Scopus 2002-2006)	14,950
Citations (Scopus 2002-2006)	72,409
Impact	4.8

Research Impact By Faculty Area

Engineering & IT	2.4
Life Sciences & Biomedicine	6.2
Natural Sciences	5.2
Social Sciences	3.3

population to no more than 11,500. It is fortunate that more than half of its Irish students have at least 500 out of a maximum of 600 points in the Irish schools' Leaving Certificate. However, it has also met its target of 15 per cent intake of non-traditional learners. At present 14 per cent of its student base are from overseas — of these 40 per cent come from outside the European Union.

People

One of its first students, James Ussher, was a notable religious scholar and since then many of its alumni have helped shape the history of Ireland and of the English-speaking world. They include George Berkeley, Jonathan Swift, Edmund Burke, Theobald Wolfe Tone, Edward Carson, Oscar Wilde, Oliver Goldsmith, and William Rowan Hamilton.

Two alumni have won Nobel prizes — Ernest Walton for physics in 1951 and Samuel Beckett for literature in 1968.

Both Mary Robinson, the former President of Ireland, and Mary McAleese, the current President, were on the staff of its law school.

What students say

The grandparents of Meghan Brown from Buffalo, New York, came from Schull, Co Cork. But it was not just sentimental attachment to Ireland that prompted her to study sociology and Spanish in Dublin. "The only way to be successful in a globalized world is to have a world-recognized degree — Trinity offers that," she says.

Good at

The arts and humanities are Trinity's top performers, with a place in the top 40 of this year's rankings. The life sciences and biomedicine are also in the top 100, with the social sciences only just missing out.

55= University of Washington

Why this university?

Some US$800 million a year in research is conducted at the University of Washington, more than at any other US public university (or any private university, for that matter, except Johns Hopkins). Much of it is linked to the entrepreneurship that has given rise to Pacific Northwest powerhouse conglomerates such as Microsoft and Boeing. And the relationship works both ways. Microsoft cofounder Bill Gates, whose parents were alumni, has made substantial financial contributions to a new law school, for scholarships to recruit outstanding students, and to pay for student research. So has Microsoft cofounder, Paul Allen, whose father was a "U-Dub" librarian and who has underwritten a new library and Center for Computer Science and Engineering.

Already home to the Cesar Pelli-designed physics and astronomy building, which includes 20 physics labs built underground to provide the most stable possible environment, the campus has added the US$74 million William H. Gates Hall at the law school, a US$90 million medical school surgery pavilion, the aforementioned US$72 million Paul Allen Center for Computer Science and Engineering, and the US$150 million William H. Foege Bioengineering and Genome Sciences Building, dedicated by Bill Gates.

Boeing, which designs and manufactures its planes nearby, uses the wind tunnels at the university's top-rated Department of Aeronautics and Astronautics to test new models. The designers of Boeing's B-52, 707, 727,

FACTFILE

University of WASHINGTON

Country	United States
Foundation Year	1861
World Ranking	55= (84)

Faculty Area Rankings

Arts & Humanities	130
Engineering & IT	81
Life Sciences & Biomedicine	42
Natural Sciences	56
Social Sciences	141

Survey Performance

Peer Review	65
Recruiter Review	247

Contact Details

Seattle
WA 98195
www.washington.edu
+1 206 543 2100

People

Student Faculty Ratio	9:1
International Faculty	11.0%
Undergraduates	26,890
Postgraduates	10,861
International Students	7.0%

Course Fees For Domestic Students

Average Undergraduate	$5,985
Average Postgraduate	$8,818

Course Fees For International Students

Average Undergraduate	$21,283
Average Postgraduate	$20,641

Overall Research Strength

Papers (Scopus 2002-2006)	151,236
Citations (Scopus 2002-2006)	1,143,231
Impact	7.6

Research Impact By Faculty Area

Engineering & IT	5.2
Life Sciences & Biomedicine	6.6
Natural Sciences	14.5
Social Sciences	4.5

747, and other planes all graduated from the University of Washington.

There are other standout departments. U-Dub has one of America's top-rated medical schools for training primary-care physicians. The departments of bioengineering and computer science and School of Social Work are at the top of their fields, and the law and business schools are highly regarded nationally; among other innovative courses of study, the business school has launched a popular technology management MBA program for working professionals in the burgeoning local high-tech industry.

There are 25,470 undergraduates at the university, and 11,763 graduate and professional students on the sprawling campus in Seattle, which was originally laid out for the 1909 world's fair, and continues to incorporate some of the original buildings; of the 3,600 faculty members, six are winners of the Nobel prize. Families that earn 65 per cent of the state's median income or less can send their children to the university tuition-free, the most generous such allowance in America. Graduate students also are eligible for stipends and health insurance, an unusual benefit.

People

Prominent alumni include the first man to fly faster than Mach 2, the men who directed the lunar orbiter program and Rockwell International's Apollo work, the head of the space shuttle program, many astronauts, actors Patrick Duffy, Dyan Cannon, and Bruce Lee, musician Kenny G. and someone whose contribution may have been even greater: the inventor of the disposable diaper.

What students say

Famously rainy Seattle is overcast 60 per cent of the time but Mathieu Fregeau, a Canadian doctoral student working on plasma generation and propulsion for space flight, doesn't mind the weather. "For me it's like paradise," he said, comparing the city with his native Montreal. "People are very laid back. I enjoy just walking on the campus and meeting everyone."

Good at

The life sciences and biomedicine provide Washington's highest placing, but the university is also in the world's top 100 for natural sciences and engineering and IT.

55= University of Wisconsin-Madison

Why this university?

A recent research project at the University of Wisconsin combined one of that state's major industries — dairy — with one of the things the university itself is famous for: intercollegiate sports. The result? A new sports drink made partly of whey protein, a byproduct of cheesemaking. The product helps athletes to refuel.

It might have gotten a lot of lighthearted attention, but this was barely a drop in the bucket of the research under way at Wisconsin. The university does just under US$700 million a year in research. It's eighth among all universities in research paid for by the national government, second in non-federally funded research, fourth in total research expenditures, and second in doctorates granted. Wisconsin is particularly highly ranked in the sciences, with an emphasis on agricultural and life sciences (it is also extremely well-regarded for its sociology and education programs). The first place where human embryonic stem cells were isolated, it's a center for embryonic-stem-cell research and the home of the National Stem Cell Bank, which licenses the use of human embryonic-stem-cell lines to researchers for nonprofit use. And it is a principal partner with the U.S. Department of Energy in seeking out new ways to produce energy and biofuels.

While some large U.S. research universities have begun dividing themselves up into smaller units to

FACTFILE

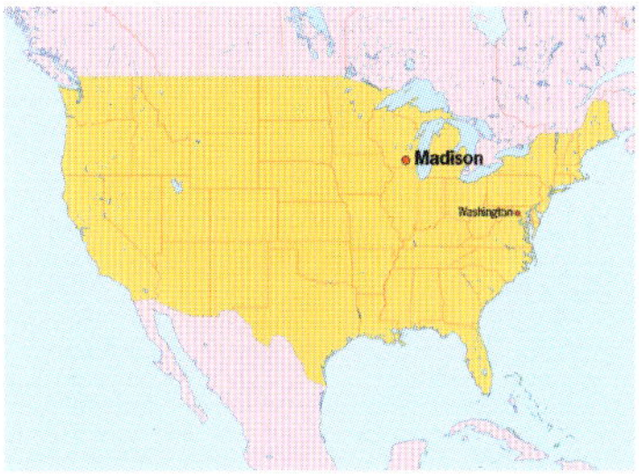

University of WISCONSIN-Madison

Country	United States
Foundation Year	1848
World Ranking	55= (79=)

Faculty Area Rankings

Arts & Humanities	67
Engineering & IT	56
Life Sciences & Biomedicine	45
Natural Sciences	39
Social Sciences	37

Survey Performance

Peer Review	42
Recruiter Review	110

Contact Details

500 Lincoln Drive
Madison
WI 53706
www.wisc.edu
+1 608 263 2400

People

Student Faculty Ratio	17.1:1
International Faculty	12.0%
Undergraduates	25,040
Postgraduates	6,470
International Students	9.0%

Course Fees For Domestic Students

Average Undergraduate	$6,730
Average Postgraduate	$9,184

Course Fees For International Students

Average Undergraduate	$20,730
Average Postgraduate	$24,454

Overall Research Strength

Papers (Scopus 2002-2006)	124,562
Citations (Scopus 2002-2006)	654,284
Impact	5.3

Research Impact By Faculty Area

Engineering & IT	3.4
Life Sciences & Biomedicine	5.7
Natural Sciences	5.9
Social Sciences	4.3

give students the feeling that they are at small colleges, Wisconsin revels in its bigness, touting the size of its library holdings (7.2 million volumes), the number of areas of study it offers (136 undergraduate majors, 155 master's and 110 doctoral programs), the variety of living arrangements, and the hundreds of student organizations. There are more than 41,400 students, 28,460 of them undergraduates and the rest in graduate and professional programs (10 per cent are international), and 2,000 faculty. Wisconsin faculty have won 17 Nobel prizes since the 1940s. Students and faculty alike take a break from their studies on autumn Saturdays, when the entire surrounding community turns red, the official color of the university, and the school's American football team takes the field.

Supported by financial contributions from its exceptionally loyal alumni, the university has recently completed a new health-sciences building, a genetics and biotechnology building, an engineering lab and office center, a pharmaceutical studies building, a chemistry research tower, a massive addition to its biochemistry building and a US$22 million renovation of its physics building.

People

Prominent alumni have included the aviator Charles Lindbergh, architect Frank Lloyd Wright, Vice President Dick Cheney, astronaut Jim Lovell, movie producers Walter Mirisch and Jerry and David Zucker, authors Joyce Carol Oates and Eudora Welty, and Major League Baseball Commissioner Allan "Bud" Selig.

What students say

Fan Yang, an undergraduate from China majoring in actuarial science in the business school, has found the classes very large. "If you're in a general course, there could be more than 100 students in a class, though I have been in more specialized courses with as few as 10," she said. But even in large classes, Ms. Yang said, the faculty "are very patient and very quick to answer questions."

There is one other disadvantage to the university's size and its obsession with athletics, Ms. Yang said. "I think this campus is very friendly, but I do talk with other international students about the distance between us and the American students. Sometimes there is trouble communicating," she said.

Good at

In the top 100 in every academic area, Wisconsin is in the top 40 for social and natural sciences.

57 University of Warwick

Why this university?

Warwick is aiming for a place in the top 50 universities in the world by the time it celebrates its 50th anniversary in 2015. It is already close to that mark, having jumped 16 places in this year's ranking. The university has carved out a place among the élite of British higher education institutions, with excellent ratings in both teaching and research and a reputation as being in the top drawer of Britain's universities after Oxford and Cambridge.

With "entrepreneurial, research-based and innovative" promoted as its watchwords, its location near unglamorous Coventry does not prevent it from attracting a substantial layer of top undergraduate and graduate students.

The university is divided into four faculties that give it genuine breadth of academic influence. The Faculty of Arts teaches everything from classics to film and television studies, whilst the science faculty teaches the key disciplines in their core forms, avoiding the trend for academic dilution. The university also has faculties of social studies and medicine, the latter only founded in 2000 after many years when Warwick concentrated on its well-established links with industry and commerce.

Warwick is one of Britain's top research universities. Six subjects are rated internationally outstanding for research — business, economics, applied mathematics and statistics, English and theatre studies — and 90 per cent of academics entered for the last research assessment

FACTFILE

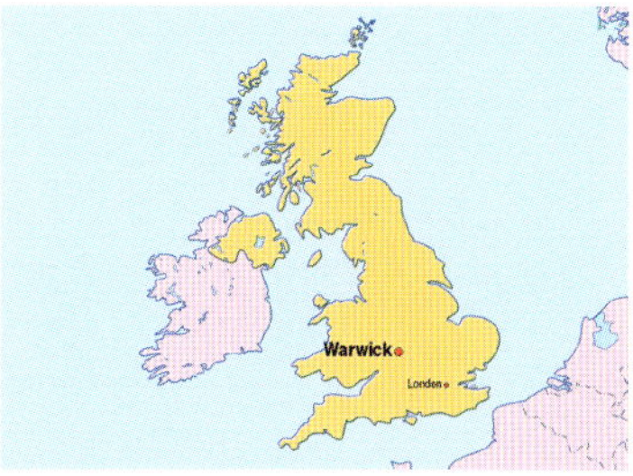

University of WARWICK

Country	United Kingdom
Foundation Year	1965
World Ranking	57 (73)

Faculty Area Rankings

Arts & Humanities	71
Engineering & IT	181
Life Sciences & Biomedicine	188
Natural Sciences	72
Social Sciences	40

Survey Performance

Peer Review	80
Recruiter Review	15

Contact Details

Coventry
CV4 7AL
www2.warwick.ac.uk
+44 24 7652 3523

People

Student Faculty Ratio	10.3:1
International Faculty	27.0%
Undergraduates	12,069
Postgraduates	4,613
International Students	27.0%

Course Fees For Domestic Students

Average Undergraduate	$2,409
Average Postgraduate	$29,879

Course Fees For International Students

Average Undergraduate	$29,366
Average Postgraduate	$33,979

Overall Research Strength

Papers (Scopus 2002-2006)	23,818
Citations (Scopus 2002-2006)	84,827
Impact	3.6

Research Impact By Faculty Area

Engineering & IT	2.3
Life Sciences & Biomedicine	4.2
Natural Sciences	4.2
Social Sciences	2.9

exercise were rated in the two highest categories. Warwick is a member of the 1994 group of research-intensive institutions, as well as the Russell Group of elite universities. Warwick's teaching standards are also excellent, with seven maximum scores in assessments.

The university has nearly 20,000 students and 2,000 academics. More than a fifth of the students are international, drawn from 102 different countries. Warwick is planning to extend its international activities by allocating a section of its campus to leading overseas institutions. It has also launched an international arm of the National Academy for Gifted and Talented Youth, which the campus hosts.

The student union is well organized and active, leading a boycott of the nationwide student satisfaction survey in its initial years. Students in languages and computing were the most satisfied when Warwick's results were published for the first time in 2007. Union facilities have been refurbished, one of many improvements to the estate enabled by £335 million of investment. The Arts Centre, the second largest in the country, was refurbished with a £33 million lottery grant.

People

Leading academics at Warwick include Lord Bhattacharyya, Director of Warwick Manufacturing Group, economics professor Andrew Oswald; and Lord Skidelsky, who recently retired as Professor of Political Economy. Famous alumni include leading politicians Baroness Amos and David Davis, and Tony Wheeler, co-founder of the Lonely Planet travel guides.

What students say

Damian King, a physics PhD student at Warwick, said: "Academically Warwick is a very strong university and in physics I have always found that staff contact time is readily available, particularly from my PhD supervisor, although other departments can differ greatly. Being a campus university Warwick won't suit all people, as many will find it isolated. However, with a strong campus life, living in Coventry in your second year and easy links to Birmingham, it's far from boring."

Good at

The social sciences produced the best position in this year's rankings, at 40th. The arts and humanities, and natural sciences are both in the top 75.

58 University of California, San Diego

Why this university?

A young school at barely 50, UCSD is modeled after old ones — Oxford and Cambridge, on which its residential colleges for undergraduates are based. Its research, however, is cutting edge, and it's had a meteoric rise in its short history.

The university was built alongside the Pacific Ocean in the southern California city of San Diego, joining the highly regarded Salk Institute and Scripps Research Institute in this onetime Navy port. Specializing in science and engineering, it has spun off more than 250 start-up companies, including 63 biomedical start-ups alone, almost singlehandedly transforming San Diego into a center of biotechnology and telecommunications. The wireless company Qualcomm was founded by a UCSD professor. One biotech firm, Hybritech, was sold to Eli Lily for US$345 million just seven years after it was established by two UCSD professors; they and their fellow scientists used the profits to establish some 60 other companies.

The university aggressively promotes the commercialization of technology developed from its research. An independent arm called UCSD Connect has been involved in starting some 900 companies, helping them raise more than US$11 billion in venture capital and navigate the wilds of planning and regulation.

UCSD is unapologetically looking toward the Pacific Rim. It is teaming up on science programs with institutions

FACTFILE

University of CALIFORNIA, San Diego

Country	United States
Foundation Year	1960
World Ranking	58 (44)

Faculty Area Rankings

Arts & Humanities	102
Engineering & IT	38
Life Sciences & Biomedicine	11
Natural Sciences	27
Social Sciences	33

Survey Performance

Peer Review	27
Recruiter Review	296

Contact Details

San Diego
9500 Gilman Drive
La Jolla
California
92093
www.ucsd.edu
+1 858 534 2230

People

Student Faculty Ratio	12.1:1
International Faculty	4.0%
Undergraduates	19,771
Postgraduates	2,866
International Students	6.0%

Course Fees For Domestic Students

Average Undergraduate	$7,446

Course Fees For International Students

Average Undergraduate	$27,066

Overall Research Strength

Papers (Scopus 2002-2006)	110,725
Citations (Scopus 2002-2006)	703,391
Impact	6.4

Research Impact By Faculty Area

Engineering & IT	3.8
Life Sciences & Biomedicine	7.2
Natural Sciences	6.2
Social Sciences	4.5

in China, India, and Singapore. The university ranks third nationally among major research schools in the number of its students who go abroad for at least a full academic year, and eighth in the number of international scholars. In all, there are 3,600 graduate students and 21,600 undergraduates, up 50 per cent in just the last 10 years. Each is assigned to one of six undergraduate colleges based on the Oxbridge system, and they study on a quarter system similar to the University of Chicago's, instead of the more typical semester scheme.

UCSD conducts more than US$730 million a year in research — the seventh-highest total in America. It's home to one of the government's two supercomputing centers and was the ninth-most-cited institution in the world based on its published research in science and the social sciences from 1995 to 2005, according to the Institute for Scientific Information. The medical school alternates between first and second in the nation in research funding per faculty member. Eight members of the faculty have won Nobel prizes, one a Fields Medal, and one the Kyoto Prize.

UCSD's biomedical engineering program, which launched many of those spinoff companies, is considered among the nation's best. Its California Institute for Telecommunications and Information Technology has also made San Diego a center for wireless technology. And it has just opened the first new business school at a major research university in decades, which will specialize in the business of technology. Called the Rady School, it will ultimately have about 65 full-time faculty members and 1,200 candidates for master's degrees in business administration.

People

Alumni include the designer of the MacIntosh computer, Nobel laureate in medicine Susumu Tonegawa, and biologist Craig Venter.

What students say

"It's in a beautiful location, 10 minutes from the seaside," said Elizabeth Blackburn, a postdoctoral research fellow in physics from Knaresborough, Yorkshire. "It's a very pleasant place to be most of the time."

Within the University of California system, Ms. Blackburn said, "San Diego has a reputation as one of the harder schools. They seem to take their studies seriously and they work quite hard."

Good at?

In the top 100 for everything except the arts and humanities, UCSD's highest placing is 11th for the life sciences and biomedicine.

59 London School of Economics & Political Science

Why this university?

The London School of Economics describes itself as "the world's leading social science institution for teaching and research". An immodest claim perhaps, but when half its departments have been rated "internationally outstanding" and the school is near the top of the world rankings, who can blame them?

The LSE is a top destination for future heads of state and Nobel prize winners. An international feel on campus, therefore, comes as no surprise. The student population of 8,800 postgraduates and undergraduates spans 24 European Union countries and 113 non-EU countries.

Half the places go to non-Britons, which puts the school in second place after Manchester University for the most applications from overseas at undergraduate level.

The school is now planning 20 per cent more places, having acquired former government buildings near its central London headquarters. A total of 44 per cent of the 768 full and part-time staff are from countries outside the UK, half of these are from the EU. Despite its name, LSE is multidisciplinary. Law, management and history have received the top rating for teaching quality. Business, economics, psychology and mathematics have also produced good results.

Research specialisms include maths, media, anthropology, communications, economic history, accounting, international relations,

FACTFILE

LONDON School of Economics and Political Science

Country	United Kingdom
Foundation Year	1895
World Ranking	59 (17)

Faculty Area Rankings

Arts & Humanities	26
Engineering & IT	257
Life Sciences & Biomedicine	260
Social Sciences	3

Survey Performance

Peer Review	49
Recruiter Review	3

Contact Details

Houghton Street
London
WC2A 2AE
www.lse.ac.uk
+44 20 7405 7686

People

Student Faculty Ratio	9.9:1
International Faculty	53.0%
Undergraduates	3,777
Postgraduates	4,114
International Students	65.0%

Course Fees For Domestic Students

Average Undergraduate	$6,294

Overall Research Strength

Papers (Scopus 2002-2006)	5,892
Citations (Scopus 2002-2006)	13,138
Impact	2.2

Research Impact By Faculty Area

Engineering & IT	1.9
Life Sciences & Biomedicine	2.6
Natural Sciences	2.4
Social Sciences	2.2

and social policy. A pan-European survey showed LSE students to be more active in student associations, more entrepreneurial and more open to working abroad than those at other leading universities.

People

Some 29 country leaders and 13 Nobel prize winners have studied there. Among them are Italian Prime Minister Romano Prodi, former Canadian Prime Minister Pierre Trudeau and Indian former President Shri KR Narayanan. The school was founded by socialist luminaries Sidney and Beatrice Webb and George Bernard Shaw. Labour Prime Minister Clement Atlee was a lecturer there. On a more modern note, the LSE is also the alma mater of Rolling Stone Mick Jagger.

What students say

Ali Dewji, from Toronto, is studying for a BSc in international relations and history. He describes the institution as an "urban and international academic powerhouse".

He said: "On any given day at LSE, I might find myself attending a public lecture given by a minister from Norway, meeting a friend for sushi and a chat about economic growth in Nigeria, practising my Spanish with some Peruvian postgraduates in an elevator on my way to a Debate Society meeting then heading back to my hall of residence to watch the latest episode of OC on TV. "When I leave LSE, I will have spent three years studying alongside some of the brightest students in the world, whose lives and experiences are themselves part of an LSE education and part of what makes LSE such a unique place to study."

Good at

The LSE is ranked third in the world for social sciences and 26th for the arts and humanities.

60 Heidelberg University

Why this university?

Eight Nobel prize winners and over 60 other famous academics have helped the University of Heidelberg ensure it remains Germany's best-known university.

A member of the League of European Research Universities (LERU) that includes just 19 others, the Ruprecht Karl University of Heidelberg, as it is known in full, has proved itself a leader in forward thinking as well as research and development since its founding in 1386.

Set up by Ruprecht I, Count Palatine of the Rhine, the university initially acted as an ecclesiastical centre for the Holy Roman Empire. However it quickly established itself as a hub for philosophers and independent thinkers and developed into a stronghold of humanism in the 15th century. Grand Duke Karl-Friedrich of Baden turned it into a state-owned institution in 1803. This revival ran parallel to the discovery of the city by poets, artists and intellectuals like Friedrich Hölderlin, Johann Wolfgang von Goethe, Joseph von Eichendorff and Robert Schumann.

In the early 20th century, the image of German university and student life entertained in the world at large was very much an image of Heidelberg. The name stood for the "embodiment of the life of the mind", a phrase coined by philosopher Karl Jaspers, who taught here until 1948. One of its outstanding features was a tradition of interdisciplinary dialogue cultivated in a variety of forums and other circles, chief among them the one presided

FACTFILE

HEIDELBERG University

Country .... Germany
Foundation Year 1386
World Ranking .... 60 (58=)

Faculty Area Rankings

Arts & Humanities 61
Life Sciences & Biomedicine 43
Natural Sciences 45
Social Sciences 78

Survey Performance

Peer Review 62
Recruiter Review 189

Contact Details

Grabengasse 1
Heidelberg
69117
www.uni-heidelberg.de
+49 62 21540

People

Student Faculty Ratio 10.6:1
International Faculty 10.0%
Undergraduates 23,062
Postgraduates 2,469
International Students 21.0%

Course Fees For Domestic Students

Overall Average $1,372

Course Fees For International Students

Overall Average $1,372

Overall Research Strength

Papers (Scopus 2002-2006) 62,873
Citations (Scopus 2002-2006) 299,754
Impact 4.8

Research Impact By Faculty Area

Engineering & IT 2.9
Life Sciences & Biomedicine 4.7
Natural Sciences 6.0
Social Sciences 3.0

over by Max Weber, the founder of the modern social sciences.

The Third Reich saw the second dark period in Heidelberg University's history when Hitler's anti-Semitic policies saw many notable professors expelled from its ranks. Turbulence arose once again in the 1960s and 1970s when links were forged between students and the left-wing terrorist organization Red Army Faction.

Today its roots are firmly planted in the sciences, but it has still managed to keep its metaphysical traditions with large theology and philosophy faculties all of which help attract students and professors from around the globe.

International Affairs professor Angelos Chaniotis added: "International students are attracted to the university not only because of its organization, infrastructure, manpower and research facilities, but also for its tradition as a leader in innovation. "We also have some of the best scientific institutes in Europe on our doorstep, which makes us very much research orientated – another reason for our success."

Included among the numerous institutes are the European Laboratory for Molecular Biology, the German Cancer Research Centre and a number of Max Planck institutes. These collaborate with the university's 12 faculties and eight of its own research institutes.

People

Weber is just one of over 70 illustrious names who studied or taught at the university. They include eight Nobel prize winners. Among them are Philipp Lenard, who won the Nobel prize for Physics for his groundbreaking work on cathode rays, Hans Jensen, who also won the Physics prize for helping to develop the shell nuclear model, and Georg Wittig, who won the Nobel prize for Chemistry in 1979. Other notables include the founder of the German Bank, Georg von Siemens, chemist Robert Bunsen, after whom the Bunsen burner was named, and former German chancellor Helmut Kohl. Nazi Minister for Propaganda, Joseph Goebbels, also attained his degree from the university in 1921.

What students say

Oksana Jurevic is just one of over 5,000 international students enrolled at the university which has a student body of around 26,000 and some 400 professors. The 28-year-old economics student from Lithuania said: "I was attracted to Heidelberg University because of its history and reputation and so far haven't been disappointed. International students must have some degree of German in order to study here, and even though I am not completely fluent, I get a lot of support from the university and its staff. We are also given plenty of opportunity for one-to-one tutorials that you just do not get at other universities, and the standard of teaching is excellent. The city itself also provides a safe and positive environment for international students."

Good at

Heidelberg's best scores in our rankings come in the natural sciences and biomedicine, both of which are in the top 50. The arts and humanities just miss the top 60, while the university is ranked 78 in social sciences.

61 Katholieke Universiteit Leuven

Why this university?

A Catholic university has existed in Leuven since 1425, although for much of its history the academic discourse in French was at odds with the Dutch spoken in the town. Dutch courses began to be given in the late Nineteenth Century, with complete bilingualism established in 1911.

However, the language divide continued to produce tensions, and following student unrest in 1968 it was decided to split the university in two. The French speakers set up a new campus, and a new town, at Louvain-la-Neuve, while the Dutch speakers remained in Leuven.

The Katholieke Universiteit Leuven is now the largest of Belgium's Flemish universities, with more than 30,000 students, around 12 per cent of whom are international. The academic staff is over 5,000 strong, spread across 14 faculties. KU Leuven also supports five hospitals, three affiliated hospitals, and a campus at Kortrijk in West Flanders, which carries out bachelor and master programs in Dutch only, plus some research.

As well as exchange programs, the university has set up a number of international academic programs aimed both at Belgian and international students, which are taught in English. Most are masters programs, although full bachelor degree programs are also offered in English for theology and philosophy students. The international masters are closely linked to the leading research areas at KU Leuven, but span

FACTFILE

Katholieke Universiteit LEUVEN

Country	Belgium
Foundation Year	1425
World Ranking	61 (96)

Faculty Area Rankings

Arts & Humanities	43
Engineering & IT	70
Life Sciences & Biomedicine	109
Natural Sciences	74
Social Sciences	54

Survey Performance

Peer Review	51
Recruiter Review	98

Contact Details

Oude Markt 13
Leuven
3000
www.kuleuven.ac.be
+32 16 32 40 10

People

Student Faculty Ratio	14.5:1
International Faculty	13.0%
Undergraduates	14,859
Postgraduates	13,583
International Students	12.0%

Course Fees For Domestic Students

Average Undergraduate	$732

Course Fees For International Students

Average Undergraduate	$6,861

Overall Research Strength

Papers (Scopus 2002-2006)	76,750
Citations (Scopus 2002-2006)	334,519
Impact	4.4

Research Impact By Faculty Area

Engineering & IT	3.0
Life Sciences & Biomedicine	5.1
Natural Sciences	4.4
Social Sciences	3.2

the whole range of disciplines, from theology and philosophy, to law and economics, pharmaceutical science and bio-engineering.

People

Leuven tempted back Catherine Verfaillie, a pioneer of work with adult stem cells, from Minnesota this year to lead a new stem cell institute. The university also has an international reputation in cryptography, and was home to Vincent Rijmen and Joan Daemen, the two researchers who developed the Rijndael advanced encryption standard adopted by the US Government.

In the 2005 round of 'Flemish Nobels', awarded every five years, Leuven faculty picked up three of the five awards. They went to Bart De Strooper (human genetics), Victor Moshchalkov (solid state physics and magnetism) and Frans Van de Werf (cardiology).

Alumni include Frank Vandenbroucke, the present education minister in Belgium's Flemish government, humanist and theologian Desiderius Erasmus; Dr A. Q. Khan, the founder of Pakistan's Nuclear Program; and cartographer Gerard Mercator.

What students say

British post-doc Simon Reeve was attracted to Leuven by the prospect of joining a research group in neurobiology being set up by an American investigator who had been persuaded to move to the university. "With him establishing a lab here, and the lab being a new place, I figured that the support, the funding, the interest would all be at a maximum." The experience has lived up to his expectations, and he has no regrets at choosing Leuven over a position in the USA. "It's a very dynamic environment," he says. "People suggest things and they go ahead." His only regret is that, in the university's English-speaking environment, there is no incentive to learn Dutch and so engage more with the local community. "From one perspective it's an advantage, but from another it's not."

Good at

Only the life sciences and biomedicine are outside the top 100 in this year's rankings. The arts and humanities produce Leuven's highest position, inside the top 50.

62 University of Adelaide

Why this university?

The University of Adelaide is Australia's third-oldest, having been established in 1874. It was the first in Australia to admit women on an equal basis with men in 1881 — well ahead of Oxford in 1920 and Cambridge in 1948 — and the first to set up a conservatorium of music.

As with other Australian universities, Adelaide is a multi-campus institution although a majority of students attend the main site in the central business district, a crowded but pleasant campus with the CBD on one side and gardens and the Torrens River on the other.

Most of Adelaide's 1,255 academics conduct research, much of it at the leading edge, and research earnings are consistently the highest per capita of any university in the country. Analysis of the impact of publications and citations has placed Adelaide in the top one per cent in the world in 11 research fields. Its major strengths are in the wine and food area, health sciences, biological sciences, physical sciences, information technology and telecommunications, environmental sciences and social sciences.

People

Because of its age and status, Adelaide attracts the biggest proportion of top-scoring school leavers although the competition with South Australia's two public and one private university has become fiercer in recent years. A large number of undergraduates go on to undertake honours and postgraduate

FACTFILE

University of ADELAIDE

Country	Australia
Foundation Year	1874
World Ranking	62 (105=)

Faculty Area Rankings

Arts & Humanities	136
Engineering & IT	149
Life Sciences & Biomedicine	100
Natural Sciences	87
Social Sciences	89

Survey Performance

Peer Review	98
Recruiter Review	86

Contact Details

The University of Adelaide
Adelaide
SA 5005
www.adelaide.edu.au
+61 8 8303 4455

People

Student Faculty Ratio	9.8:1
International Faculty	21.0%
Undergraduates	11,604
Postgraduates	3,329
International Students	27.0%

Course Fees For Domestic Students

Average Undergraduate	$5,151
Average Postgraduate	$4,763

Course Fees For International Students

Average Undergraduate	$16,847
Average Postgraduate	$16,935

Overall Research Strength

Papers (Scopus 2002-2006)	30,063
Citations (Scopus 2002-2006)	106,276
Impact	3.5

Research Impact By Faculty Area

Engineering & IT	2.1
Life Sciences & Biomedicine	3.8
Natural Sciences	4.2
Social Sciences	2.3

studies, and the university has had 101 Rhodes Scholars with 2007 the 105th year the scholarship has been awarded to an Adelaide student.

The university counts among its Nobel laureates Dr Robin Warren, who won the prize for medicine in 2005; Sir William Bragg, physics 1915, who remains the youngest Nobel prize winner ever at 25; and Lord Howard Florey, medicine 1945.

What students say

More than 20,500 local students are enrolled at Adelaide and the university also attracts 5,500 international students, 720 of whom are based off-shore. The university offers scholarships for international undergraduates that provide a waiver of full tuition fees for up to four years.

Accommodation options include university-managed places, five affiliated privately-managed residential colleges, student hostels, private rentals and share housing. Average costs vary from AU$90-AU$250 a week for private rental and shared housing, AU$165-195 for university managed accommodation, to an average AU$250 a week for fully catered and privately managed residential colleges. Last year, Adelaide opened a new city-centre facility, The Village, offering accommodation for more than 400 students with 24-hour staffing.

Zhuo Li came from Harbin in China in 2001 to undertake two years at high school before enrolling at Adelaide in a bachelor of engineering degree in mechatronics — a course combining studies in mechanical and electrical engineering. At the age of 24 he is in his final year and says he chose Adelaide because of the reputation of the university and its academics.

"The lecturers all have PhDs and good experience and skills in teaching," Mr Li says. "They are very patient and answer all the questions that students have."

He says he will apply for a permanent residency visa once he finishes the course and hopes to find work in industry or management. If he is not successful, he says he will return to China where there is a strong demand for skilled people."

Good at

A new entrant to the top 100 this year, Adelaide's top-ranked areas are the natural sciences and social sciences, although the life sciences and biomedicine also make it to the top 100.

63 Delft University of Technology

Why this university?

Delft University of Technology has chosen Prometheus' flame as its symbol, and like Prometheus the university sees itself as bringing technical knowledge to the aid of humanity. A relatively new creation, gaining university status in 1986, TU Delft is inheritor of a tradition of engineering education in the town that dates back to 1842.

Delft is a small city between Den Haag and Rotterdam, greatly influenced by the university's presence. More than 10 per cent of its 100,000 inhabitants are students and the university has attracted a large number of technology-oriented companies.

Four of the university's eight faculties cover engineering disciplines, the remainder taking on related subjects such as architecture, information technology, applied sciences and technology policy and management. It offers 16 bachelor courses, almost all taught in Dutch, and 29 masters courses, all taught in English. In 2006, there were a total of 13,400 students at the university, roughly half on bachelor courses, half on masters. Of these, 1,365 were from outside the Netherlands.

At the same time there were 2,300 scientific staff, of which nearly 200 were full professors and 700 PhD students. Just under half of the scientific staff are from outside the Netherlands, including a substantial number of PhD students.

FACTFILE

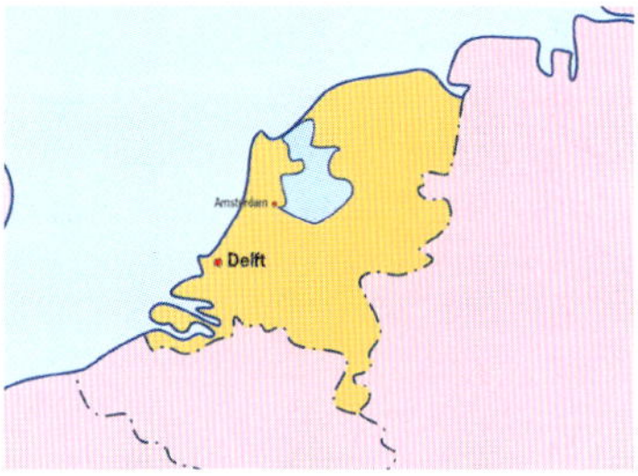

DELFT University of Technology

Country........Netherlands
Foundation Year........1842
World Ranking........63 (86)

Faculty Area Rankings

Arts & Humanities........193
Engineering & IT........17
Natural Sciences........83
Social Sciences........241

Survey Performance

Peer Review........97
Recruiter Review........112

Contact Details

Stevinweg 1
Delft
2628 CN
www.tudelft.nl
+31 15 278 9111

People

Student Faculty Ratio........9.9:1
International Faculty........24.0%
Undergraduates........9,655
Postgraduates........5,035
International Students........15.0%

Course Fees For Domestic Students

Average Undergraduate........$2,112
Average Postgraduate........$3,480

Course Fees For International Students

Average Undergraduate........$2,367
Average Postgraduate........$8,095

Overall Research Strength

Papers (Scopus 2002-2006)........43,042
Citations (Scopus 2002-2006)........138,811
Impact........3.2

Research Impact By Faculty Area

Engineering & IT........2.6
Life Sciences & Biomedicine........4.1
Natural Sciences........4.2
Social Sciences........1.7

People

The university is particularly strong in nanoscience, and in 2004 attracted substantial funding from the Kavli Foundation in the USA to establish a research institute that now has a staff of 16 professors and over 90 PhD students and postdocs. This is home to two of the university's most noted faculty, Hans Mooij, who works on quantum computing, and Cees Dekker, who received a Spinoza award (the highest Dutch honour for science) in 2003 for his work on carbon nanotubes.

The university's other Spinoza winner is René de Borst, who works in the equally strong aerospace engineering faculty. This is also home to Adriaan Beukers, who in 2006 was named the Netherlands' most entrepreneurial scientist.

What students say

The commercial relevance of Delft's courses was one of the things that attracted Nitesh Bharosa to the university from his home in Suriname, although being able to study in Dutch was also a draw. He completed his bachelor degree at Delft and is currently finishing a masters in systems engineering and policy analysis, with a focus on information and communication technologies. "Other programs mainly consist of ICT courses or programming alone, but Delft offered a lot more company-specific courses, like the economics of ICT, human skills, and the management of ICT systems. That attracted me a lot," he explains.

Delft has lived up to its promise, and even compared well to UCLA, where Nitesh followed a summer course in 2005. "The teaching methods here are more advanced, they use a lot more technology, including internet resources to provide information. Class material and so on is all on line, and that is much appreciated. Also the topics taught are really novel. When I was at UCLA, for example, they were teaching programming languages that aren't popular any more, while at Delft they teach the languages that are in demand from companies."

The one down side is that Delft does not provide much support for international students. "The university only has one small office that offers you aid in a lot of bureaucratic issues, such as housing and banking. Other universities have a much better focus on international students." However, on balance Nitesh is very pleased with the experience of studying in Delft.

Good at

Engineering and IT is easily the highest-ranked area, at 17 in world, but the natural sciences are also in the top 100.

64 University of Western Australia

Why this university?

The University of Western Australia is the oldest and richest university in the giant state where it is based. It has the most beautiful campus in WA, adjacent to Perth's most affluent suburbs, and is a mere five kilometres from the city centre. Because of its age, status and reputation, it attracts an even higher proportion of students from the top private schools than any other university in the country and enrols more than eight in ten of the state's top five per cent of school-leavers.

A member of Australia's Group of Eight research-intensive universities, UWA has a student population of more than 18,000 and provides a wide range of undergraduate and higher degree programmes that cover the arts, science and major professions across nine faculties. Research and research training are strongly emphasised and the university focuses on research into the exploration, production and development of minerals, oil and gas; the management of agricultural and natural ecosystems; the humanities and social sciences; health and bio-medicine, as well as international management and business studies.

UWA is recognised for the quality of its 1,290 academic staff who have developed strategic partnerships with Australian industry, the professions and government. Likewise, its links with international institutions are numerous and the university has hundreds of memoranda or agreements with overseas universities and research organisations.

FACTFILE

University of WESTERN AUSTRALIA

Country	Australia
Foundation Year	1911
World Ranking	64 (111=)

Faculty Area Rankings

Arts & Humanities	117
Engineering & IT	138
Life Sciences & Biomedicine	77
Natural Sciences	135
Social Sciences	157

Survey Performance

Peer Review	106
Recruiter Review	80

Contact Details

35 Stirling Highway
Crawley
WA 6009
www.uwa.edu.au
+61 8 6488 2889

People

Student Faculty Ratio	11.3:1
International Faculty	35.0%
Undergraduates	11,698
Postgraduates	2,588
International Students	17.0%

Course Fees For Domestic Students

Average Undergraduate	$12,200
Average Postgraduate	$9,350

Course Fees For International Students

Average Undergraduate	$15,300
Average Postgraduate	$16,150

Overall Research Strength

Papers (Scopus 2002-2006)	40,691
Citations (Scopus 2002-2006)	158,664
Impact	3.9

Research Impact By Faculty Area

Engineering & IT	2.0
Life Sciences & Biomedicine	4.3
Natural Sciences	3.8
Social Sciences	3.4

Because Perth is close to many south-east Asian cities and has close links with Malaysia and Singapore, many Asian students find it much nearer and cheaper to go to UWA than travel another 3000 kilometres to the other side of the country. International enrolments in 2007 totalled almost 3,400 – 600 offshore - and most of the undergraduates are from Singapore, Malaysia and Indonesia. The university has colleges adjacent to the campus which provide accommodation for approximately 700 students at a cost of around AU$300 per week.

People

Apart from Nobel laureates Professor Barry Marshall and Dr Robyn Warren who won the 2005 prize for medicine, other notable UWA graduates include a former Prime Minister, a former Opposition Leader, former WA premiers, five of the last six Australian ambassadors to China and international political leaders, including senior ministers in the Indonesian and Singapore governments.

What students say

Charmaine Kalidas is a Singaporean Indian in her third year of a bachelor or science degree in zoology. She says she had "a passion for animals from an early age" but, as there were no animal studies courses in Singapore universities, she came to Perth.

"I chose UWA because it was in the Group of Eight research universities — and also, when I asked the Perth zoo for information about working with animals, they recommended UWA as a place to study," Ms Kalidas says.

But the workload is heavy and Ms Kalidas jokingly refers to her lecturers as 'slave-drivers' because of the amount of work they require students to do. But she hastens to add that students benefit from the constant pressure because it better prepares them for the annual examinations — even if it cuts down on the opportunity to enjoy campus life.

"I would give UWA a mark of 85 out of 100 overall," she says. "And I will urge my younger sister to also come here if she wants to go abroad to study."

Good at

A new entry to the top 100 this year, UWA's best placing among the five academic areas is in the life sciences and biomedicine, where it is ranked 77th.

65= Birmingham University

Why this university?

Birmingham takes immense pride in its self-proclaimed standing as the 'Oxbridge of the Midlands', and with good reason. The university can boast two thirds of its departments as nationally or internationally outstanding, with research, especially in languages, winning the university twelve 5* ratings in the Research Assessment Exercise. Teaching also scores well, with top marks in assessments going to mathematics, biological sciences, physiotherapy and electrical and electronic engineering. It therefore comes as little surprise that eight applicants contest every student place.

The university's prestigious medical school has recently seen the largest expansion in the country with a new £11.8 million student facilities building. The engineering department has also been bolstered in recent years, now offering interdisciplinary courses combining technology with subjects as diverse as modern languages and flood management. A total of £225 million has been invested in new equipment, buildings and staff over the last five years.

The Birmingham Business School, the oldest in England, has also won a high level of respect, being one of only a dozen UK business schools in the Financial Times global top 80 for MBA rankings, with The Economist magazine giving the school top ranking in the UK for 2004-05.

Like the city itself, the university is a melting pot of cultures and nationalities. Echoing the 26.4 per

FACTFILE

University of BIRMINGHAM

Country.. United Kingdom
Foundation Year 1900
World Ranking .... 65= (90=)

Faculty Area Rankings

Arts & Humanities 181
Engineering & IT 84
Life Sciences & Biomedicine 93
Natural Sciences 166
Social Sciences 111

Survey Performance

Peer Review 112
Recruiter Review 50

Contact Details

Edgbaston
Birmingham
B15 2TT
www.bham.ac.uk
+44 121 414 3344

People

Student Faculty Ratio 10.3:1
International Faculty 24.0%
Undergraduates 17,400
Postgraduates 5,957
International Students 15.0%

Course Fees For Domestic Students

Average Undergraduate $6,294

Overall Research Strength

Papers (Scopus 2002-2006) 51,997
Citations (Scopus 2002-2006) 236,878
Impact 4.6

Research Impact By Faculty Area

Engineering & IT 2.6
Life Sciences & Biomedicine 5.2
Natural Sciences 5.2
Social Sciences 2.6

cent of Birmingham residents who self-defined as 'non-white' in the 2001 census, the university claims more than 4,000 international students from 150 countries. The university has 27,000 students in total and is a member of the Universitas 21 group of global universities.

The city, around three miles from campus, has a growing reputation amongst students, but many opt to use the plethora of bars, shops and restaurants around the university itself.

People

With a list of alumni featuring four Nobel prize winners as well as the mayor of Shanghai and the prime minister of the Bahamas, Birmingham has had its share of prestigious students. Actor Tim Curry, politician Ann Widdecombe, and zoologist and TV presenter Desmond Morris also hail from the university.

What students say

Irene Michael, a student who came from Cyprus to study physiotherapy, praised the level of support given by the university to international students. "I think it's great. The university provides a very good induction, with a student union really enabling students to develop."

Irene chose Birmingham largely due to the level of help given to her to get a place on the course in the first place. While other institutions at the time gave little or no financial support to international students wishing to get on her chosen course, Birmingham gave her funding to match the NHS bursary available for home students. "The university also gives free English courses as well as advice on visas and jobs for both students and employers," she adds. "The community here is good, but it could do better with engaging students throughout the year. The Union is playing a big part in strengthening the community."

Good at

Birmingham is in the top 100 in our rankings both for engineering and IT and the life sciences and biomedicine. The arts and humanities shared this distinction in 2006.

65= Ludwig-Maximilians-Universität München

Why this university?

Shortlisted to become one of Germany's new "elite" universities, the Ludwig-Maximilians University in Munich has a bright future ahead of it. Initially competing against more than 100 universities across the country, the LMU is now hoping to be picked as one of five "centres of excellence" from 10 remaining universities by a specialist commission set up by the government.

And as one of the strongest research universities in the country, the university in the Bavarian capital has a good chance of achieving the honour - which also comes with a multi-million euros cash injection.

Part of 26 Collaborative Research Centres funded by the German Research Foundation (DFG), of which the university hosts 14, the LMU's reputation for research and development is one of the reasons it attracts students and professors from across the globe as well as external funding to the tune of €120 million a year from both national and international sources. With degree programs available in 150 subjects in numerous combinations, the array of courses is extremely wide and it offers a well-rounded range of learning opportunities that cover all areas, whether humanities and culture studies, law, economics and sociology, or medicine and the sciences.

It is also one of the largest universities

FACTFILE

Ludwig-Maximilians-Universität München (MUNICH)

Country .... Germany
Foundation Year 1472
World Ranking .... 65= (98)

Faculty Area Rankings

Arts & Humanities 56
Engineering & IT 176
Life Sciences & Biomedicine 111
Natural Sciences 62
Social Sciences 82

Survey Performance

Peer Review 79
Recruiter Review 201

Contact Details

Geschwister-Scholl Platz 1
Munich (München)
Bavaria (Bayern)
80539
www.uni-muenchen.de
+49 89 21800

People

Student Faculty Ratio 9.4:1
International Faculty 15.0%
Undergraduates 40,697
Postgraduates 4,888
International Students 16.0%

Overall Research Strength

Papers (Scopus 2002-2006) 87,338
Citations (Scopus 2002-2006) 444,097
Impact 5.1

Research Impact By Faculty Area

Engineering & IT 3.4
Life Sciences & Biomedicine 5.0
Natural Sciences 6.3
Social Sciences 3.9

in Germany with almost 44,000 students, 16 per cent of whom come to us from abroad, 700 professors and 3,000 academic staff and has more women than men enrolled in its 18 faculties (28,000 women, 16,000 men). Rector Bernd Huber says students from across the world travel to Munich because of its unique academic diversity that covers all areas including the humanities, culture studies, law, economics, sociology, medicine and the sciences.

Although it is now known as the University of Munich, it has not always been situated in the Bavarian capital. Duke Ludwig the Wealthy of Bavaria-Landshut founded it with a Papal concession in 1472: it was called the Ingolstadt University and began with four faculties. The Faculty of Arts (today's Faculty of Philosophy) was mandatory and thus represented an undergraduate program of sorts. Its completion qualified a student for the other three faculties: medicine, jurisprudence or theology. Then it was relocated to Landshut in 1800 by Prince Elector Max IV Joseph of Bavaria. It was here that it changed its name to the Ludwig-Maximilians University after the two noblemen in 1802. Only in 1826 did the university finally move to the larger city of Munich. The main building occupied today has been in use since 1840.

Further information at www.en.uni-muenchen.de

People

Thirteen Nobel prize winners are associated with the university including Wilhelm Conrad Röntgen, who in 1895 discovered the X-ray, and Konrad Lorenz, who won the prize for medicine in 1973 for his discoveries in individual and social behaviour patterns. Interestingly all of the Nobel laureates who studied or taught at the LMU won prizes for the sciences, reinforcing its reputation as a leader in this area.

What students say

Computer Science student Xiaotian Wei, 27, from China, says he has no regrets choosing the LMU. "The LMU is one of the best universities in Germany and offers courses in almost all subjects. One of the biggest advantages to studying here is the opportunity to take part in practical research rather than just theory because of all the institutes attached to the university.

"I feel a little more support could be given to international students, particularly when it comes to things like finding accommodation in the city, although this is a minor complaint. All students, whether German or foreign, seem to be treated the same, and fees for international students seem to be less here than in many other European countries."

Good at

The university's top rating is in the natural sciences, where it is in the top 50. Biomedicine is close behind, while the social sciences are also in the top 100.

67 Technische Universität München

Why this university?

The Technical University Munich (TUM) began life in 1868 as a 'polytechnic school' thanks to King Ludwig II. It was allowed to call itself 'Technische Hochschule' as from the academic year 1877/78 and the first Principal was the former Head of the Engineering Course, Karl Max von Bauernfeind. The new designation of 'Technische Universität München' was conferred in August 1970; since then the institute has grasped its new title with both hands and has built upon the prestige of its new name ever since - becoming one of the leading technical universities in the world.

Together with the Ludwig-Maximilians University, the TUM has helped make the Bavarian capital one of the most appealing cities for students and researchers and is one of the nine largest technical universities in Germany.

The institute prides itself on its international standing, claiming that its graduates go on to careers in all corners of the globe, while its professors are diverse in origin.

At present, more than 4,000 international students are enrolled at the university which is also home to 37 foreign professors (of a total of 400) and 490 international researchers.

Part of the TUM's success is believed to be down to its continuity in leadership. Chemistry professor Wolfgang A. Herrmann, renowned in Germany for reforming higher education, has been president of the university since 1995

FACTFILE

Technische Universität MÜNCHEN

Country .... Germany
Foundation Year 1868
World Ranking .... 67 (82=)

Faculty Area Rankings

Engineering & IT 40
Life Sciences & Biomedicine 178
Natural Sciences 66

Survey Performance

Peer Review 124
Recruiter Review 150

Contact Details

Arcisstrasse 21
München
80333
www.tu-muenchen.de
+49 89 28901

People

Student Faculty Ratio 7.1:1
International Faculty 15.0%
Undergraduates 12,311
Postgraduates 9,297
International Students 19.0%

Course Fees For Domestic Students

Average Undergraduate $1,372
Average Postgraduate $1,372

Course Fees For International Students

Average Undergraduate $1,372
Average Postgraduate $1,372

Overall Research Strength

Papers (Scopus 2002-2006) 45,747
Citations (Scopus 2002-2006) 244,804
Impact 5.4

Research Impact By Faculty Area

Engineering & IT 2.5
Life Sciences & Biomedicine 6.2
Natural Sciences 6.0
Social Sciences 2.6

having being re-elected twice. It was under his initiative that fundamental structural reforms at the TUM were made, which were then followed by universities in other states as well as in neighbouring Austria.

Unlike the majority of technical universities across Europe, the TUM has also successfully managed to establish strong links with the life sciences, offering degree programs in a variety of areas including nutrition and food, biotechnology, bioinformatics and medicine, participating in European university networks and maintaining partnerships with more than 130 universities throughout the world.

Much of its innovative research and teaching has emerged from collaborations between the disciplines of its 12 faculties as well as a number of research centres. The TUM prides itself on allowing scientists freedom to experiment and in 2005 set up the 'TUM Institute for Advanced Study' that claims to add "entrepreneurial spirit" to the academic world. Projects carried out at the university range in diversity from researching innovative medicines to furthering nanoelectronic technologies and to creating ice that does not melt. The university is also heavily involved in EU projects and is actively involved in helping the bloc create a European Research Area (ERA) to promote co-operation and mobility between universities across the continent.

TU München was declared an Elite University in a joint decision taken by the Science Council and the German Research Foundation on 13/10/2006. Its success with the "International Graduate School of Science and Engineering" (IGSSE) and the two clusters of excellence hosted by TUM — "Cognition of Technical Systems" (COTESYS) and "Origin and Structure of the Universe" — paved the way to realizing the future-orientated concept of "TUM. the Entrepreneurial University".

Female students and academics are also actively encouraged at the TUM. Of the nearly 22,000 students currently enrolled more than 6,400 are female. It is the institute's goal to become the most attractive technical university for women in the country and a number of unconventional measures have been taken to create courses and work places that match the requirements of women as well as those with young families. Further information at www.tu-muenchen.de

People

Alumni include Rudolf Diesel, who invented the engine that bears his name, and the aeroplane designer Willy Messerschmitt. The TUM can count six Nobel Laureates. Of these four won the prize for chemistry, including Professor Robert Huber who was awarded a Nobel in 1988 for his work on protein structure. Other laureates at the university include Professor Heinrich Otto Wieland, Nobel prize for Chemistry 1927; Professor Rudolf L Moessbauer, Nobel prize for Physics 1961; and Professor Klaus von Klitzing who was also awarded the physics prize in 1985.

Good at

The university is best known for engineering and IT, where it is ranked In the top 40 in the world, as well as appearing in the top 100 for natural sciences.

68 University of Sheffield

Why this university?

Sheffield has been growing, both in terms of student numbers and facilities, in recent years. There are now 24,000 students from 118 countries and almost 6,000 academics.

The university has opened a new research campus and an impressive new learning facility, the £23-million Information Commons, was added in April 2007. It operates 24 hours a day, providing 1,300 study spaces and 500 computers linked to the campus network, and 110,000 books and periodicals.

The university is within walking distance of the city centre, forming a mile-long corridor of academic and residential buildings stretching into the affluent west side of Sheffield. Derbyshire's scenic Peak District is a bus ride away. The university has always had an international outlook, offering dedicated services for overseas students before many of its rivals. Its website lists more than 50 countries where prospective students can receive first-hand advice on courses and study arrangements. Sheffield International College, which offers English language and other preparatory courses for international students, is based at the university.

Three-quarters of the academics entered for the last research assessment exercise were placed in the top two categories, with starred departments in medicine, science, engineering and social science. Electrical and electronic engineering, the biosciences, politics and Russian all have maximum scores for both teaching and research. The

FACTFILE

University of SHEFFIELD

Country .... United Kingdom
Foundation Year 1897
World Ranking .... 68 (102=)

Faculty Area Rankings

Arts & Humanities 107
Engineering & IT 122
Life Sciences & Biomedicine 127
Natural Sciences 175
Social Sciences 141

Survey Performance

Peer Review 122
Recruiter Review 31

Contact Details

Western Bank
Sheffield
S10 2TN
www.shef.ac.uk
+44 114 222 2000

People

Student Faculty Ratio 9.2:1
International Faculty 23.0%
Undergraduates 18,129
Postgraduates 4,409
International Students 14.0%

Course Fees For Domestic Students

Average Undergraduate $6,294

Overall Research Strength

Papers (Scopus 2002-2006) 50,105
Citations (Scopus 2002-2006) 200,309
Impact 4.0

Research Impact By Faculty Area

Engineering & IT 2.5
Life Sciences & Biomedicine 4.5
Natural Sciences 4.7
Social Sciences 3.2

university houses national teaching centres for the arts and social sciences and for enterprise learning. Biology, physical science, maths and minority languages and area studies produced the highest satisfaction levels in the annual national student survey.

Research takes top priority in Sheffield's mission statement. An advanced manufacturing research centre has Boeing as the senior partner, which forms the hub of the new technology park. The university is the lead institution for systems engineering, smart materials and stem-cell technology in a research network of European, American and Chinese universities.

The intake is more diverse than at most leading UK universities — 83 per cent come from state schools or colleges — and one undergraduate in five comes from a working-class home. A lively social scene is based on the student union's extended facilities, which are considered among the best in Britain, but town–gown relations are much better and the crime rate lower than in most big cities.

International students are guaranteed university accommodation, most of which is within walking distance of lectures. The main halls of residence are being replaced by a £160 million student village in a phased program, which is due for completion in 2009. The university's own sports facilities have been extended recently. High-quality facilities were built by the city for the 1991 World Student Games and a £25-million regional centre for the English Institute of Sport opened in 2003.

People

Famous alumni range from pioneering aviator, Amy Johnson, to Britain's first astronaut, Helen Sharman. Nobel prize-winners include chemist Sir Harry Kroto and Richard Roberts, who took the 1993 prize for medicine. Successes in the arts include the playwright Jack Rosenthal and comedian Eddie Izzard, while business and politics are represented by former Home Secretary David Blunkett, and Penny Hughes, past president of Coca Cola.

What students say

Final-year Sri Lankan undergraduate Sajeev Jeganathan likes Sheffield so much that he hopes to find a job in the area when he completes his B Eng in Aerospace Engineering. He chose the university mainly because the broad-based nature of his course offered a variety of employment opportunities, but he would also like to take a masters degree there.

"I didn't want a big metropolitan city like London or Manchester," he says. "Sheffield is perfect for me – there is a good social life and the Peak District is really close if I want to get away. I lived in university accommodation for a year, but now I am in private accommodation close by."

Good at

Engineering and IT produced the top results in peer review by academics, with a top-100 finish in 2006. The life sciences, social sciences and the arts and humanities were all close to this mark as well.

69 Nanyang Technological University, Singapore

Why this university?

Nanyang Technological University (NTU) was founded in the last phase of colonial times in 1955 as Nanyang University. Like the National Union of Singapore, it went private on April 1 2006 but continues to receive government funding. Setting its goals very high, NTU aims, according to The Straits Times, to become "the MIT of the East".

The university occupies the Yunnan Garden campus designed by renowned Japanese architect Kenzo Tage close to the world-famous Jurong Bird Park in the west of the island. The 2-kilometre square setting is well served by the republic's reliable and extensive public transport system with both bus and Mass Rapid Transit links. Housing 13 schools and departments, including the incorporated National Institute of Education (NIE) and the Nanyang Business School, NTU can claim to have facilities of the highest physical quality right across the board, among them excellent libraries and laboratories.

Undergraduate registration figures are currently in the range of about 20,000 whilst faculty figures are a little under 1,500. Over 8,500 post-graduates are attached to the university.

Nanyang's leading role in technological innovation is widely known. For example, it was the first higher education institution in Southeast Asia to open a virtual reality theatre with its NTU Reality facility, which is

FACTFILE

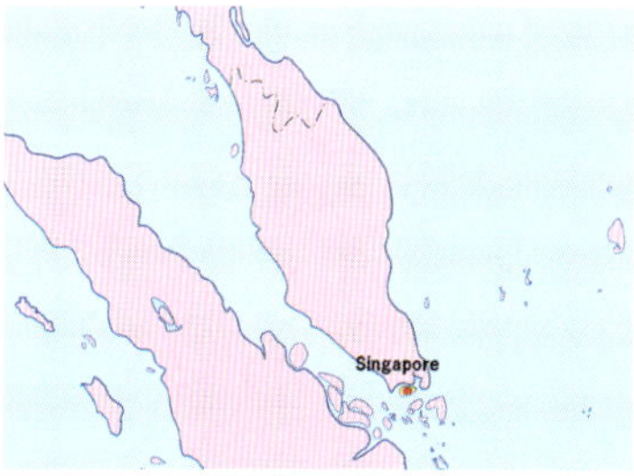

NANYANG Technological University

Country	Singapore
Foundation Year	1955
World Ranking	69 (61=)

Faculty Area Rankings

Arts & Humanities	263
Engineering & IT	25
Life Sciences & Biomedicine	102
Natural Sciences	99
Social Sciences	88

Survey Performance

Peer Review	74
Recruiter Review	106

Contact Details

Nanyang Avenue
Singapore
639798
www.ntu.edu.sg
+65 6791 1744

People

Student Faculty Ratio	15.1:1
International Faculty	49.0%
Undergraduates	19,427
Postgraduates	5,017
International Students	35.0%

Course Fees For Domestic Students

Average Undergraduate	$4,020

Course Fees For International Students

Average Undergraduate	$4,421

Overall Research Strength

Papers (Scopus 2002-2006)	60,523
Citations (Scopus 2002-2006)	148,684
Impact	2.5

Research Impact By Faculty Area

Engineering & IT	2.1
Life Sciences & Biomedicine	2.8
Natural Sciences	3.2
Social Sciences	1.9

a collaboration with SGI in the United States that highlights, amongst other things, research in biological and medical science, a field in which NTU prides itself. The university's Centre for Advanced Media Technology pursues leading-edge work in computer graphics and scientific visualization along with simulation and animation. The Reality Theatre is available to all NTU departments for teaching and research.

The Centre has been involved in a number of highly innovative projects that include the Augmented Reality Chinese Character Learning system, an example of next-generation technology. The university also plans to open a School of International Relations named after a prominent Singaporean Indian, S. Rajaratnam.

Amongst the 2006 graduates were pioneer batches in the biological sciences, a field in which NTU has invested heavily. Students, who include now a large contingent from other Asian countries, among them Vietnam, are housed in comfortable, unstressed facilities and have ample leisure and recreational facilities on offer.

People

Amongst the outstanding graduates of NTU is Adrian Yeo of the 2002 First Class honours pass from the School of Civil and Environmental Engineering who, on his own initiative, has been delivering potable water to villagers of the tsunami-stricken Indonesian province of Aceh through Water Initiative for Securing Health (WISH).

Indonesian Ardian Kristanto Poernomo, another alumnus, was the 2006 winner of the Google India Code Jam in Bangalore, India; this annual competition attracts over 14,000 contestants.

What students say

Nguyen Minh An, son of Vietnamese president Nguyen Minh Triet, joined the business school's Nanyang Fellows program, run in collaboration with MIT's Sloan School.

"It was great making friends with people from different cultures. That was a very meaningful experience for me. I attended classes and did research with experienced and devoted professors...and I was able to learn more about effective management skills."

Good at

NTU is ranked in the top 25 for engineering and IT, and is in the top 100 for both the social and natural sciences.

70 University of Nottingham

Why this university?

Nottingham University is a campus-based, research-led institution with a strong international presence and reputation. Traditionally one of the most popular universities among British students seeking places on undergraduate courses, the university also attracts a high volume of applications from overseas. There are now 24,000 home students and more than 6,000 international students from 130 different countries.

Three attractive campuses with award-winning buildings are all within easy reach of Nottingham city centre. The main 330-acre University Park campus is set around a lake with extensive greenery, and is regarded as one of the most attractive in the country. This campus is the focus of university life for most students, and includes 12 halls of residence, a conference and exhibition centre, sports facilities and an arts centre. Adjacent to University Park is Nottingham's medical school.

Jubilee campus, opened in 1999, houses the schools of education, computer science and information technology, and Nottingham's business school. A new research and innovation park is being developed here. Most biosciences students are based at Sutton Bonington campus, outside the city, which is also home to the university's new School of Veterinary Medicine and Science.

Nottingham offers overseas students a guarantee of university accommodation for the first two years of study, with over 6,000 rooms to choose from on or close to one of

FACTFILE

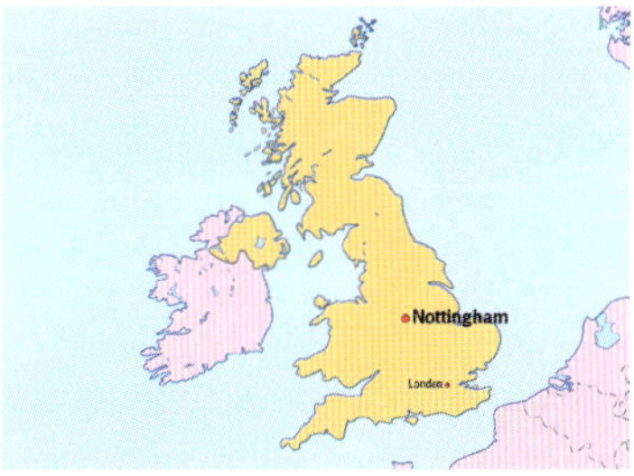

University of NOTTINGHAM

Country	United Kingdom
Foundation Year	1798
World Ranking	70 (85)

Faculty Area Rankings

Arts & Humanities	160
Engineering & IT	113
Life Sciences & Biomedicine	102
Natural Sciences	156
Social Sciences	115

Survey Performance

Peer Review	118
Recruiter Review	18

Contact Details

University Park
Nottingham
NG7 2RD
www.nottingham.ac.uk
+44 115 951 5151

People

Student Faculty Ratio	10.1:1
International Faculty	25.0%
Undergraduates	20,397
Postgraduates	4,988
International Students	21.0%

Course Fees For Domestic Students

Average Undergraduate	$6,150
Average Postgraduate	$7,575

Course Fees For International Students

Average Undergraduate	$17,382
Average Postgraduate	$17,884

Overall Research Strength

Papers (Scopus 2002-2006)	44,850
Citations (Scopus 2002-2006)	173,882
Impact	3.9

Research Impact By Faculty Area

Engineering & IT	2.5
Life Sciences & Biomedicine	4.4
Natural Sciences	4.9
Social Sciences	2.7

the university's campuses. Support for international students includes a foundation program, offered both in Nottingham and at the university's two overseas campuses, in China and Malaysia. English language tuition is provided on campus and online by a Centre for English Language Education. Meanwhile Nottingham's students' union, one of the largest in the UK, helps enrich campus social life with over 70 sports clubs and 130 societies.

Nottingham has 1,237 academic staff, including 432 professors. Its impressive academic track record, particularly in research, plays an equally important part in maintaining its international reputation. In the last Research Assessment Exercise, 26 of its departments were awarded world-class ratings, placing Nottingham in the top ten of UK institutions for research. In both teaching and research, the university is considered particularly excellent in healthcare, nanotechnology, transport engineering molecular biosciences, the built environment, philosophy, international relations and cultural studies.

People

Distinguished faculty include Nobel prize winners Sir Peter Mansfield in the field of cognitive behaviour and scanning and economist Sir Clive Granger. The novelist DH Lawrence is the most famous alumnus, but table-tennis champion Deng Yaping enjoys superstar status in her native China, while Dato Seri Najib Razak became deputy prime minister of Malaysia in 2004.

What students say

It was Nottingham's "tranquil" environment that first attracted and has impressed Julie Walabyeki, a Commonwealth Shared Scholarship Scheme scholar from Uganda who is taking a masters in public health at the university.

She said: "The university and its environment have lived up to my hopes and expectations. My course has been very intensive, but so good that I now want to do a PhD here. As a mature student, I have found the social scene at Nottingham very inclusive."

Good at

Biomedicine is the best-placed area in our rankings, just missing the top 50. The social sciences also do well.

Surprisingly, Nottingham is not in the top 100 in this year's peer review of our five subject areas. It only just missed the top 50 in the life sciences and biomedicine in 2006, when it was also 81st in the social sciences.

71= Dartmouth College

Why this university?

Dartmouth looks like a Hollywood vision of the quintessential New England university. But its size — smallest in the Ivy League, with 4,100 undergraduates and 1,600 graduate students — and picture-postcard campus shouldn't be mistaken for merely quaint.

Admission is among America's most competitive, with barely 15 per cent of applicants accepted. They can choose from some 1,600 courses in 29 departments and 10 interdisciplinary programs. They study under an unusual academic calendar divided into quarters with three vacation or leave terms and up to three terms of off-campus study during the typical run-up to an undergraduate degree. Nearly 60 per cent study abroad and more than 40 per cent are involved in research, which at Dartmouth totals US$200 million a year conducted in world-class laboratories that are benefitting as part of a US$1.3 billion renovation and expansion. (The rest of the money is going toward higher faculty salaries, more financial aid for students, and new studios, academic, and residential space.) The medical, business, and engineering schools — fourth-oldest medical school in America, first graduate school of management in the world, and first professional school of engineering in America, respectively — are considered among the best in the United States, and the university is one of the first to offer paid leave to male or female graduate students following the birth or adoption of a child.

FACTFILE

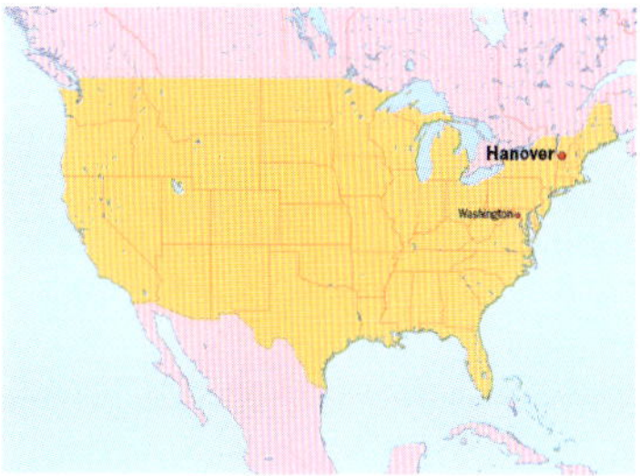

DARTMOUTH College

Country	United States
Foundation Year	1769
World Ranking	71= (61=)

Faculty Area Rankings

Arts & Humanities	139
Engineering & IT	299
Life Sciences & Biomedicine	98
Natural Sciences	251
Social Sciences	127

Survey Performance

Peer Review	161
Recruiter Review	68

Contact Details

Hanover
NH 03755
www.dartmouth.edu
+1 603 646 1110

People

Student Faculty Ratio	6.8:1
International Faculty	6.0%
Undergraduates	4,052
Postgraduates	1,604
International Students	11.0%

Course Fees For Domestic Students

Average Undergraduate	$33,501
Average Postgraduate	$33,342

Course Fees For International Students

Average Undergraduate	$33,501
Average Postgraduate	$33,342

Overall Research Strength

Papers (Scopus 2002-2006)	23,761
Citations (Scopus 2002-2006)	133,160
Impact	5.6

Research Impact By Faculty Area

Engineering & IT	3.0
Life Sciences & Biomedicine	6.4
Natural Sciences	5.0
Social Sciences	5.3

Scenic Dartmouth is also at the center of America's higher education culture wars. Home to a controversial conservative student newspaper bankrolled by leading American conservatives, it has become a lightning rod for debate about free speech and political correctness. The debate has spilled over into the ranks of alumni, who have fought over how the university's trustees are elected after several ideological conservatives won places on the governing board.

To unwind, students at Dartmouth (6.5 per cent of them are from countries outside the United States) famously party, in spite of the university's best efforts to curb social excess. Its Alpha Delta Phi fraternity was a model for the movie Animal House, and in a prank that has become a cult favorite on the website YouTube, prospective students and their parents on a campus tour are interrupted by a bell that triggers "drinking time." Students come running from all corners shouting, "Drinking time!" as the marching band appears behind a mascot modelled after a giant beer keg, all as the hapless tour guide tries to be heard above the din explaining that there's no more drinking at Dartmouth than at any other school.

People

Notable alumni include senator and statesman Daniel Webster, poet Robert Frost, and former Surgeon General C Everett Koop. In all, more than 160 Dartmouth graduates have served in the US Congress, and two on the Supreme Court. Alumni also serve or have served as the founders or heads of IBM, eBay, General Electric, NBC Television, Goldman Sachs, and the San Diego Padres baseball team.

What students say

The academic work is demanding, says Mitalee Patil, an undergraduate from India double-majoring in business and chemistry. "This is the hardest I've ever worked to get good grades. It is good preparation for dealing with the pressures of a job later on when you have deadlines and you're expected to meet them. But Ms. Patil said, "Anytime I looked lost and confused, someone would come over without my having to say anything and ask me if I needed help. There are always people tossing a Frisbee on the green. It has a very carefree atmosphere."

Good at

Dartmouth's small size does it no favours in global polling of academics. The life sciences and biomedicine account for its only top-100 finish in this year's rankings.

71= Uppsala University

Why This university?

Uppsala University, situated 40 miles north of Sweden's capital Stockholm, is the oldest university in Scandinavia, founded in 1477. With over 500 years heritage, the past weighs heavily at Uppsala and for most Swedes the university is as much associated with quaint traditions as teaching and research. For example, all Swedes don a peaked white cap when they graduate senior high school — a tradition which originated at Uppsala. But a prodigious, 40-place leap has seen Uppsala join the world's top 100 universities this year.

The university has nine faculties distributed over three so-called "disciplinary domains": Humanities and Social Sciences, Medicine and Pharmacy and Science and Technology. At present there are about 40,000 undergraduates enrolled on degree programs or short professional programs. There are about 2,400 doctoral students, many of whom receive generous stipends by other European standards. The university has a teaching staff of 3,800 out of a total of 6,000 employees. Of its annual turnover of around 4 billion SEK, approximately 60 per cent goes to graduate studies and research.

A recent research evaluation project undertaken on behalf of the university by 76 experts from 20 countries adjudged over 50 research projects at more than 20 of the university's departments to be "world leaders." Theoretical physics, surgery, and linguistics were amongst those areas singled out for special praise.

FACTFILE

UPPSALA University

Country....................Sweden
Foundation Year....................1477
World Ranking....................71= (111=)

Faculty Area Rankings

Arts & Humanities....................61
Engineering & IT....................150
Life Sciences & Biomedicine....................40
Natural Sciences....................113
Social Sciences....................102

Survey Performance

Peer Review....................61
Recruiter Review....................322

Contact Details

P.O. Box 256
Uppsala
751 05
www.uu.se
+46 18 471 00 00

People

Student Faculty Ratio....................8.1:1
International Faculty....................13.0%
Undergraduates....................22,274
Postgraduates....................1,930
International Students....................5.0%

Course Fees For Domestic Students

Average Undergraduate....................$0
Average Postgraduate....................$0

Course Fees For International Students

Average Undergraduate....................$0
Average Postgraduate....................$0

Overall Research Strength

Papers (Scopus 2002-2006)....................58,822
Citations (Scopus 2002-2006)....................284,179
Impact....................4.8

Research Impact By Faculty Area

Engineering & IT....................3.7
Life Sciences & Biomedicine....................5.0
Natural Sciences....................5.2
Social Sciences....................3.3

The picturesque university buildings are located around the historic centre of the city, close to the impressive cathedral. Recent expansion has also seen the university also occupy buildings in the south-west of the region.

Arguably the pearl in the university's crown is the university library with its extensive art and science collections. Known locally as "Carolina", the library's foremost treasure is the Silver Gothic Bible Codex Argenteus which was seized when the Swedes stormed Prague in 1648 and later donated to the university.

Student life in Uppsala is dominated by the nations. Students typically belong to one of thirteen nations, named after the provinces of Sweden. Originally this was a way of showing a student's origins. Nowadays students are free to join any nation including the Skånelandens nation which was established in the 1960s as a legal fiction to get around the compulsory membership for students who prefer not to become affiliated with the traditional nations.

In a bid to attract more international students the university has recently started offering Masters courses with teaching conducted in English. Sports play a very small role in the life of the university but music is very popular and the university has a long choral tradition.

People

Prominent alumni include eight Nobel laureates and notable scientists like botanist Carl Linnaeus (b 1707), astronomer Anders Celsius (b 1701) and founding father of physical chemistry Svante Auguust Arrhenius (b 1859). The French philosopher Michel Foucault also studied in Uppsala.

What students say

"Uppsala is a brilliant place to study," says Matthew Greig, an Australian currently studying Macro Economics. "The best thing about the university is the variety of nationalities. It's a way to really meet Swedish students as well as exchange students. The university provides a lot of information to help foreign students settle. The student website is full of tips and advice: www.uppsalastudentkar.nu"

Good at

Uppsala's top placing is 40th for the life sciences and biomedicine, while the arts and humanities only narrowly miss the top 60.

73 University of Illinois

Why this university?

More employees of the software megalith Microsoft have come from the University of Illinois than any other school, according to Microsoft founder Bill Gates — himself a Harvard dropout. The computer has a long association with this university. It was here that ILLIAC, the first computer created and owned by an educational institution, was developed. U of I's National Center for Supercomputing Applications created the browser on which Microsoft Internet Explorer is based and is at work today to build the world's fastest supercomputer, capable of performing one quadrillion calculations per second. This at a school that also is home to the world's largest virtual reality chamber at its Integrated Systems Laboratory. Its Beckman Institute for Advanced Science and Technology bypasses the traditional university hierarchy with interdisciplinary research into such things as biological intelligence and molecular and electronic nanostructures. In its Coordinated Science Laboratory, more than 450 researchers work on the development of infrastructure for information technology, including computing, communications, signal processing, and wireless transmission for applications ranging from home entertainment to disaster response. The Illinois Center for Cryptography and Information Protection is one of only four university-based cryptography centres in the world. The university also has one of the most highly regarded semiconductor and nanotechnology research facilities

FACTFILE

University of ILLINOIS

Country	United States
Foundation Year	1867
World Ranking	73 (77)

Faculty Area Rankings

Arts & Humanities	90
Engineering & IT	19
Life Sciences & Biomedicine	91
Natural Sciences	29
Social Sciences	56

Survey Performance

Peer Review	41
Recruiter Review	185

Contact Details

Box 5220
Chicago
Illinois
60680-5220
www.uillinois.edu
+1 312 996 4350

People

Student Faculty Ratio	17.9:1
International Faculty	8.0%
Undergraduates	46,644
Postgraduates	19,363
International Students	11.0%

Course Fees For Domestic Students

Average Undergraduate	$13,140
Average Postgraduate	$15,362

Overall Research Strength

Papers (Scopus 2002-2006)	156,256
Citations (Scopus 2002-2006)	702,413
Impact	4.5

Research Impact By Faculty Area

Engineering & IT	3.5
Life Sciences & Biomedicine	4.5
Natural Sciences	6.1
Social Sciences	3.4

in the United States, the Micro and Nanotechnology Laboratory. In all, U of I conducts just over half a billion dollars a year in research and holds 321 U.S. patents.

But this school on the plains of the agricultural Midwest isn't focused only on information technology. It's a principal partner in a US$500 million research institute backed by BP to study biofuels. Its academic library ranks third in size in the United States behind only Harvard's and Yale's. Its engineering library is the biggest in the country. U of I also has established a niche for itself in areas like the simulation of solid-propellant rockets in its Center for the Simulation of Advanced Rockets, set up in 1997. Its Food and Brand Lab, launched in 1992, studies why consumers buy what they buy and eat what they eat. And its Soybean Free Air Gas Concentration Enrichment program is studying the effects of atmospheric change on agriculture.

In addition to these fields, the university is highly ranked in accounting; civil, environmental, mechanical, electrical, and computer engineering; materials science; analytical science; kinesiology; and library and information sciences, including the new field of digital librarianship. Its 2,978 tenured professors include 11 Nobel laureates. (Alumni have won another 10 Nobels.)

U of I has 51, 081 undergraduate and 22,403 graduate students on its campus — more than 12 per cent from countries outside of the United States. A fifth live in fraternities and sororities in the largest Greek system in the world. Enrollment is expected to grow by another 70,000 by 2018 through an ambitious online education arm called Global Campus, despite criticism from faculty and others worried that the scheme will water down the university's reputation. Administrators have responded by agreeing to make the new division nonprofit with greater faculty input.

People

U of I alumni include Playboy magazine founder Hugh Hefner, actor Gene Hackman, director Ang Lee, architect Cesar Pelli, and the cofounders of YouTube, co-creators of Netscape, cofounders of Oracle, and inventors of the plasma display.

What students say

Hlaing Hlaing Win, a Malaysian undergraduate reading actuarial science, was drawn to the school after her older brother went there to study in the university's top-ranked accounting program. The location is the only down side, she said. Ms Win leaves often on the three-hour bus trip to Chicago (there is a train service, too, and an airport owned by the university, which is served by three commercial airlines), where her brother now lives and works. Also, she said, "the weather is too cold."

Good at

Illinois is in the top 100 in every area, with top 20 finishes in the arts and humanities and engineering and IT.

74= Emory University

Why this university?

A comparatively obscure regional school that didn't accept women until 1953 or blacks until 1962, Emory has rocketed to the top ranks of American universities. Rather than a liability, its location in the southern city of Atlanta — it was state segregation law that prohibited the school from admitting blacks until it successfully sued to reverse that policy — has become an asset as the city itself evolved into an economic powerhouse (it's home to Coca-Cola, CNN, Delta Airlines, and other major corporations). Emory was joined by neighbors including the U.S. Centers for Disease Control, the Yerkes National Primate Center (which the university runs for the National Institutes of Health), and the Carter Center, founded by former President Jimmy Carter to promote human rights around the world, with which it is a partner.

Of the US$354 million a year in research conducted at the university, US$320 million is in the health sciences, focusing on research areas including, among others, cancer, the neurosciences, immunity, cardiovascular and epithelial biology, and global health. Emory has added more than 300,000 square meters of space since the millennium for teaching, research, and healthcare, including medical science and neuroscience research buildings, a paediatrics building, a cancer institute, a vaccine research building, and a mathematics and science centre. A new medical education building is also under construction. The university plans to beef up its faculty of 3,200

FACTFILE

EMORY University

Country .... United States
Foundation Year 1836
World Ranking .... 74= (56)

Faculty Area Rankings

Arts & Humanities 95
Life Sciences & Biomedicine 51
Natural Sciences 269

Survey Performance

Peer Review 157
Recruiter Review 140

Contact Details

201 Dowman Drive
Atlanta
Georgia
30322
www.emory.edu
+1 404 727 6123

People

Student Faculty Ratio 5.2:1
International Faculty 1.0%
Undergraduates 7,136
Postgraduates 4,761
International Students 8.0%

Course Fees For Domestic Students

Average Undergraduate $32,100
Average Postgraduate $27,770

Overall Research Strength

Papers (Scopus 2002-2006) 61,228
Citations (Scopus 2002-2006) 392,139
Impact 6.4

Research Impact By Faculty Area

Engineering & IT 2.8
Life Sciences & Biomedicine 6.7
Natural Sciences 6.7
Social Sciences 4.9

and significantly increase financial aid to lure top students and plans to raise another US$3 billion to continue its expansion in Atlanta's tree-lined Druid Hills section.

There are 6,650 undergraduates and 5,700 graduate and professional students, including more than 2,000 international students and scholars. Emory claims to be the most ethnically and religiously diverse of America's top research universities.

Emory's research-intensive medical school received more than 60 applicants for every seat in one recent entering class. Its highly ranked School of Law is known for its work in child advocacy, human rights law, and environmental law, and encourages its graduates to go into lower-paying public service jobs through a tuition loan forgiveness program. And its Goizueta Business School is also top-rated, particularly for its undergraduate and Executive MBA programs.

One thing Emory does not have is an American football team, thanks to an early president who thought intercollegiate sports were evil (and, more to the point, too expensive).

People

Alumni include Alben Barkley, an American vice president; Lucius Quintus Cincinnatus Lamar, a U.S. Supreme Court justice; and astronaut Sonny Carter.

What students say

Yong Lee, an undergraduate from Indonesia, picked Emory over a smaller liberal arts school. Specializing in economics and international studies, he decided to go into public health.

"There's a lot of versatility in terms of the vast range of courses you can take," Mr. Lee said. "I had no idea what I wanted to study. I knew it was going to be business or the social sciences, but I was still up in the air, and Emory has both the liberal arts and the business programs."

Good at

Emory's best position is in the life sciences and biomedicine, where it is just outside the top 50. Emory is also in the top 100 for the arts and humanities.

74= University of York

Why this university?

Having established a worldwide reputation as a relatively small university focused on a limited range of subjects, York is now planning to grow by almost 50 per cent, adding a second campus and moving into new academic areas. The new site is adjacent to the original campus, on the outskirts of the ancient city of York, and will take its first students in 2009. Law, theatre, television and film studies will be the first subjects to be added, and the additional space will be used for research, teaching, student colleges, sport, cultural facilities and spin-out companies,

Although less than 50 years old, the university is a regular fixture near the top of domestic league tables, with a particularly good record in the UK's teaching quality assessments. Archaeology, economics, education, electrical and electronic engineering, biosciences, philosophy, physics, politics and psychology all achieved perfect scores. This is the first time that it has appeared in the top 100 of the World University Rankings, thanks partly to strong support from employers.

Computer science, psychology and English were rated internationally outstanding in the last Research assessment Exercise, when 18 of the 23 departments were placed in the top two of seven categories. Some new subjects have been added already: nursing and midwifery courses arrived with a nearby college of health studies, and medicine has been offered since 2003, in a joint initiative with Hull University. The medical

FACTFILE

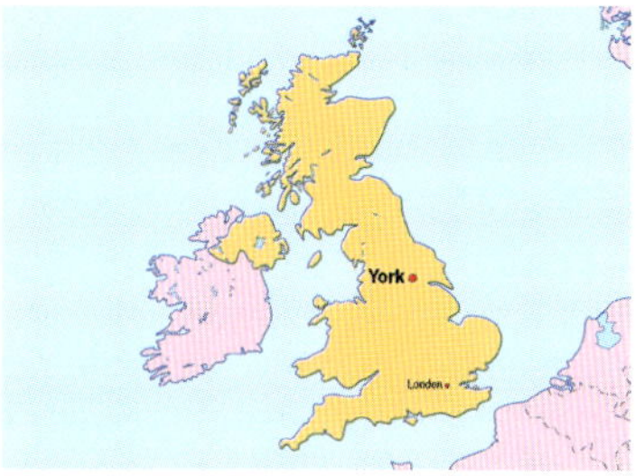

University of YORK

Country	United Kingdom
Foundation Year	1963
World Ranking	74= (124=)

Faculty Area Rankings

Arts & Humanities	70
Engineering & IT	249
Life Sciences & Biomedicine	146
Natural Sciences	242
Social Sciences	194

Survey Performance

Peer Review	148
Recruiter Review	60

Contact Details

Heslington
York
YO10 5DD
www.york.ac.uk
+44 1904 430 000

People

Student Faculty Ratio	8.5:1
International Faculty	21.0%
Undergraduates	7,802
Postgraduates	2,478
International Students	19.0%

Course Fees For Domestic Students

Average Undergraduate	$6,294
Average Postgraduate	$6,642

Course Fees For International Students

Average Undergraduate	$18,758
Average Postgraduate	$18,758

Overall Research Strength

Papers (Scopus 2002-2006)	22,880
Citations (Scopus 2002-2006)	98,807
Impact	4.3

Research Impact By Faculty Area

Engineering & IT	1.8
Life Sciences & Biomedicine	5.2
Natural Sciences	5.3
Social Sciences	3.0

school has a focus on learning in community settings.

There are nine applications to each place in most subjects, so entrance requirements are high. In 2006/7, only about one in seven of the 11,000 students were from overseas, including some 600 from other parts of the European Union. But York is a member of the Worldwide Universities Network of 16 research-led universities in Europe, North America, China and Australia. International students are guaranteed residential accommodation and most choose to live on campus.

York has been among the top performers in the UK's annual National Student Survey. Undergraduates in physics, biology, history, archaeology and psychology were the most satisfied in the latest survey. External audits have also been complimentary. Every student has a supervisor responsible for their academic and personal welfare.

The university is set in parkland, a mile from the picturesque city centre. Students join one of eight colleges, which mix academic and social roles. Most departments have their headquarters in one of the colleges, but the student community is a deliberate mixture of disciplines, years and sexes. Nursing apart, only archaeology and medieval studies are located off campus, sharing a medieval building in the centre of the city.

The city is famous for a high concentration of pubs, as well as for its historic sites. It is a favourite destination for tourists and has good transport links to the rest of the UK. The campus is the centre of social life for many students, but Leeds is within easy travelling distance for those looking for a livelier nightclub scene and more shopping.

People

Anibal Cavaco Silva, the President and former Prime Minister of Portugal, studied economics at York. Greg Dyke, former Director General of the BBC, took a politics degree and is now the university's Chancellor. Political figures include Harriet Harman, deputy leader of the Labour Party. The writer and critic Hermione Lee taught English for more than 20 years and the Marxist intellectual Alex Callinicos was Professor of Politics.

What do students say

Gong Lei, a Chinese postgraduate from Beijing, signed up for a second Masters course at York, in Computer Science, having completed one in English for speakers of other languages. She has been impressed by the level of supervision and finds the city welcoming. "I love York, which is like a small town compared with the big cities I am used to. That was one reason for staying on at the university."

Having been active in the university's Overseas Students Association, Gong Lei finds that many of her friends are from outside the UK. But clubs such as the Juggling Society bring her into contact with British students.

Good at

York is ranked 70th in the world for the arts and humanities. It has dropped out of the top 100 after a strong showing last year.

76 University of St Andrews

Why this university?

St Andrews is the oldest university in Scotland and the third-oldest in Britain, dating back to the early 15th century. Its ancient customs and enduring academic reputation have made it a favourite not just for Scottish students, but for the English and those from much farther afield — notably the United States. Almost a quarter of the intake is international, giving a cosmopolitan feel to this small, coastal community. The scenery is stunning — if windswept — and the academic standards high.

The already popular university received an extra boost while Prince William studied at St Andrews — applications shot up by 44 per cent. But its popularity has outlived the royal connection and the university is trading instead on good ratings, particularly from its own students. St Andrews was the best-liked conventional university in the last National Student Survey, which Scottish universities are not obliged to enter. The results have helped St Andrews become the top Scottish university in most UK league tables.

Students from the European Union (apart from the English, Welsh and Northern Irish) will pay no fees, under the Scottish Parliament's latest plans. Many others are visiting students on American exchange programs, while the remainder pay up to £11,000 a year for most subjects. They are guaranteed a place in university-owned residences, which accommodate more than half of all students.

St Andrews has the best teaching and research grades in Scotland.

FACTFILE

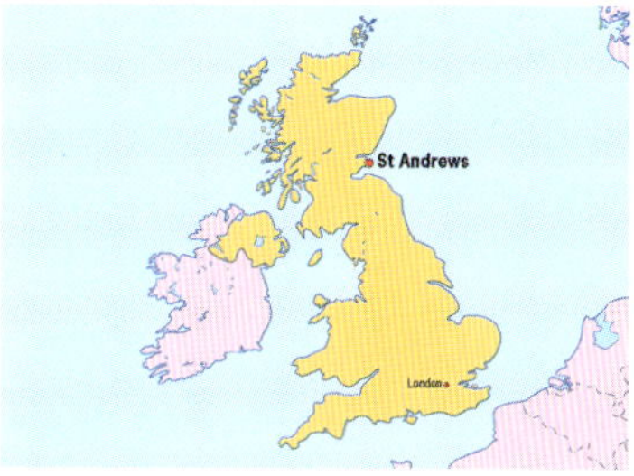

University of ST ANDREWS

Country	United Kingdom
Foundation Year	1413
World Ranking	76 (109=)

Faculty Area Rankings

Arts & Humanities	58
Engineering & IT	299
Life Sciences & Biomedicine	211
Natural Sciences	258
Social Sciences	235

Survey Performance

Peer Review	182
Recruiter Review	36

Contact Details

Fife
St Andrews
KY16 9AJ
www.st-andrews.ac.uk
+44 1334 476 161

People

Student Faculty Ratio	8.5:1
International Faculty	29.0%
Undergraduates	5,967
Postgraduates	1,161
International Students	31.0%

Course Fees For Domestic Students

Average Undergraduate	$3,557

Overall Research Strength

Papers (Scopus 2002-2006)	15,394
Citations (Scopus 2002-2006)	70,230
Impact	4.6

Research Impact By Faculty Area

Engineering & IT	2.6
Life Sciences & Biomedicine	4.5
Natural Sciences	5.7
Social Sciences	2.8

Every subject assessed has been rated either Excellent or Highly Satisfactory for teaching, demonstrating quality across the board. Psychology and English were the only starred research departments, but another 15 subjects were considered internationally excellent, putting the university into the UK top ten in terms of the average research grade per member of staff.

Although small, St Andrews offers a wide range of courses. The university's reputation has always rested primarily on the humanities, but a full range of physical sciences is taught, with sophisticated lasers and the largest optical telescope in Britain. New buildings for computer science and management opened in 2005.

The town of St Andrews is steeped in history, as well as being the centre of the golfing world. The university accounts for about a third of the 18,000 inhabitants. There are close relations between town and gown, both cultural and social. New students (known as "bejants" and "bejantines") are given third and fourth-year "parents" to ease them into university life, and on Raisin Monday give their academic guardians a bottle of wine in return for a receipt in Latin, which can be written on anything. Another unusual feature is that all humanities students are awarded an MA rather than a BA.

Many of the main buildings date from the 15th and 16th centuries, but sciences are taught at the modern North Haugh site a few streets away. Everything is within walking distance, but bicycles are common. Although apparently isolated, St Andrews is within easy reach of Dundee, with its regional airport and fast rail links.

People

As well as Prince William, the university's royal alumni included King James II of Scotland. More academic connections include Nobel prize-winners James Black and Alan McDiarmid, as well as John Napier, the inventor of logarithms. Political luminaries include Alex Salmond, First Minister of Scotland and leader of the Scottish National Party.

Good at

Arts and humanities, for which academics place St Andrews 58th in the world. The university is not close to the top 100 in the other academic fields.

77= University of Pittsburgh

Why this university?

One of America's oldest universities, the University of Pittsburgh was founded in 1797 in a log cabin on what was then the American frontier, well before many white people lived that far west. Since then, the university has continued pushing boundaries. The polio vaccine was developed there. A Pitt researcher was the first to identify the chemical structure of Vitamin C. It was at Pitt that the world's first double-transplant operation was performed, and surgeons there continue to carry out more organ transplants than at any other institution.

Pitt is still at the cutting edge. The number of applicants for places among the 17,000 undergraduates (there are also 9,000 graduate students) has doubled since the millennium, sending the quality of incoming freshmen at the university soaring. A US$500 million fund-raising campaign has proven so successful that administrators doubled the goal to US$1 billion and then doubled it again to US$2 billion, which will be used to add faculty and increase student financial aid, among other things. The university's supercomputing center operates one of the fastest non-military supercomputers in the world. Pitt was quick to carve out a particular niche for itself after the September 11, 2001 terrorist attacks by making global security a research priority. And it has vastly expanded its campus, including with a new state-of-the-art stadium it shares with the Pittsburgh Steelers professional football team.

The university conducts US$600

FACTFILE

University of PITTSBURGH

Country	United States
Foundation Year	1787
World Ranking	77= (88)

Faculty Area Rankings

Arts & Humanities	83
Engineering & IT	188
Life Sciences & Biomedicine	124
Social Sciences	176

Survey Performance

Peer Review	145
Recruiter Review	270

Contact Details

Pittsburgh
PA 15260
www.pitt.edu
+1 412 624 4141

People

Student Faculty Ratio	6.4:1
International Faculty	22.0%
Undergraduates	16,152
Postgraduates	7,866
International Students	8.0%

Course Fees For Domestic Students

Average Undergraduate	$24,000

Overall Research Strength

Papers (Scopus 2002-2006)	119,795
Citations (Scopus 2002-2006)	669,179
Impact	5.6

Research Impact By Faculty Area

Engineering & IT	2.6
Life Sciences & Biomedicine	5.8
Natural Sciences	8.0
Social Sciences	4.5

million annually in research in such trendy fields as nanotechnology, aging, biotechnology, and computer modeling. Highly regarded for drug discovery, Pitt is creating a chemical library, one of two in the country, where an inventory of chemical compounds will be stored that can be used in drug development. Like many other universities, it has added a program in the emerging field of nanoscience. And in collaboration with neighboring Carnegie Mellon University, it is investing $600 million to boost the biotechnology industry in this resurgent one-time steel town in southwestern Pennsylvania.

Pitt is aggressively undertaking academic research in the hottest topic of all — security — at its Center for National Preparedness and Matthew B. Ridgway Center for International Security, named for a Korean War-era American general.

Faculty and students specializing in public and international affairs, public health, law, medicine, and information sciences are researching such topics as bioterrorism and cyber security. Pitt lured the Center for Biosecurity away from Johns Hopkins University to be part of this effort. And Pitt researchers are already developing a system to provide quick detection of disease outbreaks by sounding an alert when there are spikes in hospital emergency visits related to a specific complaint. Within minutes of the terrorist attacks on New York and Washington, a law professor was keeping track online of the legal implications of the changed world order, and continues to monitor the balance between public security and personal rights, not only in the United States but in other countries.

About 5 per cent of Pitt's students (there are 3,800 faculty) come from other countries, mainly China, India, South Korea, Taiwan, and Turkey. It offers an unusual "certificate in global studies" for students who can select from concentrations including global health, international conflict and conflict resolution, and sustainable development.

People

Alumni include Gene Kelly, authors John Irving and August Wilson, Jaguar Cars Managing Director Bibiana Boerio, and Orient Overseas Container Line founder and owner Dong Haoyun.

What students say

Justin Chalker, a newly minted graduate who went on to Oxford to study organic chemistry on a Rhodes scholarship, chose Pitt because, he said, "they give you the freedom to pursue any interest you might have. If you're a motivated undergraduate, you're treated like a graduate student. Yet while I was focused on science for my degree, I was also able to take a lot of excellent liberal arts courses."

Good at

The arts and humanities provide Pittsburgh's only top-100 finish, as they did in 2006.

77= Purdue University

Why this university?

In late 2001, when other US universities were reigning in spending and enrollments in the slowdown that followed the terrorist attacks of that year, Purdue made a strategic decision to do the opposite.

The campus of the midwestern school, so vast it has two golf courses and one of America's only university-owned airports, erupted in a flurry of new construction. Purdue went on an US$800 million building spree, adding, among other things, a bioscience centre and a nanotechnology centre that was recognized as one of the nation's best almost as soon as it opened. A US$126 million interdisciplinary research area called Discovery Park rose from the bluffs above the Wabash River.

With 2,507 faculty to teach its 31,000 undergraduate and 7,000 graduate students — fewer than its rival institutions — Purdue went on a hiring spree, too, adding 300 new faculty in five years, many of them women and minorities. Faculty salaries were raised, class sizes were lowered, and the proportion of classes taught by faculty rather than by graduate teaching assistants was increased.

Purdue had already racked up an impressive collection of superlatives. Corporate recruiters rank it fourth in the quality of its engineering grads; its divisions of industrial, nuclear, and aeronautical and astronautical engineering are particularly highly ranked.

Its College of Technology is the largest producer of engineering technology

FACTFILE

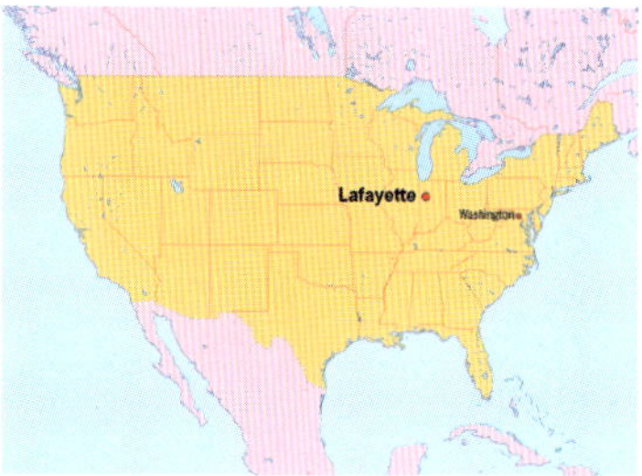

PURDUE University

Country .... United States
Foundation Year 1869
World Ranking .... 77= (127)

Faculty Area Rankings

Arts & Humanities 208
Engineering & IT 24
Life Sciences & Biomedicine 57
Natural Sciences 51
Social Sciences 130

Survey Performance

Peer Review 57
Recruiter Review 118

Contact Details

1080 Schleman Hall
West Lafayette
IN 47907-1080
www.purdue.edu
+1 765 494 4600

People

Student Faculty Ratio 20:1
International Faculty 21.0%
Undergraduates 31,266
Postgraduates 6,774
International Students 14.0%

Course Fees For Domestic Students

Average Undergraduate $6,092
Average Postgraduate $6,092

Course Fees For International Students

Average Undergraduate $18,700
Average Postgraduate $18,700

Overall Research Strength

Papers (Scopus 2002-2006) 74,150
Citations (Scopus 2002-2006) 283,151
Impact 3.8

Research Impact By Faculty Area

Engineering & IT 2.7
Life Sciences & Biomedicine 4.4
Natural Sciences 5.4
Social Sciences 2.6

undergraduate degrees among public institutions in the US. Its analytical chemistry, hospitality and tourism, and undergraduate landscape and architecture design programs are also at the top of their fields.

Purdue was the first university in the United States to establish a department of computer science, in 1962. Under its Engineering Projects in Community Service program, undergraduates use engineering and technology to solve problems for community service and educational organizations. And the university's Online Writing Lab (owl.english.purdue.edu) answers grammar and punctuation problems for more than 20 million users annually.

The university plans to increase graduate enrollment and graduate assistant stipends. It is particularly competitive in the number of international students on its campus. There are nearly 5,000 of them, from 128 countries, the second largest number in America; the biggest contingents are Indians, South Koreans, and Chinese.

People

Purdue has turned out 22 American astronauts—including Neil Armstrong, the first man to walk on the moon, and Gene Cernan, the last—more than any non-military institution outside of MIT.

What students say

Himabindu Pucha had some apprehension about going to school in West Lafayette, Indiana, about an hour from Indianapolis and two hours from Chicago ("the location does work against it, but you can't have it all," she said). But since she accepted the offer to come to Purdue, she was named one of 19 recipients of a US$10,000 national award recognizing outstanding women in engineering. She is now a doctoral student there and has done a research internship at Intel. Purdue leads the nation in the number of women engineering graduates.

"I was a little bit scared about the social environment," Ms Pucha said. "I didn't know how I would fit in. But Purdue has so many grad students and they come from so many places that I feel perfectly comfortable here."

Good at

Engineering and IT, where Purdue is in the top 25. Also close to the top 50 for natural sciences and for the life sciences and biomedicine.

79 University of Maryland

Why this university?

Maryland has a big advantage over other major public US research universities: it's close to Washington, DC, insatiable consumer of research and source of funding for it. The campus is the site of a new US$12 million government center to study what motivates terrorism and how terrorists recruit conscripts and pick targets. It leads a nationwide research program to study and control avian influenza. As the demand for Arabic speakers has skyrocketed, it has expanded its Arabic program from fewer than 30 students to more than 200. It has partnerships with or funding from government agencies including NASA, the National Security Agency, the Department of Defense, and the Department of Homeland Security. In all, Maryland conducts US$400 million a year in research, on its way to a goal of US$450 million annually.

The location of the campus wasn't always an asset. During the American Civil War, 6,000 Union troops defending Washington camped there and tore down fences for firewood. After they left, 400 confederates preparing to attack the capital arrived and were warmly welcomed. By the end of the war, the school was bankrupt.

Today's university is a vastly different place than that shaky agricultural college. Already the only public research university on the East Coast with programs in computer science, mathematics, physical science, and engineering all ranked in the top 20, it's raising US$1 billion for student aid, additional faculty, and facilities

FACTFILE

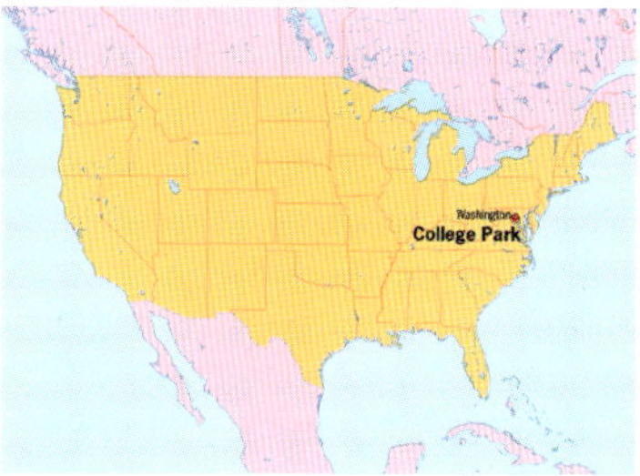

University of MARYLAND

Country	United States
Foundation Year	1856
World Ranking	79 (111=)

Faculty Area Rankings

Engineering & IT	73
Life Sciences & Biomedicine	135
Natural Sciences	59
Social Sciences	124

Survey Performance

Peer Review	110
Recruiter Review	191

Contact Details

College Park
MD 20742
www.umd.edu
+1 301 405 1000

People

Student Faculty Ratio	9.2:1
International Faculty	12.0%
Undergraduates	23,639
Postgraduates	6,192
International Students	9.0%

Course Fees For Domestic Students

Average Undergraduate	$7,906

Course Fees For International Students

Average Undergraduate	$21,345

Overall Research Strength

Papers (Scopus 2002-2006)	124,778
Citations (Scopus 2002-2006)	584,232
Impact	4.7

Research Impact By Faculty Area

Engineering & IT	3.0
Life Sciences & Biomedicine	4.9
Natural Sciences	6.1
Social Sciences	3.9

including a new bioscience research building, a new wing for the Smith School of Business, and a new home for the journalism program.

Maryland is a big place — there are 25,900 undergraduates and 10,200 graduate students, taught by 3,752 faculty — and, with an 18:1 student-faculty ratio, class sizes are large. But there are programs through which students can choose more personal attention. A division of the honors program, for example, gathers undergraduates from different disciplines to live and work together on a four-year research project, which they defend in front of a panel of experts in their final year. The College Park Scholars program places incoming students with classmates who have similar interests. In the language-immersion dormitory, students are encouraged to speak at all times in any of eight languages including Russian, French, and Spanish — but not English.

Students blow off steam watching intercollegiate athletics, at which Maryland excels, with 27 teams in the top division and as many as four national championships in a single year. Despite pressure to improve student-athlete graduation rates in the United States, student athletes at Maryland are less successful in the classroom than on the court or field. The university's basketball team in one year, for example, had no players graduate.

People

Prominent alumni have included many well-known American journalists, 2002 Nobel prize in physics winner Raymond Davis Jr., 1985 Nobel prize in chemistry winner Herbert Hauptman, NASA administrator Michael Griffin, and Muppets creator Jim Henson, of whom there is a statue on the campus. The faculty also has included four Nobel laureates.

What students say

A doctoral student specializing in supermolecular chemistry, Soumyadip Ghosh was drawn to Maryland from his native India by the standout faculty. One, Lyle Isaacs, "is one of the key players among the young generation of scientists in that area," Mr. Ghosh said. Also, he said, "The facilities that I needed to pursue my research, I have those facilities," including high-powered nuclear magnetic resonance spectrometers. "My friends in other universities, if I compare with them, I have all the facilities, I have unlimited time, and funding-wise I'm doing fine."

As a teaching assistant, Mr Ghosh said he had experienced some of Maryland's large undergraduate classes. "It depends on the section — there are large sections, small sections — but definitely there are many sections as large as 400 students. But there are 10 or 12 Tas in those classes, so you can still talk to every student, and the students are divided into smaller groups." Being close to Washington also is an advantage, he said. Not only are prestigious experts in his field nearby, but "We are near DC so we are always in touch with NIH and other big institutions, and we can communicate with them pretty easily."

Good at

Maryland's star fields are the natural sciences and engineering and IT, both of which are in the top 75 in our rankings.

80= University of Leeds

Why this university?

Only one university in the UK is more popular than Leeds, judged on the number of applications made from all over the world. More than 100 nationalities are represented among the 31,000 students, 5,000 of whom are from overseas. In addition, Leeds has links with 600 institutions outside the UK, partly through a 'worldwide network' which brings together four American and four British universities to collaborate initially on research and postgraduate degree programs. A thriving European program involves more than 100 continental partners, with students travelling in both directions.

The university is based in a conservation area, within walking distance of the city centre. The buildings are a mixture of Victorian and modern, with more being added each year as part of a £200 million building program. Student facilities are generally first rate: the 8,000 computer workstations are among the most at any British university and the library one of the biggest.

Almost 20 per cent of the students are postgraduates. Undergraduates take modular courses, enabling them to take full advantage of a growing range of interdisciplinary degrees. Almost a quarter of them now take dual honours or combinations of subjects. The university houses a national centre of excellence in interdisciplinary teaching and another in assessment and learning in medical practice settings.

Electrical and mechanical engineering,

FACTFILE

University of LEEDS

Country	United Kingdom
Foundation Year	1831
World Ranking	80= (121)

Faculty Area Rankings

Arts & Humanities	76
Engineering & IT	130
Life Sciences & Biomedicine	122
Natural Sciences	138
Social Sciences	128

Survey Performance

Peer Review	102
Recruiter Review	27

Contact Details

Leeds
LS2 9JT
www.leeds.ac.uk
+44 113 243 1751

People

Student Faculty Ratio	11.3:1
International Faculty	21.0%
Undergraduates	22,980
Postgraduates	4,972
International Students	13.0%

Course Fees For Domestic Students

Average Undergraduate	$6,294
Average Postgraduate	$6,642

Course Fees For International Students

Average Undergraduate	$19,867
Average Postgraduate	$18,680

Overall Research Strength

Papers (Scopus 2002-2006)	45,492
Citations (Scopus 2002-2006)	203,241
Impact	4.5

Research Impact By Faculty Area

Engineering & IT	2.6
Life Sciences & Biomedicine	5.6
Natural Sciences	5.1
Social Sciences	2.3

English, food science, Italian and town planning were all rated internationally outstanding for research in 2001. Teaching ratings were generally good, with education, philosophy, physics and healthcare studies achieving the best results. Ratings in the annual national student satisfaction survey have been improving, with medicine and pharmacy, English, history and archaeology producing the best scores in 2006.

Nearly a quarter of the British undergraduates come from independent schools, and there is a low proportion of working-class students — less than one in five. Students from outside the European Union and all those on exchange programs are guaranteed university accommodation throughout their course. An international office provides advice on all students' questions and organizes regular social events.

The already large students' union, famous for its long bar and big-name rock concerts, has been extended to cope with the latest phase in the university's expansion. A £4.5-million upgrade has provided a new entertainment venue, more shops and catering facilities. Town–gown relations are generally good. Leeds is a thriving city, with a lively nightlife and good shopping facilities. Many large organizations have a regional base in the city, which has allowed it to remain more prosperous than much of the north of England. Transport links are good and Yorkshire contains plenty of unspoilt countryside to explore.

People

Dame Kathleen Lonsdale, the first woman to be elected to the Royal Society: and Arthur Ransome, author of Swallows and Amazons attended Leeds. JR Tolkein taught English before writing Lord of the Rings, while EP Thompson, the social theorist and anti-nuclear campaigner, was on the extra-mural staff. Jack Straw, the Justice Secretary, was president of the students' union.

What students say

Tajudeen Ahmed, a mature student from Nigeria, who is taking an MBA, likes the cosmopolitan nature of the university and the city. He chose Leeds on the advice of academics and after comparing the value for money offered by the university's MBA with those elsewhere in the UK. "Coming from a society where the lecturer is everything in terms of program delivery, I found the very interactive class and seminar sessions revealing and ultimately rewarding," he said.

He was particularly impressed with the university's careers centre. "With its one-on-one, tailor-made meetings and several career presentations from diverse recruiters, I have fully discovered a 'new me' in terms of where the future lies once I have completed my MBA."

Good at

Arts and humanities, where academics place Leeds 76th in the world. The university is also close to the top 100 in social sciences. Natural sciences, engineering and IT achieved the next-best scores.

80= University of Southampton

Why this university?

Southampton enters the top 100 in the World University Rankings after one of the biggest rises of any university this year. A member of the Russell Group of leading UK research universities, Southampton has appeared regularly towards the top of domestic league tables and its rise reflects a growing international reputation.

Almost 10 per cent of the university's 20,000 students come from outside the UK, and it is making strenuous efforts to increase their numbers. The website has an introduction to the university in 21 languages and more than 100 nationalities are represented among the student body. Southampton is also a member of the Worldwide Universities Network of 16 research-led institutions in Europe, North America, Australia and China.

Southampton celebrated its 55th anniversary in 2007 and has expanded considerably in recent years, opening two new campuses and acquiring two others in college mergers. Its 2001 research grades were among the top ten in Britain, with the number of subjects rated internationally outstanding rising from two to eight. Uniquely among UK universities, the list included all branches of engineering, as well as physics, computer science, European studies, law and music. The proportion of income derived from research at Southampton is among the highest in Britain.

Student satisfaction rates are high, especially in law, English, modern languages, physics and history, which achieved the university's best scores

FACTFILE

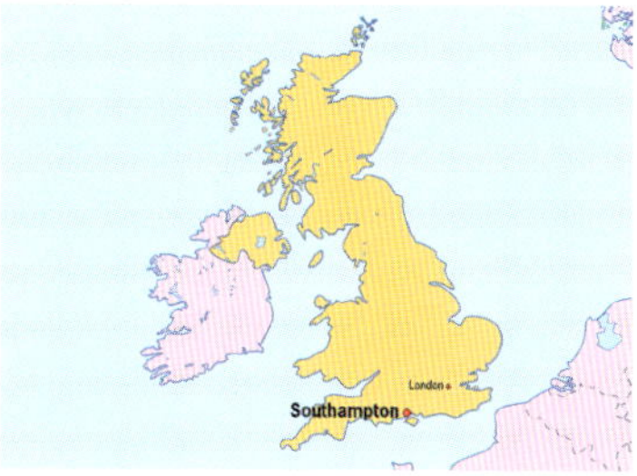

University of SOUTHAMPTON

Country	United Kingdom
Foundation Year	1862
World Ranking	80= (141=)

Faculty Area Rankings

Arts & Humanities	151
Engineering & IT	96
Life Sciences & Biomedicine	204
Natural Sciences	155
Social Sciences	266

Survey Performance

Peer Review	159
Recruiter Review	67

Contact Details

University Road
Southampton
SO17 1BJ
www.soton.ac.uk
+44 23 8059 5000

People

Student Faculty Ratio	9.2:1
International Faculty	27.0%
Undergraduates	14,032
Postgraduates	4,989
International Students	16.0%

Course Fees For International Students

Average Undergraduate	$6,294

Overall Research Strength

Papers (Scopus 2002-2006)	52,025
Citations (Scopus 2002-2006)	234,600
Impact	4.5

Research Impact By Faculty Area

Engineering & IT	2.6
Life Sciences & Biomedicine	5.5
Natural Sciences	5.5
Social Sciences	3.3

in the latest National Student Survey. Students in the highly-regarded medical school were the most satisfied in England.

The main Highfield campus, in a leafy location two miles from the city centre, has been the focus of recent development to cater for the expansion in numbers. A new student services centre provides learning support and other advisory facilities – all of which are backed up online for students in other areas of the university. The Waterside Campus, in the city's dock area, houses the National Oceanography Centre, Southampton. A £49-million joint project with the Natural Environment Research Council, it is considered Europe's finest, encompassing teaching, research and knowledge transfer facilities. Art courses are based in Winchester, 12 miles north of Southampton.

Social facilities for students have been expanded and refurbished, while sports facilities were upgraded, with the addition of an indoor sports complex and swimming pool next to the students' union and further development of the outdoor facilities. Overseas students are guaranteed a place in the university's large stock of residential accommodation, much of which has been renovated recently.

Southampton is a pleasant, if architecturally undistinguished city, on the south coast of England, little more than an hour's travelling time from London. The university's location has also encouraged strong links with Europe: France is quickly accessible by sea or air. Southampton has all the normal facilities expected in a medium-sized city and is close to unspoilt countryside and the beaches of the south coast.

People

John Denham, the UK's first Secretary of State for Innovation, Universities and Skills, was president of the students' union. Lord Plant of Highfield was Professor of European Political Thought before becoming Master of St Catherine's College, Oxford. Singer/songwriter Brian Eno studied art at Winchester, while Professor Astrid Fischel Volio, former Vice-President of Costa Rica, was one of many overseas students to make a mark after completing a Southampton degree.

What students say

Jose Beltran, a Mexican postgraduate studying environmental management and modelling, said: "This is my first experience overseas, and I'm glad that I came to Southampton. I find it has better weather than I expected and the university has a friendly and secure environment, with staff willing to help you, an excellent academic level, and approachable professors. In the masters course on which I am enrolled, I have the opportunity to live with 27 students from all over the world, and I mean 'to live with' because we live in the student halls, sharing the same building and even the kitchen in small groups of seven people. This unique experience creates the opportunity to learn beyond the lectures, to appreciate different cultures and to build friendships for the future."

Good at

Engineering and IT is the only area in which Southampton reaches the top 100 in our rankings. But oceanography is the jewel in the crown of the university's research.

82 Vanderbilt University

Why this university?

Since the millennium, Vanderbilt has led the country in the rate of increase of research funding it receives, which is approaching nearly half a billion dollars annually. The number of undergraduate applications is up more than 60 per cent during the same period of time. There are 6,378 undergraduate and 5,229 graduate students at Vanderbilt, taught by 2,700 faculty.

More than US$700 million worth of new facilities have been completed or are under construction. And while Gordon Gee, the chancellor who is credited with leading Vanderbilt to this success, has left to return to his former job as president of Ohio State University, he first helped raise nearly US$2 billion for its continued growth.

Built after the American Civil War by northern railroad tycoon Cornelius Vanderbilt for students in the South, Vanderbilt has a distinctive southern flavor. The campus itself is a designated arboretum, with more than 300 varieties of shrubs and trees, including stately magnolias framing buildings that date to the university's founding in 1873. But the bucolic campus in the laid-back southern music capital of Nashville should not be mistaken for an academic backwater. Vanderbilt's PhD program in pharmacology is rated by the National Research Council as one of the best in the nation, and its pharmacology faculty is the most cited in the world. The research council's survey of graduate programs also rates Vanderbilt's religion department as among the best. Its W.M. Keck Free-

FACTFILE

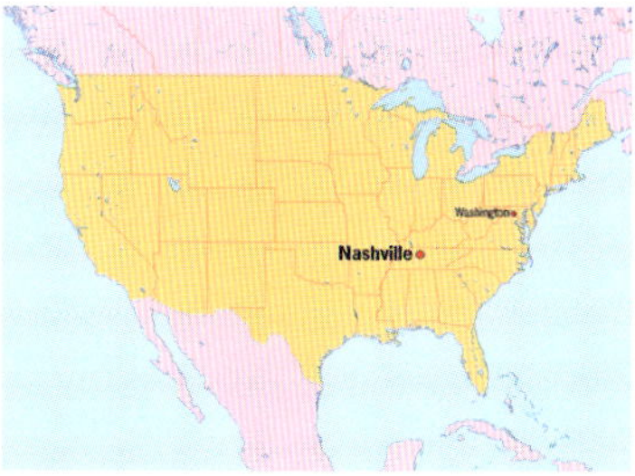

VANDERBILT University

Country	United States
Foundation Year	1873
World Ranking	82 (53)

Faculty Area Rankings

Arts & Humanities	289
Life Sciences & Biomedicine	66
Natural Sciences	224
Social Sciences	166

Survey Performance

Peer Review	192
Recruiter Review	108

Contact Details

2201 West End Avenue
Nashville
TN 37240
www.vanderbilt.edu
+1 615 322 7311

People

Student Faculty Ratio	4.8:1
International Faculty	6.0%
Undergraduates	6,329
Postgraduates	4,802
International Students	9.0%

Course Fees For Domestic Students

Average Undergraduate	$1,359
Average Postgraduate	$1,359

Course Fees For International Students

Average Undergraduate	$1,359
Average Postgraduate	$1,359

Overall Research Strength

Papers (Scopus 2002-2006)	69,346
Citations (Scopus 2002-2006)	446,619
Impact	6.4

Research Impact By Faculty Area

Engineering & IT	2.8
Life Sciences & Biomedicine	6.8
Natural Sciences	8.9
Social Sciences	3.7

Electron Laser is one of only four at a U.S. university. And its research in chemical biology helped breed a blue rose, long sought by horticulturalists.

Among the new facilities at Vanderbilt are the US$61 million Center for Otolaryngology and Communications Sciences, which houses the nation's top program in audiology. The engineering school just moved into a new US$28 million building with 50 teaching and research laboratories arrayed around a three-story atrium. The law school has undergone a US$23.5 million renovation and expansion. The Owen Graduate School of Management is also considered one of the best at a private US university.

People

Six faculty and alumni have won the Nobel prize, including alumnus and former Vice President Al Gore, whose wife, Tipper, also went to Vanderbilt. Other alumni include presidential candidates Fred Thompson and Ross Perot; the chairman and CEO of Time Incorporated; the president of USAir; the former chairman of Credit Suisse First Boston; and Muhammad Yunus, economist and founder of the Grameen Bank Bangladesh; author James Patterson; poet Robert Penn Warren; model Molly Sims; and singers Amy Grant, Rosanne Cash, Marshall Chapman, and Amy Ray of the Indigo Girls.

What students say

"The park-like setting is one of the things that drew me to Vanderbilt," said Ethel Neo, an undergraduate from Singapore. "I'm a person who just loves to sit under a tree and read a book. And Vanderbilt is perfect for that kind of thing. People are always sitting on benches and on the grass relaxing." Inside the classroom, Ms. Neo said, "My professors have become mentors to me. They've given me direction for my future."

Ms. Neo is also a fan of Nashville, a city of about 575,000 with a considerably slower pace of life than Singapore, New York, or London. "It's a small city and not crowded or crazy like New York or London. And for a college student, there are lots of cafés with great live music." Inevitably much of that music is of the genre for which the city is renowned. But as Ms. Neo puts it, "Even country music is growing on me."

Good at

The life sciences and biomedicine provide Vanderbilt's only top-100 finish, where the university is ranked 66th in the world.

83 University of Glasgow

Why this university?

Glasgow, founded in 1451, has one of the largest research bases in the UK, with more than 3,400 researchers across nine faculties. The money they raise in new research grants and contracts now passes the £100 million a year mark.

The most recent Research Assessment Exercise reported that 96 per cent of staff worked in subject areas producing international quality research. Glasgow won elite 5* ratings for English language and literature, European studies, psychology, sport-related subjects, and the infection and immunity grouping in clinical laboratory sciences, and the top research quality rating for 24 subjects, including history, physics and religious studies.

Glasgow is involved in Scotland's research pooling initiatives to bring together researchers from different universities, but for almost a decade, it has had a "Synergy" partnership with neighbouring Strathclyde University. This has created some 200 active collaborations, including a full merger of Strathclyde's department of ship and marine technology and Glasgow's department of naval architecture and ocean engineering, which Glasgow calculates has raised more than £20 million of extra funding.

The university currently has approaching 6,000 staff, almost 300 of whom are from overseas. It has just under 20,000 students, 15,500 of them undergraduates, and almost 3,000 from overseas. By 2010, it aims to have a "truly diverse student community," with an increasing

FACTFILE

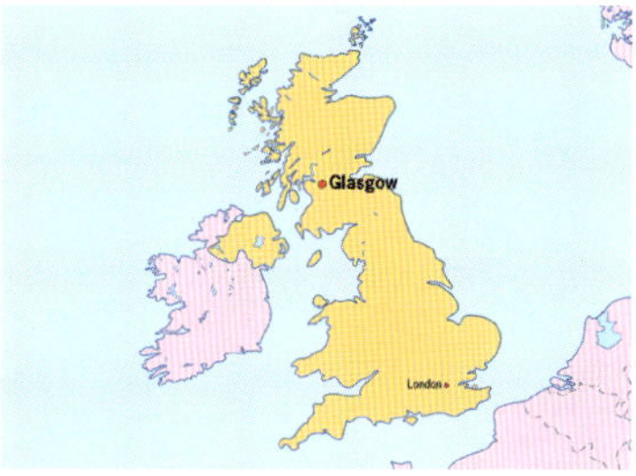

University of GLASGOW

Country .... United Kingdom
Foundation Year 1451
World Ranking 83 (81)

Faculty Area Rankings

Arts & Humanities 160
Engineering & IT 138
Life Sciences & Biomedicine 60
Natural Sciences 143
Social Sciences 166

Survey Performance

Peer Review 116
Recruiter Review 96

Contact Details

University Avenue
Glasgow
G12 8QQ
www.gla.ac.uk
+44 141 330 2000

People

Student Faculty Ratio 9.2:1
International Faculty 10.0%
Undergraduates 15,311
Postgraduates 3,462
International Students 11.0%

Course Fees For Domestic Students

Average Undergraduate $3,557

Overall Research Strength

Papers (Scopus 2002-2006) 43,673
Citations (Scopus 2002-2006) 213,267
Impact 4.9

Research Impact By Faculty Area

Engineering & IT 2.5
Life Sciences & Biomedicine 5.4
Natural Sciences 5.9
Social Sciences 3.8

proportion of both international and postgraduate students.

Glasgow has always attracted a high proportion of undergraduates from the surrounding area, and was the first of Scotland's four ancient universities to start widening access. Some 20 years ago, it launched a scheme to bring in pupils from deprived areas with non-traditional entrance qualifications.

In 2004, the university won the grading of Broad Confidence, the highest expression of satisfaction, for its teaching. Its medical faculty has been a pioneer of new teaching methods, establishing an undergraduate curriculum around problem-based learning. This introduces all medical students to clinical work from the very beginning of their education. In 1999, Glasgow faculty of veterinary medicine became only the third European school to win approved status from the American Veterinary Medical Association. It has been raising funds for a small animal hospital, not only improving care, but creating innovation, teaching and learning techniques.

The city's skyline is dominated by the university's neo-Gothic main building, but it spends around £30 million annually on building projects, and is committed to cutting energy costs and environmental pollution in the process. Its newest buildings are at the forefront of sustainable construction.

People

Glasgow has a distinguished roll of scholars, including physicist Lord Kelvin and economist Adam Smith, who were both students and professors. James Watt conducted some of his early experiments with steam power while working at the university, and John Logie Baird, a pioneer of television, was a student when the First World War intervened.

What students say

Zhaofeng Zhou, from China, is doing a PhD in competition law. He says: "There are several reasons why I chose to come to Glasgow. First, it has very long history. It is the fourth oldest university in the English speaking world. Second, many famous people are associated with Glasgow university, such as Adam Smith and Lord Kelvin. Third, it has a great reputation in regard to helping international students. For example, the university runs some subsidized trips for international students. Fourth, there are some of the best staff in my research areas within the law school. This is important for research students. Fifth, it provides excellent social events for students. It is the only British university that has two student unions. Sixth, it provides me with an excellent chance to improve my English because I work as a senior resident at Murrano street student village where most of the residents are first-year British students. Last but certainly not least, the campus is very impressive. Particularly the main building is absolutely gorgeous. The least thing I like about the university is the summer holiday because most students are at home and the university is too quiet."

Good at

Only the life sciences and biomedicine make the top 100 in our rankings, but the social sciences and arts and humanities also reached this mark last year.

84 University of Leiden

Why this university?

Legend has it that in 1575 William of Orange offered the people of Leiden a choice of rewards for withstanding a Spanish siege: they could be excused from paying certain taxes, or he would establish a university in the town.

They chose the university, thinking it would last longer than a tax cut. Whether or not the story is true, the university has endured. It is the oldest in the Netherlands, and gives a venerable academic air to a modestly-sized city, part way between Amsterdam and The Hague.

Leiden has a broad range of academic interests, from archaeology and the arts to mathematics and natural sciences. In 2006, it had approximately 17,600 students, of which 1,600 were from outside the Netherlands. The university gives a strong international push to its students, with all research masters and PhD students obliged to take a placement abroad as part of their courses.

The nine faculties offer some 50 bachelor and 70 master degree programs (most of the masters in English), while post-academic training is provided in education and environmental science. A separate campus in The Hague specializes in post-academic training in the field of law and political science.

Going into 2006 the university had 4,000 members of staff (not including those in the medical faculty who are employed by the University Medical Centre). Of these, 230 were full professors and almost 600 PhD

FACTFILE

LEIDEN University

Country	Netherlands
Foundation Year	1575
World Ranking	84 (90=)

Faculty Area Rankings

Arts & Humanities	40
Engineering & IT	287
Life Sciences & Biomedicine	72
Natural Sciences	105
Social Sciences	67

Survey Performance

Peer Review	75
Recruiter Review	187

Contact Details

Rapenburg 70
Leiden
2311 EZ
www.leiden.edu
+31 71 527 2727

People

Student Faculty Ratio	15.5:1
International Faculty	22.0%
Undergraduates	12,118
Postgraduates	4,928
International Students	8.0%

Course Fees For Domestic Students

Average Undergraduate	$2,058
Average Postgraduate	$2,058

Course Fees For International Students

Average Undergraduate	$2,058
Average Postgraduate	$15,094

Overall Research Strength

Papers (Scopus 2002-2006)	61,709
Citations (Scopus 2002-2006)	335,372
Impact	5.4

Research Impact By Faculty Area

Engineering & IT	3.2
Life Sciences & Biomedicine	5.6
Natural Sciences	6.2
Social Sciences	3.6

students. The previous year 240 doctoral dissertations were completed and nearly 2,000 master's degrees were awarded.

People

Leiden has an impressive record in the Spinoza awards, the highest Dutch academic award, with 10 winners from fields as different as clinical epidemiology and educational psychology. Strength in languages and linguistics is marked by two awards, while four have touched on mathematics and physics. This builds on a tradition that includes two Nobel prizes in physics, for Heike Kamerlingh Onnes and Hendrik Antoon Lorentz, and associations with figures such as Einstein, John Quincey Adams, ethologist Nikolaas Tinbergen and Paul Ehrenfest.

More recently Leiden has been the place of study for members of the Dutch royal family, and noted alumni include former European commissioner Frits Bolkestein and film director Paul Verhoeven.

What students say

Roosje Pertz came to Leiden from the Dutch speaking part of Belgium to take the 'book and byte' masters, a course taught in English covering book publishing and digital media. "It's very specialized, and not the sort of thing they would offer in Belgium," says Roosje, who heard of the course during an internship with a publishing house.

It lived up to her expectations, with the small size of the class and the flexibility of tutors particularly positive. "They treat you as an adult, and you can organize your own work," she explains. "At other universities, or where you are on bigger programs, you are just a number." On the other hand, this freedom was sometimes hard to deal with. "There is structure, but not a firm hand that says you have to do this or that. That is good, but it can also be a bit weird when you come from a more authoritarian university."

Good at

Leiden is strongest in the arts and humanities, which make this year's top 50. The social sciences and life sciences and biomedicine are also in the top 100.

85= Case Western Reserve University

Why this university?

Firmly rooted in the sciences, Case Western was created by the merger 40 years ago of two adjacent universities, one of them an institute of technology. Half the undergraduates specialize in engineering and the sciences, and three-quarters go on to earn advanced degrees. A recent expansion included a US$110 million research building to house 700 people studying cancer, genetic epidemiology, and other subjects, and another building to accommodate work in fuel-cell technology and structural biology. The university has also built up its faculty, expanding it by 20 per cent to 2,521. They teach 10,160 students — 40 per cent of them undergraduates including 1,200 from abroad, with a comparatively low student-faculty ratio of about 7 to 1. Case Western's Seminar Approach to General Education and Scholarship program requires undergraduates to take personalized classes of no more than 17 students.

It was at Case that scientists conducted research determining the atomic weight of oxygen, proving the nonexistence of ether, developing simulated milk formula for infants, and detecting neutrinos created by cosmic ray collisions with the atmosphere. One of those scientists, Albert Michelson, laid part of the foundation for Einstein's special theory of relativity. In 1907, Michelson became the first American to win a Nobel prize in the sciences, though by then he had gone on to the University of Chicago.

FACTFILE

CASE WESTERN RESERVE University

Country .... United States
Foundation Year 1826
World Ranking .... 85= (60)

Faculty Area Rankings

Engineering & IT 144
Life Sciences & Biomedicine 61
Natural Sciences 192
Social Sciences 265

Survey Performance

Peer Review 167
Recruiter Review 249

Contact Details

10900 Euclid Ave
Cleveland
Ohio
44106-7027
www.case.edu
+1 216 368 2000

People

Student Faculty Ratio 5.2:1
International Faculty 3.0%
Undergraduates 3,716
Postgraduates 2,763
International Students 18.0%

Course Fees For Domestic Students

Average Undergraduate $32,800
Average Postgraduate $25,400

Overall Research Strength

Papers (Scopus 2002-2006) 45,557
Citations (Scopus 2002-2006) 224,725
Impact 4.9

Research Impact By Faculty Area

Engineering & IT 2.8
Life Sciences & Biomedicine 5.1
Natural Sciences 6.2
Social Sciences 4.5

It was that kind of historical comeuppance, among other things, that prompted Case Western to embark on an ambitious spending plan and shorten its name to the simpler "Case." But deficits were soon mounting, alumni withheld their support until the decision about the name was reversed, and the faculty voted no confidence in the president, who was forced to resign. Those controversies eventually quieted, and things at the university have settled down.

In all, faculty and alumni have received 14 Nobel prizes. Case is 14th among private universities in America in government funding for research, receiving a combined US$374 million annually from the government along with other sources, much of it channelled to its highly rated medical school (which ranks 12th in government grants to U.S. medical schools). Along with engineering, it's also particularly highly regarded for its programs in biomedical engineering and management. It offers an unusual master's degree in business administration focused on sustainable development.

People

Case alumni include the first female rear admiral in the U.S. Navy, the first woman director of the U.S. Centers for Disease Control, Craigslist founder Craig Newmark, former Ecuadorian President Alfredo Palacio, U.S. presidential candidate Dennis Kucinich, several congressmen, author Richard North Patterson, and physicist Lawrence Krauss, author of the book The Physics of Star Trek.

What students say

Case feels dynamic and energetic, said Sumitha Nair, a doctoral candidate from India studying biomedical engineering. "We have new faculty and there has been a lot of construction, with much better space now than we had when I first got here. The program is very good here at Case, and very broad."

One downside is the weather in Case's hometown, the midwestern city of Cleveland. "I guess I have come to like it more now than when I first came here, but I'm from the southernmost state in India, with a tropical climate," Ms Nair said. "I had never seen snow before in my life. I have seen a lot now."

Good at

Case prides itself on excellence in engineering and technology, but its only top 100 finish this year is in the life sciences and biomedicine, where it is just outside the top 60.

85= Fudan University

Why this university

Always near the top of the Chinese university rankings, Fudan has broken into the top 100 in the world this year, with a leap of more than 20 places. Established in Shanghai by the eminent Chinese educator Ma Xiang-bo in 1905, it has been a fully-fledged university since 1917, pioneering such subjects as journalism and civil administration. After a period as a private university, it acquired the arts and science departments of ten other universities in eastern China in 1952 and expanded further after the Cultural Revolution.

Since the incorporation of Shanghai Medical School, in 2000, Fudan also has nine teaching hospitals, which serve the public as well as training student doctors and conducting research. There are 17 schools covering the full range of disciplines, while Physics, Chemistry, Macromolecular Science, and Environmental Science and Engineering are independent departments. Fudan has been introducing interdisciplinary degrees in the process of developing a distinctive curriculum. Students gain credits for extra-curricular activities such as field trips, with the aim of giving them a "sound basis, wide horizon, high ability, and active creativity".

The university has 25,000 full-time students and another 11,000 in the schools of Continuing Education and Online Education. Some 1,650 full-timers come from overseas, the second-biggest total at any Chinese university and one that is likely to rise.

Another 1,700 short-term students

FACTFILE

FUDAN University

Country	China
Foundation Year	1905
World Ranking	85= (116=)

Faculty Area Rankings

Arts & Humanities	46
Engineering & IT	115
Life Sciences & Biomedicine	53
Natural Sciences	80
Social Sciences	62

Survey Performance

Peer Review	56
Recruiter Review	30

Contact Details

220 Handan Road
Shanghai
200433
www.fudan.edu.cn
+86 21 6564 2222

People

Student Faculty Ratio	13.2:1
International Faculty	7.0%
Undergraduates	15,282
Postgraduates	9,519
International Students	6.0%

Course Fees For International Students

Average Undergraduate	$3,358
Average Postgraduate	$3,838

Overall Research Strength

Papers (Scopus 2002-2006)	73,607
Citations (Scopus 2002-2006)	149,030
Impact	2.0

Research Impact By Faculty Area

Engineering & IT	1.5
Life Sciences & Biomedicine	1.8
Natural Sciences	2.7
Social Sciences	2.0

come each year as visiting scholars. As well as Chinese language teaching, the university offers courses in Chinese literature, history, economy, philosophy and law tailored for international students. Fudan was one of the first universities in China to take foreign students, in the 1950s, and exchanges with more than 200 universities and research institutions in about 30 countries.

The 2,300 full-time teachers and researchers include 1,350 full professors and associate professors, among whom are 25 academicians of the Chinese Academy of Sciences and the Chinese Academy of Engineering. But the university prides itself on attracting outstanding young researchers and numerous award-winners on its staff.

Fudan has four campuses, including its new focal point in the new town of Jiangwan, on the northern edge of Shanghai, where a 240-acre site has been developed from scratch. Students from outside China, who have the services of a dedicated Foreign Students Office, also have access to five of their own dormitory blocks. Sport plays a big part in the life of the university: two years physical education is required for all undergraduate students. Both the university's men's and women's volleyball teams are among the nation's leading teams, but Fudan students also excel in athletics, swimming, chess, gymnastics, basketball, football and shooting.

People

Among many famous alumni are Han Zheng, the Mayor of Shanghai; Li Lanqing, a former Vice Premier of China; Professor Fujia Yang, nuclear physicist and Chancellor of the University of Nottingham; and Tong Dizhou, the pioneer of cloning fish.

Good at

In the top 100 for everything except engineering and IT, Fudan's top positions in this year's rankings are in the arts and humanities, where it is in the top 50, and the life sciences and biomedicine, where it is just outside that mark.

85= University of Vienna

Why this university?

Sited on the Austrian capital's Imperial Ringstrasse, the University of Vienna blends in with majestic surroundings that includes the 19th century Town Hall and the Austrian Parliament.

But although the main building was built at around the same time — 1877-1884 — the university's history goes back much further.

Founded in 1365 by Duke Rudolf IV, the university is the oldest university in the German-speaking world and the second oldest university in Central Europe after Prague.

At the time it was founded, religion was one of the main subjects taught across Europe, but unlike other universities Vienna did not have a theology faculty. This changed in 1384 when a theology faculty was set up to join the institute's other three faculties of law, medicine and philosophy.

The university now offers more than 130 degree programs, among them 26 bachelor programs and 47 master programs, in 17 different faculties. Its medical faculty became so popular and expanded its capacity so much that in 2004 a separate Vienna Medical University was created, which still co-operates with Vienna University's other scientific faculties and centres today.

At present 5,400 academics make up the university's scientific staff, including 2,738 women, while more than 63,000 students are enrolled at the university. It has a strong tradition of international relations and has established Erasmus partnerships with

FACTFILE

University of VIENNA

Country	Austria
Foundation Year	1365
World Ranking	85= (87)

Faculty Area Rankings

Arts & Humanities	52
Engineering & IT	167
Life Sciences & Biomedicine	56
Natural Sciences	74
Social Sciences	46

Survey Performance

Peer Review	58
Recruiter Review	115

Contact Details

Dr. Karl Lueger Ring 1
Vienna
A-1010
www.univie.ac.at
+43 1 42770

People

Student Faculty Ratio	35.7:1
International Faculty	16.0%
Undergraduates	51,255
Postgraduates	5,991
International Students	22.0%

Course Fees For Domestic Students

Average Undergraduate	$498
Average Postgraduate	$498

Course Fees For International Students

Average Undergraduate	$498
Average Postgraduate	$498

Overall Research Strength

Papers (Scopus 2002-2006)	84,925
Citations (Scopus 2002-2006)	377,524
Impact	4.4

Research Impact By Faculty Area

Engineering & IT	2.8
Life Sciences & Biomedicine	4.5
Natural Sciences	5.3
Social Sciences	3.2

311 universities, attracting thousands of international students each year from 130 different countries. It is also viewed as a gateway between east and west Europe and has been instrumental in strengthening ties with institutes and governments in South East Europe. At the moment over 16 per cent of students are from abroad.

Further information at www.univie.ac.at

People

The university has a long history of attracting top professors from around the world after Duke Albrecht III took advantage of problems within the Sorbonne and brought a number of Paris' top professors to the Austrian capital. Since then some of the best scientific minds have taught at the university, including nine Nobel prize winners, including psychiatrist Julius Wagner-Jauregg, chemist Hans Fischer, immunologist Karl Landsteiner, physicist Erwin Schrödinger and biologist Konrad Lorenz.

The university has also educated a number of other prominent people, the father of psychoanalysis Sigmund Freud being the most notable, but others include Pope Pius III, former UN Secretary General Kurt Waldheim and current Austrian Chancellor Wolfgang Schuessel.

What students say

English Literature student Tanja Maleska, 25, from Macedonia says the opportunities at Vienna are far better than in her homeland. "More money is invested in universities in Austria and a degree from the University of Vienna is more recognizable than one from the University of Skopje. There has also been great improvement in the courses on offer over the four years I have been studying here and we have many guest professors from other countries."

But she added there were problems with the university's popularity. "There are simply too many students enrolled, which means courses are quickly filled and lecture halls overcrowded. And you often get the feeling that you are on your own as professors do not have enough time for the individual."

Good at

Social sciences (34 in the world), arts and humanities (37), medicine (41).

88 Queen's University

Why this university?

Queen's University is located in Kingston, Ontario, midway between Toronto and Montreal, a city with a rich architectural heritage and spectacular waterfront, and where the St Lawrence River and Lake Ontario meet. The 166-year-old university that counted just over 16,000 full-time enrollments in 2006 — almost 3,000 of them graduate students -has programs in humanities, the arts, engineering, commerce, law and health sciences.

Some of its research centres that have been making a mark include the Queen's Institute for Energy and Environmental Policy; the Sudbury Neutrino Observatory, which groups 130 researchers across North America and Europe in a lab deep underground; the Paleoecological Environmental Assessment and Research Laboratory, which goes deep below the surface of lakes and rivers to uncover the secrets of our environmental history; PREVNet (Promoting Relationships and Eliminating Violence), an initiative with a goal to reduce bullying in schools and workplaces; and the Queen's School of Business, which not only offers a full-time, an executive, and an accelerated MBA but also the Cornell-Queen's Executive MBA, providing an international perspective to students from both sides of the Canada-US border.

Queen's has signed 110 bi-lateral exchange agreements and last year welcomed 1,003 international students to its campus, 415 of them enrolled in graduate studies.

FACTFILE

QUEEN'S University

Country .... Canada
Foundation Year 1841
World Ranking 88 (176)

Faculty Area Rankings

Arts & Humanities 86
Engineering & IT 194
Life Sciences & Biomedicine 124
Natural Sciences 198
Social Sciences 43

Survey Performance

Peer Review 100
Recruiter Review 78

Contact Details

99 University Avenue
Kingston
K7L 3N6
www.queensu.ca
+1 613 533 2000

People

Student Faculty Ratio 12.4:1
International Faculty 26.0%
Undergraduates 15,060
Postgraduates 3,017
International Students 7.0%

Course Fees For Domestic Students

Average Undergraduate $4,182
Average Postgraduate $6,033

Course Fees For International Students

Average Undergraduate $14,152
Average Postgraduate $10,143

Overall Research Strength

Papers (Scopus 2002-2006) 42,665
Citations (Scopus 2002-2006) 185,503
Impact 4.3

Research Impact By Faculty Area

Engineering & IT 2.2
Life Sciences & Biomedicine 4.6
Natural Sciences 6.1
Social Sciences 3.2

People

Among its 2,374 faculty members, physicist Art McDonald has made groundbreaking discoveries of the nature of matter and the structure of the universe; Joe Pater received the R.M.Taylor Award, Canada's most prestigious award for service in the fight against cancer; Psychologist Nikolaus Troje has become a leader in the study of visual perception by humans and animals; Sociology professor David Lyon studies how corporations and governments handle and share personal information; Philosopher Christine Overall received the Royal Society's Abbyann D Lynch Medal in Bioethics; and Queen's received three new Canada Research Chairs for 2007, for the study of greenhouse gases, dark matter, and the fight against cancer.

A couple of its more well-known alumni include celebrated author of The English Patient, Michael Ondaatje, and David Allan Bromley, former senior science advisor to President George H W Bush.

What students say

For Ruth Tearreau-Lousley, Queen's location was a big attraction. "I love the city of Kingston," says the 64-year-old from Thornton Cleveleys in the UK. "It's big enough to be interesting, but small enough to be friendly."

She is currently studying History, English Literature and Religious Studies.

For her, one of the school's strengths is that students gain an understanding of the "universality of knowledge, rather than digging deep holes in various subject areas which have no connection with anything else." All the courses she takes overlap chronologically so that one gets a sense of an inter-related world view. The level of social commitment by students also impresses her.

Socially, she says the campus is alive and buzzing for younger students, but laments that there are few opportunities for older people. "When it comes to more mature students there is no mechanism in place for us to meet up and share experiences, either scholastically or socially."

Good at

The university's best placing this year is in the social sciences, which make the top 50 in our ranking. Queen's is also in the top 100 for the arts and humanities.

89 University of Utrecht

Why this university?

Utrecht University mixes ancient and modern, boasting a heritage that goes back to the 7th Century plus an ultra-modern campus with buildings by Rem Koolhaas. It can also claim to be the largest Dutch university in terms of student numbers — 28,000 in 2007, of which 2,000 were from outside the Netherlands. They are spread over 47 bachelor programs, across all disciplines, 175 master programs, and 18 teacher-training programs. Excluding medicine, there are 640 professors and 275 professors by special appointment. Some 400 PhDs were granted in 2006.

The university has recently taken steps to further improve the quality of its intake of bachelor students, including quotas and selection processes. Once admitted, students can choose a minor subject from any of the programs offered by the university, while honours programs cater to the needs of outstanding students. International degrees are offered through University College Utrecht, an international bachelor program in economics, and almost 90 international master programs.

Graduate research programs are clustered within six schools, each covering related research masters and PhDs, the aim being to stimulate interactions between the various research areas. There are also 'prestige' master programs linked to research areas in which Utrecht holds a leading position worldwide. Students participating in these programs are closely involved in the international

FACTFILE

UTRECHT University

Country....................Netherlands
Foundation Year....................1636
World Ranking....................89 (95)

Faculty Area Rankings

Arts & Humanities....................76
Engineering & IT....................191
Life Sciences & Biomedicine....................80
Natural Sciences....................47
Social Sciences....................110

Survey Performance

Peer Review....................78
Recruiter Review....................224

Contact Details

P.O Box 80125
Utrecht
3508 TC
www.uu.nl
+31 30 253 91 11

People

Student Faculty Ratio....................10:1
International Faculty....................9.0%
Undergraduates....................17,606
Postgraduates....................10,962
International Students....................4.0%

Course Fees For Domestic Students

Average Undergraduate....................$2,058
Average Postgraduate....................$2,058

Course Fees For International Students

Average Undergraduate....................$6,404
Average Postgraduate....................$9,148

Overall Research Strength

Papers (Scopus 2002-2006)....................77,007
Citations (Scopus 2002-2006)....................379,597
Impact....................4.9

Research Impact By Faculty Area

Engineering & IT....................4.7
Life Sciences & Biomedicine....................4.9
Natural Sciences....................5.8
Social Sciences....................3.6

activities of these research groups and spend part of their program abroad.

People

Utrecht is one of the few Dutch universities that can claim a living Nobel laureate, in the form of Gerard 't Hooft. He shared the 1999 physics prize with Martinus Veltman (his former supervisor at Utrecht, who later went to the University of Michigan) for their work on the weak force, and he still works at Utrecht.

Other Nobel laureates are Nicolaas Bloembergen (physics), Peter Debye (physics), Christiaan Eijkman (physics), Willem Einthoven (physician and physicist), Tjalling Charles Koopmans (mathematician, physicist, economist), Wilhelm Röntgen (physics), Lavoslav Ruzicka (chemistry) and Martinus J.G. Veltman (physics).

English statesman Charles Spencer, 3rd Earl of Sunderland (1674-1722) studied at Utrecht.

What students say

One of the "prestige students" is Leila Kushan, from Los Angeles, who was attracted to the masters in neuroscience and cognition because of the length of the program and the opportunity of doing an internship abroad. A further factor was that the university accepts US federal student loans.

"I've been very satisfied with the program," she says. "It's research based, rather than theoretical, so I've learned many new skills and techniques. The coordinators are very helpful and there is a sense of community within the program." This has the effect of greater-than-expected involvement with the program. "Since the program is relatively small (only about 40 new students a year) the coordinators encourage student involvement both for arranging social gatherings and organising academic events like symposia and special courses."

Bureaucracy has been the main negative aspect of her experience, both in terms of coming to study abroad and the administrative problems of joining a newly established masters program.

Good at

Utrecht makes the top 50 for natural sciences. It is also in the top 100 for the arts and humanities and the life sciences and biomedicine.

90= Pennsylvania State University

Why this university?

Some of the research under way at Penn State is so advanced as to seem in the realm of science fiction. Theoretical breakthroughs made there could eventually lead to electromagnetic cloaking using nanotechnology, rendering an object invisible.

Much of what else occurs here is eminently visible. The university founded as an agricultural school and once known largely for the success of its American football team now attracts nearly US$700 million a year in research funding. It's second in the nation in the amount of research underwritten by industry, as opposed to the government. It was one of the founding members of the Worldwide Universities Network, a research collaboration among 17 universities in the United States, Asia, and Europe. It has 50 researchers on its own campus working in the field of renewable energy, and plans to add another 24 with the goal of becoming a world leader in energy science; part of the Penn State fleet already is fueled by hydrogen power from the first hydrogen refueling station on the East Coast. It plans a new Materials Science-Life Sciences Complex for its top-rated materials science program. It's home to the newly formed Center for the Study of College Student Mental Health. And its new, five-story Penn State Cancer Institute will provide cancer diagnosis and care but also research.

Penn State's business and engineering schools are particularly highly rated in supply chain management and logistics and industrial and manufacturing

FACTFILE

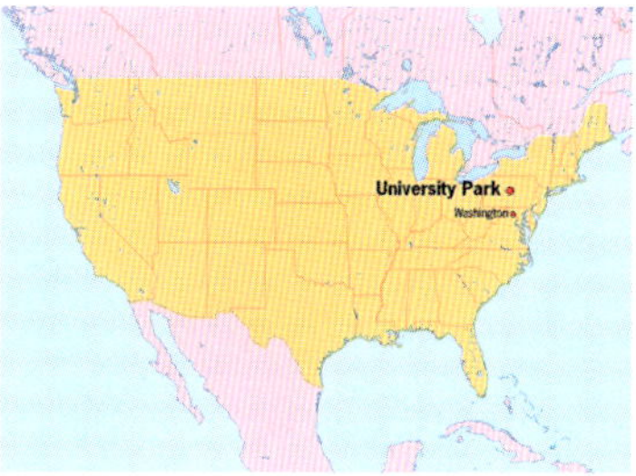

PENNSYLVANIA STATE University

Country....United States
Foundation Year....1855
World Ranking....90= (99=)

Faculty Area Rankings

Arts & Humanities....103
Engineering & IT....76
Life Sciences & Biomedicine....159
Natural Sciences....44
Social Sciences....50

Survey Performance

Peer Review....63
Recruiter Review....105

Contact Details

201 Old Main University Park
PA 16802
www.psu.edu
+1 814 865 5471

People

Student Faculty Ratio....10.2:1
International Faculty....2.0%
Undergraduates....63,996
Postgraduates....8,043
International Students....5.0%

Course Fees For Domestic Students

Average Undergraduate....$23,152
Average Postgraduate....$16,654

Overall Research Strength

Papers (Scopus 2002-2006)....100,519
Citations (Scopus 2002-2006)....473,705
Impact....4.7

Research Impact By Faculty Area

Engineering & IT....3.5
Life Sciences & Biomedicine....4.8
Natural Sciences....6.6
Social Sciences....3.1

engineering and materials, respectively; the university is first in the nation in the number of citations by its materials science faculty. One in 50 professionally licensed engineers in the United States, and one in four meteorologists, is a Penn State grad. The Design Futures Council rates its architecture program highly, and it is also well regarded in landscape architecture and nuclear engineering and for its doctoral programs in geology, hydrology, and geochemistry. The Applied Research Lab, a partner with the U.S. Defense Department, has 1,000 researchers and support staff that conducts work largely for the U.S. Navy.

With 36,815 undergraduates and 6,437 graduate students on the main campus and an equal number at the two dozen other campuses, Penn State has generally large class sizes; nearly 40 per cent of courses have 30 or more students in them. (There are 3,000 faculty.) But there is also an honors college with smaller classes and extracurricular activities tailored to the most academically talented students; applicants often choose the honors college over admission to Ivy League schools, lured in part by guaranteed scholarships for everyone who enrolls.

People

Faculty have included authors John Barth and Joseph Heller, and philosopher Ivan Illich. Alumni include Nobel chemistry laureate Paul Berg, KPMG chairman emeritus and former CEO Eugene O'Kelly, NASA space flight director Heather Rarick, and William Schreyer, chairman emeritus and former CEO of Merrill Lynch.

What students say

"The research that's going on here is top notch and the faculty are great at both the teaching and the research," said Xiaole Mao a doctoral candidate from China who is studying bioengineering. "The professors are very engaged in teaching, even though they're all quite busy with their own research projects." An aspiring teacher, Mr Mao said the university "pays a lot of attention to helping students developing teaching skills."

Good at

Penn State is in the top 50 in the world for natural and social sciences. It is also in the top 100 for engineering and IT.

90= Tokyo Institute of Technology

Why this university?

Founded in 1881 as Tokyo Vocational School, the Institute has been a national university since 1929. It is the largest higher education institution in Japan devoted to science and technology. The extensive School of Engineering has no fewer than 16 departments and there are graduate schools of decision science and innovation management, as well as the more traditional mathematical and computing sciences, bioscience and biotechnology.

There are three campuses: two in the heart of the Tokyo metropolis and one in Yokahama with a view of Mount Fuji. In 2006, there were just over 5,000 undergraduates and a similar number of postgraduates and research students. There are courses for undergraduates in the liberal arts and in health and physical education, while a special project encourages programs that will enhance students' creativity. The two libraries, in Tokyo and Yokahama, boast Japan's foremost collection of scientific and technological journals.

Sometimes dubbed the MIT of Japan, Tokyo Tech has one of the ten largest supercomputers in the world, used by more than 10,000 scientists, researchers and students. It is particularly proud of its Integrated Research Institute, established in 2005, restructuring the university's research functions to anticipate future trends and problems in collaboration with industry. The latest big initiative is the Global Edge Institute, which is designed to attract

FACTFILE

TOKYO Institute of Technology

Country........................ Japan
Foundation Year........................ 1881
World Ranking........................ 90= (118)

Faculty Area Rankings

Engineering & IT........................ 22
Life Sciences & Biomedicine........................ 175
Natural Sciences........................ 79

Survey Performance

Peer Review........................ 127
Recruiter Review........................ 84

Contact Details

2-12-1 Ookayama, Meguro-ku
Tokyo
152-8550
www.titech.ac.jp
+81 3 5734 3827

People

Student Faculty Ratio........................ 10.8:1
International Faculty........................ 8.0%
Undergraduates........................ 4,913
Postgraduates........................ 5,028
International Students........................ 9.0%

Course Fees For Domestic Students

Average Undergraduate........................ $4,465
Average Postgraduate........................ $4,465

Course Fees For International Students

Average Undergraduate........................ $4,465
Average Postgraduate........................ $4,465

Overall Research Strength

Papers (Scopus 2002-2006)........................ 77,892
Citations (Scopus 2002-2006)........................ 243,053
Impact........................ 3.1

Research Impact By Faculty Area

Engineering & IT........................ 1.8
Life Sciences & Biomedicine........................ 3.7
Natural Sciences........................ 3.9
Social Sciences........................ 1.4

young researchers from all over the world to work as assistant professors. Successful researchers will be offered tenured posts after five years.

Tokyo Tech, or Tokodai, has stressed its international ambitions in its slogan 'Leading the world in science and technology'.

There are about 1,000 foreign students, from 70 different countries. The overseas enrolment has been increasing by an average of more than six per cent a year for the last five years. Most live in private apartments, but there are two dormitories for foreign students and a separate residence for women, where students in their first year are given priority.

The International Student Centre runs Japanese language courses, as well as helping students deal with any problems.

There are cooperation agreements with 40 universities across Asia. The institute welcomed more than 200 visiting researchers in 2005, when 60 students enrolled in the international graduate course.

People

Famous alumni include Professor Hideki Shirakawa, who won the Nobel prize for chemistry in 2000 for his work on conductive polymers. Shigeo Hirose, who was awarded a PhD at the Institute and is now a professor there, is a pioneer of robotics. Naoto Kan is a former leader of the Democratic Party of Japan, while Satoru Iwata has been chief executive of Nintendo since 2002.

Good at

Tokyo Tech's main strength is in engineering and IT, where it finished just outside the world's top 20 this year. Also in the top 100 for the natural sciences.

92 Rice University

Why this university?

Comparatively small for a research university, with fewer than 3,000 undergraduates and little more than 2,000 graduate students, Rice also is very, very rich. An endowment exceeding US$4 billion makes it the fifth wealthiest university in America per student, so wealthy it once owned even Yankee Stadium, where the fabled New York Yankees play, in faraway New York. Those lucky enough to be accepted here — about one of every five students who apply — pay considerably less than the tuition charged at other private US universities. Yet they enjoy an extravagantly cozy student-faculty ratio of 5:1, and a median class size of 13. All of this on a heavily wooded, stately campus in the neo-Byzantine style, with red roofs, rose-colored brick, and elegant archways. His pan-seared chicken supreme in a porcini-mushroom sauce won the university chef the culinary competition of the National Association of College and University Food Services. No wonder Rice students have been ranked among America's happiest.

The graceful campus is in the midst of an expansion — with great pains being taken to protect those trees — as the university begins a thorough reinvention of itself. Six new buildings have shot up since the millennium, and many others have been renovated. Rice plans to fill this added space by gradually increasing its undergraduate enrolment by about 30 per cent, to 3,800, and intends especially to attract more foreign students. Though 16 per cent of all the students on the campus are from other countries, most of them attend at the graduate

FACTFILE

RICE University

Country	United States
Foundation Year	1891
World Ranking	92 (102=)

Faculty Area Rankings

Arts & Humanities	190
Engineering & IT	102
Life Sciences & Biomedicine	132
Natural Sciences	116
Social Sciences	230

Survey Performance

Peer Review	135
Recruiter Review	267

Contact Details

6100 Main
Houston
Texas 77005-1827
www.rice.edu
+1 713 348 0000

People

Student Faculty Ratio	8.2:1
International Faculty	9.0%
Undergraduates	2,851
Postgraduates	2,417
International Students	12.0%

Course Fees For Domestic Students

Average Undergraduate	$28,400
Average Postgraduate	$25,600

Overall Research Strength

Papers (Scopus 2002-2006)	22,034
Citations (Scopus 2002-2006)	138,201
Impact	6.3

Research Impact By Faculty Area

Engineering & IT	5.1
Life Sciences & Biomedicine	5.6
Natural Sciences	8.3
Social Sciences	3.7

and professional level. Fewer than 3 per cent of undergraduates are international, a proportion Rice is planning to increase with a particular focus on Asia and, given its southern U.S. location, Latin America.

Rice was promised as a gift to the city of Houston by a northern businessman, though the bequest was delayed for years by legal complications after the businessman's valet murdered him and claimed his estate under the terms of a forged will. The original charter promised a free education to any white resident of Texas. (Blacks and Jews were not allowed until 1963, when the university's governing board filed a lawsuit to change that provision.)

Already known for its standout programs in architecture and engineering (more than a quarter of students are engineering majors), Rice also excels in space science, having taken the forward-looking step of ceding part of its enormous campus to build the NASA Manned Space Flight Center, now called the Johnson Space Center, in 1962. It was at Rice that President John F. Kennedy made his famous speech on September 12 of that year calling for putting a man on the moon by the end of the 1960s.The next year, Rice opened the nation's first department of space physics. Its Rice Space Institute is today a world leader in space weather research, plasma environments of distant planets, and solar research.

The university conducts some US$72 million a year in research, an increase in funding of nearly 50 per cent in just five years. Students live in nine residential colleges (two more are planned) in the Oxbridge model, to which they are randomly assigned. Friendly though it is, Rice is academically demanding. Its students unwind by carrying forward a long tradition of pranks, including a three-times-monthly jaunt in which as many as 100 run around the campus wearing nothing but shaving cream.

People

Prominent alumni include former Newsweek editor and author William Broyles Jr, Pulitzer Prize-winning author Larry McMurtry, Sex and the City author Candace Bushnel; Howard Hughes, NASA astronauts, and former US Attorney General Alberto Gonzalez.

What students say

"I had my undergraduate degree from a public university" in her native Spain, said Rosa Dominguez, a doctoral student in environmental engineering. "I wanted to have the experience of a small private school. When I met with the faculty, they were all really friendly and helpful and really encouraging. And it's also near a big city [Houston is the fourth-largest city in the United States], so you have a lot of things to do. You're not in the middle of nowhere."

Ms Dominguez wasn't disappointed, she said. "Most of my classes have only seven or ten people," she said. "That helps the communication between you and the professor."

Good at

Only just outside the top 100 for engineering and IT, with the natural sciences the next highest in our rankings.

93= University of Copenhagen

Why this university?

Situated in a number of impressive buildings scattered around "wonderful, wonderful Copenhagen", Denmark's top university has over 100 institutes, departments, laboratories, and research centres.

The university has more than 33,000 full-time students enrolled, 2,500 part-time students and approximately 57 per cent of students are women. The average age of students enrolling at the University is 22. In general, however, students starting medicine, science and the social sciences, tend to be younger. The number of international students has risen by 63 per cent since 2000 — there were nearly 2,000 international students last year.

The university's engagement in research is evident in its commitment to both international and regional partners. The university is a menber of IARU (International Alliance of Research Universities) – a group of ten universities worldwide launched in Singapore in January 2006. The university is also a cornerstone of The Øresund University Partnership which brings together 14 universities in eastern Denmark and southern Sweden — the largest concentration of higher research and educational programs in Scandinavia. The Øresund region — comprising Copenhagen and Malmö — is currently the fastest expanding area of Scandinavia and the university partnership provides researchers and students on both sides of the Sound with improved access to expertise in Denmark and Sweden.

FACTFILE

University of COPENHAGEN

Country	Denmark
Foundation Year	1479
World Ranking	93= (54=)

Faculty Area Rankings

Arts & Humanities	67
Life Sciences & Biomedicine	62
Natural Sciences	81
Social Sciences	45

Survey Performance

Peer Review	72
Recruiter Review	224

Contact Details

Nørregade 10, P.O. Box 2177
Copenhagen K
1017
www.ku.dk
+45 35 32 26 26

People

Student Faculty Ratio	12:1
International Faculty	17.0%
Undergraduates	18,570
Postgraduates	15,282
International Students	13.0%

Course Fees For International Students

Average Undergraduate	$14,686
Average Postgraduate	$14,686

Overall Research Strength

Papers (Scopus 2002-2006)	46,472
Citations (Scopus 2002-2006)	243,762
Impact	5.2

Research Impact By Faculty Area

Engineering & IT	3.7
Life Sciences & Biomedicine	5.3
Natural Sciences	6.2
Social Sciences	3.1

The university's degree structure is divided into three levels. Three years of undergraduate studies lead to a bachelors degree, and an additional two years to a master's degree. masters degrees can be extended with three more years of postgraduate work leading to a PhD degree.

Students take on average 4.3 years to complete their bachelors, and 7.7 to complete their masters.

Together, the university's six faculties offer approximately 200 study programs in the humanities, health sciences, social sciences, law, science and theology. The university's ethos is to prepare students for a broad range of jobs in the private and public sectors. All degree programs thus promote the learning and application of specific skills as well as academic knowledge.

To appeal to an international audience, the university offers a significant number of courses in English each semester across all faculties and disciplines. However, all degree courses require Danish proficiency.

According to a new university law in Denmark tuition fees will apply to students from non-EU/EØS countries starting with the academic year 2006/07. At present, the tuition fees have not been set.

The university's research profile is focused on what it calls four major interdisciplinary research priority areas until 2007: Religion in the 21st Century, Body and Mind, BioCampus (biotechnology), and Europe in Transition. The spirit of this research is perhaps best illustrated by ground-breaking research into breast cancer. A project run by the university's Institute of Molecular Biology and the Finsen Laboratory at Copenhagen University Hospital has shown that one particular enzyme — uPA (urokinase-type plasminogen activator) — causes breast cancer to spread throughout the body.

People

Several Prime Ministers of Denmark, including Poul Nyrup Rasmussen, who served from 1993-2001; Nobel laureates include Aage Niels Bohr and Ben Roy Mottelson, who won the physics prize in 1975, and Niels Kaj Jerne, a winner in medicine and physiology in 1984; the existentialist Søren Aabye Kierkegaard; and Sir Ove Arup, the structural engineer.

What students say

Fabrizio Loce-Mandes from Perugia in Italy studied anthropology at the University of Copenhagen as a student on the Socrates/Erasmus exchange program last year. "Conditions for international students in Copenhagen are very unique. We are very close, and there are great opportunities for experiencing things and meeting new people, because everything is close by. I have become enchanted in that I, like the Danes, enjoy being able to walk safely down the street at night."

Good at

In the top 100 for everything except engineering and IT, Copenhagen's top position is 45th for the social sciences.

93= University of Montreal

Why this university?

The Université de Montréal is a large French-language university that offers a multitude of disciplines. With 273 undergraduate and 375 graduate programs, it is the largest university in Quebec and the second largest in Canada. Founded in 1878, it now counts close to 40,000 students, over 8,000 of them graduate students, and just under 2,500 professors.

The university is one of Canada's major research centres. With its two affiliated schools, the École Polytechnique, an engineering school, and HEC Montréal, its business faculty, along with its network of affiliated hospitals, it earmarks C$447 million (£227 million) for basic and applied research each year, making it Canada's second most active university in the field.

Montréal is the institution with the highest proportion of students in graduate studies in Canada (27%) and the only Canadian university that covers all the health sciences discipline.

It's one of the only non-American universities sponsored by the Bill and Melinda Gates Foundation, which has given US$15 million for a major development project to improve population and health capacity building in French-speaking Sub-Saharan Africa.

It has 203 research chairs, 142 research units and 113 Canada Research Chairs and can lay claim to some important and innovative centres, including BRAMS (Brains, Music and Sound), which combines the fields of neurosciences and music, and the

FACTFILE

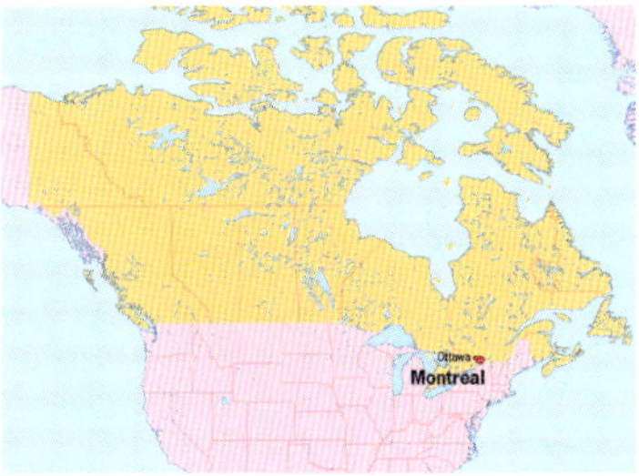

University of MONTREAL

Country	Canada
Foundation Year	1878
World Ranking	93= (181=)

Faculty Area Rankings

Arts & Humanities	57
Engineering & IT	88
Life Sciences & Biomedicine	66
Natural Sciences	93
Social Sciences	39

Survey Performance

Peer Review	53
Recruiter Review	250

Contact Details

PO Box 6128, Station Centre-ville
Montréal QC
H3C 3J7
www.umontreal.ca
+1 514 343 6111

People

Student Faculty Ratio	16.8:1
International Faculty	28.0%
Undergraduates	17,625
Postgraduates	7,156
International Students	8.0%

Course Fees For Domestic Students

Average Undergraduate	$1,668
Average Postgraduate	$2,502

Course Fees For International Students

Average Undergraduate	$11,628
Average Postgraduate	$14,067

Overall Research Strength

Papers (Scopus 2002-2006)	45,792
Citations (Scopus 2002-2006)	196,439
Impact	4.3

Research Impact By Faculty Area

Engineering & IT	2.6
Life Sciences & Biomedicine	4.6
Natural Sciences	4.9
Social Sciences	3.2

well-respected Institute for Research in Immunology and Cancer. It has researchers working in leading-edge disciplines such as pharmacogenomics, which combines the field of drugs, genomics and cardiology, and nanotechnology. It also has centres specializing in aerospace manufacturing and poultry research.

People

Some of its more famous alumni include UN High Commissioner for Human Rights, Louise Arbour; Oscar-winning filmmaker Denys Arcand; former Canadian Prime Minister Pierre Trudeau and the President of the International Criminal Court, Philippe Kirsch.

It has over 2,500 foreign students, half of whom hail from Europe and one quarter from Africa.

What students say

One of those foreign students is Brian Crane, a 34-year-old PhD candidate in Comparative Literature. The Florida native has lived in various parts of the continent but says he chose Montreal "to study in French at a world-class university in a North American city close to where I'll build my career."

The university has "a strong international community and ties to both North America and Europe," he says. Montreal is a world city on a human-scale, he says. "Anything you learn in the classroom you can live in the cafés, festivals and business milieus."

Studying abroad can be complicated and overwhelming, says Crane, but support of the school's International Student Office makes the difference, with staff that is available to help in big and small ways. "Like most large universities, Université de Montréal can seem bureaucratic when registering or paying fees — and when you are doing it in a second language, it's hard. Five minutes in the International Student Office usually works it out."

While he finds departments and services to be first-rate, the physical plant leaves much to be desired. "The old buildings look impressive perched on the side of Mount Royal, but get inside and they can seem cramped and uncomfortable. The ongoing renovations are welcome."

Good at

In the top 100 in all academic areas, Montreal's star field is social science, where it is in the top 40 in the world.

95 University of Rochester

Why this university?

In an era of large lecture courses, the University of Rochester practices what it calls "peer-led team learning" in most of its introductory science classes encouraging small groups of students to solve problems working together. The 4,940 undergraduates (there are 3,595 graduate students) can essentially study anything they want under the university's Rochester Curriculum, which has no required subjects. Students pick a major in one of three divisions — humanities, social sciences, or natural sciences and engineering — and take three or more related courses in the other two. The idea is to encourage an enduring enthusiasm for learning by letting students focus on subjects that are interesting to them. The result? Rochester ranks an impressive ninth out of 233 research and doctoral universities in the number of graduates who go on to earn PhDs, putting it in the same league as Harvard, Princeton, Yale, and Chicago. It gives many of those students an early start, too, with a program that allows the most motivated undergraduates to finish both their bachelors and masters degrees in any of ten subjects within a total of five years. Like its seminar-style introductory classes, Rochester's campus on the Genesee River in upstate New York gives the feel of a smaller school. The surrounding city of Rochester has been home to Eastman Kodak, Bausch & Lomb, and, until recently, Xerox, and the university is, not surprisingly, a center of the study of optics and imaging. Its electronic imaging programs and Institute of

FACTFILE

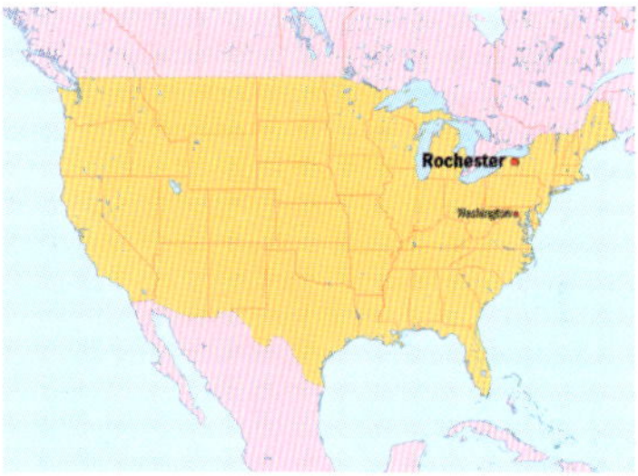

University of ROCHESTER

Country	United States
Foundation Year	1850
World Ranking	95 (48=)

Faculty Area Rankings

Arts & Humanities	206
Engineering & IT	253
Life Sciences & Biomedicine	167
Natural Sciences	194
Social Sciences	96

Survey Performance

Peer Review	171
Recruiter Review	303

Contact Details

Rochester
NY 14627
www.rochester.edu
+1 585 275 2121

People

Student Faculty Ratio	4:1
International Faculty	5.0%
Undergraduates	5,040
Postgraduates	2,810
International Students	13.0%

Course Fees For Domestic Students

Average Undergraduate	$31,297
Average Postgraduate	$31,297

Course Fees For International Students

Average Undergraduate	$31,297
Average Postgraduate	$31,297

Overall Research Strength

Papers (Scopus 2002-2006)	55,651
Citations (Scopus 2002-2006)	317,642
Impact	5.7

Research Impact By Faculty Area

Engineering & IT	4.2
Life Sciences & Biomedicine	6.0
Natural Sciences	5.8
Social Sciences	5.5

Optics, housed in the new US$37 million Robert B. Goergen Hall for Biomedical Engineering and Optics, are considered among the nation's best. They're laboring to spin off high-tech industries with opportunities that can replace the manufacturing jobs at the departed Xerox, and at Kodak, which has been shedding employees in the age of digital photography.

Rochester's Eastman School of Music, named for Kodak founder and longtime university financial backer George Eastman, also is among the best in the country. Five Eastman-trained composers have received the Pulitzer Prize in music, while others have won Grammy, Tony, and Emmy awards. The university's Laboratory for Laser Energetics is the home of Omega, the world's most powerful ultraviolet laser. Its Neurology Department is regarded as one of America's top academic centers for research into neurological conditions, and is third in the country in government-sponsored neurology research. In all, some US$350 million a year in research is conducted at the University of Rochester. Rochester faculty (there are 1,260 of them) and its alumni have collectively earned eight Nobel prizes.

The medical school is also top-rated, with a unique curriculum called the biopsychosocial model, which takes into account societal, psychological, and interpersonal influences in patient diagnosis and treatment. The concurrent double-helix curriculum weaves together strands of basic research and clinical medicine throughout the four years of physician education.

People

Prominent alumni include the dean of Harvard Medical School, the president of MIT, two astronauts, Broadway directors and composers, operatic soprano Renée Fleming, former Xerox CEO and US Deputy Education Secretary David Kearns, Pulitzer Prize-winning poet Galway Kinnell, and former US Treasury Secretary William Simon, for whom the business school is named.

What students say

Rochester still feels like a relatively small place, says Chinese-born undergraduate Christy Lang, and is especially comfortable for its 1,200 international students. Ms Lang, who planned to major in economics but also loved to paint, was attracted by the Rochester Curriculum. "I still wanted to keep my hobby," she said, by majoring in economics with a minor in studio art. Here, I get to spread out all of my interests. They're really flexible. I have the opportunity to choose whatever I want."

Good at

Rochester's only top-100 finish this year is in the social sciences, which were also its main strength in 2006.

96 University of California Davis

Why this university?

This branch of the University of California system boasts a department of viticulture and enology that helped build California's US$45 billion-a-year winemaking industry. In a pioneering model of interdisciplinary studies, faculty in this department specialize in chemistry, genetics, microbiology, engineering, horticulture, biochemistry, plant physiology, and sensory science. Together they choose varieties best suited to California growing conditions and help winemakers develop commercially successful, and often intricately crafted wines.

Agriculture is a mainstay of this school, and has been since it was established as a state training farm in 1908. But UC-Davis, which was not incorporated as a university until 1959, has quickly left those sleepy early origins behind. Some US$544 million a year in research is conducted here — the 12th-highest amount among U.S. public universities, up 85 per cent in just five years. UC-Davis leads the nation in the number of undergraduate and doctoral degrees conferred in the biological sciences. It has nearly 100 faculty engaged in research in renewable energy, alternative vehicle fuels, and lighting technology. It has one of only two centers in the country authorized by the National Institutes of Health to develop medical therapies using human stem cells. Researchers at the university also study epidemics such as avian flu and West Nile virus.

Undergraduates, who comprise 23,500 of the 30,000 UC-Davis students — an increase of 25 per cent in 10 years —

FACTFILE

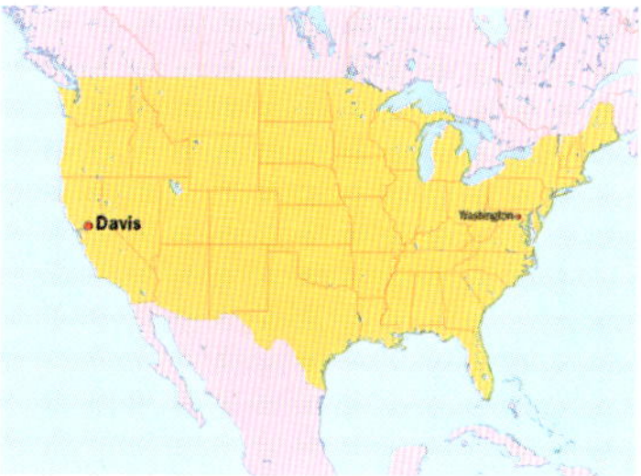

University of CALIFORNIA, Davis

Country	United States
Foundation Year	1905
World Ranking	96 (170=)

Faculty Area Rankings

Arts & Humanities	130
Engineering & IT	86
Life Sciences & Biomedicine	37
Natural Sciences	85
Social Sciences	144

Survey Performance

Peer Review	69
Recruiter Review	320

Contact Details

One Shields Avenue
Davis
California
95616
www.ucdavis.edu
+1 530 752 1011

People

Student Faculty Ratio	10.7:1
International Faculty	7.0%
Undergraduates	23,023
Postgraduates	4,547
International Students	5.0%

Course Fees For Domestic Students

Average Undergraduate	$7,446
Average Postgraduate	$14,694

Overall Research Strength

Papers (Scopus 2002-2006)	91,930
Citations (Scopus 2002-2006)	381,289
Impact	4.1

Research Impact By Faculty Area

Engineering & IT	-
Life Sciences & Biomedicine	-
Natural Sciences	-
Social Sciences	-

are involved in much of this research. (There are 4,000 faculty members.) They live and study on the largest campus of the UC system, so big it has its own airport and fire department. Students get from place to place on bicycles and in vintage double-decker buses. Halfway between San Francisco and Lake Tahoe, the picturesque school is in a small city of 64,000 people so progressive it dug an underpass so as not to disturb migration patterns of toads that were getting squashed on a newly constructed highway. (They may not have actually been getting squashed by cars, however, since environmentally conscious Davis boasts the highest number of bicycles per capita of any US city.) Residents and members of the university community share a gleaming center for the performing arts given by the Mondavi wine family.

UC-Davis is the only UC school with colleges of law, medicine, education, management, and veterinary medicine, all of them highly rated. It is about to add a school of nursing.

People

Prominent alumni include U.S. Treasurer Anna Escobedo Cabral, UNICEF head Ann Veneman, Bechtel CEO Riley Bechtel, 2002 Miss Hong Kong Tiffany Lam, author Anthony Swofford (Jarhead), Kirin Brewing Company CEO Koichiro Aramaki, and Frederick Murphy, co-discoverer of the Ebola virus.

What students say

Fernando Mardones, a student from Chile who just received his masters degree in preventative veterinary medicine now works as an epidemiologist while his wife completes the same program. Mr. Mardones does research at the UC-Davis Center for Animal Disease Modeling and Surveillance studying potential reactions to a hypothetical outbreak of hoof-and-mouth disease in the United States.

The couple was attracted to the university, Mr. Mardones said, by the quality of the program and facilities and the prestige of the widely cited faculty. They also quickly grew to like the city. "It's a very natural environment," he said. "There is a lot of green space. Everyone is biking. No one smokes. It's a very special place to live."

Good at

The main strengths are in science and technology: Davis is in the top 40 for the life sciences and biomedicine, and in the top 100 for both engineering and IT and the natural sciences.

97= University of Alberta

Why this university?

The University of Alberta is a multi-campus, public teaching and research-intensive university serving 37,000 students, including just over 6,000 in graduate studies. It employs more than 1,353 academic staff in 18 faculties and has an annual budget in excess of C$1 billion, with more than C$480 million in external research funding. Some 420 of Alberta's professors hail from outside of Canada and the university counts 4,682 international students, 2,078 of whom are graduate students.

Located atop a river valley in Edmonton, the university celebrates its centenary in 2008. Undergraduate and graduate students choose from 400 programs, including 60 doctoral programs in 300 research areas. Of note are its Native studies, the only program in Canada that boasts a faculty and not just a department. It also houses the country's only faculty of rehabilitation medicine.

The University of Alberta developed the first vaccine for hepatitis B; has made numerous discoveries in medicine and swine research, which led to the development of the Edmonton Protocol islet transplant method to treat Type 1 diabetes; and combined the fields of oncology and nanotech engineering to develop devices for faster and less expensive cancer screenings.

The University of Alberta is home to the Canadian Circumpolar Institute, which comprises more than 200 researchers focused on the North from more than a dozen disciplines. In 2007,

FACTFILE

University of ALBERTA

Country	Canada
Foundation Year	1908
World Ranking	97= (133=)

Faculty Area Rankings

Arts & Humanities	51
Engineering & IT	59
Life Sciences & Biomedicine	54
Natural Sciences	95
Social Sciences	83

Survey Performance

Peer Review	55
Recruiter Review	351

Contact Details

114 St. - 89 Ave
Edmonton
Alberta
T6G 2M7
www.ualberta.ca
+1 780 492 3111

People

Student Faculty Ratio	20.8:1
International Faculty	27.0%
Undergraduates	27,067
Postgraduates	5,274
International Students	13.0%

Course Fees For Domestic Students

Average Undergraduate	$4,484
Average Postgraduate	$3,156

Course Fees For International Students

Average Undergraduate	$15,566
Average Postgraduate	$6,592

Overall Research Strength

Papers (Scopus 2002-2006)	77,754
Citations (Scopus 2002-2006)	311,457
Impact	4.0

Research Impact By Faculty Area

Engineering & IT	2.3
Life Sciences & Biomedicine	4.7
Natural Sciences	4.2
Social Sciences	2.9

its industrial design students were the only students from Canada ever invited to participate in the International Contemporary Furniture Fair in New York. It's also home to Orlando, the world's largest textbase on British women authors that is available to scholars and readers worldwide.

People

Distinguished alumni include the Chief Justice of the Supreme Court of Canada, Beverley McLachlin, the physicist and Nobel laureate Richard Taylor and former Canadian Prime Minister Joe Clark.

Distinguished faculty include ecologist David Schindler, recipient of the Stockholm Water Prize; computer scientist Jonathan Schaeffer, whose artificial intelligence program solved the game of checkers; paleontologist Phil Currie who digs in the dinosaur badlands of Alberta; and physicians Ray Rajotte and James Shapiro, collaborators on the Edmonton Protocol.

What students say

Mohit Dang is a fourth-year Bachelor of Commerce undergrad. The 22-year-old, who came to the University of Alberta from India, chose the institution partly because of the province's oil boom, which he says promises a great deal of business and employment opportunities.

What also brought him here was the school's reputation. "The School of Business has ranked high internationally, and it offers a family business and entrepreneurship major in their Bachelor of Commerce program which was just what I was looking for."

The school's size can be a drawback: "There can be a shortage of individual study space to accommodate 37,000 students," he says. The university, spread out over 35 city blocks, is undergoing further expansion, which will address the issue of study-space shortage.

Dang says he loves the University of Alberta's increasing international presence. "The staff and students come from all walks of life, and the university has a dynamic feel with a truly international environment."

Good at

Alberta is in the top 100 in all academic areas. The arts and humanities are highest-placed, just outside the top 50.

97= Georgia Institute of Technology

Why this university?

"I'm a ramblin' wreck from Georgia Tech, and a hell of an engineer" goes what might be the world's most famous university fight song. But Georgia Tech these days is trying to move away from its perceived narrow focus on engineering, adding interdisciplinary initiatives and collaborations with its fellow Atlanta research institutions and with universities and governments worldwide. It is merging its traditional engineering strength with biology, chemistry, medicine and other fields and has already rocketed into the top tier of research centers in such areas as nanomedicine, biotechnology, photonics, high-performance computing, and cancer study. It is already landed on the list of seven "national centers of cancer nanotechnology excellence," designated by the National Cancer Institute, for work done at the cancer nanotechnology center it runs jointly with nearby Emory University.

Founded after the American Civil War to help train the leaders of a new manufacturing sector in the largely agricultural South, George Tech now is also looking to extend its reach abroad. There are research deals with the Industrial Development Agency of Ireland, for research into digital media, radio frequency identification, biotechnology, and energy, and with France's Centre National de la Recherche Scientifique to study ultra-fast telecommunications and innovative materials at its own satellite campus in Metz.

FACTFILE

GEORGIA Institute of Technology

Country	United States
Foundation Year	1885
World Ranking	97= (145)

Faculty Area Rankings

Arts & Humanities	278
Engineering & IT	8
Natural Sciences	49
Social Sciences	270

Survey Performance

Peer Review	82
Recruiter Review	131

Contact Details

Atlanta
Georgia 30332
www.gatech.edu
+1 404 894 2000

People

Student Faculty Ratio	19.6:1
International Faculty	3.0%
Undergraduates	12,000
Postgraduates	5,027
International Students	16.0%

Course Fees For Domestic Students

Average Undergraduate	$5,642
Average Postgraduate	$6,444

Course Fees For International Students

Average Undergraduate	$23,366
Average Postgraduate	$23,334

Overall Research Strength

Papers (Scopus 2002-2006)	66,248
Citations (Scopus 2002-2006)	258,046
Impact	3.9

Research Impact By Faculty Area

Engineering & IT	2.9
Life Sciences & Biomedicine	4.6
Natural Sciences	5.6
Social Sciences	3.9

This new international emphasis extends to Georgia Tech's own students in Atlanta, where the university is based. Under its International Plan, students can take courses in modern languages, global economics, and international affairs, and spend two terms abroad studying or working. There are also joint degrees offered in economics and international affairs and in global languages combined with either global economics or international affairs. The university wants to increase the proportion of its students who work or study abroad to one-third of the total.

That's one of a number of goals under a detailed and ambitious plan that has already seen the number of undergraduates increase 29 per cent in 10 years, to 11,840, and the number of graduates rise 45 per cent, to 5,300. Georgia Tech plans to increase by 50 per cent the number of undergraduates who do research, and increase the per centage of women students — two-thirds of the students are men. The school already graduates 10 per cent of all black PhDs in engineering in America, even though it's one of 320 accredited engineering programs.

Many of those students live, work, and play in buildings that were added for the 1996 Olympics, during which time Georgia Tech served as the athletes' village. In exchange, it reaped US$160 million worth of new dormitories and a huge athletics center that served as the Olympics' aquatics venue. There is also a new, four-building biotech complex and a planned nanotechnology building that will be the largest of its kind in the Southeast. In all, the university conducts US$441 million a year in research, up 84 per cent in the last 10 years.

As for the old image of the ramblin' wreck, it's still around, embodied in a 1930 Ford Model A that is part of the entertainment at football games. Alumni proved that Georgia Tech still teaches basic engineering when they hurriedly fixed it after it was in a traffic accident.

People

Prominent alumni include Nobel laureate and former President Jimmy Carter, who attended Georgia Tech although he graduated from the U.S. Naval Academy, and the CEOs of American Express, Wal-Mart, Earthlink, AT&T, and Atlanta-based Coca-Cola, along with several NASA astronauts and administrators, including former NASA administrator Richard Truly and astronaut John Young, the first commander of the space shuttle and the only person to have piloted four different classes of spacecraft.

What students say

When she was looking to study her specialty of environmental architecture, Maria Gabriela Zapata, said, "the United States had the best programs," and Georgia Tech was at the top of her list. She came there from her native Ecuador to pursue a masters degree in building ecology and emerging technologies. "I like that there is the chance to be involved very closely in research here," said Ms. Zapata. "There are so many projects here and they are open for anybody to take part in."

Good at

Georgia Tech is in the top 50 for the natural sciences, but it is in engineering and IT that it really shines, winning a place in the top ten in the world.

99 Cardiff University

Why this university?

Cardiff is the premier university in Wales and a member of the Russell Group of leading UK research universities. It left the University of Wales, believing that only full independence would enable it to compete internationally, and has since merged with the University of Wales College of Medicine. A third of the 22,000 students come from Wales, but the 3,000 from overseas testify to Cardiff's international reputation.

The university has two Nobel laureates among its academic staff since Professor Sir Martin Evans won the 2007 prize for medicine for his discovery of stem cells. Professor Robert Huber is leading the development of Structural Biology at Cardiff, having won the 1988 prize for chemistry. Seven subjects — city and regional planning, civil engineering, education, English, optometry, psychology and theology – were rated internationally outstanding in the UK's last research assessments. Almost nine out of ten researchers were placed in the top two of the seven categories, one of the best ratios in Britain.

Teaching quality is also highly rated, with 21 subjects graded as excellent, representing more than half of the university. Philosophy, theology and religious studies had the most satisfied students in the latest National Student Survey, but English, history, archaeology and biology all did well. The humanities and social sciences are the largest areas in terms of student numbers, but many undergraduate degrees share a common first year.

The university is centrally located in

FACTFILE

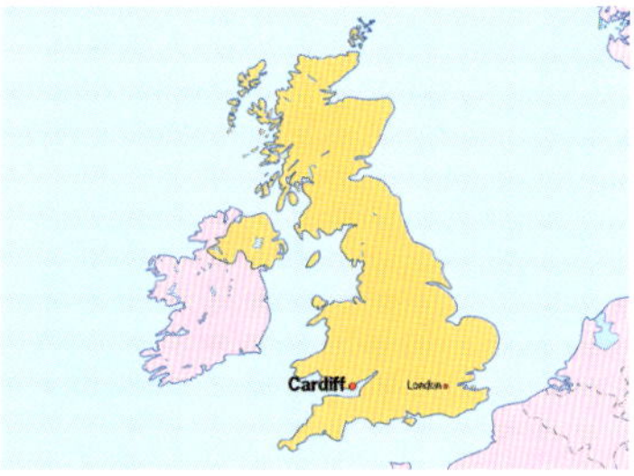

CARDIFF University

Country	United Kingdom
Foundation Year	1883
World Ranking	99 (141=)

Faculty Area Rankings

Arts & Humanities	143
Engineering & IT	206
Life Sciences & Biomedicine	74
Natural Sciences	280
Social Sciences	159

Survey Performance

Peer Review	153
Recruiter Review	95

Contact Details

Cardiff
Wales
CF10 3XQ
www.cf.ac.uk
+44 29 2087 4000

People

Student Faculty Ratio	9.3:1
International Faculty	19.0%
Undergraduates	16,923
Postgraduates	5,605
International Students	17.0%

Course Fees For Domestic Students

Average Undergraduate	$6,294

Overall Research Strength

Papers (Scopus 2002-2006)	37,217
Citations (Scopus 2002-2006)	167,933
Impact	4.5

Research Impact By Faculty Area

Engineering & IT	2.6
Life Sciences & Biomedicine	5.3
Natural Sciences	5.1
Social Sciences	3.2

Wales' capital, in the civic complex around Cathays Park. There has been significant investment in new buildings and equipment, including ongoing improvements to the university's library services. Among other developments has been a £20 million building for the highly-rated School of Optometry and Vision Sciences. Other teaching facilities are also being upgraded at the medical school, a mile away from the main campus, where the five healthcare schools share a parkland site with the University Hospital of Wales.

International students are guaranteed one of the 5,000 university-owned residential places. Most student accommodation is within walking distance of lectures, much of it featuring ensuite facilities. Rents are among the lowest in the UK. Student support services, including counselling facilities and the help offered to dyslexics, were among the features singled out for praise in an audit by the Quality Assurance Agency.

Cardiff is popular with students, offering all the attractions of a major city without such high prices as students experience in some other parts of the UK. It houses the Welsh Assembly and has undergone substantial regeneration in recent years, especially around Cardiff Bay. The main residential site at Talybont boasts a "sports village", with three multipurpose sports halls, a fitness suite and outdoor pitches. The university also runs a city-centre fitness suite. Rail and road links to other parts of the UK and by air to the rest of the world are good.

People

Apart from the university's two Nobel laureates, the academic staff includes Professor Diane Edwards, who has transformed understanding of the earliest land plants on Earth, and Professor John Pearce, a pioneer in the psychology of learning. Alumni include former Labour leader Lord Kinnock of Bedwellty, who studied industrial relations and is now the university's president. Former music student Karl Jenkins is now an acclaimed international composer. Professor Zhong Binglin, who has a Cardiff PhD in engineering, reformed teaching in China's universities as Director General of Higher Education and is now President of Beijing Normal University, while Barham Salih was Prime Minister of the Patriotic Union of Kurdistan before becoming Deputy Prime Minister of Iraq.

What students say

Sunny Li, a postgraduate journalism student from Hunan, in China, swapped the campus existence of a first degree at Stirling University for city life in Cardiff. Steered towards the university by editors whom he consulted on a work experience placement, he was attracted both by the reputation of the journalism school and the enthusiasm of the staff. "I love Cardiff," he says. "If I'm having a bad day I can go out to Cardiff Bay and take in the sea air. The Welsh are very friendly and the international journalism course gives me a lot of new perspectives."

Good at

Other academics place Cardiff 74th in the world for biomedicine and the life sciences. The university slipped out of the top 100 for the arts and humanities this year, with the social sciences producing the next-highest finish.

100 University of Helsinki

Why this university?

The University of Helsinki is the oldest university in Finland, dating back to 1640 when it was established in Turku, the then capital of Finland. The university transferred to the country's new capital, Helsinki, in 1928.

It is also the largest in the country, with nearly 39,000 students and over 7,500 staff (including PhD students, regular teaching staff and researchers who also teach). Around 10 per cent of the teaching staff are from outside Finland, mainly in the sciences, the medical faculty and the university's Biotechnology Institute. Each year, about 4,300 degrees are awarded, including almost 400 doctoral level degrees.

Helsinki University's two-year strategy for 2007-09 focuses strongly on research and internationalization. The university is one of the founding members of the élite League of European Research Universities (LERU).

There are 11 faculties and 20 independent research institutes which can quickly refocus their research on emerging fields, giving them an edge compared with their international counterparts. When measured against international quality criteria and in terms of employing the largest number of professors, the strongest research areas include information technology, international law and human rights, cognitive sciences, computational molecular science, biophysics, human genetics, structural virology, cancer biology and climate change.

FACTFILE

University of HELSINKI

Country	Finland
Foundation Year	1640
World Ranking	100 (116=)

Faculty Area Rankings

Arts & Humanities	73
Engineering & IT	188
Life Sciences & Biomedicine	89
Natural Sciences	92
Social Sciences	74

Survey Performance

Peer Review	83
Recruiter Review	270

Contact Details

P.O. Box 33
Helsinki
00014
www.helsinki.fi
+358 9 1911

People

Student Faculty Ratio	18.4:1
International Faculty	14.0%
Undergraduates	22,689
Postgraduates	3,520
International Students	18.0%

Course Fees For Domestic Students

Average Undergraduate	$0
Average Postgraduate	$0

Course Fees For International Students

Average Undergraduate	$0
Average Postgraduate	$0

Overall Research Strength

Papers (Scopus 2002-2006)	79,926
Citations (Scopus 2002-2006)	416,803
Impact	5.2

Research Impact By Faculty Area

Engineering & IT	4.0
Life Sciences & Biomedicine	4.9
Natural Sciences	7.3
Social Sciences	3.7

Helsinki fared well in comparison with other universities in Europe in an international research evaluation conducted in 2005 that gave two thirds of its 75 research units (five independent institutes and 70 faculty departments) either the highest or the second highest scores out of a possible seven.

There are currently 2,100 foreign students, representing just 5 per cent of the total. This includes over 800 undergraduate and masters level students and 525 taking doctorates. Russia, Estonia, China, Germany, Great Britain and the United States top the list of countries of origin for foreign students, although almost 100 different nationalities are represented.

At present, there are no tuition fees for foreign students, irrespective of their country of origin. However, with an average acceptance level of 23 per cent, it is not easy to gain a place. Many foreign students come to Helsinki University through the European Union's Erasmus program. There are also reciprocal arrangements with leading universities elsewhere in the world, including the University of California (Berkeley), University of Tokyo, Moscow State University and the University of Toronto.

Helsinki University aims to double the number of foreign undergraduate and doctoral students by 2009. The target is to have 1440 undergraduate students, 750 doctoral students and around 1100 non-degree students. To this end, the university plans to launch 30 additional masters level programs in English. Dedicated services aimed at foreign students such as language courses, cultural guidance and career guidance will also be improved and extended.

People

Internationally well-known former alumni include Jorma Ollila, until recently chief executive of Nokia and Linus Torvalds, developer of the Linux software system. Seven out of ten Finnish presidents have also studied at Helsinki University as have three Nobel prize winners.

What students say

Martha Vera is a Mexican student, enrolled in a masters communication degree at the faculty of Social Sciences.

"I chose the University of Helsinki specifically because of its status despite the fact that everybody I met in Helsinki told me it is very hard to get in. My study program has met my expectations although it is hard work. The main drawback is that the relevant and important information is often in Finnish only and therefore not always accessible to a first-year degree student with just a basic knowledge of the language. We get information about the practicalities of everyday life but not about how to book exams, for instance. At masters level, the compulsory Finnish language course has excellent tutors, though."

Good at

Helsinki is in the top 100 for everything except engineering and IT. The social sciences and arts and humanities are both in the top 75.

UPM
UNIVERSITI PUTRA MALAYSIA
BERILMU BERBAKTI
Universiti Putra Malaysia
Research university with a soul
Universiti Putra Malaysia (UPM), established in 1931, is one of the leading multidisciplinary, research universities in Malaysia, with commitment towards learning and research for the creation of wealth and nation building. It is dedicated towards providing its students with education that combines rigorous academic perspectives and stimulating intellectual environment.
Nurturing the brightest and the best
www.upm.edu.my

9

Top 100 universities by subject

The pages that follow list the universities regarded by scholars and researchers around the world as the best in arts and humanities, life sciences and biomedicine, natural sciences, social sciences, engineering and IT. If experts think that a specific university is good in your field, you may want to consider it and it may impress future employers. Each subject area ranking is preceded by a survey of the career options that each of these subject choices might open up for you.

Identifying the best in the world

The Times Higher-QS World University Rankings tell you the top places of learning around the world: all terrific universities. They are liked by academics and recruiters and do worthwhile teaching and research. But general rankings are of limited value if you want to choose the best university for the next stage of your career. You want to go to a university that will excite you with good teaching, where you know there are world-respected researchers, and which you know recruiters will take seriously. You don't just want a certificate at the end; you want to have transformed your skill and standing in your chosen field. This decision affects years of your life and involves spending a daunting sum of money; you need to know a lot more. There is no point crossing the world to study, mechanical engineering, if you end up at a university whose strong suit is law or literature. You need somewhere serious about technology.

The analysis in these tables comes about by looking at the peer review data in the Times Higher-QS World University Rankings. Peer reviewers are asked which subject area they are expert in, and for their choice of the best 30 universities in the world in that area. Here we show the detail of which institutions are best liked in each subject area. In addition, we show the number of times that papers in these areas have been cited in the academic literature as measured by Scopus™.

Studying arts and humanities

The arts and humanities sound like a simple enough group of subjects to grasp. They are those areas of scholarship that are essential to civilized living but which we can probably all do without, at a pinch. Look at any list of what the arts and humanities involve. Philosophy is bound to be there. While this subject has occupied many of the finest minds in history, it has not fed the hungry or cured the sick. Music and literature: people entertained themselves in song and word long before there were professors to talk about them. Archaeology and history: Fascinating, but what has the past ever done for us?

But look a little deeper and you will see that things are not quite so simple. Although there are international variations, the arts and humanities do include some subjects of unmistakable day-to-day importance. In the UK, the Arts and Humanities Research Council (AHRC) funds law research. The same applies to the National Endowment for the Humanities in the US. And in recent years, the realization has been dawning that there is money as well as intellectual stimulation in the arts and humanities. The AHRC was set up by the British parliament as recently as 2005, in recognition of their growing scale and importance. Tourism is now a larger part of the UK economy than the motor industry. That means that museum studies, theatre, art and the like all have economic clout. Publishing and the media, likewise, are growing sectors of the economy, especially online, and are powerful job creators. So, if you fancy getting involved in these burgeoning areas of the economy, don't be swayed by 20th century ideas about how engineering is 'real' work and literature is something to get interested in on your day off. A modern economy needs both.

A vast choice of subjects

Available university courses in the arts and humanities range from newer subjects such as digital media all the way to the topics taught in the world's earliest universities, such as history, literature and philosophy. A few lead directly to specific careers in subjects such as law, librarianship and languages. The high financial rewards open to lawyers are famous. While pay packets of librarians may bulge less than those of lawyers, theirs is now a high-technology trade which has been transformed by developments in information storage and retrieval, and which offers a secure and interesting career with plentiful job satisfaction. And modern languages, whatever anyone says about English as the world language, is growing in importance in line with globalization.

Another highly vocational group of subjects is in the performing and visual arts. Whether you want to sing Wagner at Bayreuth, or see your work in the Museum of Modern Art, you will need some qualifications to get started. Here you are entering a high-risk area where many people do not make it, but it is a great life if you do. If you are after a course in a specialist subject in this area, it is best to take some solid advice. Often university degrees lead to careers in teaching or administration in these areas, while future actors, performers or artists may have attended a specialist drama school, conservatoire or art college. Literature graduates have long filled the best jobs in book publishing, which, despite the rise of electronic communications continues to be a flourishing trade. However, the arts and humanities are also part of the new global economy. For example, there are now hundreds of channels of television on tap across the world. All that has to come from somewhere. Arts graduates are prominent in filling the gap.

Think creatively

But it is also worth thinking even more creatively about the arts and humanities. Archaeology: badly dressed people with embarrassing facial hair grubbing about in trenches, right? Well, perhaps, but that is only part of the story. The ways in which an archaeological site is processed and the objects it yields are identified, analyzed and dated are closer to forensic science than anything else, and learning them can open up all sorts of career doors.

And the modern world needs humanities knowledge in other ways too. An alarming number of lawyers and historians tend to end up as politicians. But in the last few years, governments have realized that cultural and religious issues are central to future political and economic alignments. They all need to know about Middle Eastern governments and central Asian religious movements, and as much as possible about cultures worldwide. They need people with skills and knowledge in these areas.

The following table shows the top 100 arts and humanities universities in the opinion of our experts around the world. But because arts subjects often do not generate papers and citations in the same way as other areas of academic life, we do not put citations data alongside it. The table shows that, in a world of diverse cultures, work in English has the highest reputation. Peking at 18 is the first ranked university that does not work mainly in English, which is also the working language of 68 universities listed here, located from Ireland to New Zealand. The message is that arts and humanities scholars, whatever language they work in, are likely to know what is happening in English.

Also, in high regard here are continental European universities, the locations of much of the world's highest-prestige art from Mozart to Picasso. But Japan, Taiwan and South Korea also appear. And it is natural to expect China, with three universities already on the list, to expand its representation, as the world's most populous country expands its cultural as well as its economic reach.

Top 100 in arts and humanities

Rank	Institution	Country	Score
1	HARVARD University	United States	100.0
2	University of California, BERKELEY	United States	96.5
3	University of OXFORD	United Kingdom	94.4
4	University of CAMBRIDGE	United Kingdom	92.3
5	YALE University	United States	84.3
6	COLUMBIA University	United States	83.3
7	PRINCETON University	United States	80.1
8	University of TORONTO	Canada	79.5
9	University of CHICAGO	United States	77.6
10	AUSTRALIAN National University	Australia	75.9
11	STANFORD University	United States	74.7
12	MCGILL University	Canada	71.3
13	University of CALIFORNIA, Los Angeles (UCLA)	United States	68.4
14	University of BRITISH COLUMBIA	Canada	67.2
15	The University of SYDNEY	Australia	66.6
16	CORNELL University	United States	64.4
17	University of MELBOURNE	Australia	63.9
18	PEKING University	China	61.2
19	University of MICHIGAN	United States	60.3
20	DUKE University	United States	58.6
21=	National University of SINGAPORE	Singapore	57.6
21=	JOHNS HOPKINS University	United States	57.6
23	NEW YORK University (NYU)	United States	56.7
24	University of TOKYO	Japan	54.7
25	MASSACHUSETTS Institute of Technology (MIT)	United States	54.4
26	LONDON School of Economics and Political Science	United Kingdom	54.0
27	UCL (University College LONDON)	United Kingdom	53.9
28	University of EDINBURGH	United Kingdom	53.5
29	Université Paris-Sorbonne (PARIS IV)	France	52.5
30	MONASH University	Australia	52.1
31	BROWN University	United States	51.7
32	The University of AUCKLAND	New Zealand	51.0
33	Ecole Normale Supérieure, PARIS	France	50.9
34	KYOTO University	Japan	50.5
35	University of NEW SOUTH WALES	Australia	49.6
36	King's College LONDON	United Kingdom	49.3
37	TRINITY College Dublin	Ireland	48.6
38	Freie Universität BERLIN	Germany	48.4
39	Hebrew University of JERUSALEM	Israel	48.0

Rank	Institution	Country	Score
40	LEIDEN University	Netherlands	47.3
41	University of AMSTERDAM	Netherlands	47.2
42	University of TEXAS at Austin	United States	46.3
43	Katholieke Universiteit LEUVEN	Belgium	45.7
44	University of HONG KONG	Hong Kong	44.9
45	University of QUEENSLAND	Australia	44.0
46	FUDAN University	China	43.2
47	University of BOLOGNA	Italy	42.9
48=	School of Oriental and African Studies, University of LONDON	United Kingdom	41.9
48=	INDIANA University Bloomington	United States	41.9
50	University of PENNSYLVANIA	United States	41.7
51	University of ALBERTA	Canada	41.3
52=	University of VIENNA	Austria	41.0
52=	University of NOTRE DAME	United States	41.0
54	BOSTON University	United States	40.9
55	WASEDA University	Japan	40.8
56	Ludwig-Maximilians-Universität München (MUNICH)	Germany	40.4
57	University of MONTREAL	Canada	40.2
58	University of ST ANDREWS	United Kingdom	40.0
59	University of MANCHESTER	United Kingdom	39.6
60	Università degli Studi di ROMA - La Sapienza	Italy	39.5
61=	HEIDELBERG University	Germany	39.4
61=	UPPSALA University	Sweden	39.4
63	RUTGERS, The State University of New Jersey	United States	39.3
64	HUMBOLDT Universität zu Berlin	Germany	39.2
65=	Université Catholique de LOUVAIN (UCL)	Belgium	38.8
65=	City University of NEW YORK	United States	38.8
67=	University of WISCONSIN-Madison	United States	38.7
67=	University of COPENHAGEN	Denmark	38.7
67=	Université PARIS I - Panthéon Sorbonne	France	38.7
70	University of YORK	United Kingdom	38.6
71	University of WARWICK	United Kingdom	38.4
72	LA TROBE University	Australia	38.3
73=	University of HELSINKI	Finland	38.2
73=	VICTORIA University of Wellington	New Zealand	38.2
75	University of CALIFORNIA, Irvine	United States	38.0
76=	UTRECHT University	Netherlands	37.1
76=	University of LEEDS	United Kingdom	37.1
78	YORK University	Canada	37.0

Rank	Institution	Country	Score
79	Universität TÜBINGEN	Germany	36.9
80	University of HAWAII	United States	36.6
81	University of OTAGO	New Zealand	36.4
82	STONY BROOK University	United States	35.9
83=	University of PITTSBURGH	United States	35.8
83=	BRANDEIS University	United States	35.8
85	University of ARIZONA	United States	35.5
86	QUEEN'S University	Canada	35.2
87	MACQUARIE University	Australia	35.1
88	University of BRISTOL	United Kingdom	35.0
89	GEORGETOWN University	United States	34.9
90	University of ILLINOIS	United States	34.4
91=	TSINGHUA University	China	34.1
91=	SEOUL National University	Korea, South	34.1
93	National TAIWAN University	Taiwan	33.9
94	Universität FREIBURG	Germany	33.6
95=	University of SUSSEX	United Kingdom	33.3
95=	EMORY University	United States	33.3
97	University of GENEVA	Switzerland	33.2
98=	CARNEGIE MELLON University	United States	33.1
98=	MCMASTER University	Canada	33.1
100=	University of WESTERN ONTARIO	Canada	33.0
100=	TEL AVIV University	Israel	33.0

Studying life sciences and biomedicine

During the 20th century, medicine was one of civilization's biggest success stories. In the 19th century, people in developed countries lived longer as their living conditions got better. But in the 20th, improved medicine drove vast improvements in the quality and length of life for people all over the rich world.

So what happens next and how do you get involved? An increasing number of observers believe that the best is yet to come. 20 years ago, it was thought that people in the rich world were bumping up against some natural limit to lifespan, but now there seems less reason to believe this. There has been a claim that half of Britain's 30-year-olds today could see their 100th birthday. Even more controversial are scientists such as Aubrey de Grey of Cambridge University, ranked here as the second most highly rated university for life sciences and biomedicine in the world. He claims that normal ageing mechanisms in the body can be stopped, opening the door to "negligible senescence" whereby we would all live to 1,000.

Global Challenges

While we need some heroic thinking like this, it is hardly answering the big concerns of most of the world's population. HIV/Aids is a health crisis in many developing world countries, and has reached such a level in parts of Africa that it is depressing economic growth and perpetuating underdevelopment. The basic facts about the HIV virus and the way it changes and spreads are well known, but decades of science lie ahead as part of the struggle to conquer Aids. This is only one of the health hazards that accompany the many benefits of globalization. Another is the near-annual arrival of new types of flu virus in Europe and North America from Asia. Again, this is a health hazard, which can only be conquered by excellent research.

Another key medical challenge in which science has a key role is the ageing of populations in the developed, and increasingly the developing, world. While planners and politicians present ageing as a problem, it is also a good sign. It happens because people are living longer and population growth is easing. Medical science has a vital role to play in ensuring that people can live longer, enjoy their extended lifespan, and perhaps remain economically active. We have a pretty good idea about the sort of exercise and diet that people need to stay physically capable. But as people live longer, they are becoming prey, in increasing numbers, to degenerative conditions such as Alzheimer's and Parkinson's diseases. These will require substantial future research on methods of alleviating and, perhaps eventually, curing them.

Accelerating knowledge

Fortunately for us all, the human race now has an unprecedented and fast-growing range of ways to attack these problems. Most conspicuous amongst these is our almost complete knowledge of the human genome and of the genetic makeup of other species. We now know that genes are not simple on-off switches. They combine in subtle ways to create the full range of human variety. But our knowledge of them is already allowing us to pinpoint genes that predispose us to specific diseases. This points the way to 'personalized medicine', in which the doctor prescribes the treatment that matches your body, not that of some average member of the population. In addition, our ability to find out about living tissue is growing fast.

Just over 100 years after X-rays were first used to see inside the human body, we now have a wide range of scanning and imaging equipment which, for example, allows us to see which part of the brain does which type of thinking, or to watch a beating heart in action. At the same time, we are finding out more about how disease works its way through society. Modern IT systems allow people to be tracked in large numbers, revealing more about the susceptibility of different groups in society to specific conditions.

This immense rate of progress is lubricated by some of the world's biggest reserves of cash, and by many of its cleverest people. Biomedical research is probably the field to which the term "publish or perish" was first applied. As the following table of the top 100 institutions shows, papers in the biomedical field have more citations than in other areas of knowledge. What it does not show is that scientists in this area also cite much newer research than others. The sheer pace is far faster than in technology or in other areas of science.

But don't be discouraged. Instead, think what you want to get out of your medical career. You can help the human condition without winning a Nobel prize.

Diversity of careers in medicine

In many countries, the range of medical occupations for which a degree has become essential is growing. At one time it was possible to become a nurse in the UK after leaving school at 16. Now nursing is largely a graduate profession. In the same way, specialist practitioners such as chiropodists and osteopaths are now mostly graduates. They can have interesting careers and make good money. While many started out wanting to be doctors, they are often happy that things worked out as they did.

Medicine has long been a magnet for talented people, so medical courses in all countries have some of the highest entry standards, as do related fields such as dentistry and veterinary science. But before trying to get on such a course, it is best to think whether it is the right route for you. Many people who have terrific careers in medical research are chemists, biochemists, microbiologists or some other type of scientist. Epidemiologists, the people who track diseases through society, need to be terrific at statistics but can get by with little knowledge of cell biology.

In most of the world, people make this outline decision while still at high school. But in the US, they do things a little differently. There, medicine is not usually taught to undergraduates. Instead medical schools (led in academic and public esteem by Harvard, number one in the list we show here) admit graduates, typically in their early twenties. Usually they have a first degree in some branch of biology, but there is the occasional mathematician, linguist or even historian curing the sick in towns across the US. The question really boils down to whether you want to treat patients directly, or think of yourself more as someone who thrives in the laboratory. But as every keen television watcher knows, even hospital or surgery-based doctors are essentially scientists, and need to be well up with emerging research if they are to avoid malpractice suits. More importantly, many medical researchers are employed jointly by hospitals and universities to treat patients, teach and carry out research.

This way of life is a highly rewarding one, but biomedicine offers other career paths too. The major pharmaceutical companies, for example, employ a wide range of life scientists in their development work. They often say that their research costs for a new drug are "a billon dollars per molecule," and a lot of that cash goes on people. However, there is a theory that the best days of global pharmaceutical companies are past. Increasingly, smaller firms, sometimes university startups and spinouts, are getting to the good molecules with streamlined processes. Few of them become big businesses in their own right, if only because the directors decide it is better value to sell out to a mega corporation. So life in a university could offer big rewards of many kinds.

If this is the direction that appeals, your best route is via a PhD rather than a medical qualification, although there are some super-studious types who get both.

Widespread excellence

The table of excellence in life sciences and biomedicine shows that the stupendous amounts of money in the US biomedical system are getting results. Most of the biggest research spenders are in the US, including the National Institutes of Health, the Veterans Health Administration, the Howard Hughes Medical Institute and a host of smaller bodies focused on specific diseases or places.

But money isn't everything. The message of this table, with ten US universities in its top 20, is that the wealth is being spent to good effect, buying the equipment and setting up the infrastructure needed to attract and support the top talent. This table also shows that you do not need a medical school to be good at biomedicine. MIT, seen here in ninth place, does not train doctors. But it does have a big stake in the life sciences research, so much so, that its people produce the world's most highly-cited biomedical research. In second place in terms of citations is CalTech, to which the same applies.

However, the table also shows that excellence in biomedicine is widespread. The UK, Canada, Singapore, Japan, Australia and China all join the US in this surprisingly diverse top 20. Just outside are establishments such as the Karolinska Institute in Sweden, a research and teaching powerhouse, which also oversees the Nobel prize in physiology or medicine. The UK is the most prominent after the US, with Cambridge and Oxford universities in second and third places and Imperial College in seventh. These have all gained from increasing government spending on medical research and from the presence in the UK of the Wellcome Trust, one of the few rivals in scale to the big US medical charities. The managers of UK medical research now realize that they have another massive advantage over their rivals in the shape of the National Health Service. It has data on 60 million patients, the biggest source of its type in the world. Many future discoveries are bound to come from mining this information.

But if you want a bet about the best direction for a possible future career in medicine, the smart money may lie in the tropics. We have an increased awareness of the problems of the developing world, and a growing realization that climate change threatens to send its diseases into Europe and the US. This has interested both governments and charities, such as the massive Bill and Melinda Gates Foundation, in tropical disease, a subject that has also been central to Wellcome's mission since the 1930s. New healthcare procedures, new drugs, and new ways of making treatments cost less are all likely to figure in a decades-long campaign to raise health standards and life expectancy in the developing world. Life scientists and biomedics are going to have plentiful career opportunities with the potential to have real worldwide impact for years to come.

Top 100 in life sciences and biomedicine

Rank	Institution	Country	Score	Citations per paper
1	HARVARD University	United States	100.0	9.1
2	University of CAMBRIDGE	United Kingdom	93.3	7.5
3	University of OXFORD	United Kingdom	87.1	7.8
4	JOHNS HOPKINS University	United States	86.7	7.1
5	University of California, BERKELEY	United States	85.4	7.7
6	STANFORD University	United States	82.0	7.7
7	Imperial College LONDON	United Kingdom	75.6	6.2
8	YALE University	United States	73.8	7.5
9	MASSACHUSETTS Institute of Technology (MIT)	United States	73.5	11.3
10	MCGILL University	Canada	70.8	5.5
11	University of CALIFORNIA, San Diego	United States	66.9	7.2
12	National University of SINGAPORE	Singapore	66.3	4.4
13	University of TOKYO	Japan	65.2	4.8
14	University of TORONTO	Canada	63.9	6.3
15	University of CALIFORNIA, Los Angeles (UCLA)	United States	63.4	5.6
16	CORNELL University	United States	62.8	5.9
17	University of MELBOURNE	Australia	61.1	4.5
18	PEKING University	China	61.0	2.4
19	DUKE University	United States	60.0	7.0
20	University of BRITISH COLUMBIA	Canada	59.5	5.0
21	CALIFORNIA Institute of Technology (Caltech)	United States	57.9	10.4
22	MONASH University	Australia	57.8	4.2
23	The University of SYDNEY	Australia	57.7	4.3
24	KAROLINSKA Institute	Sweden	55.7	5.5
25	COLUMBIA University	United States	55.1	6.8
26	UCL (University College LONDON)	United Kingdom	54.8	6.2
27	KYOTO University	Japan	54.5	4.6
28	AUSTRALIAN National University	Australia	54.4	4.9
29	PRINCETON University	United States	53.7	7.5
30	University of EDINBURGH	United Kingdom	53.2	6.0
31	University of QUEENSLAND	Australia	53.1	4.4
32	King's College LONDON	United Kingdom	52.0	5.0
33	University of MICHIGAN	United States	51.6	6.4
34	WASHINGTON University in St. Louis	United States	51.5	0.6
35	University of PENNSYLVANIA	United States	51.1	6.6

Rank	Institution	Country	Score	Citations per paper
36	University of HONG KONG	Hong Kong	50.4	5.4
37=	University of CHICAGO	United States	49.7	6.6
37=	University of CALIFORNIA, Davis	United States	49.7	4.2
39	OSAKA University	Japan	48.8	5.3
40	UPPSALA University	Sweden	48.6	5.0
41	The University of AUCKLAND	New Zealand	45.9	4.5
42	University of WASHINGTON	United States	43.7	6.6
43	HEIDELBERG University	Germany	43.1	4.7
44	BOSTON University	United States	42.9	6.6
45	University of WISCONSIN-Madison	United States	42.8	5.7
46	SEOUL National University	Korea, South	42.7	3.3
47	NEW YORK University (NYU)	United States	42.5	5.6
48	University of BRISTOL	United Kingdom	41.6	4.9
49	Université Louis Pasteur STRASBOURG I	France	40.9	4.9
50	University of NEW SOUTH WALES	Australia	40.3	4.4
51	EMORY University	United States	40.1	6.7
52	TSINGHUA University	China	39.2	2.4
53	FUDAN University	China	39.0	1.8
54	University of ALBERTA	Canada	38.7	4.7
55	Hebrew University of JERUSALEM	Israel	38.5	4.5
56	University of VIENNA	Austria	38.2	4.5
57=	PURDUE University	United States	38.1	4.4
57=	ETH Zurich (Swiss Federal Institute of Technology)	Switzerland	38.1	3.6
59	BROWN University	United States	37.5	4.9
60	University of GLASGOW	United Kingdom	37.3	5.4
61	CASE WESTERN RESERVE University	United States	37.0	5.1
62=	University of COPENHAGEN	Denmark	36.8	5.3
62=	The CHINESE University of Hong Kong	Hong Kong	36.8	4.3
64	University of MANCHESTER	United Kingdom	36.7	4.8
65	University of CALIFORNIA, Santa Barbara	United States	36.2	
66=	University of MONTREAL	Canada	35.9	4.6
66=	VANDERBILT University	United States	35.9	6.8
68	University of ZURICH	Switzerland	35.8	5.9
69=	MCMASTER University	Canada	35.3	5.3
69=	University of NORTH CAROLINA	United States	35.3	5.3
71	University of CALIFORNIA, Irvine	United States	35.0	4.8
72	LEIDEN University	Netherlands	34.8	5.6

Rank	Institution	Country	Score	Citations per paper
73	Universität TÜBINGEN	Germany	34.5	5.3
74=	NORTHWESTERN University	United States	34.4	5.6
74=	CARDIFF University	United Kingdom	34.4	5.3
76	University of DUNDEE	United Kingdom	33.8	8.0
77	University of WESTERN AUSTRALIA	Australia	33.7	4.3
78	University of MINNESOTA	United States	33.6	5.1
79	NANJING University	China	33.4	2.1
80=	University of AMSTERDAM	Netherlands	33.2	5.6
80=	HONG KONG University of Science & Technology	Hong Kong	33.2	4.4
80=	National TAIWAN University	Taiwan	33.2	2.8
80=	UTRECHT University	Netherlands	33.2	4.9
84	LUND University	Sweden	32.7	4.5
85=	University of BASEL	Switzerland	32.5	5.9
85=	University of Science and Technology of CHINA	China	32.5	2.1
87	TRINITY College Dublin	Ireland	32.4	6.2
88	TEXAS A&M University	United States	32.2	3.8
89	University of HELSINKI	Finland	31.9	4.9
90	University of OTAGO	New Zealand	31.7	3.4
91=	University of ILLINOIS	United States	31.6	4.5
91=	University of TEXAS at Austin	United States	31.6	6.2
93=	University of BIRMINGHAM	United Kingdom	31.5	5.2
93=	SHANGHAI JIAO TONG University	China	31.5	1.7
95	Universidad Nacional Autónoma de México (UNAM)	Mexico	31.4	2.3
96	TEL AVIV University	Israel	31.3	3.7
97	University of CALIFORNIA, Santa Cruz	United States	31.2	
98	DARTMOUTH College	United States	30.9	6.4
99	CARNEGIE MELLON University	United States	30.6	4.7
100=	University of ADELAIDE	Australia	30.5	3.8

Studying natural sciences

Universities are the original globalized industry. Scholars have been travelling around the world for centuries. But today, science may be the most international area of academic life. A linguist or a historian in Germany may not need to know what his or her colleagues in Australia are doing. But a big discovery in chemistry is news on a planetary scale. The structure of scientific publishing reflects this reality. Major scientific publications such as Science (US) and Nature (UK) are read around the world in a way that journals in the arts or the social sciences are not. And while scientific ideas and discoveries cross the world in seconds, the people responsible for these breakthroughs are not far behind. Scientists routinely work abroad for longer and shorter periods, and research groups in science are some of the most multinational workforces you are likely to encounter.

But while the international character of science has been apparent for many years, its structure is altering in subtle ways. International research carried out among high school students carries a striking message. The more rich and developed a country is, the less likely its students are to want to become scientists or technologists. Reasons are many. For one thing, science is hard work. Becoming a good scientist often involves long hours in the laboratory, or conquering daunting mathematical equations. For another, richer societies offer more career choices. Students cannot be blamed if they think they can have more fun and make more money after studying management or music at university than if they read physics or biology. But are students who shun science making the right decision?

The huge impact of science

The tables in this chapter separate natural science from life sciences and biomedicine. Both these fast-moving arenas of intellectual life are underlain by the same body of knowledge about the universe. They also both make use of the experimental method to test out ideas. We distinguish between them because biomedicine is a massive world scientific endeavor in its own right. It has more money than the rest of science, connects to different industries and has its own publishing culture. But in the first decade of the 21st century, science, as we define it here, is in a uniquely creative phase, showing energy that is certain to become even stronger in future years. Consider physics, in some ways the most fundamental of all the sciences. A massive machine called the Large Hadron Collider, built in a huge circular tunnel beneath the countryside of Switzerland and France, comes into use at CERN, the European nuclear physics laboratory in 2008. It is so large that just one of the magnets inside it contains more iron than the Eiffel Tower in Paris. If the nuclear collisions created within it work as they should, it will finally tell us why matter has mass, and put into a single logical system all the particles and energy forms that make up the universe around us.

If this does not excite you, pick up today's newspaper, or turn on the TV and look at the news. You will certainly find a story about climate change, an issue first raised in 1896 by a Swede called Svente Arrhenius, in a paper worrying about how the earth might warm up as industrialized countries burnt more coal. Now, governments worldwide are starting to realize he was right, as the scientific evidence has stacked up to convince them that climate change is real. Companies and individuals are also thinking about their carbon footprints and how to reduce them. Even a few years ago, the term was completely unknown. More or less overnight, people are suddenly thinking about zero-carbon homes, sustainable cities, and all the other things we might need in order to escape the worst forecasts of a warming world. This is the biggest change in mankind's approach to the future to date, and it is happening because of scientific research and the evidence it has produced.

Indeed, science has a role in most of the major problems that the human race now faces. For thousands of years, people have been developing better crops and farm animals by breeding for the characteristics they wanted. Now, our knowledge of genetics allows us to short-circuit that process, by selecting genes for properties that, for example, promise to improve crop yields. It is even possible to transfer genes between species, which makes it possible to change crops and animals faster and in new ways. Wonderful in theory, but in practice, genetic manipulation has proved bitterly divisive, especially in Europe. The scientists who are involved have had to get used to the idea that their research is political and controversial, taking them far beyond the science that makes up their core expertise. As with particle physics or climate change, science in this area is now big news. The public wants to know about it, and the bodies that pay for it expect scientists to engage with that public as well as with their professional peers.

Keeping your scientific options open

If you are thinking about a career as a scientist, you are going to need a solid base in a scientific subject. Much of the best science is now done by interdisciplinary teams, which mingle a range of scientific skills, and may also include engineers, economists or other non-scientists. But to work in this sort of setting, you will need a basic set of professional skills in some science or other. Most popular are those you might encounter in school, such as chemistry or physics. They keep your options open and can lead into industries such as electronics or chemicals. But why not also consider something you did not come across at school? Geology, oceanography or meteorology, for example, all have growing importance in an era of resource shortages and climate change. And when you are thinking where all this might go job-wise, bear in mind that industries such as aerospace or IT recruit many engineers, but they also value scientists for their understanding of the basics that underlie the businesses they are in. In any case, all the evidence shows that scientific research turns into new processes, products and even whole businesses faster than ever before. So employers need scientists as well as engineers to hand. For example, you have probably heard of nanotechnology, a new subject, building on previous experience in engineering, physics and chemistry, in which structures are assembled bottom-up, atom by atom. Although the basics are still disputed, there are already nano-products on the market, ranging from fast laptop computers to nano-trousers that include tiny dirt-repelling particles.

Once you have made a start on your life as a scientist, with a decent bachelor-level degree, choices open up. You could get a job in industry at that point, but as with most professions, the expectation is growing that you will have some sort of postgraduate qualification as well. The gold standard here is the PhD, which is often termed the driving license or even pilot's license for aspiring scientists. In the past, it was usually possible to complete a PhD in three years. But many universities, and grant awarders, now realize that science has become too complex for this and allow for PhDs to take four years. In some systems, such as the UK, researchers sometimes take a master's of research (MRes) degree after a year to prove their ability to design experiments, analyze results and otherwise be a force at the cutting edge of knowledge.

The table here will probably be of most use to you when choosing where to do a PhD. Science is expensive. The US National Science Foundation has an annual budget of about US$6 billion and is only one supporter of US science along with other big players such as NASA and the US Department of Defense. In the UK, research councils spend almost £2 billion a year on scientific research. So the big players tend to be in rich countries. The table suggests that anyone wanting a top-level PhD to kick-start is or her career as a scientist, in industry or the academic world, should head for the US. The sheer amount of money in the US system, and the mental firepower attracted to the US by the intellectual freedom on offer there, mean that it dominates this analysis. But the table shows that the UK, with seven universities listed, is also a powerful attractor of the best scientists. Australia and Canada also each have seven institutions.

The art of the scientist

The real art at the PhD stage of your career as a scientist will be finding the research group you want to belong to, and that is asking the questions in science that you want to help answer. This team could be in a specialist science university, of which the Massachusetts Institute of Technology (MIT) is the best-known. It could be in Russia, represented here by two universities, now slowly rebuilding the world position held as a scientific power in the 19th and 20th centuries. Or, increasingly, the research group you want to join might be in Asia. Japan is home to Asia's top science universities, with Tokyo and Kyoto at 12 and 17 in this table. Singapore has announced that it wants to become the science hub of South-East Asia and is putting money into universities to make it happen. The same is true of South Korea, which, like Singapore, has a stress on biology in its science planning. China is also represented by five universities, including Peking at 15 and science specialist Tsinghua at 34. It would be no surprise to find more, and better placed, Chinese institutions in this table in future years.

Top 100 in natural sciences

Rank	Institution	Country	Score	Citations per paper
1	University of California, BERKELEY	United States	100.0	9.0
2	MASSACHUSETTS Institute of Technology (MIT)	United States	97.6	7.8
3	University of CAMBRIDGE	United Kingdom	92.9	6.2
4	HARVARD University	United States	92.6	11.1
5	PRINCETON University	United States	90.2	12.2
6	CALIFORNIA Institute of Technology (Caltech)	United States	87.4	9.1
7	STANFORD University	United States	86.9	6.3
8	University of OXFORD	United Kingdom	86.7	6.3
9	CORNELL University	United States	77.4	7.2
10	YALE University	United States	72.4	8.8
11	University of CHICAGO	United States	72.0	13.8
12	University of TOKYO	Japan	70.6	5.6
13	Imperial College LONDON	United Kingdom	70.2	5.3
14	University of CALIFORNIA, Los Angeles (UCLA)	United States	67.6	7.8
15	PEKING University	China	67.5	3.2
16	University of TORONTO	Canada	66.5	6.1
17	KYOTO University	Japan	65.8	5.0
18	ETH Zurich (Swiss Federal Institute of Technology)	Switzerland	63.0	4.0
19	AUSTRALIAN National University	Australia	62.7	5.5
20	Ecole Normale Supérieure, PARIS	France	62.6	6.9
21	COLUMBIA University	United States	62.3	9.0
22	University of CALIFORNIA, Santa Barbara	United States	58.2	8.9
23	University of TEXAS at Austin	United States	56.2	6.3
24	University of MICHIGAN	United States	56.0	6.1
25	National University of SINGAPORE	Singapore	55.8	4.1
26	MCGILL University	Canada	53.6	4.4
27=	University of CALIFORNIA, San Diego	United States	53.3	6.2
27=	Lomonosov MOSCOW STATE University	Russia	53.3	2.5
29	University of ILLINOIS	United States	52.0	6.1
30	University of BRITISH COLUMBIA	Canada	51.7	5.8
31	ÉCOLE POLYTECHNIQUE	France	51.3	5.2

Rank	Institution	Country	Score	Citations per paper
32	Université Pierre-et-Marie-Curie-PARIS VI	France	49.7	4.9
33	University of MELBOURNE	Australia	49.5	5.2
34	TSINGHUA University	China	48.0	2.5
35	University of PENNSYLVANIA	United States	47.2	10.3
36	TECHNION - Israel Institute of Technology	Israel	47.1	5.7
37	JOHNS HOPKINS University	United States	46.9	10.1
38	SEOUL National University	Korea, South	45.8	4.3
39	University of WISCONSIN-Madison	United States	45.4	5.9
40=	University of Science and Technology of CHINA	China	44.6	2.5
40=	Università degli Studi di ROMA - La Sapienza	Italy	44.6	4.0
42	NEW YORK University (NYU)	United States	43.4	11.3
43	The University of SYDNEY	Australia	42.9	4.4
44	PENNSYLVANIA STATE University	United States	42.4	6.6
45=	HEIDELBERG University	Germany	42.2	6.0
45=	STONY BROOK University	United States	42.2	2.0
47=	UTRECHT University	Netherlands	42.1	5.8
47=	University of WATERLOO	Canada	42.1	3.8
49	GEORGIA Institute of Technology	United States	41.7	5.6
50	CARNEGIE MELLON University	United States	41.5	8.0
51	PURDUE University	United States	41.3	5.4
52=	HONG KONG University of Science & Technology	Hong Kong	40.6	5.0
52=	Université Paris-Sud, PARIS XI	France	40.6	4.9
54=	DUKE University	United States	40.3	6.2
54=	University of QUEENSLAND	Australia	40.3	4.2
56	University of WASHINGTON	United States	40.2	14.5
57	OSAKA University	Japan	40.0	4.3
58	University of NEW SOUTH WALES	Australia	39.9	5.4
59	University of MARYLAND	United States	39.7	6.1
60	Universität GÖTTINGEN	Germany	38.3	4.8
61	University of HONG KONG	Hong Kong	38.2	4.5
62=	BROWN University	United States	38.1	8.2
62=	Ludwig-Maximilians-Universität München (MUNICH)	Germany	38.1	6.3
64	National TAIWAN University	Taiwan	38.0	4.0
65	University of EDINBURGH	United Kingdom	37.8	6.7

Rank	Institution	Country	Score	Citations per paper
66	Technische Universität MÜNCHEN	Germany	37.7	6.0
67	Indian Institute of Technology Bombay (IITB)	India	37.4	2.0
68	MONASH University	Australia	36.9	4.2
69	BOSTON University	United States	36.7	11.6
70	UCL (University College LONDON)	United Kingdom	36.6	5.3
71	Hebrew University of JERUSALEM	Israel	36.5	5.4
72=	OHIO STATE University	United States	36.4	5.7
72=	University of WARWICK	United Kingdom	36.4	4.2
74=	University of VIENNA	Austria	36.3	5.3
74=	Katholieke Universiteit LEUVEN	Belgium	36.3	4.4
76	NANJING University	China	36.2	2.7
77	TEXAS A&M University	United States	36.1	5.3
78	The University of AUCKLAND	New Zealand	36.0	4.1
79	TOKYO Institute of Technology	Japan	35.9	3.9
80	FUDAN University	China	35.8	2.7
81	University of COPENHAGEN	Denmark	35.7	6.2
82	TOHOKU University	Japan	35.6	4.7
83	DELFT University of Technology	Netherlands	35.3	4.2
84	TEL AVIV University	Israel	35.2	4.9
85	University of CALIFORNIA, Davis	United States	35.0	5.0
86	KOREA Advanced Institute of Science & Technology	Korea, South	34.7	3.4
87=	NORTHWESTERN University	United States	34.4	7.2
87=	University of ADELAIDE	Australia	34.4	4.2
89	Ecole Polytechnique Fédérale de LAUSANNE	Switzerland	34.2	8.2
90=	Universidad Nacional Autónoma de México (UNAM)	Mexico	34.1	2.6
90=	SAINT-PETERSBURG State University	Russia	34.1	2.2
92	University of HELSINKI	Finland	33.8	7.3
93	University of MONTREAL	Canada	33.7	4.9
94	CHALMERS University of Technology	Sweden	33.6	4.9
95=	University of ALBERTA	Canada	33.5	4.2
95=	MCMASTER University	Canada	33.5	4.5
97	University of BARCELONA	Spain	32.4	5.1
98	University of BRISTOL	United Kingdom	32.2	6.3
99=	NANYANG Technological University	Singapore	32.0	3.2
99=	University of DELHI	India	32.0	2.6

Studying social sciences

Social scientists, in common with other academics, may not be the richest people on earth, but they can name the people who have the power and wealth, and explain how they got them. The subjects that social scientists study, such as economics, sociology, politics and business, are all to do with the way society operates. And those who work in the fastest growing area of the social sciences, business studies, are an elite in their own right, educating future business leaders and being paid more than any other category of academic.

The social sciences have been growing rapidly in universities since the 1960s and they certainly lead to some significant careers. The biggest social science in terms of student numbers is education. Although few teachers would identify themselves as social scientists, they are the one group of people with social science training who you cannot avoid meeting at an early stage in your life. Many universities across the world started as teacher training institutions, and many still train teachers as an important part of their mission. The numbers are huge. There are 6.2 million teachers in the US alone, or 2 per cent of the population. Just how one becomes a teacher varies from country to country. Depending on what one wants to teach and at what level, it may be necessary to have a degree in another subject first. And remember that in many countries, an increased emphasis is being put on lifelong learning. So you now have more chance of becoming a teacher without seeing any children.

Business studies and economics

But other social sciences have been growing faster than teacher training in recent years. Business studies are the obvious case. While it is possible to go to university straight from school for this subject, this is often regarded as a 'soft' option that impresses few potential employers. By contrast the MBA degree, normally taken by people with some work experience, is the world's most commercially valuable qualification, opening the door to big jobs in the private sector, consultancy and, increasingly, the public sector. Because it is intended both to broaden people's vision of the world and to give them specific skills in topics such as finance and human resources, it is also the most globalized of qualifications, with a lively international trade in ambitious students. There are many different MBAs: full or part time, or with a specific industry orientation. There are also variants such as MPA, Master of Public (rather than Business) Administration. Taking an MBA is a life decision and needs to be researched intensively. The website www.topmba.com from QS, the publishers of this book, is a very useful starting point where you will also find details of the QS World MBA Tour.

Another group of social scientists who have become more visible in recent years are economists. Once they were kept in back rooms in government departments or banks, making occasional pronouncements about such things as interest rates. Now economists have spread their wings. Investment banks pay them big money, and they are also present at all levels of government. They even show up on TV. More to the point, economics is seen as a numerical science that produces proper results and predictions, in contrast to other parts of the social sciences. It is a terrific training for analytical jobs in almost any industry. Other areas of the social sciences are closely related to the laboratory sciences, especially psychology. This subject more or less divides into a scientific and medical arm, with a stress on the brain and an affinity to other areas of neuroscience, and a social science side where the emphasis is on social interaction. While these parts of the social sciences may use methods not unlike those found in the science lab, the same is far from true of other major social sciences. Sociology, the study of social forces and in some ways the original social science, has its own methods and approaches, as do other social sciences such as politics.

But in all social sciences, more uniform data and methods are now emerging that promise to increase the validity of the claims researchers make about their subjects. Topics such as experiment design are getting hotter, while data is now being collected on a consistent basis more widely, for example by the continent-wide European Social Survey. This means that both international and national projects involving international comparisons will become more feasible. The social sciences are becoming more international in other ways too. As globalization gathers pace, we need people to look at how important it is and what it really involves. Industries globalize in different ways and at different speeds. People-intensive industries such as IT can move from place to place fairly readily, but resource-intensive ones need to be near the materials they depend upon. How does globalization work out in these two cases? Are our assumptions right about work moving to India and China from North America and Europe, or will rising wage expectations in Asia blunt its attractiveness to employers? What are the implications of the emergence of skilled but low-paid workforces in Eastern Europe as new countries join the EU?

Disciplines vital to our world

The social sciences are also vital to thinking about the future problems of the societies we live in. In many countries, people are no longer having babies at a rate adequate to replace the population. In some ways, we might applaud people being able to take decisions that allow women to have more interesting lives, and at the same time reduce the demands we make on the earth. But the social sciences take a deeper look. For example, the reduced number of children, and people's longer life spans, mean that in a few decades, all rich countries will have a significant cohort of older women with no children, and therefore no primary carer. How might societies cope with this issue?

The social sciences, especially in Europe and North America, also have a growing role in assessing how society is coping with technical change. It is social scientists that found that people who spend a lot of time on the Internet also spend more time than average socializing with the friends in the real world, disproving the generally held, but false, belief that anyone who spends all their time in cyberspace has no real life.

If you want to study the social sciences at university, you will be faced with a bafflingly wide range of possible choices. If you want to be a teacher, you probably know it already, and the way you become one will probably be determined by the national educational system in your own country. If you want to be an economist, you will need a mathematical mind as well as a strongly analytical way of thinking. For psychology, you need to be interested in biology as well as society. In addition, you will need to be ready for a lengthy professional training akin to that of a doctor if you want to work with patients.

Like other academic areas, the social sciences are in the midst of heavy diversification. There are some social scientists that study sport, and others whose interest is in terrorism. Studying sport might sound like a frivolous way to spend your life. But it is a multi-billion pound industry, it exists in every culture and it interests billions of people. So it is a natural focus for sociological interest. At the other extreme, it might seem obvious that the threat of terror facing many countries will need social science solutions. War studies, a kind of mix of politics, geography, economics and science, with its own unique knowledge on top, is a fast-growing social science. Studies of terrorism involve looking at how and why societies and cultures produce people willing to act in ways that have been unacceptable in almost all times and places. And terrorism connects to yet further issues such as surveillance. How does it alter society and how much protection does it really provide?

The table shows that large general universities such as Harvard and Berkeley are seen as powerhouses of social science research. They are joined by the London School of Economics (LSE), a specialist social science university, and by both Oxford and Cambridge universities and Chicago, home to, perhaps, the world's top economics department.

But the table also shows that a business school is the fastest way to esteem in the social sciences. Business schools are famously easier to fund than universities, as there is often a rich executive, perhaps an alumnus, willing to put money into them, sometimes in return for having his or her name over the door. The top US universities we list here all have a business school, as do Oxford and Cambridge in the shape of the Saïd and Judge business schools respectively. Business schools probably explain the appearance of MIT and Imperial College in this ranking, too. In position 83 is Bocconi, a specialist Italian business school. This table also suggests that the social sciences are an area in which Asia has so far concentrated fewer resources than it has in science, technology and medicine, though this is changing. North America, Europe, Australia and New Zealand, take up the vast majority of the places in this top 100.

Top 100 in social sciences

Rank	Institution	Country	Score	Citations per paper
1	HARVARD University	United States	100.0	5.6
2	University of California, BERKELEY	United States	93.9	5.2
3	LONDON School of Economics and Political Science	United Kingdom	83.4	2.2
4	YALE University	United States	82.8	4.3
5	STANFORD University	United States	82.2	5.0
6	University of OXFORD	United Kingdom	81.6	4.2
7	University of CAMBRIDGE	United Kingdom	81.1	4.1
8	University of CHICAGO	United States	79.6	4.4
9	PRINCETON University	United States	78.9	4.5
10	COLUMBIA University	United States	76.5	4.3
11	MASSACHUSETTS Institute of Technology (MIT)	United States	75.8	4.9
12	MCGILL University	Canada	72.1	3.8
13	University of TORONTO	Canada	71.8	3.6
14	University of BRITISH COLUMBIA	Canada	70.8	3.4
15	University of CALIFORNIA, Los Angeles (UCLA)	United States	67.8	4.9
16	AUSTRALIAN National University	Australia	66.2	2.4
17=	CORNELL University	United States	61.8	3.9
17=	University of MELBOURNE	Australia	61.8	3.7
19	University of MICHIGAN	United States	60.4	4.1
20	National University of SINGAPORE	Singapore	59.5	2.1
21	NEW YORK University (NYU)	United States	58.3	4.0
22	University of PENNSYLVANIA	United States	57.7	4.2
23	PEKING University	China	56.3	2.1
24	University of TOKYO	Japan	54.2	2.2
25	DUKE University	United States	53.9	5.2
26	MONASH University	Australia	51.8	2.1
27	The University of SYDNEY	Australia	50.7	2.7
28	CARNEGIE MELLON University	United States	48.9	4.5
29	NORTHWESTERN University	United States	48.6	3.8
30	University of NEW SOUTH WALES	Australia	47.7	3.7
31	University of HONG KONG	Hong Kong	47.2	2.1
32	UCL (University College LONDON)	United Kingdom	46.4	7.6
33	University of CALIFORNIA, San Diego	United States	45.7	4.5
34	University of QUEENSLAND	Australia	45.2	3.1
35	The University of AUCKLAND	New Zealand	45.0	2.9
36	BOSTON University	United States	44.8	4.5

Rank	Institution	Country	Score	Citations per paper
37	University of WISCONSIN-Madison	United States	44.5	4.3
38	JOHNS HOPKINS University	United States	44.1	4.1
39	University of MONTREAL	Canada	43.1	3.2
40	University of WARWICK	United Kingdom	42.3	2.9
41	YORK University	Canada	41.9	2.6
42	Université Catholique de LOUVAIN (UCL)	Belgium	41.5	2.9
43	QUEEN'S University	Canada	41.4	3.2
44	TSINGHUA University	China	41.1	1.3
45	University of COPENHAGEN	Denmark	40.2	3.1
46	University of VIENNA	Austria	39.8	3.2
47	University of EDINBURGH	United Kingdom	39.6	3.6
48=	The CHINESE University of Hong Kong	Hong Kong	39.4	2.5
48=	University of AMSTERDAM	Netherlands	39.4	3.4
50	PENNSYLVANIA STATE University	United States	38.9	3.1
51	GEORGETOWN University	United States	38.8	3.1
52=	Université Paris-Sorbonne (PARIS IV)	France	38.3	0.7
52=	University of WESTERN ONTARIO	Canada	38.3	3.7
54=	Katholieke Universiteit LEUVEN	Belgium	38.2	3.2
54=	SIMON FRASER University	Canada	38.2	2.5
56	University of ILLINOIS	United States	37.9	3.4
57=	KYOTO University	Japan	37.8	1.9
57=	SEOUL National University	Korea, South	37.8	2.6
59	MCMASTER University	Canada	37.5	4.5
60	TEL AVIV University	Israel	37.4	2.8
61	Freie Universität BERLIN	Germany	36.8	2.5
62	FUDAN University	China	36.7	2.0
63	HONG KONG University of Science & Technology	Hong Kong	36.6	3.7
64	King's College LONDON	United Kingdom	36.4	5.2
65	MAASTRICHT University	Netherlands	36.1	4.5
66	BROWN University	United States	35.8	4.5
67	LEIDEN University	Netherlands	35.6	3.6
68	University of MANCHESTER	United Kingdom	35.4	3.6
69	Hebrew University of JERUSALEM	Israel	35.1	2.9
70	CALIFORNIA Institute of Technology (Caltech)	United States	35.0	3.4
71=	STOCKHOLM School of Economics	Sweden	34.8	2.6
71=	ERASMUS University Rotterdam	Netherlands	34.8	2.7
73	Imperial College LONDON	United Kingdom	34.5	6.3
74	University of HELSINKI	Finland	34.4	3.7

Rank	Institution	Country	Score	Citations per paper
75	National TAIWAN University	Taiwan	34.3	1.8
76	Université PARIS I - Panthéon Sorbonne	France	34.1	0.9
77	University of VIRGINIA	United States	34.0	4.2
78	HEIDELBERG University	Germany	33.7	3.0
79	VICTORIA University of Wellington	New Zealand	33.1	2.1
80	OHIO STATE University	United States	32.7	3.2
81	University of TEXAS at Austin	United States	32.6	3.6
82	Ludwig-Maximilians-Universität München (MUNICH)	Germany	32.4	3.9
83=	University of ALBERTA	Canada	32.3	2.9
83=	University of NORTH CAROLINA	United States	32.3	3.6
83=	CHULALONGKORN University	Thailand	32.3	1.6
83=	Università Commerciale Luigi BOCCONI	Italy	32.3	2.3
87	WASEDA University	Japan	32.1	1.2
88	NANYANG Technological University	Singapore	31.8	1.9
89=	University of WATERLOO	Canada	31.6	2.6
89=	University of ADELAIDE	Australia	31.6	2.3
91	MICHIGAN STATE University	United States	31.5	3.8
92=	University of DELHI	India	31.3	1.3
92=	University of OTAGO	New Zealand	31.3	3.4
94	University of BOLOGNA	Italy	31.0	2.8
95	Universitat POMPEU FABRA	Spain	30.7	2.1
96	University of ROCHESTER	United States	30.6	5.5
97=	University of MINNESOTA	United States	30.5	4.1
97=	University of TOULOUSE I Sciences Sociales	France	30.5	1.2
99=	HUMBOLDT-Universität zu Berlin	Germany	30.4	3.3
99=	LUND University	Sweden	30.4	2.5

Studying engineering and IT

The five subject areas analyzed in these pages attract roughly equal numbers of students. But they differ hugely in the political attention they get. Although prime ministers tend to be trained as lawyers and economists, excellence in technology excites them most and gets them to spend money. One result of this enthusiasm is that almost every major country has one or more specialist technology universities. They are often long established, because the importance of technology has been recognized for many years. Massachusetts Institute of Technology (MIT), top of the list here, was founded in 1865. Its nearest European rival, Imperial College in London, was set up in 1907.

The TImes Higher-QS World University Rankings capture excellence in universities, not specialist colleges with a narrow agenda. So the institutions we list have to teach undergraduates and to be active in at least two of our five chosen subject areas. These criteria unfortunately exclude a number of specialist medical, business and other schools of acknowledged high quality. But, they do not exclude technology universities, prominent both in the subject ranking and in the overall World University Rankings, probably because most include science as well as technology. And a surprising number, including MIT and Imperial, have sprouted music departments, business schools and other bits of academic diversification. Many are big in medical research with associated hospitals and medical schools, such as Imperial College in London.

These universities are of growing power and importance. The new knowledge they generate and the people they produce are in a league of their own when it comes to generating jobs, in particular, well-paid, high technology jobs. This is why the European Commission has put serious thought into the idea of creating a European Institute of Technology (EIT) as a direct equivalent of MIT. This idea is not popular with European governments, as only one country would house the new institution. Nor is it popular with universities, because they would rather the money was spent on expanding their own budgets. Ultimately, EIT is likely to become a virtual university with activities on other campuses.

The changing face of engineering

Subjects within engineering and IT include many traditional subjects such as the big engineering disciplines, plus a raft of newer topics. In the first group we find mechanical, electrical, civil, production and chemical engineering. During the 20th century, electronics aeronautics and others joined these. In some universities, astronautics has been added to aeronautics. And most recently, information and communications technology has arrived on the scene. Here the hardware may be largely the province of the electronics experts, but software and systems skills are the domain of a new group of ICT specialists. But the fact that some of these subjects have been going a long time does not mean that they are out of the loop. Some have had a makeover. For example, metallurgy has turned into materials science as high-technology plastics and ceramics have grown in importance. Even subjects with unchanged names are altering the way they do things. Both the products of these industries and the way they make them have been altered by the rise of information technology and the emergence of new materials and processes. Take construction, for example. In the past, anything from a house to a massive power station was mostly built by hand on a muddy site and in the open air. Now, more and more of the key components are built in a clean factory and assembled on site. This adds to quality, cuts costs and makes for better health and safety.

In future years, traditional engineering subjects such as civil and electrical engineering are going to change even more. Governments, companies and trade bodies all over the world are alarmed that their education systems are not producing the skilled people that these industries will need. Their problem is an opportunity for the future student. Engineers are rarely out of work, and will be in more demand than ever in coming decades. One reason for this is climate change: the systems that have worked well in the past have to change radically. Take automotive engineering: fuel economy has always been regarded as desirable in vehicles, but is now a growing ecological and legal necessity. Toyota, the world's biggest car maker, has led the way in the development of hybrid cars, but these are only the first step. Electric or hydrogen-powered vehicles deriving their fuel from renewable energy or biomass will be next.

The same ethos informs the development of future buildings and cities. In the UK, new housing developments now have to derive ten per cent of their power from renewable sources, but in the longer term there are plans for buildings to use no fossil fuel and even to work in such a way that they absorb, rather than emit, carbon dioxide. These ambitious targets will mean big business for creative engineers. They could find themselves designing zero-carbon, car-free cities. They might be involved in massive renewable energy projects. We are used to seeing wind farms, but what about solar energy farms covering large expanses of the world's deserts or kilometres of devices in the ocean to suck power from the waves? Politicians and environmentalists like to talk about these ideas, but only engineers make them happen. And if these horizons seem too ambitious, climate change means opportunities for engineers nearer to home, literally. In most countries in the world, about one per cent of houses get replaced each year. So in 2050, most of us are going to be living in houses that already exist. If we are to make the transition to a more energy-efficient way of living, we are going to have to improve the buildings we have already, with smart meters to help us save energy, renewable energy devices to tap the Sun and the wind, and far higher standards of energy efficiency. So, such unglamorous arms of technology as building services engineering are going to be at the cutting edge when it comes to saving the planet.

Your engineering and IT career choices

The first thing you need to decide is the subject you want to study. Many branches of technology need a good command of mathematics and physics, which is one reason why they sometimes struggle to get enough top-quality applicants. To be a chemical engineer, you also need to be good at chemistry. So these courses are even more selective, and chemical engineers are among the best-paid engineers.

But remember, studying (say) design engineering or ICT will typecast you at an earlier age than other university choices. So it is worth taking some good advice about the branch of engineering you study. Do you want to work on a factory floor (go for production engineering), or might you be happier developing the next generation of replacement hip joints (try materials engineering)? Whatever choice you make, engineering courses are famously hard work. They involve more lectures and coursework, up to and including major projects, than almost any other subject you might study. This is partly because professional institutions maintain standards on these courses. Having a few bad historians around does not really matter, but people who build bridges or planes need to be on top of the subject.

The next problem is which university to attend, and here there are some harsh realities to face. The top technology institutions that are highly placed on this list are tough to get into. But because all governments want more engineers, there are many places to do an engineering degree where the asking price, both academic and financial, is a lot lower. Perhaps one key decision is whether you want to be at a specialist technology institution, with all that this implies for the atmosphere and the nature of the student body you will be mingling with. If that option does not sound like you, best go for a full-service university that is also good at engineering. There is plenty of choice. The rise of ICT means that California grabs places two, three and four here, just behind MIT. But even here, there is a choice between technology-oriented CalTech and generalist universities Berkeley or Stanford. But the results make it clear that both rich and developing nations are serious about engineering. Switzerland, with both of its federally funded universities here, manages to be a manufacturing power for quality goods despite its high cost base. The same applies to countries such as Sweden, Denmark, the Netherlands and Japan, which has five institutions in this top 100.

The developing world, too, appreciates that technology is the way to wealth. Four of the Indian Institutes of Technology are in this list as are two Singaporean universities including Nanyang, a technology specialist with high ambitions. There are also four Hong Kong and four Chinese universities, including three technology specialists. As always, it is worth taking time to research just where the expertise is that you want to get alongside. For example, Harvard University, 15 in this subject area ranking, has a small but very elite technology faculty. It lives in the shadow of bigger things at neighbouring MIT, but it might be just what you are looking for.

Top 100 in engineering and IT

Rank	Institution	Country	Score	Citations per paper
1	MASSACHUSETTS Institute of Technology (MIT)	United States	100.0	4.0
2	University of California, BERKELEY	United States	94.5	4.2
3	STANFORD University	United States	84.7	4.3
4	CALIFORNIA Institute of Technology (Caltech)	United States	80.0	3.7
5	University of CAMBRIDGE	United Kingdom	75.6	3.4
6	Imperial College LONDON	United Kingdom	72.1	2.7
7	CARNEGIE MELLON University	United States	71.0	3.6
8	GEORGIA Institute of Technology	United States	68.0	2.9
9	University of TOKYO	Japan	65.1	2.1
10	National University of SINGAPORE	Singapore	63.8	2.9
11	University of TORONTO	Canada	60.4	3.5
12	University of OXFORD	United Kingdom	60.2	3.7
13	ETH Zurich (Swiss Federal Institute of Technology)	Switzerland	59.6	2.5
14	PRINCETON University	United States	59.2	4.7
15	HARVARD University	United States	58.3	5.1
16	TSINGHUA University	China	58.2	1.2
17	DELFT University of Technology	Netherlands	57.7	2.6
18	University of CALIFORNIA, Los Angeles (UCLA)	United States	57.4	4.1
19	University of ILLINOIS	United States	57.3	3.5
20	CORNELL University	United States	56.7	4.4
21	University of MELBOURNE	Australia	54.1	2.9
22	TOKYO Institute of Technology	Japan	53.8	1.8
23	HONG KONG University of Science & Technology	Hong Kong	53.6	3.1
24	PURDUE University	United States	53.3	2.7
25=	TECHNION - Israel Institute of Technology	Israel	53.1	1.8
25=	NANYANG Technological University	Singapore	53.1	2.1
27	MCGILL University	Canada	52.8	2.4
28	University of NEW SOUTH WALES	Australia	52.5	2.5
29	KYOTO University	Japan	50.7	2.0
30=	University of BRITISH COLUMBIA	Canada	50.5	2.6
30=	University of TEXAS at Austin	United States	50.5	2.9
32	University of MICHIGAN	United States	50.4	3.6

Rank	Institution	Country	Score	Citations per paper
33	Indian Institute of Technology Bombay (IITB)	India	49.4	1.6
34	ÉCOLE POLYTECHNIQUE	France	48.5	2.3
35	University of WATERLOO	Canada	48.4	2.0
36	PEKING University	China	48.2	1.8
37	Indian Institute of Technology Delhi (IITD)	India	47.3	1.7
38	University of CALIFORNIA, San Diego	United States	47.0	3.8
39	AUSTRALIAN National University	Australia	46.4	2.4
40	Technische Universität MÜNCHEN	Germany	44.7	2.5
41=	The University of SYDNEY	Australia	44.5	2.3
41=	TEXAS A&M University	United States	44.5	2.4
43	University of MANCHESTER	United Kingdom	43.9	2.6
44	MONASH University	Australia	42.8	2.0
45	Virginia Polytechnic Institute (VIRGINIA TECH)	United States	42.7	2.2
46	YALE University	United States	41.7	4.5
47	Ecole Polytechnique Fédérale de LAUSANNE	Switzerland	41.6	5.3
48	KOREA Advanced Institute of Science & Technology	Korea, South	41.3	1.9
49	University of Science and Technology of CHINA	China	40.8	1.0
50	RENSSELAER Polytechnic Institute	United States	40.6	3.3
51	The University of AUCKLAND	New Zealand	39.5	2.5
52	JOHNS HOPKINS University	United States	39.0	3.8
53=	National TAIWAN University	Taiwan	38.7	2.0
53=	KTH, ROYAL Institute of Technology	Sweden	38.7	2.9
55	SHANGHAI JIAO TONG University	China	38.6	0.8
56=	University of EDINBURGH	United Kingdom	38.4	2.9
56=	University of WISCONSIN-Madison	United States	38.4	3.4
56=	SEOUL National University	Korea, South	38.4	2.3
59=	COLUMBIA University	United States	38.1	4.0
59=	University of ALBERTA	Canada	38.1	2.3
59=	Technical University of DENMARK	Denmark	38.1	3.9
62=	University of QUEENSLAND	Australia	38.0	2.0
62=	University of CALIFORNIA, Santa Barbara	United States	38.0	4.2
64	VIENNA University of Technology	Austria	37.2	2.2
65	EINDHOVEN University of Technology	Netherlands	36.9	3.0

Rank	Institution	Country	Score	Citations per paper
66	Politecnico di MILANO	Italy	36.7	1.8
67	NORTHWESTERN University	United States	36.5	4.4
68=	University of HONG KONG	Hong Kong	36.0	2.2
68=	OSAKA University	Japan	36.0	1.9
70	Katholieke Universiteit LEUVEN	Belgium	35.8	3.0
71	Universität STUTTGART	Germany	35.5	2.2
72	HELSINKI University of Technology - TKK	Finland	35.3	2.4
73	University of MARYLAND	United States	35.1	3.0
74	CHALMERS University of Technology	Sweden	34.9	3.0
75	University of MASSACHUSETTS Amherst	United States	34.8	3.4
76=	PENNSYLVANIA STATE University	United States	34.5	3.5
76=	University of SOUTHERN CALIFORNIA	United States	34.5	3.4
78	Technische Universität BERLIN	Germany	34.4	2.2
79	University of PENNSYLVANIA	United States	34.1	4.9
80	Universität KARLSRUHE	Germany	33.8	2.2
81=	University of WASHINGTON	United States	33.7	5.2
81=	Indian Institute of Technology Kharagpur (IITKGP)	India	33.7	1.6
83	Rheinisch-Westfälische Technische Hochschule AACHEN	Germany	33.6	1.8
84	University of BIRMINGHAM	United Kingdom	32.9	2.6
85	The CHINESE University of Hong Kong	Hong Kong	32.6	2.9
86=	University of CALIFORNIA, Davis	United States	31.8	3.2
86=	CITY University of Hong Kong	Hong Kong	31.8	2.7
88	University of MONTREAL	Canada	31.6	2.6
89=	BROWN University	United States	31.3	4.2
89=	MCMASTER University	Canada	31.3	2.7
91	University of CALGARY	Canada	31.2	1.5
92	Indian Institute of Technology Kanpur (IITK)	India	31.0	4.9
93	Universidad Nacional Autónoma de México (UNAM)	Mexico	30.9	1.7
94	UCL (University College LONDON)	United Kingdom	30.6	3.1
95	OHIO STATE University	United States	30.5	2.9
96	University of SOUTHAMPTON	United Kingdom	30.4	2.6
97	Lomonosov Moscow State University	Russia	30.3	1.5
98	BOSTON University	United States	29.9	5.1
99	TOHOKU University	Japan	29.8	2.2
100=	CHULALONGKORN University	Thailand	29.5	1.3
100=	QUEENSLAND University of Technology	Australia	29.5	2.4

10

The top ten study destinations

This chapter surveys the most popular study destination countries in alphabetical order: Australia, Canada, France, Germany, Japan, the Netherlands, the Nordic countries, Singapore the UK and the US. It looks at their typical types of university institutions, their international recognition, local accreditation and quality control, the prevailing attitudes towards international students and services available for students.

These country reviews also try to capture some of the non-quantitative differences, like the teaching styles in each country. For example, the style of teaching in UK institutions is different from that of many other systems of education. Where possible, there is comment on lifestyle, accommodation and availability of employment opportunities for international students and further insight is given into government grants and other subsidies for overseas students

In fact, just six countries host 67 per cent of the world's foreign or mobile students: 23 per cent in the US, followed by the UK (12 per cent), Germany (11 per cent), France (ten per cent), Australia (seven per cent) and Japan (five per cent). According to the Institute for International Education, the 25 countries which supply the most of these students to study overseas are: China, India, Korea, Japan, Greece, Germany, France, Turkey, Morocco, Italy, Taiwan, Malaysia, Canada, USA, Indonesia, Spain, Hong Kong, UK. Kazakhstan, Russia, Thailand, Singapore, Poland, Brazil and Ireland.

Students of different nationalities have different needs such as language preparation, social networks and adapting to new teaching styles. It is impossible to address all these issues in detail here, but the information in this chapter may help you narrow down the relative suitability and feasibility for you of one country as a study destination, relative to others.

Study in Australia

Things to consider

+ **Clear framework of qualifications**
+ **Reasonable costs of tuition and living**
+ **Possible to work and study**
+ **Good international reputation for degree quality**

- **Ease of gaining an entry visa**
- **High numbers of international students on some programs**

Types of institution

With 12 institutions in the top 200 of the rankings, six of which are in the top 50, Australian universities have a deserved international reputation for high quality. Australia's education system benefits from a very simple and open series of qualifications, encapsulated in the Australian Qualifications Framework (AQF). This structure enables students to move from one institution to another, even though they may be of very different types.

There are 41 universities, 38 of which are publicly funded by the Australian Government and three private, located over the entire country. The highest concentration of universities is in New South Wales, in the south east of Australia, Victoria, in the south, and Queensland, in the north east. The leading set of universities in Australia is known as The Group of Eight and covers the major research institutions of the University of Adelaide, Australian National University, University of Melbourne, Monash University, University of New South Wales, University of Queensland, University of Sydney and the University of Western Australia.

All universities offer bachelor, master and PhD programs. Like all qualifications governed by the AQF, the bachelor qualification, throughout the country, subscribes to defined learning outcomes and overall structure, ensuring that students are aware of exactly what their program should consist of and result in.

Additionally, Government funded Technical and Further Education institutions (TAFE) offer more vocationally orientated courses intended for those with more specific hands-on career goals. These institutions offer a range of qualifications from Certificates, Diplomas to Advanced Diplomas, all of which can act as alternative ways to access degree-level education. These qualifications vary in length, but tend to last between one and two years.

There is certainly a distinctive academic style in Australian institutions, where interaction with academic members of staff and fellow students is encouraged as an important part of the learning process. Like the UK system, most degree programs are based around lectures for basic instruction with smaller, follow-up classes to tackle particular themes or issues. Each course will have a set number of texts to review and term papers to submit as part of your assessment. Students are encouraged to work around their lecture subjects and develop close working relationships with other students and academic staff, where relevant.

Quality and recognition of qualifications

Australian undergraduate qualifications are considered among the leaders in the world. A robust system of quality control ensures that degrees and other qualifications all reach minimum standards, equal to international systems of quality assurance. As with other countries, the quality and recognition of qualifications from Australia forms one of the key reasons why so many international students choose to study in the country.

Unlike most other countries, Australian quality assurance is enacted through parliamentary legislation and includes four key measures: establishment of a university only through State or Federal Act, the AQF, the Educational Services for Overseas Students (ESOS) Act, which guarantees basic consumer rights to international studies following Australian qualifications and the Australian Universities Quality Assurance (AUQA), an independent organization that audits universities every five years.

Fees, finance and cost of living

Australia offers excellent value for money in terms of the costs of tuition and living. Tuition fees are set by individual universities and vary by faculty and individual program. On average, fees vary from AU$14,000 per year for an arts degree at a smaller university to AU$50,000 per year for a medicine degree at one of the country's most prestigious institutions. However, degree programs in the most popular fields for international students, such as business, law and engineering, tend to range between AU$18,000 and AU$25,000 per year.

Though there are regional variations and differences between certain cities, the cost of living in Australia is lower than in countries such as the UK and USA. On average you will require approximately AU$12,500 per year to pay for your books, accommodation, food, utility bills and entertainment.

Scholarships

There are very few scholarships offered at undergraduate level to international students. Possible sources of this kind of funding are the Australian Government, whose awards are often administered by IDP Education Australia, individual universities and private organizations. Those that are available tend to be highly competitive and therefore difficult to obtain. Details are available online at http://students.idp.com/english/study/article33.asp and the websites of individual universities.

Entry requirements

All Australian institutions set their own entry requirements, but for most university programs, 12 years of education is the minimum standard required. Additionally, if your education has not been conducted in English, you will also need to submit a recognised language qualification, the level of which will be set by the institution you are interested in. For those without appropriate qualifications, bridging qualifications are also offered by Australian institutions to enable students to qualify for degree level programs.

Undergraduate level applications to Australian institutions are made either direct to the institution in question, or via the Universities Admissions Centre (UAC), representing 16 universities throughout the country. Details of the application process through UAC are available at www.uac.edu.au.

Living and working

Australia is regarded as one of the most welcoming and friendly places in which to live, work and study. It is a country that has distinct seasons, magnificent natural scenery, beautiful and well-planned cities and a diverse population. From the cultural centres of Sydney and Melbourne, to the coastal areas and rainforests of Queensland and the preserved wilderness of Tasmania, visitors enjoy many different aspects of life in Australia.

Life in Australia tends to be very informal and is built on a very tolerant view of the world. A quarter of Australia's 20 million inhabitants was born overseas and the country boasts a varied ethnic mix. Immigration has been central to the development of modern Australia and the resulting diversity, often concentrated in the urban areas, contrasts with the ancient and indigenous culture.

The country is very large and distances between major urban centres can be very great indeed. Travel is often best undertaken by air, though long-distance bus and rail routes can be cheaper. Within individual states and cities, a range of transport options are available, the costs of which are very reasonable and often even more economical with a student discount.

Medical care is not free in Australia. All students are expected to maintain an Overseas Student Health Cover (OSHC), an insurance policy that allows them to claim back the cost of their medical treatment from their individual health funds. Many academic institutions have medical care on campus, or can, at least, recommend a local doctor or hospital.

As a full time international student you are permitted to work a maximum of 20 hours a week during term time and full time in vacations. Before applying for work, you will need to have applied for, and obtained, a work permit at the local Department of Immigration, Multicultural & Indigenous Affairs (DIMIA) office. Students are encouraged to seek employment in a field that is relevant, or at least complimentary, to their field of study, though, in reality, many seek casual employment in the popular entertainment, catering and retails sectors.

Student life

At every level of education in Australia you will find a welcoming and supporting student infrastructure to make your period of study as fulfilling as possible. Sports, social, cultural and academic clubs are all organized on or near to campus and provide an excellent way to meet other students and get to know a little more about the Australian way of life. As with other countries, these clubs tend to be organized and managed by the institution's Students' Union.

Social life in Australian institutions takes many forms and is often made more dynamic by the friendly and open manner with which many Australians welcome visitors. As a student you will benefit from discounts at restaurants, cinemas, pubs and clubs leaving you with a choice of things to do throughout the year. Additionally, should you need it, support is on hand from both academic and personal advisers to ensure that your student life is as trouble free as possible.

Study in Canada

Things to consider

+ **Good choice of institutions and programs**
+ **Reasonable costs of tuition and living**
+ **Opportunities to stay after graduation**
+ **Well regarded quality of education**

- **Smaller number of world famous universities**
- **Differences in the structure of degree programs between the provinces**

Types of institution

11 of Canada's 89 universities appear in the Top 200 of the rankings, three of which are in the top 50, demonstrating the good quality and reputation of the country's higher education system. At present the majority of Canada's institutions are publicly funded and are located across ten provinces. Additionally, Canada boasts a range of other post-secondary school education institutions, known as colleges, university colleges, institutes of technology and advanced learning, community colleges and colleges of applied arts and technology. Many of these institutions are able to grant degree-level qualifications, though many of the community colleges offer diplomas, certificates and associate degrees.

Canada's leading universities are known at the Group of Ten. These institutions are among the most research active in the country and specialize in offering joint research programs. The member institutions are the Universities of Alberta, British Columbia, Laval, McGill, McMaster, Montréal, Queen's, Toronto, Waterloo and Western Ontario. A range of other Canadian universities are equally well known and offer taught and research programs across a broad range of academic subjects.

There are over 200 universities and colleges that are currently permitted to grant undergraduate degrees in Canada. The majority of these programs are structured around three or four years of teaching, depending on the province and whether the degree is general or specialized. Honours degrees — or a baccalaureate program — indicate a higher level of academic achievement within the Canadian system, concentrating in the major subject areas. At some universities, the honours degree stream may take an additional year to complete. There are, however, small differences between institutions and provinces within the Canadian post-secondary school education system and so each individual university is the best source of information for exact specifications and requirements.

Like many other systems of higher education, the teaching and learning experience at a Canadian university is centred on a blend of teaching methods. Large lectures are common in the early stages of an undergraduate degree, with as many as 500 in some of the common, core subjects. However, as the program becomes more specialized or students become seniors, the lectures invariably get smaller. As Canadian universities offer a range of core components, students are often able to have a great deal of flexibility in their choice of subjects and so can design their own timetable to suit their tastes. Smaller classes follow up the larger lectures and enable student to develop their own ideas based on the work undertaken outside of class.

Most Canadian universities follow a trimester system with three sessions: fall, winter/spring and summer, the latter being optional for many students. Individual program courses can last one trimester, or the entire academic year, the level of credit being earned being adjusted accordingly. Assessment is based on a combination of mid-term examinations, term papers and class presentations.

Quality and recognition of qualifications

As one of the largest systems of higher education in the world, Canada has an extremely robust quality assurance and accreditation process ensuring that degree-level studies are recognised internationally. Most Canadian institutions subscribe to the Association of Universities and Colleges of Canada principles of institutional quality assurance. Adherence to these principles is renewed every five years. Further details are available at www.aucc.ca/qa/principles/index_e.html. Canadian universities also have to be in compliance with provincial or regional authorities for quality assurance, thus creating a double guarantee for students. All institutions and programs subscribe to a regular cycle of reviews by the appropriate authority. These tend to be peer-led and involve an element of self-evaluation and external review by subject experts, the results of which are made public for the sake of transparency.

Fees, finance and cost of living

Tuition fees are set by each individual institution and vary between private and public institutions and also by subject area. Undergraduate programs range from C$10,000 and C$24,000 per year depending on what and where you choose to study.

Canada has a moderate cost of living, allowing students to stretch their budgets as far as possible. Accommodation is very often provided at reasonable cost by universities in the first year of your program, at least. In subsequent years, many students seek private housing off-campus. Costs depend on the part of the country you are studying in but students are able to live reasonably well on, between, C$8,500 and C$10,500 a year.

Scholarships

Some scholarships and other forms of financial aid are available to offset the costs of studying in Canada. The best source of funds tends to be individual universities and colleges, many of whom offer a range of different scholarship types that cover tuition costs or living expenses and sometimes both. Many awards are based solely on academic merit and therefore financial aid is not taken into account through the application process.

The Canadian government also offer a range of awards for undergraduate students as do a large number of universities. A free service coordinates most scholarships and is available at www.scholarshipscanada.com. A number of scholarships that offer funds to cover tuition fees and living expenses are administered by the Association of Universities and Colleges of Canada, details of which can be found at www.aucc/scholarships/open_e.html.

Entry requirements

Canadian universities have long enjoyed educating students from all over the world and are therefore very familiar with a range of high school qualifications. The minimum entry requirements are those that lead to university entrance in your own country, though most students will have completed 12 years of formal school education before their undergraduate degree. Students apply directly to the university in which they are interested for admission, using the institution's application materials, most of which can be found online.

Each individual university sets its entry standards and these tend to vary according to the subject you are applying for. If you have not been educated in English then you will be expected to demonstrate your language ability through either an IELTS or TOEFL result. All Canadian institutions operate deadlines unique to their own requirements, but most undergraduate applications should be submitted between January and March of the year in which you wish to commence your studies.

Living and working

Canada is a vast country that offers international students many possibilities during their period of study. From the multicultural, world cities of Vancouver and Toronto to the smaller cities of Montréal and Ottawa, Canada boasts a proud and unique history that blends both British and French cultures — the country is officially bilingual — with significant minorities from Germany, the Netherlands, Greece, Poland, China, Ireland and the Ukraine.

Transport links are excellent, though the journey between some cities can take a surprisingly long time. The size of the country is something that few visitors ever quite understand, but this sense of scale and openness is an important facet in the Canadian life and character. There are six time zones in the country and, overall, Canada is the same size as the entire continent of Europe. The outdoor life is something that attracts many international students, with unparalleled opportunities for skiing and camping throughout the country.

As an international student, you are allowed to work in Canada, though you must obtain a Social Insurance Number before seeking employment. Full time students are permitted to work on campus without a work permit if they are enrolled at an appropriately recognized institution. Off campus work is also available, to a maximum of 20 hours per week in term time and full time in vacations, if certain requirements are fulfilled. These include being a full time student for six of the preceding 12 months, having a good academic record and paying the work permit application fee.

Access to medical care is dependant on the province that you are studying in. Alberta, British Columbia and Saskatchewan cover international students under their provincial health care plans. All other provinces require students to make their own arrangements and have sufficient private healthcare cover for the length of their studies.

Student life

Student life in Canada tends to be centred on events and clubs organized by on campus groups, though the social scene in towns and cities around the country is equally inviting. Most students spend between 15 and 20 hours a week in formal classes, allowing a lot of free time for other activities. Larger universities organize many activities for their students and encourage active participation in the life of the university community.

Student societies and campus groups offer a myriad of possibilities for the new student and it is not uncommon to be faced with a choice of 200 different associations to become involved with. Sports, academic, cultural, religious and purely social clubs are all available on campus and make student life rich with possibilities.

Study in France

Things to consider

+ Large number of highly reputable universities
+ Many government grants for international students
+ Many bi-lingual French/English language-based masters
+ Reasonable employment opportunities for students
+ Moderate tuition fees

- Most undergraduate courses in French only
- Moderate acceptance rate for international students
- Difficult post-study visa situation for employment
- Many private colleges of dubious quality

France is one of the world's leading destinations for foreign students: more than 245,000 choose France every year. As a spokesperson for CampusFrance points out, France has many attractions for foreign students: "France is one of the world's top tourist venues, renowned for its art and culture. France is a first-class centre for scientific and technological innovation, in such fields as aerospace, transportation, electronics, telecommunications, chemistry, biotechnology and health."

Types of institution

The traditionally high quality of French degrees is rooted in a network of internationally renowned research centres and institutions of higher education, of which there are more than 3,000, including 87 universities, 240 engineering schools, and 230 business schools. There are a further 2,000 other establishments devoted to such fields as art, fashion, design, architecture and paramedical training.

France's 87 public universities are spread throughout the country, from the Sorbonne in Paris (founded in 1179) to the high-tech campus of Nice-Sophia-Antipolis, and cover the entire range of academic disciplines Every level is represented in the awarding of national diplomas, including the licence, masters degree and doctorat (PhD).

315 doctoral schools educate 4,000 doctoral candidates in connection with more than 1,200 research laboratories (affiliated to both the universities and research organizations). French doctoral schools have always been very open to international students. The university system also stays in step with today's world, offering technological specializations and professional degrees, including:

- University engineering diplomas
- Professional qualification training via the Institutes
- Universitaires de Technologie (IUT) (a 2-year post-baccalauréat (French secondary school matriculation examination) program), offering more than 25 specializations
- A complete professional curriculum
- Management training through the Instituts d'Administration des Entreprises (IAE)
- Political Science and Economics Degrees through the Instituts d'Études Politiques (IEP)
- Journalism and Communications, with the Institut Français de Presse (IFP) and the École des Hautes Études en Sciences de l'Information et de la Communication (CELSA) or the Centre de Formation des Journalistes (CCFJ)

Studies of medicine, pharmacology, and dentistry are offered in universities in partnership with university hospitals and have their own organization and courses of study.

The Grandes Écoles are uniquely French institutions. Created in the early 19th century in parallel to the university system, they are extremely selective and offer education at a very high standard. Students are recruited either just after the baccalaureat, or at various levels, depending on their academic background. Once they get the Grande École Diploma, they can pursue doctorate studies upon specific conditions. Grandes Écoles offer diplomas at the baccalauréat + five years level, masters degrees. Graduates can follow up this degree with a specialization, such as a specialized engineering degree or a Master of Business Administration (MBA). There are also approximately 240 engineering schools, which share common characteristics; this guarantees the quality of the engineering degree, which is at masters level and covers all areas of engineering science. Grandes Écoles also exist for the study of business and management; the business schools (about 230 of them) offer specializations and training adapted to the changing economic environment and new management practices. Instruction is often structured around internships and international exchanges.

Further specialized institutions offer higher level training in specific areas such as art, design, fashion, tourism, paramedical services, social services, and so on. There are three types of art schools: the Écoles Nationals Supérieures d'Art (Grandes Écoles for art), which offer a national diploma after four or five years of study; the schools for applied art, which are supervised by the Ministry of National Education; and the schools of fine art by the Ministry of Culture, offering diplomas after three or five years of study. All have selective admission policies. Additionally, there are 20 architecture schools, overseen by the Ministry of Culture, offering the DPLG (Diplômé par le Gouvernement) architectural diploma, the only qualification in the field recognized for those working as architects in France. Studies last for six years in three cycles of two years each.

Entry requirements & admissions

French higher education is based on a common architecture (LMD), recognized at the European level, that counts the number of years of validated study following the baccalauréat The table below outlines the structure of the French system. As long as he or she meets the entrance requirements, any foreign student in an institution of higher education in his or her home country may apply for admission to a comparable French institution.

+ 9 years	• Diplôme d'État de docteur en Médecine	DOCTORAT
+ 8 years	• Doctorat	
+ 6 years	• Diplôme d'État de docteur en Chirurgie dentaire • Diplôme d'État de docteur en Pharmacie	
+ 5 years 300 ECTS	• Master recherche - Diplôme d'Études Approfondies (DEA) • Master professionnel - Diplôme d'Études Supérieures Spécialisées (DESS) • Diplôme d'ingénieur • Diplômes des Écoles de Commerce et de Gestion	MASTER
+ 4 years	• Maitrise	
+ 3 years 180 ECTS	• Licence • Licence professionnelle	LICENCE
+ 2 years	• Diplôme d'Études Universitaires Générales (DEUG) • Diplôme Universitaire de Technologie (DUT) • Brevet de Technicien Supérieur (BTS) • Diplôme d'Études Universitaires Scientifiques et Techniques (DEUST)	

End of secondary studies + baccalaureat = admission to higher education system

The 'N+I' Network is intended for students already having a bachelors degree in their own country. It brings together 60 Grandes Écoles and engineering training programs and delivers, after two years, the national engineering diploma (Masters degree). N+I covers virtually all engineering fields. For more information, visit www.nplusi.com. The advantages of this shared network are numerous:

- a single online registration and common application deadline
- shared selection of students with collective access to the student's file and common selection committee meetings
- a shared semester of training in language and study methods for all enrolled students.

Fees, finance and cost of living

International students pay the same fees as domestic students in most universities and on most academic programs. In national universities, the state pays a very large part of each student's study expenses (about €10,000 per year), keeping admission fees relatively low.

As with all EU countries, since the introduction of the Euro, the costs of basic items like food and rent have risen significantly. Cost of living indices suggest that Paris is about 15 per cent less expensive than London. Other French cities are significantly less expensive than Paris. The availability of student accommodation is generally good, though the quality tends to be somewhat variable on most campuses.

Living and working

For food and sports aficionados, France is a wonderful place to live and work. It is a racy, sexy country, which embraces modernism whilst retaining a strong sense of history and culture. Young people are allowed to be vocal and opinionated. For international students willing to learn the language, this can be a great experience.

Like all big cities, Paris can be a bit daunting, especially for those who do not speak French. It takes time to get to know local people and to break out of the international student community. Many campuses have rural settings, which can also result in a sense of isolation. For those willing to embrace the culture, it can be a life changing experience, which is why many foreign students choose to settle in France after their studies, work permits permitting.

Unlike other European countries, however, there is no easy route to working visas after a program of study has been completed. Internships are generally available, but with 20 per cent youth unemployment, there is a great deal of local competition for graduate jobs. It is not wise to be rely on a career in France to help pay for studies.

Student life

Sports facilities at most French universities are excellent. The French government has invested heavily in providing excellent track, field and stadia for sports in all, except the inner city, universities.

Student services tend not to differentiate between local and foreign students and with many students living at home, these services can be limited in scope. Generally, international students form their own groups. Political activism is common on French campuses, providing an interesting, if opinionated network. Cinema and cultural networks are also very common — great for lovers of art and theatre.

Study in Germany

Things to consider

- \+ No, or low, tuition fees
- \+ Excellent academic reputation
- \+ Familiarity with international students

- \- Procedure for admission
- \- Lack of English language taught programs

Types of institution

With more than 300 institutions of higher education throughout the country, Germany offers one of the largest university systems in Europe. Eleven German universities appear in the world Top 200 rankings, underlining the quality of both teaching and research in these institutions. German universities are well regarded internationally and, over the centuries, they have been responsible for great discoveries across the entire range of academic disciplines.

There are seven main types of institutions in Germany, all offering different types of higher education. The two main categories are universities and universities of applied sciences (Fachhochschule). Universities offer programs in which research and study are very closely aligned, with the result that graduates have a firm grasp of the theoretical nature of the subject they have studied. Universities of applied sciences offer students the opportunity to combine a basic level of academic knowledge with a more practical application relevant to the work environment. Because these institutions are orientated towards the development of students for a range of careers, members of teaching staff tend to be experienced professionals able to guide the curriculum to support their students in meeting career goals.

Other categories of institution include art and music colleges, church-sponsored universities, vocational universities in certain German states, and private colleges. The latter institutions are currently very popular in the German system, though not all of them are officially recognised. About 50 recognised colleges currently exist and offer a range of qualifications, including degree-level study, for those students willing to pay their tuition fees.

German universities offer different types of degrees, many of which are unique to the German system. The Diplom, Magister Artium and Staatsexamen all represent qualifications that are currently available in many subject areas. Most degrees should be completed in four years, or eight semesters, though the availability of courses and the volume of work often result in degrees taking a much longer period of time. However, in line with the Bologna Declaration reforms, the German system of degrees is being overhauled so that bachelors programs last three and four years and masters degrees a further one or two years. This process has already resulted in more than 2,800 bachelors programs being offered in 2007.

German university programs offer two strands of education — one general, the other specialized. General education offers students the opportunity to gain essential analytical and scientific skills relevant to their chosen area of study. On completion of an intermediate examination, students then move on to a period of study that is much more focused on their particular subject, developing an in depth knowledge and understanding of their specialization.

Like other systems of European education, German universities feature a blend of teaching methods that includes lectures, classes and seminars. Much of the work involved in attaining a German degree occurs outside of the classroom, with self-directed study, background reading and the preparation of assignments and class material contributing to a successful study experience. Tutorials and seminars are a student's opportunity to present his or her own ideas and tackle particular problems or discussions.

Quality and recognition of qualifications

German qualifications, at all levels, are regarded as being of the highest quality, based on a system of education that blends thorough theoretical knowledge with cutting-edge research, informed by contemporary technology and discoveries. The need for quality assurance among German qualifications is well recognized and is the ultimate responsibility of the Standing Conference of Ministers for Cultural Affairs (KMK), which has now implemented a number of measures to ensure adherence to agreed quality standards.

An accreditation council now implements standard procedures for all institutions of higher education that wish to have government recognition and uses additional agencies to support and enforce this process. Additionally, with many German universities moving towards the Bologna system from September 2007, quality standards that match with the rest of Europe ensure that German degree programs are internationally recognized.

Fees, finance and cost of living

One of the major attractions of studying in German is the almost universal support of all students by the state governments, meaning that there are no or very low tuition fees for international students. In most German states tuition fees are now levied for local and international students alike at a rate of €1,000 per year.

In common with many European destinations, the cost of living in Germany is relatively high, though students are able to live economically on a budget of between €600 and €800 a month. Student discounts reduce the cost associated with many things such as train travel, museum entry and some clubs and bars.

Scholarships

Because tuition fees are low, the need for financial aid and scholarships is greatly reduced. However, a range of awards exist that support students' living and study expenses in Germany. Many of these awards are offered by individual German states and are specific to the country of origin of the student applying for the award. A comprehensive database that covers all German awards and is administered by the DAAD is available at www.daad.de/deutschland/foerderung/stipendiendatenbank/00462.en.html.

Entry requirements

A major advantage of applying to study at a German university is that the application procedure is relatively straightforward. The minimum requirement is for students to have completed their country's equivalent of the German Abitur, the local high school qualification, taken after 13 years of education. However, students may also be required to take an admission assessment test (Feststellungsprüfung) that varies according to the type of institution that they are interested in. Most often, this test requires the completion of a preparatory course known as a Studienkolleg that lasts as long as two semesters.

Students also have to demonstrate knowledge of German, if the program of study they wish to pursue is taught in the local language. This is done through successful completion of the Deutsche Sprachprüfung für den Hochschulzugang (DSH) or the Test Deutsch als Fremdsprache (TestDaF) examinations. The latter examination can often be taken abroad at your local Goethe Institut. An increasing number of international programs are now being offered at German institutions. These use English as the language of instruction and you do not need to demonstrate your ability in German.

Applications are generally made direct to the university you are interested in, on forms supplied by either DAAD or the institution itself. However, more than 50 German universities now use the 'uni-assist procedure,' that allows international students to apply to a number of institutions with the same documents. Full details are available at http://www.uni-assist.de.

Living and working

As one of the largest countries in Europe, Germany offers something for everyone. With a vibrant culture and rich history, students find Germany to be a fascinating yet welcoming country in which to live and study. Though Germans have a reputation for being very serious and punctual, contemporary Germany is relaxed, open, welcoming to strangers, exciting and above all diverse. With large immigrant communities all over the country, culture and cuisine are now international yet proud of their strong German traditions.

The country itself is large, but excellent transport links — probably the best in all of Europe — allow trips of discovery whenever you have a spare weekend. From the mountains of the south, where cross-country and alpine skiing and trekking are popular, to the ports of the north, each state has a slightly different character and charm. Additionally, with its central location, Germany is a good base to explore the rest of Europe and has excellent air links to the rest of the world.

Though many people do speak English, knowledge of the German language is a definite advantage. Daily life will certainly be easier if you are comfortable with the basics of the language. The standard of healthcare is excellent in Germany and all international students are required to have public health insurance before they are permitted to register for their classes. This insurance covers all medical expenses and costs less than €50 a month. Students over the age of 30, however, are not eligible for this cover and must obtain private health insurance.

All students are allowed to work without a work permit while they study in Germany, though students from outside the EEA are limited to a fixed period of 90 days or 180 half-days throughout the year. Some local states may operate slightly different rules, but the local employment office will be able to offer the best advice. Students tend to be very popular employees in Germany, since employers are only required to pay a small element of their social welfare contributions for part-time workers.

Student life

German universities offer a range of activities for their students. Sports and social clubs are common and offer an excellent way to make friends and enjoy the local life. Additionally, many German university academic departments have a representative body that coordinates student activities and represents your interests, particularly in relation to your academic life.

Though many German universities offer large campuses few have large halls of residence, so finding accommodation and a centre for your social life is different from other countries. There are, however, many attractions available to you, irrespective of the size of town or city you are studying in, all of which are open to you as a student and students receive many discounts for attending cultural events. Bars and restaurants are very popular student destinations and the friendly nature of German social life makes for an exciting social scene.

Study in Japan

Things to consider

+ **Reputation for academic excellence throughout Asia**
+ **Generous number of scholarships for international students**
+ **Excellent support for international students**

- **High cost of tuition and living expenses**
- **Limited number of programs taught in English**
- **Lack of global reputation for undergraduate degrees**

Types of institution

Japan is the powerhouse of higher education in Asia, with 11 universities in the top 200 of the rankings and three in the top 50, all of which have risen up the rankings from last year: University of Tokyo (17th), Kyoto University (25th) and Osaka University (46th). Japanese higher education is split into a number of clearly defined sections and students can enter any one of five types of institution. These are colleges of technology, professional training colleges (senmom gakko), junior colleges, colleges and universities and graduate schools. All of these institutions fall into a further three categories, depending on their administrative status, of national, local public or private.

There are over 700 universities in Japan, the majority of which are private. The 87 national and 73 local public universities derive the majority of their funding from the government and teach across the entire range of academic subjects at undergraduate and postgraduate levels. Junior colleges offer two-year diplomas, generally vocational in emphasis, where the education is centred on developing skills for the workplace. At present, few of these programs are offered in English. Professional training colleges also provide for more vocational education, offering courses lasting between one and four years.

Undergraduate programs at universities and colleges tend to take four years to complete across most subject areas. There are some six-year programs in the fields of dentistry, medicine and veterinary science. Almost all instruction is conducted in Japanese and there are very few bachelor degrees offered in English, though some short-term programs are available. A searchable database is available at www.jasso.go.jp/cgi-bin/use/univ_search.cgi.

The style of instruction in most undergraduate programs in the Japanese system is a split between formal lectures, laboratories (where relevant) and classes. Work is monitored through examinations and each course usually requires a number of class papers to be submitted every semester. Each student is assigned a tutor from the academic staff and international students are often also provided with a student tutor to enable them to adapt to the different learning culture.

Quality and recognition of qualifications

Though the Japanese government has been deregulating higher education over the last ten years, the Ministry of Education retains the right to approve new institutions and major new academic programs. An established list of criteria is used to judge the quality of individual programs, including proposed curriculum, expected enrolments, staff-student ratio and facilities. This process ensures that Japanese higher education qualifications will conform to international standards and therefore be recognized outside the country.

Since 2004, all public and private institutions are required to be accredited by a national organization under the management of the Ministry of Education so that the quality of all programs and institutions is assured. As the accreditation system is relatively new, not all institutions have undergone a visit under the regime and it is likely to take a further three years before the entire higher education sector has been audited.

Fees, finance and cost of living

Japan is regarded as one of the most expensive countries in the world. The tuition fees for most institutions of higher education, however, are very competitively priced. Universities, language institutes, junior colleges and professional training colleges all have different fees as well as different levels of fee depending on the subject in question.

National universities charge, per year, in the region of JPY (Japan Yen) 834,800 (US$7,600); local public universities JPY950,000 (US$8,600); private universities between JPY1,118,000 (US$10,200) and JPY5,000,000 (US$45,500), depending on subject area. Junior colleges range between JPY580,000 (US$5,300) and JPY1,300,000 (US$11,800), depending on whether an institution is national, local or private. In all cases, the tuition fee is approximately 30 per cent higher for the first year of a program, than in subsequent years, as there is an admission fee.

Living expenses vary according to where you choose to study. Kanto and Tokyo tend to be the most expensive cities, though others are also quite costly. On average students spend JPY 130,800 (US$1,200) per month on living expenses, including housing, study and entertainment. The majority of this expenditure goes towards accommodation, whether in university halls of residence or private apartments.

Scholarships

Scholarships are available for many of the different types of higher education institution in Japan for international students, though they are less common in professional training colleges and language institutes. Scholarships are administered through the individual institutions where the application and selection of the award is administered.

The majority of these scholarships do not cover all expenses; rather, they meet some, or all, of the tuition fees, plus an amount for living costs. Students applying for these awards can be resident in Japan or another country at the time of application, though they should ensure that they meet all other requirements at the point of application.

Japanese government or Monbukagakusho scholarships provide up to JPY135,000 (US$1,200) a month for potential undergraduate students and are tenable for the entire period of study. Additionally, funding is available from JASSO, local government, individual educational institutions, corporate bodies and private foundations.

Entry requirements

When applying for an undergraduate degree, students must have completed 12 years of education and demonstrate their ability to this level through a recognized high school qualification. Where students have completed only 11 years of schooling, university preparatory courses are offered by some institutions to help bridge the academic gap. For international students there is a further requirement that they are 18 years of age.

Each university has its own application procedure and requirements for supporting documentation. Generally, an application form, a letter of reference, high school transcript and medical certificate will be required. Application schedules are announced in June for programs beginning in April the following year, though some universities also announce a September or October admissions procedure. Not all universities accept direct applications from international students, though approximately 100 do. Full details are available at www.jasso.go.jp.

Students must also sit and pass an entrance examination for Japanese universities. The Examination for Japanese University Admission for International Students (EJU) is administered by the Japan Student Services Organisation (JASSO) and each university sets its own timetable for this examination. At present, the exam is most commonly offered twice yearly in June and November. Additionally, some universities require non-native Japanese applicants to complete the Japanese Language Proficiency Test before admission is granted.

Living and working

Living in Japan allows a student to experience one of the most modern, dynamic and individual cultures in the world today. Ancient traditions stand side-by-side with modern technology and architecture, making Japan a feast for all. As a country, Japan enjoys a varied geographical character with four distinct seasons, all integral to the development of local art and culture. High mountains, hot springs, modern cities and a varied coastline contribute to a fascinating country.

Culturally, there is no other country quite like Japan. Rich in festivals and folk art, contemporary cinema and traditional poetry, as well deeply traditional ceremonies and unique sports, Japan also celebrates its distinctive cuisine as a central part of life. As an international student you will have the choice of living in university or private accommodation at the heart of such a culture, and approximately 75 per cent of students live in the latter. However, because of the cost and availability of housing in Japan, students can encounter some difficulty in finding a place to live. University service centres and private accommodation bureaux can help in most cases.

International students are free to work part time once they have formal permission from their university and the local immigration bureau and without the necessary documentation you may be deported. You are allowed to work a maximum of 28 hours a week during term-time and a maximum of eight hours a day in vacations, though there are certain restrictions on the kinds of work you can do. Most students obtain employment through their university careers office or private agencies.

Healthcare is offered through the national health insurance system, which all students must enrol in. Payments are made monthly under the scheme and vary according to where you live, though students tend to pay a lower premium than others. Under the scheme, students pay only 30 per cent of their medical expenses for treatment covered by the insurance.

More international students are now considering staying in Japan after graduation to work. The procedure is similar to that undertaken by local students and requires a rigorous job search through your local careers office, applications, interviews, a testing phase and final confirmation. Once employment has been secured, an international student can then apply for a change in his or her immigration status through the nearest immigration bureau. This process is normally very efficient and successful if the skills of the student and their residence record match that of the job in question.

Student life

Because of the nature of Japanese culture and society, student life can be very interesting and diverse. All institutions support their students through excellent facilities and the opportunities to meet other international and local students alike. However, student life can be daunting if there is a language barrier and so campus support networks, such as student organizations, can play a vital role in making you feel at home.

Much of your student social life will be enjoyed on campus, where many of the activities and services are subsidized. For a low annual fee, you will have access to sports, entertainment, social and arts facilities where you can meet other students on a more informal level. Some institutions offer classes in sports and languages, outside of the normal curriculum, if you have a particular skill you would like to improve.

Additionally, institutions often offer a Cooperative Society (Co-op) on campus for students to buy essential supplies. A membership organization, the Co-op serves a similar role as a Students' Union in many other countries and allows you to use services such as a travel agency, a housing association, a bookshop, food stores and restaurants.

Study in the Netherlands

Things to consider

+ **Excellent value for money**
+ **Unique problem-based learning tradition**
+ **Central location in Europe**
+ **English language teaching**

- **Difficulty in remaining to work on the completion of studies**
- **Lack of knowledge of Dutch degrees internationally**

Types of Institution

The higher education system in the Netherlands consists of two distinct types of institution — universities (universiteiten) and universities of professional education (hogescholen); the former focus on research and teaching from an academic point of view, while the latter aim to prepare students more directly for the workplace. There are also a small number of International Education Institutes intended to provide specific programs for international students. Most programs of study are offered in English throughout the Netherlands, making it a very accessible system of education for all international students.

There are currently approximately 200,000 students attending the 14 government-approved universities in the Netherlands, three of which specialize in engineering. All offer undergraduate and postgraduate programs and are fully integrated within the Bologna system of qualifications and credit transfer. It is in these institutions where the majority of research is undertaken in the Netherlands, across a full range of subjects, informing both the academic and the professional communities in the country. Of these institutions, 11 are in the Top 200 rankings in 2007, placing university education in the Netherlands amongst the highest performing in the world today.

There are a further 42 government approved universities of professional education, offering career-orientated education to more than 350,000 students a year. These institutions offer a range of qualifications, most commonly in one of seven areas — agriculture, engineering and technology, economics and business administration, health care, fine and performing arts, education (teacher training) and social welfare. In addition to lectures and classes, students are expected to complete a period of work placement as part of their period of study. Eleven International Education Institutes offer advanced courses taught exclusively in English. These focus on development-related subjects taught in small groups, comprising a range of nationalities.

Three-year bachelors degrees are arranged around lectures and tutorials — and laboratories for the more technical degrees. Learning is encouraged through a mix of theoretical, conceptual and practical approaches all of which seek to educate students to be able to think individually about, and solve, problems. Larger lectures are followed up with much smaller tutorial groups, led by an academic member of staff who leads students through specific issues and discussions. A student's performance is measured at the end of each year, either by written or oral examination, depending on the program of study. The overall style of education in Dutch universities is known as Problem-Based Learning (PBL) and is regarded as one of the best approaches to higher education in the world today.

Quality and recognition of qualifications

Dutch higher education programs have rightly secured a reputation for high quality and well organized content. The Ministry of Education, Culture and Science has responsibility for ensuring that programs meet the required international standards through a rigorous timetable of regulation, audit and accreditation. All Dutch programs are compelled to publish the status of their accreditation, making it easy for students to determine quality. In some cases, it is possible for Dutch programs to be accredited by another country's national accreditation organization.

Degree-level study has to be accredited under the 2002 Government Act, The Accreditation of Higher Education. All programs are checked against an established list of criteria to ensure consistent standards. Because of this rigorous system, Dutch degree programs are widely recognised around the world for their academic level and intellectual rigour.

Fees, finance and cost of living

Tuition fees at Dutch institutions are subsidized by the national government and so represent good value for money for the quality of the education provision. At undergraduate degree level, fees vary according to the subject, with the more popular areas such as business, economics, law and management being more expensive than literature and history, with fees anywhere between €2,000 and €12,500 a year.

The cost of living in the Netherlands is relatively expensive, though there are slight differences across the country. Many students live on between €700 - €900 a month throughout the year, with accommodation costs either in university or private residences accounting for between €300 - €450 of that budget. Student discounts and subsidized food costs at institutions can offset some of the expenses of being a student in the Netherlands.

Scholarships

There are few nationally organized undergraduate scholarships available for studying in the Netherlands, though a number of major schemes exist for postgraduate taught and research programs. Some undergraduate scholarships exist for specific countries around the world and these tend to be administered by local

Netherlands Education Support Offices (NESO). One way of locating scholarships in the Netherlands is by using the online search facility offered by Grantfinder at www.grantfinder.nl.

Some individual universities do offer scholarships to incoming international students, but these are organized, funded and awarded through the specific university.

Entry requirements

Entry requirements in the Netherlands tend to be dependent on three elements — your educational qualifications, your language skills and any specific requirements of the academic field of study you would like to pursue. As a minimum, a student will have to have the equivalent of a Dutch VWO Diploma, awarded after 13 years of education. In systems of education where only 12 years are provided for, bridging courses are available for those students wishing to study at a Dutch institution. As many programs are available in English, you will not need to demonstrate any ability in the Dutch language, though you will be expected to show competence in English through an IELTS or TOEFL examination result. The procedure for applying to universities is straightforward. Each institution requires you to complete their application materials and submit your details before the appropriate deadlines in April or May of the year in which you would like to commence your studies.

Living and working

With over 16 million citizens, the Netherlands is one of the most crowded countries in the world, yet it retains a relaxed and easy going nature that most students thoroughly enjoy. Located at the point where the cultures of Britain, France and Germany meet, the Netherlands is diverse and essentially multicultural. Because of the position of the country in Europe, the Netherlands is internationally open and this is often expressed in a willingness to accept new ideas and the famous Dutch aptitude for speaking many languages.

The Netherlands's best known city is Amsterdam. Its famous canals and traditional architecture offer something for everyone, with the enormous Rijksmuseum, Anne Frank's house, diamond factories and even the Heineken brewery. But away from Amsterdam, towns such as Leiden, Utrecht, Tilburg and Maastricht all show another side of Dutch life no less interesting and welcoming than the big city.

As a student in the Netherlands, you will enjoy the compact nature of the country and excellent infrastructure and travel links. In cities and towns, many people use a bicycle to get around, though cars, buses and trams are also plentiful. For longer journeys trains, buses and planes provide reasonably priced fares all over the Netherlands and farther afield. Because of its location, the Netherlands is an ideal base from which to explore the rest of Europe — by ferry to the UK, by plane to southern and eastern Europe or bus or train to Belgium, France and Germany.

All international students are required to obtain health insurance before they arrive in the Netherlands and this is needed in order to obtain an entry visa for the country. If a student is under the age of 30, working part-time or staying longer than three years, then the situation regarding health cover alters. Full details are available from the institution you wish to study in.

Students from outside the European Economic Area are allowed to work while they study, though they require a work permit to do so. Students have two options: a seasonal basis, full-time in June, July and August, or part-time throughout the year, working no more than ten hours per week. Students must choose one working method. The best way of finding a job is through an employment agency or your academic institution.

Student life

Being a student in the Netherlands is a little different from in other countries. Most universities and other institutions do not offer a campus environment so student life is often mixed with the life of the surrounding town or city. However, student clubs and societies are still very important and popular as a way of meeting other students. Many institutions also offer well-equipped sports facilities where you can play the sport of your choice either competitively or socially.

Student discounts allow you to travel cheaply and receive reduced admissions at museums and art galleries throughout the country. These schemes are both local to your institution and nationally available, offsetting some of your costs everywhere you go. Social life in the Netherlands can be very varied and includes the theatre and cinema, in addition to cafés, clubs and bars. Many students enjoy the liberal atmosphere of the Netherlands and most Dutch towns offer a mix of restaurants and a range of different foods, a legacy of the Netherlands being such an international country.

Study in the Nordic Countries

Denmark, Finland, Iceland, Norway & Sweden

Things to consider

- **+ High academic quality, strictly enforced and maintained**
- **+ Programs taught in English at most levels**
- **+ Active social and cultural life**

- **- High cost of living**
- **- Some difficulty with residence permits**

Types of institution

Given the small size of the respective populations and the limited number of universities in each of the five countries, the Nordic region performs remarkably well in the Top 200 rankings. Ten universities appear in the Top 200, with the University of Uppsala (Sweden) the region's best performing institution, listed at 71. Four institutions from Sweden, three from Denmark, one from each of Finland and Norway all reach the Top 200, underlining both the quality of teaching and research in the respective country systems.

The higher education systems in all five Nordic countries are organized around a very similar structure and therefore have much in common. All of the systems have adopted the Bologna structure and therefore offer three or four year bachelors degrees and one or two year masters programs. The systems are all largely state dominated, with public rather than private institutions offering degree-level education. Universities tend to offer degree level teaching while university colleges and vocational colleges offer diplomas and certificates in more vocational and practical subject areas.

The smallest of the five systems is that of Iceland, where ten institutions of higher education offer degree and vocational education programs to 12,000 students, mostly in Icelandic. The other four countries offer much larger systems of higher education, where universities and colleges teach students from all over the world in either English or the local language. Norway has the most private investment in higher education, with 29 institutions holding either program or institutional accreditation from the government. Finland boasts the largest number of English language programs in Europe taught outside of the UK, within their parallel binary system of universities (offering more academic programs) and universities of applied sciences (where the more vocational and technical subjects are taught). Sweden and Denmark offer diverse systems of higher education, where vocational and academic programs are both readily available.

The Northern European approach of larger lectures followed up by smaller classes dominates the teaching style in all of the Nordic countries. What is taught in the classroom or the laboratory is just the tip of the iceberg in the educational process and much of the emphasis of the Nordic system is on the individual student working alone or in small groups reading around the subjects at hand and developing his or her own approach to, and opinion on, the issues. Methods of assessment vary, but continuing written work through the course of the academic year augments traditional semester and yearly examinations.

Quality and recognition of qualifications

All five systems of the Nordic countries offer fully accredited programs that subscribe to international standards in the quality assessment of higher education. Each of the five countries operates a fully autonomous quality assurance agency that visits individual universities and colleges to ensure the maintenance of agreed standards. Sweden's National Agency of Higher Education evaluates all courses offered by universities and university colleges every six years, using a number of assessment methods, including a student satisfaction survey of currently enrolled students. Failure to meet the required standards results in the power to award qualifications being removed from the institution in question.

In Finland, all institutions offer a diploma supplement according to the Bologna reforms, thus making the contents of the qualifications transportable and immediately recognizable throughout the EU and farther afield. In Iceland, the Ministry of Education, Science and Culture ensure the quality of all institutions and their programs under their direction through regular and comprehensive visits based in institutions internally assessing themselves.

The qualifications offered by institutions in Denmark and Norway are similarly strictly quality controlled by national agencies through a combination of self-assessment and external visits. The resulting standards are extremely high and recognised the world over, irrespective of the individual subject offered.

Fees, finance and cost of living

One of the great advantages of higher education in the Nordic countries is that tuition fees are either reasonably priced or not yet in existence. At present, Denmark charges market-rate tuition fees and even these are on the more modest scale. Each individual university or college may charge a small administrative fee for every semester, but these amounts are nothing like as high as the tuition fees of other European countries.

However, almost without exception, the cost of living in all of the five countries of the Nordic region is high, though students have plenty of ways in which to reduce their costs as much as possible. University or private accommodation tends to be the largest single expenditure, though other aspects of living can be as cheap as in any other European country. Socializing and eating out can still be a feature of student life even on the tightest budget with some careful planning, as can travel and playing sports.

Scholarships

Scholarships are available for a number of the Nordic countries. Denmark, for example, offers a number of government schemes and additionally supports a range of EU mobility programs. Norway, similarly, administers a range of awards and scholarships through the Norwegian Centre for International Cooperation in Higher Education (SIU). A Quota Scheme also exists for 1,100 students every year from developing countries, Eastern Europe and Central Asia. Sweden and Iceland both offer scholarships to cover living costs through their national agencies and in all countries, individual universities and colleges may also offer specific awards for either certain countries or academic subject areas and details can be found at individual institutions' websites.

Entry requirements

The Nordic countries share a very similar structure in their education systems and therefore have a certain amount in common in their entry requirements. At the first degree level, secondary school education consisting of a minimum of 12 years of education is the lowest requirement for successful applications. In the case of Denmark, Finland and Norway, it is more common to award a high school diploma after 13 years of education and so this should be considered the minimum requirement for university entry. If your qualification is not sufficient to meet the required entry levels, it may be possible for you to complete a year's university preparatory course first.

Each individual university, in each of the five country systems, establishes its own application process and deadlines exist for almost all programs. Application materials are available between six and nine months ahead of registration and it is increasingly popular to apply online to the institution you are interested in.

Living and working

Each country has very different characteristics and unique aspects to offer the student wishing to live there. Sweden is a particularly diverse country that promotes equality among the sexes and the different ethnic groups that make up the country, while Finland and Iceland offer completely unique natural environments that boast lakes, glaciers and hot geysers amongst their wonderful natural attractions. Denmark is known for the equally unique aspect of the Danish character, hygge: the quality many Danes enjoy of socialising with friends or family over a drink or around a table, dining and laughing. Norway, on the other hand, is famous for its crystal clear fjords and mountains.

All of the five countries have, however, many things in common. The weather is something that the populations of each of the countries talk about. Expect long hard winters, with little and sometimes no light and plenty of snow; and then beautiful summers, with long, light filled days where people try to spend as much time as possible outside. Each of the countries offers some of the most vibrant capital cities to be found anywhere in the world — Copenhagen (Denmark), Helsinki (Finland), Reykjavik (Iceland), Oslo (Norway) and Stockholm (Sweden) —

with eclectic cultural and social scenes, known for their contemporary fashion, art and design.

Each of the countries has an excellent transport network that allows you to explore not only your place of study, but also the other Nordic countries located close by. Trains, long distance buses and an increasing number of budget airlines cater for students through various discounts and a number of ferry companies enable you to enjoy very cheap travel between Finland and Sweden in particular.

Another element of life in the Nordic countries is the excellent welfare state, offering protection for all in society. As a student from the European Economic Area (EEA) you are covered for all medical care, including emergencies, by your own medical system. Other international students are covered by the local system in Denmark (after a period of six weeks), Finland (if you are a member of the Students' Union), Iceland (if your program of study is full time), Norway and Sweden (if your program of study is longer than a year in length).

As an international student you are permitted to work in all of the Nordic countries, though each of the five have specific conditions that need to be satisfied in order for you to work legally. In most cases you are allowed to work 20 hours a week in term time and full-time during the vacation periods, subject to the status of your study visa or residence permit.

Student life

Your social life as a student in the Nordic countries very much depends on where you are located. Universities and colleges in the big cities benefit from far more facilities than those in the more rural areas. Common to all institutions is the customary range of academic, social and sporting clubs organized on or near campus by students for their fellow students. Students' Unions and Guilds are primarily political organizations, but they also offer useful resources for students in terms of discounts and various kinds of advice. Other institutions often offer social committees that organize a range of activities for all students and their varied interests. University and college halls of residence also offer great platforms for student social life.

Coffee bars, cafés and bars are all common destinations for students living in the Nordic countries. It is common for evenings to start late and continue well into the following morning, with a variety of options on offer. One of the common factors between all of the five countries is an interest in the more social side of life, making strangers feel welcome in every way possible.

Study in Singapore

Things to consider

+ Increasing international reputation
+ Reasonably priced tuition fees
+ Ability to work after graduation
+ Links to Asia

- Lack of global visibility for Singaporean qualifications
- Vast array of private colleges with unclear reputations
- Limited numbers of students from all world regions

Types of institution

The Singaporean post-secondary school education scene is particularly dynamic. Three publicly funded universities exist, two of which are included in the Top 100 of the rankings, and they attract many more applications from local as well as international students than there are places available. The National University of Singapore at 33, Nanyang Technological University at 69 and Singapore Management University, teach the entire range of academic subjects and all offer undergraduate degree qualifications, in addition to postgraduate and research programs. Singapore also has five polytechnics, offering two and three-year diplomas in many different subject areas. These institutions tend to educate students in a more vocational way, developing skills relevant to the workplace.

Additionally, Singapore plays host to both an increasingly diverse private education scene and a growing number of offshore campuses. Private institutions, which are tightly regulated by the Singaporean Ministry of Education, offer undergraduate and diploma programs that attract local and international students alike. A number of these institutions also offer qualifications with completely international curricula such as those for the Chartered Institute of Marketing and the Association of Chartered Certified Accountants. Moreover, others offer international undergraduate programs from universities in countries such as Australia, Finland, New Zealand, the UK and the US.

Sixteen universities from Asia, Europe and the US have established significant interests in Singapore, including the opening of campuses, offering a range of programs including at undergraduate level. Institutions such as the German Institute of Science and Technology offer internationalized curricula taught by local and international staff at a fraction of the cost if a student were to travel overseas for the same program. A number of international programs are also taught in Singapore through these overseas universities.

Most undergraduate programs are taught through a mix of lectures and smaller seminars, with engineering, technology and science courses requiring additional laboratory classes. A student's workload is dependent on the course of study, but is generally high, as degree-level study is demanding across all subject areas. In some cases, it is possible to take more than one subject for your degree. These programs are known as Double Degree Programs (DPP) and are popular in the fields of business, economics, engineering and law.

Quality and recognition of qualifications

Though not all of Singapore's institutions are internationally known, the effect of having two universities in the Top 100 rankings raises the profile of the entire higher education sector. The Ministry of Education directly accredits the three publicly funded universities in the country and ensures that teaching and research activities are all of an appropriate standard.

The increasing numbers of private education providers, including those that offer international partnerships, subscribe to an Education Excellent Framework. This scheme promotes excellence in academic affairs, through an accreditation program, organizational issues and student welfare and protection. The Education Services Accreditation Council gives private education providers guidelines to meet in these three areas and reviews each institution on a regular basis. Additionally, the international universities teaching in Singapore generally meet the standards required of their own national systems of quality assurance, thus making their qualifications particularly well recognized around the world.

Fees, finance and cost of living

Individual institutions set tuition fees at the undergraduate level. Fees at the three local universities tend to vary by academic subject but generally vary between SG$20,000 and SG$24,000. Exceptional programs, such as those in the medical field are priced at a much higher level and students can expect to pay anything up to SG$80,000 a year for tuition fees. Singapore's five polytechnics offer programs at a lower fee rate for their diploma programs, with annual costs of SG$12,160.

The cost of living in Singapore is very reasonable. Though there are some variations in the costs of accommodation, depending on whether you live in university or polytechnic halls of residence or elsewhere, students should budget between SG$750 and SG$1,500 a month. This estimate would cover all costs including transport, entertainment, health insurance and books.

Scholarships

Though not strictly a form of financial aid, all national and international students are free to apply to the Singaporean Ministry of Education for a Tuition Grant once they have been admitted to their program of choice. This scheme allows for a grant of between SG$14,000 and SG$16,000 for most programs to be paid against tuition fees, thus reducing the amount considerably. For programs such as medicine and music, the grant can be as much as SG$65,500 a year. However, international students are required to sign a bond in order to obtain a tuition grant, committing them to working in Singapore for three years after the completion of their university of polytechnic program.

Scholarships and bursaries are also available from either the Ministry of Education or individual universities. Such schemes include the ASEAN Undergraduate Scholarships that provide for tuition costs, SG$3,500 annual living allowance and return travel between the scholars' country and Singapore and the Singapore Technologies International Scholarships. Further details can be found at www.moe.gov.sg.

Entry requirements

Admission to both universities and polytechnics is dependent on individual program requirements. At both the university and polytechnic-levels, it is expected that a student should have completed at least 12 years of secondary education in his or her respective education system. As Singaporean institutions are used to receiving applications from international students, admissions staff are familiar with a range of high school or equivalent qualifications. For those wishing to study medicine or dentistry, an application requires grades to be presented rather than predicted, as is the case with many other subjects.

Depending on the program you are interested in, application deadlines are either at the end of December in the year before you wish to commence your period of study, or at the end of February in the year of study. Applications are made directly to the institution, usually through their own online system with supporting documents sent separately. As with many countries, the more popular a program is the more competition there is for admission.

Living and working

It would certainly be true to say that there is nowhere quite like Singapore. It is a small island state, covering an area of just over 600 square kilometres, yet boasts a population of four million people. Known as one of the great financial and trade centres of the world, Singapore has long attracted a variety of visitors and this leads to a fusion of races and cultures ideal for a unique student experience. Chinese, Malay, Indian and European cultures collide to form an exciting environment in almost every aspect.

With an excellent transport system, superb infrastructure and reputation for safety, Singapore is one of the world's favoured destinations. It offers a great variety of culinary, cultural and shopping experiences — enough to suit most tastes in an entire lifetime, let alone a period of study. From the world famous zoo to the tropical island of Sentosa, Singapore also offers an environment of natural diversity. It is also one of the most technologically advanced countries in the world today.

Singapore's location also makes it a travel hub. As a student you will have access to reduced travel costs that allow you to explore different countries in the greater region, including Australia, Cambodia, Indonesia, Malaysia and Thailand.

As a student, you have access to both university and private accommodation. The former is regarded as the best option for international students as it provides a good introduction to society and allows you to make friends very quickly. It also tends to be the most economical. Those wishing to seek housing through private apartment rentals will find Singapore to be expensive. In terms of healthcare, international students are recommended to have medical insurance for the duration of their period of study.

Full time students attending either polytechnic, university or other approved education institutions are free to seek part time employment during their period of study. Students may work a maximum of 16 hours a week during term time and full time during the vacations. In some cases the immigration status of a student prevents him or her from legally seeking employment. The latest information is available at the Ministry of Manpower's website at www.mom.gov.sg.

After graduation, those students who have accepted the Ministry of Education's Tuition Grant to fund their period of studies will be required to work in Singapore for three years. Other graduates are also free to apply for employment in Singapore, though their success is dependent on their qualification and the type of employment that they are seeking.

Student life

Singapore is an exciting place to be a student, not only because of the quality of the institutions, but because of the rich cultural mix. All institutions support their international student population though an office most commonly called International Student Services. Through this office, activities such as student orientations, cultural programs and introductions to host families are made, all adding to your student experience.

Many different kinds of student activities are encouraged outside of the classroom and are organized both on and off campus. Sporting and social clubs make up the majority of student interest groups, though various clubs representing cultural and academic interests also exist. Facilities tend to be of the highest standard in Singapore and students are free to use them for a small fee.

The Overseas Students' Association supports all international students over the age of 16 in their social, intellectual and pastoral needs. More details can be found at www.osa.org.sg.

Study in the UK

Things to consider

+ World class reputation for quality undergraduate degrees
+ English language teaching
+ Familiarity of institutions with international students
+ Varied history and links to Europe

- High cost of tuition and living expenses
- High numbers of international students on some programs

Types of institution

UK universities are regarded as being among the finest in the world. The Top 200 rankings now include no fewer than 32 UK institutions, eight of which appear in the Top 50. World famous names such as Cambridge, Imperial College and Oxford are synonymous internationally with education and learning and underline the quality of the UK higher education system. There are more than 140 institutions in the UK that are able to grant undergraduate degrees to students, in addition to a further 500 colleges that are able to offer educational programs of differing kinds.

UK universities and colleges are comprehensive and multi-faculty, offering the full range of academic subject areas from accountancy to zoology. No separate institutions exist for subjects such as business, law and medicine at the undergraduate level and these programs are offered within larger universities. Some institutions do, however, offer specific subject specializations such as the London School of Economics (social sciences), the School of Pharmacy (pharmaceutical sciences) and the Institute of Education (teacher training and education).

Almost all universities in the UK are state financed, with the exception of the University of Buckingham and a number of private colleges, though tuition fees are still payable. Until 1992, there were two types of degree-awarding institutions in the UK, the polytechnics — newer institutions that offered bachelor qualifications in technical and more vocational areas — and the universities — traditional, research-led institutions anywhere between 30 and 1,000 years old, offering bachelor qualifications across the full spectrum of subject areas. Now this division has been abandoned and all UK institutions are regarded as operating in a system of open competition for teaching students and research grants from various organizations.

Universities and colleges offer five broad types of qualification to incoming students. Colleges tend to teach for the Higher National Certificate (HNC), Higher

National Diploma (HND), Foundation Degree and Diploma of Higher Education, all lasting between one and two years and are the equivalent of the early stages of a bachelors degree in a range of subjects such as art and design, engineering, media, social studies and technology. Universities tend to teach three or four-year undergraduate degree programs that are more academic in nature and lead to a bachelors qualification. Degree programs that are four years in length tend to include a period in industry or commerce, or a period of study abroad, such as on an exchange scheme in Europe or the USA.

The style of teaching in UK institutions is different from that of many other systems of education. Bachelors degrees are taught through a mix of lectures, tutorials, laboratories (if relevant), seminars and self-directed study. Usually, very little of this structure is compulsory, as the emphasis of learning in the UK system is the individual student's responsibility. Lectures form the basis of most degrees, allowing you to gain an overall outline of a particular subject that is then detailed and discussed in seminars and tutorials. A UK lecturer will rarely tell you that an answer is right or wrong, rather they will want to seek an understanding of the structure and basis of your argument. Much of the work associated with a UK degree is conducted on your own or in small groups, developing your own ideas, point of view and appreciation of the subject matter. Regular assessment takes place through class and term papers and end of year examinations.

Quality and recognition of qualifications

Various UK agencies, independent of the universities and colleges, govern the quality of teaching and research in all UK institutions to ensure the highest standards are maintained. Most programs are subject to external assessment at least every three years in addition to the internal processes institutions impose upon themselves.

The Quality Assurance Agency www.qaa.ac.uk safeguards the standard of education provision at all universities through collaborative audit and academic review across all subject disciplines. Additionally, the quality of teaching and research are monitored by a range of audit exercises, the results of which appear on the Teaching Quality Information website www.tqi.ac.uk and in the Research Assessment Exercise www.hero.ac.uk/sites/hero/rae. In almost all cases the reports of assessment visits to individual universities and colleges are published on the web.

Fees, finance and cost of living

The UK government allows universities and colleges to set their own tuition fees. At most universities in England, students from the UK and the European Union have to pay up to £3,000 a year for tuition, while international students pay somewhere between £6,500 and £13,000 a year, depending on whether a program is classroom or laboratory based. Tuition fees also vary according to the prestige of the university.

The UK is a relatively expensive country in which to study. Costs for accommodation, utilities and books are generally high, though there are regional differences. As a very general rule, London and the south east of the UK has a higher cost of living than other parts of the country. However, as a student you will have access to discounts of all sorts that will reduce some of your expenditure. Students can expect to pay anywhere between £5,500 (outside of London and the south east) and £7,500 a year on living costs.

Scholarships

Scholarships are very difficult to obtain in the UK at undergraduate level. There are no schemes administered by government organizations and only partial funding offered by individual universities and colleges. Information is available from universities on their international office or undergraduate admissions webpages. Most schemes require you to hold an offer of admission before seeking an application for financial aid.

Entry requirements

Because UK universities and colleges are used to receiving applications from international students from all over the world, a wide range of qualifications are acceptable. Generally, students must have completed 13 years of education prior to coming to the UK and offering their local high school qualification equivalent to the UK A-levels. Acceptable entry grades are entirely dependent on the university or college you are applying to, all of whom publish explicit entry standards on their websites or in their prospectuses. Students without 13 years of education are able to apply to UK universities and colleges that offer foundation or bridging programs. These courses enable to students to upgrade their existing qualifications and reach the required standard for entry into the undergraduate system.

Applications are generally made through a central system administered by the Universities and Colleges Application Service (UCAS). Students are able to apply for up to six institutions on one form and UCAS collates all correspondence and decisions between the student and the institution concerned. Full details are available at www.ucas.ac.uk, including information on the application process and deadlines.

Living and working

Coming to the UK is both an exciting and challenging experience. The UK is a friendly, open and well-mannered society that is amongst the most multiracial in the world. When you first arrive, there will be many differences between what you are used to and what the UK offers, but you will soon get used to these. The country is well known for its traditions and colourful history, much of which is celebrated through exciting museums. As well as castles, palaces and monuments, the UK is energized with a dynamic contemporary culture of clubs, fashion and a vibrant music scene.

Because the UK is relatively small, the transport system is well developed and moderately priced for students. Train, bus and flight networks cover the entire country and allow you to travel very easily and quickly. Additionally, as a student, you will have access to free medical care if your program of study is over six months in length. You can register with a doctor close to your institution that will allow you to seek general and hospital care. Other care, such as optical and dental, will require you to pay some fees.

The opportunities for working for international students are very varied. Students from the European Economic Area (EEA) can work freely in the UK. Most other students on programs longer than six months in duration will be given a sticker in their passport on entry that allows them to work part time alongside their course. You will be allowed to work a maximum of 20 hours a week in term time and full time during the vacations. It is also possible that your spouse or partner may also be able to seek work if he or she accompanies you to the UK. Full details are available at www.dfes.gov.uk/international-students/wituk/shtml and www.ukcosa.org.uk.

Types of student employment vary. Often, temporary jobs in the retail and service sector are most common, such as waiting tables and serving in shops. However, some postgraduate students may secure employment relevant to their degree studies.

Student life

All UK universities and colleges offer a range of services for students to enjoy, such as restaurants, bars, clubs, sports facilities and special interest societies. As a student in the UK you will be eligible to join the National Union of Students, an organization that campaigns for the rights of all students and offers discounts across a wide range of services such as transport, entertainment and some retail outlets.

Universities and colleges organize cultural and sporting activities for all students. Whether you wish to compete at a college or national level, most sports will be catered for with first rate facilities and coaching staff. Other organizations offer networks for those with shared ideas and interests. Such activities can vary from the academic, debating and political societies being two examples, to the cultural, such as clubs offering a glimpse of life in places like China and Mauritius.

Restaurants and pubs are also central to student life in the UK. Both tend to be informal in nature and atmosphere and provide a great opportunity to meet other students and local residents alike.

Study in the US

Things to consider

+ Many highly reputable private and public universities
+ Streamlined online admissions processes
+ Good quality campus support services for international students
+ English language based
+ Strong employment opportunities
+ Many scholarships and financial aid for international students

- High tuition fees
- Low acceptance rate for international students
- Tough student visa requirements
- Difficult post-study visa situation for employment

Types of institution

The US has six of the world's top ten universities in the TImes Higher-QS World University Rankings this year: Harvard, Yale, Princeton, CalTech, Chicago and MIT. Only Oxford and Cambridge universities, Imperial College and University College London (UCL) have challenged the supremacy of US universities this year. However, the US's dominance of world higher education may not be as clear cut as many of their own academics would like to think. The US has 57 universities in the top 200, while Europe has 86, and this despite the fact that most citation data utilized in the rankings is based on English language papers, which can disadvantage continental European universities. Harvard and MIT, as well as being neighbours on the Charles River in Boston, are also both independent and funded entirely by income from student fees, research awards and fundraising. This structure is also shared by Yale, Princeton, Duke, Cornell, Chicago, Columbia, Pennsylvania and Stanford, all of which appear among the top 20 universities worldwide. The remainder of the Ivy League, Brown and Dartmouth, are also private, as are 75 per cent of US universities.

State funded universities, although only 25 per cent of the total, have 75 per cent of US students. The University of California, which is well funded, has five campuses within the top 200 institutions. More orthodox state universities are generally less well funded than their private rivals, a trend that has continued under the current administration, with resources being diverted away from education. These state universities have fewer high profile research groups, but this is offset by the fact that they charge lower fees.

The rankings in this book do not feature many of the private liberal arts colleges, which tend to produce fewer research papers and have a lower profile internationally. Nevertheless, in the US, schools like Williams and Swarthmore attract high caliber students who seek a broad based education, rather than a more vocational or subject focused program. A growing number of US universities now offer liberal arts degrees, which also allow this flexible, broad learning experience, almost exclusive to the US. The credit system also means that it is much easier for a student who starts out as, say a history major, to transfer to a different subject, after a year or two, without losing any time. This credit system even makes transfers between universities relatively straightforward.

Medical studies in the US differ from the rest of the world. There are no undergraduate medical degrees (Northwestern University being almost the only exception). Would-be medics take another subject in their first degree, while at the same time preparing for their MCAT (nine hours of multiple choice testing) to gain entry to medical school. Law studies in the US are similar to medical studies, in that there are no undergraduate degrees. Students take a liberal arts degree, while having to pass the LSAT test to gain entry to law school. Business education is different. The US has many of the world's best MBA programs and many of the world's best undergraduate business programs. The University of Pennsylvania's Wharton School is a good example of both a pre-eminent MBA and undergraduate business degree, attracting many international students. Harvard, Stanford and Yale feature very prominently in the social sciences subject rankings, and have very strong undergraduate business departments.

Quality and recognition of qualifications

All the universities featured in this guide are accredited. If you need to look beyond the elite group, The Council for Higher Education in Washington DC produces the definitive list of government approved US universities at undergraduate level. For business schools, there is the AACSB (American Association of Collegiate Schools of Business), which accredits about 400 institutions. The Ivy League: Brown, Columbia, Cornell, Dartmouth, Harvard, Penn, Princeton and Yale, are amongst the best-known universities but no longer dominate rankings. This grouping began as a sports league. Their reputations and attractive East Coast locations and historic campuses ensure that application ratios are amongst the most competitive in the world.

All students complete their degree with a grade point average (GPA). This is a cumulative total of each individual course grade multiplied by the course credit. Students tend to be fanatical about their GPA because it is influential in the employment marketplace. To achieve high grades requires regular attendance at lectures and consistent performance.

Fees, finance and cost of living

The elite US universities are the most expensive in the world. At the same time they can be a gateway to the most attractive employment market in the world, as well as providing value for money in terms of class time and access to professors. There is a great emphasis on tuition and access to professors. An added attraction for international students is the huge number of scholarships and financial aid packages available at many well-funded private universities, making them open to even the most disadvantaged, but bright, students. Many

US universities' financial aid departments ask for a statement of your family's financial situation. If they decide that your family can only contribute US$1,000 per year, then that is all you will have to pay — if they want you. Alternatively, they may have international student loan schemes. Those families that can afford the bills should be prepared for tuition and fees varying between US$3,500 and US$60,000 per academic year. As a guideline, average fees are about US$16,000 per year, which is usually based on a nine month academic year from September to May. Books, travel and living costs need to be added. Costs vary by city, with New York, Boston and San Francisco amongst the most expensive.

Entry requirements and admissions procedures

All US universities publish general criteria on their websites. Generally speaking, admissions offices will be familiar with grading systems in different countries. If you achieve top ten per cent grades in your country, the chances are you can gain entry to the top ten per cent of US universities, but there will be some exceptions. Some country high school qualifications are considered more advanced than US equivalents. For example, UK A-level grades can count towards credit for many US degrees, potentially taking as much as 12 months off the length of the degree. Domestic applicants have to take the SAT exam. If SAT results are a long way short of the average, it is generally not worth applying.

Living and working

American universities encourage their students to work alongside their course. There are often employment offices which offer paid work on campus, for which an international student visa will suffice. You will need to apply for a social security number, at which point you can take any campus job: as a teaching assistant, sports attendant, etc. As part of an international visa, an international student is allowed one year of optional practical training (OPT), enabling him or her to work anywhere in the US, in consulting, banking, engineering or any other field. The year can be used in batches during summer internships, or in full after your degree. There is also curricular practical training, which allows a student to find paid work as long as it relates to the subject being studied. This is most applicable for students in sciences and technology. Professors are generally amenable and there is no time limit or impact on OPT allowance.

Student life

Fraternities and sororities still form a fundamental part of student life on many US campuses. They offer a private building where you can party, or relax in smaller cohesive groups. It is a good way to get to know people and often offers alternative accommodation to university dorms. Special interest clubs and sports clubs also play a major part in the social scene at many universities. If you are good at a sport or a musical instrument, you are guaranteed a like-minded social set and lots of activities. If you enjoy a social drink you need to check out the minimum legal drinking age in each state, which can vary from 18 to 21.

11

Directory: top 500 universities worldwide

The directory that follows gives you all the basic facts and contact details you need, including web addresses, to research the top 500 universities in the world, according to the Times Higher-QS World University Rankings. The listings are presented broadly alphabetically, by country, from Argentina to Uruguay. The top 500 can also be found on www.topuniversities.com *with electronic links to their websites.*

Note

The directory includes basic facts and figures on each institution, to the extent that the data was provided as part of the research exercise behind the Times Higher-QS World University Rankings. This means that some entries are more comprehensive than others. Where possible, such gaps have been filled using publicly available sources.

While every effort has been made to ensure accuracy, collecting such a large amount of information from around the world always involves the risk of errors or omissions. This fact underlines the imperative of your own research beyond this information and the need for you to verify all data for your chosen course directly with the institution, before you take action based upon it. Any factual clarifications to the directory entries received by the publisher will be posted on www.topuniversities.com, as appropriate.

Argentina

Austral University

Contact	Statistics		Ranking	
Avda. Juan de Garay 125	**Peer review**	355	**World rank**	401-500
Ciudad de Buenos Aires	**Recruiter review**	196	**Subject area positions**	
C1063ABB	**Student faculty ratio**	11.1:1	Arts & humanities	278
Argentina	**International faculty**	4.0%		
	Undergraduates	2,497		
www.austral.edu.ar	**Postgraduates**	770		
Tel +54 11 5921 8000	**International students**	7.0%		

University of Belgrano

Contact	Statistics		Ranking	
Zabala 1837	**Peer review**	500+	**World rank**	401-500
Buenos Aires	**Recruiter review**	296		
C1426DQG	**Student faculty ratio**	7.4:1		
Argentina	**International faculty**	3.0%		
	Undergraduates	4,335		
www.ub.edu.ar	**Postgraduates**	314		
Tel +54 11 4788 5400	**International students**	25.0%		

University of Buenos Aires

Contact	Statistics		Ranking	
Viamonte 430	**Peer review**	220	**World rank**	264=
Buenos Aires	**Recruiter review**	83	**Subject area positions**	
1053	**Student faculty ratio**	10.6:1	Arts & humanities	253
Argentina	**International faculty**	6.0%	Engineering & IT	276
	Students	178,787	Life sciences & biomedicine	192
www.uba.ar	**International students**	9.0%	Natural sciences	187
Tel +54 11 4510 1100			Social sciences	186

Universidad Torcuato di Tella

Contact	Statistics		Ranking	
Miñones 2177	**Peer review**	401-500	**World rank**	401-500
Buenos Aires	**Recruiter review**	201	**Subject area positions**	
1428	**Student faculty ratio**	17.9:1	Social sciences	274
Argentina	**International faculty**	24.0%		
	Undergraduates	868		
www.utdt.edu	**Postgraduates**	524		
Tel +54 11 4784 0080	**International students**	13.0%		

Australia

University of Adelaide

Contact

The University of Adelaide
Adelaide
SA 5005
Australia

www.adelaide.edu.au
Tel +61 8 8303 4455

Statistics

Peer review	98
Recruiter review	86
Student faculty ratio	9.8:1
International faculty	21.0%
Undergraduates	11,604
Postgraduates	3,329
International students	27.0%

Ranking

World rank	62 (105=)
Subject area positions	
Arts & humanities	136
Engineering & IT	149
Life sciences & biomedicine	100
Natural sciences	87
Social sciences	89

Australian National University

Contact

Canberra
ACT 200
Australia

www.anu.edu.au
Tel +61 2 6125 5111

Statistics

Peer review	16
Recruiter review	63
Student faculty ratio	4.5:1
International faculty	18.0%
Undergraduates	7,213
Postgraduates	3,440
International students	23.0%

Ranking

World rank	16 (16)
Subject area positions	
Arts & humanities	10
Engineering & IT	39
Life sciences & biomedicine	28
Natural sciences	19
Social sciences	16

Curtin University of Technology

Contact

Kent St Bentley
Western Australia
6102
Australia

www.curtin.edu.au
Tel +61 8 9266 9266

Statistics

Peer review	215
Recruiter review	137
Student faculty ratio	21.4:1
International faculty	67.0%
Undergraduates	23,530
Postgraduates	4,280
International students	43.0%

Ranking

World rank	235 (156=)
Subject area positions	
Arts & humanities	223
Engineering & IT	197
Life sciences & biomedicine	282
Natural sciences	211
Social sciences	166

Deakin University

Contact

1 Gherinhap Street
Geelong
Victoria
3217
Australia

www.deakin.edu.au
Tel +61 3 5227 8100

Statistics

Peer review	401-500
Recruiter review	153
Student faculty ratio	20.1:1
International faculty	26.0%
Undergraduates	18,087
Postgraduates	3,607
International students	21.0%

Ranking

World Rank	374=

Flinders University

Contact

Sturt Road
Bedford Park
Adelaide
South Australia

www.flinders.edu.au
Tel +61 8 8201 3911

Statistics

Peer review	401-500
Recruiter review	286
Student faculty ratio	13.3:1
International faculty	7.0%
Undergraduates	8,955
Postgraduates	2,043
International students	19.0%

Ranking

World rank	351=
Subject area positions	
Life sciences & biomedicine	271
Social sciences	297

Griffith University

Contact

Kessels Road
Nathan
Brisbane
Queensland
4111
Australia

www.griffith.edu.au
Tel +61 7 3735 7111

Statistics

Peer review	401-500
Recruiter review	141
Student faculty ratio	16.3:1
International faculty	29.0%
Undergraduates	21,079
Postgraduates	4,095
International students	23.0%

Ranking

World rank	309=
Subject area positions	
Social sciences	235

La Trobe University

Contact

Victoria
3086
Australia

www.latrobe.edu.au
Tel +61 3 9479 1111

Statistics

Peer review	166
Recruiter review	163
Student faculty ratio	19.8:1
International faculty	32.0%
Undergraduates	10,000
Postgraduates	4,393
International students	19.0%

Ranking

World rank	205= (207=)
Subject area positions	
Arts & humanities	72
Life sciences & biomedicine	249
Natural sciences	211
Social sciences	130

Macquarie University

Contact

Balaclava Road
North Ryde
New South Wales

www.mq.edu.au
Tel +61 2 9850 7111

Statistics

Peer review	156
Recruiter review	72
Student faculty ratio	20.6:1
International faculty	25.0%
Undergraduates	15,169
Postgraduates	5,821
International students	36.0%

Ranking

World rank	168= (82=)
Subject area positions	
Arts & humanities	87
Engineering & IT	295
Life sciences & biomedicine	198
Natural sciences	236
Social sciences	103

University of Melbourne

Contact	*Statistics*		*Ranking*	
Parkville	**Peer review**	20	**World rank**	27 (22)
Victoria	**Recruiter review**	10	**Subject area positions**	
3010	**Student faculty ratio**	10.1:1	Arts & humanities	17
Australia	**International faculty**	17.0%	Engineering & IT	21
	Undergraduates	25,255	Life sciences & biomedicine	17
www.unimelb.edu.au	**Postgraduates**	8,680	Natural sciences	33
Tel +61 3 8344 4000	**International students**	26.0%	Social sciences	17

Monash University

Contact	*Statistics*		*Ranking*	
Victoria	**Peer review**	29	**World rank**	43 (38)
3800	**Recruiter review**	24	**Subject area positions**	
Australia	**Student faculty ratio**	11.8:1	Arts & humanities	30
	International faculty	43.0%	Engineering & IT	44
www.monash.edu.au	**Undergraduates**	32,072	Life sciences & biomedicine	22
Tel +61 3 9902 6000	**Postgraduates**	8,537	Natural sciences	68
	International students	34.0%	Social sciences	26

University of New South Wales

Contact	*Statistics*		*Ranking*	
Sydney	**Peer review**	31	**World rank**	44 (41)
NSW 2052	**Recruiter review**	20	**Subject area positions**	
Australia	**Student faculty ratio**	14.4:1	Arts & humanities	35
	International faculty	27.0%	Engineering & IT	28
www.unsw.edu.au	**Undergraduates**	21,601	Life sciences & biomedicine	50
Tel +61 2 9385 1000	**Postgraduates**	6,866	Natural sciences	58
	International students	23.0%	Social sciences	30

University of Newcastle

Contact	*Statistics*		*Ranking*	
Callaghan	**Peer review**	216	**World rank**	215 (207=)
NSW 2308	**Recruiter review**	151	**Subject area positions**	
Australia	**Student faculty ratio**	15:1	Arts & humanities	298
	International faculty	16.0%	Engineering & IT	174
www.newcastle.edu.au	**Undergraduates**	13,747	Life sciences & biomedicine	159
Tel +61 2 4921 5000	**Postgraduates**	2,933	Natural sciences	271
	International students	16.0%	Social sciences	182

University of Queensland

Contact

Brisbane
QLD 4072
Australia

www.uq.edu.au
Tel +61 7 3365 1111

Statistics

Peer review	36
Recruiter review	45
Student faculty ratio	9.3:1
International faculty	22.0%
Undergraduates	22,477
Postgraduates	6,205
International students	17.0%

Ranking

World rank	33= (45)
Subject area positions	
Arts & humanities	45
Engineering & IT	62
Life sciences & biomedicine	31
Natural sciences	54
Social sciences	34

Queensland University of Technology

Contact

GPO Box 2434
Gardens Point Campus:
2 George Street
Brisbane
QLD 4001
Australia

www.qut.edu.au
Tel +61 7 3138 2000

Statistics

Peer review	132
Recruiter review	82
Student faculty ratio	18.2:1
International faculty	17.0%
Undergraduates	23,193
Postgraduates	4,188
International students	13.0%

Ranking

World rank	195= (192=)
Subject area positions	
Arts & humanities	145
Engineering & IT	100
Life sciences & biomedicine	112
Natural sciences	219
Social sciences	155

RMIT University

Contact

GPO Box 2476V
Melbourne
Victoria
3001
Australia

www.rmit.edu.au
Tel +61 3 9925 2000

Statistics

Peer review	138
Recruiter review	76
Student faculty ratio	21.3:1
International faculty	20.0%
Undergraduates	24,650
Postgraduates	5,541
International students	42.0%

Ranking

World rank	200= (146)
Subject area positions	
Arts & humanities	128
Engineering & IT	107
Life sciences & biomedicine	155
Social sciences	120

University of South Australia

Contact

GPO Box 2471
Adelaide
South Australia
5001
Australia

www.unisa.edu.au
Tel +61 8 8302 6611

Statistics

Peer review	245
Recruiter review	90
Student faculty ratio	19:1
International faculty	2.0%
Undergraduates	17,993
Postgraduates	4,570
International students	30.0%

Ranking

World rank	291 (299=)
Subject area positions	
Arts & humanities	126
Engineering & IT	296
Social sciences	188

The University of Sydney

Contact	*Statistics*		*Ranking*	
Sydney	**Peer review**	25	**World rank**	31 (35=)
NSW 2006	**Recruiter review**	37	**Subject area positions**	
Australia	**Student faculty ratio**	12:1	Arts & humanities	15
	International faculty	46.0%	Engineering & IT	41
www.usyd.edu.au	**Undergraduates**	27,394	Life sciences & biomedicine	23
Tel +61 2 9351 2222	**Postgraduates**	8,580	Natural sciences	43
	International students	26.0%	Social sciences	27

University of Technology, Sydney

Contact	*Statistics*		*Ranking*	
PO Box 123	**Peer review**	193	**World rank**	259= (255=)
Broadway	**Recruiter review**	49	**Subject area positions**	
NSW 2007	**Student faculty ratio**	19.4:1	Arts & humanities	139
Australia	**International faculty**	39.0%	Engineering & IT	137
	Undergraduates	17,117	Life sciences & biomedicine	256
www.uts.edu.au	**Postgraduates**	6,495	Social sciences	144
Tel +61 2 9514 2000	**International students**	28.0%		

University of Tasmania

Contact	*Statistics*		*Ranking*	
Churchill Avenue	**Peer review**	288	**World rank**	264= (232=)
Sandy Bay	**Recruiter review**	196	**Subject area positions**	
Tasmania	**Student faculty ratio**	18.4:1	Arts & humanities	112
7001	**International faculty**	17.0%	Natural sciences	269
Australia	**Undergraduates**	11,623	Social sciences	258
	Postgraduates	1,651		
www.utas.edu.au	**International students**	22.0%		
Tel +61 3 6226 2999				

University of Western Australia

Contact	*Statistics*		*Ranking*	
35 Stirling Highway	**Peer review**	106	**World rank**	64 (111=)
Crawley	**Recruiter review**	80	**Subject area positions**	
WA 6009	**Student faculty ratio**	11.3:1	Arts & humanities	117
Australia	**International faculty**	35.0%	Engineering & IT	138
	Undergraduates	11,698	Life sciences & biomedicine	77
www.uwa.edu.au	**Postgraduates**	2,588	Natural sciences	135
Tel +61 8 6488 2889	**International students**	17.0%	Social sciences	157

University of Wollongong

Contact

Northfields Ave
Wollongong
NSW 2522
Australia

www.uow.edu.au
Tel +61 2 4221 3555

Statistics

Peer review	257
Recruiter review	71
Student faculty ratio	17.1:1
International faculty	44.0%
Undergraduates	11,679
Postgraduates	3,935
International students	35.0%

Ranking

World rank	199 (196)
Subject area positions	
Arts & humanities	269
Engineering & IT	181
Life sciences & biomedicine	244
Social sciences	223

Austria

Karl-Franzens-University Graz

Contact

Universitaetsplatz 3
Graz
8010
Austria

www.uni-graz.at
Tel +43 316 3800

Statistics

Peer review	237
Recruiter review	378
Student faculty ratio	23.1:1
International faculty	12.0%
Undergraduates	17,518
Postgraduates	2,046
International students	9.0%

Ranking

World rank	279 (284=)
Subject area positions	
Arts & humanities	251
Engineering & IT	152
Life sciences & biomedicine	231
Natural sciences	248
Social sciences	297

University of Innsbruck

Contact

Christoph-Probst-Platz
Innrain 52
Innsbruck
Tirol
6020
Austria

www.uibk.ac.at
Tel +43 512 5070

Statistics

Peer review	238
Recruiter review	401-500
Student faculty ratio	22.3:1
International faculty	18.0%
Undergraduates	15,487
Postgraduates	1,500
International students	33.0%

Ranking

World rank	225= (186)
Subject area positions	
Arts & humanities	244
Life sciences & biomedicine	224
Natural sciences	154
Social sciences	244

Johannes Kepler University Linz

Contact

Altenberger Straße 69
Linz
4040
Austria

www.jku.at
Tel +43 732 24680

Statistics

Peer review	388
Recruiter review	378
Student faculty ratio	16.7:1
International faculty	18.0%
Undergraduates	11,616
Postgraduates	536
International students	9.0%

Ranking

World rank	368 (404=)
Subject area positions	
Natural sciences	229

University of Vienna

Contact

Dr. Karl Lueger Ring 1
Vienna
1010
Austria

www.univie.ac.at
Tel +43 1 42770

Statistics

Peer review	58
Recruiter review	115
Student faculty ratio	35.7:1
International faculty	16.0%
Undergraduates	51,255
Postgraduates	5,991
International students	22.0%

Ranking

World rank	85= (87)
Subject area positions	
Arts & humanities	52
Engineering & IT	167
Life sciences & biomedicine	56
Natural sciences	74
Social sciences	46

Vienna University of Technology

Contact

Karlsplatz 13
Wien
1040
Austria

www.tuwien.ac.at
Tel +43 1 588010

Statistics

Peer review	200
Recruiter review	276
Student faculty ratio	9.6:1
International faculty	20.0%
Undergraduates	7,213
Postgraduates	7,734
International students	21.0%

Ranking

World rank	166= (138)
Subject area positions	
Engineering & IT	64
Life sciences & biomedicine	297
Natural sciences	105

Belgium

University of Antwerp

Contact

Prinsstraat 13
Antwerpen
2000
Belgium

www.ua.ac.be
Tel +32 3 220 41 11

Statistics

Peer review	282
Recruiter review	500+
Student faculty ratio	5.1:1
International faculty	15.0%
Undergraduates	5,663
Postgraduates	4,157
International students	12.0%

Ranking

World rank	187 (252=)
Subject area positions	
Arts & humanities	167
Social sciences	240

Vrije University Brussels (VUB)

Contact

Pleinlaan 2
Elsene
1050
Belgium

www.vub.ac.be
Tel +32 2 629 21 11

Statistics

Peer review	321
Recruiter review	334
Student faculty ratio	6.9:1
International faculty	2.0%
Undergraduates	4,532
Postgraduates	3,487
International students	10.0%

Ranking

World rank	229= (133=)
Subject area positions	
Arts & humanities	286
Life sciences & biomedicine	266

Université Libre de Bruxelles (ULB)

Contact

U.L.B. - CP 177
50 avenue F.D. Roosevelt
1050 Bruxelles
Belgium

www.ulb.ac.be
Tel +32 2 650 20 00

Statistics

Peer review	184
Recruiter review	240
Student faculty ratio	11:1
International faculty	11.0%
Undergraduates	10,711
Postgraduates	9,185
International students	27.0%

Ranking

World rank	154 (165=)
Subject area positions	
Arts & humanities	170
Engineering & IT	231
Life sciences & biomedicine	244
Natural sciences	122
Social sciences	200

University of Ghent

Contact

Sint-Pietersnieuwstraat 25
Ghent
9000
Belgium

www.ugent.be
Tel +32 9 264 31 11

Statistics

Peer review	141
Recruiter review	362
Student faculty ratio	7.2:1
International faculty	12.0%
Undergraduates	11,803
Postgraduates	15,654
International students	6.0%

Ranking

World rank	124 (141=)
Subject area positions	
Arts & humanities	115
Engineering & IT	146
Life sciences & biomedicine	163
Natural sciences	148
Social sciences	223

Katholieke Universiteit Leuven

Contact

Oude Markt 13
Leuven
3000
Belgium

www.kuleuven.ac.be
Tel +32 1 632 40 10

Statistics

Peer review	51
Recruiter review	98
Student faculty ratio	14.6:1
International faculty	13.0%
Undergraduates	14,859
Postgraduates	13,583
International students	12.0%

Ranking

World rank	61 (96)
Subject area positions	
Arts & humanities	43
Engineering & IT	70
Life sciences & biomedicine	109
Natural sciences	74
Social sciences	54

University of Liège

Contact

Place du 20-Août, 9
Liège
4000
Belgium

www.ulg.ac.be
Tel +32 4 366 21 11

Statistics

Peer review	287
Recruiter review	401-500
Student faculty ratio	14.3:1
International faculty	5.0%
Undergraduates	8,084
Postgraduates	7,200
International students	20.0%

Ranking

World rank	262 (201=)
Subject area positions	
Arts & Humanities	253
Engineering & IT	229
Social Sciences	277

Université Catholique de Louvain (UCL)

Contact

Place de l'université 1
Louvain-la-Neuve
1348
Belgium

www.uclouvain.be
Tel +32 1 047 24 24

Statistics

Peer review	87
Recruiter review	207
Student faculty ratio	18.2:1
International faculty	12.0%
Undergraduates	9,366
Postgraduates	10,852
International students	16.0%

Ranking

World rank	123 (76)
Subject area positions	
Arts & humanities	65
Engineering & IT	105
Life sciences & biomedicine	159
Natural sciences	189
Social sciences	42

Brazil

University of Campinas (Unicamp)

Contact

Cidade Universitária Zeferino Vaz
Campinas
São Paulo
13083-970
Brazil

www.unicamp.br
Tel +55 19 3788 2121

Statistics

Peer review	205
Recruiter review	351
Student faculty ratio	8.4:1
International faculty	10.0%
Undergraduates	9,133
Postgraduates	942
International students	2.0%

Ranking

World rank	177= (448)
Subject area positions	
Engineering & IT	123
Natural sciences	130
Social sciences	241

Federal University of Rio de Janeiro

Contact

Av. Pedro Calmon, nº 500 -
Prédio da Reitoria - 2º andar
Cidade Universitária
Rio de Janeiro
21941-901
Brazil

www.ufrj.br
Tel +55 21 2562 2010

Statistics

Peer review	286
Recruiter review	316
Student faculty ratio	14.6:1
International faculty	6.0%
Undergraduates	26,876
Postgraduates	4,897
International students	1.0%

Ranking

World rank	338 (416)
Subject area positions	
Engineering & IT	119
Life sciences & biomedicine	221
Natural sciences	200

Pontifícia Universidade Católica do Rio de Janeiro

Contact

Rua Marquês de São Vicente, 225
Gávea
Rio de Janeiro
22453-900
Brazil

www.puc-rio.br
Tel +55 21 3114 1001

Statistics

Peer review	327
Recruiter review	332
Student faculty ratio	14.7:1
International faculty	5.0%
Students	11,685
International students	5.0%

Ranking

World rank	401-500
Subject area positions	
Engineering & IT	203

University of São Paulo

Contact

Caixa Postal 66281
São Paulo
05311-970
Brazil

www.usp.br
Tel +55 11 3091 6119

Statistics

Peer review	134
Recruiter review	209
Student faculty ratio	11.9:1
International faculty	5.0%
Undergraduates	41,797
Postgraduates	18,061
International students	2.0%

Ranking

World rank	175= (284=)
Subject area positions	
Arts & humanities	185
Engineering & IT	118
Life sciences & biomedicine	141
Natural sciences	128
Social sciences	187

Canada

University of Alberta

Contact

114 St. - 89 Ave
Edmonton
Alberta
T6G 2M7
Canada

www.ualberta.ca
Tel +1 780 492 3111

Statistics

Peer review	55
Recruiter review	351
Student faculty ratio	20.8:1
International faculty	27.0%
Undergraduates	27,067
Postgraduates	5,274
International students	13.0%

Ranking

World rank	97= (133=)
Subject area positions	
Arts & humanities	51
Engineering & IT	59
Life sciences & biomedicine	54
Natural sciences	95
Social sciences	83

University of British Columbia

Contact

2329 West Mall
Vancouver
V6T 1Z4
Canada

www.ubc.ca
Tel +1 604 822 2211

Statistics

Peer review	18
Recruiter review	60
Student faculty ratio	9.3:1
International faculty	8.0%
Undergraduates	30,786
Postgraduates	7,235
International students	14.0%

Ranking

World rank	33= (50=)
Subject area positions	
Arts & humanities	14
Engineering & IT	30
Life sciences & biomedicine	20
Natural sciences	30
Social sciences	14

University of Calgary

Contact

2500 University Drive NW
Calgary
Alberta
T2N 1N4
Canada

www.ucalgary.ca
Tel +1 403 220 5110

Statistics

Peer review	126
Recruiter review	196
Student faculty ratio	18:1
International faculty	5.0%
Undergraduates	20,490
Postgraduates	4,773
International students	8.0%

Ranking

World rank	166= (266=)
Subject area positions	
Arts & humanities	204
Engineering & IT	91
Life sciences & biomedicine	116
Natural sciences	146
Social sciences	146

Carleton University

Contact	*Statistics*		*Ranking*	
1125 Colonel By Drive	**Peer review**	275	**World rank**	345= (410=)
Ottawa	**Recruiter review**	369	**Subject area positions**	
ON	**Student faculty ratio**	28.7:1	Arts & humanities	210
K1S 5B6	**International faculty**	5.0%	Engineering & IT	206
Canada	**Undergraduates**	18,301	Social sciences	173
	Postgraduates	2,511		
www.carleton.ca	**International students**	9.0%		
Tel +1 613 520 7400				

Concordia University

Contact	*Statistics*		*Ranking*	
1455 de Maisonneuve Blvd W.	**Peer review**	303	**World rank**	383= (370=)
Montreal	**Recruiter review**	221	**Subject area positions**	
Quebec	**Student faculty ratio**	22.8:1	Arts & humanities	244
H3G 1M8	**International faculty**	5.0%	Engineering & IT	194
Canada	**Undergraduates**	23,219	Social sciences	247
	Postgraduates	5,240		
www.concordia.ca	**International students**	12.0%		
Tel +1 514 848 2424				

Dalhousie University

Contact	*Statistics*		*Ranking*	
Halifax	**Peer review**	199	**World rank**	221= (270=)
Nova Scotia	**Recruiter review**	401-500	**Subject area positions**	
B3H 4R2	**Student faculty ratio**	15.3:1	Arts & humanities	178
Canada	**International faculty**	18.0%	Life sciences & biomedicine	158
	Undergraduates	11,073	Natural sciences	208
www.dal.ca	**Postgraduates**	2,911	Social sciences	173
Tel +1 902 494 2211	**International students**	8.0%		

Laval University

Contact	*Statistics*		*Ranking*	
Québec	**Peer review**	235	**World rank**	280 (412=)
G1K 7P4	**Recruiter review**	500+	**Subject area positions**	
Canada	**Student faculty ratio**	24.2:1	Arts & humanities	152
	International faculty	18.0%	Engineering & IT	244
www.ulaval.ca	**Undergraduates**	24,446	Natural sciences	297
Tel +1 418 656 2131	**Postgraduates**	7,858	Social sciences	125
	International students	11.0%		

University of Manitoba

Contact

Winnipeg
MB
R3T 2N2
Canada

www.umanitoba.ca
Tel +1 204 474 8880

Statistics

Peer review	329
Recruiter review	374
Student faculty ratio	13.7:1
International faculty	16.0%
Undergraduates	20,053
Postgraduates	2,721
International students	9.0%

Ranking

World rank	304= (424=)
Subject area positions	
Life sciences & biomedicine	247

McGill University

Contact

845 Sherbrooke Street West
Montreal
Quebec
H3A 2T5
Canada

www.mcgill.ca
Tel +1 514 398 4455

Statistics

Peer review	12
Recruiter review	25
Student faculty ratio	5:1
International faculty	20.0%
Undergraduates	17,361
Postgraduates	5,233
International students	27.0%

Ranking

World rank	12 (21)
Subject area positions	
Arts & humanities	12
Engineering & IT	27
Life sciences & biomedicine	10
Natural sciences	26
Social sciences	12

McMaster University

Contact

1280 Main St W
Hamilton
Ontario
L8S 4L9
Canada

www.mcmaster.ca
Tel +1 905 525 9140

Statistics

Peer review	67
Recruiter review	252
Student faculty ratio	17.2:1
International faculty	6.0%
Undergraduates	16,640
Postgraduates	2,163
International students	8.0%

Ranking

World rank	108 (155)
Subject area positions	
Arts & humanities	98
Engineering & IT	89
Life sciences & biomedicine	69
Natural sciences	95
Social sciences	59

Université de Montréal

Contact

PO Box 6128,
Station Centre-ville
Montréal QC
H3C 3J7
Canada

www.umontreal.ca
Tel +1 514 343 6111

Statistics

Peer review	53
Recruiter review	250
Student faculty ratio	16.8:1
International faculty	28.0%
Undergraduates	17,625
Postgraduates	7,156
International students	8.0%

Ranking

World rank	93= (181=)
Subject area positions	
Arts & humanities	57
Engineering & IT	88
Life sciences & biomedicine	66
Natural sciences	93
Social sciences	39

Ottawa University

Contact

Tabaret Hall
75 Laurier Av. E.
Ottawa
Ontario
K1N 6N5
Canada

www.uottawa.ca
Tel +1 613 562 5700

Statistics

Peer review	187
Recruiter review	351
Student faculty ratio	14.1:1
International faculty	18.0%
Undergraduates	26,567
Postgraduates	3,367
International students	6.0%

Ranking

World rank	227= (282=)
Subject area positions	
Arts & humanities	201
Engineering & IT	159
Life sciences & biomedicine	291
Natural sciences	236
Social sciences	108

Université du Québec

Contact

475 rue du Parvis
Québec
G1K 9H7
Canada

www.uquebec.ca
Tel +1 418 657 3551

Statistics

Peer review	197
Recruiter review	314
Student faculty ratio	34.9:1
International faculty	18.0%
Undergraduates	59,506
Postgraduates	13,033
International students	11.0%

Ranking

World rank	336= (482=)
Subject area positions	
Arts & humanities	275
Engineering & IT	236
Life sciences & biomedicine	151
Natural sciences	229
Social sciences	117

Queen's University

Contact

99 University Avenue
Kingston
Ontario
K7L 3N6
Canada

www.queensu.ca
Tel +1 613 533 2000

Statistics

Peer review	100
Recruiter review	78
Student faculty ratio	12.4:1
International faculty	26.0%
Undergraduates	15,060
Postgraduates	3,017
International students	7.0%

Ranking

World rank	88 (176)
Subject area positions	
Arts & humanities	86
Engineering & IT	194
Life sciences & biomedicine	124
Natural sciences	198
Social sciences	43

Simon Fraser University

Contact

8888 University Drive
Burnaby
V5A 1S6
Canada

www.sfu.ca
Tel +1 604 291 3111

Statistics

Peer review	107
Recruiter review	147
Student faculty ratio	21.7:1
International faculty	36.0%
Undergraduates	14,268
Postgraduates	3,354
International students	13.0%

Ranking

World rank	139 (282=)
Subject area positions	
Arts & humanities	116
Engineering & IT	136
Life sciences & biomedicine	149
Natural sciences	197
Social sciences	54

University of Toronto

Contact	*Statistics*		*Ranking*	
Toronto, Ontario	**Peer review**	9	**World rank**	45 (27)
M5S 1A1	**Recruiter review**	34	**Subject area positions**	
Canada	**Student faculty ratio**	22.3:1	Arts & humanities	8
	International faculty	26.0%	Engineering & IT	11
www.utoronto.ca	**Undergraduates**	50,220	Life sciences & biomedicine	14
Tel +1 416 978 2011	**Postgraduates**	10,991	Natural sciences	16
	International students	11.0%	Social sciences	13

University of Victoria

Contact	*Statistics*		*Ranking*	
3800 Finnerty Road	**Peer review**	216	**World rank**	213 (399=)
Victoria	**Recruiter review**	183	**Subject area positions**	
BC	**Student faculty ratio**	21.3:1	Arts & humanities	143
V8P 5C2	**International faculty**	22.0%	Engineering & IT	291
Canada	**Undergraduates**	12,950	Life sciences & biomedicine	288
	Postgraduates	2,294	Natural sciences	271
www.uvic.ca	**International students**	14.0%	Social sciences	121
Tel +1 250 721 7211				

University of Waterloo

Contact	*Statistics*		*Ranking*	
200 University Avenue West	**Peer review**	71	**World rank**	112= (204=)
Waterloo	**Recruiter review**	103	**Subject area positions**	
Ontario	**Student faculty ratio**	26.5:1	Arts & humanities	213
N2L 3G1	**International faculty**	16.0%	Engineering & IT	35
Canada	**Undergraduates**	21,800	Life sciences & biomedicine	182
	Postgraduates	2,600	Natural sciences	47
www.uwaterloo.ca	**International students**	10.0%	Social sciences	89
Tel +1 519 888 4567				

University of Western Ontario

Contact	*Statistics*		*Ranking*	
1151 Richmond Street, Suite 2	**Peer review**	125	**World rank**	126= (215=)
London	**Recruiter review**	64	**Subject area positions**	
Ontario	**Student faculty ratio**	17.5:1	Arts & humanities	100
N6A 5B8	**International faculty**	19.0%	Engineering & IT	216
Canada	**Undergraduates**	17,540	Life sciences & biomedicine	144
	Postgraduates	3,230	Natural sciences	273
www.uwo.ca	**International students**	6.0%	Social sciences	52
Tel +1 519 661 2111				

York University

Contact	*Statistics*		*Ranking*	
4700 Keele Street	**Peer Review**	137	**World rank**	248= (326=)
Toronto	**Recruiter Review**	84	**Subject area positions**	
M3J 1P3	**International Faculty**	18.0%	Arts & humanities	78
Canada	**Students**	20,053	Engineering & it	276
	International Students	1.0%	Natural sciences	262
www.yorku.ca			Social sciences	41
Tel +1 416 736 2100				

Chile

Pontificia Universidad Católica de Chile

Contact	*Statistics*		*Ranking*	
Avenida Libertador Bernardo	**Peer review**	243	**World rank**	239= (228=)
O'Higgins 340	**Recruiter review**	99	**Subject area positions**	
Santiago	**Student faculty ratio**	9.8:1	Arts & humanities	213
Chile	**International faculty**	5.0%	Engineering & IT	240
	Undergraduates	12,689	Natural sciences	253
www.puc.cl	**Postgraduates**	3,417	Social sciences	193
Tel +56 2 354 2000	**International students**	11.0%		

Universidad de Chile

Contact	*Statistics*		*Ranking*	
Av. Libertador Bernardo	**Peer review**	319	**World rank**	312= (277=)
O'Higgins 1058	**Recruiter review**	227	**Subject area positions**	
Santiago	**Student faculty ratio**	13.2:1	Arts & humanities	223
Chile	**International faculty**	8.0%	Engineering & IT	281
	Undergraduates	17,670	Life sciences & biomedicine	285
www.uchile.cl	**Postgraduates**	5,579		
Tel +56 2 978 2000	**International students**	5.0%		

China

University of Science and Technology of China

Contact	*Statistics*		*Ranking*	
Jinzhai Road	**Peer review**	96	**World rank**	155= (165=)
Hefei	**Recruiter review**	132	**Subject area positions**	
230026	**Student faculty ratio**	18.4:1	Arts & humanities	298
China	**International faculty**	2.0%	Engineering & IT	49
	Undergraduates	8,437	Life sciences & biomedicine	85
www.ustc.edu.cn	**Postgraduates**	8,632	Natural sciences	40
Tel +86 551 360 2949	**International students**	0.0%	Social sciences	277

Fudan University

Contact	*Statistics*		*Ranking*	
220 Handan Road	**Peer review**	56	**World rank**	85= (116=)
Shanghai	**Recruiter review**	30	**Subject area positions**	
200433	**Student faculty ratio**	13.2:1	Arts & humanities	46
China	**International faculty**	7.0%	Engineering & IT	115
	Undergraduates	15,282	Life sciences & biomedicine	53
www.fudan.edu.cn	**Postgraduates**	9,519	Natural sciences	80
Tel +86 21 6564 2222	**International students**	6.0%	Social sciences	62

University of Jilin

Contact	*Statistics*		*Ranking*	
2699 Qianjin Street	**Peer review**	401-500	**World rank**	401-500
Changchun	**Recruiter review**	500+		
130012	**Student faculty ratio**	12.1:1		
China	**International faculty**	3.0%		
	Students	56,478		
www.en.jlu.edu.cn	**International students**	1.0%		
Tel +86 431 8516 6885				

Nanjing University

Contact	*Statistics*		*Ranking*	
Hankou Road 22#	**Peer review**	101	**World rank**	125 (180)
Nanjing	**Recruiter review**	145	**Subject area positions**	
Jiangsu	**Student faculty ratio**	13.1:1	Arts & humanities	105
210093	**International faculty**	15.0%	Engineering & IT	146
China	**Undergraduates**	11,877	Life sciences & biomedicine	79
	Postgraduates	9,208	Natural sciences	76
www.nju.edu.cn	**International students**	1.0%	Social sciences	212
Tel +86 25 8359 2700				

Peking University

Contact	*Statistics*		*Ranking*	
Yiheyuan Road, Haidian District	**Peer review**	19	**World rank**	36 (14)
Beijing	**Recruiter review**	18	**Subject area positions**	
100871	**Student faculty ratio**	5.6:1	Arts & humanities	18
China	**International faculty**	7.0%	Engineering & IT	36
	Undergraduates	14,272	Life sciences & biomedicine	18
www.pku.edu.cn	**Postgraduates**	16,666	Natural sciences	15
Tel +86 10 6275 2114	**International students**	5.0%	Social sciences	23

Shandong University

Contact	*Statistics*		*Ranking*	
Shanda South Road 27#	**Peer Review**	328	**World rank**	401-500
Jinan	**Recruiter Review**	374	**Subject area positions**	
Shandong Province	**Student Faculty Ratio**	49.9:1	Life sciences & biomedicine	256
250100	**International Faculty**	9.0%	Natural sciences	280
China	**Undergraduates**	35,000		
	Postgraduates	10,000		
www.sdu.edu.cn				
Tel +86 531 8839 5114				

Shanghai Jiao Tong University

Contact	*Statistics*		*Ranking*	
1954 Huashan Road	**Peer review**	105	**World rank**	163= (179)
Shanghai	**Recruiter review**	58	**Subject area positions**	
200030	**Student faculty ratio**	14.9:1	Arts & humanities	211
China	**International faculty**	8.0%	Engineering & IT	55
	Undergraduates	17,521	Life sciences & biomedicine	93
www.sjtu.edu.cn	**Postgraduates**	16,635	Natural sciences	145
Tel +86 21 6293 2214	**International students**	0.0%	Social sciences	173

Southeast University

Contact	*Statistics*		*Ranking*	
Si Pai Lou 2#	**Peer review**	339	**World rank**	401-500
Nanjing	**Recruiter review**	329	**Subject area positions**	
210096	**Student faculty ratio**	16.9:1	Life sciences & biomedicine	217
China	**International faculty**	3.0%		
	Undergraduates	16,547		
www.seu.edu.cn	**Postgraduates**	8,317		
Tel +86 25 8379 2412	**International students**	1.0%		

Tianjin University

Contact	*Statistics*		*Ranking*	
92 Weijin Road	**Peer review**	275	**World rank**	324 (407=)
Tianjin	**Recruiter review**	236	**Subject area positions**	
300072	**Student faculty ratio**	14.7:1	Engineering & IT	237
China	**International faculty**	3.0%	Life sciences & biomedicine	145
	Undergraduates	15,094		
www.tju.edu.cn	**Postgraduates**	8,964		
Tel +86 22 2740 4167	**International students**	3.0%		

Tongji University

Contact	*Statistics*		*Ranking*	
Siping Road 1239#,	**Peer review**	283	**World rank**	401-500
Shanghai	**Recruiter review**	388	**Subject area positions**	
China	**Student faculty ratio**	17.3:1	Engineering & IT	168
	International faculty	2.0%	Life sciences & biomedicine	207
www.tongji.edu.cn	**Undergraduates**	21,973		
Tel +86 21 6598 2200	**Postgraduates**	14,248		
	International students	3.0%		

Tsinghua University

Contact	*Statistics*		*Ranking*	
Tsinghua Garden No.1,	**Peer review**	36	**World rank**	40 (28)
Haidian District	**Recruiter review**	55	**Subject area positions**	
Beijing	**Student faculty ratio**	3.7:1	Arts & humanities	91
100084	**International faculty**	3.0%	Engineering & IT	16
China	**Undergraduates**	14,127	Life sciences & biomedicine	52
	Postgraduates	3,110	Natural sciences	34
www.tsinghua.edu.cn	**International students**	7.0%	Social sciences	44
Tel +86 10 6277 2374				

Xi'an Jiaotong University

Contact	*Statistics*		*Ranking*	
28 Xianyang West Road	**Peer review**	342	**World rank**	401-500
Xi'an	**Recruiter review**	383	**Subject area positions**	
710049	**Student faculty ratio**	17.5:1	Engineering & it	178
China	**International faculty**	5.0%	Life sciences & biomedicine	251
	Undergraduates	18,466		
www.xjtu.edu.cn	**Postgraduates**	11,769		
Tel +86 29 8266 8234	**International students**	2.0%		

Zhejiang University

Contact	*Statistics*		*Ranking*	
388 Yuhangtang Road	**Peer review**	139	**World rank**	209= (239=)
Hangzhou	**Recruiter review**	323	**Subject area positions**	
Zhejiang Province	**Student faculty ratio**	11.9:1	Arts & humanities	158
310058	**International faculty**	4.0%	Engineering & IT	105
China	**Undergraduates**	24,335	Life sciences & biomedicine	120
	Postgraduates	16,542	Natural sciences	172
www.zju.edu.cn	**International students**	3.0%	Social sciences	223
Tel +86 571 8798 1358				

Colombia

Universidad de Los Andes

Contact

Carrera 1 N° 18A 10
Bogotá
Colombia

www.uniandes.edu.co
Tel +57 1 339 4949

Statistics

Peer review	401-500
Recruiter review	232
Student faculty ratio	19.2:1
International faculty	7.0%
Undergraduates	10,617
Postgraduates	1,610
International students	1.0%

Ranking

World rank	401-500

Czech Republic

Charles University

Contact

Information and Advisory
Celetná 13
Praha 1
116 36
Czech Republic

www.cuni.cz
Tel +420 224 491850

Statistics

Peer review	221
Recruiter review	401-500
Student faculty ratio	13:1
International faculty	7.0%
Undergraduates	33,574
Postgraduates	5,684
International students	14.0%

Ranking

World rank	290 (248=)
Subject area positions	
Arts & humanities	185
Life sciences & biomedicine	271
Natural sciences	120
Social sciences	277

Denmark

University of Aarhus

Contact

Nordre Ringgade 1
Aarhus C
8000
Denmark

www.au.dk
Tel +45 8942 1111

Statistics

Peer review	133
Recruiter review	401-500
Student faculty ratio	7:1
International faculty	15.0%
Undergraduates	9,059
Postgraduates	8,376
International students	8.0%

Ranking

World rank	114= (126)
Subject area positions	
Arts & humanities	120
Engineering & IT	226
Life sciences & biomedicine	142
Natural sciences	102
Social sciences	166

University of Copenhagen

Contact

Nørregade 10
P.O. Box 2177
Copenhagen K
1017
Denmark

www.ku.dk
Tel +45 3532 2626

Statistics

Peer review	72
Recruiter review	224
Student faculty ratio	12:1
International faculty	17.0%
Undergraduates	18,570
Postgraduates	15,282
International students	13.0%

Ranking

World rank	93= (54=)
Subject area positions	
Arts & humanities	67
Life sciences & biomedicine	62
Natural sciences	81
Social sciences	45

Technical University of Denmark

Contact	*Statistics*		*Ranking*	
Anker Engelundsvej 1	**Peer review**	241	**World rank**	130= (194)
Building 101A	**Recruiter review**	390	**Subject area positions**	
Kgs. Lyngby	**Student faculty ratio**	7.4:1	Engineering & IT	59
2800	**International faculty**	29.0%	Natural sciences	220
Denmark	**Undergraduates**	2,873		
	Postgraduates	2,632		
www.dtu.dk	**International students**	13.0%		
Tel +45 4525 2525				

University of Southern Denmark

Contact	*Statistics*		*Ranking*	
Campusvej 55	**Peer review**	401-500	**World rank**	317 (273)
Odense M	**Recruiter review**	401-500	**Subject area positions**	
5230	**Student faculty ratio**	11.9:1	Arts & humanities	230
Denmark	**International faculty**	21.0%		
	Undergraduates	7,234		
www.sdu.dk	**Postgraduates**	5,522		
Tel +45 6550 1000	**International students**	13.0%		

Finland

University of Helsinki

Contact	*Statistics*		*Ranking*	
P.O. Box 33	**Peer review**	83	**World rank**	100 (116=)
Helsinki	**Recruiter review**	270	**Subject area positions**	
00014	**Student faculty ratio**	18.4:1	Arts & humanities	73
Finland	**International faculty**	14.0%	Engineering & IT	188
	Undergraduates	22,689	Life sciences & biomedicine	89
www.helsinki.fi	**Postgraduates**	3,520	Natural sciences	92
Tel +358 9 1911	**International students**	18.0%	Social sciences	74

Helsinki University of Technology - TKK

Contact	*Statistics*		*Ranking*	
Otakaari 1	**Peer review**	207	**World rank**	170 (291)
Espoo	**Recruiter review**	401-500	**Subject area positions**	
2150	**Student faculty ratio**	6.4:1	Engineering & IT	72
Finland	**International faculty**	14.0%	Natural sciences	156
	Undergraduates	1,993	Social sciences	258
www.tkk.fi	**Postgraduates**	7,995		
Tel +358 9 4511	**International students**	9.0%		

University of Jyväskylä

Contact

P.O.Box 35
Jyväskylä
40014
Finland

www.jyu.fi
Tel + 358 14 260 1211

Statistics

Peer review	375
Recruiter review	500+
Student faculty ratio	12.9:1
International faculty	12.0%
Undergraduates	9,271
Postgraduates	1,183
International students	4.0%

Ranking

World rank	374= (404=)

Kuopio University

Contact

P.O. Box 1627
Yliopistonranta 1E
Kuopio
70211
Finland

www.uku.fi
Tel +358 17 162 211

Statistics

Peer review	401-500
Recruiter review	500+
Student faculty ratio	6.6:1
International faculty	7.0%
Undergraduates	4,069
Postgraduates	475
International students	2.0%

Ranking

World rank	267= (353)

University of Oulu

Contact

Pentti Kaiteran katu 1,
Oulun Yliopisto
90014
Finland

www.oulu.fi
Tel +358 8 553 1011

Statistics

Peer review	401-500
Recruiter review	500+
Student faculty ratio	9.3:1
International faculty	2.0%
Undergraduates	3,058
Postgraduates	7,074
International students	2.0%

Ranking

World rank	354= (454=)
Subject area positions	
Engineering & IT	276
Life sciences & biomedicine	288

University of Tampere

Contact

Kalevantie 4
Tampereen Yliopisto
33014
Finland

www.uta.fi
Tel +358 3 355 111

Statistics

Peer review	295
Recruiter review	401-500
Student faculty ratio	20.9:1
International faculty	9.0%
Undergraduates	2,870
Postgraduates	7,187
International students	3.0%

Ranking

World rank	319= (383=)
Subject area positions	
Arts & humanities	204
Engineering & IT	244
Social sciences	212

University of Turku

Contact

Turku
20014
Finland

www.utu.fi
Tel +358 2 333 51

Statistics

Peer review	266
Recruiter review	296
Student faculty ratio	14.4:1
International faculty	13.0%
Undergraduates	3,793
Postgraduates	7,326
International students	2.0%

Ranking

World rank	237= (317=)
Subject area positions	
Arts & humanities	275
Engineering & IT	296
Life sciences & biomedicine	197
Natural sciences	260
Social sciences	251

France

École Polytechnique

Contact

rue de Saclay
Palaiseau
91128
France

www.polytechnique.fr
Tel +33 1 69 33 33 33

Statistics

Peer review	92
Recruiter review	43
Student faculty ratio	3.7:1
International faculty	19.0%
Undergraduates	1,000
Postgraduates	1,464
International students	25.0%

Ranking

World rank	28 (37)
Subject area positions	
Engineering & IT	34
Life sciences & biomedicine	202
Natural sciences	31
Social sciences	261

École Nationale des Ponts et Chaussées - ENPC

Contact

28, rue des Saints-Pères
Paris
75343
France

www.enpc.fr
Tel +33 1 44 58 28 52

Statistics

Peer review	500+
Recruiter review	401-500
Student faculty ratio	8.2:1
International faculty	11.0%
Undergraduates	761
Postgraduates	54
International students	4.0%

Ranking

World rank	401-500

ESCP-EAP Paris

Contact

79, Avenue République
Paris
75011
France

www.escp-eap.net
Tel + 33 1 49 23 20 00

Statistics

Peer Review	500+
Recruiter Review	118
Student Faculty Ratio	27.6:1
International Faculty	34.0%
Students	2,612
International Students	44.0%

Ranking

World rank	401-500
Subject area positions	
Social sciences	263

ESSEC Business School, Paris

Contact

Cergy-Pontoise campus
Avenue Bernard Hirsch B.P.
50105
Cergy-Pontoise Cedex
95021
France

www.essec.edu
Tel +33 1 34 43 30 00

Statistics

Peer review	401-500
Recruiter review	69
Student faculty ratio	50:1
International faculty	37.0%
Undergraduates	1,204
Postgraduates	2,411
International students	12.0%

Ranking

World Rank	401-500
Subject Area Positions	
Social Sciences	133

Université Joseph-Fourier, Grenoble I

Contact

BP 53
Grenoble Cedex 9
38041
France

www.ujf-grenoble.fr
Tel +33 4 76 51 46 00

Statistics

Peer review	274
Recruiter review	351
Student faculty ratio	12.9:1
International faculty	7.0%
Undergraduates	10,417
Postgraduates	6,479
International students	13.0%

Ranking

World rank	275 (228=)
Subject area positions	
Engineering & IT	170
Life sciences & biomedicine	241
Natural sciences	177

HEC School of Management

Contact

1, rue de la Libération
Jouy en Josas cedex
78351
France

www.hec.fr
Tel +33 1 39 67 70 00

Statistics

Peer review	401-500
Recruiter review	38
Student faculty ratio	29.7:1
International faculty	34.0%
Undergraduates	360
Postgraduates	2,697
International students	24.0%

Ranking

World rank	401-500
Subject area positions	
Social sciences	157

Université des Sciences et Technologies de Lille (Lille I)

Contact

Cité Scientifique
Villeneuve d'Ascq
59655
France

www.univ-lille1.fr
Tel + 33 3 20 43 43 43

Statistics

Peer review	401-500
Recruiter review	367
Student faculty ratio	16.2:1
International faculty	11.0%
Undergraduates	8,058
Postgraduates	5,761
International students	19.0%

Ranking

World rank	401-500

École Normale Supérieure de Lyon

Contact

46, allee d'Italie
Lyon cedex 07
69364
France

www.ens-lyon.eu
Tel + 33 4 72 72 80 00

Statistics

Peer review	273
Recruiter review	270
Student faculty ratio	3.1:1
International faculty	10.0%
Undergraduates	173
Postgraduates	690
International students	12.0%

Ranking

World rank	157 (72)
Subject area positions	
Arts & humanities	250
Engineering & IT	216
Life sciences & biomedicine	285
Natural sciences	173

Université Claude Bernard - Lyon I

Contact

43, boulevard du 11 Novembre 1918
Villeurbanne
69622
France

www.univ-lyon1.fr
Tel +33 4 72 44 80 00

Statistics

Peer review	395
Recruiter review	500+
Student faculty ratio	23.9:1
International faculty	6.0%
Undergraduates	15,341
Postgraduates	13,603
International students	10.0%

Ranking

World rank	401-500
Subject area positions	
Engineering & IT	268

University of Montpellier II - Sciences and Techniques of Languedoc

Contact

Place Eugene Bataillon
Montpellier
34095
France

www.univ-montp2.fr
Tel +33 4 67 14 30 30

Statistics

Peer review	401-500
Recruiter review	401-500
Student faculty ratio	11.7:1
International faculty	11.0%
Undergraduates	7,733
Postgraduates	4,141
International students	13.0%

Ranking

World rank	301= (424=)
Subject area positions	
Life sciences & biomedicine	186
Natural sciences	280

École Normale Supérieure, Paris

Contact

45, rue d'Ulm
Paris Cedex 05
75230
France

www.ens.fr
Tel + 33 1 44 32 30 00

Statistics

Peer review	46
Recruiter review	201
Student faculty ratio	7.8:1
International faculty	16.0%
Undergraduates	242
Postgraduates	883
International students	19.0%

Ranking

World rank	26 (18)
Subject area positions	
Arts & humanities	33
Engineering & IT	102
Life sciences & biomedicine	137
Natural sciences	20
Social sciences	143

Sciences Po Paris

Contact

27, rue Saint-Guillaume
Paris CEDEX 07
75337
France

www.sciences-po.fr
Tel +33 1 45 49 50 50

Statistics

Peer review	309
Recruiter review	185
Student faculty ratio	4.8:1
International faculty	25.0%
Undergraduates	2,066
Postgraduates	3,567
International students	46.0%

Ranking

World rank	227= (52)
Subject area positions	
Arts & humanities	295
Life sciences & biomedicine	266
Social sciences	149

Université Paris I - Panthéon Sorbonne

Contact

12, Place du Panthéon
Paris
75005
France

www.univ-paris1.fr
Tel + 33 1 44 07 80 00

Statistics

Peer review	179
Recruiter review	195
Student faculty ratio	36.2:1
International faculty	7.0%
Undergraduates	19,847
Postgraduates	17,518
International students	17.0%

Ranking

World rank	369= (264)
Subject area positions	
Arts & humanities	67
Social sciences	76

Université Paris-Sorbonne (Paris IV)

Contact

1, rue Victor Cousin
Paris
75005
France

www.paris4.sorbonne.fr
Tel + 33 1 40 46 22 11

Statistics

Peer review	103
Recruiter review	180
Student faculty ratio	37.2:1
International faculty	4.0%
Undergraduates	13,803
Postgraduates	9,443
International students	17.0%

Ranking

World rank	295= (200)
Subject area positions	
Arts & humanities	29
Engineering & IT	239
Natural sciences	220
Social sciences	52

Université Paris IX - Dauphine

Contact

Place du Maréchal de Lattre de Tassigny
Paris Cedex 16
75775
France

www.dauphine.fr
Tel +33 1 44 05 44 05

Statistics

Peer review	401-500
Recruiter review	282
Student faculty ratio	30:1
International faculty	11.0%
Undergraduates	3,307
Postgraduates	4,384
International students	28.0%

Ranking

World rank	401-500

Université Paris V - Descartes

Contact

12, rue de l'École de médecine
Paris Cédex 06
75270
France

www.univ-paris5.fr
Tel + 33 1 40 46 16 16

Statistics

Peer review	381
Recruiter review	500+
Student faculty ratio	20.8:1
International faculty	15.0%
Students	25,514
International students	19.0%

Ranking

World rank	391 (432=)

Université Pierre-et-Marie-Curie - Paris VI

Contact

4, place Jussieu
Paris
75005
France

www.upmc.fr
Tel + 33 1 44 27 36 20

Statistics

Peer review	163
Recruiter review	500+
Student faculty ratio	7:1
International faculty	3.0%
Undergraduates	14,193
Postgraduates	3,630
International students	24.0%

Ranking

World rank	132= (93=)
Subject area positions	
Engineering & IT	130
Life sciences & biomedicine	104
Natural sciences	32

Université Paris VII - Denis Diderot

Contact

2, place Jussieu
Paris
75251
France

www.univ-paris7.fr
Tel + 33 1 44 27 44 27

Statistics

Peer review	334
Recruiter review	401-500
Student faculty ratio	22.1:1
International faculty	11.0%
Undergraduates	17,213
Postgraduates	8,614
International students	19.0%

Ranking

World rank	401-500
Subject area positions	
Arts & humanities	251
Natural sciences	185

Université Paris-Sud, Paris XI

Contact

15, rue Georges Clémenceau
Orsay
91405
France

www.u-psud.fr
Tel +33 1 69 15 67 50

Statistics

Peer review	267
Recruiter review	500+
Student faculty ratio	14:1
International faculty	9.0%
Undergraduates	15,392
Postgraduates	11,432
International students	15.0%

Ranking

World rank	267= (258=)
Subject area positions	
Engineering & IT	261
Natural sciences	52

University of Rennes

Contact	*Statistics*		*Ranking*	
2, rue du Thabor	**Peer review**	401-500	**World rank**	401-500
Rennes	**Recruiter review**	500+		
35065	**Student faculty ratio**	15.6:1		
France	**International faculty**	5.0%		
	Undergraduates	12,218		
www.univ-rennes1.fr	**Postgraduates**	10,847		
Tel + 33 2 23 23 35 35	**International students**	8.0%		

Université Louis Pasteur - Strasbourg I

Contact	*Statistics*		*Ranking*	
4, rue Blaise Pascal	**Peer review**	169	**World rank**	184 (161=)
Strasbourg	**Recruiter review**	183	**Subject area positions**	
67070	**Student faculty ratio**	24.2:1	Arts & humanities	222
France	**International faculty**	11.0%	Engineering & IT	257
	Undergraduates	9,548	Life sciences & biomedicine	49
www-ulp.u-strasbg.fr	**Postgraduates**	9,176	Natural sciences	166
Tel +33 3 90 24 50 00	**International students**	17.0%		

University of Toulouse III - Paul Sabatier

Contact	*Statistics*		*Ranking*	
118, route de Narbonne	**Peer review**	401-500	**World rank**	360= (401=)
Toulouse	**Recruiter review**	401-500	**Subject area positions**	
31062	**Student faculty ratio**	19.4:1	Engineering & IT	212
France	**International faculty**	17.0%		
	Students	22,325		
www.ups-tlse.fr	**International students**	19.0%		
Tel +33 5 61 55 66 11				

Germany

Rheinisch-Westfälische Technische Hochschule Aachen

Contact	*Statistics*		*Ranking*	
Templergraben 55	**Peer review**	283	**World rank**	182 (172=)
Aachen	**Recruiter review**	113	**Subject area positions**	
52062	**Student faculty ratio**	8.2:1	Engineering & IT	83
Germany	**International faculty**	13.0%	Natural sciences	147
	Undergraduates	24,843		
www.rwth-aachen.de	**Postgraduates**	5,339		
Tel +49 241 801	**International students**	18.0%		

Universität Bayreuth

Contact

Bayreuth
95440
Germany

www.uni-bayreuth.de
Tel +49 921 550

Statistics

Peer review	401-500
Recruiter review	340
Student faculty ratio	8.7:1
International faculty	12.0%
Undergraduates	9,073
Postgraduates	399
International students	7.0%

Ranking

World rank	297 (346=)

Freie Universität Berlin

Contact

Central Administration
Kaiserswerther Str. 16-18
Berlin
14195
Germany

www.fu-berlin.de
Tel +49 30 8381

Statistics

Peer review	84
Recruiter review	401-500
Student faculty ratio	17:1
International faculty	19.0%
Undergraduates	17,551
Postgraduates	5,154
International students	19.0%

Ranking

World rank	146 (149)
Subject area positions	
Arts & humanities	38
Engineering & IT	291
Life sciences & biomedicine	132
Natural sciences	102
Social sciences	61

Technische Universität Berlin

Contact

Strasse des 17. Juni 135
Berlin
10623
Germany

www.tu-berlin.de
Tel +49 30 3140

Statistics

Peer review	161
Recruiter review	261
Student faculty ratio	12.2:1
International faculty	11.0%
Students	28,200
International students	20.0%

Ranking

World rank	203= (203)
Subject area positions	
Arts & humanities	247
Engineering & IT	78
Life sciences & biomedicine	171
Natural sciences	108

Universität Bielefeld

Contact

Universitätsstraße 25
Bielefeld
33615
Germany

www.uni-bielefeld.de
Tel +49 521 10600

Statistics

Peer review	235
Recruiter review	500+
Student faculty ratio	23.7:1
International faculty	11.0%
Undergraduates	13,208
Postgraduates	2,556
International students	8.0%

Ranking

World rank	312= (329=)
Subject area positions	
Arts & humanities	183
Life sciences & biomedicine	295
Natural sciences	206
Social sciences	161

Ruhr-Universität Bochum

Contact	*Statistics*		*Ranking*	
Universitätsstraße 150	**Peer review**	341	**World rank**	333 (431)
Bochum	**Recruiter review**	401-500	**Subject area positions**	
44801	**Student faculty ratio**	16:1	Engineering & IT	264
Germany	**International faculty**	11.0%		
	Undergraduates	28,494		
www.ruhr-uni-bochum.de	**Postgraduates**	4,170		
Tel +49 234 32201	**International students**	13.0%		

Rheinische Friedrich-Wilhelms-Universität Bonn

Contact	*Statistics*		*Ranking*	
Regina-Pacis-Weg 3	**Peer review**	280	**World rank**	276= (217=)
Bonn	**Recruiter review**	401-500	**Subject area positions**	
53113	**Student faculty ratio**	15.3:1	Natural sciences	138
Germany	**International faculty**	11.0%	Social sciences	181
	Undergraduates	1,954		
www.uni-bonn.de	**Postgraduates**	27,500		
Tel +49 228 737080	**International students**	14.0%		

Technische Universität Braunschweig

Contact	*Statistics*		*Ranking*	
Pockelsstr. 14	**Peer review**	401-500	**World rank**	383= (392=)
Braunschweig	**Recruiter review**	401-500	**Subject area positions**	
38106	**Student faculty ratio**	12.1:1	Engineering & IT	247
Germany	**International faculty**	11.0%		
	Undergraduates	1,763		
www.tu-braunschweig.de	**Postgraduates**	8,978		
Tel +49 531 3910	**International students**	11.0%		

Universität Bremen

Contact	*Statistics*		*Ranking*	
Bibliothekstraße 1	**Peer review**	293	**World rank**	364= (380=)
Bremen	**Recruiter review**	401-500	**Subject area positions**	
28359	**Student faculty ratio**	20.7:1	Arts & humanities	247
Germany	**International faculty**	11.0%	Engineering & IT	291
	Undergraduates	17,618	Social sciences	211
www.uni-bremen.de	**Postgraduates**	9,172		
Tel +49 421 2181	**International students**	14.0%		

Technische Universität Darmstadt

Contact

Karolinenplatz 5
Darmstadt
64289
Germany

www.tu-darmstadt.de
Tel +49 6151 1601

Statistics

Peer review	331
Recruiter review	215
Student faculty ratio	8.9:1
International faculty	10.0%
Students	16,840
International students	21.0%

Ranking

World rank	239= (261=)
Subject area positions	
Engineering & IT	104

Universität Dortmund

Contact

Dortmund
44221
Germany

www.uni-dortmund.de
Tel +49 231 755 3720

Statistics

Peer review	401-500
Recruiter review	500+
Student faculty ratio	15.2:1
International faculty	10.0%
Undergraduates	19,620
Postgraduates	2,145
International students	14.0%

Ranking

World rank	401-500

Technische Universität Dresden

Contact

TUD-Information
Helmholtzstr. 10
Dresden
01069
Germany

www.tu-dresden.de
Tel +49 351 463 37044

Statistics

Peer review	334
Recruiter review	285
Student faculty ratio	7.8:1
International faculty	10.0%
Undergraduates	18,147
Postgraduates	3,001
International students	11.0%

Ranking

World rank	243= (386=)
Subject area positions	
Engineering & IT	202
Natural sciences	288

Universität Düsseldorf

Contact

Heinrich-Heine-Universität
Universitätsstr. 1
Düsseldorf
40225
Germany

www.uni-duesseldorf.de
Tel +49 211 8100

Statistics

Peer review	399
Recruiter review	500+
Student faculty ratio	12:1
International faculty	4.0%
Undergraduates	13,496
Postgraduates	1,967
International students	17.0%

Ranking

World rank	312= (386=)
Subject area positions	
Life sciences & biomedicine	215

Universität Duisburg - Essen

Contact	*Statistics*		*Ranking*	
Duisburg-Essen	**Peer review**	500+	**World rank**	401-500
	Recruiter review	500+		
www.uni-duisburg-essen.de	**Student faculty ratio**	12.8:1		
Tel +49 201 183 2229	**International faculty**	11.0%		
	Students	32,469		
	International students	13.0%		

Universität Erlangen - Nürnberg

Contact	*Statistics*		*Ranking*	
Schlossplatz 4	**Peer review**	369	**World rank**	270= (232=)
Erlangen	**Recruiter review**	360	**Subject area positions**	
91054	**Student faculty ratio**	12.3:1	Natural sciences	286
Germany	**International faculty**	19.0%		
	Undergraduates	14,967		
www.uni-erlangen.de	**Postgraduates**	11,402		
Tel +49 9131 850	**International students**	10.0%		

Universität Frankfurt am Main

Contact	*Statistics*		*Ranking*	
Frankfurt am Main	**Peer review**	196	**World rank**	209= (187=)
60054	**Recruiter review**	292	**Subject area positions**	
Germany	**Student faculty ratio**	14.5:1	Arts & humanities	117
	International faculty	6.0%	Engineering & IT	299
www.uni-frankfurt.de	**Undergraduates**	29,588	Life sciences & biomedicine	254
Tel +49 69 7980	**Postgraduates**	2,261	Natural sciences	192
	International students	13.0%	Social sciences	182

Universität Freiburg

Contact	*Statistics*		*Ranking*	
Fahnenbergplatz	**Peer review**	178	**World rank**	144 (219=)
Freiburg	**Recruiter review**	394	**Subject area positions**	
79085	**Student faculty ratio**	6.5:1	Arts & humanities	94
Germany	**International faculty**	5.0%	Life sciences & biomedicine	124
	Undergraduates	19,608	Natural sciences	188
www.uni-freiburg.de	**Postgraduates**	1,903	Social sciences	266
Tel +49 761 2030	**International students**	17.0%		

Justus-Liebig-Universität Gießen

Contact	*Statistics*		*Ranking*	
Ludwigstraße 23	**Peer review**	401-500	**World rank**	401-500
Gießen	**Recruiter review**	500+		
35390	**Student faculty ratio**	15.8:1		
Germany	**International faculty**	10.0%		
	Undergraduates	20,811		
www.uni-giessen.de	**Postgraduates**	1,026		
Tel +49 641 990	**International students**	8.0%		

Universität Göttingen

Contact	*Statistics*		*Ranking*	
Wilhelmsplatz 1	**Peer review**	130	**World rank**	168= (156=)
Göttingen	**Recruiter review**	500+	**Subject area positions**	
37073	**Student faculty ratio**	8.9:1	Arts & humanities	124
Germany	**International faculty**	10.0%	Engineering & IT	238
	Undergraduates	21,503	Life sciences & biomedicine	105
www.uni-goettingen.de	**Postgraduates**	3,036	Natural sciences	60
Tel +49 551 390	**International students**	11.0%	Social sciences	274

Martin-Luther-Universität Halle-Wittenberg

Contact	*Statistics*		*Ranking*	
Halle	**Peer Review**	500+	**World rank**	396= (378=)
06099	**Recruiter Review**	500+		
Germany	**Student Faculty Ratio**	11:1		
	International Faculty	11.0%		
www.uni-halle.de	**Students**	18,595		
Tel +49 345 5520	**International Students**	8.0%		

Universität Hamburg

Contact	*Statistics*		*Ranking*	
Edmund-Siemers-Allee 1	**Peer review**	203	**World rank**	216 (228=)
Hamburg	**Recruiter review**	294	**Subject area positions**	
20146	**Student faculty ratio**	11.7:1	Arts & humanities	225
Germany	**International faculty**	7.0%	Engineering & IT	212
	Undergraduates	35,338	Life sciences & biomedicine	185
www.uni-hamburg.de	**Postgraduates**	3,516	Natural sciences	161
Tel +49 40 428 384475	**International students**	13.0%	Social sciences	217

Leibniz Universität Hannover

Contact

Welfengarten 1
Hannover
30167
Germany

www.uni-hannover.de
Tel +49 511 7620

Statistics

Peer review	345
Recruiter review	401-500
Student faculty ratio	33.6:1
International faculty	5.0%
Undergraduates	21,905
Postgraduates	893
International students	17.0%

Ranking

World rank	383= (360=)
Subject area positions	
Life sciences & biomedicine	260

Heidelberg University

Contact

Grabengasse 1
Heidelberg
69117
Germany

www.uni-heidelberg.de
Tel +49 62 21540

Statistics

Peer review	62
Recruiter review	189
Student faculty ratio	10.6:1
International faculty	10.0%
Undergraduates	23,062
Postgraduates	2,469
International students	21.0%

Ranking

World rank	60 (58=)
Subject area positions	
Arts & humanities	61
Life sciences & biomedicine	43
Natural sciences	45
Social sciences	78

Humboldt-Universität zu Berlin

Contact

Unter den Linden 6
Berlin
10099
Germany

www.hu-berlin.de
Tel +49 30 20930

Statistics

Peer review	114
Recruiter review	303
Student faculty ratio	9.2:1
International faculty	11.0%
Undergraduates	33,594
Postgraduates	3,935
International students	15.0%

Ranking

World rank	126= (105=)
Subject area positions	
Arts & humanities	64
Life sciences & biomedicine	151
Natural sciences	101
Social sciences	99

Universität Jena

Contact

Jena
07740
Germany

www.uni-jena.de
Tel +49 3641 9300

Statistics

Peer review	383
Recruiter review	401-500
Student faculty ratio	10.6:1
International faculty	7.0%
Undergraduates	17,938
Postgraduates	1,140
International students	5.0%

Ranking

World rank	316 (343=)
Subject area positions	
Arts & humanities	282

Universität Karlsruhe

Contact

Kaiserstraße 12
Karlsruhe
76131
Germany

www.uni-karlsruhe.de
Tel +49 721 6080

Statistics

Peer review	256
Recruiter review	201
Student faculty ratio	9:1
International faculty	14.0%
Undergraduates	17,521
Postgraduates	1,118
International students	20.0%

Ranking

World rank	171= (222=)
Subject area positions	
Engineering & IT	80
Natural sciences	142

Christian-Albrechts-Universität zu Kiel

Contact

Kiel
24098
Germany

www.uni-kiel.de
Tel +49 431 88000

Statistics

Peer review	500+
Recruiter review	401-500
Student faculty ratio	12.1:1
International faculty	11.0%
Students	21,105
International students	9.0%

Ranking

World rank	388= (226=)

WHU Otto Beisheim School of Management - Koblenz

Contact

Burgplatz 2
Vallendar
56179
Germany

www.whu.edu
Tel +49 261 65090

Statistics

Peer review	500+
Recruiter review	103
Student faculty ratio	0.9:1
International faculty	45.0%
Undergraduates	285
Postgraduates	200
International students	14.0%

Ranking

World rank	327 (252=)

University of Cologne

Contact

Albertus-Magnus-Platz
Köln
50923
Germany

www.uni-koeln.de
Tel +49 221 4700

Statistics

Peer review	304
Recruiter review	376
Student faculty ratio	21.2:1
International faculty	12.0%
Undergraduates	42,476
Postgraduates	5,106
International students	14.0%

Ranking

World rank	319= (292=)
Subject area positions	
Arts & humanities	199
Social sciences	196

Universität Konstanz

Contact	*Statistics*		*Ranking*	
Universitätsstraße 10	**Peer review**	314	**World rank**	311 (317=)
Konstanz	**Recruiter review**	401-500	**Subject area positions**	
78464	**Student faculty ratio**	16.5:1	Arts & humanities	149
Germany	**International faculty**	14.0%	Social sciences	233
	Undergraduates	9,205		
www.uni-konstanz.de	**Postgraduates**	1,221		
Tel +49 7531 880	**International students**	9.0%		

Universität Leipzig

Contact	*Statistics*		*Ranking*	
Ritterstraße 26	**Peer review**	269	**World rank**	292= (340=)
Leipzig	**Recruiter review**	324	**Subject area positions**	
04109	**Student faculty ratio**	31.6:1	Arts & humanities	191
Germany	**International faculty**	7.0%	Life sciences & biomedicine	260
	Undergraduates	31,082	Natural sciences	240
www.uni-leipzig.de	**Postgraduates**	4,521		
Tel +49 341 97108	**International students**	8.0%		

Johannes Gutenberg Universität Mainz

Contact	*Statistics*		*Ranking*	
Saarstrasse 21	**Peer review**	401-500	**World rank**	330 (370=)
Mainz	**Recruiter review**	401-500	**Subject area positions**	
55122	**Student faculty ratio**	17.1:1	Natural sciences	208
Germany	**International faculty**	6.0%		
	Undergraduates	18,855		
www.uni-mainz.de	**Postgraduates**	1,511		
Tel +49 6131 390	**International students**	15.0%		

Universität Mannheim

Contact	*Statistics*		*Ranking*	
Schloss	**Peer review**	500+	**World rank**	392 (499)
Mannheim	**Recruiter review**	201	**Subject area positions**	
68131	**Student faculty ratio**	55.1:1	Social sciences	164
Germany	**International faculty**	4.0%		
	Undergraduates	5,705		
www.uni-mannheim.de	**Postgraduates**	6,161		
Tel +49 621 1810	**International students**	11.0%		

Universität Marburg

Contact	*Statistics*		*Ranking*	
Philipps-Universität	**Peer review**	500+	**World rank**	341= (310)
Karl-von-Frisch-Straße 4	**Recruiter review**	500+	**Subject area positions**	
Marburg	**Student faculty ratio**	9.6:1	Arts & humanities	275
35032	**International faculty**	11.0%		
Germany	**Students**	19,503		
	International students	12.0%		
www.uni-marburg.de				
Tel +49 6421 2820				

Technische Universität München

Contact	*Statistics*		*Ranking*	
Arcisstrasse 21	**Peer review**	124	**World rank**	67 (82=)
München	**Recruiter review**	150	**Subject area positions**	
80333	**Student faculty ratio**	7.1:1	Engineering & IT	40
Germany	**International faculty**	15.0%	Life sciences & biomedicine	178
	Undergraduates	12,311	Natural sciences	66
www.tu-muenchen.de	**Postgraduates**	9,297		
Tel +49 89 28901	**International students**	19.0%		

Ludwig-Maximilians-Universität München

Contact	*Statistics*		*Ranking*	
Geschwister-Scholl Platz 1	**Peer review**	79	**World rank**	65= (98)
München	**Recruiter review**	201	**Subject area positions**	
80539	**Student faculty ratio**	9.4:1	Arts & humanities	56
Germany	**International faculty**	15.0%	Engineering & IT	176
	Undergraduates	40,697	Life sciences & biomedicine	111
www.uni-muenchen.de	**Postgraduates**	4,888	Natural sciences	62
Tel +49 89 21800	**International students**	16.0%	Social sciences	82

University of Münster

Contact	*Statistics*		*Ranking*	
Schlossplatz 2	**Peer review**	365	**World rank**	339= (354=)
Münster	**Recruiter review**	401-500	**Subject area positions**	
48149	**Student faculty ratio**	13:1	Arts & humanities	208
Germany	**International faculty**	11.0%		
	Students	38,458		
www.uni-muenster.de	**International students**	8.0%		
Tel +49 251 830				

Universität Regensburg

Contact	*Statistics*		*Ranking*	
Universitätsstraße 31	**Peer review**	401-500	**World rank**	378= (358=)
Regensburg	**Recruiter review**	500+		
93053	**Student faculty ratio**	14.7:1		
Germany	**International faculty**	11.0%		
	Undergraduates	16,414		
www.uni-regensburg.de	**Postgraduates**	1,277		
Tel +49 941 94301	**International students**	8.0%		

Saarland University

Contact	*Statistics*		*Ranking*	
Postfach 151150	**Peer review**	401-500	**World rank**	345= (333=)
Saarbrücken	**Recruiter review**	500+		
66041	**Student faculty ratio**	14:1		
Germany	**International faculty**	21.0%		
	Undergraduates	12,050		
www.uni-saarland.de	**Postgraduates**	1,659		
Tel +49 681 3020	**International students**	14.0%		

Universität Stuttgart

Contact	*Statistics*		*Ranking*	
Postfach 10 60 37	**Peer review**	240	**World rank**	165 (201=)
Stuttgart	**Recruiter review**	109	**Subject area positions**	
70049	**Student faculty ratio**	9.2:1	Engineering & IT	71
Germany	**International faculty**	13.0%	Natural sciences	161
	Students	18,976		
www.uni-stuttgart.de	**International students**	22.0%		
Tel +49 711 6850				

Universität Tübingen

Contact	*Statistics*		*Ranking*	
Wilhelmstr. 7	**Peer review**	165	**World rank**	142= (170=)
Tübingen	**Recruiter review**	240	**Subject area positions**	
72074	**Student faculty ratio**	13:1	Arts & humanities	79
Germany	**International faculty**	21.0%	Life sciences & biomedicine	73
	Undergraduates	12,780	Natural sciences	201
www.uni-tuebingen.de	**Postgraduates**	13,547	Social sciences	283
Tel +49 7071 290	**International students**	14.0%		

Universität Ulm

Contact	*Statistics*		*Ranking*	
Ulm	**Peer review**	500+	**World rank**	263 (158=)
89069	**Recruiter review**	401-500		
Germany	**Student faculty ratio**	3.8:1		
	International faculty	10.0%		
www.uni-ulm.de	**Undergraduates**	5,868		
Tel +49 731 5010	**Postgraduates**	453		
	International students	11.0%		

Universität Würzburg

Contact	*Statistics*		*Ranking*	
Sanderring 2	**Peer review**	343	**World rank**	270= (296=)
Würzburg	**Recruiter review**	401-500	**Subject area positions**	
97070	**Student faculty ratio**	11.3:1	Arts & humanities	196
Germany	**International faculty**	12.0%	Life sciences & biomedicine	295
	Undergraduates	18,747		
www.uni-wuerzburg.de	**Postgraduates**	971		
Tel +49 931 310	**International students**	8.0%		

Greece

University of Athens

Contact	*Statistics*		*Ranking*	
Studies Department	**Peer review**	401-500	**World rank**	248= (508)
7, Palaion Patron Germanou str	**Recruiter review**	326		
Athens	**Student faculty ratio**	8.2:1		
10561	**Undergraduates**	7,191		
Greece	**Postgraduates**	1,127		
	International students	26.0%		
www.uoa.gr				
Tel +30 210 368 9918				

National Technical University of Athens

Contact	*Statistics*		*Ranking*	
Iroon Polytexneiou 9,	**Peer review**	401-500	**World rank**	356= (468=)
Zografou	**Recruiter review**	277	**Subject area positions**	
15780	**Student faculty ratio**	14.7:1	Engineering & IT	111
Greece	**International faculty**	0.0%		
	Undergraduates	7,052		
www.ntua.gr	**Postgraduates**	1,158		
	International students	4.0%		

Athens University of Economy and Business

Contact	*Statistics*		*Ranking*	
76, Patission Str.	**Peer review**	401-500	**World rank**	401-500
Athens 104 34	**Recruiter review**	176		
Greece	**Student faculty ratio**	44.2:1		
	International faculty	8.0%		
www.aueb.gr	**Undergraduates**	6,174		
Tel +30 210 820 3250	**Postgraduates**	1,650		
	International students	7.0%		

University of Crete

Contact	*Statistics*		*Ranking*	
Knossoou Ave.	**Peer review**	401-500	**World rank**	401-500
P.O.Box 2208	**Recruiter review**	500+	**Subject area positions**	
Heraklion	**Student faculty ratio**	15.4:1	Engineering & IT	287
71409	**International faculty**	1.0%		
Greece	**Undergraduates**	9,135		
	Postgraduates	1,644		
www.uoc.gr	**International students**	0.0%		
Tel +30 81 393				

University of Patras

Contact	*Statistics*		*Ranking*	
Rio, 26500	**Peer review**	401-500	**World rank**	401-500
Patras	**Recruiter review**	401-500	**Subject area positions**	
265 04	**Student faculty ratio**	16.1:1	Engineering & IT	181
Greece	**International faculty**	12.0%		
	Undergraduates	15,349		
www.upatras.gr	**Postgraduates**	5,438		
Tel +30 2610 991 822	**International students**	5.0%		

Aristotelian University of Thessaloniki

Contact	*Statistics*		*Ranking*	
Thessaloniki	**Peer review**	375	**World rank**	401-500
Greece 54124	**Recruiter review**	401-500	**Subject area positions**	
	Student faculty ratio	42.2:1	Arts & humanities	284
www.auth.gr	**International faculty**		Engineering & IT	268
Tel +30 2310 99 6000	**Undergraduates**	71,351		
	Postgraduates	6,947		
	International students	36.0%		

Hong Kong

The Chinese University of Hong Kong

Contact	*Statistics*		*Ranking*	
Shatin, N.T	**Peer review**	68	**World rank**	38= (50=)
Hong Kong SAR	**Recruiter review**	123	**Subject area positions**	
China	**Student faculty ratio**	8.2:1	Arts & humanities	106
	International faculty	51.0%	Engineering & IT	85
www.cuhk.edu.hk	**Undergraduates**	10,197	Life sciences & biomedicine	62
Tel +852 2609 7000	**Postgraduates**	2,863	Natural sciences	125
	International students	20.0%	Social sciences	48

City University of Hong Kong

Contact	*Statistics*		*Ranking*	
Tat Chee Avenue	**Peer review**	144	**World rank**	149= (154)
Kowloon Tong	**Recruiter review**	244	**Subject area positions**	
Hong Kong SAR	**Student faculty ratio**	14.9:1	Arts & humanities	213
China	**International faculty**	50.0%	Engineering & IT	86
	Undergraduates	10,318	Life sciences & biomedicine	275
www.cityu.edu.hk	**Postgraduates**	3,494	Natural sciences	184
Tel +852 2788 7654	**International students**	11.0%	Social sciences	101

University of Hong Kong

Contact	*Statistics*		*Ranking*	
Pok Fu Lam Road	**Peer review**	40	**World rank**	18 (33=)
Hong Kong	**Recruiter review**	66	**Subject area positions**	
China	**Student faculty ratio**	7.5:1	Arts & humanities	44
	International faculty	55.0%	Engineering & IT	68
www.hku.hk	**Undergraduates**	8,974	Life sciences & biomedicine	36
Tel +852 2859 2111	**Postgraduates**	6,792	Natural sciences	61
	International students	22.0%	Social sciences	31

Hong Kong University of Science & Technology

Contact	*Statistics*		*Ranking*	
Clear Water Bay	**Peer review**	64	**World rank**	53= (58=)
Kowloon	**Recruiter review**	106	**Subject area positions**	
Hong Kong	**Student faculty ratio**	18:1	Engineering & IT	23
China	**International faculty**	69.0%	Life sciences & biomedicine	80
	Undergraduates	5,772	Natural sciences	52
www.ust.hk	**Postgraduates**	2,488	Social sciences	63
Tel +852 2358 6000	**International students**	26.0%		

The Hong Kong Polytechnic University

Contact	Statistics		Ranking	
Hung Hom	**Peer review**	315	**World rank**	256= (-)
Hong Kong	**Recruiter review**	251	**Subject area positions**	
China	**Student faculty ratio**	20.8:1	Engineering & IT	186
	International faculty	52.0%	Natural sciences	291
www.polyu.edu.hk	**Undergraduates**	11,069		
Tel +852 2766 5111	**Postgraduates**	4,047		
	International students	11.0%		

Hungary

University of Szeged

Contact	Statistics		Ranking	
Dugonics tér 13.	**Peer review**	401-500	**World rank**	401-500
Szeged	**Recruiter review**	397		
6720	**Student faculty ratio**	13.6:1		
Hungary	**International faculty**	2.0%		
	Undergraduates	24,166		
www.u-szeged.hu	**Postgraduates**	1,298		
Tel +36 62 544 001	**International students**	5.0%		

India

University of Calcutta

Contact	Statistics		Ranking	
Senate House, 87 /1 College Street	**Peer review**	174	**World rank**	401-500
Kolkata	**Recruiter review**	234	**Subject area positions**	
West Bengal	**Students**	5,901	Arts & humanities	253
700 073			Engineering & IT	155
India			Life sciences & biomedicine	190
			Natural sciences	132
www.caluniv.ac.in			Social sciences	200
Tel +91 33 224 0071				

University of Delhi

Contact	Statistics		Ranking	
University Road	**Peer review**	95	**World rank**	254 (307=)
Delhi	**Recruiter review**	118	**Subject area positions**	
110 007	**Student faculty ratio**	378.3:1	Arts & humanities	108
India	**International faculty**	0.0%	Engineering & IT	130
	Undergraduates	306,798	Life sciences & biomedicine	105
www.du.ac.in	**Postgraduates**	18,662	Natural sciences	99
Tel +91 11 2766 7725	**International students**	0.0%	Social sciences	92

Indian Institute of Technology Bombay (IITB)

Contact

Mumbai
400076
India

www.iitb.ac.in
Tel +91 22 2572 2545

Statistics

Peer review	115
Recruiter review	180
Student faculty ratio	12.7:1
International faculty	4.0%
Undergraduates	2,036
Postgraduates	3,221
International students	0.0%

Ranking

World rank	269 (-)
Subject area positions	
Engineering & IT	33
Life sciences & biomedicine	228
Natural sciences	67
Social sciences	219

Indian Institute of Technology Delhi (IITD)

Contact

Hauz Khas
New Delhi
110 016
India

www.iitd.ernet.in
Tel +91 11 2658 2027

Statistics

Peer review	150
Recruiter review	156
Student faculty ratio	13.5:1
International faculty	0.0%
Undergraduates	2,205
Postgraduates	2,464
International students	0.0%

Ranking

World rank	307= (-)
Subject area positions	
Engineering & IT	37
Life sciences & biomedicine	183
Natural sciences	105

Indian Institute of Technology Kanpur (IITK)

Contact

Faculty Builing - 223
P.O. i.i.T Kanpur
Kanpur
208016
India

www.iitk.ac.in
Tel +91 512 2597 620

Statistics

Peer Review	311
Recruiter Review	309
Student Faculty Ratio	14.1:1
Undergraduates	2,195
Postgraduates	1,364

Ranking

World rank	401-500
Subject area positions	
Engineering & IT	92

Indian Institute of Technology Madras (IITM)

Contact

i.i.T. Post office
Chennai
600 036
India

www.iitm.ac.in
Tel +91 44 2257 8133

Statistics

Peer Review	304
Recruiter Review	401-500
Student Faculty Ratio	11.4:1
Students	4,308

Ranking

World rank	401-500
Subject area positions	
Engineering & IT	117
Life sciences & biomedicine	297
Natural sciences	206

Indian Institute of Technology Roorkee (IITR)

Contact

Roorkee
247667
India

www.iitr.ac.in
Tel +91 1332 272 349

Statistics

Peer review	380
Recruiter review	219
Student faculty ratio	13.6:1
International faculty	7.0%
Undergraduates	1,936
Postgraduates	1,985
International students	1.0%

Ranking

World rank	401-500
Subject area positions	
Engineering & IT	231
Life sciences & biomedicine	207

University of Mumbai

Contact

Fort
Mumbai
400 032
India

www.mu.ac.in
Tel +91 2265 2819

Statistics

Peer review	202
Recruiter review	189

Ranking

World rank	401-500
Subject area positions	
Engineering & IT	146
Life sciences & biomedicine	155
Natural sciences	151
Social sciences	205

University of Pune

Contact

Ganeshkhind Road
Pune, Maharashtra
411007
India

www.unipune.ernet.in
Tel +91 20 2569 1162

Statistics

Peer Review	175
Recruiter Review	303
Student Faculty Ratio	689.6:1
International Faculty	0.0%
Students	162,734
International Students	0.0%

Ranking

World rank	401-500
Subject area positions	
Arts & humanities	233
Engineering & IT	129
Life sciences & biomedicine	171
Natural sciences	143
Social sciences	251

Indonesia

Bandung Institute of Technology

Contact

Jl, Tamansari 64
Bandung
40116
Indonesia

www.itb.ac.id
Tel +62 22 250 0935

Statistics

Peer review	198
Recruiter review	159
Student faculty ratio	16.7:1
International faculty	5.0%
Undergraduates	10,546
Postgraduates	3,453
International students	0.0%

Ranking

World rank	369= (258=)
Subject area positions	
Arts & humanities	242
Engineering & IT	114
Life sciences & biomedicine	244
Natural sciences	135

Universitas Gadjah Mada

Contact

Bulaksumur
Yogyakarta
55281
Indonesia

www.ugm.ac.id
Tel +62 274 562 011

Statistics

Peer review	129
Recruiter review	308
Student faculty ratio	18.2:1
International faculty	0.0%
Undergraduates	30,030
Postgraduates	11,916
International students	2.0%

Ranking

World rank	360= (270=)
Subject area positions	
Arts & humanities	121
Engineering & IT	240
Life sciences & biomedicine	108
Natural sciences	152
Social sciences	108

University of Indonesia

Contact

Depok
16424
Indonesia

www.ui.ac.id
Tel +62 217 884 9060

Statistics

Peer review	228
Recruiter review	215
Student faculty ratio	15.6:1
International faculty	2.0%
Undergraduates	26,254
Postgraduates	10,834
International students	1.0%

Ranking

World rank	395 (250=)
Subject area positions	
Arts & humanities	201
Engineering & IT	264
Life sciences & biomedicine	198
Social sciences	150

Ireland

University College Cork

Contact

Cork
Ireland

www.ucc.ie
Tel +353 21 490 3000

Statistics

Peer review	352
Recruiter review	164
Student faculty ratio	18.3:1
International faculty	23.0%
Undergraduates	11,150
Postgraduates	2,262
International students	13.0%

Ranking

World rank	286= (386=)
Subject area positions	
Arts & humanities	284
Engineering & IT	261

University College Dublin

Contact

Belfield
Dublin 4
Ireland

www.ucd.ie
Tel +353 1 716 7777

Statistics

Peer review	185
Recruiter review	92
Student faculty ratio	17.6:1
International faculty	28.0%
Undergraduates	14,298
Postgraduates	5,711
International students	12.0%

Ranking

World rank	177= (219=)
Subject area positions	
Arts & humanities	104
Engineering & IT	243
Life sciences & biomedicine	222
Natural sciences	298
Social sciences	135

Dublin City University

Contact

Glasnevin
Dublin 9
Ireland

www.dcu.ie
Tel +353 1 700 5000

Statistics

Peer review	390
Recruiter review	155
Student faculty ratio	19.2:1
International faculty	23.0%
Undergraduates	5,492
Postgraduates	1,806
International students	13.0%

Ranking

World rank	300 (441=)
Subject area positions	
Arts & humanities	253

Dublin Institute of Technology

Contact

30 Upper Pembroke Street
Dublin 2
Ireland

www.dit.ie
Tel +353 1 402 3000

Statistics

Peer review	401-500
Recruiter review	238
Student faculty ratio	6.4:1
International faculty	4.0%
Undergraduates	12,687
Postgraduates	1,338
International students	8.0%

Ranking

World rank	351= (370=)
Subject area positions	
Engineering & IT	259

National University of Ireland, Galway

Contact

University Road
Galway
Ireland

www.nuigalway.ie
Tel +353 91 524 411

Statistics

Peer review	374
Recruiter review	259
Student faculty ratio	20.6:1
International faculty	19.0%
Undergraduates	9,804
Postgraduates	3,297
International students	13.0%

Ranking

World rank	401-500

University of Limerick

Contact

Castletroy
Limerick
Ireland

www.ul.ie
Tel +353 61 202 700

Statistics

Peer review	500+
Recruiter review	208
Student faculty ratio	29.6:1
International faculty	21.0%
Undergraduates	8,593
Postgraduates	1,775
International students	4.0%

Ranking

World rank	401-500

Trinity College Dublin

Contact	*Statistics*		*Ranking*	
College Green	**Peer review**	81	**World rank**	53= (78)
Dublin 2	**Recruiter review**	56	**Subject area positions**	
Ireland	**Student faculty ratio**	9.3:1	Arts & humanities	37
	International faculty	42.0%	Engineering & IT	211
www.tcd.ie	**Undergraduates**	9,844	Life sciences & biomedicine	87
Tel +353 1 896 1000	**Postgraduates**	2,746	Natural sciences	122
	International students	17.0%	Social sciences	103

Israel

Ben Gurion University of the Negev

Contact	*Statistics*		*Ranking*	
P.O. Box 653	**Peer review**	230	**World rank**	286= (329=)
Beer-Sheva	**Recruiter review**	401-500	**Subject area positions**	
84105	**Student faculty ratio**	15.4:1	Arts & humanities	267
Israel	**International faculty**	3.0%	Engineering & IT	216
	Undergraduates	10,707	Life sciences & biomedicine	188
www.bgu.ac.il	**Postgraduates**	5,083	Natural sciences	217
Tel +972 8 646 1111	**International students**	4.0%	Social sciences	254

Hebrew University of Jerusalem

Contact	*Statistics*		*Ranking*	
Mount Scopus	**Peer review**	60	**World rank**	128 (119)
Jerusalem	**Recruiter review**	401-500	**Subject area positions**	
91905	**Student faculty ratio**	25.3:1	Arts & humanities	39
Israel	**International faculty**	24.0%	Engineering & IT	221
	Undergraduates	11,549	Life sciences & biomedicine	55
www.huji.ac.il	**Postgraduates**	9,195	Natural sciences	71
Tel +972 2 588 2811	**International students**	2.0%	Social sciences	69

Technion - Israel Institute of Technology

Contact	*Statistics*		*Ranking*	
Technion City	**Peer review**	73	**World rank**	231= (158=)
Haifa 32000	**Recruiter review**	222	**Subject area positions**	
Israel	**Student faculty ratio**	11.9:1	Arts & humanities	178
	International faculty	1.0%	Engineering & IT	25
www.technion.ac.il	**Undergraduates**	8,700	Life sciences & biomedicine	119
Tel +972 4 829 2111	**Postgraduates**	3,354	Natural sciences	36
	International students	2.0%		

Tel Aviv University

Contact	*Statistics*		*Ranking*	
P.O. Box 39040	**Peer review**	77	**World rank**	151= (147=)
Tel Aviv 69978	**Recruiter review**	315	**Subject area positions**	
Israel	**Student faculty ratio**	19.4:1	Arts & humanities	100
	International faculty	0.0%	Engineering & IT	138
www.tau.ac.il	**Undergraduates**	13,196	Life sciences & biomedicine	96
Tel +972 3 640 8111	**Postgraduates**	7,101	Natural sciences	84
	International students	1.0%	Social sciences	60

Italy

Università Commerciale Luigi Bocconi

Contact	*Statistics*		*Ranking*	
Via Sarfatti, 25	**Peer review**	401-500	**World rank**	401-500
Milan	**Recruiter review**	9	**Subject area positions**	
20136	**Student faculty ratio**	44.7:1	Social sciences	83
Italy	**International faculty**	5.0%		
	Undergraduates	7,495		
www.unibocconi.eu	**Postgraduates**	4,357		
Tel +39 25 836 5930	**International students**	7.0%		

University of Bologna

Contact	*Statistics*		*Ranking*	
Via Zamboni, 33	**Peer review**	88	**World rank**	173= (207=)
Bologna	**Recruiter review**	171	**Subject area positions**	
40126	**Student faculty ratio**	20.5:1	Arts & humanities	47
Italy	**International faculty**	4.0%	Engineering & IT	156
	Undergraduates	53,161	Life sciences & biomedicine	113
www.unibo.it	**Postgraduates**	38,321	Natural sciences	134
Tel +39 51 209 4516	**International students**	5.0%	Social sciences	94

University of Florence

Contact	*Statistics*		*Ranking*	
P.zza S.Marco, 4	**Peer review**	226	**World rank**	329 (338=)
Florence	**Recruiter review**	401-500	**Subject area positions**	
50121	**Student faculty ratio**	32.4:1	Arts & humanities	138
Italy	**International faculty**	4.0%	Engineering & IT	286
	Undergraduates	56,123	Natural sciences	159
www.unifi.it	**Postgraduates**	7,475	Social sciences	256
Tel +39 55 275 6209	**International students**	4.0%		

University of Genoa

Contact

Via Balbi, 5
Genoa
16126
Italy

www.unige.it
Tel +39 10 20991

Statistics

Peer review	401-500
Recruiter review	500+
Student faculty ratio	25.1:1
International faculty	2.0%
Students	36,428
International students	3.0%

Ranking

World rank	401-500

Politecnico di Milano

Contact

Piazza Leonardo Da Vinci, 32
Milan
20133
Italy

www.polimi.it
Tel +39 2 23991

Statistics

Peer review	206
Recruiter review	88
Student faculty ratio	16:1
International faculty	2.0%
Undergraduates	24,169
Postgraduates	16,148
International students	4.0%

Ranking

World rank	343= (311=)
Subject area positions	
Arts & humanities	237
Engineering & IT	66
Life sciences & biomedicine	275
Natural sciences	236

University of Modena

Contact

Via Università, 4
Modena
41100
Italy

www.unimo.it
Tel +39 59 205 6511

Statistics

Peer review	500+
Recruiter review	500+
Student faculty ratio	18.4.1
International faculty	1.0%
Undergraduates	13,135
Postgraduates	276
International students	7.0%

Ranking

World rank	401-500

University of Naples - Federico II

Contact

Piazzale V. Tecchio
Naples
80125
Italy

www.unina.it
Tel +39 81 768 2232

Statistics

Peer review	345
Recruiter review	401-500
Student faculty ratio	57.8:1
International faculty	3.0%
Students	88,970
International students	1.0%

Ranking

World rank	401-500
Subject area positions	
Social sciences	288

University of Padua

Contact

Via 8 Febbraio, 2
Padova
35122
Italy

www.unipd.it
Tel +39 49 827 5111

Statistics

Peer review	229
Recruiter review	401-500
Student faculty ratio	32.8:1
International faculty	1.0%
Undergraduates	59,041
Postgraduates	6,510
International students	4.0%

Ranking

World rank	312= (370=)
Subject area positions	
Arts & humanities	169
Life sciences & biomedicine	190
Natural sciences	194

Università degli Studi di Pavia

Contact

Strada Nuova, 65
Pavia
27100
Italy

www.unipv.it
Tel +39 38 29811

Statistics

Peer review	336
Recruiter review	401-500
Student faculty ratio	17.5:1
International faculty	0.0%
Undergraduates	21,369
Postgraduates	3,529
International students	4.0%

Ranking

World rank	388= (432=)
Subject area positions	
Arts & humanities	269
Engineering & IT	249

Perugia University

Contact

Piazza dell'Università, 1
Perugia
06100
Italy

www.unipg.it
Tel +39 7 55851

Statistics

Peer review	401-500
Recruiter review	500+
Student faculty ratio	23:1
International faculty	3.0%
Undergraduates	20,600
Postgraduates	2,743
International students	5.0%

Ranking

World rank	401-500

University of Pisa

Contact

Lungarno Pacinotti, 43
Pisa
56126
Italy

www.unipi.it
Tel +39 50 221 2111

Statistics

Peer review	211
Recruiter review	401-500
Student faculty ratio	35.4:1
International faculty	0.0%
Undergraduates	44,297
Postgraduates	11,597
International students	2.0%

Ranking

World rank	325 (326=)
Subject area positions	
Arts & humanities	212
Engineering & IT	203
Life sciences & biomedicine	235
Natural sciences	112

Università degli Studi di Roma - La Sapienza

Contact

P.le Aldo Moro,5
Rome
00185
Italy

www.uniroma1.it
Tel +39 6 49911

Statistics

Peer review	85
Recruiter review	187
Student faculty ratio	37.2:1
International faculty	1.0%
Undergraduates	142,743
Postgraduates	7,759
International students	4.0%

Ranking

World rank	183 (197)
Subject area positions	
Arts & humanities	60
Engineering & IT	145
Life sciences & biomedicine	219
Natural sciences	40
Social sciences	111

Università degli Studi di Roma - Tor Vergata

Contact

Via Orazio Raimondo, 18
Rome
00173
Italy

web.uniroma2.it
Tel +39 67 259 2710

Statistics

Peer review	357
Recruiter review	324
Student faculty ratio	30.9:1
International faculty	1.0%
Undergraduates	34,984
Postgraduates	7,354
International students	3.0%

Ranking

World rank	401-500
Subject area positions	
Natural sciences	226

University of Siena

Contact

Via Banchi di Sotto, 55
Siena
53100
Italy

www.unisi.it
Tel +39 57 723 2111

Statistics

Peer review	401-500
Recruiter review	296
Student faculty ratio	29.2:1
International faculty	2.0%
Undergraduates	19,827
Postgraduates	2,864
International students	4.0%

Ranking

World rank	394 (478=)
Subject area positions	
Social sciences	247

University of Trento

Contact

Via Belenzani, 12
Trento
38100
Italy

www.unitn.it
Tel +39 46 188 1111

Statistics

Peer review	384
Recruiter review	300
Student faculty ratio	37.3:1
International faculty	5.0%
Undergraduates	12,106
Postgraduates	5,123
International students	5.0%

Ranking

World rank	401-500
Subject area positions	
Engineering & IT	259
Natural sciences	266

University of Trieste

Contact	*Statistics*		*Ranking*	
Piazzale Europa, 1	**Peer review**	306	**World rank**	374= (454=)
Trieste	**Recruiter review**	401-500	**Subject area positions**	
34127	**Student faculty ratio**	22.7:1	Arts & humanities	257
Italy	**International faculty**	0.0%	Life sciences & biomedicine	228
	Undergraduates	15,986	Natural sciences	211
www.univ.trieste.it	**Postgraduates**	5,762		
Tel +39 40 558 7111	**International students**	7.0%		

University of Turin

Contact	*Statistics*		*Ranking*	
Via Verdi, 8	**Peer Review**	377	**World rank**	401-500
Turin	**Recruiter Review**	500+	**Subject area positions**	
10124	**Student Faculty Ratio**	23.3:1	Arts & humanities	189
Italy	**International Faculty**	4.0%	Social sciences	283
	Students	60,325		
www.unito.it	**International Students**	2.0%		
Tel +39 11 670 6111				

Japan

Chiba University

Contact	*Statistics*		*Ranking*	
1-33, Yayoi-cho, Inage-ku	**Peer review**	387	**World rank**	284= (303=)
Chiba	**Recruiter review**	236	**Subject area positions**	
263-8522	**Student faculty ratio**	13.7:1	Life sciences & biomedicine	149
Japan	**International faculty**	5.0%		
	Undergraduates	11,297		
www.chiba-u.ac.jp	**Postgraduates**	3,620		
Tel +81 43 251 1111	**International students**	4.0%		

Gifu University

Contact	*Statistics*		*Ranking*	
Yanagido 1-1	**Peer review**	401-500	**World rank**	345= (332)
Gifu	**Recruiter review**	401-500		
501-1193	**Student faculty ratio**	9.8:1		
Japan	**International faculty**	5.0%		
	Undergraduates	5,956		
www.gifu-u.ac.jp	**Postgraduates**	1,580		
Tel +81 58 293 2142	**International students**	4.0%		

Gunma University

Contact

4-2 Aramaki-machi
Maebashi
Gunma
371-8510
Japan

www.gunma-u.ac.jp

Statistics

Peer review	500+
Recruiter review	500+
Student faculty ratio	6.8:1
International faculty	5.0%
Undergraduates	5,636
Postgraduates	1,356
International students	3.0%

Ranking

World rank	331= (252=)

Hiroshima University

Contact

3-2, Kagamiyama 1 chome
Higashi-Hiroshima
739-8511
Japan

www.hiroshima-u.ac.jp
Tel +81 82 422 7111

Statistics

Peer review	259
Recruiter review	265
Student faculty ratio	9.6:1
International faculty	2.0%
Undergraduates	11,048
Postgraduates	4,445
International students	4.0%

Ranking

World rank	212 (244)
Subject area positions	
Engineering & IT	222
Life sciences & biomedicine	282
Natural sciences	175
Social sciences	254

Hitotsubashi University

Contact

2-1 Naka
Kunitachi
Tokyo
186-8601
Japan

www.hit-u.ac.jp
Tel +81 42 580 8000

Statistics

Peer review	310
Recruiter review	89
Student faculty ratio	18.1:1
International faculty	3.0%
Undergraduates	4,537
Postgraduates	1,951
International students	8.0%

Ranking

World rank	401-500
Subject area positions	
Arts & humanities	213
Social sciences	114

Hokkaido University

Contact

International Affairs Division
Kita 8, Nishi 5
Kita-ku
Sapporo
060-0808
Japan

www.hokudai.ac.jp
Tel +81 11 706 2334

Statistics

Peer review	227
Recruiter review	161
Student faculty ratio	8.6:1
International faculty	3.0%
Undergraduates	11,765
Postgraduates	6,102
International students	4.0%

Ranking

World rank	151= (133=)
Subject area positions	
Engineering & IT	199
Life sciences & biomedicine	115
Natural sciences	183

Kagoshima University

Contact

8-35-1, Sakuragaoka
Kagoshima
890-8544
Japan

www.kagoshima-u.ac.jp
Tel +81 99 285 8515

Statistics

Peer review	500+
Recruiter review	401-500
Student faculty ratio	11.9:1
International faculty	1.0%
Undergraduates	9,381
Postgraduates	1,826
International students	2.0%

Ranking

World rank	401-500

Kanazawa University

Contact

Kanazawa
920-1192
Japan

www.kanazawa-u.ac.jp
Tel +81 76 264 6063

Statistics

Peer review	500+
Recruiter review	401-500
Student faculty ratio	12.5:1
International faculty	5.0%
Undergraduates	8,013
Postgraduates	2,320
International students	2.0%

Ranking

World rank	401-500

Keio University

Contact

2-15-45 Mita, Minato-ku
Tokyo
108-8345
Japan

www.keio.ac.jp
Tel +81 3 3453 4511

Statistics

Peer review	208
Recruiter review	75
Student faculty ratio	6.8:1
International faculty	5.0%
Undergraduates	28,060
Postgraduates	4,402
International students	2.0%

Ranking

World rank	161= (120)
Subject area positions	
Arts & humanities	263
Engineering & IT	192
Life sciences & biomedicine	198
Natural sciences	275
Social sciences	126

Kobe University

Contact

Kobe
Hyogo
657-8501
Japan

www.kobe-u.ac.jp
Tel +81 78 881 1212

Statistics

Peer review	218
Recruiter review	168
Student faculty ratio	10.7:1
International faculty	4.0%
Undergraduates	12,158
Postgraduates	4,898
International students	5.0%

Ranking

World rank	197= (181=)
Subject area positions	
Engineering & IT	178
Life sciences & biomedicine	136
Natural sciences	201
Social sciences	155

Kumamoto University

Contact	*Statistics*		*Ranking*	
39-1,Kurokami 2-chome	**Peer review**	500+	**World rank**	386= (232=)
Kumamoto	**Recruiter review**	401-500		
860-8555	**Student faculty ratio**	9.9:1		
Japan	**International faculty**	2.0%		
	Undergraduates	8,032		
www.kumamoto-u.ac.jp	**Postgraduates**	2,117		
Tel +81 96 344 2111	**International students**	2.0%		

Kyoto University

Contact	*Statistics*		*Ranking*	
Yoshida-Honmachi, Sakyo-ku,	**Peer review**	26	**World rank**	25 (29=)
Kyoto	**Recruiter review**	70	**Subject area positions**	
606-8501	**Student faculty ratio**	7.8:1	Arts & humanities	34
Japan	**International faculty**	7.0%	Engineering & IT	29
	Undergraduates	13,216	Life sciences & biomedicine	27
www.kyoto-u.ac.jp	**Postgraduates**	9,228	Natural sciences	17
Tel +81 75 753 7531	**International students**	4.0%	Social sciences	57

Kyushu University

Contact	*Statistics*		*Ranking*	
6-10-1 Hakozaki, Higashi-ku	**Peer review**	222	**World rank**	136 (128=)
Fukuoka	**Recruiter review**	165	**Subject area positions**	
812-8581	**Student faculty ratio**	8.1:1	Arts & humanities	175
Japan	**International faculty**	2.0%	Engineering & IT	208
	Undergraduates	11,822	Life sciences & biomedicine	186
www.kyushu-u.ac.jp	**Postgraduates**	7,071	Natural sciences	189
Tel +81 92 642 4323	**International students**	6.0%		

Mie University

Contact	*Statistics*		*Ranking*	
1577 Kurimamachiya-cho	**Peer review**	500+	**World rank**	401-500
Tsu-city	**Recruiter review**	401-500		
Mie-Pref	**Student faculty ratio**	12.5:1		
514-8507	**International faculty**	5.0%		
Japan	**Undergraduates**	6,172		
	Postgraduates	1,197		
www.mie-u.ac.jp	**International students**	3.0%		
Tel +81 59 231 9721				

Nagasaki University

Contact

1-14 Bunkyo-machi
Nagasaki-shi
852-8521
Japan

www.nagasaki-u.ac.jp
Tel +81 95 819 2043

Statistics

Peer review	401-500
Recruiter review	349
Student faculty ratio	8.7:1
International faculty	5.0%
Undergraduates	7,670
Postgraduates	1,390
International students	3.0%

Ranking

World rank	273= (277=)
Subject area positions	
Life sciences & biomedicine	256

Nagoya University

Contact

Furo-cho, Chikusa-ku
Nagoya
464-8601
Japan

www.nagoya-u.ac.jp
Tel +81 52 789 2044

Statistics

Peer review	204
Recruiter review	143
Student faculty ratio	7.8:1
International faculty	5.0%
Undergraduates	9,689
Postgraduates	5,963
International students	6.0%

Ranking

World rank	112= (128=)
Subject area positions	
Engineering & IT	125
Life sciences & biomedicine	192
Natural sciences	113

Niigata University

Contact

8050 Ikarashi 2-no-cho
Niigata City
950-2181
Japan

www.niigata-u.ac.jp
Tel +81 25 262 7000

Statistics

Peer review	500+
Recruiter review	401-500
Student faculty ratio	16.8:1
International faculty	5.0%
Undergraduates	10,570
Postgraduates	2,452
International students	2.0%

Ranking

World rank	401-500

Ochanomizu Unversity

Contact

2-1-1 Ohtsuka
Bunkyo-ku
Tokyo
112-8610
Japan

www.ocha.ac.jp
Tel +81 3 3943 3151

Statistics

Peer review	500+
Recruiter review	401-500
Student faculty ratio	14.2:1
International faculty	2.0%
Undergraduates	2,201
Postgraduates	1,076
International students	5.0%

Ranking

World rank	401-500

Okayama University

Contact	*Statistics*		*Ranking*	
1-1, Tsushima-Naka, 1-Chome	**Peer review**	401-500	**World rank**	377 (450=)
Okayama	**Recruiter review**	500+		
700-8530	**Student faculty ratio**	12:1		
Japan	**International faculty**	4.0%		
	Undergraduates	10,691		
www.okayama-u.ac.jp	**Postgraduates**	3,201		
Tel +81 86 251 7211	**International students**	3.0%		

Osaka University

Contact	*Statistics*		*Ranking*	
1-1 Yamadaoka, Suita	**Peer review**	70	**World rank**	46 (70=)
Osaka	**Recruiter review**	139	**Subject area positions**	
565 - 0871	**Student faculty ratio**	7.4:1	Arts & humanities	180
Japan	**International faculty**	2.0%	Engineering & IT	68
	Undergraduates	11,876	Life sciences & biomedicine	39
www.osaka-u.ac.jp	**Postgraduates**	7,685	Natural sciences	57
Tel +81 6 6879 7037	**International students**	6.0%	Social sciences	206

Osaka City University

Contact	*Statistics*		*Ranking*	
3-3-138, Sugimoto	**Peer review**	401-500	**World rank**	364= (232=)
Sumiyoshi-ku, Osaka-shi	**Recruiter review**	362		
558-8585	**Student faculty ratio**	13.8:1		
Japan	**International faculty**	5.0%		
	Undergraduates	7,219		
www.osaka-cu.ac.jp	**Postgraduates**	2,044		
Tel +81 6 6605 2244	**International students**	2.0%		

Showa University

Contact	*Statistics*		*Ranking*	
5-8 Hatanodai, Shinagawa-ku	**Peer review**	500+	**World rank**	318 (407=)
Tokyo	**Recruiter review**	127		
142-8555	**Student faculty ratio**	12.6:1		
Japan	**International faculty**	3.0%		
	Undergraduates	2,830		
www.showa-u.ac.jp	**Postgraduates**	421		
Tel +81 3 3784 8000	**International students**	1.0%		

Tohoku University

Contact

Public Relations Department
1-1 Katahira, 2-chome
Aoba-ku
Sendai 980-8577
Japan

www.tohoku.ac.jp
Tel +81 22 217 4848

Statistics

Peer review	201
Recruiter review	212
Student faculty ratio	5.9:1
International faculty	10.0%
Undergraduates	10,913
Postgraduates	7,188
International students	7.0%

Ranking

World rank	102= (168=)
Subject area positions	
Engineering & IT	99
Life sciences & biomedicine	204
Natural sciences	82

Tokai University

Contact

1117 Kitakaname
Hiratsuka
Kanagawa
259-1292
Japan

www.u-tokai.ac.jp
Tel +81 463 58 1211

Statistics

Peer review	401-500
Recruiter review	362
Student faculty ratio	12.7:1
International faculty	4.0%
Undergraduates	26,121
Postgraduates	1,418
International students	1.0%

Ranking

World rank	401-500
Subject area positions	
Engineering & IT	212

University of Tokyo

Contact

7-3-1, Hongo, Bunkyo-ku
Tokyo
113-8654
Japan

www.u-tokyo.ac.jp
Tel +81 3 3812 2111

Statistics

Peer review	14
Recruiter review	53
Student faculty ratio	5.9:1
International faculty	5.0%
Undergraduates	14,241
Postgraduates	15,018
International students	9.0%

Ranking

World rank	17 (19=)
Subject area positions	
Arts & humanities	24
Engineering & IT	9
Life sciences & biomedicine	13
Natural sciences	12
Social sciences	24

Tokyo Institute of Technology

Contact

2-12-1 Ookayama
Meguro-ku
Tokyo
152-8550
Japan

www.titech.ac.jp
Tel +81 3 5734 2975

Statistics

Peer review	127
Recruiter review	84
Student faculty ratio	10.8:1
International faculty	8.0%
Undergraduates	4,913
Postgraduates	5,026
International students	9.0%

Ranking

World rank	90= (118)
Subject area positions	
Engineering & IT	22
Life sciences & biomedicine	175
Natural sciences	79

Tokyo Metropolitan University

Contact	*Statistics*		*Ranking*	
1-1 Minami-Osawa, Hachioji-shi	**Peer review**	401-500	**World rank**	335 (346=)
Tokyo	**Recruiter review**	200	**Subject area positions**	
192-0397	**Student faculty ratio**	20.9:1	Natural sciences	231
Japan	**International faculty**	5.0%		
	Undergraduates	6,954		
www.metro-u.ac.jp	**Postgraduates**	1,948		
	International students	3.0%		

Science University Tokyo

Contact	*Statistics*		*Ranking*	
1-3 Kagurazaka, Shinjyuku-ku	**Peer review**	398	**World rank**	364= (468=)
Tokyo	**Recruiter review**	209	**Subject area positions**	
162-8601	**Student faculty ratio**	47.5:1	Engineering & IT	201
Japan	**International faculty**	5.0%	Life sciences & biomedicine	255
	Undergraduates	17,087	Natural sciences	222
www.sut.ac.jp	**Postgraduates**	2,934		
Tel +81 3 5228 8107	**International students**	0.0%		

University of Tsukuba

Contact	*Statistics*		*Ranking*	
1-1-1 Tennodai	**Peer review**	289	**World rank**	209= (269)
Tsukuba	**Recruiter review**	257	**Subject area positions**	
Tsukuba-shi Ibaraki-ken	**Student faculty ratio**	9.5:1	Engineering & IT	164
305-8577	**International faculty**	4.0%	Life sciences & biomedicine	280
Japan	**Undergraduates**	10,154	Natural sciences	169
	Postgraduates	6,087		
www.tsukuba.ac.jp	**International students**	6.0%		
Tel +81 29 853 2111				

Waseda University

Contact	*Statistics*		*Ranking*	
1-104 Totsukamachi	**Peer review**	123	**World rank**	180= (158=)
Tokyo	**Recruiter review**	58	**Subject area positions**	
169-8050	**Student faculty ratio**	10.1:1	Arts & humanities	55
Japan	**International faculty**	5.0%	Engineering & IT	127
	Undergraduates	45,757	Natural sciences	231
www.waseda.ac.jp	**Postgraduates**	8,471	Social sciences	87
Tel +81 3 3203 4141	**International students**	4.0%		

Yokohama City University

Contact

Kanazawa Hakkei campus
22-2 Seto, Kanazawa-ku
Yokohama 236-0027
Japan

www.yokohama-cu.ac.jp

Statistics

Peer review	500+
Recruiter review	401-500
Student faculty ratio	15:1
International faculty	5.0%
Undergraduates	3,709
Postgraduates	693
International students	3.0%

Ranking

World rank	401-500

Yokohama National University

Contact

79-1 Tokiwadai
Hodogaya-ku
Yokohama 240-8501
Japan

www.ynu.ac.jp

Statistics

Peer review	401-500
Recruiter review	180
Student faculty ratio	14.1:1
International faculty	5.0%
Undergraduates	7,856
Postgraduates	2,671
International students	6.0%

Ranking

World rank	354= (-)
Subject area positions	
Arts & humanities	295

Korea, South

Chonbuk National University

Contact

664-14 1GR Duck-Dong
Duckjin-gu Jeonju
JEONBUK
561156
Korea, South

www.chonbuk.ac.kr
Tel +81 86 251 7902

Statistics

Peer review	500+
Recruiter review	500+
Student faculty ratio	10.4:1
International faculty	5.0%
Undergraduates	7,572
Postgraduates	865
International students	4.0%

Ranking

World rank	401-500

Hanyang University

Contact

17 Haengdang-dong,
Seongdong-gu
Seoul
133-791
Korea, South

www.hanyang.ac.kr
Tel +82 2 2220 0045

Statistics

Peer review	397
Recruiter review	344
Student faculty ratio	19:1
International faculty	7.0%
Undergraduates	26,605
Postgraduates	9,248
International students	3.0%

Ranking

World rank	401-500

Korea Advanced Institute of Science & Technology

Contact	*Statistics*		*Ranking*	
373-1 Guseong-dong, Yuseong-gu	**Peer review**	136	**World rank**	132= (198=)
Daejeon	**Recruiter review**	370	**Subject area positions**	
305701	**Student faculty ratio**	10.1:1	Engineering & IT	48
Korea, South	**International faculty**	14.0%	Life sciences & biomedicine	166
	Undergraduates	2,777	Natural sciences	86
	Postgraduates	3,837		
www.kaist.edu	**International students**	5.0%		
Tel +82 42 869 2114				

Korea University

Contact	*Statistics*		*Ranking*	
Anam-dong Seongbuk-Gu	**Peer review**	208	**World rank**	243= (150=)
Seoul	**Recruiter review**	344	**Subject area positions**	
136701	**Student faculty ratio**	14:1	Arts & humanities	172
Korea, South	**International faculty**	6.0%	Engineering & IT	240
	Undergraduates	19,712	Life sciences & biomedicine	195
www.korea.edu	**Postgraduates**	8,438	Natural sciences	280
Tel +82 2 3290 1152	**International students**	17.0%	Social sciences	164

Kyunpook National University

Contact	*Statistics*		*Ranking*	
1370 Sankyuk-dong	**Peer review**	500+	**World rank**	401-500
Buk-gu	**Recruiter review**	401-500		
Daegu	**Student faculty ratio**	23:1		
702-701	**International faculty**	4.0%		
Korea, South	**Undergraduates**	20,083		
	Postgraduates	6,174		
www.knu.ac.kr	**International students**	1.0%		
Tel +82 53 950 6072				

Pohang University of Science and Technology

Contact	*Statistics*		*Ranking*	
San 31, Hyoja-dong, Num-gu	**Peer review**	372	**World rank**	233 (245)
Pohang	**Recruiter review**	344	**Subject area positions**	
790-784	**Student faculty ratio**	10:1	Engineering & IT	169
Korea, South	**International faculty**	12.0%	Life sciences & biomedicine	291
	Undergraduates	1,401	Natural sciences	242
www.postech.ac.kr	**Postgraduates**	1,489		
Tel +82 54 2793681	**International students**	2.0%		

Pusan National University

Contact	*Statistics*		*Ranking*	
Geumjeong-gu	**Peer review**	401-500	**World rank**	401-500
Busan	**Recruiter review**	401-500	**Subject area positions**	
609-735	**Student faculty ratio**	31.7:1	Life sciences & biomedicine	256
Korea, South	**Undergraduates**	17,386	Natural sciences	236
	Postgraduates	5,908		
www.pusan.ac.kr	**International students**	1.0%		
Tel +82 51 510 1105				

Seoul National University

Contact	*Statistics*		*Ranking*	
San 56-1, Shillim-dong,	**Peer review**	44	**World rank**	51= (63)
Gwanak-gu	**Recruiter review**	232	**Subject area positions**	
Seoul	**Student faculty ratio**	8.2:1	Arts & humanities	91
151 742	**International faculty**	2.0%	Engineering & IT	56
Korea, South	**Undergraduates**	17,488	Life sciences & biomedicine	46
	Postgraduates	9,789	Natural sciences	38
www.useoul.edu	**International students**	5.0%	Social sciences	57
Tel +82 2 880 2555				

Sogang University

Contact	*Statistics*		*Ranking*	
C.P.O. Box 1142	**Peer review**	500+	**World rank**	398= (531=)
Seoul	**Recruiter review**	102		
100-611	**Student faculty ratio**	12.6:1		
Korea, South	**International faculty**	9.0%		
	Undergraduates	7,838		
www.sogang.ac.kr	**Postgraduates**	970		
Tel +82 2 705 8621	**International students**	1.0%		

Sung Kyun Kwan University

Contact	*Statistics*		*Ranking*	
53 Myeongnyun-dong 3-ga,	**Peer review**	500+	**World rank**	380 (520=)
Jongno-gu	**Recruiter review**	401-500		
Seoul	**Student faculty ratio**	10:1		
110-745	**International faculty**	5.0%		
Korea, South	**Undergraduates**	18,447		
	Postgraduates	6,070		
www.skku.edu	**International students**	10.0%		
Tel +82 2 760 0114				

Yonsei University

Contact	Statistics		Ranking	
134 Sinchon-dong,	**Peer review**	301	**World rank**	236 (484=)
Seodaemun-gu	**Recruiter review**	292	**Subject area positions**	
Seoul	**Student faculty ratio**	7.7:1	Arts & humanities	263
120-749	**International faculty**	3.0%	Natural sciences	295
Korea, South	**Undergraduates**	20,844	Social sciences	203
	Postgraduates	10,582		
www.yonsei.ac.kr	**International students**	8.0%		
Tel +82 2 2123 3484				

Malaysia

Universiti Malaya (UM)

Contact	Statistics		Ranking	
Lembah Pantai	**Peer review**	131	**World rank**	246= (192=)
Kuala Lumpur	**Recruiter review**	173	**Subject area positions**	
50603	**Student faculty ratio**	14.8:1	Arts & humanities	233
Malaysia	**International faculty**	16.0%	Engineering & IT	166
	Undergraduates	19,051	Life sciences & biomedicine	107
www.um.edu.my	**Postgraduates**	10,400	Natural sciences	124
Tel +60 3 7967 4623	**International students**	8.0%	Social sciences	119

Universiti Sains Malaysia (USM)

Contact	Statistics		Ranking	
11800 Minden	**Peer review**	189	**World rank**	307= (277=)
Penang	**Recruiter review**	274	**Subject area positions**	
Malaysia	**Student faculty ratio**	16.6:1	Arts & humanities	227
	International faculty	9.0%	Engineering & IT	234
www.usm.my	**Undergraduates**	17,910	Life sciences & biomedicine	122
Tel +60 4 653 3888	**Postgraduates**	3,961	Natural sciences	161
	International students	6.0%	Social sciences	208

Universiti Kebangsaan Malaysia (UKM)

Contact	Statistics		Ranking	
Bangi	**Peer review**	158	**World rank**	309= (185)
Selangor	**Recruiter review**	316	**Subject area positions**	
43600	**Student faculty ratio**	19.7:1	Arts & humanities	233
Malaysia	**International faculty**	36.0%	Engineering & IT	192
	Undergraduates	18,450	Life sciences & biomedicine	153
www.ukm.my	**Postgraduates**	6,251	Natural sciences	116
Tel +60 3 8925 4599	**International students**	6.0%	Social sciences	146

Universiti Putra Malaysia (UPM)

Contact

Serdang
Selangor Darul Ehsan
43400
Malaysia

www.upm.edu.my
Tel +60 3 603 8946 6013

Statistics

Peer review	232
Recruiter review	266
Student faculty ratio	13.1:1
International faculty	3.0%
Undergraduates	20,694
Postgraduates	4,402
International students	4.0%

Ranking

World rank	364= (292=)
Subject area positions	
Engineering & IT	222
Life sciences & biomedicine	207
Natural sciences	165
Social sciences	233

Universiti Teknologi Malaysia (UTM)

Contact

81310 UTM Skudai
Johor Darul Takzim

www.utm.my
Tel +60 7 553 0375

Statistics

Peer review	368
Recruiter review	161
Student faculty ratio	11:1
International faculty	2.0%
Undergraduates	17,046
Postgraduates	2,779
International students	3.0%

Ranking

World rank	401-500
Subject area positions	
Arts & humanities	
Engineering & IT	
Life sciences & biomedicine	
Natural sciences	
Social sciences	

Mexico

Instituto Tecnologico y de Estudios Superiores de Monterrey

Contact

Ave Eugenio Garza Sada 2501
Col Tecnologico
Monterrey
Nuevo Leon
64849
Mexico

www.itesm.mx
Tel +52 81 8358 2000

Statistics

Peer review	369
Recruiter review	56
Student faculty ratio	14.1:1
International faculty	1.0%
Students	79,364
International students	4.0%

Ranking

World rank	401-500
Subject area positions	
Engineering & IT	157
Social sciences	241

Universidad Nacional Autónoma de México (UNAM)

Contact

Ciudad Universitaria, s/n
Ciudad de Mexico
Distrito Federal
04510
Mexico

www.unam.mx
Tel +52 55 5622 3686

Statistics

Peer review	99
Recruiter review	124
Student faculty ratio	10.1:1
International faculty	6.0%
Undergraduates	132,894
Postgraduates	20,649
International students	1.0%

Ranking

World rank	192= (74)
Subject area positions	
Arts & humanities	132
Engineering & IT	93
Life sciences & biomedicine	95
Natural sciences	90
Social sciences	170

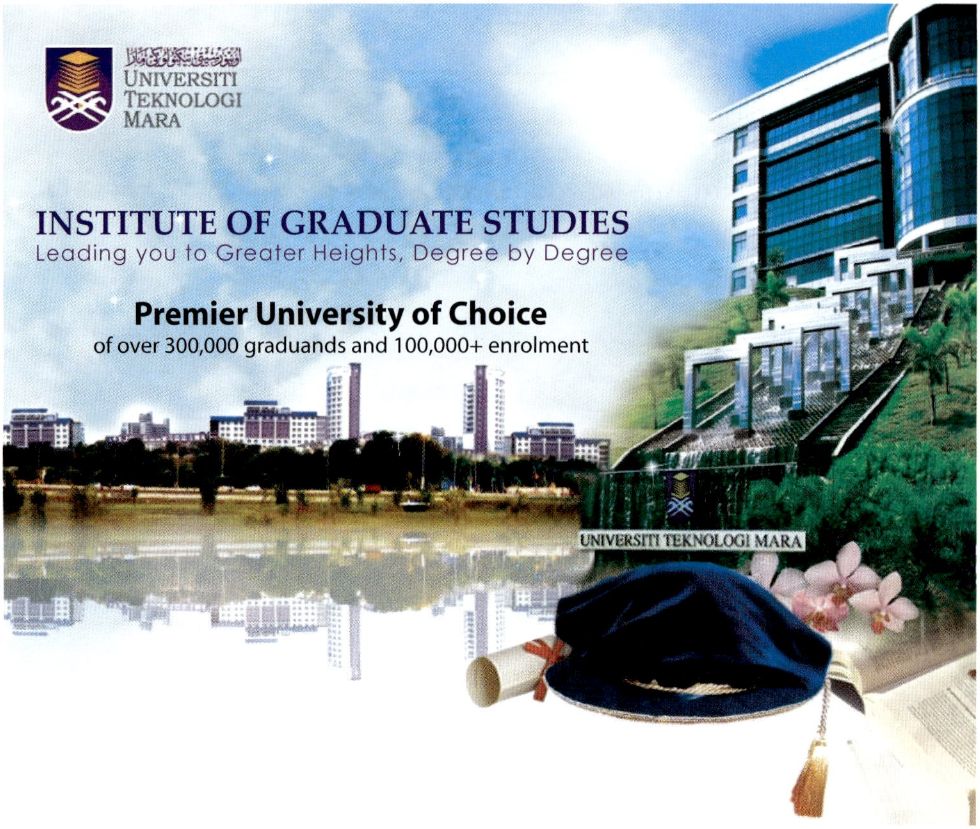

Universiti Teknologi MARA (UiTM) is the largest University in Malaysia. UiTM has been an established teaching and research-based university for the past 50 years with an ever-increasing number of programmes and student enrolment. More information on the university is available at http://www.uitm.edu.my.

At present, UiTM offers more than 90 programmes of study at Master's and Doctoral levels. These cover a broad spectrum of areas of specialisation which truly reflects the intellectual capital of its internationally trained and highly experienced faculty members.

UiTM welcomes all potential candidates who would like to pursue their postgraduate studies at this University. For more information, please visit the Postgraduate website at http://www.ipsis.uitm.edu.my.

For further details on the programmes,
please refer to our website:
www.ipsis.uitm.edu.my
or
email to:
norlidah@salam.uitm.edu.my

aryanti@salam.uitm.edu.my

Application should be addressed to:

The Dean
Institute of Graduate Studies
Universiti Teknologi MARA
INTEKMA Convention Centre
Persiaran Raja Muda Musa
Section 7, 40000 Shah Alam
Selangor, MALAYSIA

For further inquiries, please call: +(603) 5522 5340/5341/5242/5343

Netherlands

University of Amsterdam

Contact

Spui 21
Amsterdam
1012 WX
Netherlands

www.uva.nl
Tel +31 20 525 9111

Statistics

Peer review	66
Recruiter review	111
Student faculty ratio	8:1
International faculty	21.0%
Undergraduates	15,628
Postgraduates	9,450
International students	6.0%

Ranking

World rank	48 (69)
Subject area positions	
Arts & humanities	41
Engineering & IT	186
Life sciences & biomedicine	80
Natural sciences	128
Social sciences	48

Vrije Universiteit Amsterdam

Contact

De Boelelaan 1105
Amsterdam
1081 HV
Netherlands

www.english.vu.nl
Tel +31 20 598 5020

Statistics

Peer review	146
Recruiter review	253
Student faculty ratio	14.3:1
International faculty	14.0%
Undergraduates	13,338
Postgraduates	5,356
International students	5.0%

Ranking

World rank	304= (183=)
Subject area positions	
Arts & humanities	126
Engineering & IT	209
Life sciences & biomedicine	116
Natural sciences	227
Social sciences	128

Delft University of Technology

Contact

Stevinweg 1
Delft
2628 CN
Netherlands

www.tudelft.nl
Tel +31 15 278 9111

Statistics

Peer review	97
Recruiter review	112
Student faculty ratio	9.9:1
International faculty	24.0%
Undergraduates	9,655
Postgraduates	5,035
International students	15.0%

Ranking

World rank	63 (86)
Subject area positions	
Arts & humanities	193
Engineering & IT	17
Natural sciences	83
Social sciences	241

Eindhoven University of Technology

Contact

Den Dolech 2
Eindhoven
5612 AZ
Netherlands

w3.tm.tue.nl
Tel +31 40 247 9111

Statistics

Peer review	232
Recruiter review	255
Student faculty ratio	5.2:1
International faculty	16.0%
Undergraduates	6,390
Postgraduates	1,493
International students	10.0%

Ranking

World rank	130= (67)
Subject area positions	
Engineering & IT	65
Natural sciences	233

Erasmus University Rotterdam

Contact	*Statistics*		*Ranking*	
P.O.Box 1738	**Peer review**	214	**World rank**	163= (92)
Rotterdam	**Recruiter review**	28	**Subject area positions**	
3000 DR	**Student faculty ratio**	18.3:1	Arts & humanities	158
Netherlands	**International faculty**	17.0%	Life sciences & biomedicine	127
	Undergraduates	16,801	Social sciences	71
www.eur.nl	**Postgraduates**	7,970		
Tel +31 10 408 1111	**International students**	9.0%		

University of Groningen

Contact	*Statistics*		*Ranking*	
P.O. Box 72	**Peer review**	231	**World rank**	173= (232=)
Groningen	**Recruiter review**	244	**Subject area positions**	
9700 AB	**Student faculty ratio**	9.5:1	Arts & humanities	153
Netherlands	**International faculty**	16.0%	Life sciences & biomedicine	237
	Undergraduates	16,747	Natural sciences	258
www.rug.nl	**Postgraduates**	6,513	Social sciences	189
Tel +31 50 363 9111	**International students**	6.0%		

Leiden University

Contact	*Statistics*		*Ranking*	
Rapenburg 70	**Peer review**	75	**World rank**	84 (90=)
Leiden	**Recruiter review**	187	**Subject area positions**	
2311 EZ	**Student faculty ratio**	15.5:1	Arts & humanities	40
Netherlands	**International faculty**	22.0%	Engineering & IT	287
	Undergraduates	12,118	Life sciences & biomedicine	72
www.leiden.edu	**Postgraduates**	4,928	Natural sciences	105
Tel +31 71 527 2727	**International students**	8.0%	Social sciences	67

Maastricht University

Contact	*Statistics*		*Ranking*	
Minderbroedersberg 4-6	**Peer review**	268	**World rank**	111 (172=)
Maastricht	**Recruiter review**	145	**Subject area positions**	
6211 LK	**Student faculty ratio**	8.2:1	Life sciences & biomedicine	202
Netherlands	**International faculty**	18.0%	Social sciences	65
	Undergraduates	8,652		
www.unimaas.nl	**Postgraduates**	3,162		
Tel +31 43 388 5388	**International students**	33.0%		

Radboud Universiteit Nijmegen

Contact

P.O. Box 9102
Nijmegen
6500 HC
Netherlands

www.ru.nl
Tel +31 24 361 6161

Statistics

Peer review	290
Recruiter review	401-500
Student faculty ratio	8:1
International faculty	24.0%
Undergraduates	11,424
Postgraduates	5,410
International students	6.0%

Ranking

World rank	195= (137)
Subject area positions	
Arts & humanities	240
Life sciences & biomedicine	168
Social sciences	297

University of Twente

Contact

Drienerlolaan 5
Enschede
7522 NB
Netherlands

www.utwente.nl
Tel +31 53 489 9111

Statistics

Peer review	246
Recruiter review	283
Student faculty ratio	10.5:1
International faculty	20.0%
Undergraduates	4,806
Postgraduates	3,671
International students	11.0%

Ranking

World rank	185= (115)
Subject area positions	
Engineering & it	127
Natural sciences	215
Social sciences	206

Utrecht University

Contact

P.O Box 80125
Utrecht
3508 TC
Netherlands

www.uu.nl
Tel +31 30 253 9111

Statistics

Peer review	78
Recruiter review	224
Student faculty ratio	10:1
International faculty	9.0%
Undergraduates	17,000
Postgraduates	10,962
International students	4.0%

Ranking

World rank	89 (95)
Subject area positions	
Arts & humanities	76
Engineering & IT	191
Life sciences & biomedicine	80
Natural sciences	47
Social sciences	110

Wageningen University

Contact

Costerweg 50
Building no. 400
Wageningen
6700 HB
Netherlands

www.wau.nl
Tel +31 31 747 7477

Statistics

Peer review	299
Recruiter review	365
Student faculty ratio	7.2:1
International faculty	12.0%
Undergraduates	4,415
Postgraduates	1,164
International students	28.0%

Ranking

World rank	148 (97)
Subject area positions	
Life sciences & biomedicine	143
Natural sciences	210

New Zealand

The University of Auckland

Contact

Private Bag 92019
Auckland Mail Centre
Auckland
1142
New Zealand

www.auckland.ac.nz
Tel +64 9 373 7999

Statistics

Peer review	38
Recruiter review	100
Student faculty ratio	14.8:1
International faculty	59.0%
Undergraduates	23,222
Postgraduates	5,087
International students	34.0%

Ranking

World rank	50 (46=)
Subject area positions	
Arts & humanities	32
Engineering & IT	51
Life sciences & biomedicine	41
Natural sciences	78
Social sciences	35

University of Canterbury

Contact

Private Bag 4800
Christchurch
8140
New Zealand

www.canterbury.ac.nz
Tel +64 3 366 7001

Statistics

Peer review	149
Recruiter review	134
Student faculty ratio	17.3:1
International faculty	14.0%
Students	11,713
International students	14.0%

Ranking

World rank	188= (333=)
Subject area positions	
Arts & humanities	125
Engineering & IT	125
Natural sciences	141
Social sciences	135

Massey University

Contact

Massey University
Private Bag 11 222
Palmerston North
New Zealand

www.massey.ac.nz
Tel +64 6 356 9099

Statistics

Peer review	219
Recruiter review	264
Student faculty ratio	14.9:1
International faculty	42.0%
Undergraduates	15,396
Postgraduates	4,525
International students	18.0%

Ranking

World rank	242 (213)
Subject area positions	
Arts & humanities	218
Engineering & IT	281
Life sciences & biomedicine	179
Natural sciences	262
Social sciences	152

University of Otago

Contact

PO Box 56
Dunedin
New Zealand

www.otago.ac.nz
Tel +64 3 479 1100

Statistics

Peer review	117
Recruiter review	196
Student faculty ratio	14.5:1
International faculty	65.0%
Undergraduates	14,724
Postgraduates	2,725
International students	23.0%

Ranking

World rank	114= (79=)
Subject area positions	
Arts & humanities	81
Life sciences & biomedicine	90
Natural sciences	181
Social sciences	92

Victoria University of Wellington

Contact	*Statistics*		*Ranking*	
PO Box 600	**Peer review**	188	**World rank**	234 (222=)
Wellington	**Recruiter review**	134	**Subject area positions**	
6140	**Student faculty ratio**	17.8:1	Arts & humanities	73
New Zealand	**International faculty**	50.0%	Natural sciences	266
	Undergraduates	14,423	Social sciences	79
www.vuw.ac.nz	**Postgraduates**	2,227		
Tel +64 4 472 1000	**International students**	15.0%		

University of Waikato

Contact	*Statistics*		*Ranking*	
Gate 1 Knighton Road	**Peer review**	331	**World rank**	319= (340=)
Private Bag 3105	**Recruiter review**	289	**Subject area positions**	
Hamilton	**Student faculty ratio**	14.2:1	Arts & humanities	165
New Zealand	**International faculty**	22.0%	Social sciences	217
	Undergraduates	7,816		
www.waikato.ac.nz	**Postgraduates**	1,365		
Tel +64 7 856 2889	**International students**	22.0%		

Norway

University of Bergen

Contact	*Statistics*		*Ranking*	
Post box 7800	**Peer review**	239	**World rank**	225= (277=)
Bergen	**Recruiter review**	401-500	**Subject area positions**	
5020	**Student faculty ratio**	14.1:1	Arts & humanities	149
Norway	**International faculty**	24.0%	Life sciences & biomedicine	219
	Undergraduates	8,230	Social sciences	180
www.uib.no	**Postgraduates**	4,269		
Tel +47 55 58 00 00	**International students**	12.0%		

Norwegian University of Science and Technology

Contact	*Statistics*		*Ranking*	
Trondheim	**Peer review**	292	**World rank**	301= (289=)
7491	**Recruiter review**	329	**Subject area positions**	
Norway	**Student faculty ratio**	16.8:1	Engineering & IT	116
	International faculty	13.0%	Natural sciences	288
www.ntnu.no	**Undergraduates**	10,796		
Tel +47 73 59 50 00	**Postgraduates**	6,626		
	International students	7.0%		

University of Oslo

Contact	*Statistics*		*Ranking*	
Boks 1072 Blindern	**Peer review**	155	**World rank**	188= (177)
OSLO	**Recruiter review**	383	**Subject area positions**	
0316	**Student faculty ratio**	11.5:1	Arts & humanities	135
Norway	**International faculty**	13.0%	Engineering & IT	226
	Undergraduates	14,441	Life sciences & biomedicine	168
www.uio.no	**Postgraduates**	12,900	Natural sciences	181
Tel +47 22 85 50 50	**International students**	12.0%	Social sciences	117

University of Tromso

Contact	*Statistics*		*Ranking*	
Universitetet i Tromsø	**Peer review**	401-500	**World rank**	292= (401=)
Tromsø	**Recruiter review**	401-500		
9037	**Student faculty ratio**	4.8:1		
Norway	**International faculty**	13.0%		
	Students	4,784		
www.uit.no	**International students**	7.0%		
Tel +44 77 64 40 00				

Pakistan

University of Lahore

Contact	*Statistics*		*Ranking*	
1 KM Raiwind Road	**Peer review**	297	**World rank**	401-500
Lahore	**Recruiter review**	401-500	**Subject area positions**	
Pakistan	**Student faculty ratio**	11.3:1	Life sciences & biomedicine	291
	International faculty	2.0%	Natural sciences	245
www.uol.edu.pk	**Undergraduates**	2,616	Social sciences	251
Tel +92 42 541 1901	**Postgraduates**	585		
	International students	4.0%		

National University of Sciences and Technology (NUST)

Contact	*Statistics*		*Ranking*	
Tamiz uddin Road	**Peer review**	401-500	**World rank**	401-500
Rawalpindi	**Recruiter review**	383		
Punjab	**Student faculty ratio**	9.1:1		
46000	**International faculty**	3.0%		
Pakistan	**Undergraduates**	4,529		
	Postgraduates	917		
www.nust.edu.pk	**International students**	2.0%		

Peru

Pontificia Universidad Católica del Perú

Contact

Av. Universitaria 1801
San Miguel
Lima 32
Peru

www.pucp.edu.pe
Tel +51 1 626 2000

Statistics

Peer Review	500+
Recruiter Review	214
Student Faculty Ratio	10.5:1
Students	10,882
International Students	2.0%

Ranking

World rank	401-500

Philippines

Ateneo de Manila University

Contact

Katipunan Avenue,
Loyola Heights
Quezon City
1108
Philippines

www.ateneo.net
Tel +63 2426 6001

Statistics

Peer review	379
Recruiter review	79
Student faculty ratio	16.5:1
International faculty	5.0%
Undergraduates	7,533
Postgraduates	2,371
International students	6.0%

Ranking

World rank	401-500
Subject area positions	
Arts & humanities	263
Social sciences	154

University of the Philippines

Contact

Diliman
Quezon City
1101
Philippines

www.upd.edu.ph
Tel +63 981 8500

Statistics

Peer Review	242
Recruiter Review	94
Student Faculty Ratio	19.3:1
International Faculty	4.0%
Students	13,165
International Students	0.0%

Ranking

World rank	398= (299=)
Subject area positions	
Arts & humanities	139
Engineering & IT	281
Natural sciences	204
Social sciences	208

Poland

Jagiellonian University

Contact

ul. Golebia 24
Krakow
31-007
Poland

www.uj.edu.pl
Tel +48 12 422 1033

Statistics

Peer review	279
Recruiter review	366
Student faculty ratio	10.6:1
International faculty	2.0%
Undergraduates	10,157
Postgraduates	27,954
International students	3.0%

Ranking

World rank	331= (287)
Subject area positions	
Arts & humanities	145
Natural sciences	185

Warsaw University

Contact

Krakowskie Przedmiescie 26/28
Warszawa
00-927
Poland

www.uw.edu.pl
Tel +48 22 552 0000

Statistics

Peer review	275
Recruiter review	173
Student faculty ratio	20.6:1
International faculty	3.0%
Undergraduates	37,173
Postgraduates	15,577
International students	2.0%

Ranking

World rank	345= (326=)
Subject area positions	
Arts & humanities	220
Natural sciences	166
Social sciences	282

Warsaw University of Technology

Contact

Pl. Politechniki 1
Warszawa
00-661
Poland

www.pw.edu.pl
Tel +48 22 660 7211

Statistics

Peer review	351
Recruiter review	125
Student faculty ratio	11.2:1
International faculty	0.0%
Undergraduates	21,807
Postgraduates	3,626
International students	1.0%

Ranking

World rank	371= (350=)
Subject area positions	
Engineering & IT	150
Natural sciences	280

Portugal

University of Coimbra

Contact

Paço das Escolas
Coimbra
3004-531
Portugal

www.uc.pt
Tel +351 239 859 993

Statistics

Peer review	259
Recruiter review	401-500
Student faculty ratio	13.3:1
International faculty	4.0%
Undergraduates	14,190
Postgraduates	2,069
International students	10.0%

Ranking

World rank	319= (266=)
Subject area positions	
Arts & humanities	122
Engineering & IT	287
Life sciences & biomedicine	275
Social sciences	274

Universidade Nova de Lisboa

Contact

Campolide Campus
Lisbon
1099-085
Portugal

www.unl.pt
Tel +351 21 371 5600

Statistics

Peer review	338
Recruiter review	395
Student faculty ratio	13:1
International faculty	7.0%
Undergraduates	12,175
Postgraduates	2,025
International students	14.0%

Ranking

World rank	341= (277=)
Subject area positions	
Arts & humanities	244

Universidade Catolica Portuguesa, Lisboa

Contact

Palma de Cima
Lisbon
1649-023
Portugal

www.ucp.pt
Tel +351 21 726 5838

Statistics

Peer review	500+
Recruiter review	341
Student faculty ratio	9.1:1
International faculty	4.0%
Undergraduates	6,941
Postgraduates	2,191
International students	6.0%

Ranking

World rank	401-500

Russia

Lomonosov Moscow State University

Contact

GSP-2, Leninskie Gory,
Moscow
119992
Russia

www.msu.ru

Statistics

Peer Review	91
Recruiter Review	171
International Faculty	1.0%
Students	33,187
International Students	5.0%

Ranking

World rank	231= (93=)
Subject area positions	
Arts & humanities	206
Engineering & IT	97
Life sciences & biomedicine	127
Natural sciences	27
Social sciences	214

Novosibirsk State University

Contact

Novosibirsk
Russia

www.nsu.ru
Tel +7 383 339 7378

Statistics

Peer review	317
Recruiter review	401-500
Student faculty ratio	13.2:1
International faculty	4.0%
Undergraduates	5,310
Postgraduates	200
International students	5.0%

Ranking

World rank	401-500
Subject area positions	
Engineering & IT	254
Natural sciences	153

Saint-Petersburg State University

Contact

7-9,universitefskay nab
St.Petersburg
199034
Russia

www.spbu.ru
Tel +7-812 238 2000

Statistics

Peer Review	177
Recruiter Review	270
Student Faculty Ratio	7.5:1
International Faculty	0.0%
Students	30,218
International Students	6.0%

Ranking

World rank	239= (164)
Subject area positions	
Arts & humanities	172
Engineering & IT	174
Life sciences & biomedicine	213
Natural sciences	90

Tomsk State University

Contact	*Statistics*		*Ranking*	
36 Lenin Prospek	**Peer review**	500+	**World rank**	401-500
Tomsk	**Recruiter review**	401-500		
634050	**Student faculty ratio**	5.9:1		
Russia	**International faculty**	0.0%		
	Undergraduates	18,253		
www.tsu.ru	**Postgraduates**	525		
Tel +7 382 252 9852	**International students**	0.0%		

Singapore

Nanyang Technological University

Contact	*Statistics*		*Ranking*	
Nanyang Avenue	**Peer review**	74	**World rank**	69 (61=)
Singapore	**Recruiter review**	106	**Subject area positions**	
639798	**Student faculty ratio**	15.1:1	Arts & humanities	263
Singapore	**International faculty**	49.0%	Engineering & IT	25
	Undergraduates	19,427	Life sciences & biomedicine	102
www.ntu.edu.sg	**Postgraduates**	5,017	Natural sciences	99
Tel +65 6791 1744	**International students**	35.0%	Social sciences	88

National University of Singapore

Contact	*Statistics*		*Ranking*	
21 Lower Kent Ridge Road	**Peer review**	17	**World rank**	33= (19=)
Singapore	**Recruiter review**	52	**Subject area positions**	
119077	**Student faculty ratio**	16:1	Arts & humanities	21
Singapore	**International faculty**	52.0%	Engineering & IT	10
	Undergraduates	22,689	Life sciences & biomedicine	12
www.nus.edu.sg	**Postgraduates**	6,617	Natural sciences	25
Tel +65 6516 6666	**International students**	36.0%	Social sciences	20

Slovenia

University of Ljubljana

Contact	*Statistics*		*Ranking*	
Kongresni trg 12	**Peer review**	384	**World rank**	401-500
Ljubljana	**Recruiter review**	500+		
1000	**Student faculty ratio**	12.4:1		
Slovenia	**International faculty**	2.0%		
	Undergraduates	37,430		
www.uni-lj.si	**Postgraduates**	3,755		
Tel +386 1 241 85 00	**International students**	2.0%		

South Africa

University of Cape Town

Contact	*Statistics*		*Ranking*	
Private Bag	**Peer review**	194	**World rank**	200= (257)
Rondebosch	**Recruiter review**	158	**Subject area positions**	
7701	**Student faculty ratio**	18.1:1	Arts & humanities	196
South Africa	**International faculty**	6.0%	Engineering & IT	231
	Undergraduates	11,076	Life sciences & biomedicine	171
www.uct.ac.za	**Postgraduates**	3,901	Natural sciences	222
Tel +27 21 650 2696	**International students**	23.0%	Social sciences	161

University of Kwazulu-Natal

Contact	*Statistics*		*Ranking*	
Cnr. Richmond & Marianhill Rd	**Peer review**	401-500	**World rank**	401-500
Pinetown	**Recruiter review**	401-500		
3605	**Student faculty ratio**	10:1		
South Africa	**International faculty**	8.0%		
	Undergraduates	23,402		
www.ukzn.ac.za	**Postgraduates**	5,106		
	International students	6.0%		

University of Pretoria

Contact	*Statistics*		*Ranking*	
Lynnwood Road	**Peer review**	360	**World rank**	401-500
Hillcrest	**Recruiter review**	337	**Subject area positions**	
0002	**Student faculty ratio**	28.1:1	Social sciences	290
South Africa	**International faculty**	5.0%		
	Undergraduates	28,044		
www.up.ac.za	**Postgraduates**	4,905		
Tel +27 12 420 4111	**International students**	7.0%		

University of the Witwatersrand

Contact	*Statistics*		*Ranking*	
Private Bag 3, WITS	**Peer review**	300	**World rank**	282= (322=)
Johannesburg	**Recruiter review**	217	**Subject area positions**	
2050	**Student faculty ratio**	17.9:1	Social sciences	197
South Africa	**International faculty**	25.0%		
	Undergraduates	12,009		
www.wits.ac.za	**Postgraduates**	5,040		
Tel +27 11 717 1000	**International students**	9.0%		

Spain

University of Barcelona

Contact

Gran Via Corts Catalanes, 585
Barcelona
08007
Spain

www.ub.edu
Tel +34 93 402 11 00

Statistics

Peer review	120
Recruiter review	260
Student faculty ratio	21.6:1
International faculty	2.0%
Undergraduates	38,225
Postgraduates	9,327
International students	7.0%

Ranking

World rank	194 (190=)
Subject area positions	
Arts & humanities	113
Engineering & IT	159
Life sciences & biomedicine	110
Natural sciences	97
Social sciences	204

Universidad Autónoma de Barcelona

Contact

Edifici A
Campus UAB Bellaterra
Cerdanyola del Vallès
Barcelona
08193
Spain

www.uab.es
Tel +34 3 581 13 10

Statistics

Peer review	160
Recruiter review	328
Student faculty ratio	18.1:1
International faculty	7.0%
Undergraduates	31,996
Postgraduates	2,868
International students	5.0%

Ranking

World rank	258 (239=)
Subject area positions	
Arts & humanities	139
Engineering & IT	199
Life sciences & biomedicine	192
Natural sciences	203
Social sciences	115

University of Granada

Contact

Cuesta del Hospicio, s/n
Granada
18071
Spain

www.ugr.es
Tel +34 958 24 30 25

Statistics

Peer review	401-500
Recruiter review	500+
Student faculty ratio	46.9:1
International faculty	12.0%
Undergraduates	50,255
Postgraduates	8,023
International students	9.0%

Ranking

World rank	401-500

Universidad Autónoma de Madrid

Contact

Ciudad Universitaria de
Cantoblanco
Madrid
28049
Spain

www.uam.es
Tel +34 91 497 50 00

Statistics

Peer review	265
Recruiter review	320
Student faculty ratio	23.9:1
International faculty	7.0%
Undergraduates	26,827
Postgraduates	2,751
International students	5.0%

Ranking

World rank	306 (261=)
Subject area positions	
Arts & humanities	260
Life sciences & biomedicine	238
Natural sciences	178
Social sciences	263

University Complutense Madrid

Contact	*Statistics*		*Ranking*	
Ciudad Universitaria	**Peer Review**	180	**World rank**	401-500
Madrid	**Recruiter Review**	193	**Subject area positions**	
28040	**International Faculty**	7.0%	Arts & humanities	111
Spain	**Undergraduates**	69,476	Engineering & IT	266
	International Students	7.0%	Life sciences & biomedicine	204
www.ucm.es			Natural sciences	198
Tel +34 91 452 0400			Social sciences	178

University of Navarra

Contact	*Statistics*		*Ranking*	
Campus Universitario	**Peer review**	401-500	**World rank**	319= (288)
Navarra	**Recruiter review**	281	**Subject area positions**	
31080	**Student faculty ratio**	37.2:1	Life sciences & biomedicine	275
Spain	**International faculty**	26.0%	Social sciences	293
	Undergraduates	9,484		
www.unav.es	**Postgraduates**	3,845		
Tel +34 948 42 56 00	**International students**	15.0%		

Universitat Pompeu Fabra

Contact	*Statistics*		*Ranking*	
Plaça de la Mercè, 10-12	**Peer review**	323	**World rank**	339= (321)
Barcelona	**Recruiter review**	401-500	**Subject area positions**	
08002	**Student faculty ratio**	13.1:1	Arts & humanities	225
Spain	**International faculty**	37.0%	Social sciences	95
	Undergraduates	8,462		
www.upf.edu	**Postgraduates**	1,197		
Tel +34 93 542 20 00	**International students**	6.0%		

University of Salamanca

Contact	*Statistics*		*Ranking*	
Patio de Escuelas, 1	**Peer review**	399	**World rank**	401-500
Salamanca	**Recruiter review**	500+	**Subject area positions**	
37008	**Student faculty ratio**	19.9:1	Arts & humanities	199
Spain	**International faculty**	7.0%		
	Undergraduates	23,819		
www.usal.es	**Postgraduates**	1,927		
Tel +34 923 294 400	**International students**	13.0%		

Universidade de Santiago de Compostela

Contact

Praza do Obradoiro, s/n
Santiago de Compostela
15782
Spain

www.usc.es
Tel +34 981 56 31 00

Statistics

Peer review	401-500
Recruiter review	500+
Student faculty ratio	33.1:1
International faculty	7.0%
Undergraduates	26,055
Postgraduates	3,820
International students	6.0%

Ranking

World rank	401-500
Subject area positions	
Arts & humanities	236

Universidad de Sevilla

Contact

Po. de las Delicias, s/n
Sevilla
41013
Spain

www.us.es
Tel +34 954 48 12 55

Statistics

Peer review	390
Recruiter review	401-500
Student faculty ratio	27:1
International faculty	7.0%
Undergraduates	52,131
Postgraduates	3,046
International students	3.0%

Ranking

World rank	401-500

Universitat de València

Contact

Avenida Blasco Ibáñez, 13
València
46010
Spain

www.uv.es
Tel +34 963 86 41 00

Statistics

Peer review	324
Recruiter review	500+
Student faculty ratio	25.1:1
International faculty	2.0%
Undergraduates	39,947
Postgraduates	1,811
International students	6.0%

Ranking

World rank	393 (398)
Subject area positions	
Arts & humanities	221

Universidad de Zaragoza

Contact

Pedro Cerbuna, 12
Zaragoza
50009
Spain

www.unizar.es
Tel +34 976 76 10 01

Statistics

Peer review	401-500
Recruiter review	500+
Student faculty ratio	22.8:1
International faculty	2.0%
Undergraduates	32,478
Postgraduates	2,048
International students	2.0%

Ranking

World rank	401-500
Subject area positions	
Arts & humanities	260

Sweden

Chalmers University of Technology

Contact

Göteborg
412 96
Sweden

www.chalmers.se
Tel +46 31 772 1000

Statistics

Peer review	213
Recruiter review	390
Student faculty ratio	13.9:1
International faculty	20.0%
Undergraduates	1,377
Postgraduates	7,215
International students	13.0%

Ranking

World rank	197= (147=)
Subject area positions	
Engineering & IT	74
Natural sciences	94

Göteborg University

Contact

Göteborg
405 30
Sweden

www.gu.se
Tel +46 31 773 1000

Statistics

Peer review	254
Recruiter review	395
Student faculty ratio	11.6:1
International faculty	1.0%
Undergraduates	26,000
Postgraduates	2,007
International students	5.0%

Ranking

World rank	276= (284=)
Subject area positions	
Arts & humanities	164
Engineering & IT	299
Social sciences	194

Linköping University

Contact

Linköping
581 83
Sweden

www.liu.se
Tel +46 13 28 1000

Statistics

Peer review	401-500
Recruiter review	401-500
Student faculty ratio	17.2:1
International faculty	13.0%
Undergraduates	14,478
Postgraduates	1,042
International students	10.0%

Ranking

World rank	371= (322=)
Subject area positions	
Engineering & IT	188
Social sciences	297

Lund University

Contact

Paradisgatan 2
Lund
221 00
Sweden

www.lu.se
Tel +46 46 222 0000

Statistics

Peer review	93
Recruiter review	284
Student faculty ratio	13.5:1
International faculty	21.0%
Undergraduates	22,250
Postgraduates	5,291
International students	11.0%

Ranking

World rank	106 (122)
Subject area positions	
Arts & humanities	117
Engineering & IT	121
Life sciences & biomedicine	84
Natural sciences	110
Social sciences	99

KTH, Royal Institute of Technology

Contact

Valhallavagen 79
Stockholm
100 44
Sweden

www.kth.se
Tel +46 8 790 6000

Statistics

Peer review	224
Recruiter review	401-500
Student faculty ratio	12.1:1
International faculty	28.0%
Undergraduates	2,488
Postgraduates	11,335
International students	35.0%

Ranking

World rank	192= (172=)
Subject area positions	
Engineering & IT	53
Life sciences & biomedicine	297
Natural sciences	140

Stockholm University

Contact

Stockholm
106 91
Sweden

www.su.se
Tel +46 8 16 2000

Statistics

Peer review	212
Recruiter review	329
Student faculty ratio	15.6:1
International faculty	12.0%
Undergraduates	21,571
Postgraduates	1,472
International students	5.0%

Ranking

World rank	246= (261=)
Subject area positions	
Arts & humanities	193
Life sciences & biomedicine	146
Natural sciences	248
Social sciences	133

Stockholm School of Economics

Contact

P.O. Box 6501
Stockholm
113 83
Sweden

www.hhs.se
Tel +46 8 736 9000

Statistics

Peer review	401-500
Recruiter review	38
Student faculty ratio	15:1
International faculty	25.0%
Undergraduates	832
Postgraduates	488
International students	31.0%

Ranking

World rank	273= (207=)
Subject area positions	
Social sciences	71

Umeå University

Contact

Umeå
901 87
Sweden

www.umu.se
Tel +46 90 786 5000

Statistics

Peer review	401-500
Recruiter review	500+
Student faculty ratio	10.7:1
International faculty	26.0%
Undergraduates	15,270
Postgraduates	1,003
International students	11.0%

Ranking

World rank	299 (311=)
Subject area positions	
Life sciences & biomedicine	179

Uppsala University

Contact	*Statistics*		*Ranking*	
P.O. Box 256	**Peer review**	61	**World rank**	71= (111=)
Uppsala	**Recruiter review**	322	**Subject area positions**	
751 05	**Student faculty ratio**	8.1:1	Arts & humanities	61
Sweden	**International faculty**	13.0%	Engineering & IT	150
	Undergraduates	22,274	Life sciences & biomedicine	40
www.uu.se	**Postgraduates**	1,930	Natural sciences	113
Tel +46 18 471 0000	**International students**	5.0%	Social sciences	102

Switzerland

University of Basel

Contact	*Statistics*		*Ranking*	
Petersplatz 1	**Peer review**	210	**World rank**	114= (75)
Basel	**Recruiter review**	401-500	**Subject area positions**	
4003	**Student faculty ratio**	5:1	Arts & humanities	148
Switzerland	**International faculty**	27.0%	Life sciences & biomedicine	85
	Undergraduates	6,707	Natural sciences	233
www.unibas.ch	**Postgraduates**	3,580	Social sciences	271
Tel +41 61 267 3111	**International students**	18.0%		

University of Bern

Contact	*Statistics*		*Ranking*	
Hochschulstrasse 4	**Peer review**	313	**World rank**	214 (178)
Bern	**Recruiter review**	401-500	**Subject area positions**	
3012	**Student faculty ratio**	9:1	Arts & humanities	257
Switzerland	**International faculty**	34.0%	Life sciences & biomedicine	231
	Undergraduates	5,420	Social sciences	290
www.unibe.ch	**Postgraduates**	6,014		
Tel +41 31 631 8111	**International students**	9.0%		

ETH Zürich (Swiss Federal Institute of Technology)

Contact	*Statistics*		*Ranking*	
Rämistrasse 101	**Peer review**	43	**World rank**	42 (24)
Zürich	**Recruiter review**	138	**Subject area positions**	
8092	**Student faculty ratio**	10.5:1	Arts & humanities	269
Switzerland	**International faculty**	53.0%	Engineering & IT	13
	Undergraduates	6,996	Life sciences & biomedicine	57
www.ethz.ch	**Postgraduates**	6,416	Natural sciences	18
Tel +41 44 632 1111	**International students**	23.0%	Social sciences	170

University of Geneva

Contact	*Statistics*		*Ranking*	
24, rue du Général-Dufour	**Peer review**	154	**World rank**	105 (39)
Genève 4	**Recruiter review**	230	**Subject area positions**	
1211	**Student faculty ratio**	14.5:1	Arts & humanities	97
Switzerland	**International faculty**	46.0%	Engineering & IT	281
	Undergraduates	8,574	Life sciences & biomedicine	148
www.unige.ch	**Postgraduates**	2,943	Natural sciences	204
Tel +41 22 379 7111	**International students**	36.0%	Social sciences	139

Ecole Polytechnique Fédérale de Lausanne

Contact	*Statistics*		*Ranking*	
EPFL	**Peer review**	170	**World rank**	117= (64=)
Lausanne	**Recruiter review**	218	**Subject area positions**	
1015	**Student faculty ratio**	5.8:1	Engineering & IT	47
Switzerland	**International faculty**	60.0%	Life sciences & biomedicine	235
	Undergraduates	3,251	Natural sciences	89
www.epfl.ch	**Postgraduates**	2,893		
Tel +41 21 693 1111	**International students**	41.0%		

University of Lausanne

Contact	*Statistics*		*Ranking*	
Lausanne	**Peer review**	278	**World rank**	217 (89)
1015	**Recruiter review**	357	**Subject area positions**	
Switzerland	**Student faculty ratio**	13.5:1	Engineering & IT	299
	International faculty	29.0%	Life sciences & biomedicine	273
www.unil.ch	**Undergraduates**	7,204	Natural sciences	298
Tel +41 21 692 1111	**Postgraduates**	3,475	Social sciences	176
	International students	18.0%		

University of St Gallen

Contact	*Statistics*		*Ranking*	
Dufourstrasse 50	**Peer review**	401-500	**World rank**	362= (214)
St.Gallen	**Recruiter review**	42	**Subject area positions**	
9000	**Student faculty ratio**	21.3:1	Social sciences	159
Switzerland	**International faculty**	40.0%		
	Students	4,325		
www.unisg.ch	**International students**	22.0%		
Tel +41 71 224 2111				

University of Zürich

Contact

President's Office
Kuenstlergasse 15
Zürich 8001
Switzerland

www.uzh.ch
Tel +41 44 634 2211

Statistics

Peer review	111
Recruiter review	332
Student faculty ratio	32:1
International faculty	46.0%
Undergraduates	3,981
Postgraduates	19,112
International students	12.0%

Ranking

World rank	140= (109=)
Subject area positions	
Arts & humanities	132
Engineering & IT	173
Life sciences & biomedicine	68
Natural sciences	126
Social sciences	146

Taiwan

National Central University

Contact

No.300, Jhongda Rd
Jhongli
Taoyuan County
32001
Taiwan

www.ncu.edu.tw
Tel +886 3 422 7151

Statistics

Peer review	401-500
Recruiter review	357
Student faculty ratio	25.9:1
International faculty	4.0%
Undergraduates	5,452
Postgraduates	5,118
International students	1.0%

Ranking

World rank	398= (497=)

National Cheng Kung University

Contact

No.1, Ta-Hsueh Road
Tainan
701
Taiwan

www.ncku.edu.tw
Tel +886-275 7575

Statistics

Peer review	401-500
Recruiter review	261
Student faculty ratio	13.7:1
International faculty	3.0%
Undergraduates	9,843
Postgraduates	9,843
International students	1.0%

Ranking

World rank	336= (386=)
Subject area positions	
Engineering & IT	197

National Chiao Tung University

Contact

1001 Ta Hsueh Road
Hsinchu
300
Taiwan

www.nctu.edu.tw
Tel +886 3 573 1651

Statistics

Peer review	401-500
Recruiter review	360
Student faculty ratio	15.5:1
International faculty	4.0%
Undergraduates	4,788
Postgraduates	8,099
International students	3.0%

Ranking

World rank	401-500
Subject area positions	
Engineering & IT	224

National Chung Hsing University

Contact	*Statistics*		*Ranking*	
Kuo Kuang Road	**Peer review**	500+	**World rank**	401-500
Taichung	**Recruiter review**	234		
250	**Student faculty ratio**	18.1:1		
Taiwan	**International faculty**	1.0%		
	Undergraduates	7,783		
www.nchu.edu.tw	**Postgraduates**	5,278		
Tel +886 4 2287 3181	**International students**	0.0%		

National Sun Yat-Sen University

Contact	*Statistics*		*Ranking*	
70 Lien-hai Rd.	**Peer review**	401-500	**World rank**	401-500
Kaohsiung	**Recruiter review**	401-500		
804	**Student faculty ratio**	21.1:1		
Taiwan	**International faculty**	3.0%		
	Undergraduates	4,263		
www.nsysu.edu.tw	**Postgraduates**	6,052		
Tel +886 7 525 2633	**International students**	2.0%		

National Taiwan University

Contact	*Statistics*		*Ranking*	
No.1, Sec. 4, Roosevelt Road,	**Peer review**	59	**World rank**	102= (108)
Taipei,	**Recruiter review**	165	**Subject area positions**	
106	**Student faculty ratio**	14.6:1	Arts & humanities	93
Taiwan	**International faculty**	3.0%	Engineering & IT	53
	Undergraduates	17,724	Life sciences & biomedicine	80
www.ntu.edu.tw	**Postgraduates**	14,589	Natural sciences	64
Tel +886 2 3366 3262	**International students**	4.0%	Social sciences	75

National Taiwan University of Science and Technology

Contact	*Statistics*		*Ranking*	
#43,Sec.4,Keelung Rd.	**Peer review**	350	**World rank**	401-500
Taipei	**Recruiter review**	148	**Subject area positions**	
106	**Student faculty ratio**	15.4:1	Engineering & IT	276
Taiwan	**International faculty**	8.0%	Natural sciences	253
	Undergraduates	4,517		
www.ntust.edu.tw	**Postgraduates**	3,433		
Tel +886 2 2733 3141	**International students**	2.0%		

National Tsing Hua University

Contact	*Statistics*		*Ranking*	
101, Section 2 Kuang Fu Road	**Peer review**	322	**World rank**	334 (343=)
Hsinchu	**Recruiter review**	401-500	**Subject area positions**	
30013	**Student faculty ratio**	18:1	Engineering & IT	138
Taiwan	**International faculty**	4.0%	Natural sciences	217
	Undergraduates	5,186		
www.nthu.edu.tw	**Postgraduates**	5,301		
Tel +886 3 571 5131	**International students**	1.0%		

National Yang Ming University

Contact	*Statistics*		*Ranking*	
No. 155, Sec. 2, Linong St	**Peer review**	500+	**World rank**	401-500
Beitou District	**Recruiter review**	500+		
Taipei City 112	**Student faculty ratio**	4.5:1		
(R.O.C.)	**International faculty**	3.0%		
	Undergraduates	1,790		
www.ym.edu.tw	**Postgraduates**	1,944		
Tel +886 2 2733 3141	**International students**	1.0%		

Thailand

Chiang Mai University

Contact	*Statistics*		*Ranking*	
239 Huay Keaw Road, Suthep,	**Peer review**	337	**World rank**	401-500
Muang	**Recruiter review**	386	**Subject area positions**	
Chiang Mai	**Student faculty ratio**	14.5:1	Natural sciences	257
50200	**International faculty**	8.0%		
Thailand	**Undergraduates**	18,924		
	Postgraduates	6,824		
www.chiangmai.ac.th	**International students**	1.0%		
Tel +66 6822 1699				

Chulalongkorn University

Contact	*Statistics*		*Ranking*	
254 Phyathai Road, Patumwan	**Peer review**	113	**World rank**	223 (161=)
Bangkok	**Recruiter review**	152	**Subject area positions**	
10330	**Student faculty ratio**	12.9:1	Arts & humanities	136
Thailand	**International faculty**	5.0%	Engineering & IT	100
	Undergraduates	22,113	Life sciences & biomedicine	138
www.chula.ac.th	**Postgraduates**	11,870	Natural sciences	159
Tel +66 2 218 3331	**International students**	1.0%	Social sciences	83

Kasetsart University

Contact	*Statistics*		*Ranking*	
50 Phahonyothin Road,	**Peer review**	365	**World rank**	401-500
Lat Yao Subdistrict	**Recruiter review**	229	**Subject area positions**	
Bangkok	**Student faculty ratio**	12.6:1	Life sciences & biomedicine	266
10900	**International faculty**	10.0%		
Thailand	**Undergraduates**	34,176		
	Postgraduates	10,517		
www.ku.ac.th	**International students**	0.0%		
Tel +66 2 942 8500				

Mahidol University

Contact	*Statistics*		*Ranking*	
International Relations Division	**Peer review**	298	**World rank**	284= (322=)
999 Phuttamonthon 4 Road	**Recruiter review**	256	**Subject area positions**	
Salaya	**Student faculty ratio**	9:1	Life sciences & biomedicine	118
Nakhon Pathom	**International faculty**	6.0%	Natural sciences	295
73170	**Undergraduates**	15,118		
Thailand	**Postgraduates**	7,301		
	International students	2.0%		
www.mahidol.ac.th				
Tel +66 2 849 6230				

Thammasat University

Contact	*Statistics*		*Ranking*	
99 Mhu 18, Paholyothin Rd.	**Peer review**	349	**World rank**	401-500
Khong Luang	**Recruiter review**	177	**Subject area positions**	
12121	**Student faculty ratio**	12.9:1	Arts & humanities	242
Thailand	**International faculty**	1.0%	Social sciences	197
	Students	19,784		
www.tu.ac.th	**International students**	1.0%		
Tel +66 2 564 4440				

Turkey

Bilkent University

Contact	*Statistics*		*Ranking*	
Bilkent Ankara	**Peer review**	401-500	**World rank**	401-500
06800	**Recruiter review**	500+	**Subject area positions**	
Turkey	**Student faculty ratio**	11.7:1	Engineering & IT	268
	International faculty	27.0%	Natural sciences	262
www.bilkent.edu.tr	**Students**	8,771		
Tel +90 312 290 4000	**International students**	1.0%		

Istanbul Technical University

Contact	*Statistics*		*Ranking*	
Student Affairs	**Peer review**	353	**World rank**	390 (349)
ITÜ Ayazaga Kampüsü 34469	**Recruiter review**	401-500	**Subject area positions**	
Maslak-Istanbul	**Student faculty ratio**	10.1:1	Engineering & IT	157
Turkey	**International faculty**	12.0%		
	Undergraduates	10,371		
www.itu.edu.tr	**Postgraduates**	5,017		
Tel +90 212 285 3400	**International students**	3.0%		

Istanbul University

Contact	*Statistics*		*Ranking*	
Istanbul Universitesi Center	**Peer Review**	372	**World rank**	401-500
Campus	**Recruiter Review**	390		
34452 Beyazit	**Student Faculty Ratio**	10.5:1		
Eminonu-Istanbul	**International Faculty**	1.0%		
Turkey	**Students**	42,342		
	International Students	3.0%		
www.istanbul.edu.tr				
Tel +90 212 440 0000				

Sabanci University

Contact	*Statistics*		*Ranking*	
Orhanli-Tuzla	**Peer review**	401-500	**World rank**	401-500
Istanbul	**Recruiter review**	500+		
34956	**Student faculty ratio**	12.7:1		
Turkey	**International faculty**	24.0%		
	Undergraduates	2,242		
www.sabanciuniv.edu	**Postgraduates**	391		
Tel +90 216 483 9000	**International students**	1.0%		

United Kingdom

University of Aberdeen

Contact	*Statistics*		*Ranking*	
Aberdeen	**Peer review**	255	**World rank**	137= (195)
AB24 3FX	**Recruiter review**	179	**Subject area positions**	
United Kingdom	**Student faculty ratio**	8.4:1	Arts & humanities	292
	International faculty	29.0%	Engineering & IT	274
www.abdn.ac.uk	**Undergraduates**	9,035	Life sciences & biomedicine	114
Tel +44 1224 272 000	**Postgraduates**	2,044	Natural sciences	291
	International students	16.0%	Social sciences	297

Aberystwyth University

Contact	*Statistics*		*Ranking*	
Old College	**Peer review**	363	**World rank**	401-500
King Street	**Recruiter review**	401-500	**Subject area positions**	
Aberystwyth	**Student faculty ratio**	14.7:1	Arts & humanities	185
Ceredigion	**International faculty**	17.0%	Social sciences	266
SY23 2AX	**Undergraduates**	6,649		
United Kingdom	**Postgraduates**	1,219		
	International students	12.0%		
www.aber.ac.uk				
Tel +44 1970 623 111				

Aston University

Contact	*Statistics*		*Ranking*	
Birmingham	**Peer review**	386	**World rank**	266 (-)
B4 7ET	**Recruiter review**	92	**Subject area positions**	
United Kingdom	**Student faculty ratio**	16.7:1	Arts & humanities	282
	International faculty	30.0%		
www.aston.ac.uk	**Undergraduates**	6,290		
Tel +44 121 204 3200	**Postgraduates**	1,004		
	International students	18.0%		

University of Wales, Bangor

Contact	*Statistics*		*Ranking*	
Bangor	**Peer review**	401-500	**World rank**	401-500
Gwynedd	**Recruiter review**	401-500	**Subject area positions**	
LL57 2DG	**Student faculty ratio**	12.6:1	Life sciences & biomedicine	230
United Kingdom	**International faculty**	20.0%		
	Undergraduates	6,308		
www.bangor.ac.uk	**Postgraduates**	1,338		
Tel +44 1248 351 151	**International students**	10.0%		

University of Bath

Contact	*Statistics*		*Ranking*	
Bath	**Peer review**	247	**World rank**	145 (153)
BA2 7AY	**Recruiter review**	32	**Subject area positions**	
United Kingdom	**Student faculty ratio**	12.4:1	Engineering & IT	212
	International faculty	29.0%	Life sciences & biomedicine	196
www.bath.ac.uk	**Undergraduates**	8,374	Natural sciences	260
Tel +44 1225 388 388	**Postgraduates**	2,400	Social sciences	235
	International students	23.0%		

University of Birmingham

Contact	*Statistics*		*Ranking*	
Edgbaston	**Peer review**	112	**World rank**	65= (90=)
Birmingham	**Recruiter review**	50	**Subject area positions**	
B15 2TT	**Student faculty ratio**	10.3:1	Arts & humanities	181
United Kingdom	**International faculty**	24.0%	Engineering & IT	84
	Undergraduates	17,400	Life sciences & biomedicine	93
www.bham.ac.uk	**Postgraduates**	5,957	Natural sciences	166
Tel +44 121 414 3344	**International students**	15.0%	Social sciences	111

University of Bradford

Contact	*Statistics*		*Ranking*	
Bradford	**Peer review**	401-500	**World rank**	349 (307=)
West Yorkshire	**Recruiter review**	316	**Subject area positions**	
BD7 1DP	**Student faculty ratio**	16.6:1	Life sciences & biomedicine	251
United Kingdom	**International faculty**	18.0%		
	Undergraduates	7,616		
www.bradford.ac.uk	**Postgraduates**	1,737		
Tel +44 1274 232 323	**International students**	25.0%		

University of Bristol

Contact	*Statistics*		*Ranking*	
Senate House, Tyndall Avenue	**Peer review**	76	**World rank**	37 (64=)
Bristol	**Recruiter review**	12	**Subject area positions**	
BS8 1TH	**Student faculty ratio**	7.6:1	Arts & humanities	88
United Kingdom	**International faculty**	27.0%	Engineering & IT	119
	Undergraduates	12,229	Life sciences & biomedicine	48
www.bris.ac.uk	**Postgraduates**	3,590	Natural sciences	98
Tel +44 117 928 9000	**International students**	16.0%	Social sciences	121

Brunel University

Contact	*Statistics*		*Ranking*	
Kingston Lane	**Peer review**	401-500	**World rank**	292= (305=)
London	**Recruiter review**	153	**Subject area positions**	
Middlesex	**Student faculty ratio**	14.5:1	Engineering & IT	268
UB8 3PH	**International faculty**	27.0%		
United Kingdom	**Undergraduates**	9,707		
	Postgraduates	2,911		
www.brunel.ac.uk	**International students**	21.0%		
Tel +44 1895 265 288				

University of Cambridge

Contact	*Statistics*		*Ranking*	
Trinity Lane	**Peer review**	3	**World rank**	2= (2)
Cambridge	**Recruiter review**	1	**Subject area positions**	
CB2 1TN	**Student faculty ratio**	4.9:1	Arts & humanities	4
United Kingdom	**International faculty**	39.0%	Engineering & IT	5
	Undergraduates	12,699	Life sciences & biomedicine	2
www.cam.ac.uk	**Postgraduates**	5,611	Natural sciences	3
Tel +44 1223 337 733	**International students**	23.0%	Social sciences	7

Cardiff University

Contact	*Statistics*		*Ranking*	
Cardiff	**Peer review**	153	**World rank**	99 (141=)
Wales	**Recruiter review**	95	**Subject area positions**	
CF10 3XQ	**Student faculty ratio**	9.3:1	Arts & humanities	143
United Kingdom	**International faculty**	19.0%	Engineering & IT	206
	Undergraduates	16,923	Life sciences & biomedicine	74
www.cf.ac.uk	**Postgraduates**	5,605	Natural sciences	280
Tel +44 29 2087 4000	**International students**	17.0%	Social sciences	159

Cranfield University

Contact	*Statistics*		*Ranking*	
Cranfield	**Peer review**	359	**World rank**	158 (140)
Bedfordshire	**Recruiter review**	144	**Subject area positions**	
MK43 0AL	**Student faculty ratio**	3.8:1	Engineering & IT	164
United Kingdom	**International faculty**	20.0%	Social sciences	230
	Undergraduates	88		
www.cranfield.ac.uk	**Postgraduates**	2,339		
Tel +44 1234 754 171	**International students**	49.0%		

University of Dundee

Contact	*Statistics*		*Ranking*	
Dundee	**Peer review**	263	**World rank**	171= (238)
Scotland	**Recruiter review**	246	**Subject area positions**	
DD1 4HN	**Student faculty ratio**	9.9:1	Engineering & IT	296
United Kingdom	**International faculty**	24.0%	Life sciences & biomedicine	76
	Undergraduates	10,378		
www.dundee.ac.uk	**Postgraduates**	2,762		
Tel +44 1382 344 000	**International students**	14.0%		

Durham University

Contact

Old Elvet
Durham
County Durham
DH1 3HP
United Kingdom

www.durham.ac.uk
Tel +44 191 334 6328

Statistics

Peer review	168
Recruiter review	16
Student faculty ratio	12.4:1
International faculty	30.0%
Undergraduates	11,661
Postgraduates	2,696
International students	13.0%

Ranking

World rank	109 (132)
Subject area positions	
Arts & humanities	109
Engineering & IT	268
Life sciences & biomedicine	227
Natural sciences	178
Social sciences	138

University of Edinburgh

Contact

Old College
South Bridge
Edinburgh
EH8 9YL
United Kingdom

www.ed.ac.uk
Tel +44 131 650 1000

Statistics

Peer review	33
Recruiter review	14
Student faculty ratio	8:1
International faculty	19.0%
Undergraduates	15,917
Postgraduates	4,523
International students	18.0%

Ranking

World rank	23 (33=)
Subject area positions	
Arts & humanities	28
Engineering & IT	56
Life sciences & biomedicine	30
Natural sciences	65
Social sciences	47

University of Essex

Contact

Wivenhoe Park
Colchester
Essex
CO4 3SQ
United Kingdom

www.essex.ac.uk
Tel +44 1206 873 333

Statistics

Peer review	316
Recruiter review	388
Student faculty ratio	12.9:1
International faculty	37.0%
Undergraduates	6,488
Postgraduates	1,945
International students	32.0%

Ranking

World rank	272 (-)
Subject area positions	
Arts & humanities	238
Social sciences	139

University of Exeter

Contact

Devon
Exeter
EX4 4QJ
United Kingdom

www.ex.ac.uk
Tel +44 1392 661 000

Statistics

Peer review	307
Recruiter review	65
Student faculty ratio	13.5:1
International faculty	23.0%
Undergraduates	9,091
Postgraduates	2,722
International students	14.0%

Ranking

World rank	220 (224=)
Subject area positions	
Arts & humanities	191
Social sciences	271

University of Glasgow

Contact	*Statistics*		*Ranking*	
University Avenue	**Peer review**	116	**World rank**	83 (81)
Glasgow	**Recruiter review**	96	**Subject area positions**	
G12 8QQ	**Student faculty ratio**	9.2:1	Arts & humanities	160
United Kingdom	**International faculty**	10.0%	Engineering & IT	138
	Undergraduates	15,311	Life sciences & biomedicine	60
www.gla.ac.uk	**Postgraduates**	3,462	Natural sciences	143
Tel +44 141 330 2000	**International students**	11.0%	Social sciences	166

Goldsmiths, University of London

Contact	*Statistics*		*Ranking*	
New Cross	**Peer review**	345	**World rank**	401-500
London	**Recruiter review**	381	**Subject area positions**	
SE14 6NW	**Student faculty ratio**	17:1	Arts & humanities	132
United Kingdom	**International faculty**	23.0%	Social sciences	283
	Undergraduates	4,072		
www.goldsmiths.ac.uk	**Postgraduates**	2,121		
Tel +44 20 7919 7171	**International students**	20.0%		

University of Hull

Contact	*Statistics*		*Ranking*	
Cottingham Road	**Peer review**	500+	**World rank**	401-500
Hull	**Recruiter review**	500+		
HU6 7RX	**Student faculty ratio**	16.1:1		
United Kingdom	**International faculty**	22.0%		
	Undergraduates	11,596		
www.hull.ac.uk	**Postgraduates**	1,624		
Tel +44 1482 346 311	**International students**	11.0%		

University of Kent

Contact	*Statistics*		*Ranking*	
Canterbury	**Peer review**	500+	**World rank**	401-500
Kent	**Recruiter review**	356		
CT2 7NZ	**Student faculty ratio**	15.3:1		
United Kingdom	**International faculty**	29.0%		
	Undergraduates	11,478		
www.kent.ac.uk	**Postgraduates**	1,603		
Tel +44 1227 764 000	**International students**	18.0%		

University of Lancaster

Contact

Bailrigg
Lancaster
Lancashire
LA1 4YW
United Kingdom

www.lancs.ac.uk
Tel +44 1524 65201

Statistics

Peer review	223
Recruiter review	114
Student faculty ratio	9.9:1
International faculty	27.0%
Undergraduates	8,471
Postgraduates	2,167
International students	19.0%

Ranking

World rank	147 (228=)
Subject area positions	
Arts & humanities	163
Life sciences & biomedicine	239
Social sciences	105

University of Leeds

Contact

Leeds
LS2 9JT
United Kingdom

www.leeds.ac.uk
Tel +44 113 243 1751

Statistics

Peer review	102
Recruiter review	27
Student faculty ratio	11.3:1
International faculty	21.0%
Undergraduates	22,980
Postgraduates	4,972
International students	13.0%

Ranking

World rank	80= (121)
Subject area positions	
Arts & humanities	76
Engineering & IT	130
Life sciences & biomedicine	122
Natural sciences	138
Social sciences	128

University of Leicester

Contact

University Road
Leicester
LE1 7RH
United Kingdom

www.le.ac.uk
Tel +44 116 252 2522

Statistics

Peer review	311
Recruiter review	201
Student faculty ratio	10.6:1
International faculty	21.0%
Undergraduates	8,545
Postgraduates	3,788
International students	20.0%

Ranking

World rank	185= (239=)
Subject area positions	
Arts & humanities	273
Life sciences & biomedicine	239
Social sciences	219

University of Liverpool

Contact

Liverpool
L69 3BX
United Kingdom

www.liv.ac.uk
Tel +44 151 794 2000

Statistics

Peer review	191
Recruiter review	91
Student faculty ratio	9.4:1
International faculty	24.0%
Undergraduates	13,980
Postgraduates	2,529
International students	14.0%

Ranking

World rank	101 (139)
Subject area positions	
Arts & humanities	174
Engineering & IT	196
Life sciences & biomedicine	140
Natural sciences	189
Social sciences	271

Imperial College London

Contact	*Statistics*		*Ranking*	
South Kensington Campus	**Peer review**	23	**World rank**	5 (9)
London	**Recruiter review**	7	**Subject area positions**	
SW7 2AZ	**Student faculty ratio**	4.1:1	Arts & humanities	170
United Kingdom	**International faculty**	39.0%	Engineering & IT	6
	Undergraduates	7,927	Life sciences & biomedicine	7
www3.imperial.ac.uk	**Postgraduates**	4,098	Natural sciences	13
Tel +44 20 7589 5111	**International students**	37.0%	Social sciences	73

UCL (University College London)

Contact	*Statistics*		*Ranking*	
Gower Street	**Peer review**	34	**World rank**	9 (25)
London	**Recruiter review**	22	**Subject area positions**	
WC1E 6BT	**Student faculty ratio**	4.4:1	Arts & humanities	27
United Kingdom	**International faculty**	29.0%	Engineering & IT	94
	Undergraduates	11,471	Life sciences & biomedicine	26
www.ucl.ac.uk	**Postgraduates**	5,646	Natural sciences	70
Tel +44 20 7679 2000	**International students**	29.0%	Social sciences	32

King's College London

Contact	*Statistics*		*Ranking*	
Strand	**Peer review**	48	**World rank**	24 (46=)
London	**Recruiter review**	40	**Subject area positions**	
WC2R 2LS	**Student faculty ratio**	6.8:1	Arts & humanities	36
United Kingdom	**International faculty**	30.0%	Engineering & IT	154
	Undergraduates	12,554	Life sciences & biomedicine	32
www.kcl.ac.uk	**Postgraduates**	4,607	Natural sciences	102
Tel +44 20 7836 5454	**International students**	20.0%	Social sciences	64

London School of Economics and Political Science

Contact	*Statistics*		*Ranking*	
Houghton Street	**Peer review**	49	**World rank**	59 (17)
London	**Recruiter review**	3	**Subject area positions**	
WC2A 2AE	**Student faculty ratio**	9.9:1	Arts & humanities	26
United Kingdom	**International faculty**	53.0%	Engineering & IT	257
	Undergraduates	3,777	Life sciences & biomedicine	260
www.lse.ac.uk	**Postgraduates**	4,114	Social sciences	3
Tel +44 20 7405 7686	**International students**	65.0%		

Queen Mary, University of London

Contact

Mile End Road
London
E1 4NS
United Kingdom

www.qmul.ac.uk
Tel +44 20 7882 5555

Statistics

Peer review	189
Recruiter review	175
Student faculty ratio	8:1
International faculty	32.0%
Undergraduates	8,323
Postgraduates	2,192
International students	24.0%

Ranking

World rank	149= (99=)
Subject area positions	
Arts & humanities	160
Engineering & IT	224
Life sciences & biomedicine	163
Natural sciences	251
Social sciences	178

School of Oriental and African Studies, University of London

Contact

Thornhaugh Street
Russell Square
London
WC1H 0XG
United Kingdom

www.soas.ac.uk
Tel +44 20 7637 2388

Statistics

Peer review	264
Recruiter review	222
Student faculty ratio	8.5:1
International faculty	40.0%
Undergraduates	2,335
Postgraduates	1,155
International students	49.0%

Ranking

World rank	243= (70=)
Subject area positions	
Arts & humanities	48
Social sciences	111

Loughborough University

Contact

Loughborough
Leicestershire
LE11 3TU
United Kingdom

www.lboro.ac.uk
Tel +44 1509 263 171

Statistics

Peer review	340
Recruiter review	62
Student faculty ratio	12:1
International faculty	20.0%
Undergraduates	10,353
Postgraduates	2,847
International students	17.0%

Ranking

World rank	237= (266=)
Subject area positions	
Engineering & IT	178
Life sciences & biomedicine	275
Social sciences	216

University of Manchester

Contact

Oxford Road
Manchester
M13 9PL
United Kingdom

www.manchester.ac.uk
Tel +44 161 306 6000

Statistics

Peer review	50
Recruiter review	5
Student faculty ratio	8.5:1
International faculty	25.0%
Undergraduates	24,783
Postgraduates	7,499
International students	20.0%

Ranking

World rank	30 (40)
Subject area positions	
Arts & humanities	59
Engineering & IT	43
Life sciences & biomedicine	64
Natural sciences	116
Social sciences	68

Newcastle University, Newcastle Upon Tyne

Contact	*Statistics*		*Ranking*	
6 Kensington Terrace	**Peer review**	258	**World rank**	129 (133=)
Newcastle upon Tyne	**Recruiter review**	81	**Subject area positions**	
NE1 7RU	**Student faculty ratio**	8.9:1	Arts & humanities	229
United Kingdom	**International faculty**	22.0%	Engineering & IT	229
	Undergraduates	13,427	Life sciences & biomedicine	175
www.ncl.ac.uk	**Postgraduates**	3,870	Social sciences	293
Tel +44 191 222 6000	**International students**	18.0%		

University of Nottingham

Contact	*Statistics*		*Ranking*	
University Park	**Peer review**	118	**World rank**	70 (85)
Nottingham	**Recruiter review**	18	**Subject area positions**	
NG7 2RD	**Student faculty ratio**	10.1:1	Arts & humanities	160
United Kingdom	**International faculty**	25.0%	Engineering & IT	113
	Undergraduates	20,397	Life sciences & biomedicine	102
www.nottingham.ac.uk	**Postgraduates**	4,988	Natural sciences	156
Tel +44 115 951 5151	**International students**	21.0%	Social sciences	115

University of Oxford

Contact	*Statistics*		*Ranking*	
Wellington Square	**Peer review**	5	**World rank**	2= (3)
Oxford	**Recruiter review**	2	**Subject area positions**	
OX1 2JD	**Student faculty ratio**	4.7:1	Arts & humanities	3
United Kingdom	**International faculty**	36.0%	Engineering & IT	12
	Undergraduates	12,310	Life sciences & biomedicine	3
www.ox.ac.uk	**Postgraduates**	6,357	Natural sciences	8
Tel +44 1865 270 000	**International students**	27.0%	Social sciences	6

Queen's University of Belfast

Contact	*Statistics*		*Ranking*	
University Road	**Peer review**	234	**World rank**	205= (206)
Belfast	**Recruiter review**	128	**Subject area positions**	
Northern Ireland	**Student faculty ratio**	11.5:1	Arts & humanities	193
BT7 1NN	**International faculty**	35.0%	Engineering & IT	261
United Kingdom	**Undergraduates**	14,538	Life sciences & biomedicine	211
	Postgraduates	2,776	Natural sciences	255
www.qub.ac.uk	**International students**	10.0%	Social sciences	239
Tel +44 2890 245 133				

University of Reading

Contact

PO Box 217
Whiteknights
Reading
Berkshire
RG6 6AH
United Kingdom

www.reading.ac.uk
Tel + 44 118 987 5123

Statistics

Peer review	251
Recruiter review	169
Student faculty ratio	11.8:1
International faculty	22.0%
Undergraduates	8,317
Postgraduates	2,415
International students	17.0%

Ranking

World rank	180= (190=)
Subject area positions	
Arts & humanities	176
Engineering & IT	247
Natural sciences	227
Social sciences	290

Royal Holloway University of London

Contact

Egham Hill
Egham
Surrey
TW20 0EX
United Kingdom

www.rhul.ac.uk
Tel +44 1784 434 455

Statistics

Peer review	401-500
Recruiter review	401-500
Student faculty ratio	11.7:1
International faculty	32.0%
Undergraduates	5,373
Postgraduates	1,579
International students	29.0%

Ranking

World rank	401-500
Subject area positions	
Arts & humanities	218

University of Sheffield

Contact

Western Bank
Sheffield
S10 2TN
United Kingdom

www.shef.ac.uk
Tel +44 114 222 2000

Statistics

Peer review	122
Recruiter review	31
Student faculty ratio	9.2:1
International faculty	23.0%
Undergraduates	18,129
Postgraduates	4,409
International students	14.0%

Ranking

World rank	68 (102=)
Subject area positions	
Arts & humanities	107
Engineering & IT	122
Life sciences & biomedicine	127
Natural sciences	175
Social sciences	141

University of Southampton

Contact

University Road
Southampton
SO17 1BJ
United Kingdom

www.soton.ac.uk
Tel +44 23 8059 5000

Statistics

Peer review	159
Recruiter review	67
Student faculty ratio	9.2:1
International faculty	27.0%
Undergraduates	14,032
Postgraduates	4,989
International students	16.0%

Ranking

World rank	80= (141=)
Subject area positions	
Arts & humanities	151
Engineering & IT	96
Life sciences & biomedicine	204
Natural sciences	155
Social sciences	266

University of St Andrews

Contact	*Statistics*		*Ranking*	
Fife	**Peer review**	182	**World rank**	76 (109=)
St Andrews	**Recruiter review**	36	**Subject area positions**	
KY16 9AJ	**Student faculty ratio**	8.5:1	Arts & humanities	58
United Kingdom	**International faculty**	29.0%	Engineering & IT	299
	Undergraduates	5,967	Life sciences & biomedicine	211
www.st-andrews.ac.uk	**Postgraduates**	1,161	Natural sciences	258
Tel +44 1334 476 161	**International students**	31.0%	Social sciences	235

University of Strathclyde

Contact	*Statistics*		*Ranking*	
16 Richmond Street	**Peer review**	329	**World rank**	252 (307=)
Glasgow	**Recruiter review**	73	**Subject area positions**	
G1 1XQ	**Student faculty ratio**	12.9:1	Engineering & IT	254
United Kingdom	**International faculty**	18.0%	Social sciences	286
	Undergraduates	11,338		
www.strath.ac.uk	**Postgraduates**	4,914		
Tel +44 141 552 4400	**International students**	11.0%		

University of Surrey

Contact	*Statistics*		*Ranking*	
Guildford	**Peer review**	333	**World rank**	190 (258=)
Surrey	**Recruiter review**	122	**Subject area positions**	
GU2 7XH	**Student faculty ratio**	10.6:1	Arts & humanities	287
United Kingdom	**International faculty**	32.0%	Engineering & IT	177
	Undergraduates	7,397		
www.surrey.ac.uk	**Postgraduates**	2,537		
Tel +44 1483 689 249	**International students**	23.0%		

University of Sussex

Contact	*Statistics*		*Ranking*	
Sussex House	**Peer review**	171	**World rank**	121 (105=)
Falmer	**Recruiter review**	242	**Subject area positions**	
Sussex	**Student faculty ratio**	10.9:1	Arts & humanities	95
BN1 9RH	**International faculty**	28.0%	Engineering & IT	226
United Kingdom	**Undergraduates**	7,161	Life sciences & biomedicine	226
	Postgraduates	2,314	Social sciences	107
www.sussex.ac.uk	**International students**	19.0%		
Tel +44 1273 606 755				

Swansea University

Contact	*Statistics*		*Ranking*	
Singleton Park	**Peer review**	401-500	**World rank**	401-500
Swansea	**Recruiter review**	170		
SA2 8PP	**Student faculty ratio**	12.5:1		
United Kingdom	**International faculty**	23.0%		
	Undergraduates	8,811		
www.swan.ac.uk	**Postgraduates**	2,029		
Tel +44 1792 205 678	**International students**	13.0%		

University of East Anglia (UEA)

Contact	*Statistics*		*Ranking*	
Earlham Road	**Peer review**	401-500	**World rank**	356= (-)
Norwich	**Recruiter review**	290	**Subject area positions**	
Norfolk	**Student faculty ratio**	12:1	Arts & humanities	185
NR4 7TJ	**International faculty**	23.0%		
United Kingdom	**Undergraduates**	9,105		
	Postgraduates	2,493		
www.uea.ac.uk	**International students**	14.0%		
Tel +44 1603 456 161				

University of Warwick

Contact	*Statistics*		*Ranking*	
Coventry	**Peer review**	80	**World rank**	57 (73)
CV4 7AL	**Recruiter review**	15	**Subject area positions**	
United Kingdom	**Student faculty ratio**	10.3:1	Arts & humanities	71
	International faculty	27.0%	Engineering & IT	181
www2.warwick.ac.uk	**Undergraduates**	12,069	Life sciences & biomedicine	188
Tel +44 24 7652 3523	**Postgraduates**	4,613	Natural sciences	72
	International students	27.0%	Social sciences	40

University of York

Contact	*Statistics*		*Ranking*	
Heslington	**Peer review**	148	**World rank**	74= (124=)
York	**Recruiter review**	60	**Subject area positions**	
YO10 5DD	**Student faculty ratio**	8.5:1	Arts & humanities	70
United Kingdom	**International faculty**	21.0%	Engineering & IT	249
	Undergraduates	7,802	Life sciences & biomedicine	146
www.york.ac.uk	**Postgraduates**	2,478	Natural sciences	242
Tel +44 1904 430 000	**International students**	19.0%	Social sciences	194

United States of America

University of Alabama

Contact	*Statistics*		*Ranking*	
Tuscaloosa	**Peer review**	294	**World rank**	282= (217=)
AL 35487	**Recruiter review**	378	**Subject area positions**	
United States	**Student faculty ratio**	22.8:1	Life sciences & biomedicine	198
	International faculty	3.0%	Natural sciences	245
www.ua.edu	**Undergraduates**	15,603	Social sciences	286
Tel +1 205 348 6010	**Postgraduates**	2,701		
	International students	4.0%		

University of Arizona

Contact	*Statistics*		*Ranking*	
Tucson	**Peer review**	119	**World rank**	134 (224=)
AZ 85721	**Recruiter review**	220	**Subject area positions**	
United States	**Student faculty ratio**	15.1:1	Arts & humanities	85
	International faculty	6.0%	Engineering & IT	133
www.arizona.edu	**Undergraduates**	23,265	Life sciences & biomedicine	231
Tel +1 520 621 2211	**Postgraduates**	4,332	Natural sciences	121
	International students	9.0%	Social sciences	150

Arizona State University

Contact	*Statistics*		*Ranking*	
University Drive and Mill Avenue	**Peer review**	173	**World rank**	221= (270=)
Tempe	**Recruiter review**	267	**Subject area positions**	
Arizona	**Student faculty ratio**	24.9:1	Arts & humanities	257
United States	**International faculty**	8.0%	Engineering & IT	134
	Undergraduates	34,380	Life sciences & biomedicine	217
www.asu.edu	**Postgraduates**	6,364	Natural sciences	173
Tel +1 480 965 9011	**International students**	15.0%	Social sciences	135

University of Arkansas

Contact	*Statistics*		*Ranking*	
Fayetteville	**Peer review**	401-500	**World rank**	401-500
Arkansas	**Recruiter review**	401-500		
72701	**Student faculty ratio**	17.5:1		
United States	**International faculty**	5.0%		
	Undergraduates	12,555		
www.uark.edu	**Postgraduates**	2,153		
Tel +1 479 575 2000	**International students**	6.0%		

University of California, Berkeley

Contact

110 Sproul Hall
Berkeley
California
94720
United States

www.berkeley.edu
Tel +1 510 642 6000

Statistics

Peer review	1
Recruiter review	11
Student faculty ratio	10.8:1
International faculty	20.0%
Undergraduates	20,129
Postgraduates	7,277
International students	21.0%

Ranking

World rank	22 (8)
Subject area positions	
Arts & humanities	2
Engineering & IT	2
Life sciences & biomedicine	5
Natural sciences	1
Social sciences	2

Boston University

Contact

One Sherborn Street
Boston
MA 2215
United States

www.bu.edu
Tel +1 617 353 2000

Statistics

Peer review	45
Recruiter review	74
Student faculty ratio	12.4:1
International faculty	6.0%
Undergraduates	19,692
Postgraduates	6,958
International students	21.0%

Ranking

World rank	47 (66)
Subject area positions	
Arts & humanities	54
Engineering & IT	98
Life sciences & biomedicine	44
Natural sciences	69
Social sciences	36

Brandeis University

Contact

415 South St.
Waltham
MA 02454-9110
United States

www.brandeis.edu
Tel +1 781 736 2000

Statistics

Peer review	151
Recruiter review	381
Student faculty ratio	19.8:1
International faculty	5.0%
Undergraduates	3,457
Postgraduates	2,546
International students	12.0%

Ranking

World rank	208 (187=)
Subject area positions	
Arts & humanities	83
Life sciences & biomedicine	100
Natural sciences	150
Social sciences	228

Brigham Young University

Contact

Provo
UT 84602
United States

www.byu.edu
Phone+1 801 422 4636

Statistics

Peer review	394
Recruiter review	209
Student faculty ratio	24.9:1
Undergraduates	26,815
Postgraduates	2,714
International students	4.0%

Ranking

World rank	401-500
Subject area positions	
Life sciences & biomedicine	285

Brown University

Contact	*Statistics*		*Ranking*	
Providence	**Peer review**	47	**World rank**	32 (54=)
RI 2912	**Recruiter review**	130	**Subject area positions**	
United States	**Student faculty ratio**	8.9:1	Arts & humanities	31
	International faculty	21.0%	Engineering & IT	89
www.brown.edu	**Undergraduates**	5,737	Life sciences & biomedicine	59
Tel +1 401 863 1000	**Postgraduates**	1,601	Natural sciences	62
	International students	12.0%	Social sciences	66

California Institute of Technology (Caltech)

Contact	*Statistics*		*Ranking*	
1200 East California Boulevard	**Peer review**	21	**World rank**	7= (7)
Pasadena	**Recruiter review**	227	**Subject area positions**	
California	**Student faculty ratio**	2.9:1	Arts & humanities	153
91125	**International faculty**	46.0%	Engineering & IT	4
United States	**Undergraduates**	890	Life sciences & biomedicine	21
	Postgraduates	1,307	Natural sciences	6
www.caltech.edu	**International students**	23.0%	Social sciences	70
Tel +1 626 395 6811				

University of California, Los Angeles (UCLA)

Contact	*Statistics*		*Ranking*	
405 Hilgard Avenue	**Peer review**	10	**World rank**	41 (31)
Los Angeles	**Recruiter review**	54	**Subject area positions**	
California	**Student faculty ratio**	11.2:1	Arts & humanities	13
90095	**International faculty**	4.0%	Engineering & IT	18
United States	**Undergraduates**	25,423	Life sciences & biomedicine	15
	Postgraduates	9,946	Natural sciences	14
www.ucla.edu	**International students**	7.0%	Social sciences	15
Tel +1 310 825 4321				

University of California, San Diego

Contact	*Statistics*		*Ranking*	
9500 Gilman Drive	**Peer review**	27	**World rank**	58 (44)
La Jolla	**Recruiter review**	296	**Subject area positions**	
California	**Student faculty ratio**	12.1:1	Arts & humanities	102
92093	**International faculty**	4.0%	Engineering & IT	38
United States	**Undergraduates**	19,771	Life sciences & biomedicine	11
	Postgraduates	2,866	Natural sciences	27
www.ucsd.edu	**International students**	6.0%	Social sciences	33
Tel +1 858 534 2230				

University of California, Davis

Contact

One Shields Avenue
Davis
California
95616
United States

www.ucdavis.edu
Tel +1 530 752 1011

Statistics

Peer review	69
Recruiter review	320
Student faculty ratio	10.7:1
International faculty	7.0%
Undergraduates	23,023
Postgraduates	4,547
International students	5.0%

Ranking

World rank	96 (170=)
Subject area positions	
Arts & humanities	130
Engineering & IT	86
Life sciences & biomedicine	37
Natural sciences	85
Social sciences	144

University of California, Santa Barbara

Contact

3117 Cheadle Hall
Santa Barbara
California
93106-2070
United States

www.ucsb.edu
Tel +1 805 893 2277

Statistics

Peer review	52
Recruiter review	335
Student faculty ratio	19.9:1
International faculty	10.0%
Undergraduates	17,877
Postgraduates	3,317
International students	4.0%

Ranking

World rank	117= (141=)
Subject area positions	
Arts & humanities	157
Engineering & IT	62
Life sciences & biomedicine	65
Natural sciences	22
Social sciences	121

University of California, Irvine

Contact

Irvine
California
92697
United States

www.uci.edu
Tel +1 949 824 5011

Statistics

Peer review	86
Recruiter review	342
Student faculty ratio	14.7:1
International faculty	6.0%
Undergraduates	20,589
Postgraduates	4,414
International students	6.0%

Ranking

World rank	140= (198=)
Subject area positions	
Arts & humanities	75
Engineering & IT	107
Life sciences & biomedicine	71
Natural sciences	133
Social sciences	132

University of California, Santa Cruz

Contact

1156 High Street
Santa Cruz
California
95064
United States

www.ucsc.edu
Tel +1 831 459 011

Statistics

Peer review	176
Recruiter review	500+
Student faculty ratio	22.6:1
International faculty	6.0%
Undergraduates	13,694
Postgraduates	1,483
International students	3.0%

Ranking

World rank	259= (311=)
Subject area positions	
Arts & humanities	156
Engineering & IT	291
Life sciences & biomedicine	97
Natural sciences	156
Social sciences	250

University of California, Riverside

Contact

900 University Avenue
Riverside
CA 92521
United States

www.ucr.edu
Tel +1 951 827 1012

Statistics

Peer review	249
Recruiter review	401-500
Student faculty ratio	19.4:1
International faculty	8.0%
Undergraduates	14,407
Postgraduates	2,185
International students	5.0%

Ranking

World rank	298 (412=)
Subject area positions	
Engineering & IT	273
Life sciences & biomedicine	153
Natural sciences	242
Social sciences	256

Carnegie Mellon University

Contact

5000 Forbes Avenue
Pittsburgh
PA 15213-3890
United States

www.cmu.edu
Tel +1 412 268 2000

Statistics

Peer review	32
Recruiter review	41
Student faculty ratio	8.7:1
International faculty	18.0%
Undergraduates	5,359
Postgraduates	3,535
International students	27.0%

Ranking

World rank	20= (35=)
Subject area positions	
Arts & humanities	98
Engineering & IT	7
Life sciences & biomedicine	99
Natural sciences	50
Social sciences	28

Case Western Reserve University

Contact

10900 Euclid Ave
Cleveland
Ohio
44106
United States

www.cwru.edu
Tel +1 216 368 2000

Statistics

Peer review	167
Recruiter review	249
Student faculty ratio	5.2:1
International faculty	3.0%
Undergraduates	3,716
Postgraduates	2,763
International students	18.0%

Ranking

World rank	85= (60)
Subject area positions	
Engineering & IT	144
Life sciences & biomedicine	61
Natural sciences	192
Social sciences	265

University of Chicago

Contact

5801 S. Ellis Avenue
Chicago
IL 60637
United States

www.uchicago.edu
Tel +1 773 702 1234

Statistics

Peer review	15
Recruiter review	21
Student faculty ratio	4.6:1
International faculty	19.0%
Undergraduates	4,509
Postgraduates	7,228
International students	22.0%

Ranking

World rank	7= (11)
Subject area positions	
Arts & humanities	9
Engineering & IT	107
Life sciences & biomedicine	37
Natural sciences	11
Social sciences	8

University of Cincinnati

Contact

2600 Clifton Ave.
Cincinnati
Ohio
45221
United States

www.uc.edu
Tel +1 513 556 1100

Statistics

Peer review	251
Recruiter review	300
Student faculty ratio	10.9:1
International faculty	5.0%
Undergraduates	17,323
Postgraduates	5,884
International students	6.0%

Ranking

World rank	219 (367)
Subject area positions	
Arts & humanities	227
Engineering & IT	280
Life sciences & biomedicine	159
Natural sciences	285
Social sciences	293

University of Colorado

Contact

Boulder
Colorado
80309
United States

www.colorado.edu
Tel +1 303 492 1411

Statistics

Peer review	164
Recruiter review	401-500
Student faculty ratio	4.1:1
International faculty	8.0%
Undergraduates	7,567
Postgraduates	4,805
International students	6.0%

Ranking

World rank	107 (211=)
Subject area positions	
Arts & humanities	273
Engineering & IT	123
Life sciences & biomedicine	132
Natural sciences	108
Social sciences	280

Colorado State University

Contact

Fort Collins
CO 80523
United States

www.colostate.edu
Tel +1 970 491 6909

Statistics

Peer review	285
Recruiter review	401-500
Student faculty ratio	23.6:1
International faculty	7.0%
Undergraduates	20,243
Postgraduates	2,357
International students	4.0%

Ranking

World rank	326 (450=)
Subject area positions	
Engineering & IT	216
Life sciences & biomedicine	284
Natural sciences	169
Social sciences	293

Columbia University

Contact

2960 Broadway
New York
10027-6902
United States

www.columbia.edu
Tel +1 212 854 1754

Statistics

Peer review	13
Recruiter review	29
Student faculty ratio	6.3:1
International faculty	8.0%
Undergraduates	7,296
Postgraduates	11,433
International students	22.0%

Ranking

World rank	11 (12)
Subject area positions	
Arts & humanities	6
Engineering & IT	59
Life sciences & biomedicine	25
Natural sciences	21
Social sciences	10

University of Connecticut

Contact

Storrs
Connecticut
6269
United States

www.uconn.edu
Tel +1 860 486 2000

Statistics

Peer review	369
Recruiter review	399
Student faculty ratio	17.9:1
International faculty	6.0%
Undergraduates	15,530
Postgraduates	3,943
International students	7.0%

Ranking

World rank	328 (383=)
Subject area positions	
Life sciences & biomedicine	249

Cornell University

Contact

Day Hall Lobby
Ithaca
NY 14853
United States

www.cornell.edu
Tel +1 607 254 4636

Statistics

Peer review	11
Recruiter review	17
Student faculty ratio	8.8:1
International faculty	8.0%
Undergraduates	13,926
Postgraduates	4,475
International students	15.0%

Ranking

World rank	20= (15)
Subject area positions	
Arts & humanities	16
Engineering & IT	20
Life sciences & biomedicine	16
Natural sciences	9
Social sciences	17

Dartmouth College

Contact

Hanover
NH 3755
United States

www.dartmouth.edu
Tel +1 603 646 1110

Statistics

Peer review	161
Recruiter review	68
Student faculty ratio	6.8:1
International faculty	6.0%
Undergraduates	4,052
Postgraduates	1,604
International students	11.0%

Ranking

World rank	71= (61=)
Subject area positions	
Arts & humanities	139
Engineering & IT	299
Life sciences & biomedicine	98
Natural sciences	251
Social sciences	127

University of Delaware

Contact

Gainesville
Florida
32611
United States

www.udel.edu
Tel +1 352 392 3261

Statistics

Peer review	325
Recruiter review	401-500
Student faculty ratio	20.7:1
International faculty	5.0%
Undergraduates	16,919
Postgraduates	2,440
International students	6.0%

Ranking

World rank	343= (428=)
Subject area positions	
Arts & humanities	281
Engineering & IT	249
Natural sciences	286

Drexel University

Contact	*Statistics*		*Ranking*	
3141 Chestnut Street	**Peer review**	360	**World rank**	256= (365=)
Philadelphia	**Recruiter review**	368	**Subject area positions**	
PA 19104	**Student faculty ratio**	9.1:1	Engineering & IT	281
United States	**International faculty**	13.0%		
	Undergraduates	9,379		
www.drexel.edu	**Postgraduates**	3,333		
Tel +1 215 895 6700	**International students**	14.0%		

Duke University

Contact	*Statistics*		*Ranking*	
2138 Campus Drive	**Peer review**	28	**World rank**	13 (13)
Box 90586	**Recruiter review**	23	**Subject area positions**	
Durham	**Student faculty ratio**	4.4:1	Arts & humanities	20
NC 27708	**International faculty**	2.0%	Engineering & IT	107
United States	**Undergraduates**	5,452	Life sciences & biomedicine	19
	Postgraduates	4,855	Natural sciences	54
www.duke.edu	**International students**	16.0%	Social sciences	25
Tel +1 919 684 8111				

Emory University

Contact	*Statistics*		*Ranking*	
201 Dowman Drive	**Peer review**	157	**World rank**	74= (56)
Atlanta	**Recruiter review**	140	**Subject area positions**	
Georgia	**Student faculty ratio**	5.2:1	Arts & humanities	95
30322	**International faculty**	1.0%	Life sciences & biomedicine	51
United States	**Undergraduates**	7,130	Natural sciences	269
	Postgraduates	4,761		
www.emory.edu	**International students**	8.0%		
Tel +1 404 727 6123				

University of Florida

Contact	*Statistics*		*Ranking*	
Gainesville	**Peer review**	152	**World rank**	135 (226=)
Florida	**Recruiter review**	286	**Subject area positions**	
32611	**Student faculty ratio**	8.5:1	Arts & humanities	176
United States	**International faculty**	6.0%	Engineering & IT	134
	Undergraduates	33,471	Life sciences & biomedicine	179
www.ufl.edu	**Postgraduates**	13,022	Natural sciences	130
Tel +1 352 392 3261	**International students**	7.0%	Social sciences	214

Florida State University

Contact	*Statistics*		*Ranking*	
Tallahassee	**Peer review**	181	**World rank**	253 (294=)
FL 32306	**Recruiter review**	247	**Subject area positions**	
United States	**Student faculty ratio**	23.7:1	Arts & humanities	181
	International faculty	9.0%	Engineering & IT	234
www.fsu.edu	**Undergraduates**	28,723	Life sciences & biomedicine	127
Tel +1 850 644 2525	**Postgraduates**	5,902	Natural sciences	137
	International students	3.0%	Social sciences	266

George Washington University

Contact	*Statistics*		*Ranking*	
2121 I Street NW	**Peer review**	225	**World rank**	229= (168=)
Washington	**Recruiter review**	156	**Subject area positions**	
DC 20052	**Student faculty ratio**	13.6:1	Arts & humanities	129
United States	**International faculty**	2.0%	Engineering & IT	274
	Undergraduates	10,102	Life sciences & biomedicine	234
www.gwu.edu	**Postgraduates**	9,471	Social sciences	182
Tel +1 202 994 3900	**International students**	9.0%		

Georgetown University

Contact	*Statistics*		*Ranking*	
37th and O Streets, NW,	**Peer review**	182	**World rank**	102= (102=)
Washington	**Recruiter review**	43	**Subject area positions**	
DC 20057	**Student faculty ratio**	9.5:1	Arts & humanities	89
United States	**International faculty**	6.0%	Life sciences & biomedicine	265
	Undergraduates	6,503	Social sciences	51
www.georgetown.edu	**Postgraduates**	3,119		
Tel +1 202 687 0100	**International students**	16.0%		

Georgia Institute of Technology

Contact	*Statistics*		*Ranking*	
Atlanta	**Peer review**	82	**World rank**	97= (145)
Georgia	**Recruiter review**	131	**Subject area positions**	
30332	**Student faculty ratio**	19.6:1	Arts & humanities	278
United States	**International faculty**	3%	Engineering & IT	8
	Undergraduates	12,000	Natural sciences	49
www.gatech.edu	**Postgraduates**	5,027	Social sciences	270
Tel +1 404 894 2000	**International students**	16.0%		

University of Georgia

Contact

Athens
GA 30602
United States

www.uga.edu
Tel +1 706 542 3000

Statistics

Peer review	307
Recruiter review	371
Student faculty ratio	14.4:1
International faculty	12.0%
Undergraduates	23,917
Postgraduates	6,964
International students	5.0%

Ranking

World rank	295= (314=)
Subject area positions	
Arts & humanities	230
Life sciences & biomedicine	294
Natural sciences	248

Georgia State University

Contact

Atlanta
GA 30302-3965
United States

www.gsu.edu
Tel +1 404 651 2000

Statistics

Peer review	348
Recruiter review	335
Student faculty ratio	25.6:1
International faculty	10.0%
Undergraduates	17,687
Postgraduates	5,980
International students	7.0%

Ranking

World rank	396= (422)
Subject area positions	
Arts & humanities	278
Engineering & IT	8
Natural sciences	49
Social sciences	270

Harvard University

Contact

1350 Massachusetts Ave
Cambridge
MA 2138
United States

www.harvard.edu
Tel +1 617 495 1000

Statistics

Peer review	2
Recruiter review	4
Student faculty ratio	4.7:1
International faculty	31.0%
Undergraduates	3,593
Postgraduates	10,237
International students	23.0%

Ranking

World rank	1 (1)
Subject area positions	
Arts & humanities	1
Engineering & IT	15
Life sciences & biomedicine	1
Natural sciences	1
Social sciences	1

University of Hawaii

Contact

2500 Campus Road
Hawai'i Hall 202
Honolulu
HI 96822
United States

www.uhm.hawaii.edu
Tel +1 808 956 8111

Statistics

Peer review	249
Recruiter review	500+
Student faculty ratio	12.4:1
International faculty	9.0%
Undergraduates	14,345
Postgraduates	2,922
International students	10.0%

Ranking

World rank	255 (274=)
Subject area positions	
Arts & humanities	80
Natural sciences	288
Social sciences	219

University of Houston

Contact	*Statistics*		*Ranking*	
4800 Calhoun Rd.	**Peer review**	365	**World rank**	401-500
Houston	**Recruiter review**	337	**Subject area positions**	
Texas	**Student faculty ratio**	54.9:1	Life sciences & biomedicine	263
77004	**International faculty**	9.0%		
United States	**Undergraduates**	45,040		
	Postgraduates	9,245		
www.uh.edu	**International students**	5.0%		
Tel +1 713 743 2255				

University of Illinois

Contact	*Statistics*		*Ranking*	
Box 5220	**Peer review**	41	**World rank**	73 (77)
Chicago	**Recruiter review**	185	**Subject area positions**	
Illinois	**Student faculty ratio**	17.9:1	Arts & humanities	90
60680-5220	**International faculty**	8.0%	Engineering & IT	19
United States	**Undergraduates**	46,644	Life sciences & biomedicine	91
	Postgraduates	19,363	Natural sciences	29
www.uillinois.edu	**International students**	11.0%	Social sciences	56
Tel +1 312 996 4350				

Indiana University Bloomington

Contact	*Statistics*		*Ranking*	
107 S. Indiana Ave	**Peer review**	128	**World rank**	137= (232=)
Bloomington	**Recruiter review**	118	**Subject area positions**	
IN 47405-7000	**Student faculty ratio**	18:1	Arts & humanities	48
United States	**International faculty**	11.0%	Life sciences & biomedicine	138
	Undergraduates	28,640	Natural sciences	148
www.indiana.edu	**Postgraduates**	6,421	Social sciences	178
Tel +1 812 855 4848	**International students**	8.0%		

University of Iowa

Contact	*Statistics*		*Ranking*	
100 Pomerantz Center RM	**Peer review**	247	**World rank**	207 (246=)
C210	**Recruiter review**	312	**Subject area positions**	
Iowa City	**Student faculty ratio**	13.4:1	Arts & humanities	213
IA 52242-7700	**International faculty**	14.0%	Life sciences & biomedicine	127
United States	**Undergraduates**	20,774	Social sciences	223
	Postgraduates	3,167		
www.uiowa.edu	**International students**	9.0%		
Tel +1 319 335 3500				

Iowa State University

Contact

Ames
IA 50011-2011
United States

www.iastate.edu
Tel +1 515 294 5836

Statistics

Peer review	296
Recruiter review	401-500
Student faculty ratio	12.5:1
International faculty	6.0%
Undergraduates	20,900
Postgraduates	2,955
International students	10.0%

Ranking

World rank	276= (386=)
Subject area positions	
Engineering & IT	152
Life sciences & biomedicine	215
Natural sciences	262
Social sciences	244

Johns Hopkins University

Contact

3400 N Charles St.
Baltimore
Maryland
21218-2688
United States

www.jhu.edu
Tel +1 410 516 8000

Statistics

Peer review	24
Recruiter review	132
Student faculty ratio	5.5:1
International faculty	8.0%
Undergraduates	5,610
Postgraduates	10,611
International students	15.0%

Ranking

World rank	15 (23)
Subject area positions	
Arts & humanities	21
Engineering & IT	52
Life sciences & biomedicine	4
Natural sciences	37
Social sciences	38

University of Kansas

Contact

Lawrence
KS 66045
United States

www.ku.edu
Tel +1 785 864 2700

Statistics

Peer review	320
Recruiter review	355
Student faculty ratio	12.4:1
International faculty	12.0%
Undergraduates	19,253
Postgraduates	6,097
International students	6.0%

Ranking

World rank	281 (305=)
Subject area positions	
Arts & humanities	292
Life sciences & biomedicine	247
Social sciences	219

University of Kentucky

Contact

Lexington
KY 40506
United States

www.uky.edu
Tel +1 859 257 9000

Statistics

Peer review	401-500
Recruiter review	500+
Student faculty ratio	12.5:1
International faculty	4.0%
Undergraduates	17,392
Postgraduates	3,781
International students	6.0%

Ranking

World rank	378= (450=)

Louisiana State University

Contact

Baton Rouge
LA 70803
United States

www.lsu.edu
Tel +1 225 578 2311

Statistics

Peer review	401-500
Recruiter review	401-500
Student faculty ratio	18.6:1
International faculty	6.0%
Undergraduates	33,112
Postgraduates	4,352
International students	5.0%

Ranking

World rank	401-500
Subject area positions	
Life sciences & biomedicine	288
Natural sciences	291

Loyola University Chicago

Contact

6525 N. Sheridan Road
Chicago
IL 60626
United States

www.luc.edu
Tel +1 773 508 3396

Statistics

Peer review	390
Recruiter review	401-500
Student faculty ratio	12.4:1
Undergraduates	8,154
Postgraduates	2,554
International students	5.0%

Ranking

World rank	350 (343=)
Subject area positions	
Arts & humanities	269

University of Maryland

Contact

College Park
MD 20742
United States

www.umd.edu
Tel +1 301 405 1000

Statistics

Peer review	110
Recruiter review	191
Student faculty ratio	9.2:1
International faculty	12.0%
Undergraduates	23,639
Postgraduates	6,192
International students	9.0%

Ranking

World rank	79 (111=)
Subject area positions	
Engineering & IT	73
Life sciences & biomedicine	135
Natural sciences	59
Social sciences	124

Massachusetts Institute of Technology (MIT)

Contact

77 Massachusetts Avenue
Cambridge
MA 02139-4307
United States

web.mit.edu
Tel +1 617 253 1000

Statistics

Peer review	6
Recruiter review	6
Student faculty ratio	7.6:1
International faculty	8.0%
Undergraduates	4,088
Postgraduates	5,991
International students	25.0%

Ranking

World rank	10 (4=)
Subject area positions	
Arts & humanities	25
Engineering & IT	1
Life sciences & biomedicine	9
Natural sciences	2
Social sciences	11

University of Massachusetts, Amherst

Contact	*Statistics*		*Ranking*	
Amherst	**Peer review**	147	**World rank**	175= (124=)
MA 01003	**Recruiter review**	267	**Subject area positions**	
United States	**Student faculty ratio**	15.8:1	Arts & humanities	238
	International faculty	5.0%	Engineering & IT	75
www.umass.edu	**Undergraduates**	16,754	Life sciences & biomedicine	171
Tel +1 413 545 0111	**Postgraduates**	3,712	Natural sciences	211
	International students	6.0%	Social sciences	172

University of Miami

Contact	*Statistics*		*Ranking*	
Coral Gables,	**Peer review**	401-500	**World rank**	202 (211=)
Miami	**Recruiter review**	313	**Subject area positions**	
Florida	**Student faculty ratio**	6:1	Life sciences & biomedicine	266
33124	**International faculty**	15.0%		
United States	**Undergraduates**	10,105		
	Postgraduates	4,879		
www.miami.edu	**International students**	10.0%		
Tel +1 305 284 2211				

University of Michigan

Contact	*Statistics*		*Ranking*	
Ann Arbor	**Peer review**	22	**World rank**	38= (29=)
Michigan	**Recruiter review**	35	**Subject area positions**	
48109	**Student faculty ratio**	11.7:1	Arts & humanities	19
United States	**International faculty**	10.0%	Engineering & IT	32
	Undergraduates	34,001	Life sciences & biomedicine	33
www.umich.edu	**Postgraduates**	13,059	Natural sciences	21
Tel +1 734 764 1817	**International students**	11.0%	Social sciences	19

Michigan State University

Contact	*Statistics*		*Ranking*	
East Lansing	**Peer review**	142	**World rank**	159= (163)
MI 48824-0590	**Recruiter review**	148	**Subject area positions**	
United States	**Student faculty ratio**	16.1:1	Arts & humanities	268
	International faculty	17.0%	Engineering & IT	162
www.msu.edu	**Undergraduates**	32,935	Life sciences & biomedicine	222
Tel +1 517 355 8332	**Postgraduates**	7,733	Natural sciences	110
	International students	9.0%	Social sciences	91

University of Minnesota

Contact

240 Williamson Hall
231 Pillsbury Drive S.E.
Minneapolis
MN 55455-0213
United States

www.umn.edu
Tel +1 612 625 2008

Statistics

Peer review	89
Recruiter review	279
Student faculty ratio	18.3:1
International faculty	6.0%
Undergraduates	45,350
Postgraduates	7,517
International students	7.0%

Ranking

World rank	142= (187=)
Subject area positions	
Arts & humanities	123
Engineering & IT	112
Life sciences & biomedicine	78
Natural sciences	115
Social sciences	97

University of Missouri

Contact

721 Lewis Hall,
Columbia
MO 65211
United States

www.missouri.edu
Tel +1 573 882 4077

Statistics

Peer review	401-500
Recruiter review	401-500
Student faculty ratio	13.5:1
International faculty	12.0%
Undergraduates	48,254
Postgraduates	8,208
International students	7.0%

Ranking

World rank	381= (246=)

University of New Mexico

Contact

Albuquerque
NM 87131
United States

www.unm.edu
Tel +1 505 277 0111

Statistics

Peer review	358
Recruiter review	500+
Student faculty ratio	14.2:1
International faculty	8.0%
Undergraduates	16,473
Postgraduates	3,759
International students	5.0%

Ranking

World rank	358= (360=)
Subject area positions	
Natural sciences	277

New York University (NYU)

Contact

70 Washington Square South,
12S
New York
NY 10012
United States

www.nyu.edu

Statistics

Peer review	35
Recruiter review	51
Student faculty ratio	12.6:1
International faculty	7.0%
Undergraduates	21,449
Postgraduates	13,573
International students	10.0%

Ranking

World rank	49 (43)
Subject area positions	
Arts & humanities	23
Engineering & IT	205
Life sciences & biomedicine	47
Natural sciences	42
Social sciences	21

City University of New York

Contact

365 Fifth Avenue
New York
NY 10016-4309
United States

www.cuny.edu
Tel +1 212 817 7000

Statistics

Peer review	195
Recruiter review	307
Student faculty ratio	15.1:1
International faculty	4.0%
Undergraduates	165,814
Postgraduates	21,400
International students	8.0%

Ranking

World rank	358= (380=)
Subject area positions	
Arts & humanities	65
Life sciences & biomedicine	183
Natural sciences	245
Social sciences	258

University of North Carolina

Contact

CB #2200, Jackson Hall
Chapel Hill
NC 27599-2200
United States

www.unc.edu
Tel +1 919 966 3621

Statistics

Peer review	104
Recruiter review	86
Student faculty ratio	18.1:1
International faculty	4.0%
Undergraduates	63,140
Postgraduates	16,365
International students	3.0%

Ranking

World rank	151= (123)
Subject area positions	
Arts & humanities	196
Engineering & IT	172
Life sciences & biomedicine	69
Natural sciences	116
Social sciences	83

North Carolina State University

Contact

Raleigh
NC 27695
United States

www.ncsu.edu
Tel +1 919 515 2011

Statistics

Peer review	253
Recruiter review	230
Student faculty ratio	17.7:1
International faculty	5.0%
Undergraduates	21,385
Postgraduates	4,296
International students	8.0%

Ranking

World rank	248= (274=)
Subject area positions	
Engineering & IT	159
Life sciences & biomedicine	224
Natural sciences	178

Northeastern University

Contact

360 Huntington Avenue
Boston
MA 02115
United States

www.northeastern.edu
Tel +1 617 373 2000

Statistics

Peer review	401-500
Recruiter review	253
Student faculty ratio	16.9:1
International faculty	8.0%
Undergraduates	13,368
Postgraduates	3,963
International students	9.0%

Ranking

World rank	386= (468=)

Northwestern University

Contact

633 Clark Street
Evanston
IL 60208
United States

www.northwestern.edu
Tel +1 847 491 3741

Statistics

Peer review	54
Recruiter review	26
Student faculty ratio	8.5:1
International faculty	8.0%
Undergraduates	8,079
Postgraduates	6,021
International students	15.0%

Ranking

World rank	29 (42)
Subject area positions	
Arts & humanities	110
Engineering & IT	67
Life sciences & biomedicine	74
Natural sciences	87
Social sciences	29

University of Notre Dame

Contact

317 Main Building
Notre Dame
Indiana
46556
United States

www.nd.edu
Tel +1 574 631 7367

Statistics

Peer review	186
Recruiter review	76
Student faculty ratio	13.5:1
International faculty	5.0%
Undergraduates	7,538
Postgraduates	2,740
International students	10.0%

Ranking

World rank	155= (152)
Subject area positions	
Arts & humanities	52
Engineering & IT	249
Life sciences & biomedicine	266
Natural sciences	276
Social sciences	235

Ohio State University

Contact

Enarson Hall 154 W 12th
Avenue
Columbus
Ohio
43210
United States

www.osu.edu
Tel +1 614 292 5881

Statistics

Peer review	121
Recruiter review	129
Student faculty ratio	14.4:1
International faculty	18.0%
Undergraduates	37,527
Postgraduates	12,196
International students	8.0%

Ranking

World rank	120 (219=)
Subject area positions	
Engineering & IT	95
Life sciences & biomedicine	168
Natural sciences	72
Social sciences	80

University of Oklahoma

Contact

660 Parrington Oval
Norman
OK 73019-0390
United States

www.ou.edu
Tel +1 405 325 0311

Statistics

Peer review	382
Recruiter review	398
Student faculty ratio	15.9:1
International faculty	9.0%
Undergraduates	21,676
Postgraduates	7,503
International students	10.0%

Ranking

World rank	373 (418=)
Subject area positions	
Social sciences	280

University of Oregon

Contact

Eugene
OR 97403
United States

www.uoregon.edu
Tel +1 541 346 1000

Statistics

Peer review	302
Recruiter review	401-500
Student faculty ratio	20.8:1
International faculty	9.0%
Undergraduates	16,245
Postgraduates	3,470
International students	7.0%

Ranking

World rank	351= (437=)
Subject area positions	
Life sciences & biomedicine	163
Natural sciences	291

University of Pennsylvania

Contact

3451 Walnut Street
Philadelphia
Pennsylvania
19104
United States

www.upenn.edu
Tel +1 215 898 5000

Statistics

Peer review	30
Recruiter review	32
Student faculty ratio	7.2:1
International faculty	24.0%
Undergraduates	13,626
Postgraduates	9,901
International students	14.0%

Ranking

World rank	14 (26)
Subject area positions	
Arts & humanities	50
Engineering & IT	79
Life sciences & biomedicine	35
Natural sciences	35
Social sciences	22

Pennsylvania State University

Contact

201 Old Main
University Park
PA 16802
United States

www.psu.edu
Tel +1 814 865 5471

Statistics

Peer review	63
Recruiter review	105
Student faculty ratio	10.2:1
International faculty	2.0%
Undergraduates	83,998
Postgraduates	8,043
International students	5.0%

Ranking

World rank	90= (99=)
Subject area positions	
Arts & humanities	103
Engineering & IT	76
Life sciences & biomedicine	159
Natural sciences	44
Social sciences	50

University of Pittsburgh

Contact

Pittsburgh
PA 15260
United States

www.pitt.edu
Tel +1 412 624 4141

Statistics

Peer review	145
Recruiter review	270
Student faculty ratio	6.4:1
International faculty	22.0%
Undergraduates	16,152
Postgraduates	7,866
International students	8.0%

Ranking

World rank	77= (88)
Subject area positions	
Arts & humanities	83
Engineering & IT	188
Life sciences & biomedicine	124
Social sciences	176

Princeton University

Contact	*Statistics*		*Ranking*	
Princeton	**Peer review**	7	**World rank**	6 (10)
NJ 08544	**Recruiter review**	46	**Subject area positions**	
United States	**Student faculty ratio**	6.2:1	Arts & humanities	7
	International faculty	24.0%	Engineering & IT	14
www.princeton.edu	**Undergraduates**	4,783	Life sciences & biomedicine	29
Tel +1 609 258 3000	**Postgraduates**	2,012	Natural sciences	5
	International students	16.0%	Social sciences	9

Purdue University

Contact	*Statistics*		*Ranking*	
1080 Schleman Hall	**Peer review**	57	**World rank**	77= (127)
West Lafayette	**Recruiter review**	118	**Subject area positions**	
IN 47907-1080	**Student faculty ratio**	20:1	Arts & humanities	208
United States	**International faculty**	21.0%	Engineering & IT	24
	Undergraduates	31,266	Life sciences & biomedicine	57
www.purdue.edu	**Postgraduates**	6,774	Natural sciences	51
Tel +1 765 494 4600	**International students**	14.0%	Social sciences	130

Rensselaer Polytechnic Institute

Contact	*Statistics*		*Ranking*	
110 8th St.	**Peer review**	262	**World rank**	191 (255=)
Troy	**Recruiter review**	277	**Subject area positions**	
NY 12180	**Student faculty ratio**	13.3:1	Engineering & IT	50
United States	**International faculty**	19.0%	Natural sciences	161
	Undergraduates	4,529		
www.rpi.edu	**Postgraduates**	900		
Tel +1 518 276 6000	**International students**	12.0%		

Rice University

Contact	*Statistics*		*Ranking*	
6100 Main	**Peer review**	135	**World rank**	92 (102=)
Houston	**Recruiter review**	267	**Subject area positions**	
Texas	**Student faculty ratio**	8.2:1	Arts & humanities	190
77005-1827	**International faculty**	9.0%	Engineering & IT	102
United States	**Undergraduates**	2,851	Life sciences & biomedicine	132
	Postgraduates	2,417	Natural sciences	116
www.rice.edu	**International students**	12.0%	Social sciences	230
Tel +1 713 348 0000				

University of Rochester

Contact	*Statistics*		*Ranking*	
Rochester	**Peer review**	171	**World rank**	95 (48=)
NY 14627	**Recruiter review**	303	**Subject area positions**	
United States	**Student faculty ratio**	4:1	Arts & humanities	206
	International faculty	5.0%	Engineering & IT	253
www.rochester.edu	**Undergraduates**	5,040	Life sciences & biomedicine	167
Tel +1 585 275 2121	**Postgraduates**	2,810	Natural sciences	194
	International students	13.0%	Social sciences	96

Rutgers, The State University of New Jersey

Contact	*Statistics*		*Ranking*	
18 Bishop Place	**Peer review**	109	**World rank**	177= (215=)
New Brunswick	**Recruiter review**	326	**Subject area positions**	
NJ 08901-8530	**Student faculty ratio**	17.3:1	Arts & humanities	63
United States	**International faculty**	15.0%	Engineering & IT	170
	Undergraduates	35,230	Life sciences & biomedicine	213
www.rutgers.edu	**Postgraduates**	8,919	Natural sciences	127
Tel +1 732 932 7711	**International students**	4.0%	Social sciences	106

Smith College

Contact	*Statistics*		*Ranking*	
Northampton	**Peer review**	500+	**World rank**	401-500
Massachusetts	**Recruiter review**	100		
01063	**Student faculty ratio**	11.6:1		
United States	**International faculty**	4.0%		
	Undergraduates	2,694		
www.smith.edu	**Postgraduates**	467		
Tel +1 413 584 2700	**International students**	6.0%		

University of South Carolina

Contact	*Statistics*		*Ranking*	
Columbia	**Peer review**	401-500	**World rank**	362= (464)
SC 29208	**Recruiter review**	177		
United States	**Student faculty ratio**	22:1		
	International faculty	7.0%		
www.sc.edu	**Undergraduates**	25,370		
Tel +1 803 777 7000	**Postgraduates**	6,433		
	International students	4.0%		

University of South Florida

Contact	*Statistics*		*Ranking*	
4202 E. Fowler Avenue	**Peer review**	500+	**World rank**	401-500
Tampa	**Recruiter review**	500+		
FL 33620	**Student faculty ratio**	23.9:1		
United States	**International faculty**	2.0%		
	Undergraduates	29,001		
www.usf.edu	**Postgraduates**	6,226		
Tel +1 813 974 2011	**International students**	7.0%		

University of Southern California

Contact	*Statistics*		*Ranking*	
Los Angeles	**Peer review**	143	**World rank**	119 (101)
CA 90089	**Recruiter review**	134	**Subject area positions**	
United States	**Student faculty ratio**	11.8:1	Arts & humanities	155
	International faculty	5.0%	Engineering & IT	76
www.usc.edu	**Undergraduates**	17,639	Life sciences & biomedicine	210
Tel +1 213 740 2311	**Postgraduates**	13,143	Natural sciences	224
	International students	18.0%	Social sciences	197

Stanford University

Contact	*Statistics*		*Ranking*	
Montag Hall	**Peer review**	4	**World rank**	19 (6)
Stanford	**Recruiter review**	7	**Subject area positions**	
CA 94305-3020	**Student faculty ratio**	9.8:1	Arts & humanities	11
United States	**International faculty**	5.0%	Engineering & IT	3
	Undergraduates	5,785	Life sciences & biomedicine	6
www.stanford.edu	**Postgraduates**	9,132	Natural sciences	7
Tel +1 650 723 2300	**International students**	25.0%	Social sciences	5

Stony Brook University

Contact	*Statistics*		*Ranking*	
Stony Brook	**Peer review**	94	**World rank**	224 (165=)
NY 11794	**Recruiter review**	390	**Subject area positions**	
United States	**Student faculty ratio**	11.8:1	Arts & humanities	82
	International faculty	18.0%	Engineering & IT	163
www.sunysb.edu	**Undergraduates**	14,069	Life sciences & biomedicine	155
Tel +1 631 632 6000	**Postgraduates**	5,068	Natural sciences	45
	International students	21.0%	Social sciences	152

Temple University

Contact	*Statistics*		*Ranking*	
1801 North Broad Street	**Peer review**	378	**World rank**	401-500
Philadelphia	**Recruiter review**	401-500	**Subject area positions**	
PA 19122	**Student faculty ratio**	19:1	Social sciences	247
United States	**International faculty**	4.0%		
	Undergraduates	21,265		
www.temple.edu	**Postgraduates**	6,595		
Tel +1 215 204 7000	**International students**	5.0%		

University of Tennessee

Contact	*Statistics*		*Ranking*	
Knoxville	**Peer review**	401-500	**World rank**	289 (370=)
Tennessee	**Recruiter review**	275		
37996	**Student faculty ratio**	10.2:1		
United States	**International faculty**	6.0%		
	Undergraduates	18,925		
www.utk.edu	**Postgraduates**	5,186		
Tel +1 865 974 1000	**International students**	4.0%		

University of Texas at Austin

Contact	*Statistics*		*Ranking*	
1 University Station	**Peer review**	39	**World rank**	51= (32)
Austin	**Recruiter review**	48	**Subject area positions**	
Texas	**Student faculty ratio**	21.4:1	Arts & humanities	42
78712	**International faculty**	17.0%	Engineering & IT	30
United States	**Undergraduates**	34,172	Life sciences & biomedicine	91
	Postgraduates	11,442	Natural sciences	23
www.utexas.edu	**International students**	10.0%	Social sciences	81
Tel +1 512 471 3434				

Texas A&M University

Contact	*Statistics*		*Ranking*	
College Station	**Peer review**	90	**World rank**	122 (150=)
TX 77843	**Recruiter review**	142	**Subject area positions**	
United States	**Student faculty ratio**	18.5:1	Arts & humanities	278
	International faculty	10.0%	Engineering & IT	41
www.tamu.edu	**Undergraduates**	33,234	Life sciences & biomedicine	88
Tel +1 979 845 3211	**Postgraduates**	6,807	Natural sciences	77
	International students	8.0%	Social sciences	192

Tufts University

Contact

Medford
MA 02155
United States

www.tufts.edu
Tel +1 617 628 5000

Statistics

Peer review	272
Recruiter review	125
Student faculty ratio	10.5:1
International faculty	11.0%
Undergraduates	4,967
Postgraduates	4,532
International students	9.0%

Ranking

World rank	159= (130=)
Subject area positions	
Arts & humanities	168
Life sciences & biomedicine	175
Social sciences	208

Tulane University

Contact

6823 St. Charles Avenue
New Orleans
LA 70118
United States

www.tulane.edu
Tel +1 504 865 5000

Statistics

Peer review	390
Recruiter review	115
Student faculty ratio	11.1:1
International faculty	25.0%
Undergraduates	7,515
Postgraduates	4,243
International students	9.0%

Ranking

World rank	218 (243)

University of Utah

Contact

Salt Lake City
UT 84112
United States

www.utah.edu
Tel +1 801 581 7200

Statistics

Peer review	317
Recruiter review	401-500
Student faculty ratio	10.6:1
International faculty	12.0%
Undergraduates	19,938
Postgraduates	5,863
International students	6.0%

Ranking

World rank	261 (265)
Subject area positions	
Arts & humanities	295
Natural sciences	216

Vanderbilt University

Contact

2201 West End Avenue
Nashville
TN 37240
United States

www.vanderbilt.edu
Tel +1 615 322 7311

Statistics

Peer review	192
Recruiter review	108
Student faculty ratio	4.8:1
International faculty	6.0%
Undergraduates	6,329
Postgraduates	4,802
International students	9.0%

Ranking

World rank	82 (53)
Subject area positions	
Arts & humanities	289
Life sciences & biomedicine	66
Natural sciences	224
Social sciences	166

University of Virginia

Contact

P.O. Box 400132
Charlottesville
VA 22904-4132
United States

www.virginia.edu
Tel +1 434 924 7923

Statistics

Peer review	139
Recruiter review	47
Student faculty ratio	11.9:1
International faculty	4.0%
Undergraduates	13,946
Postgraduates	7,288
International students	7.0%

Ranking

World rank	110 (130=)
Subject area positions	
Arts & humanities	184
Engineering & IT	185
Life sciences & biomedicine	120
Natural sciences	240
Social sciences	77

Virginia Commonwealth University

Contact

901 West Franklin Street
P.O. Box 842527
Richmond,
Virginia
23284-2527
United States

www.vcu.edu
Tel +1 804 828 0100

Statistics

Peer review	401-500
Recruiter review	401-500
Student faculty ratio	16:1
International faculty	3.0%
Undergraduates	18,157
Postgraduates	6,035
International students	4.0%

Ranking

World rank	401-500

Virginia Polytechnic Institute (Virginia Tech)

Contact

Blacksburg
VA 24061
United States

www.vt.edu
Tel +1 540 231 6000

Statistics

Peer review	244
Recruiter review	239
Student faculty ratio	13.9:1
International faculty	12.0%
Undergraduates	19,584
Postgraduates	5,211
International students	9.0%

Ranking

World rank	248= (248=)
Subject area positions	
Engineering & IT	45
Natural sciences	268

Wake Forest University

Contact

1834 Wake Forest Road
Winston-Salem
NC 27106
United States

www.wfu.edu
Tel +1 336 758 5255

Statistics

Peer review	401-500
Recruiter review	159
Student faculty ratio	4.8:1
International faculty	8.0%
Undergraduates	4,005
Postgraduates	1,446
International students	3.0%

Ranking

World rank	203= (111=)
Subject area positions	
Life sciences & biomedicine	263

University of Washington

Contact

Seattle
WA 98195
United States

www.washington.edu
Tel +1 206 543 2100

Statistics

Peer review	65
Recruiter review	247
Student faculty ratio	9:1
International faculty	11.0%
Undergraduates	26,890
Postgraduates	10,861
International students	7.0%

Ranking

World rank	55= (84)
Subject area positions	
Arts & humanities	130
Engineering & IT	81
Life sciences & biomedicine	42
Natural sciences	56
Social sciences	141

Washington University in St. Louis

Contact

One Brookings Drive
St Louis
MO 63130-4899
United States

www.wustl.edu
Tel +1 314 935 6000

Statistics

Peer review	107
Recruiter review	191
Student faculty ratio	4.5:1
International faculty	6.0%
Undergraduates	6,847
Postgraduates	5,251
International students	10.0%

Ranking

World rank	161= (48=)
Subject area positions	
Arts & humanities	145
Engineering & IT	209
Life sciences & biomedicine	34
Natural sciences	233
Social sciences	161

Washington State University

Contact

PO Box 641067
Pullman
WA 99164-1067
United States

www.wsu.edu

Statistics

Peer review	326
Recruiter review	401-500
Student faculty ratio	10.8:1
International faculty	13.0%
Undergraduates	16,963
Postgraduates	2,901
International students	6.0%

Ranking

World rank	286= (299=)
Subject area positions	
Engineering & IT	266
Life sciences & biomedicine	241

College of William & Mary

Contact

Williamsburg
VA 23187-8795
United States

www.wm.edu
Tel +1 757 221 4000

Statistics

Peer review	401-500
Recruiter review	193
Student faculty ratio	11.9:1
International faculty	0.0%
Undergraduates	5,714
Postgraduates	1,918
International students	7.0%

Ranking

World rank	303 (336=)

University of Wisconsin-Madison

Contact	*Statistics*		*Ranking*	
500 Lincoln Drive	**Peer review**	42	**World rank**	55= (79=)
Madison	**Recruiter review**	110	**Subject area positions**	
WI 53706	**Student faculty ratio**	17.1:1	Arts & humanities	67
United States	**International faculty**	12.0%	Engineering & IT	56
	Undergraduates	25,040	Life sciences & biomedicine	45
www.wisc.edu	**Postgraduates**	6,470	Natural sciences	39
Tel +1 608 263 2400	**International students**	9.0%	Social sciences	37

Yale University

Contact	*Statistics*		*Ranking*	
P.O. Box 208236	**Peer review**	8	**World rank**	2= (4=)
New Haven	**Recruiter review**	13	**Subject area positions**	
CT 6520	**Student faculty ratio**	3.4:1	Arts & humanities	5
United States	**International faculty**	24.0%	Engineering & IT	46
	Undergraduates	5,218	Life sciences & biomedicine	8
www.yale.edu	**Postgraduates**	4,383	Natural sciences	10
Tel +1 203 432 4771	**International students**	16.0%	Social sciences	4

Yeshiva University

Contact	*Statistics*		*Ranking*	
500 West 185th Street	**Peer review**	500+	**World rank**	381= (172=)
New York	**Recruiter review**	399		
10033	**Student faculty ratio**	4.9:1		
United States	**International faculty**	9.0%		
	Undergraduates	2,186		
www.yu.edu	**Postgraduates**	1,282		
Tel +1 212 960 5400	**International students**	5.0%		

Uruguay

Universidad ORT Uruguay

Contact	*Statistics*		*Ranking*	
Cuareim 1451	**Peer review**	500+	**World rank**	401-500
Montevideo	**Recruiter review**	357		
11100	**Student faculty ratio**	5.3:1		
Uruguay	**International faculty**	6.0%		
	Undergraduates	2,596		
www.ort.edu.uy	**Postgraduates**	188		
Tel +598 2 902 1505	**International students**	2.0%		

Index

Top Universities Guide is a reference work and many chapters contain information listed in an index-like way. For example, the worldwide information sources on page 22 and the international higher education data sources on page 93. These entries are not duplicated in the following three indexes.

Index to universities

This first index lists all the institutions mentioned in this guide. The reference to specific sections about a university (profiles or directory entries) are shown in **bold**. Many universities have very complicated names and the priority has been to list them in such a way that they will be easily found according to how they are well known. Extensive use of abbreviations has been made for reasons of space and clarity. For example, University (or its equivalent in other languages) has been omitted or left as 'U' when it belongs in the centre of a name or is an integral part of it (eg University College London UCL). Commonly occurring words such as Technology, Institute, School etc, or their equivalents in other languages, have been abbreviated Tech, Inst, Sch etc.

Index of topics

The second, non-exhaustive, index of topics gives pointers to some of the other institutions and subjects in the editorial chapters of this book.

Index of advertisers

Top Universities Guide is grateful to its sponsors and advertisers and the third index lists the positions of their advertisements.

A

B

C

I

J

K

L

M

A

B

C

D

E

F

G

R

S

T

U

V

W

Index of Advertisers

NOTES